F

THE ROOTS OF INDIVIDUALITY

Modern Applications in Psychology

under the editorship of

Joseph D. Matarazzo
UNIVERSITY OF OREGON MEDICAL SCHOOL

Judson S. Brown
UNIVERSITY OF IOWA

THE ROOTS OF INDIVIDUALITY

Normal Patterns of Development in Infancy

BY SIBYLLE K. ESCALONA
ALBERT EINSTEIN COLLEGE OF MEDICINE,
YESHIVA UNIVERSITY

ALDINE PUBLISHING COMPANY / Chicago

First published 1968 by
ALDINE Publishing Company
320 West Adams Street
Chicago, Illinois 60606

Library of Congress Catalog Card Number 67-27392
Designed by David Miller
Printed in the United States of America

IN MEMORY OF THREE TEACHERS
WHO WERE MY FRIENDS:
Kurt Lewin
David Rapaport
and John Benjamin

PREFACE

Preparation of this book took place over a span of twenty years. During much of that time work on the book took second place to other professional activities, yet could not have progressed without the support and encouragement received from the institutions where I was employed.

For a number of years a grant from the Foundation's Fund for Research in Psychiatry made it possible to devote substantial time to this work, and also provided research assistance for three years. Later yet, a career investigator grant[1] again provided that most precious of commodities—time to write. I am deeply indebted to those who provided funds, and wish to express special appreciation of the flexible use I was enabled to make of the grant from the Foundation's Fund.

The research project that provided our data was made possible by the interest and active support received from the Menninger Foundation, and by a grant from the National Institute of Mental Health. Full acknowledgment of all who aided the first project[2] was made in earlier publications.

The Child Study Center of Yale University and the Department of Psychiatry of the Albert Einstein Medical School were most generous in their support. They provided more than administrative facilitation. Dr. Milton Senn, then Director of the Child Study Center, and Dr. Milton Rosenbaum, as well as Dr. Morton Reiser, both of the Albert Einstein College of Medicine, showed unfailing interest in the work at hand, and patient understanding of the difficulties it entailed.

So many friends and colleagues helped by critical discussion of the material that it is impossible to make more than collective acknowledgment. However, I wish to express particular appreciation to Dr. Mary Varley Kuhn and Dr. Beverly Birns who rendered valuable research assistance, to Mrs. Bonnie Seegmiller who checked and double checked the endless tables, and to my friend and colleague Dr. Harvey Corman who shared each step in the preparation of the text. Mrs. Ann Smith also earned my gratitude for more than ordinary efforts required in the typing of the manuscript.

Finally, Martha Crossen Gillmor, in her capacity as editor, made a substantial contribution. Her suggestions lent structure to the book and emphasized the importance of a concrete and direct style of writing.

To these persons, and to my family who bore with years of preoccupation, goes my gratitude.

[1] National Institute of Mental Health, U.S. Public Health Service.

[2] *Early Phases of Personality Development* (Escalona, Leitch, *et al.*, 1953).

CONTENTS

PART I

○ ○
○

METHODS AND THEORY

Within the covers of a single book we have combined a number of separate but related approaches to the problem of better understanding what takes place during the first half year of normal development in human beings. This book is an account of the experience of a single investigator over a span of twenty years. The thoughts and facts reported here derive from a body of core data that were used to articulate a conceptual framework within which it is possible to ask and answer relevant questions about the interactional effects of many variables that play a role in shaping the early phases of the developmental process.

Part One provides a summary of where we began and where we ended: in other words, we shall describe the core data upon which the work was based, the methods used in the analysis of these data, and a condensed account of the theoretical formulation at which we finally arrived. Part Two reports on the results of one branch of this research venture; namely, a comparison of the behavior and development of two groups of infants differing from each other in one primary reaction tendency—that of activity level. Part Three reports on the results of a very different mode of dealing with the same data. Comparisons among the infants are now based on a determination of stable patterns of experience, as derived from the assessment of large constellations of determinants, of which activity level is but one.

Thus, this book about the developmental processes is developmental in its structure. The only way we know of communicating the hypotheses and concepts that emerged is to acquaint the reader with the raw data, with the shortcomings of each of several modes of approach, and with the sequence of transformations that led to the final formulations. Thus, as with any history, much that is said at the beginning will be documented and applied much later, yet the final form of the research data is intelligible only in light of that which went before.

ONE

CURRENT TRENDS IN RESEARCH

The work on which this book is based was begun in 1944 and ended in the mid-1960's. In the United States and elsewhere, this time span coincides with a period of renewed interest in the field of infant and early child development. Inevitably, our work derives its meaning from what preceded it and from publications that appeared while it was in progress. A sketch of dominant trends in this area of research should place our effort in perspective and clarify its relevance to widely shared concerns.

The last two decades have been so productive of empirical research in child development, and of theoretical elaboration, that a review of the literature would require a book in its own right. A complete review would also be gratuitous, since a number of excellent summaries and source books have appeared within recent years.[1] What we shall do instead is to offer some comments about issues and problems that play a large role in current thinking about early phases of human development.

Interest in the Neonate and Earliest Infancy

Until fairly recently the human neonate was described in textbooks as a functionally decorticate organism, imperfectly equipped to discriminate (or even to receive) sensory stimulation, and essentially passive and vulnerable in its relationship to the physical and social environment. In consequence, developmental psychologists seldom chose to study neonates[2] and frequently ignored earlier reports of relatively complex and adaptive neonatal behavior.

Within about the last fifteen years, an impressive body of experimental and observational work on neonates and young infants has profoundly

[1] See, for instance, Casler (1961); Foss (1961, 1963, 1965); Hoffman and Hoffman (1964); Kessen (1963); Lipsit and Spiker (1963); Tanner and Inhelder (1953, 1955, 1956); and Yarrow (1961).

[2] During the late 1920's and early 1930's the behavioral characteristics and capacities of newborns were studied extensively. At that time these purely descriptive studies were not effectively linked to developmental theory and, perhaps for this reason, interest waned.

altered our conception of what tiny babies are like. We now know that the neonate can register and discriminate sensory input in all modalities. He can focus and engage in fleeting visual pursuit, and he shows discrimination among visual stimuli.[3] He responds differentially to sound not only in terms of volume but also in terms of pitch.[4] Both the tactile sensitivity of newborn infants [5] and their responsiveness to thermal stimuli were confirmed (Bridger and Reiser, 1959; Birns, Blank, and Bridger, 1966). After a long series of failures due to methodological difficulties, the existence of olfactory discrimination now seems to have been established also (Engen, Lipsit, and Kaye, 1963; Lipsit, Engen, and Kaye, 1963).

All behaviors that can be observed in neonates came in for more precise observation and for measurement. Many of the simple reflex activations were described anew. However, the earlier extensive literature on neonatal reflexes tended to focus on their clinical significance and their prevalence, whereas more recent studies have emphasized the adaptative and developmental role of reflex activations. The change in point of view is nicely reflected in the fact that up to 1940, the largest proportion of publications in this area were devoted to the Babinsky reflex, whereas after 1950 the greatest research interest was in the rooting and the orienting reflexes. For instance, extensive study found that the rooting reflex facilitates food intake not only because it brings the mouth to the nipple, but because it elicits from the caretaking adult responsive accommodations of the position of breast or bottle, and is among the mechanisms mediating one of the earliest interactions between the newborn and his mother.[6] Similarly, the facial movement destined to become a social smile was studied extensively. It occurs during the first few weeks of life, and at that time it can be elicited by a variety of stimuli, though not with great regularity.[7]

Other studies dealt with such behaviors as hand-mouth contact and sucking: their incidence, their relationship to the infant's state of arousal, and their functional consequences for the infant's subsequent behavior.[8] Neonatal movement patterns were restudied, and not only were earlier reports confirmed, but it was also possible to discover certain rhythms and regularities as well as striking individual differences in the activity of babies.[9] Among other things it was learned that while the newborn is drowsy or asleep, spontaneous startles occur with fair regularity, but during alert but inactive states, they occur in response to sudden stimuli but

[3] See Berlyne (1958); Bower (1966); Brazelton (1961); Fantz (1961, 1965); Fantz, Ordy, and Udelf (1962); Korner and Grobstein (1966); Wertheimer (1961); Wolff (1965); and Wolff and White (1965).

[4] See Bridger (1961, 1962) and Steinschneider, Lipton, and Richmond (1966).

[5] See Bell (1964); Bell and Darling (1965); Lipsit and Levy (1959); and Rosenblith and DeLucia (1963).

[6] See Blauvelt and McKenna (1960, 1961, 1962); Gunther (1961); and Prechtl (1958).

[7] See Wolff (1959, 1963a).

[8] See Bridger (1966); Hendry and Kessen (1964); and Williams and Kessen (1961).

[9] See Bridger and Reiser (1959); Gordon and Bell (1961); Kessen, Hendry, and Leutzendorff (1961); and Wolff (1959, 1966).

otherwise appear to be replaced by activity (chiefly gazing) focused upon an aspect of the environment.

The cumulative effect of a great many studies was to draw attention to the importance of physiologic state as a determinant of behavior. Responsiveness to sights, sounds, touch, and thermal stimuli was found to vary greatly, depending upon the degree to which the infant is aroused, as shown by autonomic indices (heart rate and respiration being favored measures).[10] Similarly, not only the amount of movement but also particular activations such as sucking proved to vary in close association with excitation level as reflected by autonomic measures. Thus, consistencies in neonatal response to different stimuli could be detected if state was controlled or otherwise accounted for, but when state was disregarded the same responses showed little regularity.

A second important fact that emerged from combined psychophysiological and behavioral study of very young infants was that, for reasons still unknown, normal infants differ from one another in excitability. The degree to which external stimuli elicit changes in the autonomic nervous system and in behavior differs among babies, and these differences were shown to be relatively stable, at least during early infancy.[11] It may be that excitability is a biological property of the organism which accounts for many observed differences and which co-determines the course of subsequent development.

The attention devoted to the adaptive aspects of neonatal behavior, and the emphasis upon reciprocal exchanges between the infant organism and the environment (primarily the caretaking adult), gave new impetus to the study of learning and development during the early months of life. Currently, it is not so much behavior changes as a function of age that are being studied as it is the processes and mechanisms that constitute developmental change, and the demonstration that learning takes place at a very early age.

Experimental studies as well as systematic observations of behavior under different environmental conditions have shown that maturational advances are dependent on the infant's self-generated activities; that is, his responsiveness to perceptual stimulation in the immediate environment. For instance, the development of visual-motor coordination depends on the degree to which babies have occasion to regard objects, to swipe at them, to reach for them, and finally to manipulate suitable objects. The frequency with which infants show spontaneous behaviors of this sort, and the particular behavior integrations they acquire, are clearly related to the degree to which the immediate environment provides impetus and opportunity for these activities. One group of studies (White, 1963; White,

[10] See Bell (1960); Birns and Blank (1965); Bridger and Reiser (1959); Brown (1964); Escalona (1962); Richmond and Lipton (1959); and Wolff (1959).

[11] See Birns (1965); Bridger, Birns, and Blank (1965); Lipton, Steinschneider, and Richmond (1961a, 1961b); Lustman (1956); and Richmond and Lipton (1959).

Castle, and Held, 1964) showed that infants living in an impoverished environment (an institutional setting) learn to regard their own hands and to reach for objects at a later age than do infants reared at home. However, when the institutional infants were provided with both daily periods of playful attention and suitable objects within easy view and reach, the rate and course of the acquisition of visual-motor coordinations was altered. Those babies to whose cribs stimulating equipment had been attached showed *less* hand regard and hand play than is otherwise observed, but the development of reaching and grasping was accelerated by about six weeks. Apparently, the coordinated movements directed toward objects tended to replace the hand regard and hand play.

The relationship between developmental sequences and the amount and kind of stimulation offered was studied in a great many ways.[12] The amount of social smiling and of vocalizing at the sight of another person was found to be related to the degree to which caretaking persons reciprocate or initiate such social interactions by smiling at the infant, talking to him, and otherwise making and maintaining contact with him. In fact, these social behaviors can be altered by experimental means. That is, infants (again in impoverished institutionalized settings) could be made to smile or coo more regularly on seeing another person if, for a period of weeks, they were played with regularly (Rheingold, 1956), or if each time they smiled or cooed during an experimental session they were "rewarded" with answering social attention, or even with an impersonal but apparently welcome stimulus such as the chiming of a bell (Brackbill, 1958; Rheingold, Gewirtz, and Ross, 1959b; Weisberg, 1963).[13]

In this kind of research the focal interest has been to determine what continuity exists between learning processes during the early months of life and learning processes at later ages. Both classical and operant conditioning have been cited as the primary laws that govern learning. Pavlovian conditioning can be induced by the age of 4 or 5 months (some investigators think very much earlier), but it is widely recognized that classical conditioning fails to account for much of the learning that is observed in nature (Harlow, 1953a). However, operant conditioning, which occurs when certain of the spontaneous behaviors shown by the organism are consistently reinforced, can readily be demonstrated in infants as young as 12 weeks of age. One influential trend of thought is to explain the relationship between different patterns of environmental stimulation and developmental behavior sequences as entirely the result of operant conditioning. In pure form this theoretical approach defines the task of comprehending developmental changes as simply the identification of appropriate reinforcers for each relevant behavior—nothing else is needed.[14]

[12] See, among others, Ambrose (1963); Gewirtz (1965a, 1965b); and Richmond and Lipton (1959).

[13] See also Papoušek (1965) and Rheingold (1963).

[14] For an uncompromising exposition of this point of view see Skinner (1965).

What it is about the environmental input that lends it power as a reinforcer, or what goes on within the organism as the behavior repertoire expands and new functions arise on the basis of ever-changing sets of reinforcers, then appears irrelevant or is considered to fall within the province of neurophysiology. Like all closed theoretical systems, the commitment to operant conditioning as *the* key to early learning has an element of circularity: that which elicits and perpetuates particular behaviors on the infant's part is defined as a reinforcer, and this designation implies that reinforcement is the mechanism that explains the association between the stimulus conditions and the behavioral response. In our view, the theory of operant conditioning provides a useful language in which to describe empirical relationships. However, it tends to close the door to inquiry directed at a structural analysis of developmental change and to the study of the organism's contribution to the process—at least on the level of changing behavior organization and changes in mental content.

The majority of experimental studies that deal with learning during the first year of life use conditioning techniques, but go beyond the theory of conditioning in order to account for additional and fascinating components of the developmental process. One such component is the observation that infants seek out stimulation; that they expend effort to perform behaviors that are their own reward, in the sense that these behaviors take place even in the presence of obstacles or negative consequences imposed by the environment (White, 1959; Stott, 1957). The phenomenon has been described under the heading of curiosity, mastery, or an innate drive toward competence. Hebb's formulations (1949, 1955), often referred to as the incongruity hypothesis, made it possible to explore the phenomenon in terms of more specific dimensions. Hebb proposed that perceptual experience leaves patterned traces and that exposure to novel perceptual input sets up conflicting impulses within the nervous system. If the discrepancy between the familiar stimulus configuration and the new stimulus is great, the resulting neural excitation is large and leads to avoidance and/or fearfulness. If the discrepancy is relatively small, the resulting excitation leads to approach, interest, and active efforts to transform the novel into a familiar category. Experimental evidence lends support to the incongruity hypothesis. It has been shown, for instance, that very young infants devote more visual attention to novel and complex patterns than to familiar ones, and that novel stimuli and the pursuit of novel tasks produce greater excitation (in the autonomic nervous system) than do familiar ones.[15]

The idea that novelty and complexity constitute a source of motivation that is independent of primary need states has also been applied to developmental sequences in the social and affective realm. For instance, the emergence of fearfulness in response to strangers has been thought to co-

[15] See Berlyne (1959, 1966); Fantz, Ordy, and Udelf (1962); Hunt (1963b); and Lewis, Bartels, Fadel, and Campbell (1966).

incide with advances in perceptual discrimination to a point at which the sight of a very familiar person is an altogether different category of perceptual event than the sight of an unfamiliar one (Hunt, 1960). However, the work of Schaffer (1966b), Benjamin (1963), and others (Tennes and Lampl, 1964) has shown that discrimination of a stranger is typically observed several months before the fear of strangers begins. It would appear that discrimination between strange and familiar persons is a necessary precondition for the emergence of both stranger anxiety and a strong selective tie to the mother, but that it is not a sufficient condition for the emergence of these behaviors.

As research focused more and more on the manner in which the child's behavior influences the environment and thereby helps to shape the course of his experience and his learning, a large body of earlier research on development became relevant to the work of experimentally minded developmental psychologists. We have in mind especially Piaget's work on cognition, but also the descriptive studies of infancy and early childhood that flourished during the 1930's and before.[16]

When the first volumes of Piaget's monumental series became available in English (between 1926 and 1950), they were largely either ignored or misunderstood. His theory that thought develops in an invariant sequence of stages, and that functioning at each stage restructures the interaction between the child and the environment in such a way as to produce the next stage, was misunderstood, as though Piaget had proposed a preformed and built-in sequence that unfolds in the course of maturation and is independent of experience. The manner in which developmental psychology (especially in the United States) first responded to Piaget's theory lends itself to interpretation in light of the incongruity hypothesis. His basic dialectic notion that cognitive structures are created by the child in consequence of his actions (rather than acquired) violated the then-rigid view of maturation as an autonomous process. It was also incongruent with the then-prevailing conception of environmental forces *acting on* the organism. In consequence, developmental researchers in the United States tended to avoid Piaget's work.

But as soon as experimental work with animals and humans made it necessary to think in terms of reciprocal processes and of structures, the incongruity was reduced and Piaget's work began to draw a good deal of attention. In part through the efforts of Flavel (1963) and Hunt (1961), the essential content of the theory was recognized and found to yield a rich supply of testable hypotheses. Throughout this book we shall have occasion to discuss Piaget's theory (at least of sensorimotor intelligence) in detail. Here we need do no more than point to the fact that his con-

[16] For instance, Irwin's studies of neonatal activity (1930, 1934, 1941); Shirley's pioneering studies (1931, 1933a, 1933b); and even the diaries of Darwin (1877) and Preyer (1890), all of which are cited more frequently in recent publications.

tribution has been assimilated into the mainstream of developmental research and has led to significant reformulations about the nature of the learning process.

Essentially the same phenomena of infant life that have been studied in terms of learning theories, ethological concepts, and Piaget's theory of cognition have become increasingly important in psychoanalytic theory and research. Psychoanalysis is the only major personality theory that, from the beginning, assigned central importance to early infancy and specified distinct needs and distinct patterns of functioning for that developmental stage. Until fairly recently, the psychoanalytic conception of infancy was based entirely on reconstruction from clinical facts that become observable only much later in life. And psychoanalytic theory was couched in abstract and obscure terminology. These circumstances made it almost impossible to apply empirical research methods to psychoanalytic propositions—at least for the great majority of behavioral scientists who lack specific and intensive training in the theory of psychoanalysis. Both these impediments to constructive interaction between psychoanalysis and other developmental theories still exist. However, within about the last twenty years, as part of the increasing emphasis on psychoanalytic ego psychology, psychoanalitic scholars have acquired an interest in formal empirical research. In its most extreme form, this new emphasis seeks to transform psychoanalysis into an encompassing theory of human behavior, and to validate this broader theory by accepted scientific methods. Even those psychoanalysts who are not prepared to accept the ego-psychoanalytic frame of reference in its entirety now agree that, at least with respect to infancy and early childhood, psychoanalytic hypotheses require factual support that must be obtained by direct observation of behavior.

Psychoanalytic research on infancy has taken place in one of two ways. Some psychoanalysts have become experimentalists, conducting their research in a manner indistinguishable from that of psychophysiologists. A good deal of the work dealing with patterns of excitation in the autonomic system, to which we have referred, has been done by psychoanalysts.[17] They differ from their counterparts among behavioral scientists only in the theoretical context in which they place their work. They are likely to speculate about the significance of different patterns of arousal for the fate of object relations, for the choice of defense mechanisms, or for vulnerability to anxiety. At the time of this writing, psychoanalysts who use laboratory methods in the study of young infants have not yet attempted to investigate directly the link between infantile patterns of arousal and later psychological development.[18]

[17] For instance, Bridger and Reiser (1959); Lipton, Steinschneider, and Richmond (1961a, 1961b); Lustman (1956).

[18] The work of Peter Wolff is a significant exception. However, Wolff relies primarily upon direct observation of behavior under ordinary life conditions, and uses experimental techniques in a supplementary fashion.

Another group of researchers stayed closer to the subject matter of psychoanalysis and attempted to translate abstract psychoanalytic concepts into behavioral terms. Using chiefly the method of systematic observation, along with the techniques of psychological testing and the experiment, these investigators sought to elucidate and document the behavioral phenomena that reflect the emergence of ego functions and of advances in libidinal development as centered in the mother-child relationship. The greatest impact of this research has been its demonstration of the destructive consequences of institutionalization in infancy and of the effects of separation from the mother during the early years of life.[19] Less widely known, but quite as important, are investigations concerned with regular changes in the behavior and capacity of infants as they reflect such developmental landmarks as separation between the self and the environment, the development of a relationship with another human being, the emergence of volitional behavior and hence the functions of anticipation, memory, and goal-striving.[20] In this book infant behavior and development are regarded primarily within the framework of psychoanalytic ego psychology, and later we shall refer frequently to the last named group of investigations.

Although this chapter does not discuss issues and findings, it must include a general comment about the context in which our work took place. By and large, there has been no rapprochement between the main body of academic developmental research and the more sophisticated ego-psychoanalytic research under discussion. Analyst investigators have borrowed methods and occasionally concepts from learning theory or from ethology without integrating them with basic psychoanalytic postulates. Academic psychologists, on the other hand, do on occasion seek to confirm or to refute psychoanalytic hypotheses. Yet, with a few notable exceptions, communication between psychoanalysts and other behavioral scientists has been unsatisfactory. This is true even of the *definition* of phenomena under discussion. For instance, the notion of "stranger anxiety," as used by psychoanalysts is frequently equated with "fear of the stranger" by psychologists; most of the academic work on the topic fails to recognize that what is postulated by psychoanalysts is a fear of losing the mother which manifests itself in the response to strangers under certain—and only certain—conditions. Similarly, the psychoanalytic concept of "object relations" has specific connotations, quite different from the definition of "attachment behavior" as the term is used by psychologists. The two terms refer to related but not identical phenomena, yet we encounter in the research literature an assumption that what is learned about attachment behavior has direct application to the concept of object relations.

[19] See, among others, Bowlby (1951, 1958, 1960); Spitz (1945, 1946); and Spitz and Wolf (1946b, 1946c).

[20] See Benjamin (1950, 1959, 1961a, 1963); Hartmann, Kris, and Loewenstein (1946); Spitz (1949b, 1957, 1965); Spitz and Wolf (1946a); and Tennes and Lampl (1964).

The Impact of Large Environmental Differences upon Developmental Outcome

We have known for a long time that children born to poverty, neglect, and family disintegration tend to be less able intellectually and to run greater risk of psychological impairment than children from stable and nurturing backgrounds. For many years this discrepancy was ascribed to genetic inferiority on the part of some ethnic and low socioeconomic groups, as well as to poor nutrition, harassing life conditions, and poor medical care.

Recent changes in both social climate and developmental theory refocused the old problem and led to a great deal of research that tried to clarify the relationships of social background and early experience with developmental outcome. Perhaps the single most important change in the approach to this problem was that the critical importance of the first few years of life was recognized. Spitz's work on the devastating consequence of institutionalization in infancy and Bowlby's monograph summarizing research on this topic played an important part in bringing about this change of focus.[21] So did the fact that in recent decades psychoanalytic findings about the mother-child relationship as the single most important element of early experience became more widely accepted. Last, but not least, research activity in this area was stimulated in the United States by dissatisfaction with a society that, despite unprecedented affluence, subjects large portions of the population to severe developmental handicaps. The combined effect of these influences led to research aimed at discovery of the specific aspects of early experience that can be proven (rather than inferred) to hinder intellectual and personality development. Almost for the first time, child development research asked the question of why the same social, economic, and familial circumstances affect some children more seriously than others, while leaving still others apparently unscathed.

The amount of work that has been done on this topic is so vast that any reference to trends is somewhat arbitrary; a few comments will nonetheless be offered. The aggregate of empirical research and clinical observation has isolated some specific factors and raised some central issues. For instance, residence in institutions during the first years of life (and to some extent during all of childhood), as well as separation from the mother at an early age, has been shown to exert significant adverse effects upon development.[22]

Since hospitalization and residential care during early childhood ordinarily involve separation from the home, the task of distinguishing the

[21] See Spitz (1945, 1946); Spitz and Wolf (1946b, 1946c); and Bowlby (1951).

[22] See, for instance, Bowlby (1951); Damborska and Stepanova (1962); Dennis and Najarian (1957); Dennis (1964); Klackenberg (1956); Provence and Lipton (1962); Schaffer (1958); Schaffer and Callender (1959); Skeels (1966); and Spitz (1945, 1949b).

effects of separation from the mother from the effects of institutionalization has not yet been completed. Both of these noxious elements of early experience were at first reported as *always* and *severely* damaging; but further, more sophisticated research, while confirming the importance of institutionalization as an experience variable, showed its effects as less universally severe and modifiable by other coexisting elements of experience.[23] More recent studies of children reared (in part) in institutions tend to emphasize that variations in personality patterns and in social achievement are very great within this group. A shared early aspect of experience does not lead to similarity in outcome. Similarly, the immediate consequences of separation from the mother at an early age have been confirmed, but the severity and duration of the effect depend on many factors.[24] These include the quality of the mother-child relationship prior to separation, the type of care provided during separation, the age of the child, and many others.

In the course of investigating the detrimental effects of institutionalized existence, the amount and kind of perceptual stimulation provided for the infant emerged as an independent and important aspect of early experience. The developmental retardation of infants living in institutions can be alleviated, at least in some respects, when drab surroundings are enriched by providing toys, interesting sights and sounds, and free opportunity for age-appropriate activity.[25] So much is this the case that it has become difficult to locate the type of institution reported by Spitz and by Dennis, which will produce massive impairment. Reports showing no significant differences between children raised in institutional residences and those reared in their family (for instance, Przelacnikowa, Buterlewicz, and Chrzanowska, 1963) have come from studies made in countries where residential institutions for children are not regarded as a social evil and where children in institutions receive highly personalized care and rich perceptual stimulation.

Some investigators have suggested that the critical factor is not primarily the affective bond with one or a few selected caretakers, and that the stimulation ordinarily provided by the family can be matched by appropriate equipment and by programmed activity. This is an extreme position which might well be the result of the tendency to overemphasize the importance of a new discovery, as though it rendered null and void previous and independent findings. Actually, we do not yet know the long-range effects of enlightened group care. In addition, it is difficult to separate the amount and kind of perceptual stimulation from the social variable of prolonged intimacy with a limited number of parental figures.

[23] See Bowlby, Ainsworth, Boston and Rosenbluth (1956); Hellman (1962); Maas (1963); Schaffer (1965); and Sayegh and Dennis (1965).

[24] See Williams and Scott (1953) and Yarrow and Goodwin (1961).

[25] See especially Sayegh and Dennis (1965) and Schaffer (1965). Additional relevant references are listed in the first section of this chapter.

Institutions that provide rich and appropriate stimulation are also institutions that provide individualized care by a relatively small number of adults with whom the children do in fact develop intense personal relationships. The few instances in which children from such model institutions could be compared with family-reared children tended to show subtle but possibly important differences.[26] It would seem that development in the areas of language, social behavior, and coping with the stress of novelty is impeded by group care in infancy.

The more searching the study of the impact of early environmental influences upon development, the more unprofitable does it seem to investigate global environmental conditions (such as social class, broken family, race, multiple mothering, and the like [27]) in correlation to developmental outcome. The evidence suggests that it is the interaction between numerous aspects of a particular social milieu and such intrinsic factors as age, endowment, previous experience, and inborn reaction tendencies that account for the variable consequences for development of any one aspect of experience.

Specific Antecedent Variables and Personality Development

Partly because the conglomeration of conditions associated with global environmental variables failed to account for much of the variability in the development of children, much child development research of the last two decades has been directed toward specific aspects of early care as they relate to mental health and personality development of children. Clinical studies and common sense observation suggest a number of variables that would seem centrally important. Among them are breast versus bottle feeding, the feeding schedule, the timing and techniques employed for weaning and for toilet training, parental attitudes, and many more. The net result of a great many studies can be compressed into a single sentence: When child-rearing techniques of this order are treated as the independent variable, no significant relationship can be shown to exist between child-rearing techniques and later personality characteristics. Some parental attitudes do relate to child characteristics at school age and in adolescence, but no significant relationships have been demonstrated between parental attitudes toward a child during the first three or four years of life and the child's later characteristics.[28]

[26] See Damborska and Stepanova (1962); Freud and Burlingham (1944); Freud (1951); and Przelacnikowa, Buterlewicz, and Chrzanowska (1963).

[27] Benda *et al.* (1963); Caldwell *et al.* (1963); Fairweather and Illsley (1960); Frank (1965); Gilliland (1951); Knobloch and Pasamanick (1958); and Lesser, Fifer, and Clark (1965).

[28] See Beres and Obers (1950); Heinstein (1963); Kagan and Moss (1962); Orlansky (1949); Peterson and Spano (1941); Richmond and Caldwell (1963); Ross, Fisher, and King (1957); Schaefer and Bayley (1963); and Yarrow (1954).

The failure to establish a relationship between any one specific aspect of child care and any later personality characteristic (of those that have been studied up to this point) can be interpreted in either of two ways: It can be concluded that child-rearing techniques and parental attitudes are in fact of little consequence, at least for development during the preschool years; or it can be concluded that the same child-rearing technique (such as a relaxed or a rigid feeding schedule, or an indulgent versus a controlling mode of dealing with the baby) may be applied in totally different ways by different parents and may occur as part of widely different family atmospheres. In that case, what is important is not so much the particular child-rearing technique as the manner in which it is implemented, and perhaps also the total pattern of parental practices of which it is a part. This view implies that what was found to be true for the long-range consequences of global environmental differences is equally true for the effects of specific child-rearing practices: namely, the interactions among environmental antecedents and between the environmental factors and reaction tendencies of the infant are so important that the study of single environmental antecedents (or small groups) is not likely to be productive.

The emphasis on interactional effects gained support from a number of studies that focused on the relationship between certain aspects of maternal care and the infant's concurrent developmental and behavior characteristics. The more such studies directed themselves to the particulars of what caretaking persons do with and for the baby, the frequency of these actions, and the degree to which the adult's activities are responsive to behavior clues given by the baby, the more clearly could a relationship between maternal practices and child behavior be demonstrated.[29] For instance, Yarrow and Goodwin (1965) found that the more a mother flexibly adapted her behavior to the infant's momentary state, as reflected in his overt behavior, the better the baby could cope with stressful situations. Other maternal variables, such as the amount and variety of stimulation provided for the infant, and patterns of need gratification and of soothing, also proved to be related to the infant's behavior characteristics; however, these factors appeared to have more influence on the rate of developmental progress than on adaptation to stress. Similarly, it has been shown that patterns of stimulation provided to the "only" and the "youngest" child in a family differ in kind and amount, and that corresponding differences exist in the behavior of the infants (Gewirtz and Gewirtz, 1965). Most of the studies of infant learning to which we referred earlier in this chapter are also relevant, for they demonstrated that social attentiveness to the infant as well as other forms of perceptual stimulation affect the rate of developmental change.

It seems that there is ample evidence to show that what caretakers do

[29] See Benjamin (1963); Brody (1956); Schaffer (1963); Schaffer and Emerson (1964); Wolf (1953); Wolff (1963a); and Yarrow (1963).

and fail to do in relation to the infant has an impact upon the child's behavior and development at the time, although long-range effects of closely related variables cannot be demonstrated (always excepting the effects of massive and multiple deprivation).

INTRINSIC DETERMINANTS OF DEVELOPMENT AND CONSTITUTIONAL VARIATIONS

It has always been assumed that species-specific properties of the organism determine major developmental changes, though internal and external conditions can retard, enhance, and modify the course of development. Since the late 1940's, efforts have been made to specify some of the built-in determinants of human development. To the old question of how experience can affect potential, recent research has added the new question of how intrinsic propensities of the organism can modify experience.

The notion of developmental stages is as old as child psychology. Stages used to be derived from behavior norms that were shown to be typical for successive age groups, making the concept of stage purely descriptive. More recently the term "developmental stage" has been applied not so much to patterns of overt behavior as to more central regulatory mechanisms and dynamic constellations that are thought to be dominant during a given stage. Extending the psychoanalytic theory of stages in libidinal development, Erikson (1963) proposed that at each stage certain body functions impose their primary pattern upon all behavior and upon psychic organization in general. In consequence, specific modes of behavior are dominant at each stage, and the modes of functioning acquired during any one stage remain significant components of adaptation throughout life. For instance, taking in and ejecting are held to be the primary modes of early infancy (deriving from the vital use of the mouth to accept and to reject food), while the issue of autonomy assumes primary importance when skilled use of the body musculature and locomotion are at the core of developmental change. The behaviors, the needs, and the affective qualities that constitute stage-specific modes are met by each culture and family setting in a manner that either supports or suppresses some components of the constellation. For instance, in the United States autonomy and resistance to coercion are positively valued. The manner in which adults deal with the young child's efforts to achieve self-determination tends to encourage autonomy. In some Oriental cultures, on the other hand, submission to superior authority and control over impulses is valued highly. Correspondingly, child-rearing practices in such countries tend to encourage the acceptance of coercion without loss of face, at the expense of self-determination.

Such a view of developmental stages implies that the same environmental influences will have a different impact upon the child's development, depending on the stage in which they are brought to bear. It also implies that enduring attitudes and personality characteristics derive from experience during each developmental stage, and that the mature personality integrates and combines the dimensions of feeling, the coping patterns and defenses, and the modes of functioning that first emerged during each stage. This epigenetic view of personality [30] has become influential in current theories of child development, though it does not lend itself to validation except by clinical descriptive methods.

The notion of intrinsically programmed stages, especially of critical stages, has also been productive in the context of experimental work. For instance, it has been proposed that a primary attachment to a maternal figure must take place within a given developmental stage or it cannot occur at all, at least with the intensity believed to be optimal (Bowlby, 1958 and 1960). Such attachment to the mother was likened to the phenomenon of imprinting in birds in that it requires a convergence between maturational readiness and appropriate environmental support. Similarly, the effectiveness of certain varieties of stimulation is far greater at some developmental levels than at others. For instance, visual-motor coordinations appear to be most plastic to environmental stimulation between about 1½ and 5 months of age (White, 1963; White, Castle, and Held, 1964), whereas social responsiveness (cooing and smiling) are readily reinforced by appropriate stimulation after the age of 3 months, but probably not before (Lenneberg, Rebelsky and Nichols, 1965). In general, much of the work on early learning to which we have referred in another context suggests that new behavior integrations are bound to a biological timetable in such a way that when these new behaviors are learned with inappropriate delay, they are learned less effectively and prove more vulnerable to impairment under stress.

Critical periods may be defined in terms of heightened sensitivity to supportive or noxious environmental stimulation, or in terms of resistance to external influence; but in any case the concept refers to especially important interactions between a given developmental level and a specific aspect of experience. Investigations guided by this notion seek to determine differences in the effects of the same environmental variables upon behavior and development as a function of developmental stage during which these variables impinge upon the organism (Caldwell, 1962; Scott, 1963).

The importance of intrinsic factors for behavioral and psychological development has been approached also from quite a different point of view. From clinical and descriptive data it was inferred that some biological characteristics of the organism may modify the child's responsiveness to experience and therefore constitute a predisposition toward particular per-

[30] It will be apparent that Erikson's view of developmental stages has intrinsic similarities to Piaget's theory of cognition. Both are epigenetic theories.

sonality characteristics at later ages. Among the inborn behavior tendencies that have been proposed, research has dealt primarily with *activity level* and *zest* or *excitability* (which as defined by various authors seem to refer to much the same reaction tendency).[31] Two of the major longitudinal studies of normal children (Kagan and Moss, 1962; Schaefer and Bayley, 1963) reported that behavior during infancy did not correlate with later characteristics, with the single exception of a behavior attribute that is at least a close cousin to activity level—rapidity of movement in one case, passivity in the other. Earlier reports to the effect that activity level tends to remain stable from infancy through adolescence (Fries and Woolf, 1953; Fries, 1954) could not be confirmed. However, the importance of activity level for behavior and development within a narrower time span has repeatedly been documented.[32]

Another intrinsic reaction tendency that has received a good deal of attention is response to unfamiliar situations. On the basis of very detailed longitudinal observations, Meili (1957) found that the manner in which infants below the age of 3 months respond to a visual stimulus foreshadows their response to the unfamiliar at later ages. Meili found a strong correlation between many of the adaptive and social characteristics of 4-year-olds and the same children's behavior style during exposure to novel stimuli in infancy, which latter he regards as "primary perceptual transactions." Similarly, Thomas *et al.* (1963) found that the response to novelty remains highly stable during the first several years of life in terms of a consistent tendency to respond with either withdrawal and distress or a confident approach. These investigators regard the response to novelty as one of several primary reaction tendencies, along with others such as distractability, intensity, prevailing mood, and rhythmicity. Many descriptive studies have adduced evidence to show that the effect of child-rearing techniques upon the behavior of the infant varies as a function both of the child's endowment and of intrinsic reaction tendencies.[33]

The bases on which primary reaction tendencies arise have as yet barely been investigated. One study showed that early social behavior, especially the response to strangers, is far more similar for identical than for fraternal twins, suggesting that this behavior characteristic is subject to hereditary control (Freedman and Keller, 1963; Freedman, 1965). Another study showed that activity level (in neonates) is correlated with the length of labor, suggesting that this reaction tendency may be an acquired biological characteristic (McGrade, Kessen, and Leutzendorff, 1965).

A large body of research dealing with the development of children who as neonates or very young infants showed minor and inconclusive

[31] Fries (1954); Escalona and Heider (1959); Escalona (1963); Thomas *et al.* (1963); Kessen *et al.* (1961); and Maccoby, Dowley, and Hagen (1965).

[32] Ritvo *et al.* (1963); Schaffer (1966); and Escalona (1965).

[33] See, for instance, Wolf (1953); Escalona and Heider (1959); Ritvo *et al.* (1963); Escalona (1965); and Schaffer (1966).

signs of brain damage has also served to emphasize the contribution of biological equipment to intellectual and personality development. Minimal brain damage is associated with a higher incidence of developmental and behavior problems than found in normal children (Prechtl, 1963). Similar results have been reported for premature infants, in whom the incidence of intellectual and social difficulty relates less to birth weight than to the number and severity of postnatal complications (Braine *et al.,* 1966). Typically, minimal signs of central nervous system deficit at birth and prematurity show a statistical relationship to socioeconomic deprivation and to poor physical health in other members of the family. This congruence between physical, social, and familial impediments to normal development is again understood in terms of complex interactions between poverty, insufficient medical care in the parent generation, poor nutrition, and the psychological consequences of social and material deprivation.

THE DESCRIPTIVE STUDY OF INTERACTION BETWEEN INFANT AND SOCIAL SETTING

In one respect, all the research we have discussed so far has led to the same conclusion: the observed phenomena and relationships do not prove orderly and comprehensible when isolated antecedent variables are related to isolated later developmental measures or behavior characteristics. Whether the antecedent variables be intrinsic (prematurity, minimal brain damage, activity level) or extrinsic (institutionalization, social class, ordinal position, child-rearing techniques), all well-controlled investigations have shown a wide disparity among children subject to the same antecedent conditions. Even when a statistical relationship emerged—which was by no means always the case—differences within a group tend to be nearly as large as differences between the groups. It has been suggested more than once that the road to an understanding of developmental processes will be the systematic study of multiple interactions among an assortment of heterogeneous variables.

This recognition forced investigators to reconsider methodology in terms of research design and techniques for the measurement of environmental conditions as well as of the child's behavior characteristics. Several investigators have stressed the advantages of direct observation. For instance, in a review of research dealing with the discrepancy between parental attitudes and parental behavior, Hoffman and Hoffman (1964) conclude, "It is only when the level of observation is macroscopic that one can speak of a disparity between attitude and overt behavior. When the level of observation can deal with smaller units, then the behavior output from a severe method-warm mother and a severe method-cold mother will not be coded as the same behavior." Similarly, a study in which interview data and direct observation were obtained for the same population showed that scores obtained when the same variables were assessed separately on the basis of each type of data correlated very poorly. Beyond this, the author concludes that "we need measurements of when and how behavior occurs perhaps more than we need an 'average' or a summary of it in each mother" (Radke-Yarrow, 1963). Technological developments have made it feasible to record and process observations of environmental input and behavior output over prolonged periods of time.[34] These research experiences also led to an emphasis upon recording patterns of environmental stimulation in terms not only of their objective frequency and intensity, but also of their demonstrable effect upon the child's behavior. Yarrow and Goodwin (1965) coined the term "effective environment" in this connection, and Gewirtz (1965) suggested that only those extrinsic variables that are "functional" are important.

Discussions of research strategy designed to capture and identify interaction effects have, for the most part, led to the conclusion that no one design can include all relevant dimensions. Neither longitudinal nor concurrent nor prospective studies, neither experimental nor observational nor measuring techniques are sufficient to permit encompassing generalizations. Many methodologists of child development research now consider that the lawful regularities of the developmental process are capable of articulation only if the results of different types of study are integrated and consolidated.[35]

Finally, the fact that the impact of extrinsic and intrinsic variables on behavior and development appears to be contingent on a host of antecedent and concurrent factors has lent new importance to purely descriptive contributions. Nursery life as inferred from constrained conditions of investigation (the experiment, the interview, or the test) and nursery life as derived from abstract theory (psychoanalysis, learning theory) are totally unlike nursery life as observed directly. This confrontation with the gap between theoretical constructions and the reality to which they refer has dramatized the fact that much that happens to the young child—as well as much of what the young child does—is at present unknown territory. Many descriptive studies of developmentally relevant phenomena have been published. For instance, patterns of interaction between infants and caretakers in institutions have been described, as have patterns of interaction between infants and their natural mothers.[36] Developmental patterns have emerged from observation of changes in the nature of mother-child interaction at successive stages (Sander, 1962). Similarly, patterns of interaction between different mother-baby couples have been described in

[34] See among others Rheingold (1960, 1961); Wolff (1963a); Gewirtz (1965b); Moss (1965); and Barker (1965).

[35] For relevant discussions see Benjamin (1950); Bell (1959/60); Yarrow (1961); Escalona (1962); Wenar and Wenar (1963); Wolff (1964); Kessen (1966); and Spiker (1966).

[36] See, for instance, Escalona (1953); Brody (1956); Blauvelt and McKenna (1960); Gunther (1961); Murphy (1962); Schaffer (1963); and Ainsworth (1964).

formal terms and found to be quite stable.[37] In addition, the interaction between some presumably congenital attributes and specific environmental constellations have been traced by means of detailed studies of single cases.[38]

Our own work, both in the past and as reported here, belongs in the category of descriptive research and seeks to demonstrate that the formulation of adequate hypotheses depends upon extensive and specific information about the phenomenology of infant behavior. The more recent descriptive work to which we have referred differs from the informal accounts that constituted the beginnings of child psychology. It focuses on overt behavior rather than impressionistic judgments; it is more encompassing and systematic; and in most instances observations follow a prestructured program so that comparisons can be made on the basis of comparable information.

Our survey of major trends in child development research during the last two decades indicated changes in the direction of a greater readiness to abandon tightly knit and abstract formulations in favor of conceptualizations closer to observable phenomena, as well as a greater readiness to depart from a single model of scientific procedure in favor of an array of techniques and approaches with greater flexibility. In other words, investigators recognize that validation of developmental theories will take the form of convergence among numerous and diverse items of information, in contrast to the exclusively experimental model which relies on the reduplication of phenomena. There is also a greater readiness to abandon the view that extrinsic and intrinsic factors act upon the organism to produce behavior change in favor of the view that the organism's activity (motoric, perceptual, affective) shapes and constructs the events that constitute developmental change. Last, the survey tends to show a greater readiness to accept focused and systematic descriptions of the phenomenology of behavior as a necessary and contributory research activity.

One might expect that a new research discipline would begin by delineating the phenomena that require explanation, and only afterward develop theories and methods that become more complex as the science advances. The actual history of child development research—at least the history of research concerning development during the first few years of life—was otherwise. It was the failure of encompassing theory to account for observable fact, and the failure of hypotheses derived from constrained conditions of investigation to predict measurable effects, that forced investigators to retrace their steps and to describe and define the subject matter of their science. It is to this task of relating overt phenomena of behavior to meaningful theoretical dimensions that this book hopes to make a contribution.

[37] Marschak (1960); Appell and David (1965); and Call and Marschak (1966).
[38] Wolf (1953); Boyer (1956); Escalona (1955, 1963); and Ritvo *et al.* (1963).

TWO

DIMENSIONS OF INFANT BEHAVIOR

In the chapters to follow we shall describe the behavior of active and inactive infants in some detail and compare it systematically. A comparative analysis requires that the mass of infinitely varied behavior which took place under widely different circumstances be divided into categories of some sort. Unless something remains the same in the behavior episodes compared, it is impossible to specify in what *respect* active and inactive infants differ from one another. In this chapter we shall describe the major categories or dimensions of behavior chosen for comparison in Part Two and for the delineation of individual adaptation syndromes in Part Three.

The selection of aspects of behavior is a compromise between those aspects of behavior organization and daily experience that appear to us especially important, and the limitations of the data. In the original records some features of infant behavior were clearly recorded and amply documented, but others could not be ascertained with equal accuracy under the conditions of observation that characterized the study. Adequate information could not be secured about each infant's experience with family members other than the mother, or about recurrent events on which observers could not intrude, such as the baby's awakening in the morning, and his behavior in the late afternoon, when in many homes children are at their most demanding, as fathers are returning from work, and mothers are busy with preparations for the evening meal.

Within these limits, we selected for comparison the situations and behaviors most likely to reflect stable and recurring aspects of the baby's experience, as well as individual differences in adaptive style. Last, we elected to report in detail some behaviors that are universally observed in healthy infants, but that have special relevance to central aspects of the developmental process.

Eight major areas or dimensions of behavior were finally selected. The term "dimension" is appropriate because each provides a different focus or perspective on substantially the same behavioral events. Two of these dimensions refer to patterns of reactivity that characterize each infant and that appear to be intrinsic to the organism; namely, *activity level* and *perceptual sensitivity*. Two others refer to specific patterns of behavior activation (*motility* and *bodily self-stimulation*), while the remainder refer to each infant's characteristic responsiveness to certain aspects of the environment or to certain states: behavior in response to inanimate objects; social behavior; behavior while hungry or fatigued, and behavior in the course of spontaneous activity—that is, when the infant is awake, alert, and left to his own devices.

It is apparent that these are overlapping categories. Any behavior episode can be scrutinized from the point of view of the motility patterns shown by the infant or the degree to which he is responsive to different sensory stimuli, or with a focus on self-stimulating behaviors that he displays. As we hope to show in the descriptive material that is to follow, most of these dimensions are designed to abstract from the behavior stream certain aspects that can be stated in formal terms. By analyzing behavior relevant to any one of these dimensions, it is possible to make a statement that applies to the infant's behavior in its totality. In other words, these eight dimensions of infant behavior supply the framework for a structural analysis of the fluid behavior stream.

Before presenting the results of behavior analyses in terms of these dimensions, we should like to define each of them, giving a rationale for its selection in terms of its relevance to the developmental process.

Activity Level

Unlike the other dimensions, the assessment of each infant's activity level does not derive from the behavior analyses to be presented, but was built into the selection of the sample. As described in Chapter 4, each of the infants included in an earlier study of a larger group of infants was rated on activity level at the time the original observations were made. For the intensive study presented in these pages we selected from that pool of subjects the most active and the least active subjects at each age level.

As a result of this preselection, the notion of activity level will loom large in all subsequent discussions, and requires a defining statement in advance:

We define "activity level" as the amount and vigor of body motion *typically* shown by a given infant in a wide variety of situations.[1] An infant is designated as having a "high" activity level if he is one who, in comparison with the majority of peers, and under comparable circumstances, tends to move more often, more extensively, and more forcefully. A "low" activity level reflects the opposite behavior tendency, and a rat-

[1] See Ch. 4 for the techniques employed in rating activity level.

ing of "medium" (rare in our sample) means that the extent and forcefulness of movement shown by an infant does not differ markedly from that seen in most infants.[2]

Individual differences in activity level have been reported by many investigators for neonates and for older children. It is a behavior characteristic that has especially interested psychoanalytic students of development. In a pioneering study of its kind Fries (1954; Fries and Woolf, 1953), observed a group of children from birth to puberty. Her observations led to the conclusion that activity level tends to remain constant from earliest infancy well into young adulthood. Fries emphasized that activity level, which she regards as an inborn characteristic, is influential in molding patterns of the early mother-child relationship, that it is associated with a predisposition for the development of certain among the defense mechanisms, and that it contributes to the vicissitudes of instinctual development, especially aggressive strivings.

Other investigators[3] were unable to confirm the constancy of activity level throughout childhood, but all agree that it is an identifiable behavioral characteristic and an important variable in relation to development.

Drawing largely on previous research, we view activity level as an organismic characteristic that codetermines behavioral response at all times, and thus exerts an influence on the course of development and on individual styles of adaptation. Available research findings suggest that while activity level remains constant for some children, in general it tends to converge towards the mean. In other words, whereas in early infancy activity level shows an approximately normal distribution in unselected samples, toward the end of the preschool years extremely high and extremely low levels have become less frequent. With Spitz and Benjamin,[4] we believe that a child's activity level affects the developments that take place while it remains unchanged, and that fluctuations in activity level are one determinant of the developmental process. In other words, if an infant were markedly inactive during the first year of life, the developmental patterns formed during the first year would be in part determined by this low activity. If the same infant shifted to a higher activity level during the second year, his patterns of development during that year would be affected by his increased proclivity for forceful motion. Yet since development during the second year builds on patterns acquired earlier, his development during the second year would bear the stamp of his previous low activity level. The importance of activity level as a determinant of development is in no way tied to the stability of this behavior attribute.

[2] In the original study of 128 infants, activity level ratings from "low" to "high" showed a normal distribution (Escalona and Leitch, 1952).

[3] Thomas *et al.* (1963); Escalona and Heider (1959); Spitz (personal communication); Benjamin (personal communication).

[4] Personal communication.

The influence of activity level upon some of the developmental sequences that occur during the first year of life will be traced in subsequent chapters. We expect to demonstrate that not only the development of motor skills, but also precursors of cognitive functions and early varieties of affective and social behavior, tend to develop in a different manner in active and inactive infants.

The claim that activity level demonstrably affects the course of development does nothing to define the processes or mechanisms that account for variations in the intensity and frequency of motor action. Schematically speaking, it is possible to assume that active infants differ from inactive ones primarily because they are subject to more frequent and more intense arousal. But it is equally possible to assume that active and inactive infants are subject to impulses and excitations of equal strength, and that they differ chiefly due to variations in the effectiveness of controlling mechanisms.[5] For the time being, based exclusively on behavior data, the assumption that differences in activity level depend on differences in the processing of excitation (rather than its intensity) yields a more coherent picture of the observable phenomena. As we present other aspects of behavioral response to external and internal stimulation, it will be seen that markedly inactive infants can reflect in their behavior the impact of excitation quite as much as active ones, but these behavior alterations do not include as much activation of the large musculature. We make the tentative assumption that the activation of the large musculature, or the release of movement, may be governed by a threshold that differs among babies. Our data permit the inference that a given excitatory stimulus may in some infants lead to intensified mouth activity (a body activation of the small musculature not leading to the displacement of the body in space), in others to gross movement responses, and in still others to a change in the kind and organization of movement, rather than in the amount.[6]

As a working hypothesis, we shall assume that observable differences in activity level of infants below the age of eight months can be attributed to differences in the threshold for the release of movement. We will try to envision some of the regulatory principles that make observed behavior differences intelligible. It is therefore not necessary to postulate an actual physiological or structural entity within the organism that performs this function. We use the term "threshold" in relation to the occurrence of movement as a hypothetical construct, which should become unnecessary when the relevant neurophysiological facts have been established.

[5] In principle it should be possible to decide the issue by empirical means, when physiological and behavioral methods of study are combined. The strength of an excitatory impulse could be traced by means of autonomic and other measures, and concurrently the intensity of overt response could be determined by behavioral methods.

[6] It is likely that in some infants autonomic activations, such as changes in respiration, in tonus, and in heartrate, replace in part response to excitation in the form of movement.

Perceptual Sensitivity

The term "perceptual sensitivity" has been used by me and by others to denote the degree to which an infant is reactive to sensory stimulation in general, and to specific stimulation in the various sensory modalities. An infant who responds relatively strongly (compared with other infants of like age) to sights, sounds, touch, and other stimuli is described as highly sensitive. An infant who behaviorally ignores slight stimuli and whose response to moderate or strong stimuli is less intense than that of the majority is described as possessing low sensitivity.[7]

In addition to varying in their general tendency toward greater or lesser reactivity to external stimulation, the majority of infants react more to some varieties of stimulation than to others. One infant may typically react to even slight sounds, may respond fairly strongly to moderate sounds, and may be massively aroused by very loud sounds. In comparison, the same infant's reactivity to vision or to touch may be consistently less marked. We would describe such an infant as distinctly sensitive in the auditory sphere, and less sensitive in the other modalities. The implication is that infants respond differentially to external stimuli of identical physical nature, receiving greater or lesser doses of stimulation as a function of a biologically rooted characteristic of the perceiving organism.

The dimension of perceptual sensitivity will be dealt with primarily in Part Three. Indirectly, it also enters the comparison between active and inactive infants in Part Two, primarily in terms of the relative effectiveness of the distance modalities (sight and sound) in evoking overt responses. To anticipate the results of that comparison, in this sample we found no association between activity level and perceptual sensitivity. These two organismic characteristics appear to have independent origins; and concrete patterns of experience arise in part from the different combinations of activity level and perceptual sensitivity that happen to characterize each infant.

In previous publications we and others have attributed differences in perceptual sensitivity to differences in sensory thresholds. For many reasons we now consider this view of the matter as untenable. It is impossible to differentiate threshold from response by behavioral methods. If an infant responds overtly to a perceptual stimulus, it may safely be concluded that the stimulus has been registered by his nervous system. But if he fails to respond, it is impossible to know whether the stimulus failed to

[7] Bergman and Escalona (1949) reported on a group of children who in early infancy showed marked hypersensitivity, and who in childhood developed psychiatric illness or deviant development. They suggested that such infants lacked an effective "stimulus barrier," so that ordinary levels of stimulation proved overwhelming to them. In speaking of high and low perceptual sensitivity in the present context, we refer only to variations within the normal range.

enter the nervous system or whether it was perceived but not responded to overtly. Thus the notion of sensory threshold to account for varying reactivity becomes circular.[8] For want of better understanding, we shall accept the existence of differences in perceptual sensitivity as a fact, and turn our attention to the manner in which specific patterns of reactivity facilitate the occurrence of some experiences and behaviors, and tend to reduce the probability for the occurrence of certain others.

A word is in order about what little is known about the developmental aspects of the phenomenon in general:

Neonates and very young infants differ from older babies in that they are both more and less reactive to sensory stimulation. A quiescent but alert and awake neonate may startle or show random motion in response to almost any sudden stimulus, whether it be sound, touch, vibration or a bright light. Certain very slight stimuli, such as a small sound or a gentle touch on any portion of the skin will at times lead to circumscribed responses, such as flexion or extension of one finger or one toe, head rotation, facial grimacing, or a change in arm or leg position. In neonates, such responses to the onset of external stimulation do not occur with regularity. In many states, even fairly strong stimulation may elicit no visible response, or may lead to transient quieting instead of activation. With ongoing development, after the age of about 12 weeks, infants can behaviorally ignore many sorts of incidental stimulation and are less massively aroused by sudden stimuli of moderate intensity. It is for this reason that tiny infants are usually kept in a shielded environment, whereas after the age of about 4 months they can usually adapt to ordinary conditions of family life.

Although reactivity diminishes in some respects, it increases over the same time span in that the range of external stimulation capable of evoking a response expands during the first few months. All but distinctly irritable neonates and tiny babies are adequately protected in a buggy or a crib, shaded from bright lights and not jarred by vibratory stimuli, even though all manner of activity may take place at a distance; however, beginning at about the age of 4 or 5 months, most infants will not go to sleep if there is too much going on in the same room, nor will they ignore distant stimuli while awake and alert.

Development during the first half year brings lesser vulnerability to many external stimuli on the one hand, but leads to expanded receptivity to a larger variety of stimuli on the other hand, bringing new sorts of vulnerability.

Another universal developmental trend concerns the relative dominance

[8] This is another problem urgently requiring study by combined neurophysiological and behavioral methods. Except in earliest infancy, where the conditioning of autonomic responses remains a controversial issue, it should be possible to establish sensory thresholds by using conditioning techniques, and to compare them with thresholds as manifested by overt behavior.

among the various modalities. Neonates and young infants are capable of responding to stimuli in any modality. However, a very large proportion of behavioral response to external stimuli is mediated by touch and by passive motion. If our data are representative, very young infants are somewhat more responsive to auditory than visual stimuli.[9] In the course of development, the relative importance of the distant receptors increases markedly, and by the age of about 5 months much of overt behavior is responsive to visual and auditory components of the environment. In stressing the shift in dominance from near to distant receptors, we do not mean to imply that touch and other body feelings lose in importance, but rather that they become coordinated to and integrated with both vision and sound. For instance, between the ages of 2 and 3 months, the ubiquitous schema of hand regard consists of arm motions that happen to bring the hand into the visual field, whereupon the infant focuses his gaze on it, but then loses visual contact as his arms continue to move. A little later, arm and hand motions are guided by vision as the infant brings his hands into the visual field and keeps them there until another sort of activation or a diverting stimulus disrupts the episode.[10] It is in this sense, in terms of the degree to which behavior adapts to and is guided by visual or auditory components, that the distant receptors achieve dominance.

The perception of external events is best described not as a distinct registration of separate sense impressions, such as touch, sight, or sound, but as a unitary sensorimotor episode. To a 4-week-old baby, such events as being held, being covered by a blanket, or sucking at a nipple are likely to differ from one another only in how they make him feel. He does not yet connect the sight of the mother or the nipple with a cluster of previously experienced sensations. His behavioral response to external stimulation remains specific to its immediate impact. While he is almost certainly not aware of being touched as distinct from hearing or from seeing, he responds directly to the sensation, and not to perceptions proper, which imply a degree of recognition and therefore also of anticipation. Thus, in very early infancy, sense impressions received through various modalities may overlap and merge, but the responses (which are indistinguishable

[9] On theoretical grounds some authors believe olfaction to be of primary importance at very early stages of development. Our data do not yield information on this point, as in most life situations smells accompany other sensory stimulation; for instance, when a baby is approached and held by a person, or when food is brought close to his face. All we can say is that our younger subjects did not respond differentially to persons who must have carried with them a distinct aura of perfume, soap or recent smoking. In 6- and 7-month-old subjects it is possible, but by no means certain, that some differential response to the initial approach of various investigators could have been due to this factor.

[10] Some experimental support for the notion that intentional or directed hand regard follows upon a stage where it is incidental to movement impulses is provided by Held and White (1963). These investigators provided infants with mobiles and other visual stimuli, some within reach and others not. They found that when objects were located convenient to the infant's eyes and hands, the schema of hand regard was far less prominent than in the control group, who had not been exposed to the regular presence of the equipment. They also found that, in the experimental group, arm and hand motions became directed and coordinated but were oriented chiefly toward the equipment.

from the act of perceiving or of sensing) do not yet include coordination among the various modalities. Somewhat later, beginning usually during the fourth month, infants coordinate tactile with visual, auditory with visual, and tactile with auditory schemas in such a way that stimulation in any one of these modalities is closely tied to a sensorimotor constellation that involves other modalities as well. For instance, a baby's response to his mother's approach may come to be determined more by the fact that the "stimulus" is the familiar and recognized mother than by whether he initially perceives her through tactile, auditory, or visual channels. Should the infant first hear the mother's voice, he is likely to turn around and bring her into visual focus. Should he first feel her touch, he is likely to do much the same.

Despite the facts that external events are nearly always registered through multiple sensory channels and that behavioral response is made to the totality of perceptual input and not to its components, differential patterns of perceptual sensitivity can be demonstrated on the basis of a sufficiently large aggregate of behavior observations. In our data, individual differences in the degree of response to stimulation of various sense modalities are most readily discernible for the youngest group (4 to 12 weeks). Some infants are consistently more (or less) responsive to touch (or vision or sound) than are others. Among the youngest infants, patterns of perceptual sensitivity provide the most powerful demonstration of individual differences. At later ages, the reactivity to stimulation in different sense modalities could be determined,[11] and could be shown to be an important component of individual differences in developmental course and style of adaptation. However, in infants of 24 weeks and older, overall differences in behavior can best be described in terms of relatively more complex and patterned behaviors, rather than in terms of primary characteristics of reactivity.

As is the case with each behavior characteristic discussed, our intent is to show its consequences for the totality of the infant's experience and its relationship to developmental course and adaptation. On the assumption that the experience of infants will be modified by the degree to which they are responsive to external stimuli, and also by the degree to which they respond more acutely in one or another modality, perceptual sensitivity becomes a major aspect of the effort to delineate adaptation syndromes for each baby. As will be shown later (Part Three), the functional importance of reactivity to perceptual stimuli depends in large measure upon the dosages of stimulation provided for each infant in his particular milieu.

From the analysis of our data we learned that mothers differ in the sense modalities they emphasize during contact with their babies. For

[11] See Ch. 10 for a detailed account of behavioral criteria employed in determining perceptual sensitivity.

instance, some mothers rarely approach their babies without also speaking to them, and these tend to be the same mothers who also make a variety of noises to entertain the baby in play and who often sing or hum as they attempt to soothe him. Other mothers emphasize touch in the same manner, or vision, or even passive motion. In addition, mothers may by their behavior establish links between certain sensory modalities and certain feeling states and situations. For instance, some mothers we observed spoke or sang to the baby only during two situations—when they soothed him, or when they restrained and scolded him. Rarely did they utter sounds in the baby's direction while he was content or while playing with him. Other mothers rarely touched their babies (beyond the necessary manipulations) except as a means of comforting and soothing when the infants were in acute distress. Where this was the case, the infants experienced the mother's touch frequently while they were in a state of distress, and very rarely while they were in alert and comfortable interaction with her.

In summary, we regard individual differences in perceptual sensitivity as an independent organismic characteristic that contributes to the shaping of day-by-day experience. Yet the effects of perceptual sensitivity upon experience, behavior and development become apparent only when scrutiny is directed toward the combination of reactivity with typical and recurrent patterns of stimulation. In general, an important aspect of the construction of adaptation syndromes was to discern the various patterns resulting from combinations such as the following: low reactivity–massive stimulation (which would be experienced by the baby as only moderate in intensity); high reactivity–massive stimulation (experienced by the baby as exceedingly intense stimulation); low reactivity–minimal stimulation (experienced at a very low level of intensity and, at times, to judge by overt behavior, not experienced at all).

Similarly, it proved rewarding to identify patterns of convergence and divergence between mother and infant in terms of preferred (or underemphasized) modalities. An infant highly sensitive to touch whose mother handles him very little is an example of divergence, in that a modality to which the infant is highly reactive is evoked minimally by the events of his daily life. An infant who is far more reactive to auditory stimuli than to vision, and whose mother emphasizes speech and sounds to the comparative neglect of vision, is an example of convergence, in that the mother frequently evokes the modality to which the infant happens to be most reactive.

Motility

Movement patterns provide the primary data for the analysis of any and all behavioral dimensions. Yet, how much a baby moves, the manner in which he does so, and the conditions under which movement increases, decreases, or alters in pattern are also a source of individual differences, and a dimension of behavior in their own right. The term "motility" here refers not to any and all neuromuscular activations, but only to those that lead to *displacement in space.* It refers to both the quantitative and the qualitative aspects of body movement.

The infant's capacity to move, as well as the fact that he is under periodic necessity to move, occupies a central place in developmental theory and in most theories of personality. From the early diaries of Darwin (1877) and Preyer (1890), through the numerous normative studies of the type represented by the work of Gesell and his associates, to the sophisticated analyses of sensory motor sequences reported by Piaget, the gradual transition from reflexive and apparently random motion to increasingly coordinated and voluntary movement has been viewed as a central index to the developmental process as a whole.

Aside from its role in the development of cognitive structure, the significance of body movement has been of central concern in all dynamic theories of personality development. Freud postulated that in earliest infancy, massive body motion is the primary—if not the only—channel for the discharge of tension. Psychoanalytic theory further implies that at later stages of development, and in maturity, the adaptively necessary discharge of instinctual tension is closely linked to the activation of the skeletal muscle system. In particular, gross muscle activity is thought of as a preferred channel of discharge for aggressive energies. Other developmental theories, which do not necessarily postulate specific instincts or drives as sources of motivation, nonetheless treat movement responses as the vehicle of tension discharge. Gestalt psychology assumes that need states or goal strivings give rise to tension within the organism, and that such tension is discharged by motoric action.

Similarly, all varieties of learning theory make the primary assumption that accumulating drive tension necessarily evokes behavior—that is, activation of the body. In learning theory it is assumed that the patterning of behavior, its increasing differentiation and complexity—in short, the process of development—is made possible by the fact that in the course of the activity aroused by need tension, the organism learns which patterns of behavior lead to a reduction of tension and are thus effective and rewarding.[12]

Apparently it is impossible to theorize about the source and the role of body movement except by reliance (explicit or implicit) upon the homeostatic model. Even Piaget, who holds that motivation falls beyond the scope

[12] These few sentences clearly fail to describe the substance or the true nature of either learning theory or Gestalt psychology. Both have much to say about the role of maturation, about complex relationships between past experience and subsequent patterns of learning, and about the neural mechanisms that underlie behavioral development. In the present context, our sole purpose is to call attention to the fact that in theories that otherwise make widely different assumptions, bodily activation is systematically linked to the increase and decrease of excitation or of tension.

of his theory, makes use of the concept of equilibrium. The mathematical abstraction he employs leaves untouched the basic assumption that, in infancy, sensori*motor* activation results from a dissonance or lack of equilibrium between the behavior schemas available to the infant and their effectiveness or fitness when applied to the appropriate component of the environment. In other words, the continuous and simultaneous process of accommodation and assimilation cannot be envisioned except on a dynamic basis that involves waxing and waning states of tension in the infant organism. In Chapter 4 we shall discuss the conceptual inadequacies of the homeostatic model, as well as our reasons for employing it nonetheless. Our use of data dealing with fluctuations in motility will in part concern itself with patterns of coordination that reflect maturation and the operation of early cognitive functions, and in part with the amount and quality of body movement as the primary (but not the only) index of changes in the infant's state of behavioral arousal or excitation. Our interest is in the study of development in its own right, not whether infant behavior is capable of confirming or expanding a general theory of personality. A description of patterns of motility observed in our infant subjects is given prominence because, during infancy, responsiveness to stimulation from within or without is nearly always reflected in the form of movement. The interactions between organism and environment take place on many levels, but movement is the primary instrument of change. An adaptive behavior episode may consist of a change on the infant's part to better accommodate to the environment, as when a baby rotates his head to maintain contact with the nipple. Or it may consist of an action that changes the environment to better fit the infant's momentary state, as when a baby reaches for a distant toy and brings it to his mouth. It is in this sense that we regard body movement as a primary medium of adaptive behavior.

Bodily Self-stimulation

Among the many movement patterns observable in infants, one category is those movements that deliver direct stimulation to a body zone. In the clinical literature these activities, which include the familiar patterns of thumbsucking and rocking, have been labeled as "autoerotic." In later chapters, behavior of this sort is to be described and compared in the same manner as the other dimensions of behavior, and we prefer the more neutral and more inclusive term "bodily self-stimulation."

From the first day of life, infants tend to bring the hand to the mouth, which leads to sucking for as long as the hand-mouth contact lasts. In the course of the first half year of life, a great variety of other self-stimulating behavior patterns emerge, sharing the characteristic of all other movements in that they become increasingly differentiated, coordinated, and voluntary in nature. Mouthing and sucking are expanded into a large repertoire of oral behaviors, so that for babies between 24 and 32 weeks of age we were able to distinguish 24 different varieties of recurrent oral activation. Tactile self-stimulation during the first 8 weeks or thereabouts is limited to rubbing the sole of one foot along the ventral surface of the opposite leg, and to grasping loose portions of the skin. Somewhat later it comes to include stroking, fingering, pinching, poking, and pulling at protuberances such as ears or hair. And, in our sample, infants may also provide themselves with kinesthetic stimulation, beginning at about the age of 4 months. This consists of rolling the head or trunk from side to side in a sustained fashion, bouncing with motion originating in the pelvic region, or swinging back and forth on the abdomen with legs extended and raised from the surface. By the time babies are able to maintain the creeping posture, it often consists of what mothers call "cradle rocking"—a rhythmic back-and-forth motion on hands and knees.

Bodily self-stimulation may occur under many different circumstances, and will therefore be a part of the comparison between active and inactive infants, whether comparisons are made during need states, during spontaneous activity, or under any other circumstance. At the same time, it is a variety of self-generated behavior that has special relevance to the core of moment-by-moment experience, in that it reflects the infant's state of arousal and is closely interwoven with the rhythm of waxing and waning excitation.

As we shall show in later sections, babies can and do soothe themselves by sucking or by rocking. Bodily self-stimulation may also be one component of rising discomfort and excitation, as when hungry or sleepy babies chomp or bite at their hands, rock forcefully, or pinch, rub, and stroke their skin. At other times, all varieties of bodily self-stimulation may occur when the baby is alert, content, quiescent, and in a situation of relative perceptual monotony.

It is well known that infants differ from one another in the amount and intensity of self-stimulation they tend to show, and also in the particular modality of self-induced body stimulation that is most prominent. There are infants who suck and mouth a great deal, but who never rock or stroke their skins. There are others who show some non-nutritive mouthing, but who generate tactile or kinesthetic sensations for themselves far more often and more intensively than oral ones. Within preferred modalities, as well as in all of them together, there are babies who seldom engage in bodily self-stimulation, while other babies occupy large portions of their waking time in that manner.

All human infants have a tendency to provide for themselves varieties of bodily sensation that they have received at the hands of caretaking persons on other occasions. Not only are sucking and mouthing somehow related to the baby's bodily experience during feeding, but touching his own skin and rocking bear a similar relationship to his sensations as he is touched, moved from place to place, and rocked or swayed by the mother. Many authors have pointed to the probable importance of bodily self-stimulation in connection with infantile sexuality and with the infant's capacity to cope with states of stress. It has been regarded as an important component in the developing perception of the body ego, and has been considered in its relationship to those behaviors that serve mastery. Finally, bodily self-stimulation has been shown to play a role in the developing mother-child relationship; at least, excessive self-stimulation has often been reported as a typical syndrome in motherless children, or in those who for other reasons (such as brain damage) cannot participate in a sustained and reciprocal relationship with a mother person.

Our purpose here is to introduce this dimension of behavior, and to provide a general background for the descriptive material that follows. Cross-sectional data are not likely to yield much information about the genesis of particular patterns of self-stimulation. Yet it was possible to describe for each infant the variety of self-stimulating behaviors he showed, the modalities involved, and the context in which the behavior occurred. When this information was related to other behavior characteristics of the infant, to the patterns of stimulation he received from the mother, and to what we have learned about the specific consequences of behavior activation in various body systems, some suggestions emerged about the determinants of individual difference in self-stimulation behavior patterns.

We came to the conclusion that three separate factors play a necessary role and account for much of the behavior variation we observed. These factors are: (1) the actual biological characteristics of each modality; (2) the mother's habitual practice in terms of the modalities she emphasizes in stimulating and in soothing her infant; (3) the infant's differential reactivity to stimulation in each of the relevant modalities.

Whenever one encounters a ubiquitous feature of human behavior, it is plausible to assume that the biological construction of the organism directly supports and even requires it. Actually, the human infant is a creature capable of generating sensory stimulation for itself in all modalities. Babies cry or babble and receive auditory feedback; they move their hands or feet or a toy and provide for themselves visual spectacles; and they stimulate their mouths, their skin, or the kinesthetic system in the ways we have mentioned. Yet only the near receptors [13] (mouth, skin, and kinesthetic) are involved in the development of fairly stable and autonomous patterns that occur in direct association with waxing and waning excitation. The term "autoerotic" has been used to label these behaviors partly because of their link to excitatory states and partly because of their self-absorbed, inwardly focused quality.

[13] Auditory and visual feedback and self-stimulation play an important role in cognitive development and are discussed elsewhere.

If one inspects the infant's response to stimulation in various modalities when it is provided by the mother, it turns out that the near receptors possess greater power to reduce excitation than do the distant ones. A brief survey of each modality from this point of view will clarify the point:

Among infants below the age of 8 months, the *visual* system does not appear at all in the context of excitation and soothing. An irritable infant may be diverted by means of visual stimulation, but in such situations the change of mood is not coincident with a reduction in excitation. Rather, in response to the diverting stimulus, such as the sight of an animated face, a toy, or even patches of sunlight on the wall, the infant is apt to show an animated response. Similarly, massive excitation never leads an infant to intensify looking or gazing. Rather, it prevents the baby from focusing on visual stimuli.

At first glance the *auditory* modality would appear to have a significant potential for soothing. Distressed infants often stop crying and thrashing about at the onset of a loud sound, and singing or humming is frequently a part of maternal soothing. Closer inspection of the phenomena suggests otherwise. When a very young baby is exposed to fairly intense sound while aroused, he ordinarily arrests movement and crying temporarily, but his posture and physiognomy reflect a high level of muscular tension. Typically, when the sound stops, or when the baby has adapted to it, he resumes crying as before.[14] As to the effect of sound as an accompaniment to rocking, patting or swaying, it is difficult to know how much it may contribute to the soothing effect. However, we have never seen an aroused baby quiet more than momentarily in response to being sung to if he was not also touched or moved about. In babies up to the age of 8 months, the auditory modality does not play a central role in reducing excitation, though it does have the power to briefly inhibit the usual manifestations of excitement.

Tactile and *kinesthetic* stimulation both play a major role in the excitation and relaxation cycle. In soothing infants up to about the age of 3 months, mothers typically combine the two by holding, swaying, rocking, and patting the baby all at once. However, we have seen infants as young as 4 and 8 weeks who could be soothed by rocking without touch (as by rhythmic motion of the crib or buggy) and by touch without passive motion (as when the mother places her hand on the baby's back). The tactile and kinesthetic modalities, singly and in combination, do enter the excitation-relaxation syndrome in that external stimulation in these modalities can reduce excitation. Of the two, only the kinesthetic modality is also activated in the course of excitation, as large movement resulting from excitation generates kinesthetic sensations.

[14] Neurophysiological research with neonates has shown that continuous sound, as well as other varieties of stimulation, does have a quieting effect and may induce a state resembling sleep. Whatever mechanism underlies this phenomenon, it appears to be effective only while the nervous system is very immature. (See Brazelton, 1962.)

Oral stimulation has a tactile component, though the important element appears to be the activation of the mouth musculature that follows. Certainly small infants, even neonates, become relatively quiet when they begin to mouth or suck, not when the finger or nipple first touches the mouth. Oral activation frequently occurs as part of generalized excitation; it is by far the most effective soothing mechanism when provided through the environment; and oral self-stimulation is the most frequent and pervasive of the observable varieties. It is present at birth, though at first it is incidental to reflex activations. However, the hand-mouth schema is among the earliest to be acquired as a coordinated movement, and becomes available at will no later than during the third month. The most familiar commercial quieting device—the pacifier—derives both its name and its popularity from its power as a soothing agent.

The very construction of the human organism thus provides a variety of modalities for the registration of excitation, and for its processing and regulation. In their functional power to affect the state of the organism, these modalities are hierarchically ordered. In terms of experience during the first eight months of life, only some modalities belonging to the near receptor system have the property of reducing excitation when they are activated from the outside. It is those same modalities that infants activate at moments of stress and that come to serve as self-soothing devices.

The other two determinants—the mother's habitual practice of activating certain modalities in dealing with her baby, and the infant's differential reactivity to such stimulation—have already been discussed in connection with perceptual sensitivity. Their relevance to the amount and kind of bodily self-stimulation that an infant tends to show is as follows: A baby may have the potential for being soothed by passive motion, yet his mother may make a point of not rocking him when he is distressed, for fear of spoiling him. In this baby's experience, being rocked will not have been a prominent component of relief from distress or of the transition toward relative quiescence. If what we observed in this small sample proves to be generally true, such a baby is unlikely to develop rocking as one of the prominent self-stimulating behaviors. The same circumstances may apply to touch, which may or may not be a regular feature of an infant's experience as his mother succeeds in calming him. There are some infants in our group whose mothers used patting, stroking, and the like a great deal while tending their babies, yet some of these infants were not highly reactive to touch, and soothing occurred because of other components of the stimulation that the mother offered. Under these conditions, tactile self-stimulation did not become prominent in the behavior of the infant, presumably because, although the experience was provided for him, it had little impact on his state. Oral self-stimulation was the only variety observed to at least some degree in *every* infant. We believe that this is so because the habitat of the human infant demands that the experience of need satisfaction be mediated by oral activation, as infants must be fed to be kept alive.[15]

Our hypothesis, to be documented later, may be summarized as follows: If an infant shows prominent and fairly intense bodily self-stimulation, it will take place in that modality to which he was relatively most reactive when stimulation was provided by the mother, but *only* if the mother did in fact offer this variety of stimulation.

We have spoken of what determines the choice of self-stimulating modalities, but not of what determines the relative intensity of self-stimulation. Neither the theories of underlying motivation, in terms of biopsychological needs or acquired drives, nor the interaction between the type of stimulation received and the intrinsic reaction pattern, suggest why some babies stimulate their own bodies intensively and often, while other babies do so only occasionally.

The construction of adaptation syndromes provided a number of hypotheses about patterns of experience that generate more than the usual baseline levels of excitation, or that fail to provide sufficient opportunities for relief from high states of arousal. The determinants of unusually intense bodily self-stimulation are discussed in the adaptation syndromes (Part Three), though much of the relevant descriptive data is contained in the comparison of active with inactive infants in Part Two.

Spontaneous Activity

The dimension we have called "spontaneous activity" is the first to be defined by the situation in which it takes place, not by the behavior of the baby. It refers to situations during which the infant is awake and alert, not subject to somatic discomfort, and not exposed to specific and focused stimulation from without. That is, the times when an awake and content baby is left to his own devices, though of course exposed to variable background stimulation. The capacity to sustain a state of wakeful animation is, of course, a maturational phenomenon. Infants of 4 and even 8 weeks show spontaneous behavior in our sense relatively seldom and for only brief periods of time—and a degree of drowsiness may prevail even then. Infants vary in the age at which they begin to spend more than brief moments awake and alert, "entertaining themselves," as mothers often put it. The proportion of the day so spent begins to be appreciable for most babies

[15] Engels and Reichsman studied intensively a small series of children with gastric fistulas who were not fed by mouth. It was not possible to draw conclusions about the effects of the absence of sucking because too many other factors in the experience of these children also differed from the usual. However, it is of some interest that at least one of these children, Monica, showed an excessive interest in and dependence upon oral intake (of water, candy, and the like) years after normal feeding had been implemented (Reichsman, Engel, Harway, and Escalona, 1958).

after the third month, though we have seen some babies at prolonged spontaneous play as early as 12 weeks.

However, once the infant organism is capable of spending time in this way, the mother's customary practices and the general nature of the household will determine how much opportunity he has to do so. Some of our infant subjects had mothers who were almost constantly doing things with and for the baby. When not giving routine care or grooming, they would speak to him, hold and carry him, offer toys, and in other ways directly stimulate him. Where this was the case, spontaneous activity occupied a far lesser proportion of the infant's waking time than for babies whose mothers tended to intervene only when they needed care. Similarly, the presence of siblings who are permitted free access to the baby severely limits the frequency and duration of spontaneous behavior; so does the style of life in some extended families, where relatives are constantly about, vying for the baby's attention. Nonetheless, in our sample (and probably in general) all babies spent some time each day in this situation.

When behavior during spontaneous activity is analyzed for the movement patterns of each baby at times when this activity is not the immediate response to a specific excitatory stimulus, individual differences become particularly clear. Aside from the obvious fact that some babies spend much of their time in forceful and extensive motion, while others are given to gentle motions of only part of the body, the organization and complexity of self-generated behavior vary greatly. This aspect of behavior lends itself to description in terms of recurrent sensorimotor schemas, as defined by Piaget. For infants below the age of 8 months, it proved to be a fact that certain schemas tend to dominate an infant's behavior at a given time. Thus, when the object-to-mouth schema is prominent, almost any available thing will be so employed; when banging, or regarding his own hand, or any other specific behavior integrations dominate, the baby will apply these schemas during spontaneous activity to the relative neglect of other behavior patterns that are demonstrably within his repertoire. Describing spontaneous behavior in terms of schemas makes it possible to assess the relative maturity or complexity with which an infant functions in the absence of specific stimulation. By comparing an infant's behavior during spontaneous activity with his behavior during times such as developmental testing (and also with his test results), an additional variety of individual differences can be demonstrated; namely, that some infants when left to their own devices will engage in behavior that comes close to the most mature integrations of which they are capable. Others limit spontaneous activity to what are for them easy, well-learned schemas, while in response to specific prodding (as when mother plays with them or when they are tested) their behavior becomes a great deal more complex.

Similarly, what might be called the content or direction of behavior differs widely under this condition. After the age of 3 months some babies direct most of their attention to things in the environment. They gaze alertly at ceiling lights, people passing at a distance, and so forth. Others direct most of their behavior toward their own body, by playing with their hands and feet, experimenting with position changes, and the like. Or they may devote large portions of their time to bodily self-stimulation, by sucking, rolling about, rocking or patting, pinching and rubbing their own skin. Although they are not unaware of things about them, their activity is much less focused on the environment, which lends their behavior an absorbed, self-contained quality.

An assessment of the variety of behavior schemas seen during spontaneous activity, and a description of the relative prominence of each of these patterns, proved to be a useful baseline against which to assess the impact of other and more specific stimulating conditions. In describing an infant's response to hunger or fatigue, to social stimulation, or to anything else, we compared his behavior under this condition with his behavior when alert, content, and left to his own devices. For instance, many infants engage in massive whole-body motions while hungry or while being dressed. Some of these infants rarely or never show such movements spontaneously, and it may be said that for them hunger and manipulation lead to a marked increase in activity. Other babies who are just as active while hungry or while being dressed are merely continuing a behavior equally prominent during spontaneous behavior. For them an association between hunger or manipulation and activity increase does not exist.

Finally, the events and states typicaly present while the baby is alert, content, and unattended are an important part of daily experience that is worthy of description in its own right. To our way of thinking, what a baby does during spontaneous activity both determines and reflects ongoing developmental processes.

Self-generated behavior in the absence of need pressure or other compelling stimulation has received much discussion in the psychological literature, chiefly because it is then that human infants tend to exercise those behavior integrations that are in the process of being learned and that are necessary stepping stones to the next and more advanced behavior patterns on the developmental schedule. This spontaneous tendency to engage in learning activity, and to derive pleasure from so doing, has been accepted as an essential component of normal functioning in infancy and childhood. Whether it is attributed to an instinct for mastery (Hendricks, 1942), the presence of autonomous ego energies (Hartmann, 1952, 1958), an inborn pleasure in function (Bühler, 1930), curiosity (Harlow, 1953), or a need for competence (R. White, 1959), all agree that early cognitive development can proceed normally only in its presence.[16] Thus the study of be-

[16] It has been shown that institutionalized babies, those otherwise deprived, and infants suffering from some forms of organic pathology show a much reduced tendency for mastery behavior.

havior during spontaneous activity, when combined with other information about the child's experience and life circumstances, ought to be illuminating in the study of the conditions that facilitate and retard developmental advance.

In summary, behavior during spontaneous activity serves to describe individual differences in motility and in the organization of behavior schemas. It also provides a method of assessing the impact of specific stimulation by describing behavior in response to known and fairly strong stimuli as contrasted with the baseline of spontaneous behavior. Last, patterns of spontaneous activity are descriptive of the experience pattern of each child, and are one of several dimensions of behavior that provide direct clues to the specific actions that mediate developmental progress.

Somatic Need States and Need Gratifications

Another dimension that is determined by the situational context, not by the infant's behavior, is the recurring changes in state that result from cyclic bodily need states. Among these, hunger and fatigue, the corresponding consummatory activities of eating and sleeping, and the subsequent changes that constitute a return to a relatively stable waking state are the most prominent.

Somatic need states, especially hunger and its satisfaction, have been the subject of considerable study and extensive speculation. Frequently, the recurring sequence of hunger/discomfort–perception of mother and food intake–cessation of unpleasure (or positive pleasure) has been treated as a prototype of all arousal due to inner needs.

Psychoanalytic theory proposes that the very young infant is impelled to a first awareness of the discrepancy between the self and a surrounding field when unpleasure excitation due to hunger does not subside at once, so that the infant is forced to register the fact that food and satisfaction reach him from the "outside." In Freud's original formulation, recurring need states and delay in satisfaction are the biological agents by which the differentiation of an ego from the undifferentiated, wholly autistic id is set in motion. From this first step, Freud derived the complex series of structural changes in the organism that are necessary for the emergence of the first and decisive object relation (to the mother); the differentiation of the perceptual, cognitive, and motoric apparatuses that are first mobilized in the active search for need gratification; and, in fact, the entire process of ego development.

In the later psychoanalytic literature, Freud's basic formulations were expanded and elaborated. The degree to which mothers are able to provide need satisfaction, as well as the manner in which they do so, came to be viewed as centrally important not only as a mediator of ego development, but also as a determinant of the particular quality of later object relations and of basic early orientations (destined to become attitudes) such as "trust" or "optimism" and their counterparts. Psychodynamic theories of early development, influenced by psychoanalysis but not of it, lent even more specific and far-reaching significance to the patterns of maternal care. Both popularly and in the realm of the behavioral sciences, there crystallized a system of beliefs to the effect that the particulars of maternal care in early life have a powerful impact on the infant's well-being and future mental health.

Still more recently, ego psychoanalytic formulations offered by Hartmann, Kris, and Loewenstein (1946), by Spitz (1957, 1965), and by Benjamin (1963), have introduced important modifications of the central paradigm. These authors do not regard the cyclic need states and delay as the single source of ego differentiation. Rather, delay of need gratification is held to be a necessary but not a sufficient condition for the earliest emergence of precursory ego functions. Inborn biopsychological regulatory mechanisms and maturational processes are considered independent determinants that interact with the experiental factors. These investigators tend to view hunger and being fed as one of many important and recurring interactions between mother and infant, but not necessarily the prototype of all others.

In view of the great importance attached to this aspect of the young child's life experience, it is somewhat surprising that the behavioral manifestations of hunger and other bodily need states have received little attention in the literature. Far more has been said about maternal practices and attitudes than about the infant behavior that compels mothers to feed their babies in one way or another. Nor has a systematic effort been made to determine how hunger compares with other need states in the frequency and intensity of arousal it occasions. For this small sample, we shall make good the omission and provide a picture of the variety and the intensity of behavior alterations associated with some bodily need states.

Our primary interest in tracing the different patterns of recurring excitations due to need states is descriptive. We wish to know what happens to infants when they feel hunger and fatigue. This includes not only the degree to which displeasure is experienced, and how it manifests itself, but also such questions as the following: In the age range with which we are dealing, is the onset of hunger and fatigue sudden or gradual? Once excitation and/or displeasure have set in, are they manifested continuously or intermittently during the period of delay—that is, until food intake begins or the infant falls asleep? While hungry or sleepy, does an infant continue to respond to sights and sounds in the same manner as before, or does the excitation block responsiveness to outer stimuli? Do movement patterns become less complex, less integrated and coordinated, and does bodily self-stimulation increase or decrease? Correspondingly, what happens to motility, to affect and responsiveness during feeding and during sleep? Does relative quiescence always follow need satisfaction? And, during feeding, to what degree and in what manner is the infant's behavior focused on the mother or on other aspects of the environment? As will be shown, all of these and other alterations of behavior do occur, but there are great individual differences not only in the degree of such change but also in the widely different behavior manifestations of the need state. We think that it must make a difference to early development how these periodic need states affect an infant's functioning; and indeed, individual differences in this respect will be shown to be related to other aspects of the child's behavior.

As would be expected, the impact of hunger and fatigue changes with age. For our sample it can be said that, by and large, hunger is more disruptive and massive in its effect on babies below the age of about 12 weeks than on older infants, and that it plays a very minor role in the day-by-day experience of many babies over 6 months of age. Fatigue, on the other hand, is manifested in only some of our 4- and 8-week-olds, because young infants are often capable of sinking into drowsiness and sleep without delay, provided they are free from vegetative distress at the time. After this age, and especially after the age of 20 weeks, fatigue proved a source of excitation and distress for an increasing proportion of our subjects, often much more so than hunger. Among our older subjects (those between 5 and 7 months), some experienced very little difficulty in falling asleep. Fatigue became observable only when some external circumstance (for instance, being taken from home in order to serve as a research subject) interfered with the customary schedule. But a large number of these older babies regularly spent portions of each day in a state of acute fatigue, though the duration and intensity varied. The only general statement that can be made is that the fatigue syndrome was somewhat more apparent in those between 12 and 20 weeks than it was in 4- and 8-week-olds, and that it was conspicuous in babies between 24 and 32 weeks old.

For this and other reasons, it was found most useful to describe and analyze separately the behaviors occurring with hunger and with fatigue. The two need states have different characteristics and present very different problems to the mother. Gratification of hunger depends upon one thing only—the offer of suitable food. Those mothers who feed their babies at the slightest sign of discomfort that might conceivably be due to hunger, effectively prevent massive arousal and excitation. Other mothers, who follow a schedule or who fail to discern hunger discomfort until it has reached massive proportions, may thereby establish a pattern of experience for their babies that includes marked excitation/displeasure at periodic intervals. In this small sample we had occasion to confirm an observation also made in other contexts: most babies over 16 weeks who were fed on a regular four-hour schedule showed minimal signs of hunger, or none at all, yet they accepted food with eagerness when it was given. We offer the opinion that such relative absence of hunger distress does not reflect primarily the infant's capacity to adapt his biological rhythm to a fixed schedule. Although this may contribute, in the light of other observations it is more plausible to assume that these well-adapted schedule babies are among those who on physiological grounds experience hunger at longer intervals. That is, they are similar to those babies who, on a self-regulated schedule, show hunger at intervals of four to five hours.

In any case, the descriptive study of hunger and eating situations offers an opportunity to assess an important portion of the infant's daily experience, and one of the recurring states of disequilibrium to which he must adapt. However, because maternal practices can determine the course of hunger, this need state proved less useful for the purpose of describing *intrinsic* reaction characteristics of each infant.

We find it difficult to relate the behavioral data on hungry infants to the theoretical abstractions referred to earlier. Descriptive behavioral data can neither confirm nor disprove the hypothesis that it is the excitation during the interval between the onset of hunger and the beginning of food intake that mediates something like a dim awareness of an outer reality, and that leads to early forms of perceptual and affective recognition of the mother as a need-gratifying object. Behavioral data can and do testify to the fact that breast or bottle, and the attendant proximity of the mother, are among the earliest situations that elicit selective responsiveness, affective behavior, and early signs of the recognition-memory-anticipation combination which, by definition, signifies the emergence of rudimentary ego functions.

As behavior under the conditions of hunger and satiation is described for our infant subjects, discussion will be limited to the implications or consequences these experiences may have for the infant's total pattern of adaptation, and to the variety of mother-child interactions that typically arise in this situational context.

The need for sleep recurs as regularly as the need for food and, as has been said, can lead to acute distress and to massive arousal. In the youngest age group, perhaps the most common impediment to the infant's well-being (and to the mother's also) arises from conditions that prevent the baby from sleeping. Gastric disturbances, inadequate food intake, and other irregularities of vegetative functioning are disruptive to the baby chiefly because they keep him from sleeping normally, and thus also from experiencing the periods of relative quiescence short of sleep, which normally occur during the brief times when the young infant is neither sleeping nor hungry nor eating. In older infants, fatigue as a distinctive state frequently occurs in perfectly healthy, well-functioning babies. Unlike the state of hunger, there is very little that the mother or anybody else can do to meet the baby's need for sleep. As will be described, many mothers devise special techniques to induce sleep. However, whether or not a baby typically undergoes a period of distressed arousal before he falls asleep, and the length of time it lasts, is only slightly influenced by maternal ingenuity.

It is impossible to "put baby to sleep"; at best, it is feasible to create conditions under which the baby can fall asleep most easily.[17] In our sample, at any rate, marked difficulties in falling asleep are not associated with other signs of maladaptation, nor do they seem to be related to any particular features of the mother-child interaction. It is more plausible to view the occurrence of massive excitation with fatigue as a by-product of neurophysiological maturation.

In the light of what has been learned about the physiology of sleep (Kleitman and Enselman, 1953), it is probable that, prior to smooth neural integration, antagonistic physiological processes are at work simultaneously, causing the fatigue syndrome. In any case, the management of a desperately tired baby who cannot go to sleep is one of the most taxing aspects of maternal care. In view of the fact that fatigue that does not yield to sleep is such a common problem during the first and second year of life, it is surprising to find that it is rarely mentioned in the clinical literature or in research reports, though the amount of sleep has been a popular variable.

Behavioral changes with fatigue and during sleep will be described in terms of the same varieties of individual difference mentioned for hunger. In other words, for different babies at the same age, and for successive age groups, we shall compare the intensity and duration of fatigue, and the prominent aspects of manifest behavior in this state. This includes increases and decreases in activity (sometimes alternating), changes in motility (usually in the direction of a loss of coordination), the appearance of visible muscle tension and bodily self-stimulation, and the amount and intensity of crying. Further, it includes the abrupt or gradual nature of the onset of fatigue, the continuity or discontinuity of displeasure excitation with fatigue, and how much the infant continues to respond to external stimuli as well as how much he can respond to maternal soothing.

The comparison between active and inactive subjects will be limited to behavior during hunger and fatigue. Behavior during feeding and sleeping will be described as part of the adaptation syndromes, as it lends itself better to qualitative description than to the rating of behavior attributes and their frequency.

To summarize, the uses to which we expect to put our data concerning the behavioral manifestations of two somatic need states, hunger and fatigue, and the corresponding consummatory processes are: (1) to describe the impact of such excitation and of its disappearance on motility, on responsiveness to a variety of external stimuli, and on the stimulation infants

[17] By emphasizing the impossibility of providing immediate and direct gratification of the need to sleep, we do not mean to suggest that the capacity for going to sleep is independent of the mother-child interaction as a whole. However, it is one thing to say that a mother's inability (for any reason) to maintain for her baby a comfortable rhythm of existence may also lead to sleep difficulties, and quite another thing to say—as we do for hunger—that the consummatory activity can be directly offered (or withheld) by the mother. (See also Nagera, 1966.)

provide for themselves (bodily self-stimulation); (2) to describe the varieties and intensities of affect expression at these times, as well as those kinds of mother-child interaction regularly associated with the need states; (3) to compare the impact of need states upon behavior for successive age groups, in order to define some of the consequences of developmental advance for the organization of behavior.

Object-related Behavior

We define object-related behavior as the totality of behavioral events in which the infant responds to the perception of objects or things in the environment, as distinct from his response to the perception of human beings. The decision to discuss responses to objects separately from responses to persons is somewhat contrived, for the same behavior integrations are activated in both contexts, further, in the baby's experience, things are responded to as part of a social encounter quite as often as otherwise. Yet an infant's transactions with the world of things tend to elicit and make manifest with special clarity certain aspects of developmental change.

In infants of 4 weeks (the age at which our observations begin) there is no behavioral discrimination between socially mediated stimulation and stimulation that comes from things. It is the observer who classifies the mother's touch as "social," and the touch of a blanket as "impersonal" and emanating from a thing. In the course of the first several months, infants do begin to discriminate among types of stimulation that reach them from the outside. Reciprocal interactions with various things begin to differentiate so that behavior elicited by the sight of a bottle differs from that elicited by the sight of a rattle or the sight of a smiling countenance. These differentiations come about as the child repeatedly experiences the consistent differences in body feeling and in perceptual awareness caused by the actual physical properties of various stable components of the environment. A rubber nipple feels different to the mouth than a plastic rattle or a woolen blanket; more important, it sets in motion different body activations accompanied by different constellations of sensation.

Soon, discrimination is aided by the fact that each manipulatable object (or each group) proves to possess different action potentials. Toys strung across the crib can be gazed at, touched, and set in motion—they cannot be brought to the mouth. Shaking a rattle produces sound reliably; shaking a zwieback or a squeaky rubber toy fails to do so. And, of course, smiling at another human being brings results very different from smiling at the sight of a moving light or at a sound. A large number of sensations, actions, and interactions occur only during contact with another human being. In our experience, with these data and in general, most infants make some clear distinctions—in terms of consistently differentiated behavioral response—between different objects earlier than they distinguish between different human beings. We find this not surprising, because in their impact on the baby's immediate experience, adults do not differ as sharply from one another in their response to young infants as things do. Persons smile, talk, lift, and hold babies, as the situation seems to indicate. Their responses to the behavior of the infant have a great deal more in common than the "responses" of widely different things. This discrimination between "social" and "thing" aspects of the environment occurs about as early as, if not earlier than, the discrimination among objects, and for the same reason—namely, that contact with people has such different experiential characteristics from contact with things.

After about the age of 16 weeks, an infant's manner of dealing with objects clearly reveals changes in perceptual discrimination, changes in the degree of coordination of directed movement, an increasing differentiation of behavior, and changes in the degree to which the infant's behavior is dictated by and adaptive to the physical/perceptual properties of the outer world, rather than his own state. These changes as a whole are those that in psychoanalytic theory are thought of as reflecting early stages of ego development and as heralding and promoting the development of the reality principle. In the discussion of spontaneous behavior we have referred to the fact that these behaviors are generally regarded as forerunners or early stages in the development of cognition. It is necessary to return to this point here, as behavior with objects lends itself to a more detailed account of the development of specific early ego functions.[18]

Among the object manipulations that exemplify early sensorimotor stages of cognition, we may mention a widely used test item in which the infant must use a stick in order to obtain a toy that is beyond his reach. Earlier stages may be exemplified by such items as the ability to ring a bell holding it by the handle (*i.e.*, to treat it differently from a rattle and other toys); or to place a small object into a container (*i.e.*, to bring two objects into appropriate relationship to one another); or, earlier yet, to transfer an object from one hand to the other (*i.e.*, to displace an object in space with hand motion guided by visual clues, so that the object is not lost to the child's awareness in transit).

Piaget provided the most extensive and detailed account of successive stages in the infant's manner of dealing with things. He went beyond the normative studies of the same phenomena in that his interest lay in discerning systematic changes in the patterns of behavior or, as he put it, the "operations" performed by the child. In his view, each reorganization of behavior, or each schema employing an operation not available to the

[18] Certain aspects of the developmental process have to be discussed in relation to all of the dimensions of infant behavior. A degree of apparent redundancy is unavoidable if one wishes to trace the converging and interacting variables which, in their totality, mold behavior and development.

child before that time, constitutes an advance in cognitive development that plays a role in later thought processes, when the same operation takes place on the level of mental representation rather than on the level of sensorimotor action. Detailed observation of his own three children led Piaget to conclude that certain major stages of behavior organization occur in an invariant sequence, and that each stage is a necessary step for the acquisition of the next more complex stage, inextricably tied to later verbal and symbolic mental operations. Piaget views these behavior transformations as the product of continuous reciprocal interactions between the organism, which changes constantly as the result of these transactions, and an environment that possesses stable physical characteristics. In other words, Piaget holds that by virtue of successive patterned activations of the sensorimotor apparatus, the child literally creates or constructs for himself a reality that contains permanent objects, that possesses the dimension of space, that operates by means of causal laws, and that can be altered and to some extent controlled only as thought and comprehension enable him to adapt his actions to the actual laws that govern physical phenomena.

In the analysis of our data, the infant's actions in response to physical aspects of the outer world are given prominence because we believe that during early phases of development, this aspect of experience mediates centrally important learning processes, including, but not limited to, cognition. We also think that early patterns of behavior are strongly influenced by the manner in which objects are utilized as components of the social interaction between mother and child (here, as elsewhere, we use the term "mother" to designate any person who participates in the baby's care and performs maternal functions). For instance, some mothers, in playing with their babies or comforting them, characteristically limit their approach to the more primitive, body-focused varieties of stimulation. They hold their babies close and swing, bounce, or rock them; they cultivate body games such as tickling, kissing gestures, or encouraging the baby to manually explore the mother's face. Toys and other objects are then offered in place of human contact, as consolation or a counterattraction to make cessation of the social contact painless. Other mothers also provide these body stimulations, but use them to rouse the baby's interest in the environmental field. They offer and playfully withdraw toys; they play short-lived hiding games such as peek-a-boo; they attract the baby's attention to his own feet or booties as something to grasp; they perform interesting movements with their hands for the baby to watch, and in general stimulate outer-directed attention and behavior activation. Most infants are responsive to available objects whether or not this type of activity has been imbedded in pleasurable interaction with the mother. However, ego development in the direction of an increasing affective investment in outer reality as a source of pleasurable activity, and in the direction of increasing capacity for reality testing, may well be related to the degree to which mothers tend, by their behavior, to animate and, as it were, illuminate objects in the environment.[19]

For this dimension of behavior, as for all others, our interest is directed toward the variety of object transactions that infants show during the first half year of life, and toward differences observed among infants of like age. We encountered some typical differences in this respect between active and inactive babies, as well as wide individual differences that were unrelated to activity level. Various levels and patterns of behavior in response to inanimate components of the environment will be described and related to the following more general issues: (1) the emergence of mastery behavior and of early ego functions in general; (2) the role of these patterns in the context of the child's social experience and especially the relationship with the mother; (3) as one among several varieties of externally mediated arousal which is part of each infant's stable patterns of experience, and provides clues for each infant's manner of dealing with induced tension and therefore constitutes an approach to an important element of adaptation.

Social Behavior

Few would doubt that what happens to young babies as they perceive the mother and other people has profound consequences, not only for the development of the all-important first relationship to another human being (that with the mother), but also for the set of expectations and feelings that will dominate their orientation to the environment as a whole and toward themselves and their place in the scheme of things. The child's experience during contact with other human beings is probably the most important of our dimensions.

In Chapter 3 we shall discuss the fact that time-limited observations of overt behavior are ill-suited to the study of emerging relationships with other human beings. Our material does lend itself, however, to a systematic account of the interaction patterns that regularly occur as a part of infant care. It also provides a description of wide varieties of maternal style and of the consequences of such different styles for the infant's immediate experience. These limited varieties of information are relevant to at least two different issues of more general importance.

[19] Spitz (1965) and others have made a similar point by saying that it is the infant's cathexis of the mother object that enables him also to cathect things and observable phenomena in the surrounding field. From a dynamic point of view it might not matter whether the infant's early cathexis of the mother is established with or without the involvement of inanimate objects. Indeed, some of our subjects who received almost no "object stimulation" from their mothers proved intensely responsive to such stimulation when it was provided by the investigators. However, these infants, who became markedly excited with exposure to suitable toys, were less advanced and skillful in their object manipulations than those whose mothers had actively cultivated behavior of this kind.

At present, the literature tells more about maternal attitudes and practices in general than about the particulars of maternal behavior. For instance, numerous studies have dealt with the antecedents and the consequences of bottle versus breast feeding, but very few studies have dealt with *how* mothers behave when they feed their babies, regardless of the method.[20] It seems to us that more detailed knowledge of *what* mothers actually do with and for their babies, how they do it, and how their actions influence the immediate experience of their infants, is a prerequisite to a systematic understanding of the relationship between maternal behavior and infant development.

Second, previous studies of infant behavior have provided little information about differences among normal babies in their response to the varieties and dosages of social attention they receive. "Social stimulation" is an awkward term, but we shall use it because it allows scrutiny of the behavior data in ways parallel to the analysis of other dimensions of behavior. It is true in social situations, as in others, that infants differ in how strongly they respond to "social stimuli" of different intensity. For instance, some infants make maximal responses to moderately intense social stimulation. They are apt to smile and vocalize at the mere sight of a face, and may make their most intense and complex responses when someone speaks to them smilingly from close by. Other babies respond socially in proportion to the intensity of provocation. The sight of a face may lead to only visual regard, and being smiled at may elicit only a smile in return; a maximal response in terms of vocalizing, chuckling, or laughing occurs only in the course of sustained and active play initiated by the adult.

What we now know about the vital role of mothering in early infancy and about the connection between maternal attitudes and feelings as related to the child's subsequent development and adaptation [21] will become more intelligible as we understand which maternal actions, at what times and with what frequency, elicit which varieties of response from infants. It would appear to be the combination of the infant's reaction patterns, his total experiences, and the varieties of social experience provided by his milieu that hold the key to better understanding of how the mother's inner motivations (and the social climate of the family) intervene and shape the course of his development.

A few concrete examples may illustrate our approach in describing differences in the social experience of young babies. Some mothers take care of their young infants as though they were valuable and fragile things. In holding, feeding, dressing, and otherwise manipulating them, such

[20] Brody's *Patterns of Mothering* (1956) and a series of recent articles are notable exceptions. See, for instance, Appell and David (1965); Marschak (1960); David and Appell (1961); Yarrow (1963); and Gewirtz and Gewirtz (1965).

[21] See Ch. 1.

mothers are highly task-oriented. They do not invite smiles or cooing and behave much as one might in performing any delicate task, such as arranging flowers in a vase or wrapping a package. For such mothers, and therefore for their infants, social episodes are separate from routine care. They occur, whether frequently or seldom, at times when the mother's entire attention is focused on eliciting a social response from the baby.

Other mothers never lose awareness of the baby as a social partner. Even with infants as young as 4 weeks of age, they are under some necessity to lend social meaning to the contact by maintaining a constant stream of conversation while encouraging the baby to look at them. Such mothers typically attribute to the baby's behavior far more communicatory meaning than it could possibly possess. They say and apparently believe that their baby knows in advance that clean diapers will make him feel better; they consider that the baby is "scolding" them for a delay in feeding; and they take for granted that the baby means to be naughty when he spits out his food. Such cognitive misapprehension by a mother exerts considerable influence on her transactions with the baby. She is constantly responding to him as she believes him to respond to her, and this leads her to react to his sounds, his movements, and his facial expression with earnest efforts to discern his meaning.

Such differences in the mother's dealings with her baby were found to have quite different consequences for the infant's social experience, depending on his pattern of reactivity. Babies who are ready to smile and coo at the mere sight of mother's face tend to experience every routine caretaking episode as social, even if the mother fails to show social awareness of the baby at such times. Other infants, those who do not smile or coo except in response to specific provocation from the partner, may lie impassively as they are diapered or groomed, or may focus their attention on something other than the social partner. In the latter case, the mother's failure to treat the baby consistently as a social partner will have a relatively greater impact on the baby's social experience with her, in comparison with the baby who reacts more strongly to social stimuli.

So far we have mentioned social responsiveness only in its pleasurable aspects. Equally important are differences in the experience of infants concerning the occurence of displeasure in a social context. All infants perceive their mothers (and other persons as well) in association with displeasure. A distressed baby whimpers or cries and often, though not always, someone approaches and attempts to remedy the situation. We were interested in learning the patterns of frequently recurring experience of this sort among our subjects. Some of them had more occasion to become aware of the mother's presence while they were distressed than at any other time, because of the mother's tendency to leave the baby alone unless he needed something. Of these subjects, some typically remained in contact with their mothers while discomfort disappeared, as while being fed, or being rocked and soothed successfully. Others of these babies commonly regained a comfortable state while the mother was not in the perceptual field, as by taking a propped bottle, being rocked or pushed in the buggy, or by merely being placed in a more comfortable position. Still others of these subjects frequently remained in close contact with the mother while distress continued unabated. This was true, for instance, in infants who suffered from gastric distress, or who experienced intense and prolonged fatigue before falling asleep.

It is self-evident that the different practices just mentioned are not necessarily a function of maternal attitude or competence; that is, what a mother does when her baby cries or while she cares for him does reflect her feelings, attitudes, and convictions, but similar maternal practices can occur in the presence of widely different qualities of feeling toward the baby. For instance, some mothers seldom soothe their babies simply because there is no need for it. This is the case with some healthy babies who are fed before hunger distress becomes acute, who go to sleep easily, and who simply do not experience acute distress. These babies lack, in their pattern of experience, the element of perceiving mother as the agent of relief from distress. In other babies the same element of experience may also be absent, but because the mother is unable or unwilling to provide relief. Thus, it need not be true that babies cared for by indulgent and protective mothers have ample opportunity to experience her as the need gratifier and agent of relief from distress. If the early mother-child relationship grows from the baby's dawning recognition of mother as a need satisfier, its emergence and intensity may be determined more by the opportunity he has to experience her in that connection than by her attitude.

In comparing active with inactive children we shall report primarily upon patterns of social responsiveness observed in our babies. The adaptation syndromes in Part Three will focus on differences in maternal and familial style and on the different constellations of experience that result from the interaction between what the environment provides and how the child reacts.

These few comments about social experience are intended to do no more than to convey both the uses to which our data on social behavior can be put and the limitations of the data in this particular area. In summary, we shall analyze different patterns of infants' social responsiveness to very similar or identical social stimulation from the mother, from the investigators, and from any other person observed in direct contact with them. We shall also describe differences among the mothers in the intensity, frequency and manner of their social contacts with their babies. Finally, other characteristics of the infant, such as activity level, will be explored for the influence they exert upon his experience in the social realm.

THREE

○○
○

STABLE PATTERNS OF EXPERIENCE AS DETERMINANTS OF DEVELOPMENTAL COURSE

Research in child development differs from that in other psychological and behavioral fields because it concerns itself with changes in functioning and abilities that occur before the organism has reached maturity. It does not seek to elucidate the processes of cognition, perception, communication and the like in their own right, but rather to discern the mechanisms that propel developmental change in any and all areas in which change occurs as a correlate of chronological age. One of the features that sets child development apart from other kinds of research inquiry is that while the results of developmental change can be described and measured in a systematic fashion, the process itself can hardly be induced and studied under controlled conditions.[1] Yet developmental changes take place in an orderly fashion and show a high degree of regularity—so much so, that the notion of normal development is of great heuristic value. It is possible to ascertain for any child the degree to which his developmental acquisitions conform to the rate and pattern observed among the great majority of children.

Certain premises underlie any systematic effort to investigate the nature and the determinants of developmental change. It is assumed that the human organism is so constructed (biologically) that at birth it contains the potential for all universal human abilities and modes of behaving, though perhaps in unequal degree. It is further assumed that developments that occur early in life are the necessary forerunners and foundations of later developmental changes, and therefore are of critical importance for the course and outcome of the entire developmental process. Recently, behavior and development during the first and most formative years of life have become an important topic of research, chiefly because of the belief that experience and development during infancy have lasting effects, some of which cannot be undone at later ages. It therefore seems

[1] The study of the learning process is a partial exception, in that learning of certain kinds can be induced, studied in process, and modified in rate and effectiveness by providing different conditions of learning. As will be discussed more fully later in this chapter, the laws of learning derived from experimental work fail to account for much of the learning that takes place in the course of development.

of great importance to learn what factors in the environment, as well as what intrinsic factors, play a major role in maintaining and supporting development during the early years of life.

By comparison with other sciences, and by comparison with psychological research in other areas, child development research has so far been disappointing in its power to test hypotheses and to generate theories that are firmly anchored in empirical knowledge. It has become a truism to say that those concepts and hypotheses that have the widest application and that address themselves to the most important elements and determinants of child behavior are also those that cannot be confirmed or disproved by acceptable scientific means; whereas the areas of child behavior that have been subjected to rigorous empiric test tend to be trivial, in the sense that they concern peripheral aspects of human functioning. In other words, a large body of empirical research has yielded relatively little enlightenment about central aspects of human development, and little tested knowledge that is directly applicable to uncontrolled life events.

Many efforts have been made to direct research inquiry toward those determinants of human functioning and development that are of great practical importance though not subject to experimental manipulation. Variations in the circumstances under which children are reared have been treated as though they were experiments of nature. By comparing children reared in institutions with those reared in families, by comparing first-born children with those in other ordinal positions, by comparing children whose families belong to different socioeconomic or ethnic groups, it was hoped to identify aspects of early experience that have predictable effects upon development. Most of the facts and much of the theory in the area of child development have derived from this research approach.[2]

By and large, research of this nature has been successful in demonstrating a relationship between fairly extreme conditions of deprivation or of trauma and the *absence* of normal development. The association between intellectual retardation and socioeconomic deprivation, and the association between personality disorders and the virtual absence of stable mothering during the early years of life, are familiar examples. Thus, gross deviations from the pattern of existence usual and normal in our culture are known to yield developmental deficits and distortions for a significant proportion of children subject to such atypical experience. However, little progress has been made in learning which aspects of early experience affect which components of the developmental process. In other words, we do not yet know in what manner socioeconomic deprivation or the absence of mothering alters the developmental process—which is but a way of saying

[2] Clinical studies conform to the same model, except that it is usually a communality in developmental outcome that leads the clinician to search for explanatory communalities in the past experience of individuals who have in common a particular form of maldevelopment or psychopathology.

that we do not know what facilitates normal development in integrated families, or what devoted mothers do that sustains normal development. In consequence, no one knows how it comes about that among children who experience insufficient early care, some are damaged much more seriously than are others. By the same token, it is difficult to reconcile what we know about the effects of disorder and negligence in early life with the well-documented fact that outstandingly able and competent personalities have emerged from a background that conforms to the classic textbook description of deprived and brutalizing environments.

The difficulty in establishing specific links between particular aspects of early experience and subsequent development is even more apparent when the environmental variables concern child-rearing techniques (see Chapter 1). Neither breast versus bottle feeding, nor a relaxed versus a stringent feeding schedule, nor a disciplinarian versus an indulgent mode of child-rearing has proved to be a valid antecedent or correlate of specific individual differences in the development and functioning of the child. When the independent variables concerned intrinsic characteristics of the biological organism, we have fared only slightly better. For instance, efforts to relate body build or activity level to specific personality characteristics have not produced compelling evidence. And, as is also the case with gross environmental deficits, even global organic factors such as prematurity or brain lesions do not have the same cognitive or other psychologic consequences for all children. Again, we do not know how, or by what mediating mechanisms, activity level or a brain lesion affects the child's experience and development.

Yet, paradoxically, each study of the significance of an extrinsic or intrinsic variable that affects the lives of young children deepens the conviction of its relevance, even while it fails to tie the variable to a specific developmental outcome. *Retroactive* or *concurrent* study always shows that the factor selected as the independent variable has in fact played a role in shaping the course of personality development or of some of its components. But when the same variables, such as child-rearing practices, parental attitudes or activity level, are made the subject of prediction or of cross-validation, they prove ineffective. It always turns out that the same environmental factor (or psychobiological attribute) is also present in the lives of many children whose development and functioning is unlike what would have been predicted on the basis of the original study.[3]

In short, research concerned with developmental processes, especially that concerned with the determinants of individual differences within and beyond the normal range, has frequently failed to achieve its major aim—if

[3] This statement applies only to those developmental determinants that have been submitted to stringent empirical test. A great many hypotheses about the developmental consequences of certain antecedent conditions, especially in the interpersonal realm, have not been put to critical test.

by "major aim" one means that such research ought to make explicit the mechanisms or the mediating processes that constitute developmental change, as well as the manner in which developmental transformations depend on the presence of identifiable necessary and sufficient conditions. What child development research has accomplished is to specify the capacities and patterns of functioning that are normally found at different levels of maturity. We know the progressive changes in neuromuscular coordination, in social behavior, in cognition, and in other dimensions that occur with time. We do not know how one "stage" of behavior is transformed into the next, nor do we know how to account for differences in the rate of developmental progress. We know a good deal about the antecedents of developmental deficit and of deviant personality functioning, but we cannot predict the nature or the degree of maldevelopment that will occur as the result of grossly depriving or traumatic conditions of existence during the early years of life.

Our description of the shortcomings of developmental research applies only to empirical research, and the principles or general laws that were derived from research that used the experimental method.

Psychological theories of development have of course been generated. Until fairly recently, they concerned the relative importance assigned to autonomous maturational factors and to the environment. At one extreme are those theories that see the developmental process as essentially the overt reflection of bioneurological maturation—the role of the environment being merely to facilitate the unfolding of inherent capacities, or in varying degrees, to stunt and limit the actualization of potentialities. At the other extreme are the so-called tabula rasa theories which assume that, given a normal intact organism, all developmental changes and all variations in the structure and functioning of the mature personality are the product of environmental forces acting upon the plastic organism. Neither of these assumptions, nor their combination in a middle-of-the-road position that postulates the participation of both maturational and environmental factors, has shed much light on the particular determinants of developmental events and of individual differences. Perhaps this was partly because neither the maturational processes nor the way they interact with environmental factors could be specified concretely.[4]

More recently, and under the influence of concepts that have become dominant in both natural and social sciences, developmental theory has come to regard the organism not as the vehicle or the locus of development, but as an active agent that itself generates developmental change. Most theories of development now assume that childhood experience is not imposed on the organism. Rather, whatever happens to the growing child

[4] R. Spitz in *No and Yes* (1957) has gone further than most in specifying particular cognitive changes (which he treats as autonomous maturational phenomena) that must converge with certain developments in the interpersonal sphere (which he treats as dependent on environmental factors) in order for the next more mature phase of ego development to occur.

is regarded as the result of continuous interaction between him and the conditions and events to which he actively and selectively responds. Children—even newborn infants—have the power to influence and change their environments. It is further assumed by many developmental theoreticians that children differ even in their response to unalterable aspects of the environment, by virtue of biological endowment and of characteristics they have acquired in the course of past experience. This new look at development has directed attention to development as a *process,* rather than as a static product of unspecified prior events.

The interactional point of view can be applied to child behavior and to the problem of the genesis of individual differences more readily than the more static theories. The work of Piaget and Inhelder, as well as much work within the framework of psychoanalytic ego psychology, addresses itself to central aspects of the developmental process as it takes place in life situations; it has succeeded in encompassing a wide variety of observed facts within a coherent conceptual frame of reference. However, with the exception of Piaget and his associates (upon whose work I lean very heavily), the interactional approach has taken the form of a combination of description and plausible speculation. The problems mentioned at the outset have remained unsolved. It is one thing to accept the interactional view of child development and the importance of biological factors in determining the nature of those interactions, and quite another thing to apply this view to the systematic study of development in behavioral and psychological terms.

In my judgment, the difficulty in establishing consistent and reliable relationships between particular biological or environmental determinants and developmental events and outcomes is largely due to two related circumstances. The first of these is that, at least for development during the early years, we lack sufficiently detailed and extensive knowledge of the relevant phenomena. The behavior of infants and toddlers has been studied from the point of view of changing abilities and capacities, while experience during the early years has been assessed in terms of global aspects. To quote ourselves (Escalona and Leitch, 1953), "The range of behavior displayed by infants during early phases of development is largely unknown, as is the range of environmental conditions under which such behavior occurs." In any science, significant abstractions (which can arise from creative but unsystematic observation) have led to testable hypotheses and to scientific confirmation only on the basis of systematic and highly specific phenomenological observation. I believe that in the psychological and behavioral study of early phases of development, we have moved too quickly from description (except of isolated functions under controlled conditions) to abstractions and hypotheses that have remained resistant to stringent empirical test.

An analogy from another research area may be helpful in clarifying the issue. Current efforts to identify relationships between early experiential factors and developmental outcome have much in common with studies of the genesis of disease made when biochemistry and related fields were still in early stages of their development. For example, the symptoms of beriberi were familiar before the turn of the century. Since it was known only that the disease occurred most severely in certain parts of Asia and among sailors, it was as plausible to ascribe it to climatic factors as to nutrition. On a strictly descriptive basis the illness was then linked to diets consisting largely of polished rice. Soon after, experimentation with this diet led to the notion of a dietary deficiency consisting of the absence of a then purely hypothetical substance called "vitamin" (I. Funk, 1911). And so matters stood until much later, when in a different context, the vitamin B_1 complex was isolated. With this step, many separate facts fell into place. It was only after the structure of Vitamin B_1 had been discovered that it became apparent that beriberi is not caused by polished rice (any more than cognitive retardation is caused by socioeconomic deprivation), but by the *absence* of certain substances in the rice diet. The specific link between certain diets and the disease became comprehensible in terms of underlying processes. This new knowledge proved as illuminating for normal functioning as for disease.

The second circumstance that makes it difficult to acquire tested knowledge about developmental processes and their determinants is also best stated in epistemological terms. As has been said, the scientific models that find ready acceptance among behavioral scientists are derived from the most advanced sciences, notably physics and the mathematical models being applied in all the natural sciences. Yet these models require experimental manipulation; they require sophisticated measurement of part-processes; and they require control over all relevant coexisting variables. The relevant phenomena in child development, even insofar as they have been identified, resist such manipulation and control.

The phenomena of child development are by definition unlike those studied by the physicist; they resemble instead the phenomena in the domain of general biology. Biology shares with the psychological study of personality development a number of intrinsic and recalcitrant features. It deals with changes over time; it deals with complex organisms in changeable milieus; it deals with the manifold interactions between the organism and its environment; and it addresses itself to the study of what occurs as the result of innumerable and diverse constellations of extrinsic and intrinsic variables. Biology and the behavioral study of development also have in common that the phenomena under study come about as the result of events of widely different order. The chemist concerns himself only with the behavior of chemical substances, labeling but not investigating the structure or the action context in which they occur. The physicist deals with forces and particles, and measures consequences on the same level.

But the biologist deals with living organisms in their habitat. He cannot ignore the fact that organisms are subject to physical laws and that their existence is mediated by continuous chemical processes. Biology addresses itself to the consequences of physical, chemical, geological, and even sociological facts for the organism or the species. Precisely the same is true of child development, which equally deals with psychological, biological, physical, chemical, and social factors as they converge on the growing child.

Biological phenomena have lent themselves to description and theoretical elaboration in terms of such concepts as adaptation, state, system, structure, potential, emergence, activation, suppression, and extinction. They have also been described in terms of general and relative concepts such as stages, primitive versus complex, and hierarchical patterns of organization. In comparison with the concepts and terms used in physics (and in biochemistry, which is indifferent to the organism as a whole), the language of general biology lacks sharpness of definition and formal elegance. Yet it conveys the content of empirical observation, and it has been the vehicle for powerful theoretical formulations, the theory of evolution being the most distinguished example.

We are of the opinion that much of the research in child development has suffered from the fact that psychologists chose to adopt strategies and concepts analogous to physics rather than to biology. In point of fact, we consider that the psychological and behavioral study of human development falls within the scope of general biology.

This point of view has repeatedly been expressed by biologists.[5] It has also been the basis for psychoanalysis, one of the most productive theories of personality development, and for outstandingly enlightening research on cognitive development; namely, the work of Piaget, Inhelder, and their associates. Both Freud and Piaget were biologists before they became involved in the study of psychological phenomena, and both defined their approach and basic premises as rooted in the tradition of biology. If a theory is judged by the degree to which it encompasses a large proportion of the phenomena observed in nature, and by the degree to which it brings to light new facts and new relationships among facts, both psychoanalysis and Piaget's work on cognitive development are remarkably successful theories.

The major purpose of this book is to propose an approach to the study of human development, especially to the study of the genesis of individual differences, that may be useful in achieving a better understanding of the *process* of development, and that may enable us to discover invariant and consistent relationships between experience during the early years of life and individual characteristics of behavior and functioning that become manifest at later ages. It will become apparent that our work derives

[5] See, for instance, Dubos (1965) and Burgess (1966).

largely from biological theory and from those psychological theories that acknowledge a close kinship with biology.[6]

A commitment to studying early development in terms of the behavior of the organism as a whole in the context of the relevant field conditions is no more than a general background for a specific research venture. We shall now turn to a description of the specific goals of this undertaking and the specific research strategies we shall use to implement them.

Our primary interest has been (1) to identify differences in the behavior and reaction tendencies of infants up to the age of eight months; (2) to study the genesis of these differences; and (3) to establish whether behaviorally manifested differences in early life *make a difference; i.e.,* whether they may account in part for observable differences in the rate and course of development and differences in adaptive style or personality functioning at later ages. In the course of earlier work [7] we observed that two organismic variables—activity level and perceptual sensitivity [8]—seemed to account for much of the variation in behavior that we were able to observe among a carefully studied sample of normal infants. This fact led us to the speculation that the same environmental conditions are likely to have a different impact upon infants who differ from one another in a biological characteristic, such as an inherent tendency to activate the large muscle system frequently, or strong (or weak) reactivity to external stimulation through one or several of the sensory modalities. For one organismic characteristic, activity level, we propose to investigate in detail the consequences of high or low activity level, not only for stable behavioral characteristics, but also for responsiveness to any and all conditions encountered by the infant in the course of daily life. In other words, we shall attempt to construct a detailed account of what happened to each of the active and the inactive infants in the course of moment-by-moment and day-by-day experience, and how they responded to the particular situations and patterns of stimulation that came their way. The systematic analysis of what infants are observed to do and the circumstances under which they do it forced us to find a way of dealing with the obvious fact that the behavior of active babies, for instance, is highly consistent—yet it varied enormously because of the different environmental conditions to which the active infants were required to adapt. For example, all the

[6] A split exists within biology itself. Microbiology is far closer (in its methods and its theoretical formulations) to the physical-mathematical sciences than to general organismic biology. The exact counterpart exists within psychology, in the continuous debate between those who rely exclusively on the experimental model (or who seek to submit psychological data to contemporary mathematical models) and those who attempt the study of the "organism as a whole." In both controversies the author is aligned with those who consider the investigation of underlying micro-processes to be essential, but who consider that the behavior of the organism (or the species or other natural groups) requires study in its own right, and cannot be comprehended by reduction to the underlying biophysical events.

[7] See Escalona (1952, 1953, 1959, 1963).

[8] Activity level and perceptual sensitivity were defined and discussed in Chapter 2.

highly active infants tended to show excitation and distress when ongoing body movement was restrained, in contrast to the markedly inactive infants, who tended to accept with equanimity the restraining interruption in the execution of a movement impulse. On the other hand, excitation and distress in response to restraint had relatively little significance in the early experience of those active infants whose mothers seldom restrained movement. For other active infants, however, the same behavior characteristic was a powerful determinant of day-by-day experience, because in the course of routine caretaking situations and other mother-child interactions, restraint was regularly imposed and distress followed with equal regularity.

In observing infants in their milieu in this manner, in noting the regularities and patterns of behavior that make up the texture of their lives, in noting the different courses that development can take even within the first half year of life, in identifying organismic characteristics, and in trying to relate the empirical observations to hypotheses and theories now available, we think that we have come to recognize at least one reason for the failure to demonstrate consistent relationships between specific aspects of early experience and developmental outcome.

We have come to think that the fault may not lie with the hypotheses being tested, but with an inappropriate selection of criteria that are taken to reflect qualities or aspects of early experience.

In most of the more rigorous and formal research on the effects of experience variables upon development, these variables have been selected with seeming objectivity in terms of the actual properties or characteristics of the environment. That is, if affectionate and highly personalized care was predicated as an important factor in shaping early experience, the index or measure of the presence of such care was maternal attitude, or reports by the mother as to the child-rearing techniques employed; the seemingly plausible assumption was that a warmly loving mother would provide for her infant a pattern of experience characterized by such features as much gratifying body contact, protection from discomfort, and so forth. Even in more recent studies in which direct observation of maternal behavior served as the criterion, it has tacitly been assumed that if we know the objective properties of the environment, they will serve as a valid index of the nature of the child's experience. But to assume that the same external condition or the same variety of stimulation will provide the same quality and intensity of experience for all children is to run counter to the interactional point of view, which holds behavior and what actually happens to the infant to be the result of an interaction between the organism and its milieu.[9] We have concluded that in many instances

[9] Within recent years some investigators (Yarrow, 1963; Yarrow and Goodwin, 1965) have turned to the direct observation of infant behavior as an index of the nature of infantile experience. They did so because they questioned the validity of objective assessments of the environment for much the same reasons as those discussed above.

the model that guides thinking about behavior and development is quite different from the model that guides research strategy.

We propose that behavior in the context of the conditions to which it is responsive can provide a valid and yet objective index of infantile experience. And we further propose that when behavior-in-context is used as the independent variable of experience, consistent relationships with the dependent variables of developmental outcome will be demonstrated, and the determinants of individual differences will be better understood.

Figure 3.1 is a schematic representation of the difference between the traditional research design and the model we propose as more congruent with the interactional theory of child development.

Model One is a schematic approximation of the view that environmental and organismic factors combine to produce the actual behavioral events that characterize early experience. Since the effect of any single factor (or any selected group of factors) is qualified and altered by all other coexisting intrinsic and extrinsic factors, one would not expect an invariant and direct relationship between organismic (A factors) or environmental (B factors) variables and developmental outcome (D). However, if one succeeded in assessing or measuring the significant components of early experience (C), these should show a consistent and direct relationship to developmental outcome (D).

Model Two provides a schematic approximation of what has been done in most child development research. Selected A and B factors were related directly to developmental outcome (D). The implied assumption is that some of the environmental and intrinsic factors are so powerful in their effect upon early experience that they will be reflected in developmental outcome despite the widely varying dispersion of coexisting A and B factors. Such short-circuiting of the experience patterns themselves or, to put it another way, the *indirect* assessment of experience variables, explains both the successes and the failures of much developmental research. The theoretical model implies, as does common sense, that when an element of experience is objectively lacking, this deficit must make itself felt in actual experience, regardless of all other relevant circumstances or conditions. And in fact, such factors as the virtual absence of maternal care or the absence of sufficient perceptual stimulation were shown to have a demonstrable relationship to developmental outcome when the research strategy was as described in Model Two. But the specific nature and extent of developmental effects could not be accounted for in terms of the specific B factor without reference to many of the coexisting other variables, and even then not in a systematic manner.

Our suggestion for a profitable way of investigating the relationship between experience during the most formative early years and individual differences in developmental outcome is to bring the design of empirical research into accord with the theoretical model. The child's experience

FIGURE 3.1. TWO MODELS OF RESEARCH DESIGN.

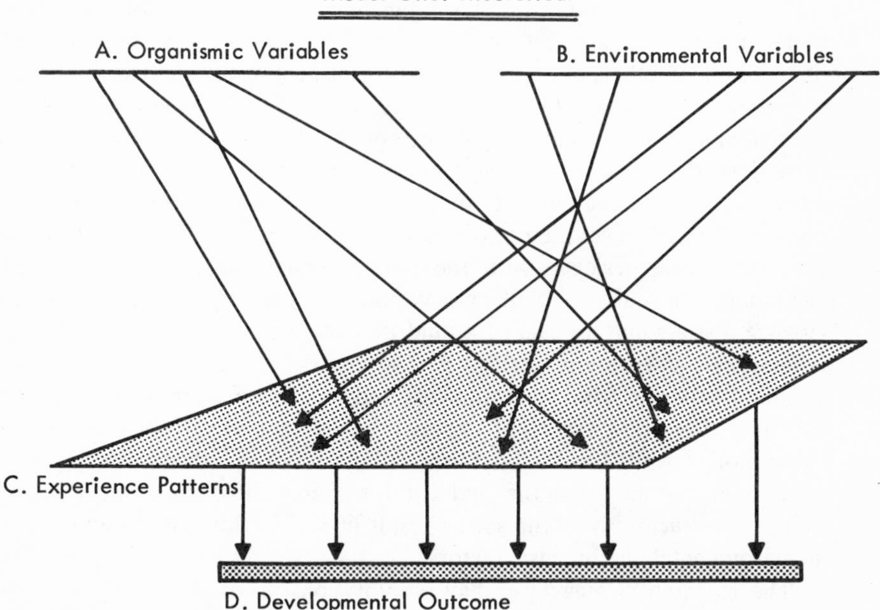

Early experience is the resultant of multiple interactions between organismic and environmental variables. Developmental outcome is a function of early experience.

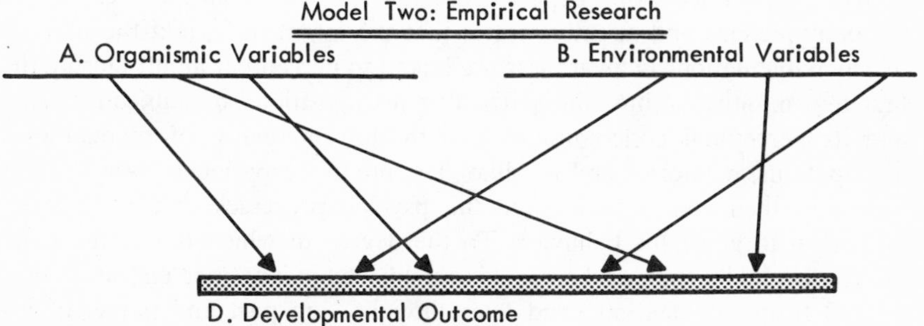

Early experience is assessed or measured by single or multiple organismic and/or environmental factors, which are directly related to developmental outcome.

itself, the particular impact that the combination of existing A and B factors has upon the child's state and behavior, would then have to be regarded as an *intervening variable.* This intervening variable links the determinants of experience to developmental outcome. That is, if attention were focused upon the developmental consequences of variations in the quality and amount of interaction that takes place between the infant and his mother, one would assess this aspect of the child's experience by looking at the interactions themselves, and not by looking only at what the mother's attitudes and feelings are, or at what she does or fails to do for and to the infant. If in interaction with the mother, the infant frequently experiences a change in state from excitation and distress to quiescence and the cessation of distress, this is a demonstrable and objective feature of his experience with the mother—but it is not an automatic consequence of maternal skill or devotion. For instance, some infants experience distress and arousal of a kind that cannot immediately be relieved by maternal intervention, such as gastric distress or painful ear infections. An infant suffering from such ailments and tended by an indulgent mother may thus share one aspect of experience with a perfectly healthy infant whose mother waits too long before feeding him or in other ways typically does not intervene to soothe and comfort him. Thus, the *same kind of actual experience* may occur as the result of widely different combinations of environmental and intrinsic factors.

The research strategy we shall employ consists of describing and assessing the intervening variables of experience in their own right, and to relate them to developmental outcome. To continue with the same (and grossly oversimplified) example, we should be inclined to explore the hypothesis that those experience patterns in early infancy in which the association of perceiving the mother's presence with relief from distress is lacking will have similar consequences for developmental outcome, however dissimilar the reasons for the lack.

By "experience" or "experience patterns" we mean the sensations, the body feelings and affective states that the infant feels, and the manner in which fluctuations in awareness are linked to perceptual input. During the first few months of life, the particular juxtapositions of subjective state and its perceptual concomitants lead to the emergence of recognitions, anticipations, memories and the like. The infant's experience, as we define the term, then comes to include the psychic processes that accompany and begin to guide his behavior. To the degree to which this is the case, the young child's goals and fears, his established inclinations and aversions, and all forms of ideation (and later thought) are part and parcel of his experience. For example, for a 3-week-old infant the experience of being held, smiled at, and patted by his mother and the experience of being handled in precisely the same manner by an unfamiliar person, may be very much alike, to judge by his behavior at such times. For a 5-month-old baby, the identical ministrations performed by the mother and by the stranger will provide a very different experience, for his behavior reflects the fact that his awareness now includes a sense of familiarity with the mother and the perceptual discrimination of unfamiliar persons. Thus, the aspect of experience that concerns an infant's exposure to direct contact with strangers (a B factor) will have different significance at the age of 5 months than at the age of 3 weeks. Still, the particular quality and intensity of the 5-month-old's experience during contact with the stranger varies from one infant to the next, as well as from time to time.

The intervening variable of experience is by definition highly subjective, which probably accounts for the fact that most psychologists have shied away from it. And indeed, experience and experience patterns can never be assessed directly—they must be inferred. We have said earlier that in most child development research, the nature of early experience is inferred on the basis of objective characteristics of the environment (Fig. 3.1, Model Two).[10] And we have expressed the opinion that, for many reasons, the assessment of experience by means of such objective criteria (the A and B factors in our diagram) is inadequate. The example of an infant's response to direct encounter with a stranger may serve to illustrate the point.

Children's experiences will differ because of the objective fact that some are cared for and dealt with almost exclusively by the mother, while others have direct contact with many strangers. The effect of this difference upon at least some aspects of the child's experience is not likely to emerge by simply comparing groups of children who have or have not been exposed to strangers frequently. If one knows how a child behaves during contacts with strangers, compared with his behavior with familiar persons, one will note the particulars of the difference in experience that occur because of this environmental variable. For infants who cry on such occasions, frequent exposures to strangers may safely be said to add to the number of occasions when distress and arousal are experienced in a social context. For infants who merely fail to respond with the pleasure and animation they show to the mother, it may safely be said that frequent encounters with strangers affect experience by reducing the frequency of pleasurable social interaction. The B variable of relatively frequent exposures to strangers is likely to have some effect in all instances. But the kind of effect and its magnitude—and hence the consequences for subsequent development—will depend on how this environmental factor alters behavior (and,

[10] The experimental study of selected aspects of early experience upon selected aspects of developmental outcome constitutes a partial exception. For instance, the effect of preschool attendance upon I.Q., or the effect of specific social stimulation on the infant's rate of vocalization, or the effect of providing stimuli to encourage grasping on the development of reaching and grasping have all relied on providing specified varieties of experience and testing the consequences for a narrowly defined aspect of development.

The problem that concerns us arises when one seeks to determine how relationships that can be produced experimentally operate under uncontrolled life conditions.

by inference, experience), how extensively it does so, and what behaviors it affects.

Our approach to the study of behavior and development has only one distinctive feature—the emphasis on direct and consistent relationships between the behavioral events that comprise the infant's experience, and the consequences of these events for the subsequent course of development. Yet, when the premise is applied to specific research issues, it has major consequences in terms of the hypotheses it generates. For instance, a backward glance at Fig. 3.1, Model One, reveals two implicit assumptions: (1) diverse constellations of organismic and environmental factors may produce similar (in theory identical) patterns of concrete experience; and (2) identical environmental conditions or events may generate quite different patterns of experience for different infants.

A further example may help to clarify the point. The environmental conditions under which two infants live may differ sharply with respect to one variable—the frequency and intensity with which the mother approaches the infant and, in one way or another, manipulates him. One mother holds him often, speaks to him frequently, and in general maintains direct contact with him during most of his waking hours. She also tends to touch him vigorously, to speak or sing to him fairly loudly, and to be generally energetic in her dealings with him. The other mother holds and touches her infant only when it is necessary, leaves him alone unless he appears to be in bodily discomfort, and also happens to be very gentle in her approach. She is a mother who speaks softly, touches the baby gingerly, and so forth. The environments of these two infants differ in that one exposes the baby to frequent and fairly intense maternal ministrations, whereas the other offers the same type of stimulation only rarely, and then at a lower level of intensity. In terms of an objective description of what is provided by the milieu, they are at opposite extremes (a B factor in our scheme).

However, the experience generated for each of these infants in the course of contact with the mother may be very similar if the babies differ markedly in terms of one organismic variable—sensitivity to perceptual stimulation (an A factor). If experience is judged by the infant's behavior while the mother deals with him, then it can be described in terms of the behavior changes that typically occur. These may be in the direction of arousal and excitation, as when the infant kicks, waves his arms, vocalizes, and otherwise becomes more active than before maternal stimulation began. They may also be in the direction of pleasure or displeasure, as when the infant smiles, chuckles, frowns, whimpers, or cries in response to maternal ministrations.

Further, maternal ministrations may set in motion particular behavior integrations such as visual focusing upon the mother's face, coordinated reaching, and participation in reciprocal interchanges that provide feedback for the infant, as he vocalizes and is "answered" by similar sounds directed toward him by the mother, or as he smiles and perceives her smiling face. If the impact of maternal ministrations upon the infant's experience is judged by behavioral criteria of this sort, the organismic difference between our two hypothetical [11] infants can affect their responsiveness to their mothers so as nearly to cancel out the difference in maternal style. If the infant cared for by the mother who provides a great deal of handling were relatively insensitive to perceptual stimulation (*i.e.,* behaviorally ignores very slight stimulation, and responds with moderate intensity to even fairly strong sound, touch, or other stimulation), his behavior as the mother handles him would range from no change during brief and slight contacts, to mild responses of the gazing, vocalizing sort, and occasional spurts of more massive behavior activation in response to intense and prolonged stimulation by the mother.

If the infant whose mother comparatively seldom engaged in direct contact with him were markedly sensitive to perceptual stimulation, even brief and gentle contact in the course of being handled would evoke marked behavior alterations. In other words, by behavioral criteria, the subjective experiences of responding to direct contact with the mother with pleasure, arousal or distress can be very similar in kind and frequency for the sensitive, highly reactive infant who receives relatively little manipulation and personal attention and the robust, not markedly reactive infant who is exposed to an unusual amount of such stimulation.

The experience of each of these babies would be different if they were cared for in a different style. The highly sensitive infant, if stimulated a great deal, would experience intense arousal very frequently and thus, in fact, be overstimulated. The fairly impassive and perceptually robust infant, if stimulated seldom and very gently, would experience a minimum of arousal in contact with the mother, and in fact be understimulated.

The model we propose is applicable to any study of the relationship between an aspect of past or present experience and a behavior characteristic or aspect of developmental outcome. Whether one's interest is in the rate of intellectual development as reflected on test performance, or in individual characteristics of personality functioning—such as fearfulness, aggressivity, or frustration tolerance—the independent variable(s) would always be relevant aspects of the child's experience as reflected by behavioral criteria. To give one last example, if one sought to determine the relative effectiveness of reward and punishment upon an aspect of subsequent development, such as independence, it would not be enough to know parental practices in terms of the controlling devices they employ. In order to describe the relevant experience one would have to know both what the

[11] These are in fact schematized condensations and not inventions. The individual case studies presented in the Adaptation Syndromes (Chs. 13, 14, 15) contain examples for each of the extremes mentioned in the text above.

parents did and how the child responded. A measure used by the parents as reward may not be perceived as such by the child if he does not derive enjoyment from what he is given, or if he fails to see the connection between the reward and his behavior. Punishing actions may not constitute punishment if the child is gratified by the attention he thus receives.

It will be recognized that the assumptions we have made go beyond the mere substitution of behavior-in-context as an objective measure of subjective experience for the independent measure of external or intrinsic factors. In our view (again, as depicted in Fig. 3.1, Model One), the behavior stream viewed over time—that is, the aggregate of experience over weeks, months, and years—is simultaneously the determinant of development, the process of development, and the result or product of development.[12] "Development" is an abstraction and refers to changes in behavior insofar as they reflect the manner in which the organism changes in its responsiveness to objectively unaltered situations. The change from cooing to speech in words; the change from being able to move only body segments to the ability to locomote in space; the change from behavioral response only to immediate perceptual input to behavior dictated by memories, goals, and anticipations; and all other developmental sequences reflect changes in how the growing child behaves and responds. Developmental change is therefore conceptualized as an alteration within the organism. New patterns of functioning signal the emergence of new structures, or of more complex integration of previously acquired capacities and structures.

In many areas, the sequence of new behavioral adaptations that constitute development is regular, orderly, and similar for all children. The very notion of "normal development" is based on the fact that certain patterns of behavior are so regularly seen at certain ages that their failure to emerge on time (or their appearance ahead of schedule) is a significant exception. The great regularity of many developmental sequences rests on what we have called organismic characteristics, which include the structure of the nervous system and all biological attributes of the species. However, our model would not permit ascribing any developmental sequence to "maturation," if by that term is meant the mere unfolding of completely prestructured and internally programmed actualization of inherent capacities. Rather we think that by virtue of organismic similarities and also common features in the physical and social environment for all infants, many elements of experience are similar or identical for all. We assume that all

[12] While this formulation may appear so sweeping as to blur the boundaries between antecedent conditions or events and consequent or subsequent events, this is not the case. Any process viewed in time perspective has the same property. What exists or what happens at a given point in time can always be regarded as the result of what preceded it, as an example of ongoing process, or as the antecedent of what is to occur. It is the abstracting and organizing function of the investigator that imposes structure, and it is the definition of the particular research problem that dictates which aspects of behavior are selected to serve as antecedent variables, and which behavioral events may prove to be dependent on the particular independent variable chosen.

infants have in common a great many patterns of experience, by virtue of the fact that given identical features of the nervous system and the environment (in terms of the physical surroundings and the biosocial necessity that infants must be fed and cared for by adults) yield the same experience patterns.

When deviance occurs, we seek its causes in environmental and intrinsic factors, and therefore scientific curiosity has been directed primarily at the obstacles to normal development, almost as though normal development itself required no explanation, much as the phenomenon of falling objects did not demand an explanation until the law of gravity made it relevant to an understanding of the universe. The focus on experience as reflected by behavior-in-context requires that every aspect of developmental change, however regular and ordinary, be comprehended as the result of specifiable necessary and sufficient antecedents.[13]

Not all aspects of developmental change are regular and normative; individual differences in the rate of development and in its pattern occur within the realm of normative behavior. Such differences within the normal range are attributable to variations in experience patterns. Further, the term "development" includes not only bodily coordinations and cognitive skills, but also affective experience and the control of impulse, attitudes, and interests, preferred styles of adaptation, and a host of behavior attributes subsumed under such terms as personality, character, or temperament. We take it that a child or an adult who is timid and unassertive has acquired these characteristics in the course of his development, just as he has acquired attitudes, value structures, or any of the other characteristics in which persons differ from one another. Our suggestion is that the more variable portions of developmental outcome—the characteristics that may be rare or frequent, but are by no means normative—are determined by the highly variable aspects of experience. The same assumption has been made by all who investigated personality type or structure as a function of different cultures (by nation, by ethnic groups, by socioeconomic status, etc.). In our view it applies also to differences within the same cultural milieu. If within the same family or the same culture one child proves to be outgoing and another seclusive, one is given to affect storms and another is controlled, one prefers books and the other athletics—we judge these differences to be the result of demonstrable differences in each child's experience.

A research venture that began with the modest aim of describing individual differences in the behavior of young infants and relating them to differences in intrinsic biological characteristics and environmental variations led to a formulation that applies to the regular and invariant aspects of development quite as much as to the genesis of individual differences. Re-

[13] For certain aspects of cognitive development, Piaget's work is the outstanding example of the contribution made by this approach.

search operations performed with data obtained from a cross-sectional study led to a central hypothesis that can be tested only by longitudinal methods.

Finally, a research focus on the functioning and development of normal infants led to an approach that is equally applicable to the study of the genesis of developmental deviation and psychopathology. Yet, as we have tried to describe in this chapter, radical changes in how developmental processes may best be studied are proposed, without proposing a single new substantive hypothesis or constructing a new theory of development. What we have done instead is to select among the existing developmental theories those that appear most illuminating and most applicable to the phenomena of child behavior and development as they occur in nature; these theoretical approaches have leaned on concepts and methods closely allied to general biology. By contrast, much of the academic child development research has selected concepts and methods akin to those used in the advanced natural sciences (specifically nineteenth-century physics). We have further examined prevalent research strategy from the point of view of its congruence with prevalent developmental theory, and concluded that the failure to either disprove or confirm hypotheses about early experience as a determinant of individual differences is the result of a discrepancy between, on one hand, the substantive premises of interactional theories of development and, on the other, empirical research procedures. The facts and ideas reported in this book constitute a first attempt to explore the behavior and development of infants by methods that are consistent with the interactional and "organismic" view of child development and designed to meet the need for more precise phenomenological description of infant behavior and of developmental changes in behavior during the all important first few months of life.

FOUR

○○
○

BASIC DATA AND METHODS OF DATA ANALYSIS

In an earlier research project [1] the author, in association with a group of colleagues, undertook to describe individual differences in the behavior of 128 normal infants, all of whom were reared by their natural parents in normally functioning intact families. This book is based upon the intensive analysis of 32 infant subjects who were members of that original larger study. The raw data for this book are entirely material collected as part of the earlier project; this is but one of a number of publications based on the data collected in the original study.

Some acquaintance with the methods of data collection employed in the first study is necessary. The project, entitled *Early Phases of Personality Development,* was a complex enterprise. It was intended to provide a pool of factual information about infants and their families in the hope that such information would lend itself to varied research purposes. In order to avoid the awkwardness of having to describe the sample, the research procedure, and the techniques anew each time, the first project publication was a monograph giving the background information for all subsequent research reports.[2]

The project was directed by the author and codirected by Mary Leitch, M.D., a child psychiatrist and psychoanalyst. These two designed the study and participated in data collection throughout. At all times, the research staff included additional experienced personnel, most of whom were psychologists by training.[3] The study took place in a midwestern city of modest size, and all infant subjects were enrolled by their parents voluntarily. It was explained to the families that not enough is known about the behavior of normal infants, and that an opportunity to observe babies under natural circumstances would result in better understanding of how and why infants grow up to become distinct and individual personalities. No compensation

[1] *Early Phases of Personality Development,* supported (in part) by a grant from the National Institutes of Health, USPHS (1947–1951).

[2] For a detailed account of how our data were obtained, the reader is referred to this monograph (Escalona and Leitch, 1953).

[3] The following persons participated in the project and share responsibility and credit for what was accomplished: Anna Kulka, M.D. (1947–48); Margaret McFarland (1948–49); Sylvia Brody (1949–50); Grace Heider (1949–51); and Irene Hollingsworth (1950–51).

or reward attached to participation in the study (even the results of developmental testing were not communicated), unless a gift to the parents of photographs of their children were to be so regarded. As fully described in the earlier publication, participating mothers appeared to enjoy the research sessions, and many new enrollments occurred informally as study mothers referred us to their friends and relatives.

The population of the original study consisted of eight boys and eight girls at each monthly (lunar) age level, beginning at age 4 weeks and continuing through age 32 weeks: 128 infants in all. In order to obtain the best possible picture of the *range* of normal behavior, a cross-sectional approach was chosen, so that each of the 128 infants was studied only once, for a period of about one week.[4] The socioeconomic status of study families ranged from above average (35 per cent) to below average (22 per cent). The ordinal position of infant subjects ranged from first to fifth, with 41 per cent being firstborn babies. Despite considerable variation in socioeconomic status, religious affiliation, the age of the mother, and other respects, these families lived in a fairly homogeneous cultural and social climate, at least by comparison with urban samples. All were settled members of a community that could be described as stable and conventional in its customs and—at that time—relatively unaffected by the uncertainties and upheavals that characterize a society in transition.

The primary research method was direct observation of each infant and his mother by multiple trained observers. In the course of pilot studies that extended over years, the investigators developed observational skills and techniques to assess the reliability of their protocols. Each new staff member was entrusted with responsibility for data collection only after she had met the same criteria of reliability. In addition, once a year a reliability check was carried out among all observers. When indicated, a series of retraining sessions (using filmed records) followed, during which observers reconciled their differences in terminology.[5]

The study of each infant yielded the following records and types of information:

1. Description of initial contact with each family.

2. A full description of the interview[6] with the mother, which took place while mother and infant spent half a day at project quarters.

3. Running record: during the four- to five-hour session at research quarters, a record was kept, providing a detailed log (by 5-minute inter-

[4] Lois Murphy and associates conducted a longitudinal study on another small sample of these subjects.

[5] It may also be relevant to mention that during the last year of the project, all case files were examined for the quality of the records and for agreement among the different observations covering the same time intervals. If records were incomplete, or if agreement was less than good, the case was dropped and another infant of like age and sex was studied and included instead.

[6] Interview material was used in this book only in the Adaptation Syndromes (Chs. 13, 14, 15) and there to a minimal degree. For a description of interview techniques and content, please see the earlier publication (Escalona and Leitch, 1953).

vals) of the events occurring during the entire session. The protocol kept track of where each person was in space and of what they were doing. It described the conditions prevailing during each 5-minute interval, including incidental noises, notable changes in temperature, or any other thing that might have affected the behavior of any person in the room. Insofar as possible, the running record also contained detailed behavior data on both mother and infant.

4. Detailed observational records: these consisted of narrative records focused upon a sequential and detailed account of the behavior of the infant, including as much as possible about the immediate and specific perceptual input (*i.e.,* mother's touch, sounds, etc.), although the behavior of the mother and the observers was covered in the running record.

5. Descriptive protocol of home visit: home visits were made within ten days of the session at research quarters. The primary purpose was to observe the baby's behavior in his usual surroundings, for additional information and for comparison with his behavior during the session at our quarters. The home visit also provided an opportunity for additional interviewing of the mother, and, in many instances, for supplementary interviews with other members of the family.

6. Test protocols and interpretative write-ups of two developmental tests (Cattell Infant Intelligence Scale; Gesell Developmental Schedules).

7. Record of pediatric examination and physical growth measurements.

8. A series of special ratings, performed independently by all observers. These included activity level before and after feeding, during a 5-minute interval while alert and content, and for the entire session; as well as ratings of tissue resistance, leg resistance, and strength of grip. Cardiac and respiratory rates while awake and asleep were also obtained.[7]

9. Kymograph tracings and counter readings of activity before and after feeding (obtained by means of a stabilimeter).

10. Filmed records of behavior during feeding and spontaneous activity (usually about 500 ft. each).

11. Questionnaire. Upon completion of the study, each mother filled out a questionnaire designed to reveal maternal attitudes. It asked mothers to define a series of words frequently used in connection with infant care (*i.e.,* spoiling, neglecting, etc.).

The general issue of the advantages and limitations of direct observation as a research tool has been amply discussed in the literature.[8] In our view, the usefulness of the method depends upon the degree to which the resulting data lend themselves to systematic analysis, and the degree to which such analysis points to phenomena and relationships that prove of interest. The reader will form his own opinion on this point.

[7] The techniques are described in the monograph by Escalona and Leitch (1953).

[8] See among others: Barker and Wright (1949); Wright and Barker (1950); Benjamin (1950); Escalona and Leitch (1952); Barker (1963); Escalona (1963); Radke-Yarrow (1963); Wolff (1964); Barker (1964); Gewirtz and Gewirtz (1965); and Moss (1965).

If it is granted that narrative records by multiple observers can accurately reflect a large proportion of the behavior that took place, a cross-sectional study of the kind we have described still has many limitations. What we obtained was an extended time sample of the experience and behavior of each infant subject, augmented by sufficient information about the baby's history and about the family to place the time-limited data in perspective. The study was designed to elicit information about the immediate behavioral response of young infants to events and circumstances that are recurrent and stable components of their daily life. It was designed also to provide information about maternal styles and practices as shown during direct encounters with the infant. Lastly, it was designed to identify and describe infant behavior tendencies that manifest themselves in a wide variety of situations (individual differences). Such an aggregate of descriptive data lends itself only to exploratory research. In other words, it can lead to the discovery of phenomena, and it allows for the construction of hypotheses on an empirical basis.

The Small Sample

In order to highlight individual differences among normal infants (and to reduce the amount of data to manageable proportions) a smaller sample of subjects was selected for intensive study. When the data were being collected, activity level was a variable of special interest and was assessed very carefully. Therefore, the small sample was selected to include the extremes of high and low activity level that occurred at each age level in the original sample. Thus, from among the sixteen 4-week-old infants we selected the two who had received the highest activity level ratings and the two who had received the lowest. The same procedure was followed for each age level, yielding a group of 32 subjects for the intensive study.

At the time of the original study overall activity level was rated for each subject on a three-point scale as follows:

1 = *Relatively small amount of activity,* frequently of low intensity, but within the normal range [9] (does not exclude occasional periods of energetic movement under strong stimulation).

2 = *Medium amount of activity.* Covers a wide range in that it applies to all infants who are neither conspicuously active nor conspicuously inactive.

3 = *Large amounts of activity,* frequently forceful, but within the normal range [9] (does not exclude brief periods of low activity or quiescence).

To the reader who has never applied this type of rating to infant behavior, the above definitions may appear to be vague. However, differences

[9] Hyper- and hypoactive infants were assigned ratings of 3+ and 1− respectively, and were eliminated from the sample as failing to meet our criteria of normalcy.

in activity level among young infants are marked and consistent, and experienced observers encounter no difficulty in arriving at such a judgment. In our research group, rater reliability on this item ranged from 97 to 99 per cent. In fact, though it was not originally planned, the research staff refined the scale by attaching a plus or minus sign to the rating of those infants who fell close to the upper or lower limits within their activity group. The resulting 7-point scale proved reliable; agreement among at least three observers ranged from 85 to 92 per cent. The final activity level values as reported in these pages consist of pooled ratings of three independent judgments (a plus or minus sign was given a weight of .3).

Table 4.1—The Sample by Age, Sex, Activity Level, Socioeconomic Level, and Ordinal Position

Active Subjects	Age	SEX M	SEX F	Ordin.	Socio-economic Level[a]	Inactive Subjects	Age	SEX M	SEX F	Ordin.	Socio-economic Level[a]
I	4		1	1	UM	I	4		1	4	UL or LL
II	4	1		1	UM	II	4	1		2	UL
III	8		1	1	LM	III	8		1	2	LM
IV	8		1	1	LL	IV	8	1		1	UM
V	12	1		1	LL	V	12		1	2	UL
VI	12		1	1	UM	VI	12	1		4	LM
VII	16	1		2	LM	VII	16		1	3	LM
VIII	16		1	2	UL	VIII	16	1		2	LM
IX	20		1	1	UM	IX	20		1	3	LL
X	20	1		2	UM or LM	X	20		1	3	LL
XI	24	1		1	LM	XI	24		1	2	UM
XII	24	1		1	LM	XII	24		1	2	UM or LM
XIII	28	1		2	UM	XIII	28		1	1	LM
XIV	28		1	1	UM	XIV	28	1		3	LM
XV	32	1		2	UL	XV	32		1	3	UM
XVI	32	1		1	UL or ML	XVI	32	1		2	LL
N Subjects		9	7					6	10		

[a] Classification of socioeconomic status according to Warner (Warner, Meeker, and Eels, 1949).

Legend:
UM = Upper middle class
MM = Middle middle class
LM = Lower middle class
UL = Upper lower class
ML = Middle lower class
LL = Lower lower class

Table 4.1 describes the small sample in terms of the infant's activity level, age, sex, and ordinal position, as well as the socioeconomic status of the family. The table shows that activity level was not equally high (or equally low) at all age levels. By chance, there were fewer very active infants in the 16- and 20-weeks levels of the original study than in the older or younger groups. The direction of the difference between infants at each age level was identical for all, but the magnitude of the difference varied. Our procedure also yielded an imbalanced distribution of the sexes (fifteen boys and seventeen girls), and in several other ways this small sample is not fully representative of the much larger research population from which it was drawn.[10] Since no attempt is made to generalize from our small sample to the population as a whole, these partial inequalities are of little consequence.

Procedures of Data Analysis

Narrative records are a heterogenous assembly of events that overlap and occur simultaneously. To transform written observations into research data requires that elements or aspects of the material be abstracted and then ordered in terms of these abstractions. The material in our case files has been treated to such manipulations in many ways. Each new element that was isolated led us to the perception of behavior attributes or possible relationships that we had not thought to explore before. The methods and techniques used for the presentation of material in this book are a distillation of many years of work with the same raw data. These methods survived because they came closest to the goal of going beyond mere description in the account of behavior regularities. Going beyond mere description means, in this context, that for each assertion we performed manipulations of the data to test whether or not it was compatible with *all* the available information. In other words, we took pains to find in the material all instances and circumstances where behavior differed from what had been asserted, or where a relationship between phenomena that had been described was not manifest. Before turning to a discussion of the methods of data analysis that were found ultimately useful, we will briefly review the major prior steps in organizing the material, to show how we arrived at the final format.

THE CASE ANALYSIS

In the course of collecting data for the major project we developed a set of categories that came to be referred to as the "case analysis." Individual differences in the behavior of the infants and in the environmental conditions to which they were exposed were made explicit by means of this instrument. It took the form of a schedule with fifteen major topics, each with a large number of subheadings. It moved from the areas of physical growth and somatic functioning to the sensorium, and from there to the child's responsiveness to recurrent need states (hunger, fatigue) and their satisfaction. Developmental attainments (neuromuscular coordination, vocalizations) were specified next, and then motility. The tempo of all behavior (from respiratory rates to the speed of food intake) was a transitional category, leading to an enumeration of more qualitative and psycho-

[10] For instance, Table 4.1 suggests a strong association between high activity level and being the firstborn child. In the larger sample a trend existed in the same direction, but it was not of the same magnitude.

logically descriptive headings. These included persistency and effort expended in self-initiated activity; the manner in which the child dealt with and responded to the inanimate environment; and a category we labeled as "reaction to and use of own body."

The child's response to and interaction with other human beings was an especially important heading. The last categories dealt with affect manifestations, and with an assessment of the social and physical environment in its direct effect on the infant. Nearly anything that can be observed about an infant found a place in this scheme, although milieu factors were dealt with on a very global level.

The case analysis proved a valuable background for later and more detailed assessments. Entries under each heading consisted of a summary of the behavior episodes observed with page references to locate each of these episodes in the case folder. A separate section summarized or quoted relevant parental reports and comments (again with page references to the source). The case analyses made it possible to compare any of the infants with respect to a large number of behavior characteristics.

THE SYNDROME ANALYSIS

In the form of case analyses, the material lent itself to the identification of behavior aspects that varied greatly from one infant to the next, in contrast to those behaviors that tended to be fairly uniform. However, it did not provide a means of assessing overall central characteristics of each baby, nor did it facilitate a study of the interrelationships among different behavior tendencies noted in the same child.

Previous work had led to the belief that it is possible to construct a typology of infant behavior, in that certain characteristics tend to go together. For instance, cumulative observation had suggested that one such *behavior syndrome* (a term we prefer to "type") consists of the simultaneous presence of these characteristics: high activity level, low tolerance for frustration and restraint, relatively undifferentiated social responsiveness, and a tendency to experience gastric distress, although food is typically accepted with eagerness. By contrast, the behavior syndrome associated with low activity level was thought to include a tendency to develop skin rashes (including those of allergic origin), notably high discrimination and sensitivity in response to the social environment, and a tendency to experience feeding difficulties (poor appetite, inefficient sucking, resistance to solid feedings, etc.), though gastric disturbances are rare.

The syndrome analysis was designed to discover clusters or patterns among widely different characteristics of behavior and functioning in the same child. It completely disregarded the conditions to which each child had to adapt, and sought for consistency only in terms of the infant's stable behavior patterns and reaction tendencies. The syndrome analysis took the form of a topically indexed card file for each subject. The entries constituted an entirely new organization of the raw data, in that they documented judgments concerning such variables as social sensitivity, perceptual sensitivity, frustration tolerance, and lability in the functioning of various body systems. As in the previous analysis, documentation consisted of the enumeration of specific behaviors or other facts, complete with page references to the source.

It was possible to demonstrate for this sample that activity level tends to be associated with certain behavioral and somatic proclivities, as had been hypothesized. However, this fact alone proved to be of scant interest, since, in comparing sixteen active with sixteen inactive infants, the occasional exceptions were quite as impressive as the consistencies. Far more important than the positive findings was the recognition that a behavior (or somatic attribute) is of interest only when viewed in the light of its functional consequences for the infant's experience. It was while working with the syndrome analyses that we learned how a given characteristic, such as high activity level, may increase or decrease the occurrence of distress in a baby's life; and how the same characteristic may facilitate or retard developmental progress—always depending on the environmental circumstances and on other and independent reaction tendencies. It was also in the course of working with the syndrome analysis that waxing and waning states of excitation were recognized as a central issue. When the focus of interest shifted to the description of the adaptive consequences of particular behavior characteristics, it became all important to investigate each variety of behavior as it was linked to body states and to the conditions of external stimulation to which it was responsive. Hence, we undertook a new and still more detailed assessment of the contents of the original case files.

The Final Methods

As described in Chapter 3, we decided to use the research data for two major purposes: (1) to describe the phenomenology of normal infant behavior during the first eight months of life and to formulate hypotheses about the relevance of particular behavior activations to ongoing developmental changes; and (2) to explore the possibility that individual differences among normal infants are consistently related to experience patterns that are prominent and stable components of the infant's day-by-day existence. Accordingly, the report on results is divided into two major sections. In Part Two, phenomenological description is combined with the demonstration of behavioral differences between markedly active and markedly inactive babies; in addition, developmental changes during the first half year of life are discussed. Part Three delineates for each infant certain recurrent patterns of experience. These experience patterns are derived from particular constellations of organismic and environmental factors. The relationships between different patterns of experience and differences in the infant's developmental and adaptive status are examined.

The methods of analysis used in Part Two are entirely different from those employed in Part Three. Procedures and techniques will be described in the text; an appendix to each chapter (*Supplementary Material*) contains a complete account of criteria and procedures used for the various ratings, as well as most of the quantitative results.

We shall discuss methodological choices and issues in more general terms here, and in particular define the method in terms of its virtues and its limitations.

BEHAVIOR EPISODES AND THE DISTINCTION BETWEEN STIMULUS CONDITION AND BEHAVIORAL RESPONSE

Behavior is continuous; it consists of sequential changes that occur simultaneously on several levels and in a number of qualitatively different ways. The systematic analysis of overt behavior under uncontrolled conditions is a difficult research tool. That it can be used at all is due to the fact that behavior is also structured; it falls into natural divisions in the form of behavioral events or episodes.

For instance, an infant may be seated in his crib, and his glance may be attracted to a toy at some distance. While regarding it he may begin to stir and to vocalize, and soon he may shift into the hand-knee posture and creep toward the toy. Upon arrival he may grasp it and bring it to his mouth. From the moment when he first looked at the toy to the moment when he brought it to his mouth, his behavior was governed by his awareness of the toy. Or rather, his behavior was governed by the action impulses that were evoked by his perception of the toy. When behavior is analyzed from the point of view of the child's response to and engagement with objects in the environment (which is one of the dimensions discussed in Chapter 2), the sequence we have described constitutes a single episode.

The same sequence also lends itself to analysis in terms of many other dimensions of behavior. It furnishes information about the infant's responsiveness to visual components of the environment, because it was the *sight* of the object that initiated the episode. Similarly, it enters the description of the infant's vocal behavior, for he responded to the sight of the object first by brief cooing, accompanied by a slight increase in activity, but ceased to vocalize as he locomoted toward the object and reached it. The sequence is equally relevant for an assessment of motility. It yields four instances of coordinated voluntary movement (shift from sitting to hand-knee position; creeping; reaching for an object; bringing it to his mouth) and one instance of diffuse random motion (the stirring at first sight of the toy). Each of the component movement episodes can be classified with respect to intensity, tempo and degree of coordination (for instance, the initial stirring lacks coordination; creeping may be wobbly and not yet smoothly integrated; reaching and grasping may be performed with delicate precision).

When analysis is directed to the conditions that elicit activity increases, the same sequence furnishes an instance in that the sight of the toy roused the infant to a greater level of bodily activity than before. The sequence further contributes to information about non-nutritive oral behavior (bringing toy to mouth) which can be further classified in terms of the oral activation that ensued (sucking, licking, biting, etc.). It may also contribute to the description of affective behavior if, for instance, the baby smiled on seeing the toy, or if transient distress was shown as the infant encountered difficulty in creeping. Finally, the episode occurred during what we have called "spontaneous activity," and will contribute to an account of the behavior activations that occur (frequently or rarely) in that situation.

The relevant external conditions include the fact that the infant was in the crib, yet free to move (not confined by clothing or by blankets), and that there was a toy in sight, but not in reach. Further, the infant's state while engaged in spontaneous activity is also a variable that requires specification (awake/alert; fatigued; subject to teething discomfort, etc.). This example is an illustration to show how all behavior sequences were analyzed in different contexts to yield the data that will be reported.

Since we are interested in the degree to which particular behaviors or behavior attributes are linked to the conditions of stimulation (or perceptual input), and the degree to which they are determined by the infant's state, it was necessary to perform separate analyses of what might be called behavior output (movements, affect expressions, vocalizations, etc.) and of the input factors (the content of the perceptual field); and then a separate analysis in terms of the infant's state (alert, fatigued, etc.). When the behaviors themselves (output) were the primary focus of analysis, the situational and state variables were always included. In analyzing stimulus conditions or states, the behavior output that occurred under particular stimulus conditions was always specified. This principle of "double entry" is the main feature of the methods used to trace the determinants and the fate of specific behavior activations.

It may not be immediately apparent why it should be necessary to ascertain the combination of stimulus condition and behavior twice: once by listing all the conditions under which a behavior occurred, and once by listing all the behaviors that occurred under a single stimulus condition. An example may clarify the point. In studying the behavioral consequences of bodily need states, we tabulated all of the behaviors these babies showed before feeding and before falling asleep. Under both of these conditions, many babies sucked their fingers and engaged in other forms of mouthing.

need states, it might have been concluded that hunger and fatigue induce oral behavior. However, when the records were scrutinized for each instance of oral behavior and the situations and states in which it occurred, we found that many of the babies showed equally intense and frequent oral behavior at other times as well—for instance, during spontaneous activity while alert and content, or in the wake of events that initially evoked displeasure (when mother left after playing with them or when a toy dropped from their hand). So for the infants who showed as much oral behavior at other times as they did when hungry and fatigued, it would not be accurate to say that in their experience bodily need states were linked to oral behavior.

The comparison of active with inactive infants in each of the eight dimensions of behavior was thus based on the result of analyzing behavior episodes for all infants by the double entry method. The actual procedure (which is fully described in Part Two) was to carry out frequency counts and assessments of a single variable for all subjects in a given age group. For instance, to obtain ratings on how each subject responded to the offer of an object (brought into his visual field by another person), we went through at least eight case files (belonging to one age group, see p. 83) and recorded all instances where the infant responded to a proffered toy or other object, noting whether he gazed at it, reached for it, or responded in any other way. This yielded lists and tabulations enumerating particular responses to the sight of a proffered object, along with the frequency of each for individual subjects, for the active group compared with the inactive group, and for the age groups as a whole. The next step was to begin anew and scrutinize the same records in terms of the frequency with which toys were presented to each baby and the way he responded on each occasion (including instances when the infant ignored the proffered toy although he had clearly seen it). This yielded tabulations reflecting differences among infants and among groups of infants in terms of the frequency with which they were exposed to the stimulus condition.

It was not feasible to follow the usual custom of having independent raters perform these procedures, largely because no one but the author could be expected to tolerate the tedium involved, but also because the cost would have been prohibitive. A number of safeguards were employed to reduce the influence of the rater's anticipations and memories to a minimum. Since the assessments were based on counted episodes, and each instance of a relevant behavior or situation was listed, rigid adherence to the predetermined scoring criteria was enforced. Further, the rule of performing tabulations for a single variable on at least eight subjects in succession served to reduce the so-called "halo effect." When we looked for a particular behavior in the record of a given subject, we were totally unable to recall the result of ratings he might have received on other variables because so many similar behavior episodes had been reviewed.

Our methods are not original, though some of the built-in controls for consistency and accuracy are innovations. Among those investigators [11] who rely on direct observations as a primary research tool, Barker, Wright, and their associates have published most extensively about ways in which narrative material can be transformed into quantifiable data.[12] They developed criteria to determine the onset and termination of behavior episodes, and they devised means of denoting the hierarchical structure of behavioral events. Barker and Wright were able to demonstrate compelling relationships between what they call "behavior settings" and the behavior each setting is likely to elicit. A large proportion of individual differences can be described in terms of the fact that different children have access to different behavior settings and with greater or lesser frequency.

Our analysis of the behavior stream in young infants has a good deal in common with the ecological method as used by Barker and Wright.[13] Because of these similarities, it is important to point out the differences. In psychological ecology as developed by these authors, the structure of an episode is derived from the goals that shaped the behavior. For instance, if a child decides to eat an apple, the relevant behavior episode might begin as he asks for permission and end as he takes the first bite. The goal or the intention that shapes an action is recognized by verbal communication by the subject and/or by the end result. Thus, if a child is seen to run in a certain direction, it is assumed that he intended to go in that direction (or to go away from where he was), although the child may not provide an explanation.

Even if one were to accept the assumption that behavior in older individuals is always guided by its consequences, infant behavior is frequently not structured in this manner. At least during the first half year of life, what babies do can often be understood as a reaction to a state or to certain conditions of stimulation, but there is no reason to assume that the behavior is based on anticipation of the end result. On the contrary, the emergence of the capacity for voluntary and intentional action is a hallmark of early stages of development. In our analysis of infant behavior, episodes were structured by the criterion of *behavior change* and by the *functional accompaniments* and *consequences* of the infant's action. If a baby lay fairly quietly and then began to kick and wave his arms, only to subside again, the spurt of body activation would be regarded as an episode. If a mother made playful approaches to her baby, and the infant cooed and smiled while these lasted but ceased smiling as the mother

[11] See, for instance, Meili (1957a); Radke-Yarrow (1963); Gewirtz and Gewirtz (1965); Marschak (1960); Moss (1965); and Yarrow and Goodwin (1965).

[12] See Barker and Wright (1949); Barker (1963a, 1963b, 1965); Wright and Barker (1950).

[13] The fact that independently we developed similar techniques may have a good deal to do with the fact that we share an earlier professional experience; namely, close association with Kurt Lewin.

withdrew, we should regard this as an episode of social interaction. Intentional and goal-directed action of a simple sort constituted but one of many kinds of event structures with which we dealt.

A second important difference between our approach and that of Barker and Wright is our interest not only in *what* was done, but in *how* it was done. In psychological ecology, verbal explanation, physiognomic expression, the speed of movement, etc., are used to infer the underlying structure of the situation; they are not studied in their own right. To return to the previous example, a child may eat an apple because he feels like it or he may eat it because he has been told that he must. The difference between a situation of unimpeded goal striving (eating for pleasure) and one of social compulsion would be assessed by ecological methods, and the discrimination would be made on the basis of how the child performed the action, his facial expression, and the quality of his movements (as well as by what he said). In this approach, slow and reluctant movements, many pauses, a facial expression of disgust, or a verbal expression of dislike would be *equivalent* to one another in that each indicates a situation in which the child performs an action contrary to his own inclination. In our analysis of the same episode, similar inferences would be made about the distinction between self-generated activity and social compulsion. But the manner in which the child shows eagerness or reluctance (by words, by quality of motion, by tone of voice, etc.) would also become a variable, to be assessed in its own right as a dimension of individual differences. Correspondingly, the parents' manner of securing obedience would be of primary importance as an individual difference in the environment.

We have used a somewhat absurd example in order to make the point that the same series of behavior episodes, observed and recorded in the same manner, can be viewed so as to yield lawful regularities of different sorts. If the analysis be ecological, what will be assessed is behavior as a function of environmental context or behavior setting. If the analysis be directed at the psychological study of individual differences, what will be assessed are consistencies in the behavior of a single child across a wide variety of situations or behavior settings, as well as the different forms that the same basic event structure can assume. Needless to say, neither approach can be carried out in pure form. In what is to follow, we shall report a good deal about the compelling power of behavior settings, but chiefly as a background against which to measure the range of individual differences.

THE COMPARISON OF ACTIVE WITH INACTIVE INFANTS

The enumeration of behavior tendencies for each member of an active and an inactive group of infant subjects cannot be used immediately to compare the groups. The behaviors that were observed, classified, and counted varied as a function of many factors besides activity level.

One basic principle was to compare the behavior differences between active and inactive infants under very similar conditions of stimulation. For instance, if social responsiveness was the subject of comparison, it had to be based upon the behavior of active or inactive babies at times when the nature and intensity of "social stimulation" were similar. That is, one infant could be compared with another at times when stimulation was the sight of the mother's smiling countenance at a distance, or when the social partner was close by, or when laughter or speech as well as touch were part of the mother's playful approach.

Even when comparisons are made separately for behavioral response to highly similar states and situations, it is not possible to compare the entire active group of infants with the entire group of inactive ones because the behavioral capacities of babies less than 3 months of age are altogether different from those of older babies. In the age group that concerns us here, each month brings so much developmental change that comparison of the entire group in terms of specific behavior situations becomes meaningless. To meet this intrinsic difficulty, the demonstration of behavior characteristics associated with activity level required cumbersome manipulations which will be briefly summarized below (for a full description see Part Two).

THE CONTRAST ANALYSIS

The basic model of the analysis was the comparison of pairs of subjects, each member of the pair being of the same chronological age, but differing in activity level. The 32 subjects were grouped into sixteen pairs, which were numbered in order of chronological age; there were two pairs at each age level. Individual subjects will be identified throughout in terms of their pair membership. Active I (Ac I) refers to the most active 4-week-old in the sample, and Inactive I (In I) to the least active infant of the same age. Pair II (Ac II and In II) refers to the second most active and second least active 4-week-old. Carrying this system through, then, Pair XV designates the most active and inactive 32-week-old infants, and Pair XVI the second most and second least active infants in the same age group.

The comparison of active with inactive subjects for any single aspect of behavior rests upon a series of sixteen comparisons. These comparisons were arrived at on the basis of yet another extensive set of documents, to which we refer as the *Contrast Analyses*.[14] For each pair of infants the contrast analysis provides information about the same aspect of behavior or the same components of environmental stimulation, on parallel columns

[14] The Contrast Analysis is described in a previous publication (Escalona, 1963).

of the same page (see *Supplementary Material* for an outline). The Contrast Analysis provided a new and systematic review of each individual case; it was focused on the separate assessment of behavior and of the conditions to which behavior was responsive. Such an arrangement not only brought together the required data for all subjects, but also led to the identification of behavior differences encountered among individual pairs. Each difference observed in a single pair could then be looked for in all other pairs, and thus become a hypothesis for group differences to be tested on the sample as a whole.

All subsequent elaborations and regroupings of the data were based on the detailed account of relevant information contained in the Contrast Analyses. Nevertheless, it was occasionally necessary to return to the original file to check for items of which we became aware at a later time.

PAIR AND CROSS-PAIR COMPARISONS

In establishing the behavioral correlates of high and low activity level, the small number of pairs was a real limitation. Since the sample contained four subjects at each age level, it was possible to test more critically the association between a given behavior tendency and activity level. If the difference between Ac I and In I was due to the activity level variable, Ac I should differ from In II (also a 4-week-old) in the same direction, and the difference between Ac II and In I should also conform. Such realignment or cross-comparison for each set of pairs yielded a total of 32 comparisons on each variable, always pairing an active infant with an inactive one of the same age.

COMPARISON BY AGE GROUPS

A comparison limited to a series of single pairs conveys only a narrow range of the behaviors that, in aggregate, provide evidence for the consequences of activity level for behavior. Further, it provides no opportunity for exploring the possibility that activity level may influence behavior only for the youngest or only for the oldest babies. Since the range of behavioral capacities and situational contexts overlaps for adjacent age levels, we divided our subjects into three groups:

Group One: Pairs I through VI, ages 4, 8, and 12 weeks, 12 subjects.

Group Two: Pairs VII through X, ages 16 and 20 weeks, 8 subjects.

Group Three: Pairs XI through XVI, ages 24, 28, and 32 weeks, 12 subjects.

For most behavior variables we shall present tables that compare all active infants in one age group [15] with inactive ones in the same age group.

[15] The term "age group" will be used to designate the three groups of children at similar ages, and "age level" will designate chronological age in weeks.

Insofar as our data concern differences between activity level groups, we have assumed that a behavior difference is a function of activity level (at least in this sample) if, and only if, the following conditions are met: (1) A significant majority of individual pair comparisons and of cross-pair comparisons must manifest the same difference. (2) The comparison of the active infants with the inactive ones, within an age group, must confirm the difference noted in the original pairs.

WEIGHTED SCORES, RELIABILITY, AND TESTS OF SIGNIFICANCE

Special care was taken to assure accuracy of the recorded observations (as explained at the beginning of this chapter), but in view of human limitations it cannot be assumed that every portion of every record was factually correct. Once a behavior sequence has taken place, it is lost for all time, which means that the usual techniques for testing reliability—determining the degree to which repeated measurements of the same phenomenon yield the same result—cannot be applied to the direct observation of ongoing behavior sequences. (Filmed records very nearly preserve the original material and, as mentioned earlier, we made use of them in establishing and maintaining reliability. However, only tiny portions of the behavior of each infant could be photographed.) Independent observational records that are produced by several observers and cover the same time span do provide some assurance on this point. Accordingly, agreement among the different records describing the same behavior sequence was crucial in determining which portions of the raw data could be used with confidence.

During the original data collection, three observers made independent records covering the same time span. But each one had been instructed to concentrate on one aspect of the total situation, and then to include as much as possible of all the rest. (One focused on the mother's behavior, one on a detailed account of the infant's behavior, and the running record gave a full account of all that occurred, in proper context, and so was not as detailed.) The procedure in determining the nature of any one behavior sequence was to read all three accounts of the particular episode.

If the three accounts contained incompatible discrepancies, the particular behavior episode was *not included* in the analysis, since it was impossible to know which observer was correct. (For example, in one record: "Mother smiled as she leaned over the crib and wiped the baby's cheek with a diaper." Another record: "Mother bent down and cleaned the baby's face using a diaper in an impersonal and efficient manner.")

If the same episode was described in greater detail by one observer than by another, but there were no incompatibilities in the material, the episode was used. For example, in the running record: "The baby now made strenuous efforts to pull herself to the standing position against the side of the crib." Observational record: "The baby had crept close to the cribside. She grasped the bar first with one hand, and stiffened her legs against the mattress, while pulling herself upright. She succeeded in raising the trunk off the mattress, but soon flopped down again. Next, she grasped the side of the crib with both hands, tensed the entire body, and very nearly reached the full standing posture. She was flushed, looked intent but not displeased. However, she stood at such an angle that once upright she collapsed again, as her feet began to slide."

A third variety of discrepancy occurred when an episode was described by only some of the observers. If two of the three records contained a description, and both accounts agreed, the episode was used even if the third observer had omitted it. If an episode was in the record detailing the infant's behavior, but was omitted in the other two, it was used in the analysis if the other two records contained nothing that seemed incongruous or incompatible. But an episode mentioned only in the running record or only in the record of maternal behavior was *not included* in the analysis. The information contained in our tables and descriptions thus had to meet the test of agreement among the observational records.

A more difficult problem than merely assuring accurate observation was finding a technique that would allow for meaningful comparison. It will be remembered that behavior characteristics and patterns were compared primarily as they occurred under approximately equal conditions of stimulation. Since the observations were made under uncontrolled life circumstances, the same states and the same situations did not occur with equal frequency among the different babies, nor for equal lengths of time. Therefore, a simple frequency count of how often each baby behaved in a certain way under a specified condition would not convey the relevant information (though frequencies are reported where this seemed appropriate).

For instance, one child might often be observed being smiled at and spoken to gently by the mother, and another only occasionally. To report that one infant smiled and cooed fifty times in response to this variety of social stimulation while another did so only twenty times fails to reflect either child's consistent and regular response to such stimulation. The infant who was smiled at and spoken to fairly seldom might show the same behavioral response each time, so that smiling and cooing was for him invariably associated with the stimulating condition. The other infant might often have smiled and cooed in response to the same maternal approach, but at other times he might have merely gazed or even behaviorally ignored the same stimulation. From the point of view of each child's characteristic pattern of experience, the fact that one was smiled at and spoken to by his mother much more often than the other, is an important difference in its own right. But when the aim is to compare responses to a particular situation, the absolute frequency with which a response was seen to occur is irrelevant.

We therefore used the lists and tables of what each infant did in a given situation, and how often, to rate the *prominence* of a particular behavior. The prominence rating took into account the duration and frequency of the stimulus conditions observed, as well as the consistency with which the infant responded to the same situation. Prominence was assessed on a three-point scale. A prominence rating of 1.0 meant that the behavior occurred, but was overshadowed by other behaviors that also occurred in response to the same situation. A rating of 3.0 meant that the behavior *invariably* occurred in the particular situation and was predominant over other behavior activations that may also have occurred. A prominence rating of 2.0 applied when the behavior usually occurred in the situation, but could not be regarded as one of the infant's conspicuous and dominant behavior activations. (Specific rating criteria and a great many examples will be found in Part Two.)

The technique of weighted scores was applied also to other aspects of behavior. For instance, many behaviors can be performed at different levels of intensity. A particular movement such as kicking can be executed gently or with great vigor, as can vocalizations and many other components of behavior.

The comparison of the behavior of these infants was expressed in numerical form in several ways. A behavior or behavior aspect was reported as occurring under a given stimulus condition at a particular level of prominence and also at a particular level of intensity. The pair and cross-pair comparisons were based on prominence and intensity ratings, but in the form of "greater than," "equal" or "less than." Thus, if Ac I had received a prominence rating of 3.0, and In I a rating of 1.0, this was expressed as Ac I > In I. If AC III was given a prominence rating of 2.0, and In III did not show the behavior (prominence = 0), it was equally true that Ac III > In III. In view of the fact that we dealt with ratings and not with measured values, the simplest possible quantitative statement is also the most appropriate. A series of differences in the same direction have quantitative meaning. Whenever data are presented in the form of pair and cross-pair comparisons, tests of significance of the difference are provided.

Comparisons between groups were based on the sum of the prominence ratings received by each member of the group. Technically it would have been possible to test the significance of these group differences, but to do so would have been to exceed the limitations of the data. Available tests of significance that are applicable to small samples require a number of assumptions. Most nonparametric tests of significance assume complete independence of the data subject to comparison, as well as equidistant intervals between adjacent numbers and the existence of a zero point. These assumptions cannot be made about the behaviors we report and about the ratings that reflect them.[16] Except for the series of pair comparisons, this exploratory study employs the method of *quantitative description,* rather than of statistical manipulation.

The Construction of the Adaptation Syndrome

In Part Three we shall apply the research design that seeks to establish direct relationships between patterns of experience and indices of developmental status and adaptation. We also wish to illustrate the manner in which organismic and environmental factors interact to yield relatively stable patterns of experience.

Therefore, the ratings and assessments utilized in Part Three are of four different kinds for each infant: (1) certain organismic characteristics; (2) certain conspicuous and recurrent features of the child's environment; (3) stable patterns of experience; and (4) developmental status and some other indices of adaptation.

The concepts and operational definitions that guided all of these assessments are fully described and discussed in Part Three. In this chapter, however, we are considering methodological issues in broader terms, particularly some of the inherent limitations of our method and their effect on the interpretation of results.

THE CONCEPTUAL SHORTCOMINGS OF THE HOMEOSTATIC MODEL

In Chapters 2 and 3 it was frequently mentioned that behavior activations and their adaptive consequences can be described in terms of waxing and waning excitation. It was not difficult to arrive at behavioral criteria for various degrees of arousal and excitation that are applicable to all infants in all observable situations—at least for subjects less than eight months of age. However, when behavior is judged and assessed by such criteria, and when individual differences are described from this vantage point, much is implied that ought to be made explicit.

To speak of excitation and of states of relative equilibrium is to invoke the principle of homeostasis. In so doing, we are in good company, for most theories of development imply the homeostatic model. The descriptive psychologists of development, from Stern to Gesell, assume that behavior

[16] An appreciable number of the group differences appear to be significant when tested by Chi-Square techniques. However, quasi-rigor is the plague of psychological research, and we are anxious to avoid this pitfall.

occurs in response to excitation. So much is this taken for granted that it is treated as a primary fact not requiring theoretical elaboration. In psychoanalytic theory homeostasis is a central principle; and psychoanalytic metapsychology is devoted to an explication of homeostatic mechanisms in the regulation of human behavior, albeit on a purely speculative level. Most academic learning theories assume that drives or tissue tension arouse behavior activation and that energy or force is expended in the consequent behavior.[17]

More recently, many developmental theorists have stressed the importance of novelty and complexity as arousers of behavior, postulating that such stimuli set in motion conflicting neural excitations because of the dissonance between the unfamiliar perceptual input and perceptual traces stored on the basis of previous experience. In this and similar conceptions, disturbances of equilibrium are seen not as psychic forces nor as biological drives, but as biophysical neural energies. The model shares with its predecessors the assumption of a link between excitation, arousal, and behavior activation, and the implication that although a state of total equilibrium or rest does not occur in living organisms, behavior reflects the rise and decline of excitation. Piaget takes pains to exclude motivation from his theory of cognitive development, yet he relies heavily on the concept of equilibrium.[18]

Thus, many, if not all, theories of human behavior and development have found it necessary to assume that behavior changes are contingent on a state of disequilibrium that generates or releases energy or forces. This primary event may be referred to hypothetical constructs such as "drive" or "instinct," it may be conceptualized in terms of neural excitation, or it may be referred to vaguely as a biologically given "reservoir of energy" or "élan vital."

The application of the homeostatic principle to human behavior on the psychological level is beset with conceptual difficulties that at present seem insoluble. Psychoanalysis and other dynamic theories view the organism as a closed system, in the sense in which this concept was defined in nineteenth-century mechanics. It implies the proposition that systems

[17] Psychophysiological studies of behavior and development also evoke the homeostatic principle. Developmental changes as well as individual differences are treated in terms of the amount, gradient, and duration of autonomic arousal in a cycle that moves from excitation to discharge and a return to equilibrium. See, for instance, Brazelton (1961); Bridger and Reiser (1959); Bridger (1962); Bridger (1966); Papoušek (1965); Steinschneider, Lipton, and Richmond (1966); and Bridger, Birns, and Blank (1965).

[18] Piaget attempts to separate the concept of equilibrium from that of homeostasis (and in fact from all energy concepts) by treating the processes of cognitive development in terms of information and game theory. Cognitive events are seen as structural changes, whereas the energic aspects of developmental change are referred to an undefined realm of "affectivity." Nonetheless, the constant process of equilibration that yields equilibrium when cognitive structures are formed cannot be envisioned except as it occurs on the basis of either neural excitations or psychological "affective" forces (see Tanner and Inhelder, 1956).

have an inherent tendency to maintain relative stability by behaving in such a way as to counteract the accumulation of tension above tolerable levels. In physical terms this means that systems have the property of reacting to stress (excitation, tension) by discharge processes that preserve the boundary of the system, and hence preserve it as a coherent entity.[19] When applied to behavior in relation to psychological events, such a conceptualization seems less than adequate, in part because the forces or energies involved in the assumed energy transformations are entirely hypothetical. Psychic forces cannot be seen, measured, or made concrete in any way, and so the energic aspects of such theories cannot be tested by empiric means. In addition, the conception of the organism as a closed system is arbitrary and out of keeping with prevailing models of thought. Indeed, the concept of homeostasis in the narrow sense has become obsolete in physics, and it is no longer a central notion even in biology.

Therefore, many behavioral scientists and some psychoanalysts have rejected the principle altogether; for instance, Colby (1955) provided cogent arguments to document its theoretical shortcomings. In the theory of human development and human behavior, the dilemma has been met in one of two ways. Either some processes of energy transformation and motivation have been postulated, but not accounted for by specific hypotheses concerning their laws or mechanisms of operation; or else behavior and *psychological* structures and functions have been derived from energic transformations in the nervous system. The latter choice has the great advantage that neural excitations are a physical phenomenon subject to measurement. The disadvantage is that the reduction of psychological events to physiological (and ultimately physical) processes closes the door to investigation of psychological events in their own right. Ultimately, the reductionist approach implies that ideation, perception, thought, affect qualities, and the like are epiphenomena, and of no further interest to the student of behavior, once underlying "real" events are fully understood. (For an uncompromising exposition of this view see Skinner, 1953). Yet a primary characteristic of the human species would appear to be the high degree to which the organization and regulation of behavior, including the developmental process, is mediated by psychological events that are not identical with, nor reducible to, the physiological processes on which they rest.

Despite the fact that in our judgment the homeostatic model is unsatisfactory, and despite our belief that behavioral and psychological events will be describable in the language of probability theory once the primary data are better understood, much of our material will be presented

[19] The extension of this model to include continuous feedback processes as one of several mechanisms of regulation does not significantly alter the assumption (see Tanner and Inhelder, 1956).

in the context of waxing and waning excitation. This choice was made because we found no other way of noting and describing behavior regularities and their determinants in infancy. However, this decision to employ a concept that is outmoded in other disciplines is congruent with the thoughts we presented in Chapter 3. The psychological phenomena relevant to human development are still recorded and measured either globally or in isolated fragments. Even where quantitative treatment of the data is sophisticated, the quanta themselves tend to be either inexact or somewhat arbitrary. This applies to the material reported here, just as we think that it applies to behavioral research that utilizes the experimental method or relies on standard scales and tests. A century ago, when the raw data of the physical and biological sciences still had similar limitations, the concept of homeostasis served these sciences exceedingly well. It helped to order diverse phenomena, and it permitted the discovery of physical laws that could not otherwise have emerged. In our opinion, the homeostatic model still fulfills this function in the psychological study of human behavior.

THE DIFFICULTY OF DESCRIBING INTERACTIONS WHILE SEPARATING "STIMULUS" FROM "RESPONSE"

Our techniques of describing the behavior and experience of young babies entail another paradox. We maintain that each behavioral event is to be viewed as an interaction—in purist language, as a transaction—between the organism and the surrounding field; that is, the forces and conditions by which the organism is affected. Yet we report the stimulus conditions as distinct from behavioral response, as though the two were separated as proposed by classical S-R theories.

If we knew a *systematic* method of treating behavior data in a manner that links what the organism does with what takes place in the surrounding field, and that yet does justice to the unity of the resulting process or event,[20] we would gladly have adopted it. Once again it was necessary to adjust our sights to what is *possible*. However, it is important to keep in mind that when we speak of "social stimulation" or of the "response to hunger," these designations are intended to label certain components of a total event. We use the words "stimulus" and "response" in a general and descriptive manner, quite different from the way in which these words are defined in academic learning theories.

In summary, in preceding chapters we pointed to the discrepancy often

[20] Piaget, through his emphasis on simultaneous processes of accommodation and assimilation, has succeeded in formulating such an approach. However, this was possible because he focused on universal developmental transformations, ordered by the temporal dimension. When his concepts are applied to specific behavioral events and to individual differences among children, the integral unity between all participating forces and conditions can no longer be maintained.

found between the conceptual models that guide the investigator's thinking and the research operations that are performed. We proposed a model for empirical research that is more congruent with the dynamic and interactional view of human development. Yet, in the course of a first attempt to apply the new model, we recognized that our techniques also suffer from a gap between the logical properties of preferred conceptualizations and the relative crudeness of the data, as well as from the imperfect tools available for manipulating them. Limitations and inconsistencies that cannot be helped must be borne, but they should be recognized. In the case of the research venture described in these pages, the consequence of the methodological shortcomings is a severe limitation on the generalizations that can be made on the basis of our findings.

To be specific: We can say with certainty that the behaviors described did in fact take place under the conditions described. We can further say that *among the children in this sample* certain relationships existed between activity level and some behavioral characteristics of the infants. In addition, we can demonstrate, for this sample, a relationship between certain stable components of each infant's day-by-day experience and certain characteristics of development and functioning. On the basis of these findings, hypotheses suggest themselves about the determinants of selected aspects of development and about the genesis of individual differences. Yet our data are insufficient to either prove or disprove their validity.

One last word must be said about our methods. Compared with the more commonly used techniques of behavioral research, ours are cumbersome and laborious. This imbalance came about because the raw data were not gathered for the specific purposes to which they were put. Therefore, the selection of variables and their definition—which usually takes place before a research project is begun—became an important part of the research itself. The necessity for teasing out behavior units, behavior attributes, and relevant aspects of the stimulus conditions accounts for the lack of elegance and the redundancies involved in the rating procedures.

We believe that it was important to scrutinize infant behavior in such detail and in so many contexts in order to discover which of the elements involved will be most useful and relevant for later more selective studies. (We thought of our efforts as parallel, on a much smaller scale, to what Linnaeus did for botany.) Each of the variables we extracted in retroactive fashion can now be chosen in advance for investigation in more systematic manner. In the course of endlessly reviewing our records, we were irked by the inefficiency of the procedure, but took heart from the thought that if we succeeded in delineating important aspects of infant experience, future studies would gain in precision and relevance, with the expenditure of far less effort.

SUPPLEMENTARY MATERIAL TO CHAPTER 4

The Contrast Analysis: Topic Outline

The term "observed behavior" refers to a complete account of relevant episodes, accompanied by page references, specifying the general situational context, the specific conditions of stimulation, the person(s) or object(s) involved, the infant's state, and whatever affect manifestations were present. Although the major category headings remained the same for all infants, subcategories were added when necessary to include all relevant behavior episodes.

Background:	Description of family, cultural and socioeconomic characteristics, developmental history of infant.

Bodily Need States and Gratification

Background facts:	Method of feeding, schedule, etc.
Hunger:	Description of observed behavior, parental report.
Breast or bottle feeding:	Description of observed behavior, parental report.
Nipple loss:	Observed behavior.
Semisolid feedings:	Observed behavior, parental report.
Drinking from cup:	Observed behavior, parental report.
First nursing:	Parental report.
Termination, bottle or breast feeding:	Observed behavior.
Termination, semisolid feeding:	Observed behavior.
Fatigue:	Observed behavior, parental report.
Sleep:	Observed behavior, parental report.
Awakening:	Observed behavior, parental report.

Summary—Bodily Need States and Gratification: Narrative summary, comparing two infants.

Body Manipulations

Diaper changes:	Observed behavior.
Being dressed and undressed:	Observed behavior.
Ratings and pediatric examination:	Observed behavior.
Other:	Observed behavior.

Summary—Body Manipulations: Narrative and comparative summary.

Bodily Need States and Gratification

Active	Inactive
Background facts:............	Background facts:.........
....	....
....	....
Hunger:	
Observed: p. 12, line 3	Observed: p. 10, paragraph 2....
....	....
....	....
....	....
P. 7, line 2:.................	P.23, line 5:.................
....	....
....	....
Reported (Pp 16, 5, 11):.......	Reported: (Pp 16, 2, 31):......
....	....
Breast or Bottle Feeding:	
Observed:	Observed:

FIGURE 4.1. SCHEMATIC REPRESENTATION OF A PAGE OF THE CONTRAST ANALYSIS.

Object Stimulation

Stationary objects nearby:	Observed behavior.
Moving object nearby:	Observed behavior.
Object offered by person:	Observed behavior.
Object in hand:	Observed behavior.
Loss of an object:	Observed behavior.
Distant objects:	Observed behavior.
Toy preferences:	Observed behavior.
Other:	Observed behavior.

Summary—Object Stimulation: Descriptive and comparative summary.

Social Stimulation

Gentle social stimulation:

Sight of person not attending infant:	Observed behavior.

Sight of mother not attending infant:	Observed behavior.
Being smiled at and spoken to by mother:	Observed behavior.
Being smiled at and spoken to by person:	Observed behavior.
Being smiled at, spoken to, briefly touched by mother:	Observed behavior.
Being smiled at, spoken to, briefly touched by person:	Observed behavior.

Moderately strong social stimulation:

All instances of active but not overly forceful contact made by others, separately for mother and other persons:	Observed behavior.

Strong social stimulation:

All instances of forceful contact or manipulation, separately for mother and other persons:	Observed behavior.

Learned imitative games:

Where present, each instance:	Observed behavior.

Communication:

If present, all instances:	Observed behavior.
Response to strangers:	Observed behavior whether or not stranger reaction present.
Discriminatory social responses:	All instances, observed behavior.

Summary—Social Stimulation: Narrative and comparative summary.

Sensory Modalities: Vision

Minimal visual stimuli:	All instances, observed behavior.
Response to photo lights and other strong visual stimuli:	Observed behavior.
Visual discrimination:	All instances, observed behavior.
Intent gaze in social context:	All instances, observed behavior.
Response to mirror image:	Observed behavior.

Summary—Vision: Narrative and comparative summary.

Sensory Modalities: Auditory

Slight sounds:	Observed behavior.
Moderate or loud sounds:	Observed behavior.
Noises during sleep:	Observed behavior.

Response to human voice:	Observed behavior.
Imitation of sounds:	Observed behavior.
Self-generated sounds:	Observed behavior.

Summary—Auditory: Narrative and comparative summary.

Sensory Modalities: Tactile

Gentle touch by mother:	Observed behavior.
Gentle touch by observer:	Observed behavior.
Gentle touch by object:	Observed behavior.
Moderate or strong touch by mother:	Observed behavior.
Moderate or strong touch by observer:	Observed behavior.
Strong prolonged touch by observers:	Observed behavior during ratings of muscle tonus, leg resistance and pediatric examination.
Self-generated touching of mother:	Observed behavior.
Self-generated touching of objects:	Observed behavior.

Summary—Tactile: Narrative comparative summary.

Sensory Modalities: Kinesthetic (and tactile/kinesthetic)

Gentle passive motion:	Observed behavior.
Moderate and strong passive motion:	Observed behavior.
Self-generated kinesthetic stimulation:	All instances of rocking, bouncing, etc., initiated by infant, observed behavior.

Summary—Kinesthetic: Narrative comparative summary.

Non-nutritive Oral Behavior

All varieties of oral behavior:	All instances, observed behavior.
Varieties of oral schemas:	Enumeration of different oral schemas shown, and relative frequency.

Summary—Oral Behavior: Narrative comparative summary.

Delay and Frustration

Frustration:	All instances, observed behavior.
Delay:	All instances where significant delay between perception of stimulus and overt response occurred.

Summary—Delay and Frustration: Narrative, comparative summary.

Activity Increases and Decreases (*infants up to 24 weeks only*)

Activity increases:	All situations in which activity increase *typically* occurred, description.
Activity decreases:	All situations in which activity decreases *typically* occurred.
Representative activity:	Selected portions of raw data, exemplifying motility and activity level during spontaneous activity.

Summary—Activity Increases and Decreases: Narrative, comparative summary.

PART II

COMPARISON OF ACTIVE AND INACTIVE INFANTS

Describing the behavior of infants selected to reflect extremes of activity level is a device to highlight the qualities and ranges of behavior that characterize infants at these ages. We found that although some behavior tendencies were associated with high and low activity, many others seemed to be independent of this dimension. Furthermore, behavior differences among active infants and among inactive infants are as great as those between the groups, and are of equal interest. But, for two reasons, we chose this method of describing variable behavior patterns. In the first place, it is easier to focus on specific behavior attributes by describing contrasting patterns rather than commonalities.[1] In the second place, the activity level variable offered an opportunity to demonstrate in some detail our conception of the manner in which any single determinant of behavior interacts with all others. We assume that the same factor may have different and even opposite effects upon behavior, and that patterns of association among diverse behavior attributes are not separate traits that can ultimately be reduced to a single determining source. Rather, we think that relatively constant and repetitive experiences—that is, constellations of external and internal conditions that produce specific behaviors —lead to the formation of stable reaction tendencies in each infant. In principle, the variable influence upon behavior of a single determining factor could be demonstrated equally well

[1] The case files on these 32 infants had been studied in many different ways before the technique of "contrast analyses" occurred to us. Once the comparison of individual babies in this manner was under way, we discovered many behavior aspects and patterns that had previously not been differentiated and recognized in their own right.

if we had selected infants by any other criterion. In the section on adaptation syndromes, the same conceptual approach will be applied simultaneously to a large number of variables. The discussion of adaptation syndromes presupposes acquaintance with concrete behavior manifestations, which are provided by the comparison of active with inactive infants. Because we are concerned with *all* behavior variations, the tables and discussions will include not only those behavior aspects that tend to vary with activity level but also those that do not.

The material to be reported is based primarily on the Contrast Analyses, which compared the behavior of a single active infant with that of a single inactive one, each such pair consisting of babies of like age, as described in Chapter 4. In these analyses, each statement about the behavior of an infant in a given situation was accompanied by references to the original case file. The following material, consequently, was drawn from both the Contrast Analyses and these case files.

During the first half year of life, behavior patterns change with great rapidity. Although some directions and tendencies of difference remain constant throughout the period, the specific behavior adaptions of a 4-week-old bear no resemblance to those of a 28-week-old. The data are, therefore, presented separately for three age groups: *Group One,* the twelve infants from 4 to 12 weeks of age (pairs I through VI); *Group Two,* the eight infants who were 16 and 20 weeks of age (pairs VII through X); and *Group Three,* twelve infants from 24 to 32 weeks old (pairs XI through XVI).

Typical and recurrent aspects of behavioral response to specific conditions of stimulation were compared for each pair (one active and one inactive baby) and for the group of active babies as contrasted to the group of inactive ones in each age group. Since the behavior repertoire of all infants at a given age level has a great deal in common, the chief difference was that, under comparable conditions, certain behavior patterns were shown more frequently or more prominently by either the active or the inactive infants.

The primary data consist of a large number of episodes and ratings of behavior observed in a small number of subjects. It was our best judgment that group differences in a small sample could be attributed to the activity level variable *only* if it could be demonstrated that all or most of the individual subjects contributed to the difference. Thus, for most behaviors under scrutiny, it was necessary to compare the infants in each pair in all possible alignments, in order to see whether behavior differed *in the same direction* for each pair comparison. A behavioral difference was tentatively assumed to be related to activity level only if it emerged in any combination of active and inactive subjects of like age.

The description of findings that require such cumbersome manipulations is in constant danger of becoming tedious. Yet our purpose is not merely to illustrate the basis for our general conclusions but to document them. The best solution we found was to limit the main text to descriptive condensations and discussion of the observations; with more detailed information about the original ratings, their distribution, and the defining criteria appended to each chapter in sections called *Supplementary Material.*

FIVE

GROUP ONE: 4- TO 12-WEEK-OLDS

Spontaneous Activity

In the lives of 4- to 8-week-old babies, moments when they are awake, alert, and not subject to specific environmental stimulation are rare and transient. For the most part, the infants drowse or sleep—unless hunger, other bodily discomfort, or manipulations by the mother keep them awake. At 12 weeks, most of our subjects spent some time each morning and each afternoon "playing by themselves," as mothers put it. Nonetheless, even our youngest subjects had frequent brief periods, lasting for as little as three minutes but not for more than ten minutes, during which they were not asleep and not uncomfortable. Among some 12-week-olds, episodes of spontaneous activity could last up to 34 minutes. The frequency with which spontaneous activity was observed ranged from six to twelve episodes per baby.

At later ages, the condition of spontaneous activity affords an excellent opportunity to note whatever patterns are set in motion when behavior is not in response to compelling stimulation. Individual differences then emerge with greatest clarity in this state. For infants below the age of 3 months, behavior during spontaneous activity could be described primarily in terms of characteristic patterns of motility, and secondarily in terms of the absence or presence of vocalizations and of transient attentiveness to aspects of the immediate environment.

MOTILITY

Moment-by-moment movement patterns shown by these infants could be classified in terms of the body segments involved and the intensity or forcefulness of movement. Once each movement had been classified, it was rated for its prominence in the behavior of each infant during spontaneous activity. Prominence ratings were based on *relative frequency* and ranged from "absent" (prominence score 0) through "rare" (0.5), "occasional" (1.0), and "medium" (2.0) to "frequent" (3.0). The prominence ratings in numerical form are used as a matter of convenience. Each numerical value is to be understood as a *documented descriptive judgment* on the author's part. It is not a measurement, partly because a rating of "frequent" or "rare" was relative to the time interval involved and to the frequency distribution of other movement activations during the same time interval. For instance, if a baby was observed during eight periods of spontaneous activity, each of which lasted no longer than three minutes, and the baby was observed to bring his hand to his mouth six to eight times during each brief period, the hand-mouth pattern would be rated as frequent and highly prominent in his behavior. Another baby, observed for only two time periods, each lasting close to half an hour, might receive a rating of "occasional" if he showed the same number of hand-mouth activations. (See *Supplementary Material* to this chapter for a full description of each movement category and its definition.)

During spontaneous activity, active babies exceeded inactive ones in forceful whole-body and part-body motions and in muscle tension. Inactive babies exceeded active ones in gentle part-body motions. Table 5.1 reflects for each infant in Group One the prominence rating he received for each type of movement. Table 5.2 summarizes the results for the group as a whole, in terms of a pair and cross-pair comparison. Table 5.3 also summarizes group results, but in terms of summed prominence ratings received by each group for each type of movement activation.[1] (See Chapter 4 discussion of pair and cross-pair comparisons.)

There is nothing remarkable about the fact that infants preselected to represent differences in activity level should differ in the amount and forcefulness of their movement patterns. The original ratings of activity level were made on the basis of each infant's total behavior in a great many different situations. It is of some interest to learn that infants who were originally judged to be markedly active or inactive in their response to various excitatory stimuli showed the same difference during spontaneous activity alone—especially in this youngest age group, for whom spontaneous activity was a small fragment of their waking time.

Typical patterns of motility vary widely among active infants and moderately among inactive ones. Table 5.1 shows that among active infants, each movement category may occur at any level of prominence. For instance, among active infants ratings for "forceful whole-body movement" ranged from "occasional" (1.0) to "frequent" (3.0). Muscle tension was sometimes absent in active babies, but also occurred with "medium" (2.0) prominence. The variability among inactive babies was somewhat narrower. For instance, "gentle whole-body movements" were limited to either "me-

[1] We chose to present the same data in three different ways in order to demonstrate the method of checking each observed behavior difference by using both absolute ratings, and comparisons between pairs which disregard the absolute prominence. In connection with behavior differences less clear-cut than those in motility, these different modes of analysis will be seen to yield information of a different order.

dium" (2.0) or "occasional" (1.0), and "forceful whole-body movements" were, in inactive babies, never more than "rare" (0.5).

A horizontal reading of Table 5.1 yields for each infant a profile of characteristic movement patterns. It shows that in this sample the patterns of being active were strikingly different, while the inactive babies' patterns showed greater similarity to one another. For instance, subject Ac III showed forceful whole-body motions only occasionally (1.0), but forceful part-body activations were "frequent" (3.0); gentle whole-body motions were rated as "medium" (2.0), and quiescent intervals did not occur at all. By contrast, subject Ac II showed "frequent" (3.0) forceful whole-body motions and "medium" (2.0) forceful part-body movements. However, he showed frequent intervals of complete quiescence, and muscle tension was fairly prominent, receiving a rating of "medium." Inactive infants differed chiefly in that some (for instance, In IV and In VI) showed no gentle whole-body motions at all, though gentle part-body motions were quite prominent. Some inactive babies, like In VI, were never entirely still, but others, like In IV, typically had quiescent intervals.

For infants below 3 months of age, the determination of individually characteristic patterns of motility is a primary means of constructing a picture of the baby's sensorimotor experience at times of alert and not uncomfortable wakefulness. Surely it makes a difference to the infant's pattern of existence if he can be relaxed and apparently resting during spontaneous activity, rather than in a state of fairly constant excitation. It is equally of interest to know that some infants, during spontaneous activity, often experience the sensations that accompany such activations as massive movement, stiffening of the body and tremorous motion, or leisurely and confined motion of a leg or an arm. This aspect of the matter is important for gauging the impact of various other conditions. For instance, for a baby who shows considerable muscle tension during spontaneous activity and also fans his toes or arches his back during feeding, the feeding situation is not markedly different from other occasions with respect to *this particular component* of body feeling. For another infant, who shows muscle tension during spontaneous activity but complete muscular relaxation during feeding, the feeding situation is markedly different from other times, as mediated by a change in accompanying body feelings.

BEHAVIOR DIFFERENCES OTHER THAN MOTILITY

Tactile exploration of a nearby surface, visual focusing on a nearby impasssive face, and non-nutritive oral behavior were more prominent in the behavior of inactive infants. Tables 5.4, 5.5, and 5.6 describe certain qualitatively specific behavior patterns of the infants in Group One. Two of these patterns—oral behavior and vocalization—involve the activation of a single body system; while in other behaviors—focusing on his own hand, on a nearby face, or on a toy suspended above the crib—the infant's behavior is oriented toward an aspect of the environment. Tactile exploration of a nearby surface is, at these ages, an isolated behavior in the sense that it is not coordinated with vision, and a baby will grasp, finger, or scratch any surfaces that the hand happens to encounter in the course of generalized movement—the sheet or blanket or his shirt in the region of chest or abdomen. As Piaget does, we regard the infant's tendency to re-create hand-object contacts in response to chance occurrence as an early schema in a series that ultimately leads to prehension. It is similar to visual focusing and following, in which a chance visual contact is actively prolonged and repeated by the infant's response.[2] Seen in the light of this assumption, both tactile exploration and visual focusing are early adaptive responses to aspects of the surrounding field.

The observation that regard of a nearby face, tactile exploration, and oral behaviors are prominent among inactive babies, while fleeting hand regard is equally prominent in both groups, can be interpreted to mean that activity level does not determine the degree of responsiveness to external stimuli. In the general discussion of spontaneous behavior (see Chapter 2), it was mentioned that although certain behaviors occur more conspicuously in one activity group than in another, we are not inclined to postulate a direct link between activity level and the behavior associated with it. Instead it appears to us that being markedly active or inactive affects the *probability for the occurrence* of certain behaviors, for practical reasons that have nothing to do with the infant's capacity to perform the behavior in question. Active infants in Group One typically engaged in massive movement—they squirmed or simultaneously waved their arms and kicked. These gross movements preclude more contained behaviors such as visual focusing and scratching.[3] In a manner of speaking, the active infants have less time and less opportunity for the more limited behaviors.

The relative prominence of more narrowly confined behaviors is not always a function of activity level. Tables 5.4 and 5.5 show that in two of the six original pair comparisons (and also in two of the six cross-pair comparisons) the active subject showed oral behavior more prominently than did the inactive one. Such a reversal of the more usual association between activity level and a behavior tendency does not necessarily run counter to our hypothesis about the explanation for the group difference. For instance, Ac III showed oral behavior more prominently than did In III. However, Ac III was an infant who (as indicated in Table 5.1)

[2] Piaget refers to behaviors of this order as primary circulary reactions that necessarily precede the coordination among several sensory modalities.

[3] For neonates, much the same idea was proposed by Wolff (1965).

showed forceful whole-body activations only occasionally, whereas forceful part-body movements were frequent. Since her dominant movement schema was kicking along with raising and lowering the legs, this pattern, though distinctly active, did not prevent her from also bringing the hand to the mouth. In addition, In III was the only one of the inactive babies in Group One who showed no oral behavior at all during spontaneous activity. Our hypothesis is that energetic gross motion interferes with the frequent or prolonged execution of confined behavior activations, and that low levels of activity *permit* the execution of oral or other limited behavior activations. As it happens, the behavior of In III supports this notion, for she was a baby who frequently engaged in tactile exploration. Similarly, the reversal shown by pair VI is in harmony with the hypothesis. Ac VI showed oral behavior only occasionally, and In VI was another inactive baby whose tactile exploration was rated as frequent, while his oral behavior during spontaneous activity was rare.[4]

We have interpreted our findings to mean that activity level plays a role in that it influences the *probability* for the occurrence of certain behavior patterns; for instance, the absence of predominantly massive movement is regarded as a necessary condition for prominent oral behavior in early infancy, but not as a sufficient condition or as a correlate. In this context, a reversal of an association between activity level and specific behavior tendencies can serve either to support or negate the underlying hypothesis. The apparent reversals discussed above were shown to support the underlying hypothesis and to illustrate the limitations inherent in the technique of pair-comparisons made on only the "greater than" or "smaller than" relationship. Because of these limitations, ratings of prominence and comparison between the groups in absolute, rather than in relative, terms are also provided.[5] In summary, during spontaneous activity the behavior of these twelve subjects between 4 and 12 weeks of age showed pronounced individual differences. Some of these differences were associated with activity level: forceful body movements, muscle tension, the tendency to focus visually on an immobile face, tactile exploration of nearby surfaces, and non-nutritive oral behavior.

[4] The same circumstances account for the reversal with respect to focusing upon a nearby impassive face on pair V. In V did not show the behavior at all, and Ac V did so only rarely.

[5] We are dealing here with a hypothesis that consists of a probability statement, although the procedure for testing the truth of the statement is not a statistical test of probability. The usual situation in psychological research is that the hypothesis proposes a common determinant for diverse behaviors or a causal link between behaviors. In these more usual instances the hypothesized relationship is assumed to exist without exception, whereas the test of the hypothesis rests on probability theory. Our hypothesis concerning a relationship between activity level and the likelihood of prominent gazing, sucking, etc., during spontaneous activity can be confirmed (at least tentatively) only if it is in accord with every comparison or other finding. In our case, the hypothesis conforms to the formal pattern of relationship between a law and the relevant phenomena that K. Lewin designated as "Galilean" (by contrast to "Aristotelian") logic.

Hunger and Fatigue

In babies less than 3 months of age, bodily need states such as hunger and fatigue are accompanied by massive alterations in overt behavior. Nonetheless, recording behavior in detail on these occasions proved difficult for the observers. In many instances, the case files for the situations of hunger and fatigue are not as detailed as they are for many others. This was clearly due to a degree of confusion as babies cried, mothers heated bottles or tried to soothe their babies, and preparations for movie photography were under way. Our criteria for reliability, as described in Chapter 4, permitted the rating of behavior changes associated with needs in the following respects: changes in the amount of activity, crying, whimpering, and other distress vocalizations; changes in oral behavior; and whether distress was manifested continuously or intermittently. The criteria by which these aspects of behavior were assessed are described in *Supplementary Material* at the end of this chapter.

Hunger leads to more intense excitation and distress in active than in inactive infants. Figure 5.1 summarizes for the two groups the behavior changes associated with hunger or, at any rate, with prefeeding behavior at times when the mother judged the baby to be hungry and when the baby accepted normal amounts of food once it was offered.[6] Table 5.7 provides the ratings of behavior during hunger for each subject. Severe crying or screaming typically occurred in five (of six) active babies, and in only one (of six) inactive ones. Further, for five active babies, crying and/or movement increases were continuous from the onset of hunger until food was provided, whereas only one of the inactive babies cried continuously.

During fatigue, inactive babies showed almost as much excitation and distress as did the active ones. Figure 5.2 and Table 5.8 show behavior changes associated with the presleep period for the groups as a whole and for each infant individually. Intense crying and unremitting distress were more frequent among the active children in this situation as well, but the difference between the groups is less pronounced. A comparison of Table 5.8 with Table 5.7 suggests that, in this sample, active infants tended to respond somewhat more strongly to hunger than to fatigue, whereas several inactive babies were more distressed during fatigue than during hunger.

In assessing this important aspect of recurrent experience in the life of infants, it is of interest to note that hunger and fatigue may imply a

[6] Some instances of prefeeding behavior were excluded, although the mother judged the baby hungry. These were the few occasions when an infant failed to accept food with eagerness; that is, when he consumed no more than about an ounce, or when he did not suck at the breast with any steadiness. In each of these instances we had occasion to see the same baby at least twice at a time when, to judge by his consumption, he was in fact hungry.

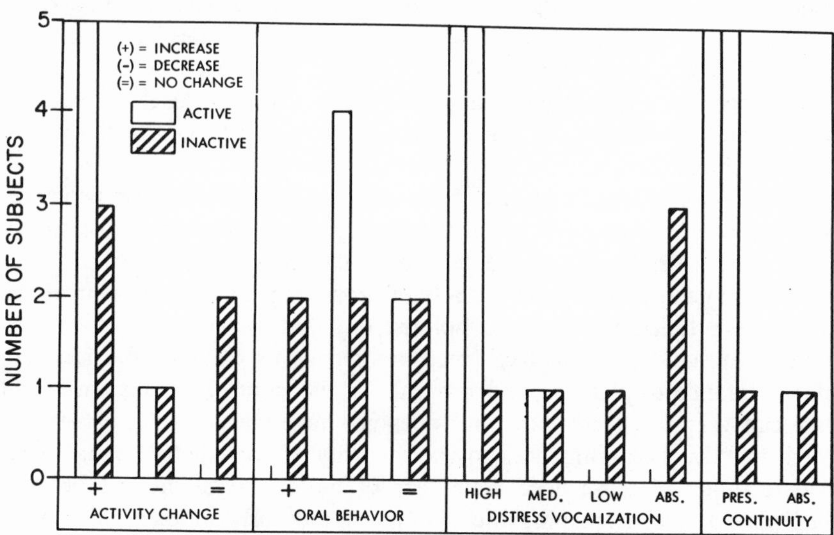

FIGURE 5.1. MANIFESTATIONS OF HUNGER.

NOTE: Number of subjects = 12 for each category except continuity, which could not be rated in four subjects.

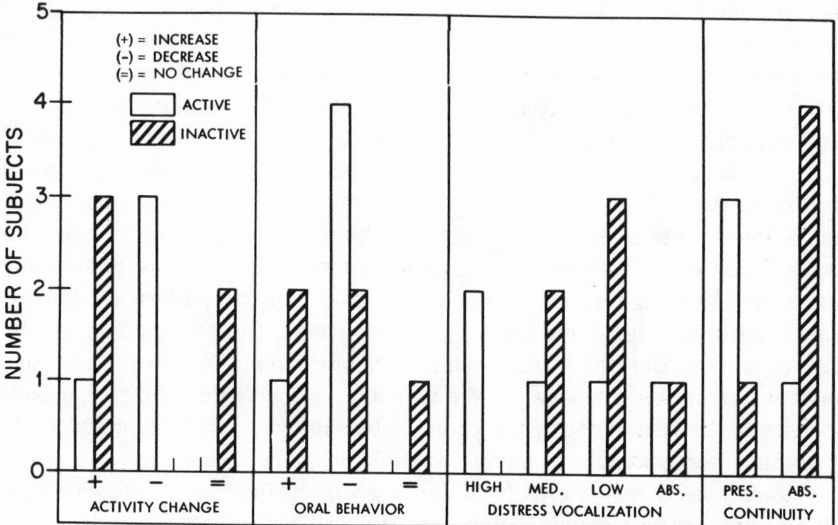

FIGURE 5.2. MANIFESTATIONS OF FATIGUE.

NOTE: One subject (Ac VI) was asleep at the beginning of each observation. Five active and six inactive subjects were rated, but records did not permit judgments on each variable (see table 5.8).

wide variety of states, ranging from no visible behavior change to maximal arousal. Further, for some babies, fatigue regularly brings moderate distress, while hunger does not. Moreover, for some—but not all—babies, both hunger and fatigue are sharply demarcated in experience, as each of these states, several times each day, leads to heightened activity and severe crying.

In the discussion of bodily need states as a dimension of behavior, we mentioned the possibility that the perception of discomfort due to delayed need satisfaction may be related to the infant's early awareness of an environment, and thus play a role in propelling the development of the earliest ego functions. We also pointed out that, in the case of hunger, maternal practices can in large measure reduce or enhance the intensity of the infant's displeasure and arousal. In the case of fatigue, maternal care can vary in effectiveness, but does not have the power to satisfy the need directly. The differences in the intensity of each baby's usual reaction to either of these need states are of more general interest because they play a role in shaping the pattern of the early mother-child interaction.

For babies such as Ac I, Ac IV, In IV and Ac V, the mothers' best efforts to keep them comfortable at all times were of no avail during fatigue. This not only meant recurrent distress for the babies, but also placed their mothers in a situation where they expended loving efforts without the immediate gratification of seeing the babies respond. Maternal feeling and behavior depend heavily on the mother's perception of herself as someone who knows what is best for the baby and who knows herself effective in tending and satisfying his needs. A deeply rooted feeling of essential competence comes about in part as the mother proves herself capable of so managing the baby's care that prolonged distress is a rare occasion. Thus, women who are inexperienced or plagued by anxiety for reasons unrelated to the baby's behavior can be greatly hindered in acquiring a sense of basic competence if the infant happens to be one who reacts intensely to fatigue and does not respond well to the usual soothing measures. In such circumstances, an intrinsic reaction pattern on the infant's part may have far-reaching consequences for the quality of the subsequent mother-child relationship. Yet our sample, small as it is, also contains examples to document the fact that mothers who bring great confidence to the task of caring for young babies may be nearly immune to the disruptive consequences of having a "difficult" baby to care for.

During need states, oral behavior is no more intense or frequent than during spontaneous activity. Non-nutritive oral behavior will be described in some detail in a later section. However, in the assessment of behavior during hunger and fatigue, and during spontaneous activity, a single rating was made for the prominence of oral behavior at these times.

Oral behavior during need states was assessed for each baby only in comparison with the prominence with which the same baby showed such behavior during spontaneous activity. In Tables 5.7 and 5.8 and Figs. 5.1 and 5.2, an increase means that oral behavior was more prominent or intense during the need state than during spontaneous activity; decrease means that oral behavior during the need state was reduced in comparison with spontaneous activity.

Contrary to what might have been expected, only a small minority of these babies showed sucking, mouthing, and the like more prominently while hungry or sleepy than they did while alert, awake, and content. With hunger, only two of twelve babies intensified oral activity beyond the level shown during spontaneous activity. With fatigue, oral behavior was shown with greater prominence by three of the twelve. At the very least, one may conclude that in infants less than 3 months of age, hunger and fatigue do not generally lead to non-nutritive oral behavior of greater intensity or prominence than that shown at some other times.

In fact, four active and two inactive babies typically showed less oral behavior in the presence of either of these need states than they did when awake and alert. The psychological literature has often suggested that mouthing and sucking are behavioral expressions of hunger, as though the infant organism activated schemas most closely associated with the relevant need-gratifying activity. The fact that in our sample oral behavior showed no closer association with hunger than with a number of other states does not support this notion—nor does it disprove it. As will be shown in the material to follow, many of these babies did activate oral behavior during need states, some at high levels of intensity. It is plausible to assume that in these instances the oral behaviors were a manifestation of bodily tension created by hunger or fatigue. However, for the great majority of these infants it is possible to demonstrate that other varieties of internal and external stimulation have equal power to activate the oral schemas.[7]

RESPONSE TO VISUAL STIMULI AND RESPONSIVENESS BY MEANS OF VISION

Infants between 4 and 12 weeks of age are rarely capable of coordinated responsiveness to objects, as differentiated from perceptual input that emanates from persons or from visible parts of their own body. Therefore it would not be meaningful to present for the younger subjects a section on their behavior during "Object Stimulation" (as discussed in Chapter 2). A survey of the behavior of the youngest subjects under all observed conditions suggested that, between the ages of 4 and 12 weeks, responsiveness

[7] Our results are in keeping with those reported by Bridger (1966), who found that for neonates hunger did increase the intensity and duration of sucking behavior. However, when excitation of comparable levels was produced experimentally, while the infants were *not* hungry, the intensity of sucking behavior increased to the same degree. He concluded that a state of heightened arousal leads neonates to intensify sucking, and that the association between hunger and sucking is so frequently observed merely because hunger is a frequent cause of arousal.

to external stimuli is manifested chiefly by visual attentiveness and secondarily by motor coordinations that are guided by visual stimuli.

Some visually oriented behaviors were noted to occur during spontaneous activity. However, infants below the age of 3 months turn their attention to external stimuli mostly when something in the environment impinges forcefully on their awareness. It is when a baby is approached and spoken to and perhaps touched that he usually gazes at a person. And it is when objects such as rattles are invitingly placed in the visual field and moved about that he is likely to respond to them.

Vision plays a unique role in mediating the differentiation between self and a surround, and in mediating sensorimotor discrimination among components of the environment. Vision differs from all other sense modalities because it is both a receptor system and a primary response modality, and its activation in response to any stimulus serves to orient the organism and inform it about the objective properties of the stimulus. It provides the only way in which young infants can by their behavior directly influence the amount of information they receive about the environmental field. When an infant, in response to an external auditory, tactile, or other kind of stimulation, moves his body or vocalizes such activation of proprioceptive or auditory modalities does not lead directly to further information about the external object. It is by *looking* at his mother or the rattle that the infant comes to behaviorally recognize the difference between mother's voice and other sounds. By looking at such things as bottles, clothing, blankets, and his own feet and hands, he is able to coordinate the feel of certain textures with visual characteristics and thus again achieve discrimination among objects. Vision, therefore, has special significance for the development of early ego functions that hinge on achieving a distinction between self and the surrounding field and a distinction among components of the outer world.

On the basis of clinical observation of the development of congenitally blind children, Sandler (1963) proposed a very similar hypothesis. She attributed the developmental retardation seen in blind children to the fact that, due to their lack of vision, their experience as infants remains fragmented for a long time. It is vision, she points out, that unifies and integrates sensorimotor experience, because most environmental stimuli in other modalities are, at the same time, visible. Normal infants learn to recognize and anticipate events and to establish simple causal connections between them by means of the continuity that only vision can provide.

For instance, babies usually see the bottle before the nipple arrives at the mouth, and therefore the bottle is recognized very early. It is much more difficult for blind infants to link an anticipation of satisfaction with perception of the bottle, since they can perceive the bottle only by touch. On this basis, Sandler designated vision as "a prime neutralizing agent," meaning that it is essential for the creation of a distance between self and nonself, for the construction of an environment, and hence for the neutralization of drive energies.[8]

Inactive infants were more responsive in the visual modality then were active ones. For infants in Group One, it was possible to identify 12 combinations of stimulating situations and responses in which vision played a crucial role. The behavior of each infant and of the active and inactive subjects as a group is reflected in Tables 5.9 and 5.10. Briefly, the type of observation that is summarized in these tables is this: The first two categories (aversion to photo lights and visual discrimination) refer to discriminatory behavior on a purely visual basis, and could be rated only as absent or present. The infants' reactivity to the bright photographic lights was noted in the course of taking movies several times during each observational session. Some of the babies made no response at all; others blinked, grimaced, averted their heads, or whimpered briefly.

The category of visual discrimination refers to each infant's responsiveness to visual aspects of a variety of standard objects to which he was exposed during the developmental test. These included bright red objects, various toys in pastel shades, a large and very shiny metal cup, and a mirror. A number of subjects responded differentially to shiny objects such as the cup, showing, for instance, greater excitation or aversion. When this (or any other visual discrimination) occurred, it was standard practice to expose the infant repeatedly to the shiny cup and to objects of similar size but less reflectiveness. We rated such discrimination as present only if the differential response could be elicited with regularity.

The other visual criterion situations concern the intensity of visual responsiveness, and/or the relative frequency with which certain visually oriented coordinations occurred. These categories were assessed for each infant in terms of prominence ranging from "rare" (0.5) to "frequent" (3.0). The categories are self-explanatory, except for the intensity dimension, which may be illustrated for the situation we have called "intent regard as social response." Most infants gaze at a person who comes close and speaks to them with animation. But only some babies become so completely absorbed in visual regard that gazing becomes an activity in its own right, during which movement is arrested and even smiling and vocalizing do not begin until the visual regard is broken and the child lets his gaze travel over the mother's face and body. Such intense visual regard is easily distinguished from casual looking, which more often accompanies a body activation. And it is altogether different from the autistic staring occasionally seen in tiny babies. (For a detailed description of rating criteria on these variables, see *Supplementary Material.*)

Tables 5.9 and 5.10 both show that while some visual-motor coordinations were equally prominent among active and inactive infants, a

[8] The detailed investigation of search behaviors of blind children reported by Fraiberg, Siegel, and Gibson (1966), provides excellent documentation of this point.

much larger proportion of the visually oriented behaviors were more prominent among inactive babies. To summarize these results, of a total of 53 comparisons between an active and an inactive baby, the inactive one was the more responsive in 28 comparisons, or 53 per cent; the reverse was true in 8 (15 per cent) of the comparisons. (On cross-pair comparison, the corresponding values were 27 comparisons [51 per cent] in which the inactive baby exceeded the active one and 12 [or 23 per cent] in which the active baby was the more responsive.)

Table 5.9 shows that all of these visually mediated responses were seen among active subjects as well as inactive ones. The difference is merely that some occurred in a larger proportion of inactive babies or were more prominent in their behavior. The magnitude of differences reflected in Table 5.10 is moderate, perhaps in part because the method of pair comparison somewhat obscures actual differences when it is applied to behaviors that some among the subjects do not show at all. Table 5.11 provides summed prominence scores and average prominence scores for those visual behaviors that discriminated between the activity level groups. It shows that the summed weighted score for the intensity and frequency of these visual behaviors among inactive infants is more than twice that for the active group. And the average prominence scores for those members of each group that showed the behavior to any degree (that is, omitting subjects who received zero scores) were consistently higher for the inactive group.

As these behaviors are just emerging among infants of this age, and they must therefore also be a function of different developmental levels, we are impressed by the consistency of these differences.

Differences in the visual behavior of active and inactive infants were limited to behaviors that can occur only in the absence of other body movement. It has previously been suggested that several of the behavior differences between active and inactive babies can be understood in light of the fact that energetic movement precludes certain of the more limited and contained behaviors. Tables 5.9 through 5.11 indicate that the visual responsiveness of active and inactive babies did differ primarily on behavior items (those included in Table 5.11) that are not compatible with movement activations. A small infant cannot maintain visual contact with a stationary or a moving object unless the relationship between head position and the stimulus remains reasonably constant, which requires that no motion displace the head or intervene between the visual stimulus and the baby's gaze. On the other hand, the visual coordinations that can occur transiently and in the course of body movement (fleeting regard of toy in hand, reaching for and contacting object) were approximately equal in both active and inactive children. Similarly, immediate visual responses that do not require prolonged gazing were no different for the two groups. One such response is the regard of an immobile person (but not intent regard), with an accompanying activity decrease. Others are visual discrimination, which was seen in three active and only one inactive infant, and an aversion to the photographic lights, which was seen chiefly, but not exclusively, in inactive infants.

The fact that a strong tendency of inactive babies to respond visually holds true for only some visually oriented behaviors is in harmony with our assumption. Indeed, the underlying hypothesis was derived from findings of this nature, obtained in many different contexts and for a large variety of behavior patterns.

Behavior in Contact with People

In describing the behavior of infants up to three months of age, we prefer not to use the term "social," since for the most part we are dealing with situations that are still in the process of becoming social. However, we were interested in the behavior and experience of our subjects at times when the mother or another person made herself felt in their awareness. As was said in the section on social behavior as a dimension of experience (Chapter 2), it is more than probable that the specific quality of feeling and expectation that comes to be connected with the mother, and to some extent with people generally, is established by means of recurrent sequences of experience that have in common the infant's perception of another person's presence.

The qualitative description of patterns of mother-infant interaction is more appropriate to the presentation of adaptation syndromes and will be found in later chapters. However, it was possible to compare active and inactive infants while they were in direct contact with another person in terms of some relatively formal aspects of behavior. The choice of situations we were able to include in this analysis was, of course, limited by our opportunity to observe them. Many relevant recurrent situations of direct contact with another person could not be included. For instance, being bathed is one of the frequent recurrent interactions between mother and infant, but, although we were able to observe one bath for more than half of our subjects, there were no opportunities for repeated observations.

In our data for the youngest age group, ten situations were observed frequently enough to allow an assessment of the infant's response. Table 5.12 provides a schematic overview of response characteristics of active and inactive subjects to each of these ten situations, as well as a description of criteria for each response category. Since this variety of behavior data does not lend itself to rating, but is best summarized in words, the table is included only to enable the reader to assess the specific observations that underlie the more general descriptions. Our summary below, and Table 5.12, need some explanation.

Of the ten situations, five are very frequent in the experience of all young infants. These are feeding, diapering while content and while discontent, and dressing while content and while discontent. The other five—gentle playful approach, moderately intense playful approach,[9] gentle soothing, moderately intense soothing, and very intense soothing—were represented almost as much in the body of observational data, but their frequency in the experience of a particular infant varies greatly. The frequency with which soothing occurs depends partly on how irritable the infant is. A few of our subjects almost never required soothing because they simply did not cry or fuss. Soothing also depends on maternal style, in that some mothers of irritable infants provide a pacifier, and such soothing does not involve direct contact with the mother. Similarly, the frequency with which a baby experiences playful contacts with another person varies greatly as a function of maternal style and general family atmosphere.

In order to limit our assessment to relatively stable patterns of the infant's response, we included only such contacts between mother and infant (or another person and infant) as could be observed repeatedly. Similarly, we included only those aspects of the infant's behavior that were *typically* shown in the particular situation.[10] For example, if it is reported that an infant reduces activity during gentle play, this indicates that he reduced activity on *each* of many occasions when gentle play was observed. We are reporting only *typical* responses to specific situations for those subjects in whom the relevant situation and response was observed often enough to make this possible.[11] Independent of the degree to which what we observed was representative of the infant's behavior in general, the responses about to be reported constitute some of the ways in which infants behave in these situations.

[9] Intense playful approaches were not made to infants of this age, but only to older infants.

[10] As described fully in *Supplementary Material,* some infants responded variably to the same situation on different occasions. This variability is reflected in Table 5.14 by assigning to the infant a score of 0.5 for each of the response patterns observed. This was useful only in the instances where a component of response, such as smiling or an increase of movement, occurred sometimes but not always, while other aspects of response behavior remained constant. One infant who suffered from fluctuating gastric distress while under observation was so variable that no assessment could be made.

[11] What we could observe of a situation, such as playful contacts or diapering, constitutes but a tiny fragment of the infant's behavior and experience in this context. As discussed fully in Ch. 4, we assume that each subject may respond to the same situation differently at other times. Insofar as consistencies and consistent individual differences in response tendency emerge in sample situations, we consider that they reflect the operation of some central regulating mechanisms. These central regulating mechanisms are likely to play a role in shaping the infant's behavior at other times as well. It is not overt behavior for which our small sampling of behavior episodes can be considered as representative. However, underlying stabilities and consistencies may tentatively be regarded as possibly representative examples of behavioral determinants. In each instance we also obtained from the mother a description of how the infant usually behaved in those situations. The mother's report was included in the Contrast Analyses, but was never used in the reporting of behavior tendencies. Generally, it was in substantial agreement with what was observed.

During feeding, activity level is reduced only for active infants. Gazing at the mother is rare, as are other modes of specific response to her person. All of the active infants reduced activity as soon as feeding began, whereas only one inactive baby showed this change. The four remaining infants [12] did not alter the amount of movement they showed. The difference occurs, of course, because active infants typically engaged in forceful gross body movement during hunger, while inactive ones did not. In this youngest age group only, all infants typically were quiet during feedings, apparently totally absorbed by the activities of sucking and swallowing and the attendant body feeling. It is still interesting that the *only* situations in which active infants were quiescent were being fed (all of them) and being asleep (most of them), whereas most inactive babies showed similar degrees of relaxation at other times as well—for instance, while in the mother's arms or during spontaneous activity.

Our observations also suggest that in very young infants such awareness of the mother as they may feel during the feeding process must be mediated chiefly by touch, and possibly also by sound, thermal stimuli and smell. Only two of these eleven babies were seen to gaze at their mother's face during feeding, and none moved their hands to touch the mother's body. Very young infants (in our sample, those 4 and 8 weeks of age) tend to close their eyes or move them in an incoordinated manner or to engage in autistic staring while they feed. Among the 12-week-old babies, there was often a degree of contact with nearby things, as the infant's hand traveled over the bottle, over the mother's hand and arms, or over his own chest. Babies at this age also sometimes focused on movement in the visual field or on a stationary object during feeding. The mother's face did not become the visual focus, largely because it was obscured by her arm or breast as the baby was held in a half-reclining position.

Of the eleven subjects, eight were fed by bottle and three at the breast. Among these babies, neither the degree of body relaxation nor the minimal tendency to focus upon the mother visually were affected by the feeding method. To judge not only by this sample, but by observation of the feeding process in a very large number of young infants, it is probable that below the age of 3 months the reciprocal aspects of the mother-child encounter during feeding take place almost entirely on a physiological level. The child adapts to the size, position, and movement of the nipple, while the mother in turn adjusts her own position, and that of the baby to the speed and rhythm of his sucking. Although babies in this age range are capable of looking at the mother and of smiling and cooing responsively, these more explicit and externally directed responses to the social partner rarely emerge during feeding.

[12] Ac V received his bottle propped in the crib and was therefore excluded from this analysis.

Being diapered while content elicited focused social responses from most infants above 4 weeks of age. It altered activity level for approximately half the sample. This situation was observed with sufficient frequency in ten infants.[13] Ordinarily the baby is lifted by the mother and put down on a table or her lap as she removes the diaper, sometimes cleans or powders the baby, and then fixes the new diaper securely. Almost invariably this routine brings mother and infant face-to-face, as she bends down over him. Whether or not the mothers made this situation an occasion for social play, all but one of the babies above 4 weeks of age at least gazed at their mother's face, and about half of them also smiled or cooed. One 12-week-old smiled and occasionally cooed, though his gaze merely grazed the mother's face and person. Two of the 4-week-olds transiently but clearly focused on the mother's face during diapering. It appears that a caretaking routine that does not involve gratification of a vital need but does necessitate body stimulation while preserving some physical distance between mother and child is well suited to elicit such specific responses to another person as very young infants can achieve.

In five of the ten babies, the diapering situation always brought a change in activity level; the change was almost as often a decrease as an increase, but remained consistent in direction for each infant.

Being diapered while discontent never elicited social responses, even if it led to the cessation of overt unpleasure. Seven babies in this sample were repeatedly observed as they were being diapered at a time when, for any reason (other than hunger or severe fatigue), they had been crying or mildly irritable, as manifested by restless whimpering. Three of them responded to diapering as a soothing maneuver, in that their distress vocalizations ceased although activity level did not alter. However, even after they had quieted, none of these babies regarded the mother's face nor did they smile responsively. Two other infants were clearly irritated by the procedure, though neither of them had shown discomfort when it took place while they were content. Both of these babies increased their crying and restless activity. They appeared oblivious of the mother's presence, or at least none of their behavior could be seen as responsive to her. The two remaining infants continued to behave much as they had before diapering, also failing to respond specifically to the mother.

The implications of the diapering situation for the infant's experience depend on his initial state—an observation that seems both obvious and trivial. Yet, as an occasion for the baby to gaze at another person and to acquire practice in behavior integrations that lead to recognition of the mother, maternal practices during diapering can make a real difference. If a mother whose baby is irritable and often discontent tends to diaper him at such times, then day in and day out he has fewer chances to inter-

[13] Two active babies were seldom changed unless they cried or whimpered, as their mothers did not believe in "keeping up with the diapers."

act with her than does an infant whose mother changes his diaper just as often, but usually while he is content.

Being dressed while content elicited outwardly focused social responses from most babies and was irritating to some. Ten infants were observed often enough in this situation. The remaining two (one active and one inactive) always cried or fussed during this procedure, even when they had been perfectly content before. Both of them returned to a state of pleasant responsiveness as soon as the procedure was completed. Being dressed differs from being diapered because it involves more forceful and prolonged manipulations. Depending somewhat on the mother's skill and the baby's sensitivity, being dressed has relatively greater power to arouse the infant. Probably for this reason, none of the babies reduced activity on these occasions, while a few typically increased motility. The infants who did not respond adversely to being dressed gazed at the mother's face and smiled and cooed about as much as when being diapered.

Being dressed while discontent was never soothing, was never accompanied by social responses, and sometimes led to an increase in the intensity of distress. Seven subjects were observed repeatedly being dressed while discontent. Of these, three always became more distressed in the course of the procedure than they had been at the beginning, and a fourth occasionally reacted in this way. The other babies continued to cry or fuss as they had before. None of the babies looked at their mothers or registered in overt ways any responsiveness to them as external objects.

Gentle play, when it was not combined with caretaking manipulations, elicited focused social responses from all infants. We have defined as "play" those situations in which the mother, or anybody else, makes contact with the baby for no other purpose than to arouse a pleasurable social response. For a very young infant, gentle play consists of speaking softly to him (or making slight sounds in his direction) from some distance. Often this is interspersed or combined with slight patting, or lightly resting the hand on a portion of the baby's body. The mothers of five active and four inactive babies were repeatedly observed to do this. The other mothers either played with greater intensity or not at all.

The infants responded to gentle play by gazing at the other person (the sole exception was a 4-week-old). The older babies (12 weeks) always smiled, and the active ones also cooed. In other words, given the same kinds of playful attention, in a situation of play for its own sake, the infants *always* responded socially; whereas when the play was combined with body manipulations, like dressing, they *often* did so (see Table 5.12).

Active infants responded to moderately intense play [14] *in the same man-*

[14] It can be said for this sample, as well as for the much larger original study, that mothers do not usually attempt to distract irritable babies by means of social play until after the babies are at least 5 months old. We understand this as an appropriate adaptation on the mother's part to the young infant's incapacity to respond socially while markedly distressed.

ner as to gentle play. Inactive babies responded more strongly. Ten infants in Group One frequently experienced fairly intense playful stimulation. The mother (or another person) spoke to the baby in a compelling manner from close by, often while holding him in her arms; or she might hold the baby's hand or foot and move it about fairly vigorously. Table 5.12 shows that most babies responded to such play by smiling and gazing, as they did to gentle play. However, cooing—the most intense and the developmentally most advanced social response of which 8- and 12-week-olds are capable—appeared among inactive infants only in response to fairly strong social stimulation.

Infants less than 3 months of age respond differently to play as an elaboration of routine care and play for its own sake. For the majority of our youngest infants, play by itself evoked social responsiveness most readily and most intently. The slight indication that the intensity of social stimulation affects the intensity of response more noticeably among inactive infants is mentioned only because it foreshadows consistent and clear-cut differences found among the older babies.

Gentle soothing was provided for all active infants, but for only a minority of inactive ones. Soothing refers to situations in which the infant shows distress and the mother (or anybody else) intervenes to comfort him in ways other than feeding or providing a pacifier. We classified soothing as gentle if it was limited to patting a baby lightly, speaking softly to him, humming, or merely holding him (without rocking, swaying, talking, or singing). Such maternal soothing was offered regularly to all the active infants, but to only two of the inactive ones. This difference may be largely understood as a maternal adaptation to the infant's pattern of reactivity. Active infants are, at these early ages, more irritable than inactive ones and so more frequently require soothing. It was also true for this small sample that the mothers of active infants used soothing more readily because they knew their babies were likely to become exceedingly distressed if allowed to remain uncomfortable for any length of time. Inactive babies, on the other hand, very rarely reached high peaks of unpleasurable excitation. They might whimper, fret, or cry for a short time, yet subside even if left unattended.

However, to judge by what we were able to observe, maternal efforts to prevent prolonged or intense distress in active babies were not especially effective. Two of the active infants always remained uncomforted, one always showed increased distress, and only two were actually soothed.

Moderately intense soothing generally reduced the intensity of the baby's distress, though it failed to restore a quiet and contented state.

Fairly intense soothing was given to all infants when they were markedly distressed from fatigue or hunger (in the latter case, babies were soothed while the bottle was made ready). There was no real difference between active and inactive infants' reactions to moderate soothing measures such as being held and walked about, patted, spoken to, swayed, and the like. The great majority cried and whimpered less (though vocalizations of distress rarely disappeared altogether), and most subjects also reduced activity. Two inactive subjects were resistant to such soothing (one always and one sometimes), and one of the active infants could be calmed only occasionally.

Intense soothing was rarely offered to infants in this age range, and its effectiveness was more than questionable. Massive stimulation is not a customary way of soothing tiny babies. Four of the mothers (two for each activity group) did rock the baby in their arms vigorously, and combined or alternated this with such actions as energetic bouncing of the baby, holding him very tightly to their bodies and, in one instance, patting so energetically that observers thought it ought to be described as "pounding." In every instance, these strong and somewhat frantic measures were taken in an effort to get desperately tired babies off to sleep. The fact that three of the four infants did become calmer may have been due to fatigue and not to the soothing (as was probably also true in some instances of moderate soothing), but certainly their relative quiescence came about in the presence of the mother's forceful stimulation. The one inactive infant who did not relax at all seemed to us to be actually roused by his mother's stimulation, which was ill adapted to her avowed purpose of soothing the baby.

Among young infants, soothing does not mediate awareness of the mother as an outer object. Focusing upon the mother's face occurred very rarely, and the two infants who did so began only after they had become fairly quiet, though the mother continued to soothe as before. Smiling or cooing did not occur at all, not even at the end of these episodes. Nonetheless, it is an important component of the infant's experience whether the mother approaches to soothe him when he is distressed, and whether her soothing is effective or not. The indications are that, by and large, active infants require soothing (from mothers who are inclined to provide it) more often than inactive ones. And it also appears that when soothing is provided for inactive infants, they are more often able to respond by quieting.

The recurring transactions that routinely take place between a mother and her young infant are unequal in their power to compel the infant's awareness of the mother as a distinct component of the environment. The concrete descriptions of some of the recurrent encounters between very young infants and their mothers yielded only slight differences in the typical behavior and experience of active and inactive infants. However, they are relevant to our interest in describing those concrete events that mediate an awareness of the mother in small infants. Individual differences in the baby's typical response come to be important as they are related to differences in maternal style, and will be fully discussed in the chapters on adaptation syndromes (Chapters 13, 14, 15). In the present context, we wish to emphasize that the degree to which individual babies have the opportunity to respond to the mother as a distinct component of the environmental field varies widely as a result of *what* mothers do, *when* they do it, and *how* the infant tends to respond to specific sets of stimulating conditions. Among the situations we were able to observe, among infants up to the age of 12 weeks, being fed, being dressed or diapered while distressed, and being soothed do *not* appear to enhance the infant's awareness of the mother as an external object. But gentle and moderate social play, as well as diapering and dressing while content, *do* provide opportunity for responding to her as a component of the environment.

It is possible that this aspect of early ego development—the awareness of persons as distinct from inanimate objects in the environment and the recognition of mother as a distinguished object—depends to some extent on the frequency and intensity with which young infants experience encounters with the mother that elicit outwardly directed responses. The mother's behavior with the infant then assumes prime importance in determining these early differentiations. However, her impact upon the baby does not stem entirely from either the attitudes and feelings that dictate her behavior or the skill and appropriateness of her techniques. For instance, an infant who has good tolerance for the manipulations involved in being dressed, diapered, or bathed may have ample scope to develop an awareness of the mother, even if she never approaches him in a playful manner. On the other hand, an infant who tends to be unpleasurably aroused by such procedures, and who is rarely played with, will have much less occasion to respond to the mother as a separate entity.

The same relationships can have a bearing on the developmental process in quite a different way. For instance, a mother who is skillful in her manipulation of the infant can make a social encounter of every routine procedure. A less skillful mother, or one whose attention remains focused on just one portion of the baby's body (rather than on the baby as a person), may—even if the baby is not disturbed by the procedures—in no way enhance the baby's awareness of her person. Thus maternal skill and style may make the difference as to whether or not the same number of encounters (of the sort conducive to interaction) provide the same impetus to growth.

Finally, we think that describing what mothers do and how infants behave in consequence may be of help in defining the objective content of the range of behaviors known as "mothering." It seems to us that the reciprocal relationship between mother and baby is more complex and subtle than the interactions that young infants have with things and with their own bodies simply because mothers are more complex and subtle, and show greater variability in their behavior.

During the first two months, each transaction between mother and infant may be viewed as a phenomenon of the same order as the infant's transactions with the environment as he observes the play of light and shadow on the wall, regards toys strung across the crib, or begins to grasp one hand with the other. The difference lies in the fact that such encounters with visual spectacles or with the movement potentials of his own body are a far less prominent and vital aspect of what we have called the effective environment. Alterations in state, strong body feelings, and vivid perceptions calling forth maximal response typically occur during the very young infant's contact with maternal figures. They seldom occur in the course of his transactions with inanimate aspects of the surrounding field. When regarded in this light, the profound importance of the very early mother-child relationship is understood as the result of the prominence, the frequency, and especially the intensity of the child's experience in contact with the mother. Such a view makes it unnecessary to think of the early mother-child relationship as possessing special and powerful attributes that make it qualitatively different from other interactive situations in the infant's experience.[15]

Bodily Self-Stimulation

Bodily self-stimulation was defined as patterned and directed movement that serves to provide direct stimulation of the infant's body. In discussing this dimension of behavior, we mentioned that coordinated movement in general emerges during the first three months of life, and that tactile and kinesthetic self-stimulation are, therefore, manifested clearly only during the fourth month and beyond. In our group of 4- to 12-week-old infants, tactile self-stimulation occurred in four infants, all 8- and 12-week-olds. The behavior was transient, except for one inactive baby who showed it with enough prominence to receive a rating of "medium." Kinesthetic self-stimulation, as previously defined, was not observed in Group One subjects. The comparison of active and inactive babies for this dimension is therefore limited to non-nutritive oral behavior.

Inactive babies showed more oral behavior than did active ones. The material on behavior during spontaneous activity included a rating of the prominence of oral behavior. Here our interest is in the variety of oral behaviors shown by each subject under all circumstances. As was done for most other behavioral dimensions, we noted each oral pattern and its prominence in the behavior of each subject.

Tables 5.13 and 5.14 show that among this group of infants (4 to 12 weeks of age) it was possible to discern eleven different oral patterns. Table 5.13 indicates the prominence of each of these in the behavior of each baby. It also shows for each infant an "oral score," which consists

[15] A similar idea was advanced by others; for instance, Rheingold (1961) and R. W. White (1963).

of the sum of prominence ratings he attained. With the exception of pair VI, inactive infants exceeded active ones in terms of total oral scores.

Table 5.14 describes the frequency and prominence of each oral pattern for the group as a whole, as well as the age range within which each pattern was observed. It shows that ten of the eleven patterns had greater prominence among inactive babies. Another way of summarizing the difference between the groups is to say that the total of oral prominence scores received by the group was 89.5. Of this total 57.0, or 63.6 per cent, was contributed by the inactive infants. Table 5.14 suggests that many oral patterns were shown by an equal number of active and inactive infants, so that differences between the groups reflect primarily the tendency of inactive infants to engage in intense and prolonged mouthing (as Table 5.15 confirms). An oral schema was rated "frequent" (3.0) only twice among active subjects, but eleven times among inactive ones. Lesser ratings were distributed almost equally among active and inactive subjects.

Finally, the same difference was assessed by the method of pair and cross-pair comparisons. Table 5.16 shows that of twelve possible comparisons, in terms of total oral score, inactive babies exceeded active ones in nine instances, whereas the active babies showed more oral behavior on only two comparisons.

Infants show individually different styles and patterns of oral behavior. The varieties of oral activation are of interest because what infants do to stimulate the oral zone differs widely and not as a function of activity level. Licking the hand or an object, which occurs as early as 4 weeks, provides quite different sensations in and about the mouth than does sucking the hand, which also occurs at this early age. Similarly, simply touching one's own lip (which begins at 4 weeks) provides far less intense sensations than does rubbing the lips against the hand, as another 4-week-old was apt to do. Some of these oral behaviors create contact between the mouth and another portion of the body; others are mouth movements that create contact only between the lips, gums and tongue (such as diffuse mouthing and empty sucking), while still others create contact with an inanimate object.

Another sort of difference has to do with the degree to which oral behavior is differentiated. Diffuse mouthing and touching or rubbing of the lips are the most primitive varieties, requiring a minimum of coordination. Articulated tonguing (which involves protrusion of the tongue beyond the lips), sucking the hand or an object, and licking appear to be the earliest coordinations. Sucking the thumb or finger, which requires that one digit be inserted, and mouthing a nearby object demand relatively advanced motor coordinations.

From Table 5.13, read vertically for each subject, it can be seen that most of our subjects cultivated oral schemas at a particular level and of a particular intensity. For instance, Ac I chiefly showed diffuse mouthing, and engaged in occasional brief but avid sucking of the hand. In I supplemented the diffuse mouthing (which was common to all twelve infants) by resting her hand on her lip. Neither of these babies was given to a great deal of oral behavior, but for each the characteristic intensity of body activation was shown by the preferred oral schema. For another example, In V showed every one of the four schemas that employ a sucking movement, three of them frequently; whereas Ac V rarely and gently sucked his hand, but otherwise specialized in articulated tonguing. In the material dealing with older infants it will be shown that the variety of mouthing preferred by different infants may well have a bearing on the use to which oral activations are put. At these later ages, when oral schemas are combined with vision and with other modes of dealing with one's own body and with objects, some oral activations lend themselves to exploration of the environment, whereas others lend themselves chiefly to the arousal of bodily sensations that, for the time being, counteract outward direction of attention.

Although cross-sectional data yield no information on this point, it is likely that infants change in the selection of preferred oral schema as a function of development in general, as well as of teething. However, insofar as differences in the style of oral activation are similar for different age groups, we speculate that the oral experience of individual babies also shows continuity and unity to some extent.

SUPPLEMENTARY MATERIAL TO CHAPTER 5

Criteria for Rating Categories of Motility

Forceful whole-body motion:

Overall motions such as stretching, squirming, rolling, simultaneous kicking of legs and flailing of arms.

Gentle whole-body motion:

As above, but limited in extent, slow, "lazy."

Forceful part-body motion:

Energetic motion of body segments, such as vigorous kicking, windmill motion of arms, elevating rigidly extended legs, etc.

Gentle part-body motion:

Movements of very small body segments, such as fingers only, toes only, rotation of ankle or of wrist, slow and limited lateral motions of head, etc.

Muscle tension:

Gross tremors, exceptionally jerky motions, very rigid extension of a limb (often described as "freezing"), fanning of toes or fingers, severe arching of back.

Quiescent intervals:

Periods during which there occurred no perceptible displacement of the body in space, and during which muscle tension was *not* present.

Table 5.1 (Group One)—Types of Movement during Spontaneous Activity: Individual Prominence Scores

	FORCEFUL WHOLE-BODY		GENTLE WHOLE-BODY		FORCEFUL PART-BODY		GENTLE PART-BODY		MUSCLE TENSION		QUIESCENT	
Pair	*Ac*	*In*	*Ac*	*In*	*Ac*	*In*	*Ac*	*In*	*Ac*	*In*	*Ac*	*In*
I	2.0	0.0	2.0	2.0	3.0	1.0	0.0	3.0	2.0	0.0	0.5	1.0
II	3.0	0.5	0.5	1.0	2.0	0.0	0.0	3.0	2.0	0.0	3.0	2.0
III	1.0	0.0	2.0	2.0	3.0	0.0	1.0	2.0	0.0	0.0	0.0	3.0
IV	1.0	0.5	3.0	0.0	3.0	1.0	2.0	2.0	0.5	0.0	3.0	2.0
V	1.0	0.0	0.0	1.0	3.0	0.5	1.0	3.0	0.0	0.0	0.0	0.0
VI	3.0	0.0	0.0	0.0	3.0	1.0	0.0	3.0	2.0	0.0	0.0	0.0
Totals	11.0	1.0	7.5	6.0	17.0	3.5	4.0	16.0	6.5	0.0	6.5	8.0

Ratings: 3.0 = frequent; 2.0 = medium; 1.0 = occasional; 0.5 = rare; 0.0 = absent.

Table 5.2 (Group One)—Types of Movement during Spontaneous Activity: Pair and Cross-Pair Comparison of Prominence Scores

	Ac > In		Ac < In		Ac = In		NEITHER		N COMPARISONS [a]	
Movement Type	*Pair*	*Cross-Pair*	*Pair*	*Cross-Pair*	*Pair*	*Cross-Pair*	*Pair*	*Cross-Pair*	*Pair*	*Cross-Pair*
Forceful whole-body *	6	6	0	0	0	0	0	0	6	6
Gentle whole-body	1	3	2	2	2	1	1	0	5	6
Forceful part-body *	6	6	0	0	0	0	0	0	6	6
Gentle part-body *	0	0	5	5	1	1	0	0	6	6
Muscle tension *	4	3	0	0	0	0	2	3	4	3
Quiescent	2	1	2	2	0	1	2	2	4	4

[a] Does not include those falling into the "Neither" category.
* Significant at or below p = .05 to a one-tailed sign test (Siegel, 1956).

Table 5.3 (Group One)—*Types of Movement during Spontaneous Activity: Summed Prominence Scores for Active and Inactive Infants*

	N. Ratings	FORCEFUL		GENTLE		MUSCLE TENSION	QUIES-CENT
		Whole-body	Part-body	Whole-body	Part-body		
Active	30	11.0	17.0	7.5	4.0	6.5	6.5
Inactive	30	1.0	3.5	6.0	16.0	0.0	8.0

Table 5.4 (Group One)—*Behaviors during Spontaneous Activity: Pair and Cross-Pair Comparisons of Prominence Scores*

Behavior Category	Ac > In		Ac < In		Ac = In		NEITHER		N COM-PARISONS	
	Pair	Cross-Pair	Pair	Cross-Pair	Pair	Cross-Pair	Pair	Cross-Pair	Pair	Cross-Pair
Oral	2	2	4	4	0	0	0	0	6	6
Vocalizing	2	2	1	0	3	4	0	0	6	6
Hand regard	3	3	1	2	2	1	0	0	6	6
Tactile exploration *	0	0	4	3	0	1	0	0	4	4
Focusing on face **	1	0	4	4	0	1	1	1	6	6
Focusing on suspended toy	1	0	0	0	0	1	0	0	1	1

* Significant at or below p = .05 to a one-tailed sign test (Siegel, 1956).
** p = .050 to 0.55 (doubtful significance).

Table 5.5 (Group One)—*Behaviors during Spontaneous Activity: Comparisons of Prominence Scores*

Pair	ORAL		VOCALIZING		HAND REGARD		TACTILE EXPLORATION		FOCUSING ON FACE		FOCUSING ON SUSPENDED TOY	
	Ac	In	Ac	In	Ac	In	Ac	In	Ac	In	Ac	In
I	1.0	3.0	2.0	2.0	0.5	0.0	0.0	0.0	0.0	1.0	–	–[a]
II	1.0	3.0	2.0	2.0	0.5	0.5	0.0	0.0	0.0	0.0	–	–
III	2.0	0.0	1.0	0.0	1.0	0.0	0.0	3.0	0.0	1.0	–	–
IV	1.0	3.0	1.0	1.0	0.5	0.0	0.0	1.0	0.0	1.0	–	–
V	2.0	3.0	2.0	3.0	0.0	2.0	0.0	1.0	0.5	0.0	–	1.0
VI	1.0	0.5	2.0	0.5	1.0	1.0	1.0	3.0	1.0	2.0	1.0	0.0
Sum	8.0	12.5	10.0	8.5	3.5	3.5	1.0	8.0	1.5	5.0	1.0	1.0

Ratings: 3.0 = frequent; 2.0 = medium; 1.0 = occasional; 0.5 = rare; 0.0 = absent.
[a] – indicates no opportunity for behavior to occur.

Table 5.6 (Group One)—*Behaviors during Spontaneous Activity: Summed Prominence Scores and Average Prominence Scores*

Behavior Category	SUM OF PROMINENCE SCORES		N Subjects: ALL		N Subjects: NUMBER SHOWING BEHAVIOR		Average Score: ALL		Average Score: NUMBER SHOWING BEHAVIOR	
	Ac	In	Ac	In	Ac	In	Ac	In	Ac	In
Oral	8.0	12.5	6	6	6	5	1.33	2.08	1.33	2.50
Vocalization	10.0	8.5	6	6	6	5	1.66	1.44	1.66	1.70
Hand regard	3.5	3.5	6	6	5	3	0.58	0.58	0.70	1.16
Tactile exploration	1.0	8.3	4		1	4	0.25	2.0	1.00	2.00
Focusing on face	1.5	5.0	6	6	2	4	0.25	0.83	0.75	1.25
Focusing on suspended toy	1.0	1.0	1	2	1	1	1.00	0.50	1.00	1.00

Criteria for Assessment of Behavior Changes during Hunger and Fatigue

Activity level:

Increase (+), decrease (−), and no change (=) were judged by comparing activity level during the need state with activity level during the 5-minute interval before the need state became recognizable to the observers (and usually also to the mother).

Oral behavior:

Increase (+), decrease (−), and no change (=) were judged by comparing the prominence of oral behavior during spontaneous activity with its prominence during the need state. For instance, if an infant sucked his hand while hungry or fatigued yet hand-sucking was equally prominent during spontaneous activity, he received a rating of "no change."

Distress vocalizations:

Ratings for this category reflect the intensity of crying or fussing as follows: High (3.0) = intense loud crying, screaming, or squalling; Medium (2.0) = crying or squalling of moderate intensity; Low (1.0) = whimpering, fussing, all sounds expressing displeasure that are less intense than crying.

Continuity:

Present: if distress vocalizations and agitated movements were continuous from the onset of the need state until the beginning of the need satisfaction (feeding or falling asleep).

Absent: if, between the onset of the need state and the beginning of need satisfaction, distress vocalizations and agitated movements alternated with periods during which the infant did not overtly express discomfort.

Table 5.7 (Group One)—Behavior Changes: Effects of Hunger on Activity Level, Oral Behavior, Distress Vocalization, and Continuity of Distress

	ACTIVITY LEVEL						ORAL BEHAVIOR						DISTRESS VOCALIZATION RATING		CONTINUITY OF DISTRESS			
	+		−		=		+		−		=				+		−	
Pair	Ac	In	Ac	In	Ac	In	Ac	In	Ac	In	Ac	In	Ac	In	Ac	In	Ac	In
I	v	v								v	v		3	3	v			v
II			v[a]			v		v	v				3	0	v			−[b]
III	v			v					v			v	3	0			v	−[b]
IV	v					v			v	v			2	1	v			−[b]
V	v	v							v			v	3	0	v			−[c]
VI	v	v						v			v		3	2	v	v		
Totals	5	3	1	1	0	2	0	2	4	2	2	2	17	6	5	1	1	1

Symbols: (+) = increase; (—) = decrease; (=) = no change; (v) = behavior present.

[a] Ac II showed pronounced muscle tension.

[b] No continuity judgment possible since no visible excitation present.

[c] Records equivocal.

Table 5.8 (Group One)—Behavior Changes: Effects of Fatigue on Activity Level, Oral Behavior, Distress Vocalization, and Continuity of Distress

	ACTIVITY LEVEL						ORAL BEHAVIOR						DISTRESS VOCALIZATION RATING		CONTINUITY OF DISTRESS			
	+		−		=		+		−		=				+		−	
Pair	Ac	In	Ac	In	Ac	In	Ac	In	Ac	In	Ac	In	Ac	In	Ac	In	Ac	In
I			v			v			v	v			3	0	v			–[b]
II		–[b]	v				v			v			1	1		v	v	
III			v			v		v	v				0	1	–[b]			v
IV		v	v						v			–[b]	3	2	v			v
V	v	v							v			v	2	2	v			v
VI[a]		v						v						1				v
Totals	1	3	4	0	0	2	1	2	4	2	0	1	9	7	3	1	1	4

Symbols: (+) = increase; (—) = decrease; (=) = no change; (v) = behavior present.
[a] Ac VI was asleep at the beginning of each observation period.
[b] No rating possible.

Criteria for Rating Response to Visual Stimuli

Aversion to photo lights:

Illumination for movie photography was turned on gradually (over 30 seconds) by means of a variac. If on each occasion (there were from six to ten for each baby) the infant blinked, grimaced, or responded in other ways, a rating of "present" was made. If the infant so responded only at some times and not at others, or if he regarded the photo lights undisturbed as he might look at ordinary ceiling lights, or if he paid no attention to the photo lights, a rating of "absent" was given.

Visual discrimination:

For a rating of "present" to be given, it was required that the infant display a discriminatory response whenever the relevant objects were presented, provided that the examiner succeeded in attracting the infant's attention to the stimulus. In all cases but one, the discrimination consisted of an aversion to bright and shiny objects.

Regard immobile face:

As the babies were in the crib, the mother and several observers always sat close by and, depending upon the infant's position, were in his view at a distance from about 2 to 5 feet. As mothers conversed with the interviewer, or did some sewing they had brought along, they frequently paid no attention to the baby. Observers usually maintained impassive physiognomic expressions as they watched the infant. Ratings were assigned on the basis of a combination of the intensity and frequency with which the baby focused on the face of a nearby person as follows: High (3.0) = If baby focused intently many times, or if baby focused fairly often but always for an unusual length of time.

Medium (2.0) = If the baby focused often enough and intently enough for this behavior to be one of the dominant and recurrent patterns.
Occasional (1.0) = If, in comparison with other behavior activations taking place during the same time span, the baby showed focused regard of an unresponsive face at least twice during short intervals (2 to 4 minutes) and with proportional infrequency during longer intervals of time.
Rare (0.5) = If the behavior pattern was observed, but only once or twice.

Follow moving object or person:

Self-explanatory except for the fact that the behavior was rated only if it was the *movement* within the visual field that attracted the infant's attention. When a baby had already focused on a stationary object or person, and then showed visual pursuit as it began to move, the behavior was not scored. Judgments of frequency were made by the same criteria as described for the regard of an immobile person. In addition, judgments of frequency were made relative to the number of occasions when a movement occurred in the infant's field of vision that he *could* have noted, in terms of his position at the time.

Selective regard, distant object:

This behavior was not seen in infants less than 12 weeks of age. In the situation described for the preceding items, or while held quietly on mother's lap, some infants fixedly regarded such objects as a doorknob 6 or 7 feet away, the mother's purse on a table similarly distant, a coffee pot or some such thing. We excluded the regard of ceiling lights, bright windows, and other conspicuous visual spectacles at a distance (because regard of such features of the environment is nearly universal). Visual regard of distant objects had to be intent enough for the narrative records to state that while it lasted, other behaviors disappeared or were greatly reduced. Ratings from 3.0 to 0.5 ("high" to "rare") were assigned on the basis of the relative frequency with which the behavior occurred (as described for "Regard immobile face").

Regard of toy in hand:

Ordinarily this behavior does not occur until the age of 12 weeks, though it was noted in one 8-week-old. Only one subject repeatedly performed this action (In VI), and his rating of 2.0 reflects moderate frequency combined with high intensity.

Reach for, contact object:

This is another item seen at 12 weeks at the earliest. A rating was assigned only if the baby reached toward the object at mere sight of it; *i.e.*, if it was not in motion nor brought to the baby's attention by another person.

Activity decrease, regard person:

Refers to the regard of an unresponsive person as described earlier, but the present rating concerns activity decrease as a conspicuous aspect of the behavior. Infants who each time became immobile as they gazed at persons, and who remained so for the duration of such regard, received a rating of 3.0 (high). Those who showed the same behavior on numerous occasions, but who were also seen regarding a person without reducing their activity, were rated as 2.0 (medium). Ratings of 1.0 and 0.5 signified that the behavior was observed, but was "occasional" or "rare," respectively.

Intent regard as a social response:

When the infant's gaze was attracted to someone who was addressing him, that is, when a person smiled at him and talked to him, the *sole* response of some babies was to gaze at the social partner, not smiling, moving, or vocalizing. When this occurred he received a rating under this heading. Ratings from 3.0 (high) to 0.5 (rare) were assigned on the basis of relative frequency and duration (since high intensity defines this behavior).

Smile, vocalize at sight of object:

Self-explanatory except for the fact that the response had to be made to the sight of only an object, not a person and an object. This was accomplished by suspending an object from a string and presenting it while remaining out of the baby's sight, or by placing an object in the baby's field of vision while the infant's gaze was directed elsewhere. Again, ratings of prominence were based primarily on relative frequency (from smiling and/or cooing each time an object was shown to responding in this manner only occasionally), and secondarily on duration and intensity of the response.

Intensity of interest at sight of object:

On seeing an object (presented as described above), some infants registered excitement and absorption by intense gazing, increasing or decreasing activity, or flushing and breathing rapidly. Their facial expression at such times reflected tension or strain more than pleasure. Here again a combination of relative frequency and intensity was used to assign prominence ratings from 3.0 (high) to 0.5 (rare).

Mouthing, gaping at sight of objects:

Some infants who may or may not gaze or activate the body when objects are presented as described above open the mouth in a gaping fashion. Other babies show, as part of their response to the sight of an object, a movement of the lips and jaws (repeated contraction and lateral motion of the lips that does not resemble sucking). If such behavior commenced at the sight of an object it was scored, but only if there had been no similar oral activation during the minute or two before the object was presented. In this instance relative frequency and duration (not intensity) determined prominence scores from 3.0 (high) to 0.5 (rare).

Table 5.9 (Group One)—Visual Responsiveness: Pair Comparisons of Individual Ratings

	I		*II*		*III*		*IV*		*V*		*VI*	
Behavior Pattern	*Ac*	*In*	*Ac*	*In*	*Ac*	*In*	*Ac*	*In*	*Ac*	*In*	*Ac*	*In*
Aversion to photo lights	−	+	−	+	−	−	+	−[a]	−	+	−	+
Visual discrimination	−	+	−	−	−	−	+	−	+	−	+	−
Regard immobile person					0	1	3	0	0	1	2	2
Follow moving person					2	1	1	2	0	2	1	3
Selective regard: distant object									3	0.5	0.5	0.5
Regard toy in hand					0.5	0	0	0	0	0	0	2
Reach for, contact object									0	0	1	1
Activity decrease: regard person	0	2	2	2	2	3	0.5	0	0	0	0	0
Intent regard as social response					1	2	0.5	3	2	3	0	3
Smile, vocalize at sight of object	0	1	0	0	0	0	0	1	0	1	0.5	2
Intense interest at sight of object	3	3	1	1	2	3	1	2	1	3	2	3
Mouthing, gaping at sight of object					1	2	0	0	0.5	2	0.5	2
Totals	3.0	6.0	3.0	3.0	8.5	12.0	6.0	8.0	6.5	12.5	7.5	18.5

Symbols: (+) = present; (—) = absent.
Ratings: 0.5 = rare or minimal intensity; 1 = occasional or weak; 2 = medium; 3 = frequent or maximal intensty.
[a] Insufficient data for rating.

Table 5.10 (Group One)—Visual Responsiveness: Pair and Cross-Pair Comparisons of Ratings

Behavior Pattern	Ac > In		Ac < In		Ac = In		NEITHER		TOTAL N COMPARISONS		Age Range in Weeks
	Pair	*Cross-Pair*	*Pair*	*Cross-Pair*	*Pair*	*Cross-Pair*	*Pair*	*Cross-Pair*	*Pair*	*Cross-Pair*	
Aversion to photo lights [a]	0	1	4	4	1	0	0	0	5	5	8–12
Visual discrimination [a]	3	3	1	1	2	2	0	0	6	6	8–12
Regard immobile person	1	2	2	1	1	0	0	1	4	3	8–12
Follow moving object, person	1	0	3	2	0	2	0	0	4	4	8–12
Selective regard: distant object	1	1	0	0	1	1	0	0	2	2	12
Regard toy in hand	1	1	1	1	0	0	2	2	2	2	8–12
Reach for, contact object	0	1	0	1	1	0	1	0	1	2	12
Activity decrease, regard person	1	1	2	2	1	1	2	2	4	4	4–8
Intent regard as social response *	0	0	4	4	0	0	0	0	4	4	8–12
Smile, vocalize at sight of object *	0	0	4	4	0	0	2	2	4	4	4–8
Intense interest at sight of object	0	1	4	4	2	1	0	0	6	6	4–8
Mouthing, gaping at sight of object	0	1	3	3	0	0	1	0	3	4	8–12
Totals	8	12	28	27	9	7	8	7	47	46	
Percentage of total comparisons [a]	15%	23%	53%	51%	17%	13%	15%	13%			

Number of Comparisons

* p = <.05 (Siegel, 1956)

[a] For categories rated only as "absent" or "present,' absence in both members of the pair was judged as "equal" rather than "neither."

Table 5.11 (Group One)—Visual Responsiveness: Summed and Average Prominence Scores

	SUM SCORE		N RATINGS		Average Scores: WHOLE GROUP		Average Scores: SUBJECTS SHOWING BEHAVIOR	
Behavior Pattern	*Ac*	*In*	*Ac*	*In*	*Ac*	*In*	*Ac*	*In*
Follow moving object, person	4.00	8.00	4	4	1.00	2.00	1.33	2.00
Intent regard as social response	3.50	11.00	4	4	.87	2.70	1.16	2.70
Smile, vocalize at sight of object	.50	5.00	6	6	.08	.83	.50	1.20
Intensity, interest at sight of object	10.00	15.00	6	6	1.66	2.50	1.66	2.50
Mouthing, gaping at sight of object	2.00	6.00	4	4	.50	1.50	.66	2.00
Totals	20.00	45.00	24	24	4.11	9.53	5.31	10.40

Table 5.12 (Group One)—Social Responsiveness: Changes in Activity, Distress Vocalization, and Social Responses

	N SUBJECTS OBSERVED			Activity: +		Activity: −		Activity: =		Distress Vocalization: +		Distress Vocalization: −		Distress Vocalization: =		Distress Vocalization: NOT PRESENT		Social Responses: SMILE		Social Responses: TOUCH		Social Responses: FOCUS		Social Responses: COOING	
Situation	*Ac*	*In*	*State*	*Ac*	*In*	*Ac*	*In*	*Ac*	*In*	*Ac*	*In*	*Ac*	*In*	*Ac*	*In*	*Ac*	*In*	*Ac*	*In*	*Ac*	*In*	*Ac*	*In*	*Ac*	*In*
Feeding	5	6	content	0	0	5	½	0	5½	0	0	0	0	0	0	5	6	0	0	0	0	1	1	0	1
Diapering	4	6	content	1	2	1	1	2	3	0	0	0	0	0	0	4	6	1	2	0	0	2	3	1	1½
Diapering	4	3	discontent	1	2	0	0	3	1	1	1	1	2	1	1	0	0								
Dressing	6	5	content	1	2	0	0	5	3	1½	1	0	0	0	0	4½	4	1	1	0	0	2	2	1	1
Dressing	4	3	discontent	2	1	½	0	1½	2	2½	1	½	0	1	2	0	0	½	0	0	0	½	1	0	0
Gentle play	5	4	content	0	0	2	1	3	3	0	0	0	0	0	0	5	4	2	2	0	0	5	3	2	0
Moderate play	5	5	content	0	0	1½	1	3½	4	0	0	0	0	0	0	5	5	3	3½	0	0	4	3	3½	2
Gentle soothing	6	2	distressed	0	0	1½	1½	3½	½	1	0	2½	2	2½	0	0	0	0	0	0	0	1	1	0	0
Moderate soothing	2	2	distressed	0	0	2	1	0	1	0	0	2	1	0	1	0	0	0	0	0	0	0	0	0	0
Totals	47	42		5	7½	18	10½	22	24	6	3	11½	9½	5	4	23½	25	7½	8½	–	–	16½	14½	7½	5½

Symbols: (+) = increase; (−) = decrease; (=) = no change.
Note: The ½ score represents subjects who showed a behavior, but not on all occasions.

Criteria for Rating Oral Behavior Patterns

Diffuse mouthing:

Defined as irregular and limited activation of the lips and sometimes of the tongue, not patterned, and therefore unlike sucking, chewing, or licking. Diffuse mouthing almost always occurs together with more general body movement and is ubiquitous among infants below the age of 3 months. Prominence ratings from 3.0 (high) to 0.5 (rare) were based on the relative frequency and duration of such episodes.

Hand sucking, avid:

In infants of 12 weeks and younger, the hand is usually sucked in the region of the knuckles except when the baby is in the supine position, when the hand is likely to rest on the mouth, palm up. In the prone position, the mouth is lowered until it touches the hand, which rests on the mattress. This rating was assigned only when sucking at the hand was intense. Prominence ratings from 3.0 (high) to 0.5 (rare) reflect the relative frequency and duration of this behavior.

Hand sucking, mild:

As above, except that a rating was assigned only when hand sucking lacked force and was intermittent.

Hand touches lip, no activation:

Defined as more than momentary contact between the hand and lip, during which the mouth musculature remains at rest so that stimulation of the mouth is purely tactile and of low intensity. Among young infants this pattern is rarely seen; it occurs with moderate frequency after the age of 3 months. Prominence ratings were assigned as for all other categories of oral behavior and ranged from "high" (3.0) to "rare" (0.5).

Licking hand or finger:

An oral movement was defined as "licking" if the tongue protruded between the lips and moved along a surface which was not inserted into the mouth. In infants below 3 months of age, tongue movement is well articulated but the lips and jaws participate. At later ages licking becomes more differentiated in that the tongue moves while the lips remain at rest. Prominence ratings were assigned as described for previous categories.

Licking proximal object:

As above, except that the tongue is applied to sheet, blanket, or any other inanimate object that happens to be close to the infant's mouth. Prominence ratings were assigned as for the other categories.

Rubbing mouth against hand or object:

This pattern refers to a vigorous lateral motion of the head while the mouth is pressed against any surface or against the infant's hand. Prominence ratings reflect the frequency and duration of this behavior, as for the other categories.

Empty sucking:

Defined as a well-articulated sucking motion executed while neither the hand nor any object is in contact with the mouth. Prominence ratings were assigned in the manner described for the other categories.

Thumb or finger sucking:

This familiar pattern differs from hand sucking by the fact that a single digit is inserted into the mouth, with the lips closed around it. This pattern is seldom seen before the age of 8 weeks. Prominence ratings were based on the same criteria as those described for other oral patterns.

Mouthing proximal object:

We define as "mouthing" all behaviors that consist of approaching an object with the mouth, partially closing the lips around it, and then activating jaws, lips, and tongue. The mouth action depends upon the shape and texture of the object, but is scored here only if it is not sufficiently well defined to resemble either chewing, biting, or sucking. Prominence ratings were assigned in the manner described for previous categories of oral behavior.

Table 5.13 (Group One)—Oral Behaviors: Pair Comparisons of Prominence Scores and Summed Ratings

	Pair												Σ RATINGS		
	I		II		III		IV		V		VI				
Behaviors	Ac [a]	In	Ac	In	Ac	In	Ac	In [a]	Ac [a]	In	Ac	In	Ac	In	Both
Diffuse mouthing	2	2	1	3	2	3	3	3	3	3	2	2	13.0	16.0	29.0
Hand sucking, avid	1	0	2	0.5	0	0	0	1	0	3	0.5	0	3.5	4.5	8.0
Hand sucking, mild	0	0	2	3	2	0.5	2	2	0.5	1	0.5	2	7.0	8.5	15.5
Hand touches lip, no activation	0	2	0.5	0	0	0	0	0	0	0.5	0	0	0.5	2.5	3.0
Licking hand or finger	0	0	0	3	0.5	1	0	0	x	x	x	x	0.5	4.0	4.5
Licking proximal object	0	0	0	1	0.5	0.5	0	0	x	x	x	x	0.5	1.5	2.0
Rubbing mouth against hand/object	0	0	0	3	x	x	x	x	x	x	x	x	0.0	3.0	3.0
Articulated tonguing	0	0	0	2	2	3	0.5	0.5	2	2	0.5	0	5.0	7.5	12.5
Empty sucking	x	x	x	x	0	1	1	0	0	3	0	0	1.0	4.0	5.0
Thumb/finger sucking	x	x	x	x	0	0	0	2	0	3	0	0	0.0	5.0	5.0
Mouthing proximal object	x	x	x	x	x	x	x	x	0.5	0.5	1	0	1.5	0.5	2.0
Oral Score	3.0	4.0	5.5	15.5	7.0	9.0	6.5	8.5	6.0	16.0	4.5	4.0	32.5	57.0	89.5

Symbols: x = not applicable to age.
Ratings: 3.0 = frequent; 2.0 = medium; 1.0 = occasional; 0.5 = rare; 0 = absent.
[a] child was given pacifier (at times not included in these ratings).

Table 5.14 (Group One)—Oral Schemas: Age Range, Frequency of Behaviors, and Summed Prominence Scores

Schema	Age Range (in weeks)	N Subjects: Showing Behavior Ac	N Subjects: Showing Behavior In	N Subjects: Within Age Range Ac	N Subjects: Within Age Range In	Σ Prominence Scores Ac	Σ Prominence Scores In	Σ Prominence Scores All
Diffuse mouthing	4–12	6	6	6	6	13.0	16.0	29.0
Hand sucking, avid	4–12	3	3	6	6	3.5	4.5	8.0
Hand sucking, mild	4–12	5	5	6	6	7.0	8.5	15.5
Hand touches lip, no activation	4–12	1	2	6	6	0.5	2.5	3.0
Articulated tonguing	4–12	4	4	6	6	5.0	7.5	12.5
Rubbing mouth against hand/object	4	0	1	2	2	0.0	3.0	3.0
Licking hand/fingers	4–8	1	2	4	4	0.5	4.0	4.5
Licking proximal object	4–8	1	2	4	4	0.5	1.5	2.0
Empty sucking	8–12	1	2	4	4	1.0	4.0	5.0
Thumb/finger sucking	8–12	0	2	4	4	0.0	5.0	5.0
Mouthing proximal object	12	2	1	2	2	1.5	0.5	2.0
Totals						32.5	57.0	89.5

Table 5.15 (Group One)—Oral Schemas: Frequency of Prominence Ratings and Summed Prominence Scores

Prominence Rating	N Ratings Ac	N Ratings In	N Ratings Both	Σ Prominence Scores Ac	Σ Prominence Scores In	Σ Prominence Scores Both
Frequent	2	11	13	6.0	33.0	39.0
Medium	9	8	17	18.0	16.0	34.0
Occasional	4	5	9	4.0	5.0	9.0
Rare	9	6	15	4.5	3.0	7.5
Absent	26	20	46	0.0	0.0	0.0
Totals	50	50	100	32.5	57.0	89.5

Ratings: 3.0 = frequent; 2.0 = medium; 1.0 = occasional; 0.5 = rare; 0.0 = absent.

Table 5.16 (Group One)—Oral Behavior: Pair and Cross-Pair Comparison

Pair	Ac > In	Ac < In	Ac = In	N Comparisons
Original	0	5	1	6
Cross	2	4	0	6

SIX

GROUP TWO: 16- TO 20-WEEK-OLDS

Spontaneous Activity

Infants between 4 and 6 months of age are apt to spend considerable portions of their waking time unattended, in a contented and animated state. At this age, behavior is far more varied and differentiated than earlier, so that individual characteristics emerge with clarity. This applies not only to motility but also to the degree to which each baby tends to engage in complex mastery behaviors, the degree to which he spontaneously directs behavior toward inanimate objects, and the like.

Yet, for various reasons, our data on children 16 and 20 weeks of age afford only limited opportunity for a comparison of active with inactive infants. Group Two has eight subjects, allowing only four comparisons among active and inactive infants (and, in addition, four cross-pair comparisons). Further, Group Two happens to include no active subjects who were rated as coming close to the extreme, although the inactive end of the continuum is well represented. All active subjects in Group Two had overall activity ratings of either 2.2 or 2.3, whereas in Group One overall activity ratings ranged from 2.3 to 2.7, and in Group Three from 2.5 to 3.0. In short, this sample fails to include behavior patterns characteristic of very distinctly active infants.[1]

A further complication arises from the fact that major developmental changes occur during the fourth and fifth months, so that behavior differences at one level were difficult to compare with differences at the next. Although our findings on Group Two will be reported within the format of a comparison of active with inactive infants, the nature of developmental changes during this age span and individual differences not necessarily associated with activity level are of greater interest.

[1] See Ch. 4 for a full description of the sample, which was selected to include the most active and least active infants at each age level in the much larger population of infants from which the present sample was selected.

Motility

As with the youngest infants, typical patterns of motility could be recognized most clearly during spontaneous activity. Movement patterns were categorized and rated in the same manner as for the infants in Group One.

Active infants showed a great deal more forceful movement of the whole body and of body parts than did inactive ones. Gentle part-body movement was shown much more by the inactive babies, and only they typically had quiescent intervals. Table 6.1 indicates for each infant the prominence with which he showed each type of movement during spontaneous activity. Table 6.2 summarizes these findings for the group as a whole. The results are altogether similar to those obtained for Group One and require no additional discussion.

Patterns of motility differ widely among active infants and less so among inactive ones. Table 6.1 may be read horizontally to yield a profile of relatively more and less prominent movement activations for each baby. Some active infants (Ac VII and Ac IX) seldom moved the entire body in a forceful manner, but instead showed a great deal of forceful part-body activation; whereas others (Ac VIII and Ac X) engaged in a fair amount of forceful whole-body motion in variable constellation with other types of movement. By contrast, all inactive babies received ratings of frequent for gentle part-body motions, and rarely more than a rating of occasional for any other type of movement. As was also true for the younger babies, a classification in terms of active and inactive does not adequately describe individual styles of motility, which, particularly among active babies, can vary widely.

SPECIFIC PATTERNS OF BEHAVIOR, THEIR DIRECTION AND COMPLEXITY

Beyond the age of 4 months, differences in the amount and forcefulness of motion that infants show during spontaneous activity are clear-cut, but they fail to describe the sensorimotor content of behavior at such times.

In order to determine what these infants actually did while alert, awake, and unattended, the observational records were scrutinized in terms of specific behavior patterns or schemas that occurred and their relative prominence in the behavior of each baby.

During spontaneous activity, infants of Group Two showed 29 different behavior schemas. Of these, more than half were coordinated, and approximately half were oriented toward a component of the immediate environment. Because of our interest in the qualitative aspects of behavior during spontaneous activity, and its developmental relevance, each of the observed behavior patterns was classified in a number of ways. One was whether the behavior in question was "coordinated" or "primitive," referring to the degree of patterning and integration relative to that expected at the age. For instance, "rolling" was classified as primitive, and "articulated kicking" and "regard of object in hand" were classified as coordinated.[2] The same schemas were also classified as to whether they were "self-contained" or "outer-focused," indicating whether or not the baby's attention was directed toward a specific component of the immediate environment.

For very young infants, some segments of their own body, such as the hand or the foot, are clearly parts of the environment. For example, we classified "articulated kicking" and "tactile self-stimulation" as self-contained, while "reach for and contact object" and "hand regard" were considered to have an outer focus. Behaviors that mediate awareness of components of the environment can be directed toward different aspects of the surrounding field. They were classified in terms of whether attention and movement were directed at a portion of the body ("grasping foot"; "hand regard"); at an environmental object ("reaches for, contacts toy"; "regards distant object"); or at a person ("regards moving person"; "regards immobile person"). Lastly, some of the schemas activated chiefly or entirely a single sensory modality or a single body system. These schemas were classified as being "tactile," "visual," "vocal," and "oral" in nature.

Table 6.4 gives all behavior schemas noted during spontaneous activity in Group Two, the classification of each, and the frequency with which each behavior occurred in the sample as a whole.[3] It indicated that of the 29 schemas, 11, or 38 per cent were "primitive," and the remaining 18 (62 per cent) were judged to be "coordinated" for infants of this age.

Figure 6.1 shows that slightly more than half (58.6 per cent) of the 29 schemas were outer-focused, while the rest were self-contained. Most of the former were focused either on a part of the body (27.5 per cent) or on an inanimate object (24.2 per cent). Only two schemas (7 per cent) had a social focus. Among the youngest infants of Group One, we were able to distinguish only six behavior patterns during spontaneous activity (see Tables 5.4 and 5.6). Of these, three had an outer focus (fleeting hand regard, focusing upon an impassive face, and focusing upon suspended toys). In Group One all these behaviors were exceedingly rare and, by definition, transient. A comparison of Tables 5.4 and 5.6 with the data on spontaneous activity for Group Two illustrates the massive developmental changes that take place during the fourth and fifth month of life. These data also specify, to some extent, the nature of these changes. They consist of increasing differentiation (from 6 to 29 patterns) and a greatly

[2] Two behaviors—"squealing" and "grasping, tactile exploration of object"—are considered as "coordinated" at 16 weeks and as "primitive" at 20 weeks.

[3] Table 6.5 specifies the behavior schemas shown by each infant, as well as their prominence.

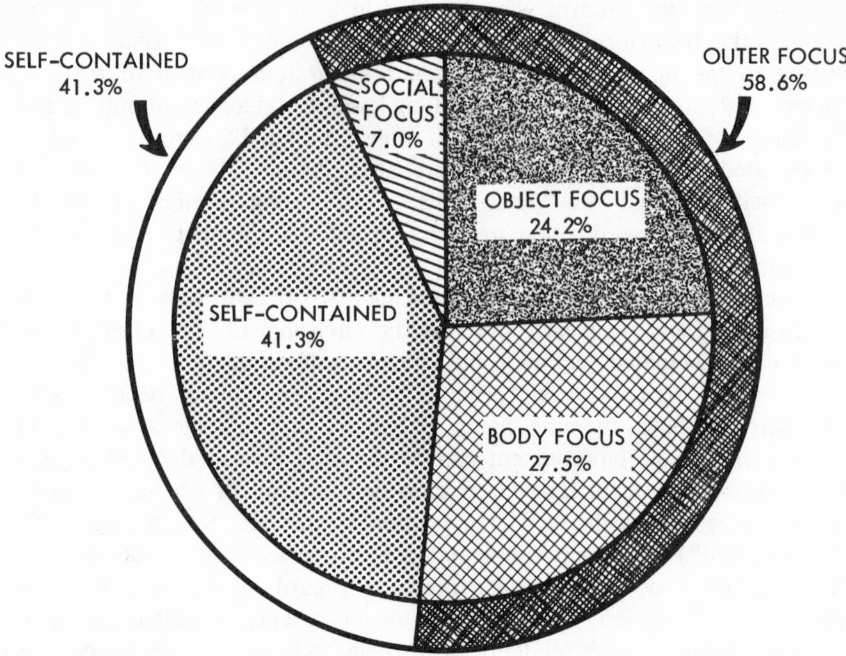

FIGURE 6.1. SCHEMAS DURING SPONTANEOUS ACTIVITY: RATIOS OF SELF-CONTAINED TO OUTWARDLY FOCUSED SCHEMAS.

increased capacity to orient and focus behavior on a component of the immediate environment, which in turn reflects the emergence of the capacity for directed and voluntary movement.

We have specified the diversity of behavior schemas, but have not yet dealt with the prominence of each type of schema in the behavior of these babies. Table 6.6 shows that for the sample as a whole, the distribution of prominence scores yields a picture almost identical to that obtained from the classification of each schema. For the entire sample, 60 per cent of all prominence scores were contributed by ratings received for coordinated schemas. Similarly, about one-half of all prominence ratings (52.2 per cent) were contributed by ratings received for outwardly focused behavior patterns.

Inactive babies showed primitive and self-contained behaviors more prominently than did active ones. They also directed behavior more prominently toward parts of their own body, while active babies' behavior was directed more toward inanimate objects. A comparison between the behavior patterns of active and inactive infants during spontaneous activity is provided in Table 6.6 for the group as a whole, and on Tables 6.7 and 6.8 for each infant. Throughout, differences between the groups are so small that they might easily be due to chance. However, Table 6.9 compares for each pair (and each realignment on cross-pair comparison) the percentage of the total prominence score received by each infant, contributed by behavior in each classification for which a group difference had been found. This table shows that in the great majority of instances, the difference between individual pairs is in the same direction as the group difference. Specifically, of 24 comparisons of the original pairs, 20 were in the same direction as the group difference; and in cross-pair comparison, 19 of 24 conformed to the group difference. These consistencies are significant, and may be taken to mean that inactive babies in this sample tended to show, during spontaneous activity, behavior somewhat more primitive, more self-contained, and more focused upon their own body.

Individual infants may show a pattern atypical of their activity level group. Table 6.8 shows that all reversals from the group pattern were contributed by pair VII. Ac VII rarely focused his attention on an object, and his behavior was self-contained to a much larger degree than that of any other active baby. In VII, on the other hand, was the only inactive baby who oriented an appreciable portion of her spontaneous behavior toward objects. It so happened that Ac VII spent almost his entire waking time in the supine position, strapped to a bassinette. In VII had a mother who not only moved the baby a good deal, but who regularly placed a rattle in her hand, endlessly restoring the toy when the baby lost it. Ac VII thus had little scope for activity and little to look at but the ceiling. Accordingly, his prominent behaviors (see Table 6.5) were squirming, stiff extension of the limbs, kicking, clasping his hands (above his chest and not in the visual field), indistinct vocalizing, and regarding an immobile person. In VII, who spent a fair amount of time sitting upright (propped against pillows), and who was frequently handed a toy, engaged primarily in arm waving, lateral head motions, tactile exploration of nearby objects, reaching for and contacting nearby objects, and hand regard (guided by vision).

In this instance, as in others, we are interested in determining whether the actual behavior of the infant whose pattern deviates from the majority is nonetheless in accord with the characteristic reaction tendencies of his activity level group. For the two 16-week-olds just referred to, we conclude that the type of activity each showed while left to his own devices conformed to what was typically seen in active and inactive babies. The spontaneous behavior of Ac VII reffects the fact that he received minimal environmental support for exploratory behavior. In VII, on the other hand, was provided with more than ordinary enticement to complex action, even when not in direct contact with her mother. It will be remembered that we understand the group differences on the basis of a typical difference in reactivity that appears to be associated with activity level—the tendency of active infants to mobilize much of their behavior repertoire in response to minimal stimulation. By contrast, inactive infants tend to mobilize more complex and intense behavioral responses only when external stimulation is at least moderately strong. In VII, because of her usual sitting position, by proximity to toys, and by frequent disruptions of spontaneous activity as the mother gave back lost toys, was indeed responding to a degree of external stimulation even when left to her own devices.

Individual differences in the nature of spontaneous behavior are pronounced, even among children in the same activity level group. Quite aside from the consequences of activity for the organization of behavior, individual differences are pronounced in terms of what these babies did while unattended. As shown in Tables 6.7 and 6.8 in this small sample, these differences cannot be ascribed to markedly different developmental level, for the proportion of coordinated schemas is very similar in all (except Ac IX, whose I.Q. was 144; 75 per cent of her spontaneous behavior was coordinated).[4] But the variety of coordinations set in motion differed widely. One inactive baby (In VII) paid as much attention to nearby objects as to her own body, while two others never focused on objects at all. One active baby (Ac VII) directed as much as 50 per cent of his behavior toward the mere sight of a person whereas this behavior was minimal in other active babies. Preoccupation with body-focused activity ranged, among all babies, from 5 per cent (Ac IX) to 71 per cent (In X). Clearly, what these babies experienced as they were left to their own devices was widely different in terms of the content of perceptual awareness, the intensity and complexity of behavior, and the degree of animation and effort they expended.

It is one thing to document the fact that well-developed infants of like age spend their "free time" in widely different ways, and quite another thing to demonstrate that such behavior differences play a role in shaping the course and pattern of development. For the most part, discussion of this point is reserved for the chapters dealing with adaptation syndromes (Part Three). Here we should like to call attention to the fact that what infants are capable of doing by themselves, and what they are likely to do when unattended, alters to some extent the acquisition of behavior adaptations that reflect spatial extension of the effective environment.

Overall, our observations of spontaneous behavior in 16- and 20-week-old infants suggest that at these transitional ages, a relatively higher activity level tends to make babies more aware of and more responsive to physically distant aspects of the environment. Table 6.10 reflects the prominence

[4] In general, the degree to which spontaneous behavior was coordinated, or the complexity of coordination, was in keeping with the results of developmental testing. However, for the markedly accelerated infants, many coordinated behaviors were in fact well-learned and simple schemas, as shown by contrast with their most advanced behavior integrations as displayed at these and other times. The I.Q.s for the other seven babies in Group Two ranged from 90 to 119.

ratings received by active and inactive babies for behaviors that clearly demonstrate either awareness of the more distant environment (regard or reaching), or a greater distance between subject and object, in that an object is manipulated rather than approached or perceived (transferring object from hand to hand with visual regard). The same table shows that the differences between inactive and active babies were much greater for these specific responses than for the classes of behavior reported in the earlier tables. During the time span when development consists chiefly of the emergence of voluntary and directed movement, which presupposes some differentiation on the sensorimotor level between the acting subject and the acted-upon object, and of adaptive and specific (rather than diffuse) responsiveness to more than the proximal environment, activity level probably plays a role in determining the relative pace of these developmental acquisitions.

Bodily Need States: Hunger and Fatigue

The states of hunger and fatigue were observed repeatedly in each member of Group Two. In 16- and 20-week-old babies both of these conditions are demarcated more clearly from other waking states than in the younger babies, simply because the intervals between feedings and between naps are longer, and because these older infants remain awake for a larger number of daytime hours.

For active infants, hunger leads to more intense distress and greater agitation than it does for inactive ones. Fatigue, however, is associated with nearly equal signs of overt distress in both activity level groups. As a first assessment of the impact of hunger and fatigue upon behavior, we noted changes in activity, oral behavior, and distress vocalizations in the same manner as we had for infants of Group One. We also noted, for each baby, whether motoric agitation and distress were continuous, or whether the discomfort arising from the need state was intermittent. Figs. 6.2 and 6.3 indicate these behavior changes for hunger and for fatigue. More active than inactive babies cried severely while hungry; more of the active ones cried continuously; and all active ones increased activity. Most of these signs of discomfort were seen also among inactive babies, except that none of them showed continuous distress, nor did any of them cry or scream at a high level of intensity. In the case of fatigue there was very little difference between the groups, except that two inactive babies showed no distress at all, while all of the active subjects did.

Tables 6.11 and 6.12 give an account of the typical behavior with hunger and fatigue for each member of Group Two. The material on these tables is provided because, when read in conjunction with the parallel tables concerning other dimensions of behavior, it makes it possible to

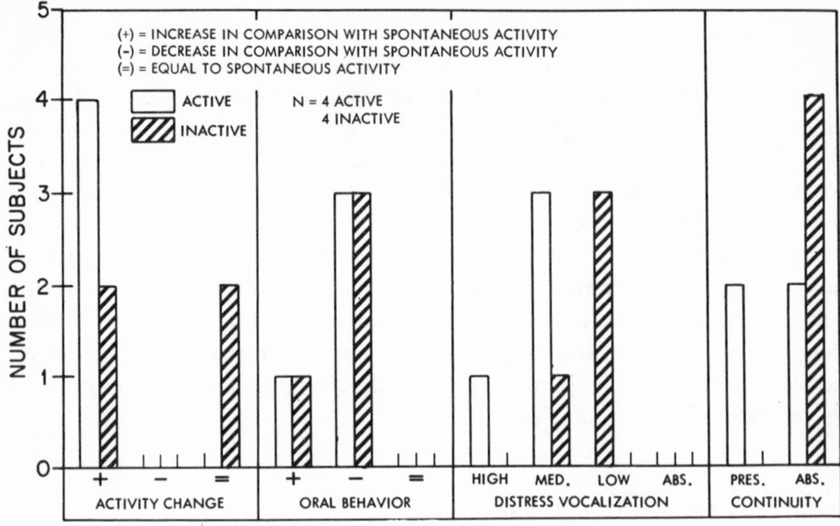

FIGURE 6.2. MANIFESTATIONS OF HUNGER.

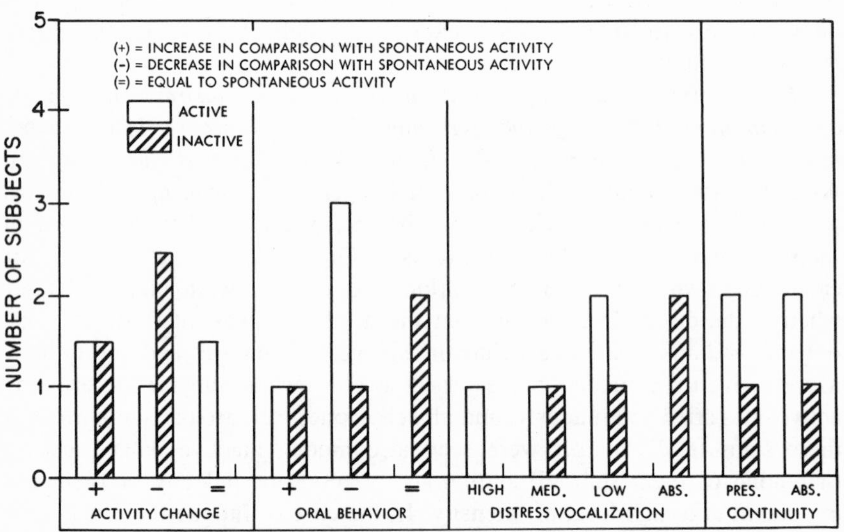

FIGURE 6.3. MANIFESTATIONS OF FATIGUE.

NOTE: Two inactive subjects showed no distress, hence continuity during rating was not applicable. Several subjects showed a different activity pattern during early stages of fatigue and later stages; they received a score of ½ for each activity change.

determine for each baby typical behaviors under a variety of conditions. These and similar tables will serve as background material for the discussion of adaptation syndromes.

For most babies, neither hunger nor fatigue led to more intense oral behavior than they showed during spontaneous activity. Non-nutritive oral behavior will be described in greater detail in a later section. The data reflected on Figs. 6.2 and 6.3 merely compare the prominence of oral behavior while the baby was hungry or fatigued with its prominence while the same baby was contented, alert and left to his own devices. Only two of the eight infants showed more intense oral behavior during need states than during spontaneous activity. This does not mean that these babies did not mouth or suck while hungry and while sleepy, but it does mean that while alert and contented, they showed much the same behavior to an equal degree. In fact, six of the eight babies showed less oral behavior while they were hungry, and four showed less oral behavior while sleepy than during spontaneous activity. It appears that many of the babies were so aroused by the need state that it was difficult for them to sustain the degree of coordination and the relatively low level of motility that are necessary for prolonged oral activation.

The complexity of behavior organization and the responsiveness toward the environment are profoundly altered during hunger and fatigue. Anyone acquainted with infant behavior knows that a hungry or a sleepy baby behaves quite differently from when he is awake and content, and that crying and changes in motility do not describe the difference. While uncomfortable from such causes, the baby "is not himself," as mothers often put it. It seemed important to delineate the effects of hunger and fatigue in terms of changes in the organization of behavior. In babies 16 and 20 weeks of age, behavior remains patterned during need states (which is not the case with 4- and 8-week-olds). Therefore, these infants' behavior while hungry and fatigued was scrutinized and classified in terms of behavior patterns, using the same criteria used in the analysis of spontaneous activity. For each infant we could thus determine which, if any, of the behavior patterns that were typical for him during spontaneous activity altered during need states. Further, we could specify for each infant those behavior patterns that occurred during need states but had not been observed at all while he was alert and content.

Other than distress vocalizations (from whimpering to screaming), the behaviors noted only during bodily need states were limited to tactile self-stimulation (five infants), rolling (one), squirming (two) and kicking (one). These are all self-contained behaviors and, with the exception of kicking, are primitive and undifferentiated body activations. Massive changes in behavior did occur with bodily need states largely because many behavior patterns disappeared while others either increased or decreased in prominence.

Table 6.13 shows that in both hunger and fatigue, the coordinated and the outer-focused schemas tended to be lost, and only primitive and self-contained varieties of behavior increased in number. Table 6.14 indicates for each infant the relative prominence of primitive and self-contained behaviors during hunger and fatigue as compared with the prominence of such behavior during spontaneous activity. In nearly every subject, behavior during need states was entirely self-contained and generally primitive.

In other words, when the impact of bodily need states is assessed in terms of *functional changes,* we find that hunger and fatigue have equally massive effects on active and inactive infants.

The alternation between periods of optimal behavior integration and periods during which relatively mature coordinations are lost may play a role in mediating developmental progress. In the discussion of bodily need states as a dimension of behavior, we mentioned the psychoanalytic hypothesis that a first awareness of outer reality emerges, wholly or in part, out of the repetitive experience of need tension and a delay in need gratification. The hypothesis does no more than propose that delayed need gratification is a necessary condition for the subsequent emergence of rudimentary ego functions; it does not specify that awareness of an environment distinct from the body self comes about *during* need states. However, speculations on the subject have occasionally presumed an association in time between the experience of hunger and the recognition of an outer reality.

Our elaborate classification of behaviors noted in hungry and sleepy babies merely restates common knowledge; namely, that strong excitation and distress deprive the infant of such integrative capacities as he may possess during states of equilibrium or in response to lesser degrees of excitation. Our statement that during need states the (partial) differentiation between self and non-self disappears raises an intriguing question. If the delay in need gratification does not by itself mediate an awareness of the environment, then in what situations and states do infants show by their behavior that some orientation toward an external environment exists?

From the description of spontaneous activity, we know that 4- and 5-month-old babies can and do focus upon the environment. For infants up to 12 weeks of age, such a rudimentary awareness of something in the environmental field is likely to occur during recurrent encounters between mother and infant. However, the fact that a behavioral differentiation between self and non-self appears at times when infants are alert and when external stimulation is of low or moderate intensity does not mean that there is no relationship between this differentiation and the recurrent experience of need-tension and of delay in need gratification.

Tentatively we suggest that it is the *recurrent loss* of the relatively most integrated patterns of function, *alternating* with contented and animated states during which new and more mature patterns can be mobilized, that may be necessary for developmental progress. In other words, if patterns of behavior integration at a given developmental level were never disrupted, they might stabilize so much as to counteract their replacement by new and more mature sensorimotor schemas.[5]

Certain clinical facts are in good accord with our view. Infants who deviate from the normal in that their early development is retarded or grossly distorted are known to be either hyperirritable or lethargic during the first year of life and beyond.[6] Lethargic and irritable babies have in common that their experience lacks a regular alternation between states of marked excitation, states of relative quiescence, and states of mild and moderate animation. In hyperirritable infants, relatively high levels of excitation are chronic, and relaxation tends to be an all-or-none affair. Whether the developmental deviation is due to demonstrable pathology of the central nervous system or to other causes, hyperirritable infants are seen predominantly in one of two states: they are drowsy or asleep, or else their excitation and discomfort are strong enough to limit behavior to the primitive and self-contained varieties described earlier as being associated with bodily need states in normal babies. What such babies seldom or never experience are the in-between states of alert responsiveness.

Lethargic infants also have far less opportunity to experience the entire range of states of excitation. Much of the time they behave like some of our inactive subjects during spontaneous activity, not using any but the simplest schemas, and thus not driven to encounters with things in the outer world, including perceptible and manipulatable parts of their own body. Their experience differs from that of normal inactive babies in that, by virtue of their pathology, the usual varieties of mildly excitatory stimulation do not penetrate sufficiently to rouse them to more focused and active responsiveness. Excitation is for them a matter of extremes: it requires pain, hunger or other massive stimulation to mobilize their active responses, which then tend to be poorly focused and primitive in nature. Autistic infants, about whom little is yet known, are an extreme instance: their vegetative functions proceed with singular smoothness so that bodily distress is rare; they show many of the usual developments in neuromuscular coordination; and their behavior is extraordinarily self-contained. These are the very infants whose pathology in early childhood includes a striking lack of ability to consistently maintain a separation between the self and the surrounding field.

We suggest that what may be a necessary condition for earliest ego

[5] Indeed, theories of mental retardation that emphasize the pathological and premature rigidity in the functioning of feebleminded children (Lewin, 1935; Werner, 1948) have made essentially the same assumption.

[6] See, for instance, Foss (1963, pp. 53–60).

differentiation is the experience of a delay in need gratification *as part of a regular sequence* that also includes an adequate range of moderate excitations and relative quiescence. According to this hypothesis the relative lack of *any* of the three degrees of excitation should have the effect of retarding the development of early ego functions. Similarly, the lack of such a combination of experiences should have the same consequences although in some instances the experiential deficit has organic causes and in others it may be due to gross environmental deficit.

Object Stimulation

By "object stimulation" we mean those situations in which the mother or another person takes active steps to interest a baby in inanimate objects. Such stimulation may range in intensity from merely presenting a toy in an inviting manner, to moving it about and shaking or squeaking it before placing it within the baby's reach, to very animated talking to the baby while performing with the toy, or touching the baby's hands with it. Developmental testing involved the most prolonged and usually the most intense object stimulation we had occasion to observe in these subjects. However, many of the mothers frequently enticed their infants to play with toys, sometimes to divert them, sometimes to demonstrate to us a behavior they had reported, and very often for the fun of it.

In contrast to the youngest age group, infants 16 and 20 weeks of age have begun to discriminate among inanimate components of the environment. They are capable of a variety of behavior integrations that are specifically adapted to the physical properties and location of a particular object. It will be recalled that, during spontaneous activity, 8 of 29 behavior schemas were object-oriented (Table 6.4) and 24.2 per cent of the combined prominence score for the group was contributed by object-focused behaviors (Fig. 6.1).

Object stimulation increases the number and complexity of object-focused behaviors. Following our usual procedure, we listed for each infant all object-related behavior patterns noted during object stimulation and assigned a prominence rating to each pattern for each baby (see Table 6.15). For Group Two as a whole, object stimulation elicited seventeen different object-related behavior schemas, or twice as many as were noted during spontaneous activity. Of these seventeen schemas, ten were observed only during object stimulation. In large part, these were among the most complex and articulated behaviors of which babies are capable at this age, for instance, shaking a rattle with attention to the resulting sound, banging objects, moving objects about, and attempting to regain objects that had dropped from their hands.

The contrast between the variety and prominence of object-related and usually coordinated behavior when babies are left to their own devices and when their attention is playfully drawn to nearby things suggests a clue to one of the many experiences that is provided by mothering, but minimized or absent in the lives of institutionalized infants and of those babies who, for whatever reason, do not enjoy effective maternal care. The data on even this exceedingly small sample strongly suggest that to direct their behavior and attention to specific components of the environmental field and, especially, to respond with relatively mature and novel modes of coordination, infants need to be in a state of comfortable animation—not compelled by strong body needs or by very forceful external stimulation, and not distressed. But even in this optimum state, specific prodding is necessary to elicit the more complex behaviors that are in the process of being acquired.

Such special playful prodding at times when babies are content and animated comes about primarily because, in ordinary home environments, adults and older children derive pleasure from such play and from the baby's response. Institutional personnel are rarely free to indulge in more than transient play. Similarly, mothers who cannot establish an easy intimacy with their babies usually derive little pleasure from such play and therefore lack the motivation to provide it.

We are not suggesting that it is merely the deficiency of perceptual richness and stimulation for infants in an institutional setting (or its emotional equivalent) that retards the precursors of cognition and other early ego functions. In that event, supplying mobiles, automatic music or rhythmic sound, or a multitude of available objects (which in that context are manipulanda rather than toys) would adequately compensate infants deprived of intimate maternal attention. But observation of the contrast between self-generated play and reciprocal play (for this sample and in general) highlights the fact that the actual physical or sensorimotor experience of the infant is quite different in the two situations. A person who plays with a baby, using toys or objects treated as toys, is specifically responsive to behavior clues given by the baby. The object is either held within the baby's reach and moved as his position changes, or moved provocatively just beyond reach, inviting the baby's efforts to obtain it. If the baby looks displeased or loses interest, the toy is brought closer or another type of playful approach is instituted. If the baby responds (by reaching, "giving back" the toy, shaking the rattle, etc.) the adult partner smiles, laughs, hugs the baby, and the like. In short, object stimulation provided by a social partner is specifically attuned to the infant's momentary state and movement pattern; it is appropriately varied in tempo and intensity; it is imbedded in a back-and-forth flow of social interaction; and thus it facilitates novel behavior adaptations in a manner that even sophisticated programmed automatic stimulation cannot be expected to approximate.[7]

Object stimulation greatly altered the behavior of inactive subjects, while active babies showed comparatively little change. Table 6.16 shows the number and prominence of object-related behaviors noted for each baby during object stimulation, as well as the number and prominence of such behaviors during spontaneous activity. The striking difference between active and inactive babies during spontaneous activity altogether disappeared when object stimulation was provided. For the inactive babies as a group, the total prominence score for object related behaviors rose from 4.5 during spontaneous activity to 33.0 during object stimulation. For the active babies, the total prominence score changed from 27.0 to 36.5. Similarly, the total number of ratings for different object schemas rose, for inactive babies, from 6 during spontaneous activity to 26 during object stimulation; the corresponding values for the active group being 15 for spontaneous activity and 29 for object stimulation. This difference in the response to object stimulation was pronounced in three of the four pairs,[8] and one active baby (Ac VIII) showed object-focused behavior less prominently with special stimulation than without.

This finding is but one of many that lead to the hypothesis that motorically inactive infants are generally just as able as active ones to perform the coordinated behaviors appropriate to their age, but that they depend far more on external stimulation. From this we have inferred that maternal stimulation must play a different role in the experience of active and inactive infants. Between the third and ninth month of life, when these coordinations first emerge, inactive babies rarely practice them unless engaged in animated play by someone else, whereas active infants generate such behaviors without specific provocation, as long as they are free to move and there are manipulatable objects within sight and reach.[9]

Object stimulation not only raised the complexity of object-related behavior of inactive babies to the same level as that attained by the active ones, but also eliminated qualitative differences between the groups. During spontaneous activity certain schemas were shown to be typical for active and for inactive babies. Table 6.15, however, shows that during object stimulation the prominence of particular schemas in individual children was unrelated to activity level. Certain coordinations were most

[7] Another piece of evidence for the specific properties of social object play is the commonplace observation that the eager efforts of preschool age siblings to play with the baby usually end in tears. A 4-year-old bent on amusing the infant lacks awareness of the baby's responsive behavior and so fails to make the adaptations without which a young infant cannot sustain the situation for long.

[8] The exception, pair VII, was discussed on page 141.

[9] This hypothesis was advanced in an earlier publication (Escalona, 1963). Subsequently Schaffer (1966a) compared the effects of hospitalization upon developmental progress for active and inactive infants in this age range. He found that hospitalization impeded developmental advance significantly more for inactive than for active infants. An independent study on a very different population thus lent support to the hypothesis.

frequent in the sample as a whole, and all of them were seen about as often among active babies as among inactive ones. These were, in order of frequency: bringing a toy to the mouth; regarding a toy held in the hand; reaching for and grasping an object; and transferring an object from one hand to the other.

The disappearance of differences in behavioral style under conditions of fairly strong and specific stimulation was encountered in many contexts, and is not surprising. In general, the more intense and/or the more specific the stimulation, the narrower the range of possible behavioral responses. At the age when simple modes of approaching and manipulating objects are in the process of developing, appropriate stimulation has compelling power. In observing babies of this age as they perform these responsive actions, one has the impression that—provided one succeeds in focusing their attention—they *have* to gaze, grasp, bring to the mouth, transfer, or perform whatever schema happens to be dominant. This observation has been made by many students of infant behavior, and has been discussed under the heading of "stimulus-boundedness." The term means that, under appropriate conditions, the infant's visual-motor response to object stimuli is directed but not entirely voluntary. It is as though the responding infant had no true alternative, so that gazing, reaching and the like are very nearly automatic, in the same sense that a startle or an exclamation in response to sudden pain is not an entirely voluntary action. One aspect of development is precisely the fact that, with advancing age, infants acquire greater freedom not only to withhold response but also to respond in increasingly varied and modulated ways.

Babies differed markedly from one another in their social and motoric response to object stimulation, but these differences were totally unrelated to activity level. The description of behavior during object stimulation is not limited to the number and kind of object-focused schemas shown by each child. To some babies the situation remains primarily a social one, and their attention is divided between the partner and the toys. Other babies, once their attention has focused upon an object, are so absorbed that they neither smile nor coo nor gaze at the partner. Some babies become markedly excited, others never show more than a very moderate degree of animation. And some babies immediately initiate a motoric response at the sight of objects; while others typically gaze at the toy for some time before moving to touch it.

Table 6.17 summarizes these behaviors for subjects of Group Two. During object stimulation, these babies showed excitation and involvement to varying degrees, but the differences were not related to activity level. One might think that both social responsiveness and the degree of excitation could be accounted for by differences in the style and intensity of the playful stimulation provided by the adult. However, this was not the case. Our assessment was based primarily on behavior during the developmental tests, which were invariably administered by one of two staff members, always in the same manner. Behavior during episodes when the mother or another person used objects playfully was checked independently. We were surprised to find that, if play was at all sustained, each baby behaved in a manner consistent with his behavior during developmental testing.

Social responsiveness during the testing situation (and on similar occasions) appears to depend on the degree of excitation evoked by the presentation of toys. As shown in Table 6.17, those babies who showed high or medium levels of muscle tension and visible autonomic signs of tension (such as heavy irregular respiration and paling or flushing) were unable to sustain social responsiveness at more than minimal levels.[10]

Specific displeasure when a toy was removed occurred only among the 20-week-old babies. This response is among the very earliest to reflect the operation of the function of memory, for the infant is responding to the discrepancy between the preceding pleasurable situation and the immediate situation, which, though in no way noxious in itself, lacks the toy. It is included in Table 6.17 to illustrate that early cognitive development may progress as rapidly in inactive as in active subjects. In addition, the capacity to respond affectively to something that is *not perceptually present* also alters the quality of the baby's experience at moments of environmental change, and will therefore play a role in the delineation of characteristic patterns of experience for each infant.

Three of the infants in Group Two typically showed a marked delay between focusing on a proffered object and the responsive motoric action (usually reaching). Such apparent inhibition of response is interesting in relation to our hypothesis about activity level itself; namely, that the threshold for the release of movement is comparatively low in active infants and relatively high in inactive ones. Here, we merely note that the phenomenon was seen in moderately active babies at the age of 16 weeks (both Ac VII and Ac VIII had activity ratings of 2.2); it will be discussed in the next chapter, where we see that it occurred at later ages only among inactive infants.

In summary, our analysis showed that, among all babies in Group Two, object stimulation elicited a larger number and a greater prominence of relatively complex object-related behaviors than appeared during spontaneous activity. Further, these behaviors occurred with equal complexity and equal prominence in both active and inactive infants. Finally, where behavioral differences did occur among the infants—in the degree of social responsiveness they maintained during object-oriented play; the degree of motoric and autonomic excitement they showed; the tendency to delay between perception and motoric response; and the tendency to show dis-

[10] Ac X is an exception, but he alternated between vivid social responsiveness and excited responsiveness to the toys. The report of the psychological test findings comments that the examiner provided intermittent episodes of social play because she felt that unremitting object stimulation would have been overly exciting to the infant.

pleasure when a toy was taken away—the behavior differences were not related to activity level.

Social Behavior

Our primary interest in the youngest group of infants had been to discern those situations that tend to elicit attentiveness toward persons in the environment, as shown by changes in activity and by intent regard, smiling, and occasional cooing. By 16 and 20 weeks, outwardly focused attention prevails during a fair portion of the infant's waking time; it may be lost under certain conditions, but it no longer requires a special state and certain environmental conditions. The social experience and behavior of babies during the fourth and fifth months can now be assessed in terms of the intensity of behavioral response as a function of different sorts of social stimulation.

In comparison with the younger babies of Group One, only a very few new social responses had emerged at 16 and 20 weeks. In Group Two, individual differences lay chiefly in the manner in which components of social response were combined, and in differences in intensity. To describe the social responsiveness of our subjects, we classified each observed episode during which the infant was in perceptual contact with the mother or another person in terms of the intensity of social stimulation it involved. Thus a continuum was constructed, beginning with "sight only," indicating that the infant saw another person who, at the moment, paid no particular attention to him. Next in order is "gentle" social stimulation, which included situations in which the mother or someone else looked at the baby in a smiling or animated fashion, spoke to the baby from a distance or briefly from close by; or interspersed task-oriented actions (such as diapering) with an occasional word or smile to him. The last category of social stimulation was, for this age group, designated as "moderately strong" because in our sample we did not observe truly intense social stimulation until the children were more than 20 weeks old. Moderately strong social stimulation included sustained interactions during which the mother (or anybody else) spoke to the baby warmly and intensively and, in many instances, touched him as in gentle tickling or rolling or bouncing him in her arms.

A similar ranking was made of the intensity of the infant's response, which was classified as "weak," "medium," or "strong." As for other behaviors, a prominence rating was made for each variety of response under each condition of social stimulation for each baby. Our criteria of reliabilty (see Chapter 4) permitted only a distinction between "prominent" (scored as 2) and "peripheral" (scored as 1). A pattern was rated as prominent if it was observed on *every occasion* when social stimulation occurred at the level defined; if it was seen on no less than two occasions among such episodes, it was rated as peripheral. Table 6.18 lists each pattern of social response as classified, as well as the frequency and prominence of its occurrence in Group Two.

In addition to gazing, smiling, and cooing, all of which were present in Group One, most of these older infants also showed chuckling, laughing and squealing. A very few of our Group Two subjects turned to look at someone who spoke outside their visual field, or they reached toward the partner and touched her. The different patterns of social response listed in Table 6.18 are largely different combinations of the same behavioral elements. A baby may smile in response to the sight of his mother's smiling face, but not alter his behavior in any other way. Or he may rivet his visual attention on his mother's face and be so absorbed that body movement decreases or ceases altogether. Or a baby who perceives his mother's face may begin to squeal or chuckle while also waving his arms or kicking his legs. Another baby may only smile as he sees the mother's face, but add body movement and laughing or cooing if she speaks to him or touches him.

By and large, active and inactive infants showed the same varieties of social response. The most frequent and most prominent social responses among the 16- and 20-week-old infants were the following: gazing only, smiling only, laughing, chuckling, or squealing with activity increase, and a combination of gazing and smiling.

Social responses of medium and strong intensity were made more often and more prominently by active babies than by inactive ones. Inactive infants were less responsive to conditions of minimal social stimulation. Once again, our subjects did not differ a great deal in *what* they did, but there were some differences in the conditions that typically elicited a given level of responsiveness. Table 6.19 indicates for each group the frequency and prominence of weak, medium and strong social responses at different levels of intensity of social stimulation.

In response to minimal social stimulation (the mere sight of a person),[11] active infants responded prominently in ways we classified as being of medium intensity, while inactive babies made fewer responses to the situation, and most of these were of low (weak) intensity. The total prominence score of active babies for "sight only" social responses was 16, compared with a total prominence score of 8 for the inactive ones. However, when social stimulation was fairly strong, active and inactive babies responded with much the same intensity. All together, and under all conditions of stimulation combined, the inactive babies received more ratings for weak responses than did the active ones (ten and six respectively); and they

[11] The condition of "sight only" includes spontaneous activity but goes beyond it. It also includes moments when the baby was held quietly on mother's lap, but not facing the mother, who was conversing with investigators. In this situation, babies saw observers as they wrote or busied themselves otherwise and did not focus their attention on the baby.

received fewer ratings, with lower prominence, for behaviors of medium and strong intensity.

In Group Two, the magnitude of differences in social responsiveness between active and inactive babies is very small. When every active baby was compared with every inactive one of like age, differences were in the same direction as those between the groups, except for pair VII.[12] More important is the tendency of inactive babies to be relatively more dependent on external stimulation, which was found also for responsiveness to inanimate objects; especially because the same difference between activity level groups was present at all three age levels. The slight tendency indicated in Table 6.18 and 6.19 is thus worth reporting primarily because it is in harmony with numerous other and independent findings. (Its implications were anticipated in the discussion of the variable effects of object stimulation.)

Assuming that reciprocal smiling and vocalizing toward another person play a role in the development of such functions as discrimination among persons in the environment, communication, and the development of a special tie to the mother and to other significant individuals, how much opportunity the child is given to engage in these behaviors may be important. If our findings are confirmed on larger samples, one can conclude that at the ages of 16 and 20 weeks, inactive infants are more dependent than active ones on the mother's inclination to treat her baby as a social partner and to play with him. Indeed, the more detailed study of patterns of social interaction found at this age level and the next supports the suggestion that somewhat more mature patterns of social responsiveness prevail among active babies, though this is qualified in instances where mothers of inactive infants are given to frequent and fairly intense social stimulation. However, such a relationship between activity level and the emergence of new patterns of social responsiveness concerns only the *time* of emergence. We do not imply that the infant who, relatively early, laughs responsively or squeals or reaches for his mother necessarily develops in a healthier or otherwise superior fashion. Nor have we reason to believe that such socially advanced babies are necessarily in a better position to develop an intense affective bond to maternal figures.

A backward glance at reports for Group One may illustrate the difference between the timing of developmental events and their effective integration. It will be recalled that even 8- and 12-week-old active babies were somewhat more able to respond specifically to aspects of the environment—especially objects—than were their inactive peers. Yet, the data on the behavior of 16- and 20-week-olds showed that behavior patterns that required special stimulating conditions in order to emerge at all among the

[12] The same two babies failed to show the parallel difference during spontaneous activity and in response to object stimulation. The probable reasons for this reversal are discussed on page 141 and apply to social responsiveness as well.

12-week-olds were frequent components of spontaneous activity among infants in Group Two. This was true equally for active and inactive infants. As the material on Group Three will show, many behaviors that Group Two inactive babies tend to show only under special stimulation are freely available to inactive babies in the next older group. Although the course of development for active and inactive babies is somewhat different, in terms of timing as well as in terms of the specific experiences that mediate the learning, our data do not suggest that developmental outcome is affected by the somewhat later appearance of certain behavior integrations among the inactive babies.

Discriminatory social responses and displeasure at the termination of a social interlude are developmentally advanced behaviors for this age group; they are unrelated to activity level. The presence and prominence of specific patterns of social response is but one aspect of these infants' social behavior. Table 6.20 describes aspects of behavior not previously included: soothability (that is, the degree to which these babies responded to maternal soothing); behavioral discrimination between mother and other persons; responsiveness to the encounter with strangers; behavioral discrimination among different observers after the stranger effect had disappeared; and response to termination of a social interaction. Except for soothability, the social behaviors listed in Table 6.20 were not present among the infants of Group One. They are new emergents of social responsiveness that are noted in only a minority of our 16- and 20-week-old infants. Ratings for each subject are provided because the first acquisition of new behavior organizations is an especially interesting aspect of individual difference to which we shall return in the discussion of adaptation syndromes.

Since the literature does not include a full description of these social behaviors among 4- and 5-month-old infants, the phenomena referred to in the table are summarized below.

The response to strangers shown by three of eight subjects is qualitatively different from full-blown "stranger anxiety," as this phenomenon has been described by Spitz, Benjamin, and others.[13] We were somewhat surprised to find that babies of 16 and 20 weeks could show distinct discomfort at the first sight or approach of a stranger (a response seen also in the original sample, which had 32 infants at this age level). The 16-week-olds failed to smile or otherwise respond to cautious and gentle contacts made by the observers during the first few minutes, although they responded fully to their mothers. In addition, the babies gazed at the observers with special intensity, and only after an exposure of ten to twelve minutes did they respond to the observers as they did to the mothers, simultaneously discontinuing the intense, selective visual regard. While no overt displeasure was noted, the babies' expressions lacked animation and could be described as somewhat tense while the stranger response lasted. The one 20-week-old

[13] Spitz (1957, 1965); J. Benjamin (1963).

in whom the stranger response occurred showed the same behavior. Unlike the younger babies (who remained impassive), she began to cry when an observer came moderately close and spoke to her softly.[14]

The baby's discrimination of his mother from other women could be noted only after he had begun to respond pleasurably and easily to the observers. In both instances, the baby made his strongest social responses only to the mother and responded more strongly to slight stimulation from her than to moderately strong stimulation from an observer; in one instance, the baby could be soothed by the mother, but not by any of the observers.

Clinical studies of the emergence of the discrimination between the mother and all other persons have focused on the age of 6 months as a critical period. It has been assumed that by approximately this age several ego functions (particularly perception, memory, and anticipation) have sufficiently matured so that, in combination, they lead to behavioral discrimination of the mother. Despite the fact that some of our 4- and 5-month-old infants showed a fleeting stranger response and a more lasting selective responsiveness to their mothers, our observations are in good accord with those reported in the literature. Other authors have focused on anxiety and displeasure at contact with unfamiliar persons as the criterion for sensory-affective (not necessarily cognitive) recognition of the mother. None of the babies in Group Two showed behavior of this sort. We believe that a transient uneasiness in response to strangers and a higher level of responsiveness to the mother may be regarded as precursors of true stranger anxiety.

Previous experience had left us unprepared for what appeared to be preferences and/or aversions on the baby's part among the three (and sometimes four) observers. The infant might show a special fascination with one member of the staff or might respond more or less well and readily to one than to the others. For instance, Ac VII reacted negatively to one of the three observers, and though this baby could smile at her briefly, he did not learn to tolerate her close approach during the four hours of the observation period. It is difficult to know on what basis very young infants make such discriminations among unfamiliar people, but in these instances we know, from the reactions of more than a hundred other infants, that they were not reactions to a style of behavior inappropriate or unacceptable to infants in general. Nor did it seem to us that the person selected for avoidant behavior was more unlike or more like the mother than the other strangers were. Such aversion or preference among unfamiliar persons was seen only in two 16-week-old infants, and in one 24-week-old. This isolated behavior observation seems worthy of mention because it may be one of the transitional behaviors that ordinarily escape attention. In general, as a new function or capacity emerges, it is applied or manifested in a particularly intense manner, as though the child were "sharpening his tools" for

[14] For similar observations, see Meili (1957a, 1957b) and Schaffer (1966).

later more adaptive use. This is a familiar phenomenon in the area of early cognitive behavior (the incessant practice of new skills), and may exist for other functions also. We suppose that an infant who is still uncertain in his recognition of important and familiar figures regards each human countenance with strained attention, showing a hypervigilance that will disappear when discrimination of the mother has become confident and effortless.

Two of these eight subjects whimpered, and one of them always sucked her thumb when either mother or observer terminated a playful episode. This response is commonly noted among babies above 6 months of age. Much like displeasure at the disappearance of a toy, it implies memory for a recent state, in that displeasure occurs when a pleasurable situation ends, although no other noxious event occurs.

The incidence of these behaviors is so small that even if they were related to activity level, the material would be insufficient to reflect the association. Nor is there any reason to suppose that discriminatory functioning should be more important or accelerated in one of the two groups, since neither visual discrimination among inanimate objects nor auditory discrimination was shown to be associated with activity level. The one exception is discrimination of the mother, which we saw only in inactive infants (two 16-week-olds) in Group Two, and which proved to be more pronounced and frequent among inactive babies in Group Three as well.[15]

During recurrent contacts with caretaking adults, inactive babies showed activity increase more often than did active ones. Affect and motility changes were associated more often among inactive babies than among active ones. The social experience of infants is not limited to occasions when someone plays with them or attempts to soothe and comfort them. Routine care, such as feeding, diapering, and dressing, accounts for a large proportion of the infant's direct contact with other human beings. The degree to which these contacts are associated with an alteration in the infant's state, with pleasure or displeasure, and with active responsiveness to the other person varies as a result of maternal practices and style and the infant's reaction patterns. On a descriptive level it seems worth knowing how much contact each infant has with the mother (and other constant persons in the environment), what form these contacts take, and what affective and other behavior alterations tend to occur on these occasions.

Figure 6.4 summarizes for the group changes in affect and motility that typically accompanied recurrent contacts with the mother (or other constant caretaking persons). We included all varieties of mother-child interaction that we knew were a stable component of the baby's daily life, provided they had been observed with sufficient frequency to allow an assessment of the infant's typical response. Thus for each infant we made a single set of ratings for each relevant situation (such as being diapered or being fed).

[15] The possible connection between activity level and early discrimination of the mother is discussed in the next chapter.

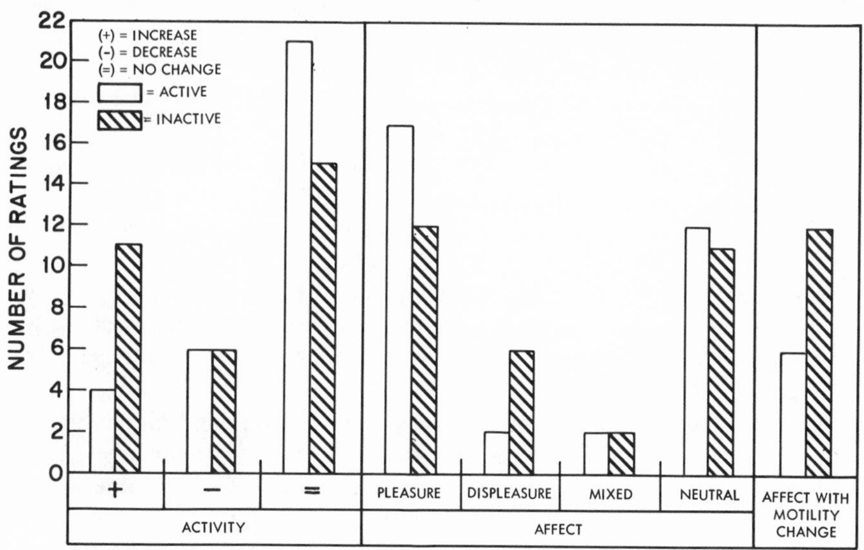

FIGURE 6.4. CHANGES IN AFFECT AND ACTIVITY DURING RECURRENT CONTACTS WITH PEOPLE.
NOTE: Number situations rated—32 active; 32 inactive.

Each rating was based on repeated observation of the same situation, so that the number of ratings on Fig. 6.4 refers to the number of *different situations* during which a particular behavior change occurred with regularity. The 63 ratings shown are based on the analysis of more than 300 separately observed behavior episodes.

For the sample as a whole, about two-thirds of the recurrent encounters with the mother tended to evoke affect, and pleasure far outweighted displeasure for both groups. For inactive infants, direct contact with a mother person led to an increase in activity more often than it did for active ones. Similarly, it was for the inactive babies that overt signs of affect (smiling, whimpering, chuckling, crying, and the like) were more often associated with changes in the amount of movement.

In presenting this material, we are, once again, not primarily interested in the group differences, which may or may not be found in larger samples, but in aspects of the infant's behavior and experience that seem relevant to the development of central ego functions and regulatory mechanisms. The term "affect" is usually taken to refer to a body state as well as to a subjective quality of feeling. Since the association between body states and emotion remains very close even in maturity, it is plausible to assume that in early infancy overt signs of affect are the direct expression of perceived body feelings; in other words, affect will be felt and expressed as the result of altered bodily sensations. During the first half year of life, autonomic functions and motility are very highly correlated. That is, wide fluctuations in respiratory or circulatory rates, in GSR, or in other autonomic measures are almost always accompanied by movement. At later ages, movement and autonomic arousal continue to correlate, but marked autonomic fluctuations can occur even in the absence of movement.[16]

In speculating about the development of pleasure and displeasure as subjective qualities of feeling, it is interesting to look for clues to bodily arousal as they may coincide with affect signs. In the youngest age group, where affect is limited to smiling or to whimpering or crying, smiling was always associated with low levels of activity, whereas displeasure signs (except minimal fretting while fatigued) were generally associated with movement increases. By the age of 16 weeks, both pleasure and displeasure can be accompanied by a movement increase. Pleasure has become an excitatory phenomenon, though motoric agitation still tends to be more intense with negative affect. The capacity to smile and laugh or whimper and cry without changes in motility is one sign of increasing differentiation, and hence constitutes developmental advance. Our active subjects showed this differentiation somewhat more than the inactive ones; in a larger number of situations (15 of 32, compared with 9 of 31 in inactive subjects) they typically displayed affect without changes in the amount of movement.

The data provided on Fig. 6.4 make explicit some differences in these babies' reactions to certain combinations of state and external conditions of stimulation. However, this material does not describe differences in the stable aspects of day-by-day experience. The situations included were selected by only two criteria; namely, that the original case file contained a sufficient number of relevant episodes, and that the situation was one that occurred repeatedly in the baby's daily life. However, the frequency of each situation in the baby's experience varied widely. For instance, two infants—each of whom regularly showed pleasure and increased activity while being held and gently spoken to—received the same ratings for their responsiveness to moderate social stimulation. However, one of them was held and played with by mother and other relatives a large part of each wakeful period each day, while the other usually had this experience only during the last hour before he was put to sleep at night (after father had returned from work and while mother fixed the evening meal). Though the two babies were alike in some aspects of responsiveness, the first one had frequent social contacts, and so smiled, chuckled and activated his limbs while focusing on another person many times each day. The second baby had this experience on limited occasions. Thus, moderate social stimulation con-

[16] It was reported (Lipton, Steinschneider, and Richmond, 1960, 1961) that when neonate movement is prevented by tight swaddling, autonomic changes occur in the absence of motility. But this is recognized as an experimentally induced departure from patterns of functioning under ordinary life conditions.

tributed a great many pleasurable episodes to one baby's life, and a much smaller number to the other's.

Table 6.21 lists only those recurrent mother-baby contacts that were frequent in the experience of each baby. Four of eight situations were frequent for all of the infants, whereas the other situations were frequent for some babies but not for others. The table shows that gentle play and being diapered or dressed while content evoked pleasurable affect from the great majority of infants, while other frequently recurring situations failed to do so. Essentially, those mother-child contacts that elicited socially oriented behavior from the tiny infants in Group One also most regularly evoked optimal social responsiveness from 4- and 5-month-olds. The table appears to indicate that among the frequent encounters between mother and baby, the proportion that elicit changes in motility and specific affects is approximately equal for active and inactive babies in this small sample. It needs to be remembered that many of the frequently recurring contacts are not included in the table, for lack of opportunity to observe them. We have no way of estimating the degree to which the eight situations are representative of all of the frequent mother-child interactions for each couple.

In summary, a comparison of social responsiveness showed that active subjects tended to respond often and at greater levels of intensity than did inactive ones, whereas inactive subjects exceeded active ones in the number and prominence of "weak" social responses. It was also found that this difference is pronounced in situations that provide minimal social stimulation, such as the mere sight of another person. In situations that involve moderately low intensity of stimulation (what we have called "gentle play"), differences in the intensity of response by active and inactive subjects are small, and under conditions of moderately strong stimulation the intensity was equal. Finally, the two groups differed in that in direct contacts with the mother (or other persons in the environment), inactive infants more often showed signs of affect (both pleasure and displeasure) combined with a change in activity level. In other words, although subjects in both groups had acquired the capacity to show affect *without* altering the level of motility, active subjects displayed the capacity much more often.

When the social behavior of 16- and 20-week-old infants in this sample is compared with that of younger infants, the major changes revealed are these: Attentiveness to another person in the immediate environment was a relatively rare and isolated occurrence among the youngest infants, whereas at 16 and 20 weeks it was always present unless the baby was subject to compelling and disruptive excitation (hunger and sometimes fatigue) or greatly altered bodily state (as during bottle or breast feeding and late stages of fatigue). Only a limited number of qualitatively new social responses had been added to the repertoire; they consisted of chuckling, laughing, touching the partner and turning to locate visually the source of a voice.

However, important new social discriminations were in the process of emerging at the ages of 16 and 20 weeks—behaviors that were not seen at all in Group One, but were seen in a minority of subjects in Group Two. These new behaviors were (1) a transient response to the sight and approach of strangers; (2) a sustained behavioral discrimination between the mother and other persons after the stranger effect had disappeared; (3) a sustained discrimination among the unfamiliar observers; and (4) an unpleasurable response to the termination of pleasurable social interaction. Lastly, for all babies in the sample it was found that more than half of the recurrent contacts with the mother (or other caretaking persons) evoked signs of affect—the great majority of these being situations that evoked pleasure. Individual differences, including those unrelated to activity level, lay chiefly in the intensity of affective response, the particular situations that elicited pleasure or displeasure, and last, but most important, the maternal practices rather than the infant's pattern of response.

Bodily Self-Stimulation

Unlike the younger infants, subjects in Group Two showed bodily self-stimulation in all three modalities. By the fifth and sixth months, neuromuscular coordination has matured sufficiently to allow for patterned movements that directly stimulate the skin or provide kinesthetic sensations. It is therefore possible to describe separately self-stimulating behaviors in each of three modalities. Table 6.22 provides an overview of the prominence of self-stimulating behavior in each modality and for each child. It shows that for this sample neither a relatively strong tendency to engage in bodily self-stimulation nor a preference for any one modality is at all related to activity level. Disregarding activity level, we see that these babies tended to differ more in terms of how much bodily self-stimulation (of any sort) they showed than in terms of dominant modalities. The babies in whom oral behavior was high or (in one case) medium in prominence received similar ratings for tactile and kinesthetic self-stimulation. Ac X, who showed a great deal of oral self-stimulation and very little of the other varieties, was the single exception.

TACTILE SELF-STIMULATION

Among the tactile patterns of self-stimulation, only rubbing of a body surface was frequent among infants in Group Two. Table 6.23 lists the eight different patterns of tactile self-stimulation noted in the 16- and 20-week-old babies. It also shows the frequency with which each pattern occurred among the active and the inactive infants, and at what levels of intensity. Of the eight babies, seven rubbed the face, the abdomen, or the hands with either medium or low intensity. All other patterns were characteristic of only one or two babies in the whole sample. It would seem, therefore, that tactile self-stimulation can be an important and prominent aspect of behavior for some infants at this age (Ac VII and In IX in this sample), but it is not among the behaviors that are generally prominent.

Table 6.23 also shows that when tactile self-stimulation did occur, it was seldom low in intensity. Of the sixteen ratings contributed by eight babies, only three were for the occurrence of a tactile pattern at low intensity; all three concerned the ubiquitous pattern of rubbing the skin.

In most subjects, tactile self-stimulation occurs only during bodily need states. In the discussion of bodily self-stimulation as a dimension of behavior, it was indicated that this variety of self-generated activation is of interest primarily in terms of its functional consequences. Has it the capacity to excite or soothe the baby? Does it further his awareness of the outer world, or does it hinder outwardly directed attentiveness? Does it bear a relationship to the modality conspicuously involved in his interactions with the mother? We were therefore especially interested in *when* babies tend to engage in tactile self-stimulation, and in its effect on their subsequent behavior. Table 6.24 lists for each baby the situational context in which tactile self-stimulation occurred. For all babies except In IX, rubbing, scratching, poking, and all other patterns were conspicuous only during need states.[17] In other words, many of these babies tended to provide for themselves fairly intense bodily sensations at the very times when they were feeling acute bodily discomfort. Considering that kinesthetic and oral self-stimulation also were increased during need states (though in both of these latter modalities, other situations could equally evoke self-stimulation), it may be said that the infant organism has a tendency to stimulate itself in response to unpleasant stimulation originating from within.

In the case of tactile self-stimulation (and for many infants this also held true for kinesthetic and oral behavior during need states), self-stimulation was anything but soothing in its effect. As these babies scratched, rubbed, and pulled at their own skin, they kicked and thrashed about and also squealed unhappily or cried. In searching for an explanation, we were reminded that at times of extreme pain, a similar behavior tendency can be noted in older children and adults. Tightly grasping the hands or arms, biting the lips or gritting the teeth, and other forms of, as it were, feeling one's own body are common devices to make pain endurable with relative composure. In adults, such behavior is also noted during anxiety in the absence of physical pain. In adults, forceful self-stimulation at such times appears to serve as a counterirritant, overshadowing or distracting from the primary focus of pain. In addition, the confined motor action may partially release

[17] Ac VII showed such a pattern during social stimulation at high intensity, but during need states his tactile self-stimulation was more extensive and varied, and equally high in intensity.

the impulse to respond to pain with diffuse motor action; the self-inflicted pain acts as a kind of safety valve in the face of mounting painful tension.

With infants less than 8 months of age, the self-induced heightening of bodily awareness during need states is regularly present, but clearly does not serve as a controlling device. However, it can be speculated that, even in infants, a localized bodily sensation that the child can produce by his own movement is qualitatively different from the diffuse discomfort of hunger and fatigue. To judge by the nature of behavior changes during these need states, the diffuse but intense discomfort during hunger and fatigue leads to a loss of awareness of surrounding things and also, therefore, to a loss of the rudimentary awareness of the own body as a cohesive entity. The additional self-induced bodily sensations may then serve to counteract such primitivization by producing familiar and predictable feelings localized at the body boundary.

The primitivization of behavior seen in infants during need states presumably reflects the fact that high levels of excitation temporarily prevent the operation of the developmentally more mature mechanism of neural integration. The infant is then left with a behavior repertoire not much different from that available to him during the early weeks of life, before more advanced coordinations had been achieved. The nearly universal tendency to engage in bodily self-stimulation during need states (and states of distress from other causes, such as gastric pain) can thus be understood as the automatic consequence of the neurophysiological processes that lead to the loss of higher controlling mechanisms. The involuntary self-stimulation that ensues may be regarded as one of many built-in biopsychological adaptive mechanisms, in that it reinforces the awareness of body boundaries. The universal adult mechanism of enduring pain by means of adding self-inflicted pain may therefore be viewed as deriving from the matrix of early body memories. It becomes a means of maintaining "a hold upon oneself" in order not to "let oneself go."

The behavior of one infant (In IX) did not conform to what was seen in all the others. In IX was given to more than the ordinary amount of bodily self-stimulation, both oral and tactile; when she rubbed or scratched herself, or pulled her hair, she often did so with an intensity not seen in any of the other infants. However, this baby showed such behavior prominently during spontaneous activity and in response to social stimulation. During need states she engaged in intense oral behavior, but never once touched her own skin. (In IX showed a somewhat unusual pattern of adaptation in general, and will be discussed at length at a later time.) During spontaneous activity she never once focused upon an object; a relatively large proportion of her behavior was primitive, and such coordinated behavior patterns as occurred were largely focused on parts of her own body (see Tables 6.6 and 6.7). Although her behavior during need states was similar to that of the other infants, it was relatively less different from what she did during spontaneous activity. For her, tactile self-stimulation during spontaneous activity was associated with an increase in generalized excitation. At least, while it lasted, she was more animated and lively than at other times, and her facial expression suggested a state of pleasurable animation. She was the only Group Two baby in whose behavior tactile self-stimulation appeared in the same contexts that, in other inactive babies, were characteristically associated with increases in oral behavior.

KINESTHETIC SELF-STIMULATION

In Group Two, kinesthetic self-stimulation was rare, occurring chiefly during spontaneous activity. Only three different patterns of kinesthetic self-stimulation were observed in this age group; Table 6.25 summarizes all relevant data. Insofar as it was seen at all, kinesthetic self-stimulation occurred as part of the self-contained and primitive varieties of body play during spontaneous activity, or as part of presleep drowsiness.

In this age group, kinesthetic self-stimulation was never seen as part of an excitatory syndrome. During spontaneous activity it did not appear to affect the infant's level of animation, and during drowsiness it coincided with other signs of impending sleep, such as slower respiration and intermittent closing of the eyes. If fatigue was accompanied by distress, neither head-rolling nor other kinesthetic patterns were seen. Though kinesthetic self-stimulation was an insignificant component of behavior in our 16- and 20-week-old infants, it is reported to provide a contrast with the older infants of Group Three, for whom it plays a role somewhat similar to that of oral and tactile patterns.

ORAL BEHAVIOR

By the age of 4 and 5 months non-nutritive oral behavior has reached its maximal level of differentiation. Among the younger infants of Group One we were able to identify eleven different oral patterns. When each episode of non-nutritive oral behavior was delineated for the babies in Group Two, it was possible to discern 31 different oral activations (see Table 6.26). This striking difference in the degree of differentiation of movements involving the mouth zone runs parallel with the greater coordination and sharper articulation of other kinds of movement, such as object-oriented behaviors.

However, oral patterns at the age of 4 and 5 months differ in two ways from patterns involving other body regions. In the first place, at the ages of 16 and 20 weeks, but not later, oral movements are more diversified than other kinds of movement. Even hand movements, which are destined to achieve the highest possible degree of differentiation, are at these ages limited to a relatively small number of patterns (mainly contact, stroking, whole-hand grasping, crude release and poking). Secondly, oral coordinations differ from all others in that the differentiation seen at the ages of 4 and 5 months is the maximum within the age range under study. Other patterns, such as whole-body movements and postures, object-oriented behaviors, vocalizations, and social responses, show a regular increase in the number of different patterns from Group One to Group Two, and again from Group Two to Group Three. However, the diversity of oral behavior *decreases* from Group Two to Group Three. As will be shown in the next chapter, oral patterns among the older babies shrink in number because certain basic schemas achieve dominance, and a great variety of mouth movements are replaced by only a few patterns—chiefly sucking, chewing, biting, licking, and a few others. If similar findings are obtained on other samples, it may be said that the pervasive developmental trend of increasing differentiation followed by reintegration and consolidation (involving the abandonment of less effective patterns) takes place in the oral zone chronologically earlier than in other areas of body movement.[18]

Active and inactive infants generated for themselves essentially the same kinds of sensations in the oral zone. Each oral schema was classified in terms of what the mouth touched (see Table 6.26). By an "empty" oral pattern we understand one in which there is contact only between the lips, gums, and tongue. Other oral patterns mediate contact with an object, as when a baby mouths a toy or stuffs cloth into his mouth, or with another body part, as in finger-sucking. In Group Two, fourteen, or 45.2 per cent, of all oral patterns involved another body part. Ten patterns, or 32.3 per cent, were of the kind that brings the mouth into contact with an object, and the remaining 22.5 per cent were empty; that is, portions of the mouth musculature moved so as to provide sensations within the oral zone.

As one attempts to specify what babies actually felt during episodes of oral behavior, the nature of the activation may be more important than its place of application. In order of frequency, the basic activations were sucking (eight schemas); deep insertion with pressure (four schemas); lip contact without activation (four); chewing (three); and licking, rubbing, biting, articulated tongue or lip motions, and diffuse activations (each of which contributed one or two patterns).

Table 6.26 shows that the frequency distribution of particular oral patterns was nearly identical among active and inactive infants.

In contrast with the younger infants, Group Two infants varied greatly in the prominence of oral behavior, but the variation was not associated

[18] Mouth movements and mouth-hand coordinations are prominent in neonates, and even at their most developed level they remain primitive in comparison with many other aspects of behavior. The speculation that mouth movements mature earlier and reach final stages of development in advance of most other coordinations is in keeping with many observations in the field of comparative and developmental psychology. In both phylogeny and ontogeny, it is generally true that more primitive functions and structures mature more rapidly and stabilize earlier than do the more flexible and complex higher functions, which re-

with activity level. For each infant we assessed both the number and prominence of oral patterns that appeared in his behavior. Table 6.27 provides a summary for the active and inactive infants as a group. It shows that inactive babies received a somewhat larger number of "frequent" ratings, which reflect very high prominence for a particular oral pattern. "Medium" ratings were more frequently assigned to active infants, but the summed oral prominence ratings were nearly identical for the groups.

Our explanation for the difference between active and inactive Group One babies was that high levels of total body movement prevent the emergence of the smaller and coordinated motions that are required for most oral behaviors. We also thought that somewhat older infants are better able to combine oral activation with body motion because of their more advanced neuromuscular coordination. In Group Two, the similarity in the behavior of active and inactive infants cannot be attributed to the maturational factor. At 16 and 20 weeks, babies are not yet able to mouth a toy or their hand and simultaneously move about or change posture, as older infants often do. Rather, the fact that active and inactive infants in Group Two could show equally prominent oral behavior is in keeping with the circumstance that comparisons here are actually between *moderately* active and inactive infants. None of the active babies in Group Two showed forceful whole-body movements to the same degree as the active babies of Group One and Group Three.

Nonetheless, in some of these babies, oral behavior was inconspicuous and peripheral, while it was an outstanding and dominant feature of behavior in others. Table 6.28 shows for each baby in Group Two the number of oral patterns and his oral score, which, as before, consists of the summed prominence ratings received for oral behavior. Although babies differed widely in the prominence of oral behavior, the number of different patterns was very similar for all except the most intensely oral baby (In X).

Intense oral behavior during spontaneous activity was seen only in inactive subjects. Self-soothing by means of sucking was observed in a minority of babies and was unrelated to activity level. It was mentioned earlier that oral behavior can intensify and diminish in a variety of contexts. It may be one of several manifestations of generalized excitation due to inner or outer causes; it may occur as a variety of animated behavior during spontaneous activity; it may have a soothing effect upon a previously irritable baby. We determined for each infant the circumstances under which oral behavior waxed and waned in prominence, as well as the associated behavior changes in terms of fluctuating states of excitation and of relative quiescence.

To present these data in the form of tables would be tedious in the extreme; instead, we shall summarize the recurrent and clear-cut sequences observed. Regular and striking fluctuations in oral behavior as a function of situational context were not observed in babies whose total oral score was low. Subjects In VII and Ac IX fall into this category (with oral scores of 7.0 and 7.5 respectively). Neither of these infants reflected excitation by marked changes in oral behavior, nor did mouthing serve to induce quiescence, nor in fact did they show really intense oral behavior at any time. In VIII, with an oral score of 8.0, occasionally sucked his fingers avidly and showed some other oral patterns very casually. This occurred while he was content and left to himself, often following a spurt of what was for him rather active motoric play. During hunger, but not during fatigue, this baby inserted his fist deeply into his mouth, bit his thumb, and sucked, but these forceful oral activations did not relieve discomfort even transiently.

In this sample, all but one subject decreased or ceased oral activations in response to external stimulation such as social play, developmental testing, or the pediatric examination. In such contacts with the animate environment, these babies tended to orient all behavior toward the things and the people to which their attention was drawn. They occasionally brought an object to the mouth, but these were transient episodes (unlike the sustained oral use of objects seen during spontaneous activity). The exception was Ac X, who became inordinately excited when stimulated vigorously by another person. This led to marked primitivization of behavior, including bubble blowing and diffuse mouthing, as well as a strong tendency to approach objects by mouth rather than following his usual pattern of grasping them with his hands.

When excitation was due to bodily need states, the majority of subjects did engage in diffuse mouthing, sucking or chewing motions. However, as reported earlier, oral behavior at these times was less intense than during spontaneous activity or about the same (except for two babies, Ac VII and In VIII; see Tables 6.11 and 6.12).

Only inactive babies showed the tendency to engage in intense oral behavior while comfortable, previously relaxed, and not specifically stimulated (all but In VII, who did not show intense oral behavior at any time). As these babies lay in the crib or were held in mother's arms, they typically alternated between gazing, slight moving, and recurrent spells of intensive sucking, biting, chewing, and other forms of mouthing. One received the impression that, in these babies, mouth movements registered fluctuations in general state much as minimal and extensive motions of the total body reflect such fluctuations in other infants. At any rate, none of the moderately active babies in this sample ever showed spurts of intense oral activation while relaxed, alert and content.

In this group of eight babies, five showed the capacity to soothe themselves by oral means. One active baby (Ac VIII) sucked his thumb avidly while fatigued. As soon as he started to suck, he ceased restless movements and irritable crying, only to resume when he lost his thumb. One of the inactive babies (In X) had perfected the technique of oral self-soothing to an impressive degree. Due to eczema, she was a generally irritable infant. She sucked her thumb while sleepy, but never lost it, and during the intervals from being put down to falling asleep (which could be as short as 8 minutes and as long as 25), she neither moved nor made a sound except for sucking motions and the attendant smacking noises. However, In X brought her fingers or a toy to the mouth on nearly every occasion when discomfort was observed. Over and over again we saw her fuss on the mother's lap, then begin to mouth and look better pleased; when the finger-sucking was disrupted she began to fret, but soon brought her hand to her mouth again, becoming content as soon as sucking was resumed. In the same manner, whenever a toy was taken from her hand, she first cried, then took to sucking and seemed contented.

The other three babies (two inactive and one active) showed similar behavior, but less consistently and with less success. When uncomfortable for any cause, they frequently relaxed and ceased plaintive noises once they began mouthing. However, oral activation in their case never led to lasting changes in state. It is worth noting that all the babies for whom oral activity did possess soothing power—whether regularly or occasionally—engaged in a variety of oral activations, often interspersed with sucking. Only sucking (of finger, thumb or object) was ever seen to soothe; chewing, licking, engulfing, and all the others either had no visible effects or appeared to be part of an excitation syndrome.

Babies who showed prominent oral (and tactile) self-stimulation during spontaneous activity showed less focused and environmentally oriented behavior at those times. We had speculated earlier that if bodily self-stimulation dominates during spontaneous activity, it may counteract the occurrence of environmentally focused behavior, especially object-oriented mastery activities. Among the subjects of Group Two, oral or combined oral and tactile self-stimulation were prominent and intense during spontaneous activity in subjects In VIII, In IX, and In X. In Table 6.8 we presented the proportion of spontaneous activity each baby devoted to object-focused behavior activations. When all members of the sample were ranked in terms of this variable, the three subjects most given to oral and tactile self-stimulation occupied the three lowest positions on the rank order for object-related behavior. However, the only baby who prominently engaged in kinesthetic self-stimulation during spontaneous activity (Ac VIII) showed the second highest percentage of object-related behaviors. Kinesthetic self-stimulation, at least of moderate degree, apparently did not affect the tendency to direct attention and coordinated behavior towards objects in the environment.

In summary, among the 16- and 20-week-olds in this sample, oral self-stimulation was common for all infants. It occurred in the tactile mode for a good many, but was rarely shown in the kinesthetic mode. Differences among babies were primarily in the prominence and intensity of self-stimulating behaviors, and secondarily in the modalities employed. Some babies regularly showed bodily self-stimulation during need states; only inactive babies engaged in intense oral behavior during contented and relaxed moments; and five of eight infants could soothe themselves by self-initiated sucking.

In general, kinesthetic self-stimulation, when it occurred, was a component of contented and animated play during spontaneous activity. Tactile self-stimulation was typically associated with bodily need states, though in inactive babies it was also seen during spontaneous activity and social play. Oral behavior could occur in almost every situation, but there were consistent individual differences in the conditions associated with its waxing and waning. However, nearly every infant regularly decreased (or discontinued) oral behavior during social stimulation of more than slight intensity.

SUPPLEMENTARY MATERIAL TO CHAPTER 6

Table 6.1 (Group Two)—Types of Movement during Spontaneous Activity: Individual Prominence Scores

	WHOLE-BODY				PART-BODY				Muscle Tension		Quiescence	
	Forceful		Gentle		Forceful		Gentle					
Pair	Ac	In	Ac	In	Ac	In	Ac	In	Ac	In	Ac	In
VII	1.0	0.0	2.0	0.5	3.0	0.0	0.5	3.0	1.0	0.0	0.5	0.0
VIII	2.0	0.0	2.0	1.0	2.0	0.5	1.0	3.0	0.0	0.0	0.0	2.0
IX	0.5	0.0	2.0	1.0	3.0	1.0	3.0	3.0	0.0	0.0	0.0	1.0
X	2.0	0.0	1.0	2.0	3.0	0.5	2.0	3.0	0.0	0.0	0.0	1.0
Totals	5.5	0.0	7.0	4.5	11.0	2.0	6.5	12.0	1.0	0.0	0.5	4.0

Ratings: 3.0 = frequent; 2.0 = medium; 1.0 = occasional; 0.5 = rare.

Table 6.2 (Group Two)—Types of Movement during Spontaneous Activity: Summed Prominence Scores for Active and Inactive Infants

		FORCEFUL		GENTLE			
Group	N Ratings	Whole-body	Part-body	Whole-body	Part-body	Muscle Tension	Quiescence
Active	24	5.5	11.0	7.0	6.5	1.0	0.5
Inactive	24	0.0	2.0	4.5	12.0	0.0	4.0

Table 6.3 (Group Two)—*Types of Movement during Spontaneous Activity: Pair and Cross-Pair Comparison of Prominence Scores*

	Ac > In		Ac < In		Ac = In		NEITHER		N COMPARISON	
Movement Type	*Pair*	*Cross-Pair*	*Pair*	*Cross-Pair*	*Pair*	*Cross-Pair*	*Pair*	*Cross-Pair*	*Pair*	*Cross-Pair*
Forceful whole-body *	4	4	0	0	0	0	0	0	4	4
Gentle whole-body	3	2	1	0	0	2	0	0	4	4
Forceful part-body *	4	4	0	0	0	0	0	0	4	4
Gentle part-body	0	0	3	3	1	1	0	0	4	4
Muscle tension	1	1	0	0	0	0	3	0	1	1
Quiescence	1	0	3	3	0	0	0	1	4	3

* p = <.05 (Siegel, 1956).

Table 6.4 (Group Two)—*Behaviors during Spontaneous Activity: Frequency and Classification*

Behavior	*Age Range (in Weeks)*	*Frequency*	*Classification*
Stretching, squirming, or extension/flexion whole body	16	1	Primitive, self-contained
Stiff extension arm(s) or leg(s)	16–20	7	Primitive, self-contained
Rolling	16–20	4	Primitive, self-contained
Arm waving	16–20	3	Primitive, self-contained
Tactile self-stimulation	16–20	4	Primitive, self-contained, tactile
Head rotation or elevation	16–20	3	Primitive, self-contained
Uncoordinated arm and leg motion	16	2	Primitive, self-contained
Scratching sheet or crib side, no vision	16–20	3	Primitive, tactile, self-contained
Grasping, tactile exploration nearby object	16–20	4	16 weeks: coordinated; 20 weeks: primitive, tactile, object
Indistinct vocalization	16–20	6	Primitive, self-contained, vocal
Squealing	16–20	3	16 weeks: coordinated; 20 weeks: primitive, self-contained, vocal
Articulated kicking	16	3	Coordinated, self-contained
Hands clasp at midline	16–20	5	Coordinated, body-focused
Reach for, contact, move objects	16–20	6	Coordinated, object-focused
Lifting dress, blanket toward face	16	1	Coordinated, object-focused
Regard immobile person	16–20	8	Coordinated, social focus, vision
Regard distant stationary object	16–20	4	Coordinated, object-focused, vision
Regard moving person	16–20	8	Coordinated, social focus, vision
Hand regard	16–20	6	Coordinated, body-focused, visual
Regard object in hand	16–20	3	Coordinated, object-focused, visual
Grasping own foot	16–20	5	Coordinated, body-focused
Re-erect to sitting	20	1	Coordinated, body-focused
From prone to creeping posture	20	1	Coordinated, body-focused
Strained reaching, distant toy	20	3	Coordinated, object-focused
Transfer object hand to hand	20	2	Coordinated, object-focused
Approach object by mouth	20	2	Coordinated, object-focused
Foot to mouth	20	1	Coordinated, body-focused
Manipulating own leg	20	2	Coordinated, body-focused
Oral self-stimulation	16–20	8	Self-contained, primitive

N Behaviors = 29

Table 6.5 (Group Two)—Behaviors during Spontaneous Activity: Prominence Scores and Summed Ratings

	Prominence Ratings								Sum for Groups				Total	
	VII		VIII		IX		X		N		PROMINENCE			
Behavior	Ac	In	Ac	In	Ac	In	Ac	In	Ac	In	Ac	In	N	Prom.
Stretching, squirming, extension/flexion	2	0	0	0	0	0	0	0	1	0	2	0	1	2.0
Stiff extension arm(s) or leg(s)	2	0	1	1	2	1	3	0.5	4	3	8	2.5	7	10.0
Rolling	0	0	2	0	0.5	0	2	2	3	1	4.5	2	4	6.5
Arm waving	0.5	2	0	0	0	0	0	3	1	2	0.5	5	3	5.5
Tactile self-stimulation	0	0.5	0.5	0	0	0.5	0	0.5	1	3	0.5	1.5	4	2.0
Head rotation or elevation	0	2	0	2	0	2	0	0	0	3	0	6	3	6
Uncoordinated arm and leg motion	0	0	2	1	0	0	0	0	1	1	2	1	2	3
Scratching, sheet, crib, no vision	0	0	0	3	0	0.5	1	0	1	2	1	3.5	3	4.5
Tactile exploration nearby object	0.5	3	0	0	3	0.5	0	0	2	2	3.5	3.5	4	7.0
Indistinct vocalization	3	0.5	0.5	1	0	0.5	0	0.5	2	4	3.5	2.5	6	7.0
Squealing	1	0	0	3	3	0	0	0	2	1	4	3	3	7.0
Articulated kicking	3	0	2	1	0	0	0	0	2	1	5	1	3	6.0
Hands clasp at midline	3	1	0	0	0	0.5	2	2	2	3	5	3.5	5	8.5
Reach, contact, move object	0.5	2	3	0	3	0.5	2	0	4	2	8.5	2.5	6	11.0
Lift dress, blanket toward face	0	0	2	0	0	0	0	0	1	0	2	0	1	2.0
Regard immobile person	3	1	3	3	3	2	3	1	4	4	12.0	7	8	19.0
Regard distant stationary object	0.5	0.5	0.5	0	0	0	2	0	3	1	3	0.5	4	3.5
Regard moving person	1	1	0.5	2	3	2	1	1	4	4	5.5	6	8	11.5
Hand regard	0	2	1	2	0	2	0.5	2	2	4	1.5	8	6	9.5
Regard object in hand	0	0.5	3	0	3	0	0	0	2	1	6	0.5	3	6.5
Grasping own foot	0	0	3	0	0.5	2	1	1	3	2	4.5	3	5	7.5
Re-erect to sitting	0	0	0	0	0.5	0	0	0	1	0	0.5	0	1	0.5
From prone to creeping posture	0	0	0	0	0	1	0	0	0	1	0	1	1	1.0
Strained reaching, distant toy	0	0	0	0	3	0.5	0.5	0	2	1	3.5	0.5	3	4.0
Transfer toy hand to hand	0	0	0	0	3	0.5	0	0	1	1	3	0.5	2	3.5
Approach object by mouth	0	0	0	0	0.5	0	0.5	0	2	0	1	0	2	1.0
Foot to mouth	0	0	0	0	0	0.5	0	0	0	1	0	0.5	1	0.5
Manipulate own leg	0	0	0	0	0	1	1	0	1	1	1	1	2	2.0
Oral self-stimulation	2	1	3	1	2	3	2	3	4	4	9	8	8	17.0

N Schemas = 29

Table 6.6 (Group Two)—Behaviors during Spontaneous Activity: Frequency, Prominence Scores, and Percentage of Prominence Scores

Behavior Classification	N RATINGS			PROMINENCE SCORES			% PROMINENCE SCORES		
	Ac	*In*	*Both*	*Ac*	*In*	*Both*	*Ac*	*In*	*Both*
Coordinated	36	28	64	66.0	38.5	104.5	65.7	51.3	60.0
Primitive	20	24	44	34.5	36.5	71.0	34.3	48.7	40.0
Outer-focused	32	26	58	57.0	34.5	91.5	56.7	46.0	52.2
Self-contained	24	26	50	43.5	40.5	84.0	43.3	54.0	47.8
All Schemas	56	52	108	100.5	75.0	175.5	100	100	100

Note: Percentage prominence scores represent the proportion of all prominence scores contributed by each type of behavior.

Table 6.7 (Group Two)—Behaviors during Spontaneous Activity: Number, Summed Prominence Scores, and Percentage of Prominence Scores of Primitive and Coordinated Behavior

Behavior Classification	*VII*		*VIII*		*IX*		*X*	
	Ac	*In*	*Ac*	*In*	*Ac*	*In*	*Ac*	*In*
Primitive								
Number	6	6	6	6	4	6	4	6
Σ Prominence	10.0	9.0	9.0	9.0	7.5	9.0	8.0	9.5
% Prominence	45.5	52.9	33.3	45.0	25.5	41.8	37.2	57.6
Coordinated								
Number	7	7	9	5	10	11	10	5
Σ Prominence	12.0	8.0	18.0	11.0	22.5	12.5	13.5	7.0
% Prominence	54.5	47.1	66.6	55.0	75.0	58.1	62.8	42.4
All Schemas								
Number	13	13	15	1	14	17	14	11
Σ Prominence	22.0	17.0	27.0	20.0	30.0	21.5	21.5	16.5

Note: Percentage prominence reflects the proportion of the sum of all prominence ratings contributed by primitive or coordinated schemas for each subject.

Table 6.8 (Group Two)—Behaviors during Spontaneous Activity: Number, Summed Prominence, and Percentage of Prominence of Self-contained and Outer-focused Behavior

Behavior Classification	VII		VIII		IX		X	
	Ac	In	Ac	In	Ac	In	Ac	In
Self-contained								
Number	8	6	7	8	5	6	4	6
Σ Prominence	14.0	9.0	11.0	13.0	10.5	9.0	8.0	9.5
% Prominence	63.6	52.9	40.7	65.0	35.0	41.8	37.2	57.6
Outer-focused								
Number	5	7	8	3	9	11	10	5
Σ Prominence	8.0	8.0	16.0	7.0	19.5	12.5	13.5	7.0
% Prominence	36.4	47.1	59.2	35.0	65.0	58.1	62.8	42.4
Body-focused								
Number	1	2	2	1	2	6	4	3
Σ Prominence	3.0	3.0	4.0	2.0	1.0	7.0	4.5	5.0
% Prominence *	37.5	37.5	25.0	28.6	5.1	56.0	33.3	71.4
Object-focused								
Number	2	3	4	0	5	3	4	0
Σ Prominence	1.0	3.0	8.5	0	12.5	1.5	5.0	0
% Prominence *	12.5	37.5	53.1	0	64.1	12.0	37.0	0
Social Focus								
Number	2	2	2	2	2	2	2	2
Σ Prominence	4.0	2.0	3.5	5.0	6.0	4.0	4.0	2.0
% Prominence *	50.0	25.0	21.9	71.4	30.7	32.0	29.6	28.6

* Percentage based on sum of outer-focused prominence scores.

Table 6.9 (Group Two)—Behaviors during Spontaneous Activity: Pair and Cross-Pair Comparison of Prominence Scores

Behavior Classification	Ac > In		Ac < In		Ac = In		N COMPARISONS	
	Pair	Cross-Pair	Pair	Cross-Pair	Pair	Cross-Pair	Pair	Cross-Pair
Primitive *	0	0	4	3	0	1	4	4
Coordinated *	4	3	0	0	0	1	4	4
Self-contained	1	0	3	3	0	1	4	4
Outer-focused	3	3	1	0	0	1	4	4
Body-focused	0	1	3	3	1	0	4	4
Object-focused *	3	4	1	0	0	0	4	4
Totals	11	11	12	9	1	4	24	24

Note: Comparison was based on percentage of each subject's total prominence score contributed by ratings received for each behavior category. See Tables 6.7 and 6.8.

* $p < .05$, one-tailed test (Siegel, 1956).

Table 6.10 (Group Two)—*Behaviors during Spontaneous Activity: Summed Prominence Scores in Relation to Expansion of Effective Environment and Complexity of Object Manipulation*

Behavior	PROMINENCE (Σ Ratings)	
	Ac	*In*
Reach for, contact object	8.5	2.5
Regard immobile person	12.0	7.0
Regard distant object	3.0	0.5
Regard object in hand	6.0	0.5
Strained reaching distant toy	3.5	0.5
Transfer toy from hand to hand	3.0	0.5
Total	36.0	11.5

Note: Σ Ratings are sum of prominence ratings in each category by all active or inactive subjects.

Table 6.11 (Group Two)—*Behavior Changes: Effects of Hunger on Activity, Oral Behavior, Distress Vocalization, and Continuity of Distress*

	ACTIVITY LEVEL						ORAL BEHAVIOR						DISTRESS VOCALIZATION (rating)		DISTRESS CONTINUITY			
	+		−		=		+		−		=				+		−	
Pair	*Ac*	*In*	*Ac*	*In*	*Ac*	*In*	*Ac*	*In*	*Ac*	*In*	*Ac*	*In*	*Ac*	*In*	*Ac*	*In*	*Ac*	*In*
VII	v	v					v			v			3	1	v			v
VIII	v					v		v	v				2	2			v	v
IX	v					v			v	v			2	1			v	v
X	v	v							v	v			2	1	v			v
SUM	4	2	0	0	0	2	1	1	3	3	0	0	9	5	2	0	2	4

Symbols: (+) = increase; (—) = decrease; (=) no change; v = behavior present.

Ratings for distress vocalizations: 3 = screaming, very intense crying; 2 = crying and distressed squealing; 1 = soft crying, distressed whimpering.

Table 6.12 (Group Two)—Behavior Changes: Effects of Fatigue on Activity Level, Oral Behavior, Distress Vocalization, and Continuity of Distress

	ACTIVITY LEVEL						ORAL BEHAVIOR						DISTRESS VOCALIZATION[a] (rating)		DISTRESS CONTINUITY				FATIGUE[b] DURATION (minutes)	
	+		−		=		+		−		=				+		−			
Pair	Ac	In	Ac	In	Ac	In	Ac	In	Ac	In	Ac	In	Ac	In	Ac	In	Ac	In	Ac	In
VII	½[c]	v	½[c]				v			v			1	1	v	v			20	20–25
VIII				v	v			v	v				1	0			v	ϕ		
IX	v			v					v			v	3	0	v	ϕ		ϕ	10–15	10–15
X		½[c]	½[c]	½[c]	½[c]				v			v	2	2			v	ϕ	20–30	8
Total	1½	1½	1	2½	1½	0	1	1	3	1	0	2	7	3	2	1	2	1		

Symbols: (+) = increase; (—) = decrease; (=) = no change; v = behavior present; (ϕ) = no distress, hence no rating.

[a] For ratings of distress vocalization, see Table 6.11.
[b] Duration refers to observed occasions.
[c] Infant showed different activity pattern during early and late stage of fatigue.

Table 6.13 (Group Two)—Behavior Changes: Number of Behaviors during Hunger and Fatigue Compared with Spontaneous Activity

		Number of Patterns							
		PRIMITIVE		COORDINATED		SELF-CONTAINED		OUTER-FOCUSED	
Condition	Pattern Change	Ac	In	Ac	In	Ac	In	Ac	In
Spontaneous activity (Baseline distribution)		20	24	36	28	24	26	32	26
Hunger	Lost[a]	7	6	18	13	8	6	16	13
	Decreased	5	4	3	0	4	3	2	0
	Retained	0	1	1	1	1	2	0	0
	Increased	5	5	0	1	6	3	0	1
	New	7	7	1	1	8	7	0	0
Fatigue	Lost[a]	3	6	17	14	6	5	15	12
	Decreased	3	2	1	0	5	2	1	0
	Retained	1	0	0	1	1	1	0	0
	Increased	5	4	1	1	5	2	0	0
	New	10	8	0	0	10	9	0	0

[a] Patterns seen during spontaneous activity but not during need state.

Table 6.14 (Group Two)—Behavior Changes: Comparison of Behaviors during Hunger or Fatigue with Spontaneous Activity

Condition	Behavior Category	Ratings	VII		VIII		IX		X	
			Ac	*In*	*Ac*	*In*	*Ac*	*In*	*Ac*	*In*
Spontaneous activity	**Primitive**	Σ Prominence	10.0	9.0	9.0	9.0	7.5	9.0	8.0	9.5
		% Prominence	45.5	52.9	33.3	45.0	25.0	41.9	37.2	57.6
	Self-contained	Σ Prominence	14.0	9.0	11.0	13.0	10.5	9.0	8.0	9.5
		% Prominence	63.6	52.9	40.7	65.0	35.0	41.8	37.2	57.6
Hunger	**Primitive**	Σ Prominence	9.0	7.5	8.0	5.0	7.0	5.0	10.5	11.0
		% Prominence	82.0	72.4	100	71.4	100	100	84.0	100
	Self-contained	Σ Prominence	11.0	7.5	8.0	5.0	7.0	5.0	10.0	11.0
		% Prominence	100	71.4	100	100	100	100	80.0	100
Fatigue	**Primitive**	Σ Prominence	17.0	9.0	5.0	4.5	8.0	3.0	10.0	7.0
		% Prominence	89.4	82.0	100	100	89.0	100	83.3	100
	Self-contained	Σ Prominence	19.0	11.0	5.0	4.5	9.0	3.0	10.0	7.0
		% Prominence	100	100	100	100	100	100	83.3	100

Note: % Prominence is that portion of the total prominence score, under each condition, that was contributed by primitive or by self-contained behavior.

Table 6.15 (Group Two)—Behavior Schemas during Object Stimulation: Frequency and Prominence Scores

Behavior	Pair								Activity Groups				TOTAL		Age Range (in weeks)
	VII		VIII		IX		X		N RATINGS		Σ RATINGS				
	Ac	In	Ac	In	Ac	In	Ac	In	Ac	In	Ac	In	N	Σ Prom.	
Visual regard, arms activate	0.5	0.5	0.5	1.0					2	2	1.0	1.5	4	2.5	16
Directed reaching, no grasp	0.5	1.0	0.5	0	0	0	1.0	0.5	3	2	2.0	1.5	5	3.5	16–20
Reaching and grasping, retaining [a]	3.0	1.0	0	0	3.0	3.0	1.0	3.0	3	3	7.0	7.0	6	14.0	16–20
Toy to mouth [a]	1.0	1.0	0.5	0.5	3.0	3.0	2.0	3.0	4	4	6.5	7.5	8	14.0	16–20
Regards toy in hand [a]	0.5	0.5	0.5	2.0	3.0	0	0.5	2.0	4	3	4.5	4.5	7	9.0	16–20
Transfer object hand to hand [a]	0.5	0	0.5	0	3.0	1.0	0	0.5	3	2	4.0	1.5	5	5.5	16–20
Shake rattle, apparently listening	0	0.5	0	0	0	0	0	0	0	1	0	0.5	1	0.5	16
Bring mouth to object	0	0.5	0	0	0	0	3.0	0.5	1	2	3.0	1.0	3	4.0	16–20
Pull at object or move it aimlessly	0.5	0.5	0	0	0	0	0.5	3.0	2	2	1.0	3.5	4	4.5	16–20
Visual regard only, no activation [a]	0.5	1.0	0	0	0	0	0	0	1	1	0.5	1.0	2	1.5	16
Holding object no regard or activity	0	0	0.5	0	0	0	0	0	1	0	0.5	0	1	0.5	16
Hcld and bring together two objects	0	0	0	0	0.5	0	0	0	1	0	0.5	0	1	0.5	20
Tries or succeeds to resecure lost object					2.0	0	0	2.0	1	1	2.0	2.0	2	4.0	20
Persistent reaching distant object [a]					3.0	0	0	0.5	1	1	3.0	0.5	2	3.5	20
Intent regard, fingering (no grasping)					0	0.5	0	0	0	1	0	0.5	1	0.5	20
Banging object					0	0	0.5	0	1	0	0.5	0	1	0.5	20
Grasping nearby object (not offered) [a]					0.5	0.5	0	0	1	1	0.5	0.5	2	1.0	20
N Schemas = 17	7.0	6.5	3.0	3.5	18.0	8.0	8.5	15.0	29	26	36.5	33.0	55	69.5	

[a] Behavior also noted, in some subjects, during spontaneous activity.

Table 6.16 (Group Two)—Behavior Changes: Number and Summed Prominence Scores during Spontaneous Activity and Object Stimulation

	Spontaneous Activity				Object Stimulation			
	N SCHEMAS		Σ RATINGS		N SCHEMAS		Σ RATINGS	
Pairs	*Ac*	*In*	*Ac*	*In*	*Ac*	*In*	*Ac*	*In*
VII	2	3	1.0	3.0	8	9	7.0	6.5
VIII	4	0	8.5	0	6	3	3.0	3.5
IX	5	3	12.5	1.5	8	5	18.0	8.0
X	4	0	5.0	0	7	9	8.5	15.0
Totals	15	6	27.0	4.5	29	26	36.5	33.0

Table 6.17 (Group Two)—Behaviors during Object Stimulation

	Pair							
	VII		VIII		IX		X	
Behavior	*Ac*	*In*	*Ac*	*In*	*Ac*	*In*	*Ac*	*In*
Social awareness during object stimulation	minimal	very high	very high	moderate	moderate	none	moderate	none
Muscle tension or strong autonomic response	high	none	minimal	low	minimal	very high	high	medium
Delay between perception and response	frequent	none	frequent	none	none	frequent	very rare (once)	none
Response to loss of toy	none	not observed	none	none	marked displeasure	occasional minimal	minimal	marked displeasure

Table 6.18 (Group Two)—Social Responsiveness: Number and Summed Prominence Scores

		ACTIVE		INACTIVE		TOTAL	
Behavior	*Intensity*	*N*	Σ Prominence	*N*	Σ Prominence	*N*	Σ Prominence
Gazing only	Weak	3	5	6	7	9	12
Smile only	Weak	2	4	4	7	6	11
Touch partner, no visual regard	Weak	1	2	0	0	1	2
Gazing, activity decrease	Medium	2	4	1	2	3	6
Gazing, activity increase	Medium	0	0	1	2	1	2
Gazing, smiling	Medium	3	6	2	3	5	9
Gazing, soft vocalizing	Medium	2	2	1	1	3	3
Smiling, activity increase	Medium	2	3	2	2	4	5
Smiling, soft vocalizing	Medium	3	4	2	2	5	6
Turns to locate voice	Medium	2	2	0	0	2	2
Gazing, smiling, vocalizing	Strong	2	2	0	0	2	2
Laughing, chuckling, squealing	Strong	3	6	2	2	5	8
As above, activity increase	Strong	4	5	4	6	8	11
Touch partner, smiling and cooing	Strong	1	1	0	0	1	1
N Schemas = 14		30	46	25	34	55	80

Note: Prominence was rated as "prominent" (2.0) or "peripheral" (1.0). Prominence scores reflect all ratings received by active or inactive infants for each pattern.

Table 6.19 (Group Two)—Social Responsiveness: Frequency and Prominence in Relation to Degree of Social Stimulation

Degree of Social Stimulation	Weak Responses				Medium Responses				Strong Responses				Totals					
	Ac		In		Ac		In		Ac		In		Ac		In		BOTH	
	N	Σ Prom.	N	Σ Prom.	N	Σ Prom.	N	Σ Prom.	N	Σ Prom.	N	Σ Prom.	N	Σ Prom.	N	Σ Prom.	N	Σ Prom.
Sight only	3	5	4	5	6	9	2	3	2	2	0	0	11	16	6	8	17	24
Gentle	2	4	4	6	6	9	5	6	2	5	3	3	10	18	12	15	22	33
Moderately strong	1	2	2	3	3	3	2	3	5	7	3	5	9	12	7	11	16	23
Total	6	11	10	14	15	21	9	12	9	14	6	8	30	46	25	34	55	80

Symbols: N = number of behaviors scored. Prom = prominent (2) or peripheral (1) in infant's behavior under stated condition.

Table 6.20 (Group Two)—Social Responsiveness: Comparison by Behavior Characteristics

Behavior Characteristics	VII		VIII		IX		X	
	Ac	In	Ac	In	Ac	In	Ac	In
Stranger response	+ mild	—	—	+ mild	+ marked	—	—	—
Discrimination of mother	—	+ mild	—	—	—	—	—	+ marked
Discrimination among observers	+	—	very slight	—	—	—	—	—
Response to termination	—	+ marked	+	—	—	—	—	—
Soothability	low	high	medium	medium	medium	ϕ	high	medium

Symbols: (+) = present; (—) = absent; (ϕ) = no opportunity for behavior to occur.
Note: The notations below the + sign refer to intensity and/or prominence of the characteristic.

Table 6.21 (Group Two)—Social Responsiveness: Activity and Affect Changes

Situation	N SUBJECTS OBSERVED		Activity: +		Activity: −		Activity: =		Affect: POSITIVE		Affect: MIXED		Affect: NEGATIVE		Affect: NEUTRAL	
	Ac	*In*	*Ac*	*In*	*Ac*	*In*	*Ac*	*In*	*Ac*	*In*	*Ac*	*In*	*Ac*	*In*	*Ac*	*In*
Bottle or breast feeding	4	4	½ [a]		2½ [a]	1	1	3	0	0	1	0	0	0	3	4
Being diapered	4	4	1	2	0	1	3	1	2	2	0	0	0	1	2	1
Being dressed	4	4	0	3	1	0	3	1	2	3	1	1	1	0	0	0
On lap, content, not attended	2	2	0	0	0	0	2	2	0	0	0	0	0	1	2	1
On lap, discontent, not attended	1	3	0	0	0	1	1	2	0	0	0	1	0	0	1 [b]	2 [b]
Gentle play	4	3	2	0	0	2	2	1	4	3	0	0	0	0	0	0
Moderately intense play	2	1	0	0	0	0	2	1	2	1	0	0	0	0	0	0
Soothing	2	3	0	0	2	1	0	2	0	0	1	2	0	0	1 [b]	1 [b]
Totals	23	24	3½	5	5½	6	14	13	10	9	3	4	1	2	9	9

Symbols: (+) = increase; (—) = decrease; (=) = no change.
[a] One infant alternated between activity increases and decreases, scored ½ each.
[b] Irritability stopped, child's affect remained neutral on lap.

Table 6.22 (Group Two)—Bodily Self-Stimulation: Overall Prominence Ratings

	Modality					
	ORAL		TACTILE		KINESTHETIC	
Pair	*Ac*	*In*	*Ac*	*In*	*Ac*	*In*
VII	High −	Low	Medium +	Low −	Low	Low +
VIII	Medium	Low +	Medium −	Low	Medium −	Low +
IX	Low	High −	Low −	High	Absent	Absent
X	High −	High +	Low	Medium −	Low	Absent

Table 6.23 (Group Two)—Tactile Self-Stimulation: Frequency at Each Prominence Level

	Intensity								
	HIGH		MEDIUM		LOW		COMBINED		BOTH
Behavior Patterns	*Ac*	*In*	*Ac*	*In*	*Ac*	*In*	*Ac*	*In*	
Rubbing face, abdomen, hands	0	0	2	2	2	1	4	3	7
Rubbing one leg against other	0	0	1	1	0	0	1	1	2
Clutching head tightly	0	1	0	1	0	0	0	2	2
Hands tightly clasped	1	0	0	0	0	0	1	0	1
Pulling, scratching ears	1	0	0	0	0	0	1	0	1
Holding foot prolongedly	0	0	1	0	0	0	1	0	1
Scratching various body parts	0	1	0	0	0	0	0	1	1
Pulling hair	0	1	0	0	0	0	0	1	1
Totals	2	3	4	4	2	1	8	8	16

Table 6.24 (Group Two)—Tactile Self-Stimulation: Patterns and Intensity by Situation

Situation	*Subject*	*Pattern*	*Intensity*
Spontaneous activity	Ac VIII	Holding foot prolongedly	medium
	In IX	Rubbing face, abdomen, hands	medium
	In IX	Rubbing one leg against other	medium
	In IX	Pulling hair	high
	In IX	Clutching head	high
Hunger and/or fatigue	Ac VII	Rubbing face, abdomen, hands	medium
	Ac VIII	Rubbing face, abdomen, hands	medium
	Ac IX	Rubbing face, abdomen, hands	low
	Ac X	Rubbing face, abdomen, hands	low
	In VII	Rubbing face, abdomen, hands	low
	In VIII	Rubbing face, abdomen, hands	medium
	In X	Rubbing face, abdomen, hands	medium
	In X	Clutching head	medium
	Ac VII	Pulling, scratching ears	high
	Ac VII	Rubbing one leg against other	medium
Social stimulation	Ac VII	Tight clasping hands	high
	In IX	Scratching various body parts	high

Table 6.25 (Group Two)—Kinesthetic Self-Stimulation: Patterns and Intensity by Situation

Situation	*Subject*	*Pattern*	*Intensity*
Spontaneous activity	Ac VIII	Rolling whole body	medium
	Ac X	Rolling whole body	low
	In VIII	Rolling whole body	low
	In VIII	Swinging on abdomen	low
Fatigue	Ac VII	Head rolling	low
	In VII	Head rolling	medium

Table 6.26 (Group Two)—Oral Behavior: Frequency by Age Range and Classification of Patterns

	Frequency							
	16 WEEKS		*20 WEEKS*		*TOTAL*			
Behavior Patterns	*Ac*	*In*	*Ac*	*In*	*Ac*	*In*	*Both*	*Classification*
Diffuse mouthing	2	2	2	2	4	4	8	Empty
Bubble blowing	0	1	2	0	2	1	3	Empty
Tonguing	1	1	0	2	1	3	4	Empty
Tongue protrusion	0	0	1	1	1	1	2	Empty
Pulling lower lip beneath upper lip	1	0	0	0	1	0	1	Empty
Empty chewing	0	1	0	0	0	1	1	Empty
Tongue sucking	1	0	1	0	2	0	2	Empty
Hand(s) inserted, no activation	0	1	1	1	1	2	3	Own body
Sucking hand	2	2	1	0	3	2	5	Own body
Sucking finger(s)	2	0	1	2	3	2	5	Own body
Hands move over mouth zone	0	0	1	1	1	1	2	Own body
Finger, thumb inserted, no activation	2	2	1	1	3	3	6	Own body
Licking hand	1	0	0	1.	1	1	2	Own body
Active thumbsucking, brief	2	1	1	2	3	3	6	Own body
Active thumbsucking, prolonged	0	1	0	2	0	3	3	Own body
Moving thumb in mouth while sucking	0	0	0	1	0	1	1	Own body
Chewing, gnawing, thumb, finger	1	1	0	2	1	3	4	Own body
Biting thumb	0	1	0	0	0	1	1	Own body
Foot pushed into mouth	0	0	0	1	0	1	1	Own body
Rubbing gums with hand	0	0	1	0	1	0	1	Own body
Mouth resting on hand, prone	0	0	0	1	0	1	1	Own body
Sucking mother's body, hand, or arm	0	0	1	0	1	0	1	Object
Sucking sheet	0	0	1	0	1	0	1	Object
Approach object by mouth	0	0	1	1	1	1	2	Object
Object held at mouth, no activation	2	1	2	2	4	3	7	Object
Sucking object	1	0	1	1	2	1	3	Object
Chewing object	0	0	2	2	2	2	4	Object
Mouthing object	0	1	1	1	1	2	3	Object
Licking object	0	0	1	1	1	1	2	Object
Rubbing mouth against surface	0	1	0	0	0	1	1	Object
Toy deeply inserted, no activation	0	0	1	0	1	0	1	Object
N Patterns: 31	18	17	24	28	42	45	87	

Table 6.27 (Group Two)—Oral Behavior: Comparisons of Frequency and Prominence Scores

	N RATINGS			PROMINENCE SCORES		
Prominence Rating	*Ac*	*In*	*Both*	*Ac*	*In*	*Both*
Frequent	3	5	8	9.0	15.0	24.0
Medium	9	4	13	18.0	8.0	26.0
Occasional	11	19	30	11.0	19.0	30.0
Rare	19	17	36	9.5	8.5	18.0
Absent	7	6	13	0.0	0.0	0.0
Totals	49	51	100	47.5	50.5	98.0

Ratings: 3.0 = frequent; 2.0 = medium; 1.0 = occasional; 0.5 = rare; 0.0 = absent.

Table 6.28 (Group Two)—Oral Behavior: Number of Patterns and Oral Scores

	N PATTERNS		ORAL SCORES [a]	
Pair	*Ac*	*In*	*Ac*	*In*
VII	9	10	14.0	7.5
VIII	10	7	12.0	8.0
IX	11	11	7.0	15.0
X	12	17	14.5	20.0
Totals	42	45	47.5	50.5

[a] Oral score is the sum of prominence ratings for oral patterns received by each infant.

SEVEN

GROUP THREE: 24- TO 32-WEEK-OLDS

Spontaneous Activity

During the sixth, seventh, and eighth months of life, babies spend a considerable portion of each day awake, alert, and not specifically stimulated. The data on behavior during spontaneous activity for Group Three thus represent a larger portion of each infant's behavior day (to use R. Barker's phrase) than in the earlier age groups. Since behavior is also more highly organized and varied than before, observations made during spontaneous activity provide information about a larger number of behavior attributes than could be discerned for the younger ages. These infants also provided our best opportunity to contrast the behavior organizations found in active and inactive subjects because their overall activity level ratings include both extremes of the continuum. The average overall activity level for the active infants in this group was 2.8 (range: 2.5 to 3.0), and that for the inactive infants was 1.5 (range: 1.1 to 2.0).

Motility

Beginning at about the age of six months, the motility of infants differs more in directedness and quality than in the extent and force of motion. Therefore, the rating of movement patterns in terms of gross categories (such as were presented for the younger age groups) becomes less descriptive of the behavior stream. Nevertheless, this group's behavior during spontaneous activity was first assessed in terms of the kind and extent of body activation it involved; the results were entirely harmonious with those obtained for younger infants.

Active infants engage in forceful whole body and part body motions much more than do inactive ones; conversely, inactive babies engage primarily in gentle motions of either the whole or part of the body. Table 7.3 shows this difference for the group as a whole in terms of summed prominence ratings for each child and each type of movement. The differences are to be found in each of the pairs both in terms of absolute ratings (Table 7.1) and in terms of pair and cross-pair comparison (Table 7.2).

Quiescent intervals were more frequent and more conspicuous among inactive subjects, and muscle tension was no longer seen during spontaneous activity. In infants of Group Two quiescent intervals were also more characteristic of inactive infants, but among the youngest babies (Group One) this behavior did not discriminate among the activity groups. However, it was noted at all ages that even very active infants can and do achieve nearly complete quiescence at times, while some inactive subjects are never still during spontaneous activity. The disappearance of muscle tension—arching, stiffening, fanning of toes, and grossly tremorous movement—is to be regarded as a developmental phenomenon. As will be reported, infants up to 7½ months of age still show these behaviors at moments of marked excitation, but when they are not particularly roused, more advanced motor coordinations ordinarily suppress or replace these very primitive behaviors.

SPECIFIC PATTERNS OF BEHAVIOR, THEIR DIRECTION AND COMPLEXITY

Infants beyond the age of 5 months are capable of a large variety of behaviors during spontaneous activity, which vary in terms of many different dimensions. They may be directed toward an aspect of the environment (inanimate objects or persons), toward achieving feats of motor coordination (pulling the body to an upright kneeling or standing position or creeping), or toward the child's own body (rocking, bouncing, oral behavior, etc.). Any of these behaviors may be more or less complex and of different intensities; and of course, they may involve different body systems. It would be unwieldy to classify each one simultaneously in all respects. Therefore, we first described each behavior pattern in terms of its descriptive attributes, reflecting the general quality and, as it were, the sensorimotor content. This yielded a list of various *types* of behavior, in addition to a list of specific activations. Each of these types of activation, as well as each specific action, was again rated for its prominence in the spontaneous behavior of each child. On this basis, a first comparison could be made between the self-generated behavior of infants between the ages of 24 and 32 weeks and the younger infants of Group Two, and also between the spontaneous behavior of active and inactive members of Group Three.

In comparison with the younger age groups, all subjects in Group Three showed more active, more varied and more complex spontaneous behavior, reflecting the expected developmental changes. Table 7.4 lists 28 different behavior patterns, their frequency in this sample, and their prominence. For the sample as a whole, the most frequent and most prominent behavior activations were the following: complex position changes (often to and from a sitting position), reaching for and contacting objects, manipulating objects, regarding objects in the hand, persistent efforts to elicit social response from an impassive person (by physical approach, squealing or laughing in a provocative manner), squealing (both joyously and impatiently), and multisyllabic babbling. Many of these behaviors also occurred in infants 16 to 20 weeks old (compare Tables 6.4 and 6.5) but much less often. At this later age, the behaviors have become readily available.

Many new patterns are noted also, and most of them reflect the expansion of the effective environment and an increase in the degree to which these babies tend to behave so as to change their environment. These actions upon the environment include situations in which the infant becomes the agent or cause of an external event (such as making noises, causing objects to fall or move, causing other persons to respond to them, etc.). They also include situations in which the infant's environment and opportunities for action are altered because he has effected a change in his position or in his location in space. Creeping across the room to make contact with a person or a thing changes the baby's immediate environment, causing that which was distant to be nearby. The same kind of change in the perceptual surroundings is achieved when he attains an upright position, changes from the creeping to the sitting posture at will, and makes other position changes.

These behaviors confirm well-known developmental trends. They are described in some detail in order to point to the large variety of ways in which infants can and do become active agents of change, and thereby acquire a primitive but definite awareness of the self or the body ego. In subsequent discussion of individual differences we hope to show that seemingly very different behaviors may serve the identical developmental gain. For instance, an infant may acquire a sense of effectiveness in relation to the environment by the increasing certainty with which he is able to push an object along a surface, cause it to fall in an intended (or at least anticipated) direction, or bring two objects into precise contact with one another in mid-air. Another baby may experience himself as the cause of actual change chiefly in terms of his increasing capacity to move in space and to exert force against resistance (as in pulling himself up to a standing position, working against gravity). Yet another may come to feel himself as independently active primarily by compelling others to smile, laugh, or approach him as he creates intense and varied sounds directed to a person in sight, screams or squeals when someone leaves him, or tugs at mother's skirt until she lifts him to her lap.

The literature on child development has shown that many of these steps in the development of gross and fine neuromuscular coordination, as well as in the acquisition of socially directed behaviors, are necessary and invariant components of normal development. During the middle and latter portion of the first year (or later), *all* children learn to move about in space, all acquire a primitive "vocabulary" of sound and gesture, and all act upon manipulatable objects. However, infants may achieve any one of these developmental landmarks relatively early or relatively late. Once they make these skills part of the behavior repertoire, they may use any one of them frequently or rarely.

These variations of developmental progress have also been described, but chiefly in terms of variable developmental speed. The point we emphasize is that, with respect to some central developmental acquisitions, widely different behaviors may be regarded as *developmental equivalents.* We suggest that putting small objects into a container may mediate the experience of the body self as a causal agent to much the same degree as does creeping across the room or pulling at the drapes. At the same time, we should like to explore the possibility that differences in the behavioral route or the particular behavior sequence by which the same new level of development is attained may contribute to more lasting individual differences in adaptive style, in later patterns of learning, and in the aspects of experience that lead to the arousal of interest, of pleasure and displeasure, and of anxiety.

During spontaneous activity the behavior of active babies is more intense, ranges over space more freely, produces more noise, and is more complex in organization. Tables 7.4 and 7.5 indicate those spontaneous behavior patterns that were shown predominantly or exclusively by active and inactive members of the sample. The group differences shown on Table 7.4 were examined by pair and cross-pair comparisons; Table 7.5 shows that, with one exception (reaching for a distant object), what was true for the groups was true also for the great majority of individual pairs. We infer that, in all likelihood, these behavior differences are associated with activity level for infants in this sample. Based on these tables, a composite description of the characteristic spontaneous behavior of each group can be constructed. The active babies moved about a great deal, alternately pivoting, scooting, or creeping. They made frequent persistent efforts to achieve upright kneeling or standing postures, and some of them bounced and jumped vigorously, both while seated and while standing with support. They manipulated two objects simultaneously (more often than inactive subjects) and were persistent in their efforts to provoke a social interaction with initially unresponsive persons. They also squealed and babbled a great deal, often not directing these sounds to a person, but simply accompanying motor or manipulatory activity.

The inactive babies by and large tended to remain where they had been placed. Creeping, pivoting, and scooting were rarely seen, nor did they strive to attain the upright posture unaided. Instead they were likely to change position (not location) by rolling from prone to supine (and vice versa) and by alternating between horizontal and sitting postures. They cooed pleasantly and occasionally whimpered in annoyance, but squealing and babbling were inconspicuous. Inactive babies were more likely to spend time visually exploring diverse aspects of the environment, and some of them were given to rhythmic rocking on hands and knees.

Active and inactive babies differed from each other in that the former directed more attention to the environment and the latter devoted relatively more attention to parts of their own body. The behavior patterns listed in Table 7.4 were classified in terms of whether they were directed toward an aspect of the environment (things or people) or toward the body or the creation of specific bodily sensations. All subjects in the sample showed both kinds of behavior, but the active babies showed a somewhat larger proportion of environmentally focused behavior patterns and engaged in them somewhat more prominently (Tables 7.6 and 7.7). The inactive babies, on the other hand, excelled the active ones in the number and prominence of body-oriented behaviors. The absolute difference between the active and inactive group is small, but it is highly consistent and significant when individual pairs are compared.[1]

Outwardly directed behavior may be focused on either a person or inanimate objects. During spontaneous activity social behavior was necessarily restricted. Each subject showed either one or two such patterns, and differences in prominence were minimal (the inactive subjects were slightly more inclined to direct attention to people in sight). Thus, the real difference between active and inactive subjects was that the former had a greater tendency to act with and on thing-aspects of the environment.

Active babies engaged more often and more prominently in complex object schemas than did inactive ones. During the sixth, seventh, and eighth months infants learn to perform a large number of different actions using objects. These range from very simple schemas, such as reaching for a thing or mouthing it, to what are complex integrations for babies at this age, such as repeatedly throwing toys and creeping to retrieve them, or discovering how to rotate a swivel chair. In the younger age group it was the active infants who tended to show relatively more complex object schemas during spontaneous activity. From all of the behavior patterns noted during spontaneous activity among the Group Three infants, we selected those that utilized objects. Table 7.8 lists the 38 different object schemas noted and their classification as either "simple" or "complex" for the age group.[2] For each baby, each of these behavior patterns was rated as being "absent" (0), "prominent" (2), or "peripheral" (1) during spontaneous activity. In this manner it was determined which of the object schemas each baby had shown during spontaneous activity were simple

[1] Inspection of the raw data shows that pair XVI proved atypical in that both infants showed an almost identical proportion of behaviors directed toward the environment and toward their own bodies.

[2] Behaviors classified and rated under a single heading on Table 7.4 were separately noted on Table 7.8.

or complex, and how many of these schemas occurred prominently and peripherally. While left to their own devices, the active babies showed thirteen complex object schemas prominently, whereas only two complex object schemas were rated as prominent in the behavior of the six inactive babies during at least ten hours (total time) of spontaneous activity (Table 7.9). Table 7.10 compares the number and prominence of complex and simple object schemas for all possible combinations of active and inactive infants of like age (pair and cross-pair comparison). Of 24 comparisons concerning either the number or the prominence of *complex* object schemas, 16 conformed to the pattern of the group data.[3]

The tendency to engage in complex object schemas during spontaneous activity can be suppressed or increased by factors other than activity level. In accordance with our view that activity level does not correlate directly with any one behavior tendency, but does enhance the probability for the occurrence of certain behaviors, we were again interested in identifying the factors associated with reversals in group trends. The behavior of two subjects (In XI and Ac XIII) accounts for all of the instances where, on pair comparison, the inactive babies showed more, or more prominent, object schemas (either complex or simple). In XI was the one inactive baby in the sample who, during spontaneous activity, showed nearly as many complex as simple object schemas. Yet, like all other inactive babies in Group Three, the prominence of *all* object schemas (simple and complex combined) in her spontaneous activity was very moderate. The range of total object prominence ratings in the sample was from 8 to 25 (median = 17), and In XI had a total prominence rating of 13. On both developmental tests In XI proved accelerated. At the age of 28 weeks her behavior conformed to normative standards for 32-week-olds and, in some items, for 36-week-olds. We have previously noted (Chapter 6) that complexity of behavior during spontaneous activity is generally related to developmental level. Superior endowment is likely to account, at least in part, for the difference in the spontaneous behavior of In XI as compared with the other inactive subjects. However, we are inclined to attach at least as much importance to another factor. In XI was played with very little. Her mother was of the opinion that babies should not be given much attention except when they are in distress or need. At the same time, partly to keep her baby content, the mother provided an exceptionally large array of toys, as she had done since the baby's early infancy. She also made a point of moving the baby about, explaining that she wanted to "keep the baby from being bored." In XI was shifted from crib to playpen to floor to sofa, and with each change was given additional or different toys. Thus, it is not surprising that this well-endowed child, who in all other re-

[3] These differences were not significant (except for total prominence scores), but the comparisons between the number and prominence of simple schemas between active and inactive subjects received p levels ranging from .073 to .194, suggesting a real trend.

spects showed the reaction tendencies noted in inactive babies, showed an unusually large number of complex object activations, even when not specifically stimulated to use them.

Ac XIII was also a child whose developmental level exceeded average standards by at least four weeks. Yet during spontaneous activity, he engaged in only a single complex object schema, and that peripherally. He was an exceedingly active baby and, when we knew him at 28 weeks, he was intensely motivated to practice motor skills. Incessantly he crept, pulled himself to the upright kneeling posture or to exceedingly wobbly standing positions, and experimented with many other perilous postures. Each time he succceeded, especially in getting upright, he looked excited and turned toward his mother, vocalizing in a manner described by each observer as "triumphant." His play with objects was almost always secondary to these motor feats and therefore tended to be simple. He would hold or mouth a toy while creeping or while exploring the crib side with both feet and supporting himself on one extended arm. Characteristically, the one complex object schema he employed was to throw a toy deliberately in order to follow it on his hands and knees. His behavior during spontaneous activity was typical of active infants in that it was well integrated and complex. The manipulation of objects played a very secondary role because at the time of observation he was preoccupied with the mastery of gross locomotor skills.

Previously, we related the behavioral differences between active and inactive infants to the more general hypothesis that the perception of action opportunities (in the absence of more specific stimulation) is likely to rouse active infants to their most integrated and rather intense behavior activations, whereas inactive infants tend to require stronger stimulation in order to mobilize comparable behavior responses (Chapter 6). The behavior of Ac XIII was entirely in accordance with the hypothesis; in him, the high responsiveness to low-level stimulation merely took a somewhat different form than in the other active babies. The behavior of In XI would also be in keeping with the same hypothesis if the behaviors classified as complex for the age group were for her simple well-learned schemas that did not require special stimulation. This assumption is supported by the fact that the data on behavior during "object stimulation" (to be reported in a later section) shows that, like all other inactive subjects, In XI engaged in more complex object schemas while specifically stimulated than she did during spontaneous activity.

Inactive and active infants are equally capable of performing complex object manipulations during spontaneous activity; they differ in how often they do so. What has been said about active infants having a larger proportion of complex object manipulations than inactive ones holds true only for prominent behavior patterns. When it comes to the object schemas these babies showed only occasionally during spontaneous activity (those receiving a prominence rating of peripheral), we found that each activity group displayed twelve complex object schemas. In other words while the inactive subjects did not require special stimulation to be able to perform many complex object schemas, spontaneous activity did not provide sufficient incentive for these schemas to become dominant.

Bodily Need States: Hunger and Fatigue

In the younger infants hunger and fatigue were excitatory states that, for most babies, were associated with overt distress. Crying and signs of motoric agitation tended to be more intense among the active babies, especially during hunger. However, when the impact of hunger and fatigue on behavior was assessed in terms of changes in the quality and organization of behavior, it was seen that these need states altered patterns of behavior quite as much for inactive as for active subjects. In general, even when discomfort was not overt, outwardly focused and complex behaviors disappeared, and were replaced by primitive and self-contained behavior patterns.

For our subjects between the ages of 5 and 7½ months, findings were very similar. A comparison of need state behavior in subjects of Group Three with that of the younger subjects of Group Two suggests two developmental trends in relation to the impact of these need states.

At these later ages hunger does not necessarily evoke excitation or even significant behavior change. Of the twelve infants in Group Three, four showed no overt behavior changes before feeding, though they accepted food when it was offered at the customary times. A fifth baby, who was on a three-meals-a-day schedule, and whom we did not see before her feedings, was reported to play contentedly until she actually saw the approaching food. Although these babies failed to show overt signs of hunger, it was evident that the need state was present, for they accepted normal quantities of food with avidity. It would seem that whatever sensations hunger generated, they were not sufficiently intense to have visible effects on behavior.

In the somewhat older infants fatigue brings distress and marked behavior changes to an even greater extent than in the younger infants. All twelve subjects of Group Three manifested fatigue by massive alterations of behavior; only one of these babies failed to register overt displeasure by crying, squealing unhappily, screaming or at least whimpering. Five of the twelve subjects experienced fatigue and accompanying distress for long periods of time (from 30 to 90 minutes), not only when we saw them, but quite regularly, according to mothers' reports.

Figures 7.1 and 7.2 indicate these findings for the groups as a whole. With respect to gross aspects of behavioral change, the observations on

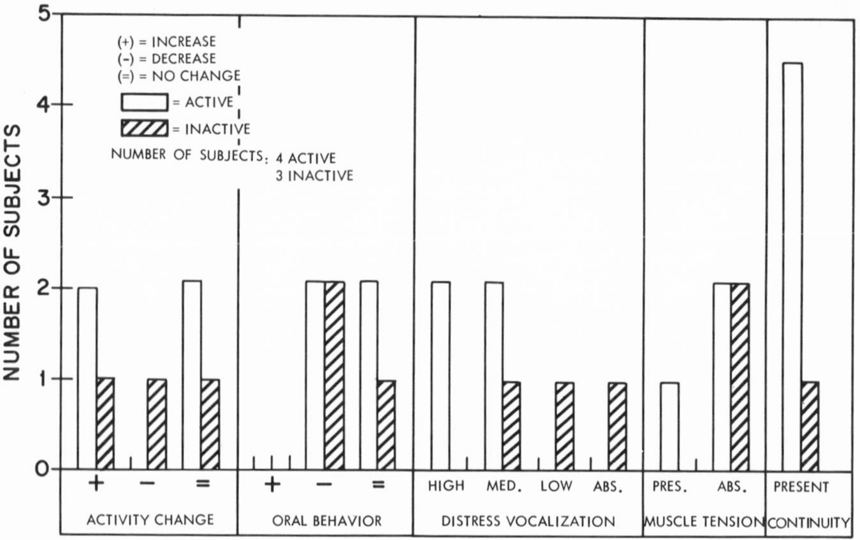

FIGURE 7.1. MANIFESTATIONS OF HUNGER IN ACTIVE AND INACTIVE INFANTS, GROUP THREE.

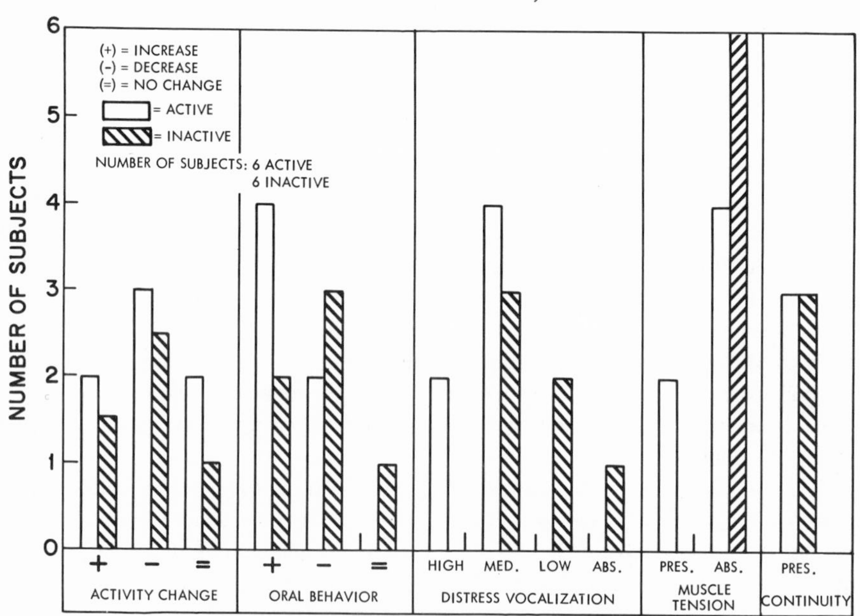

FIGURE 7.2. MANIFESTATIONS OF FATIGUE IN ACTIVE AND INACTIVE INFANTS, GROUP THREE.

NOTE: A score of ½ was assigned to both activity increase and decrease for the three subjects who typically showed a different activity pattern during early and late stages of fatigue.

Group Three are very similar to those reported for Group Two. They may be summarized as follows:

The major difference between active and inactive babies in their response to hunger and fatigue was that only active babies showed extreme distress and, occasionally, muscle tension. In most respects, differences in the response to bodily need states were not associated with activity level. During hunger, oral behavior tended to decrease in comparison with spontaneous activity, or else to remain at much the same level. Fatigue, on the other hand, did affect the amount of oral behavior shown by these babies. In some it markedly increased, but in others it markedly diminished.

As was true to some extent even for the younger subjects, behavior during need states retained sufficient patterning to permit description of what these babies actually did while hungry and while sleepy, allowing comparison of such need state patterns with those prevailing during spontaneous activity.

Behavior during need states tends to be self-contained and primitive and to generate strong bodily sensations. Behavior alterations during hunger and fatigue proved to be very similar. The ratings here combine what was observed under both conditions. The best description of the quality of behavior at these times is obtained by looking at the patterns that were observed in each baby during one or both need states, but which had not been shown at all during spontaneous activity. These are listed in Table 7.11 according to their frequency. Behaviors shown by infants of Group Three only during need states resemble the spontaneous behaviors of the youngest infants (Group One) and, to a lesser extent, of the 16- and 20-week-olds (Group Two). In other words, a primitivization of behavior takes place during need states.

Some babies showed the same behavior patterns during spontaneous activity that other members of the sample showed only while either hungry or fatigued. This was true of such behaviors as oral and tactile self-stimulation, cradle rocking, and squealing. We have already pointed out that during spontaneous activity the active children tended to direct more of their behavior toward objects in the environment, while inactive ones spent more time in behavior focused on their bodies. In other words, for inactive subjects hunger and fatigue tended to bring body-oriented behavior schemas into greater prominence than in spontaneous activity; active subjects tended to show the same kind of body-oriented behaviors during need states, but they had not usually shown such behavior during spontaneous activity.

The impact of need states on behavior organization was equally great for active and inactive subjects, as reflected by the loss of complex and environmentally focused patterns of behavior. Of the behavior schemas shown during spontaneous activity, between 70 and 84 per cent disappeared during hunger and fatigue for the activity groups as a whole (Table

7.12). The behavior patterns lost during bodily need states were, without exception, the ones that had been most frequent and most prominent while the infants were alert and content—namely, those directed toward the environment or toward achievement of a complex motor coordination. It was therefore unnecessary to assess the relative complexity or developmental level of behavior organization during the two conditions—the retained or modified behaviors were, like the new patterns listed on Table 7.11, relatively primitive and almost exclusively body-focused. Except for the fact that active subjects added more new patterns during need states, active and inactive infants did not differ in the degree to which need states altered the organization of behavior.

Vulnerability to behavior alteration due to hunger and fatigue varies widely among individual babies. Table 7.13 shows for each infant the number and proportion of behavior patterns present during spontaneous activity that disappeared with hunger and with fatigue. The percentage of patterns previously available that were lost during either hunger or fatigue varied from 23 per cent (in In XII with hunger) to 100 per cent (in In XVI with hunger). Four of the babies in this sample lost only between 23 per cent and 55 per cent of the spontaneous patterns, though the majority lost upwards of 75 per cent. Similarly, some infants showed no behavior patterns that were "new" during hunger and fatigue, in the sense that they had not also been present during spontaneous activity. These infants merely discontinued the complex outer-focused activities previously present. At the other extreme, especially during fatigue, some babies showed as many as thirteen new patterns.

Although the group differences are also reflected in the comparison of individual pairs (Table 7.13) for the percentage of spontaneous patterns lost and the number of new patterns added during need states, variations within each group are as great as those between the two groups.

In terms of each baby's experience in the course of recurring need states, the impact of hunger or fatigue may be reflected in the amount of excitation and overt distress shown at these times (Figs. 7.1 and 7.2), and/or in the degree to which the nature and complexity of behavior are altered (Tables 7.11, 7.12, and 7.13). We are interested in the fact that many of these infants did not register acute distress or excitation, which may be interpreted to mean that the sensations of discomfort or of pain were less intense for them than for those who cried severely. Yet most of the babies who seemed relatively undisturbed by hunger or fatigue were incapable of functioning in their usual manner at those times. In terms of developmental primitivization, the disruption of the ordinary behavior stream was for them quite as severe as it was for their more demonstrative peers. (The exceptions were those five babies whose behavior did not alter before feeding, though their behavior during feeding indicated that hunger must have been present.)

Here is another example of the manner in which infantile reaction patterns are likely to determine maternal practices, at least in part. The observation of these and other mother-baby couples led us to believe that a baby who fails to show overt distress when hungry is more likely to be kept waiting. In terms of daily experience over weeks and months, he is thus likely to spend a relatively larger proportion of his day in a state short of acute distress but far from alert and contented animation. On the other hand, these babies are often spared the peaks of unhappy excitation that punctuate the days of more highly reactive infants. For the baby who shows less overt distress when fatigued, though usual behavior patterns are severely disrupted, the consequences are somewhat different. Less overtly reactive infants seldom elicited maternal soothing at these times; however, the duration of fatigue discomfort was of the same order (varying in this sample from 8 to 90 minutes) among babies who were and were not soothed. The infants' reaction pattern did play a role in determining the amount of direct contact with the mother at such times, but it is an open question whether the amount of maternal soothing necessarily affected the intensity or the duration of the need state.[4]

At times of bodily discomfort, infants activate behaviors that provide direct body stimulation. All the material on behavior during need states (especially Table 7.11) describes for Group Three a behavior tendency that was discussed at length in Chapter 6: at times of bodily distress, the infant organism supplies itself with tactile, kinesthetic and oral self-stimulation. The more extensive observations on the older babies show with special clarity that, as a result of primitivization, hungry and sleepy babies are likely to intensify those self-stimulating behaviors that are a part of their behavior also at some other times. For some babies bodily self-stimulation during need states can reduce excitation and distress, although for the majority, it remains a component of general arousal. However, as stated earlier, even babies who are not soothed by such activity may, by means of self-stimulation, counteract the diffuse feelings of distress and attendant loss of cohesiveness by providing for themselves predictable and localized bodily sensations.

Object Stimulation

Babies more than 5½ months old can manipulate objects in a great variety of ways (see Table 7.8). Even in the absence of special prodding, these older infants are more inclined to direct their behavior toward inanimate things than to engage in body play, though both kinds of activation are noted when they are left to their own devices.

[4] This contrasts with the effectiveness of self-generated soothing behavior, as described on pp. 219.

The developmental testing situation was the best opportunity for noting the effects of sustained object stimulation upon behavior. Most of the material reported here refers to the behavior of our subjects during the test, but ten of the twelve infants were also observed as the mother (or another person) drew their attention to toys during vigorous play. (The remaining two babies were also seen in that situation, but their mothers played with them in this way only when the babies were somewhat irritable, in an effort to improve their mood.) Each infant's response to vigorous play of this sort was very similar to his response during the testing situation, as had also been true for the younger babies.

Object-related behavior during object stimulation was less varied but more complex than in spontaneous activity. Table 7.14 lists all object schemas shown by each infant during object stimulation, and the prominence of each in his behavior. The sample as a whole generated 32 different schemas, of which 18, or 56 per cent, were complex integrations. The corresponding data on schemas shown during spontaneous activity (Table 7.8) list 38 different schemas, of which only 13, or 34 per cent, were complex. Again, as in Group Two, special prodding led to an increase in complex and more highly integrated patterns of behavior.

During object stimulation the behavior of inactive infants was as complex and as developmentally advanced, as the behavior of active infants. During spontaneous activity the inactive babies showed complex patterns less frequently and much less prominently than active ones did. However, this difference disappeared when the infant's attention was energetically drawn to objects—that is, during object stimulation. The occurrence and the prominence of simple and complex object schemas for each subject during spontaneous activity and during object stimulation are shown in Table 7.15. Table 7.16 summarizes for the group as a whole the number and prominence of simple and complex object-related behavior patterns during object stimulation. Both tables show that special stimulation greatly increased the number and prominence of complex schemas for inactive babies. Some of the active ones showed small changes in the same direction; others, none at all. Figure 7.3 summarizes the same information in the form of pair and cross-pair comparisons. Of the twelve possible alignments between active and inactive subjects of like age, eleven pairs differ in the same direction. In this age group, the impact of object stimulation upon the complexity of object schemas is clearly related to activity level.

This finding is in accord with what has been reported for the younger age groups. Throughout, the behavior of inactive subjects was altered much more by energetic and appropriate stimulation than was that of active subjects. We have discussed elsewhere the significance of this reaction tendency as it affects the importance of maternal stimulation in facilitating developmental progress.

The complexity of object-related behavior during object stimulation is

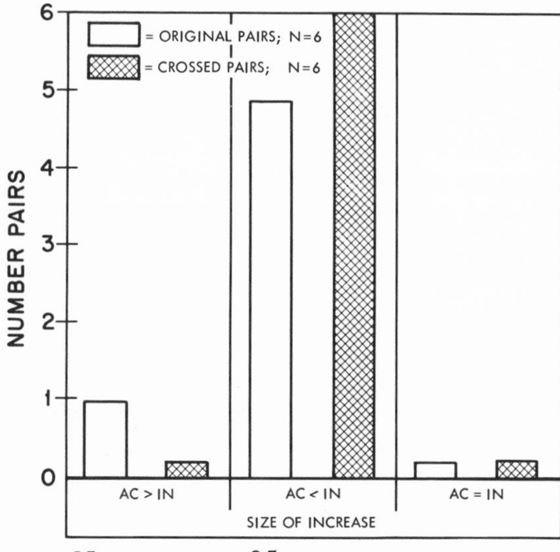

NOTE: p = < .05.

FIGURE 7.3. INCREASES IN THE PROMINENCE OF COMPLEX OBJECT SCHEMAS FROM SPONTANEOUS ACTIVITY TO OBJECT STIMULATION, PAIR AND CROSS-PAIR COMPARISON, GROUP THREE.

highly variable among children with the same activity level. The number of complex schemas during object stimulation varied from three to eleven among active babies, and from four to ten among inactive ones. Similarly, the active subjects' prominence ratings for complex schemas ranged from 3 to 14, and those of inactive subjects ranged from 6 to 13 (Table 7.15). Individual differences within groups were just as great as those between groups.

Each infant's tendency to engage in object manipulations, the degree to which these tend to be complex, and even the particular schemas that become dominant in his behavior are characteristics that are subject to multiple determinants. In the discussion of adaptation syndromes, it will be shown that the following factors are among those related to the nature of object behavior: developmental status, maternal practices, particular constellations of perceptual reactivity, the degree to which the infant tends to engage in bodily self-stimulation, and the degree to which he is responsive to social stimulation. With few exceptions, these determinants fluctuate from week to week and from month to month. For instance, many babies go through a phase when any opportunity for social interaction is so attractive that, for the time being, it reduces their interest in inanimate objects. Similarly, most infants go through phases when the accomplishment of new motor skills absorbs most of their energy at the expense of object manipulations. The individual differences in the quality and quantity of object behavior, both with and without special stimulation, are attributed to variations of this nature. By the same token, we take for granted that the prominence and nature of object schemas shown by individual infants will fluctuate from week to week, and certainly over a period of months. This aspect of behavior organization, like many others, is not considered an attribute or characteristic of the individual child, but the fluctuating resultant of the interaction between stable reaction tendencies and many more variable influences.

What remains relatively stable in the behavior organization of infants is not overt behavior, but the direction and extent of behavior change in response to different states and external conditions. All active infants in Group Three, as well as most of the active babies in Groups One and Two, showed relatively less behavior alteration with increasingly strong stimulation than did the inactive infants. Yet, at the same time, and for the very same behaviors, the patterns within both the active and the inactive groups were markedly dissimilar.

In the study of individual differences, behavioral scientists generally recognize that stable aspects of behavior organization can be demonstrated when each subject is compared with himself, and that such differences can be obscured when subjects are compared with one another. However, in research seeking to discover the effect of one or several variables upon developmental progress, this principle is often disregarded.[5] In our view, the method of comparing each subject with himself is appropriate not only to the study of individual differences but also to the investigation of the effects of any variable on the course of development.

For instance, many recent studies have dealt with the impact on development of differences in socioeconomic status.[6] The predominant research design has been to compare groups of children from deprived backgrounds with groups of children from middle class populations. Comparison was made in terms of test performance or of behavior attributes under comparable situations. Striking differences were found in both the abilities and the characteristic behavior attributes of these groups during the third and fourth year of life (and, of course, beyond). But during the nonverbal stages of development, culturally and economically deprived children were not found to differ significantly from middle class infants and toddlers. Some authors have concluded that these sociocultural variables affect cognitive and personal development not earlier than the third

[5] In psychophysiological research the comparison of subjects with themselves has become the preferred model, even in the elucidation of group differences.

[6] See, among others, Lesser, Fifer, and Clark (1965); Knobloch and Pasamanick (1958); Gilliland (1951); and Benda *et al.* (1963).

year. However, our experience (and that of others) in directly observing infants whose background deviates from the American middle class does not support this conclusion. Although their scores on developmental tests do not necessarily reflect the difference, children from deprived or restricted backgrounds do function and develop in a different manner.

For instance, beginning at about the age of 11 or 12 months, children from disadvantaged families often fail to engage in spontaneous exploratory behavior, though with patient inducement they can at length be motivated to perform much the same manipulations of test materials as are performed readily and easily by most middle-class children. Similarly, many babies from deprived backgrounds (or from families whose child-rearing customs deviate greatly from the dominant American pattern, such as lower middle-class Italian-American or Spanish-American groups) fail to repeat newly learned behavior schemas spontaneously, as we have come to expect from the middle-class babies on whose behavior our developmental psychology is largely based. Thus, having learned how to ring a bell, how to empty a container, or how to throw and retrieve objects, an infant "typically" will initiate these schemas over and over again, show glee and excitement in the process, and resist obstacles to such activity (Stott, 1961). But many babies from a markedly different milieu will perform the actions in question if induced to do so, will smile briefly at accomplishment or at playful recognition from the adult, and will then drop the toy and look about, content to wait for whatever happens next.

These and many other observations make it appear likely that the spontaneous development of mastery or competence takes a different form in children from different socioeconomic and cultural groups. Possibly the differences between socioeconomic groups demonstrated among preschool children are the result of experiential differences during the first years of life. If this is so, the effects of cultural deprivation occur long before they are manifested by comparing achievement levels of the groups. Such antecedent effects could be uncovered, however, if the research design were to compare groups of subjects in terms of the variability of each subject's performance under different conditions.

Only inactive infants diminished social responsiveness during object stimulation and showed marked delay between perception and response. When behavior other than the direct response to objects was examined during object stimulation, some differences between active and inactive infants were seen. For the younger babies in Group Two, it was reported that during testing (and in similar situations), active babies remained as socially responsive as they were at other times. However, some inactive babies focused upon inanimate objects to the exclusion of any responsiveness toward the person who presented the objects or toward the mother. A similar difference occurred in Group Three though, again, it was not a regular phenomenon (Table 7.17). The social responsiveness of one of the six active subjects diminished during object stimulation. Of the six inactive babies, two ceased all overt social responsiveness and one reduced it noticeably, while the other three remained as responsive as they were at other times. It would appear that between the ages of 5 and 8 months, markedly inactive children can become so absorbed in object manipulation that they lose awareness of social aspects of the situation, but they may also be able to sustain both varieties of interaction.

A minority of the babies in Group Two tended to focus intently on a visual stimulus, but reach for the object only after some delay. Perhaps because activity level differences were not extreme in Group Two, this behavior characteristic did not appear to be related to activity level. But in this group a marked delay between perception and motoric response was noted in four of the inactive babies and in none of the active ones (Table 7.17).

The capacity (or the necessity) to delay movement in response to excitation is of considerable interest, in that fine coordinations and deliberate problem solving are impossible in the absence of delay. Psychoanalytic ego psychology, as well as other developmental theories, have emphasized that the acquisition of the capacity to inhibit immediate motoric response is a necessary condition for the emergence of thought and ideation, for the modulation of affect, and for impulse control. In short, all of the important ego functions are based upon delay capacity. It has been speculated by this author and by others [7] that activity level may be a predisposing factor, in that children of low activity level may have the ability to delay earlier than children of high activity level. The interval between intent focus upon a stimulus and adaptive motor response may be a transient inhibition, and hence involve delay.

However, it is also possible that in some inactive children the appropriate movement impulse not only arises less forcefully but also requires more time to emerge. Descriptively speaking, the infant is not hesitating or delaying a felt impulse, but is simply waiting for the impulse to arise. This notion is congruent with our tentative hypothesis that low activity level is due to a high threshold for the release of movement. The phenomenon of actual delay between perception and response is also of interest in relation to other behavior characteristics of inactive infants, some of which have already been described: the less frequent occurrence of high peaks of excitation and affect expression in their experience, their relatively greater capacity to return to a comfortable state after disruptive episodes (self-soothing), and the greater prominence of behaviors that consist solely or chiefly of visual regard.

The results of developmental testing included another relevant finding that will be discussed fully in the section on adaptation syndromes. Among

[7] Escalona and Heider (1959); Wolf (1953).

the inactive subjects, regardless of absolute developmental status, those test items that required delicate coordination of hand movement and/or responsiveness to small detail were frequently among the infants' most mature behaviors. In active children, the ability to manipulate larger objects and to control the posture and movement of the entire body tended to be more mature than the ability to perform fine movements. The increasingly complex behavior integrations that constitute developmental progress may be described as a gradual change from immediate reactivity to increasingly mediated responsiveness. These findings, then, would indicate that behavior tends to be relatively more immediate in many spheres when activity level is high; so that those functions that specifically depend on a degree of distance between impulse, perception, or excitation and the adaptive or coordinated response are impeded. When activity level is low, the mediation processes emerge more easily, yet the impetus for them or for any other activation is comparatively less strong and less frequent, at least in the absence of fairly frequent and appropriate stimulation.

In summary, the material on behavior change in response to object stimulation showed that most infants in Group Three responded to playful prodding by performing complex object schemas more prominently than at other times. Such special stimulation produced marked increases in object-related behaviors among inactive subjects, and comparatively small increases among active ones. Further, during object stimulation (but not during spontaneous activity) active and inactive babies showed very similar object schemas, though there were marked individual differences in the amount and kind of object-related behavior. Consistent differences as a function of activity level concerned only the degree of change resulting from different conditions of stimulation. A delay between perception and response was seen almost exclusively in inactive subjects, as was the diminution or absence of social responsiveness during object stimulation. Overt distress at loss of a toy during object stimulation was characteristic of most active babies, but was seen in only one inactive subject.

Social Behavior

Above the age of 5½ months, babies have become social creatures; they can freely initiate social interaction and can sustain their share of reciprocal interactions longer and more flexibly than before; they respond to the social components of almost any situation; and conventional communication signals emerge in rudimentary form.

In comparison with that of the younger infants of Group Two, social behavior has become more differentiated, more complex, and more often initiated by the infant. Table 7.18 lists all patterns of social behavior noted in Group Three, their frequency among the active and inactive babies, and their prominence in both groups. While Group Two (Table 6.19) had exhibited only fourteen different patterns, we noted 29 among these older infants. The basic components of social response are still gazing, smiling, laughing, chuckling, and squealing. However, among these older babies one finds more varied combinations of these elements; more importantly, they are elicited by a much wider range of circumstances. Thus, babies in Group Three moved toward the mother or another person, and they remembered their mother's position in the room when she was out of sight and were able to turn toward her at will. The older ones were also able to participate in playful rituals of the peek-a-boo variety. Some of these babies played an active role in what Table 7.18 lists as "active reciprocal love games," by which we mean situations in which babies elaborate intimate play with their mothers—putting their arms around her head or neck in a hugging gesture, burying their faces in her neck, poking or grasping her nose, mouth or other body parts, making kissing gestures they have been taught—initiating such activities themselves in an active, lover-like way.

Most of the social responses occurred among both active and inactive infants. However, the social responses of active babies tended to be more directed in space and more specific; those of inactive babies tended to be more diffuse and were relatively more responsive than initiatory. Of the 29 social behavior patterns, five were shown exclusively or predominantly by active infants: persistent effort to obtain response; smile, vocalize and touch partner's face; turn to remembered position of mother; active reciprocal love games; locomote toward partner while vocalizing. Six different patterns were exclusive or predominant among inactive infants: gaze and vocalize; smile only; activity increase and smile; touch partner without smile or sound; prolonged, intent, "puzzled" regard; smile at voice out of sight without turning.

Active babies were more responsive than inactive ones to minimal social stimulation, but less responsive to medium levels of social stimulation. In response to different degrees of social stimulation, the inactive infants as a group made fewer responses of the kind classified as "strong," and with less prominence, than did the active ones (see Table 7.19). However, differences in social responsiveness occurred under only two conditions: (1) the mere sight of a person, when active babies tended to respond more strongly than inactive ones; and (2) social stimulation of medium intensity, to which inactive babies were a good deal more responsive.[8] The total number and summed prominence ratings of social behavior patterns were very similar for the two groups.

As has been reported for Groups One and Two under conditions of social stimulation, and as was found for Group Three in response to object

[8] Table 7.19 appears to indicate that inactive infants also were more responsive to strong stimulation than were active ones. But the next table (7.20) shows that this group result is an artifact due to the circumstance that more inactive babies received strong social stimulation.

stimulation, active and inactive infants can and will respond at equal levels of intensity. However, each comparison also proved that active babies were most responsive to minimal and low levels of stimulation. Inactive babies, on the other hand, typically showed high levels of responsiveness when stimulation was of medium intensity, and sometimes when it was very strong.

Not all babies in this sample were exposed to social stimulation so intense as to be classified as "strong." Four active and three inactive infants were never played with in such a vigorous manner, while three mothers never went beyond gentle social stimulation. It was therefore necessary to see whether the differences shown in group comparison also existed between individual pairs in which both infants received the same variety of stimulation. Active infants always responded more strongly and more often to minimal social stimulation than did inactive ones (Table 7.20). On the other hand, responses of medium strength to medium levels of stimulation tended to be more prominent among inactive babies (in five of seven possible comparisons).

The differential impact of similar types of stimulation on active and inactive babies has been discussed in previous sections, and needs no further amplification. However, one general aspect of this finding is demonstrated better in this material than in preceding portions, though it has been reported throughout.

During social interaction, strong stimulation tends to suppress maximum responsiveness. Table 7.19 shows that both the number and prominence of different social responses were relatively small in response to strong stimulation, in comparison with all other conditions. From the way babies of this age behave when their mothers jiggle and bounce, toss and tickle, and vigorously kiss them, it is apparent that although the babies may enjoy these occasions, they are also somewhat overwhelmed by them. Smiling, laughing, and chuckling are the only responses that occur, and even these are often brief and slightly explosive in character. Sustained *interaction* between mother and young baby is only possible when the baby's responses are given time to emerge, and when the mother's play is attuned to whatever behaviors the infant may initiate or prolong.

We believe that the regulation of the intensity of social play in accordance with this "law of diminishing returns" is an important part of skillful mothering. Most mothers and most other women automatically adapt the intensity of their approach to whatever level elicits optimal responsiveness from the baby. Many fathers (and men in general) are less empathic in this respect. Hence, playful episodes when fathers or older siblings are in charge run more risk of overexciting the baby; at the least, they often reduce the baby to the role of respondent rather than participant. In the total adaptation of infants within the family, the more provocative and less sheltering contacts with people are probably important in facilitating tolerance for more intense arousal; they promote growth just because they combine high points of pleasure with a degree of discomfort.

This suggestion finds support from general clinical observation. For instance, it is often noted that young children reared exclusively by the mother, or in entirely female households, tend to be somewhat fragile and ill equipped to cope with stress. This observation is often linked to the explanation that in fatherless homes the child is likely to receive overly intense emotion from the mother, which may alter the quality of relationship in an unhealthy direction. Generally, the explanation for the fragility and vulnerability of children reared in feminine environments is formulated in terms of the effect of specific maternal attitudes and feelings on the emotional life of the infant and toddler. The issue is a good example of the manner in which the intervening variable of concrete experience can clarify and unify phenomena that otherwise require several and separate explanations.

If our inference is correct, states of arousal (short of disruptive excitation) created by highly accommodating maternal behavior bring to the fore developmentally advanced forms of social interaction; the more forceful (and still pleasurable) forms of social play also contribute developmental impetus, but chiefly toward enlarging the infant's tolerance for external stimulation. These assumptions account for similarities in developmental outcome under seemingly different environmental circumstances on the basis of similarities in the child's concrete experience.

A balance between what we may call specifically "maternal" types of interaction (rousing but only moderately excitatory) and the more forceful, less accommodating social encounters (those we think typical of loving fathers) can come about in different ways. If the infant is an active one, variations in social experience ranging from the mere sight of persons to gentle social stimulation are maximally accommodating, in the sense that they elicit strong and varied responses. Occasional medium stimulation would provide more intense provocation and the necessity to accommodate to forceful stimuli. If the child is an inactive one, the same balance in social experience will exist only if medium stimulation is frequent and strong stimulation occurs occasionally.

This formulation would imply that infants reared by their mothers only (or receiving only the accommodating "maternal" variety of social stimulation) seldom experience the push of forceful stimulation and, therefore, tend to become markedly differentiated in the social realm, yet lack the ability to withstand stress and novelty.[9] Infants whose mothers are not empathic as described, and whose social experience is thus often too intense to permit optimal response or too slight to be arousing, lack a significant component of mothering. Their concrete experience in this respect is similar to that of children reared in institutions, who typically show delay

[9] The biographies of numerous poets and imaginative writers—for example, Dickens and Proust—strongly suggest this syndrome.

or impoverishment in social development.[10] We suggest that similar shortcomings in social development noted in children who lack mothering of the empathic kind can be explained on the basis of similarities in this aspect of early experience.

The suggestion that features of adaptation and developmental course are related to specific patterns of experience is not intended to replace the hard-won knowledge of the effects of maternal attitudes, needs, and conflicts on the affective life of young children, and on the constellations of conflict and defense that will emerge in their development. Rather, it is an attempt to specify some of the behavioral consequences for the infant of the motivations of the adults who raise him. If further research succeeds in delineating developmentally significant patterns of concrete experience, it should be possible to find explanations for the fact that similar maternal and familial constellations yield widely different syndromes of adaptation and development, because of differences in the mother's (and any caretaking person's) behavioral style, and in the infant's reaction tendencies.

Our description of specifically "maternal" varieties of social interaction, as contrasted with other, more intrusive patterns, is highly schematic. It is in the nature of a model or a paradigm and is not intended as an adequate description of the relevant phenomena. Nearly all mothers offer most varieties of social experience to their babies; many fathers are exquisitely "maternal" in the sense in which we have used the term; and each baby's experience with all other persons, from relatives to the most casual passers-by, can be placed on the continuum from greatest to least accommodation to the baby's momentary state and action readiness.

Discriminatory social behavior and rudimentary communication vary greatly among infants; they do not appear to be related to activity level. Some characteristics of social behavior are not encompassed in the description of particular patterns; they were rated separately on the basis of the totality of each infant's behavior during the observation periods. For the babies of Group Three the following characteristics could be assessed: response to first contact with strangers; differential behavior toward mother and other people after stranger response had abated; differential response to different observers after stranger response had disappeared; soothability; distractibility; response to termination of a social interlude; and communicatory behavior that suggested the presence of an intention or the comprehension of a verbal sign.

Table 7.21 lists the presence and relative strength of each of these behavior aspects for all infants in Group Three. Comparison with Table 6.20, which provides parallel information about the younger babies in Group Two, shows that the stranger response, discrimination of the mother,

[10] The adaptation syndromes of our normal subjects include some instances of inactive babies, either understimulated or stimulated frequently but at very low intensity, whose social development was somewhat retarded.

and response to the termination of a playful interlude were shown by a larger proportion of the older babies. These behaviors begin to emerge as early as 24 weeks, are acquired by many infants during the seventh and eighth months, but do not appear in some babies until after the eighth month. All of the younger infants responded to soothing, at least to some degree; half of the subjects of Group Three, however, no longer had the experience of being soothed. After a baby is more than 5 months old, many mothers no longer rock, pat, or otherwise attempt to induce quiescence when he is distressed. They are more likely to engage the baby in an activity designed to arouse his interest and improve his mood. The category labeled "distractibility" refers to the infant's typical response to the attempt to cheer him by diversion, and varies in much the same way that "soothability" does for younger infants.

Beginning at the age of 28 weeks, in this sample, babies behaved in ways clearly reflecting their intention or anticipation of inducing their mothers to act in a certain way. For instance, when unable to achieve a desired position change or obtain a distant toy, they turned *away from the goal* and vocalized toward the mother in a manner understood by parents and by the observers as "pleading," "coaxing," "demanding," or otherwise communicating a request. Similarly, some of these babies could respond to verbal signals in a specific manner. Several could perform the motions conventionally associated with the games of "pat-a-cake" and "so big," and would do so without imitation; that is, in response to the mother's verbal request unaccompanied by gestures. An interesting borderline situation was also noted in these babies' response to purely verbal restraint or direction. Two of our subjects, when creeping at a considerable distance from the mother, could be halted in their tracks by a compellingly uttered maternal "no, no." They would look toward the mother, away from the attractive goal, and desist from motion as long as the mother continued to repeat her prohibition. One 32-week-old also approached his mother when he was called, though his facial expression and his repeated deflections from the straight course clearly indicated that he did not wish to come; still, he was unable to ignore the mother's call.

The capacity to participate in the exchange of conventionally patterned communication signals and to use established behavior patterns (such as babbling or squealing) as a means of communication profoundly alters the nature of an infant's social experience. Before it is acquired, reciprocity between the infant and his social partner consists of mutually responsive actions in the *immediate* situation: the infant smiles or coos at the sight or sound of a person, is responded to, alters his behavior in accordance with his partner's fluctuating changes of expression, movement and sound, all of this being dictated by his state and by the immediate perceptual input. Mutual imitation enters the process, but the baby is always oriented (visually and bodily) toward something he is perceiving at the moment.

After communication signals become available and understood, social behavior begins to acquire the cognitive organization of a means-end structure. A baby who turns from looking at and reaching for a toy to vocalize demandingly to the mother has not lost interest in the desired toy. On the contrary, he is anticipating that, in response to his sounds and gestures, she will make the toy accessible. Spitz (1957) and other authors have emphasized that a truly reciprocal relationship between mother and child presupposes that the infant's behavior recognizes the mother's existence as a separate object; his turning toward her in the manner described is an example of such recognition.

The question has been raised as to whether the requisite degree of cognitive maturity must be achieved before the baby can develop a true object relation (in the psychoanalytic sense); or whether, on the contrary, the development of such a relationship enables the child to recognize inanimate objects as independent and constant objects (in the everyday sense).[11]

Our data on behavior organization in transactions with inanimate objects and with other persons suggest that a means-end structure underlies behavior directed at things before such a cognitive structure is manifest in social interactions. All the infants of Group Three and all 20-week-olds in Group Two were able to perform an action as a means to achieve an end. An infant who grasps a bell by the handle and moves it to produce a ringing sound does so with the sensorimotor anticipation that his movement will have specific consequences; the younger infant merely grasps the bell and waves or moves it as he does other objects, although he may incidentally produce the sound. The same is true of babies who throw toys in order to retrieve them, or who turn completely around in order to find a toy previously used and remembered.

To define the manner in which social and affective aspects of development are intertwined with perceptual, cognitive, and neuromuscular development, it seems to us important to separate the *first emergence* of some ego functions in the course of an immediate response from their *application* in various behavior contexts. "Application" of a function here means situations in which self-generated behavior (such as turning from the toy toward the mother, or dropping and retrieving a toy) is guided by a mental function. We suggest the tentative hypothesis that several of the early ego functions *first emerge* during interactions between infant and maternal figures, but are *applied* earlier in the infant's transactions with inanimate objects than in social transactions. For instance, both anticipation and perceptual discrimination appear very early. The best-documented behavior reflecting the presence of both these functions is the hungry baby's ability to stop crying at the mere sight of the mother and/or bottle, before the nipple has

[11] See Gouin-Decarie (1965).

been brought to the mouth. If the infant remembers the visual percept of the mother-breast or bottle constellation, as being closely linked to remembered satisfaction, then he is responding to the preliminaries to feeding as an indivisible part of the entire feeding situation. He has, as Freud put it, begun to make use of "purposes remembered in advance" (Freud, 1958). Yet, at ages when many infants show discrimination and anticipation in these rudimentary forms, their spontaneous behavior with objects is still indiscriminate and does not use anticipation. At the age of 16 weeks the majority of infants "know that food is coming," but, in relation to objects, they still perform almost automatically. That is, as the baby reaches for an object, his hand and finger positions do not adapt to the visually perceived size of the object, but change only when it is actually grasped; his behavior with objects already grasped does not vary to suit the actual properties of the object. Everything is waved, brought to the mouth, or fingered—whether it be a rattle, clothing, the mother's finger, or a zwieback.

During the next several months self-generated behaviors are adapted increasingly to the physical properties of objects or of the body. Anticipation, discrimination, and, presumably, memory begin to organize these behaviors; as anticipation is further developed and a variety of sensorimotor schema become freely available, a means-end structure emerges. Only after the means-end mode of functioning has been part of the child's repertoire for some time does it appear in the context of purely social behavior; *i.e.,* social play and communication. This idea would be in keeping with Freud's original theory that the early ego functions differentiate of necessity, as the infant experiences delay in need gratification and develops vigilance for signs of impending gratification. For human infants, need gratification is necessarily provided by a person, and it involves direct contact between the giver and the recipient. Yet, as was suggested in previous discussions of mastery, the process by which new functions and capacities are coordinated and lead to more complex behavior integrations takes place in relatively neutral situations that involve more constant and manipulatable segments of the environment.

The same routine caretaking situations provide widely different patterns of mother-child interaction. By far the most constant part of each infant's experience in direct contact with the mother occurs during routine caretaking situations. But what actually takes place as mothers care for their infants is not at all the same from one family to the next, even apart from each child's pattern of reactivity. Among the many recurrent contacts between mother and infant, we were able to observe only a few often enough to assess both the characteristic features of the mother's behavior and the relatively stable aspects of the child's response. Before describing differences between the typical experiences of active and inactive infants at such times, we shall describe the extent of variations in the nature of these situations, as apparent in even so small a group of infants. These differences seem the more impressive because, from a sociocultural point of view, ours was a fairly homogeneous population.

The situations included in our analysis of this aspect of the infant's life were the following: maternal interventions as the infant was hungry or fatigued; bottle (or breast) feedings; solid (or cup) feedings; diapering; dressing; and, where it occurred frequently, mother's play with the baby aside from caretaking situations. In order to demonstrate the variable nature of these situations, we shall briefly summarize the constellations observed during breast or bottle feeding.

Two babies in Group Three, Ac XIII and Ac XVI, were still fed at the breast. Both babies were very active in the mother's arms, so much so that they often lost the nipple and then briefly cried or squealed. However, Ac XIII was intensively responsive to the mother, as she was to him. He not only grasped the mother's breast and clothing but, between spells of vigorous feeding, he also fingered her face, put his hand into her mouth, clutched her nose, pinched her neck, laughed, smiled, and babbled at her while keeping his eyes on her face. However, especially during the first half of the feeding, he also arched his back and thrashed about so actively that his mother had to hold him very firmly to prevent him from falling off her lap. Frequently, his motions caused him to lose the nipple, at which he screamed and cried. Even the periods of actual nursing were not relaxed; he clung to nipple and breast and, as the mother put it, "gulped his food as if he were afraid to lose it." However, each time we could observe a feeding, it was followed by an interval of intense but more relaxed play of the kind we previously described as "active reciprocal love games." Throughout, the mother's attention was riveted on the baby.

Ac XVI also lunged at the breast, also occasionally lost the nipple and cried until it was restored, and also sucked vigorously. He was playful, especially during the second half of feeding, but though he was responsive to the mother, his attention was not focused on her face or person. The nature of the interaction was pleasurable and casual on both sides. No intense mutual gazing or smiling occurred, his hands did not explore the mother's body, and neither mother nor baby seemed absorbed by the situation, which both of them enjoyed.

Four of the babies were always held during bottle feeding. In one instance (Ac XII) the situation was similar to the first of those described above—highly sociable and playful, accompanied by absorbing and intimate mutual body play, mutual gazing and the like. This baby also moved about enough to lose the nipple and depended on his mother to restore it. One baby (In XII) was very quiet but fully oriented toward her mother. Neither mother nor baby was the least bit playful, but mutual gazing was very prominent and each participant seemed absorbed in the situation to the point where observers felt that neither one was aware of their presence. Two other babies (Ac XIV and In XVI) were held on the lap, accepted food eagerly and efficiently, and seemed entirely content, but oblivious of the mother and everything else. Though encircled by their mother's arms, neither child looked at her face (their eyelids drooped), nor did their hands make contact with her body. Neither of these mothers looked at the baby more than casually, or created body contact with the baby beyond comfortably holding him.

Five babies (Ac and In XV, In XIV, Ac and In XI) received their bottle propped in the crib or on the bassinette. All of them took the bottle well and seemed entirely content. Three mothers left the baby, merely checking from time to time and staying close enough to hear him should he register discomfort. All three of these babies moved about some during feeding, and two of them paid attention to the sights and sounds about, cooed, and engaged in secondary play with the crib side, the blanket, or a toy. The third was very nearly motionless, with eyes nearly closed, apparently oblivious of all but the sucking activity itself. Two of the mothers sat close by and watched the baby. In each case, their attention was on his behavior, they often gazed at his face and even smiled, but he could not see the mother's face. One infant seemed oblivious of his mother's presence, though he looked at various objects and movements in his visual field and vocalized as his gaze encountered that of an observer. The other baby was very quiet, but he repeatedly interrupted sucking, turned his head to find the mother's face, and there was intense and prolonged gazing and smiling between them. Each time it was the baby who both initiated such social episodes and terminated them in order to resume sucking.

These brief summaries may serve to illustrate the fact that the amount and kind of mother-child interaction during feeding does not necessarily depend on the feeding method. Equally great differences were found during soothing, diapering, dressing, solid feeding, and play periods. The remaining material on the differences in these infants' experience during recurrent contacts with their mothers is based on observation of such variations in all of the relevant situations.

Among active infants, a larger proportion of recurrent contacts with the mother are excitatory or involve unpleasure or mixed affect than among inactive ones. For each infant we selected those daily recurring contacts that could be observed repeatedly, and that the mother assured us were typical of his behavior on these occasions. A situation was considered excitatory if, during the contact, the baby regularly showed excitation, either due to or despite the mother's manipulation of him. Thus, for infants who continued to cry and thrash about even during mother's efforts to soothe them, soothing was considered as excitatory because while the direct mother-child contact took place, the infant was usually aroused. In infants who responded well to soothing, the same situation was classified as not excitatory, because once soothing began, the infant was typically calm while it lasted. The assessment of affective states involved the same prin-

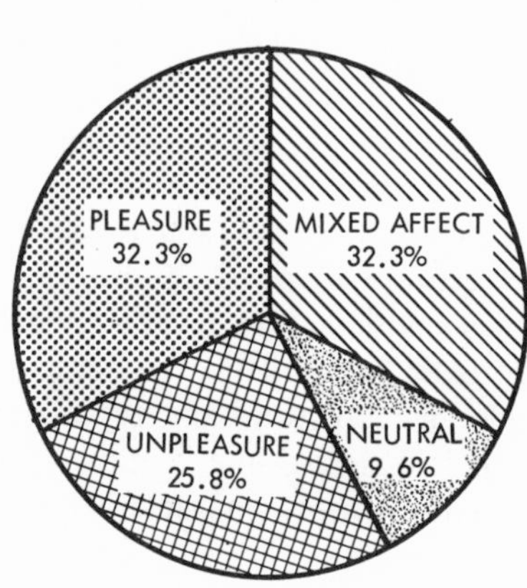

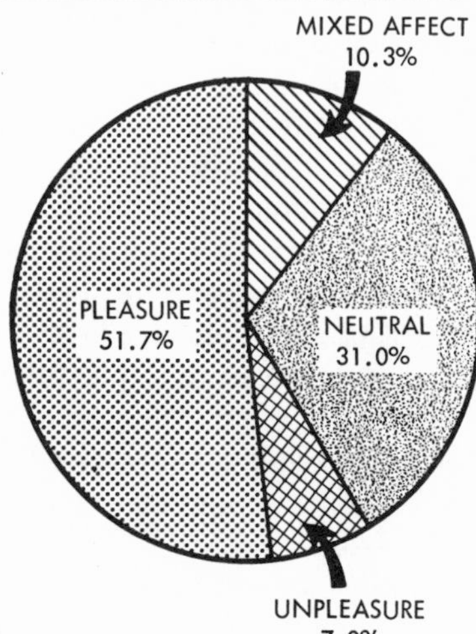

FIGURE 7.4. THE PERCENTAGE OF RECURRENT SOCIAL INTERACTIONS THAT TYPICALLY EVOKE VARIOUS AFFECTIVE RESPONSES FOR ACTIVE AND INACTIVE SUBJECTS OF GROUP THREE.

ciple, although pleasure or displeasure were usually responsive to whatever the mother did with and for the baby. It is important to keep in mind that the relevant tables and Figure 7.4 do not state the frequency with which we observed these responses. All the situations occurred several times each day in the baby's life and were typically combined with the behavioral responses indicated.[12]

During the recurrent contacts with the mother, active babies responded with unpleasure or mixed affect to 58.1 per cent of the situations, and the inactive babies only 17.3 per cent (Fig. 7.4). (Another finding apparently shown on Fig. 7.4—that a larger proportion of the situations led to pleasure for the inactive babies—proved to be an artifact due to the variation in the absolute number of situations included for each infant.) Pair and cross-pair comparisons confirmed the association between activity level and behavioral group differences (see Table 7.23). In eleven of twelve possible comparisons between babies of like age, the proportion of recurrent contacts that involved marked excitation and either unpleasure or mixed affect was higher for the active member of the pair. Similarly, the proportion of situations accompanied by overt displeasure was greater for the active member of the pair in eight of ten comparisons. The proportion

[12] A great many of the recurrent situations in each baby's life could not be observed more than twice and so are not included in these tables. For some subjects the number of different situations was very small because, although we observed several instances of a situation, the mother assured us that the baby's behavior had been atypical.

of situations involving pleasure was not consistently associated with activity level. In six of twelve comparisons, inactive babies showed pleasure more often than active ones; in three of twelve comparisons, active babies showed pleasure more often, and in the remaining three pairs no difference existed.

The relatively greater affectivity and excitation of active children during routine contacts with the mother could be anticipated on the basis of their behavior characteristics in other situations. The mixed affective state (very rare among inactive infants) almost always occurred as the active babies reacted with displeasure to the movement restraint involved in dressing, diapering, and solid feeding. Yet, the babies continued to respond with intermittent pleasure to playful maternal efforts to divert them. In addition, some social interactions occur regularly only because the baby regularly becomes excited and distressed and thus compels maternal intervention. We already know know that this sequence of events is more characteristic of active babies.

Individual differences in experience during recurrent social contacts with the mother were nearly as great within activity level groups as between them. As was true for many other variables, the presence of consistent differences between active and inactive babies does not necessarily lead to great similarity in the reaction patterns of members of the same activity level group. In order to highlight these individual differences, Table 7.22 provides the original assessments of the response to recurrent social situations for each member of Group Three. Among active infants, the proportion of excitatory contacts varied from as high as 80 per cent (Ac XIII) to as low as 20 per cent (Ac XVI), and similar variation was present in all other types of response except that of neutral affect, which was absent or rare in all active infants.

Among inactive infants also, some kinds of response were highly variable; others were not. For one baby (In XV) all recurrent social contacts were accompanied by pleasure, but In XVI responded so to only one of five situations. However, these individual patterns are not an adequate description of what each of these babies experienced during routine contacts with their mothers. Such almost universally pleasurable situations as the bath or the first feeding in the early morning were necessarily excluded, and some babies' responses to similar events varied greatly with their state (and possibly with the mother's). Still, most daily routines were included for each baby, and these partial data support the suggestion that studies that include all regular caretaking situations probably would lead to similar results.

In summary, analysis of the social behavior shown by infants of Group Three illustrates the expected increase in the number and complexity of social responses and of discriminatory social behavior. It also illustrates the changes in the pattern of interaction made possible by very early forms of denotative communication. Active and inactive infants differed primarily not in the overt behavior patterns they showed, but in the conditions that elicited maximal social response.

Bodily Self-Stimulation

The frequency, prominence and intensity of bodily self-stimulation in Group Three was very similar to that in Group Two. As a first approach to the description of self-stimulating behaviors in Group Three, we assessed for each baby the prominence of such behavior in each of the three relevant modalities. Table 7.24 summarizes this information. Comparison with Table 6.23, which provides the parallel data for Group Two, shows that the incidence and prominence of self-stimulating behaviors do not differ appreciably for the two age levels. All infants showed some non-nutritive oral behavior, and the great majority also engaged in tactile and/or kinesthetic forms of self-stimulation. The only change, in terms of this global assessment, is that kinesthetic self-stimulation was shown more among the older infants and perhaps more prominently among the active subjects. There was no striking association between activity level and the prominence of bodily self-stimulation in either group (see Tables 6.23 and 7.24).

TACTILE SELF-STIMULATION

All members of Group Two had shown tactile self-stimulation of one sort or another, though most only with low prominence. This was not true of the older subjects, five of whom never touched their own skin except incidentally as part of some other movement.

Patterns of tactile self-stimulation were nearly identical in kind and intensity for infants in both Group Three and Group Two. Table 7.25 specifies the patterns of tactile self-stimulation observed in subjects of Group Three, and the frequency and prominence of each among active and inactive subjects. Comparison with Table 6.24, referring to Group Two, proves that the particular patterns and the overall incidence [13] of tactile self-stimulation were about the same in both age groups. Rubbing of the face and of other body portions was among the most frequent and prominent patterns at both age levels. In addition, the older babies showed a new pattern with relatively high frequency—the forceful slapping or banging of the thigh with the hand or a toy.

Differences between active and inactive subjects were minimal, though the most frequent patterns of tactile self-stimulation were more strongly represented among inatcive infants. Table 7.25 shows that of the nine patterns, only four occurred in at least three of the twelve babies. All

[13] Eight subjects had a total of sixteen ratings for tactile self-stimulation in Group Two, and twelve subjects in Group Three had a total of 23 such ratings.

these more common varieties of tactile self-stimulation were also more prominent among inactive subjects. Although absolute differences were small, a comparison of those forms of tactile self-stimulation shown by inactive subjects with those shown more often (or only) by active ones suggests a consistent difference in the quality of bodily sensations these babies tended to provide for themselves. In one or another of the active babies, but no inactive ones, we saw tight clutching of the head with both hands, tight clasping of the hands, clasping one foot with both hands, bumping the head against the crib side (not as a part of rocking), rubbing the heels against the base of the Teeter-Babe while seated, and scratching the face or chest. Inactive babies, on the other hand, showed these patterns prominently or exclusively: rubbing or stroking the body, rubbing the face, rubbing the legs against one another, and forcefully and repeatedly banging a hand or toy against the thigh.

It appears that, comparatively speaking, active infants were more likely to exert tactile pressure on one portion of the body, clasping or bumping it, while inactive babies were given to repetitive stimulation of the surface of the skin, primarily with rubbing and stroking motions. Possibly the clutching, head bumping and rubbing the heels against the base of the infant seat were primarily muscular activations that produced tactile sensations incidentally, whereas repeated motions of the hand over body surfaces were more unequivocally behaviors directed to yield purely tactile sensations.

Tactile self-stimulation occurs chiefly during somatic need states, though inactive babies may show it during spontaneous activity. As had been found for the younger infants in Group Two (see Table 6.25), it was during the discomfort of hunger or fatigue that these older babies tended to stimulate their own skin (Table 7.26). Some inactive babies also engaged in tactile self-stimulation while content and alert, though generally only briefly and peripherally in comparison with the prominence of other behaviors. The tendency of infants to provide bodily self-stimulation for themselves at times when they presumably feel unpleasurable awareness of internal bodily sensations has already been discussed (Chapter 6). Table 7.26 shows that among the older babies as well, tactile self-stimulation usually accompanied behavioral arousal from internal causes. In no infant at any age level did it fulfill the function of self-soothing.

KINESTHETIC SELF-STIMULATION

Kinesthetic self-stimulation was about equally prominent among active and inactive babies, and it was at least as prominent during spontaneous activity as during need states. Tables 7.27 and 7.28 describe the frequency and prominence of kinesthetic self-stimulation and the conditions under which it occurred. The basic movement patterns involved are rocking, bouncing, rolling, and a variation that we described as "swinging." In this age group, rocking and bouncing are possible in various positions; that is, seated, standing, supine, or in the hand-knee creeping position. Rocking always had a marked rhythmic quality, while rolling and bouncing did in some children, but not in others. The tables indicate that infants inclined to show kinesthetic self-stimulation ordinarily do so at medium or high levels of intensity; only rolling (and in one situation, for one baby, swinging on the abdomen) was seen at a low prominence level. Unlike tactile self-stimulation, the kinesthetic variety was activated as much during spontaneous activity, as a form of motor play, as during the discomfort associated with fatigue or hunger.[14] In fact, those infants who showed patterns such as rocking, rolling, or bouncing during spontaneous activity tended to behave in the same way during hunger and fatigue.

Among the kinesthetic patterns, only cradle rocking served the function of self-soothing. Two inactive babies (In XI and In XIII) cradle rocked in an animated and fairly vigorous fashion while content, and both increased the vigor and the prominence of rocking while in somatic distress. In both of these children the rocking while distressed had a visible effect in that they stopped crying, looked absorbed rather than discontent, breathed more evenly, and generally appeared comforted and less excited than before. One active baby (Ac XIII) was observed to cradle rock while hungry and fatigued, though during contented play he liked to swing on his abdomen or to roll. As he rocked while distressed, his overt expressions of displeasure decreased (from crying to intermittent whimpering), but his facial expression, posture, respiration, and quality of motion led observers to conclude that the activity was only minimally soothing, perhaps not at all.

ORAL SELF-STIMULATION

Oral behavior was as prominent among the older Group Three infants as among those in Group Two, but there were qualitative differences between the age groups. Table 7.29 lists all oral behavior schemas observed in Group Three, as well as the frequency and prominence of each schema among active and inactive subjects. In Group Two, eight infants produced 31 different oral schemas (see Table 6.26);[15] in Group Three, only 23 different oral patterns were shown by twelve subjects. All of the oral schemas found only among the younger subjects were either of the kind we called "empty" (mostly activations of the tongue only), or movements of the hand around the oral zone (such as moving the hand over the mouth zone, rubbing the gums with the hand, resting the mouth on the hand while prone). Since the older infants showed only two patterns not

[14] Many of the babies in Group Three did not manifest distress during hunger.

[15] Table 6.26 does not list the prominence ratings for each schema because no differences existed between active and inactive subjects in Group Two; in that sample, prominence was a function of frequency.

seen among the younger ones (playful respiratory games such as bubble blowing, and a snapping motion of the mouth toward an object), it would seem that non-nutritive oral behaviors differentiate chiefly during the first five months of life. Older infants may apply the same basic oral activations to an increasing number of external objects, and under different conditions than before, but the activations do not change in nature. One of the developmental changes appears to be that more oral behavior involves objects (48 per cent of oral schemas in Group Three compared with 32 per cent in Group Two), with a corresponding decrease in the proportion of oral schemas in which the mouth contacts the baby's own body (from 45 per cent in Group Two to 30 per cent in Group Three). A listing of the schemas that received the highest prominence (and also frequency) ratings in each group illustrates the changes in preference:

Group Two

(1) Diffuse mouthing
(2) Object at mouth, no activation
(3) Sucking hand or fingers
(4) Insertion thumb or finger, no activation
(5) Thumbsucking

Group Three

(1) Chewing, chomping object
(2) Mouthing object as primary activity
(3) Approaching object by mouth
(4) Object at mouth, no activation
(5) Sucking object (other than pacifier or nipple)

Another developmental change in oral behavior is shown in Table 7.30. In Group Two, oral behavior was relatively prominent during need states in most babies and during spontaneous activity only in a few inactive babies; it tended to diminish or disappear during external stimulation such as being played with or being dressed, or during the developmental test. Among many of the babies beyond the age of 4½ months, oral behavior was relatively inconspicuous during need states. It was prominent during spontaneous activity for most babies, and for many (though not all) it *increased* in response to external stimulation.

All these changes are probably related to the older babies' generally greater responsiveness to the environment, and in particular, to the process of teething. Most babies in Group Three already had at least one tooth, though only about half of them were in an acute phase of teething (as judged by the appearance of their gums). We were surprised to find that the intensity and frequency of oral behavior were not related to acute teething in these infants. However, in view of the fact that energetic stimulation of the gums (as in chomping, gnawing, biting, and exerting pressure by pushing the hand or a toy deeply into the mouth) played a large role in the behavior of these babies, we are inclined to think that some physiologic tension in the gum zone is perceptible to infants even before the gums redden and swell before a tooth erupts.

Although there were only small differences between active and inactive infants in the frequency and intensity of mouthing, differences in the quality of oral behavior and its relationship to situational context were consistent.

Oral behavior was somewhat less conspicuous in active babies than in inactive ones, as indicated by Tables 7.29 and 7.30. The active babies exceed the inactive ones for only four types of oral activation: chewing objects, chewing their fingers, sucking the hand or finger, and mouthing an object as a primary activity. On the other hand, twelve oral schemas—licking toy, approaching an object by mouth, pressing lips against surface, rubbing lips or gums with an object, inserting fingers or foot into the mouth without active mouthing, both brief and prolonged thumbsucking, moving thumb in mouth, diffuse mouthing, drawing lips in and out, snapping motions directed at an object, and bubble blowing or playful smacking sounds—occurred more prominently among inactive infants. For some of the inactive babies, they were the only schemas employed.

The data on Group Three suggest, as did those for the younger babies, that the role of oral self-stimulation within the excitation/relaxation cycle tends to be different for active and inactive babies. As reflected in Table 7.30, only among some of the inactive babies was oral behavior at its most intense during spontaneous activity rather than in need states or during external stimulation. Consistently effective self-soothing by oral means occurred only in two inactive infants. In other words, only among inactive babies (and not in all of them) was oral self-stimulation instrumental in either raising (during spontaneous activity) or lowering (during distress) the baby's general state of behavioral arousal.

Oral self-stimulation as a component of generalized excitation was more characteristic of the active babies, though it occurred in both groups. Among the active subjects, external stimulation tended to elicit oral behavior greater than in spontaneous activity (in four babies), or equal to it; this was only true of two inactive babies, both of whom were not particularly given to oral self-stimulation in general (In XI and In XV). A decrease in oral activity with the onset of external stimulation was regularly observed in three of the six inactive subjects (In XII; In XIII; In XIV), and did not occur in any of the active babies.

What difference there was between active and inactive subjects in patterns of oral self-stimulation and its relationship to the infant's state, lay in the fact that, among active babies, any excitation beyond the general background level (due to need states or to active stimulation from without) was likely to produce increased behavioral arousal in terms of motility, vocalization, and respiration simultaneously with enhanced oral activity. Oral behavior could be a component of generalized arousal among inactive babies, but it could also be a relatively more autonomous behavior system (during spontaneous activity); and in four of the six inactive babies it was seen to alter the infant's general state toward increasing or decreasing behavioral arousal, or both at different times.

Individual differences in the prominence and the pattern of oral behavior were as great within activity level groups as between them. As in the younger age groups, the oral behavior of both active and inactive babies differed greatly within activity groups (see Table 7.31). Among the active babies, total oral scores ranged from 4.0 to 15.0 (with a mean of 10.4), and in inactive babies this value ranged from 9.0 to 22.0 (with a mean of 13.0). During spontaneous activity some active babies showed next to no oral behavior (Ac XV and Ac XVI), but one (Ac XIII) showed as much as he did during external stimulation. Similarly, oral behavior could be absent during need states (Ac XIV), or these could be the only situation in which it was intense (Ac XV). The differences among inactive babies are similar, though somewhat less extreme (see Table 7.31).

It was reported for Group Two that those babies who showed oral self-stimulation very prominently during spontaneous behavior showed relatively few complex object-related behaviors at that time. The same relationship was found for the older babies as well. The single active baby who showed oral behavior prominently during spontaneous activity (Ac XIII) also showed by far the lowest proportion of complex object schemas —6 per cent (for the other active babies this value ranged from 22 per cent to 48 per cent). For the three inactive babies most given to oral behavior during spontaneous activity (In XII, In XIII, In XIV), the proportions of complex object schemas were 25 per cent, 13 per cent, and 19 per cent, respectively, whereas the proportions for the other inactive children were 31 per cent and 38 per cent.[16]

In summary, the data on bodily self-stimulation reflect some developmental changes. These were an increase in the number and prominence of kinesthetic and tactile patterns of self-stimulation; an increase in the occurrence of kinesthetic and oral self-stimulation during spontaneous activity; and a change in the prominent oral patterns, from primarily mouthing and oral stimulation of parts of the child's own body to the chewing, chomping and sucking of objects, as well as a tendency to approach objects by mouth (instead of by hand).

Although individual differences were marked within each activity level

[16] No comparable value is available for In XV because, while under observation, he was handled or played with by the mother so much that his behavior during spontaneous activity could not be assessed.

group, certain consistent differences in bodily self-stimulation appeared to be related to activity level. Four of six inactive subjects in Group Three could regularly soothe themselves in this manner (two by rocking and two by thumbsucking), whereas no active babies showed this capacity. Inactive babies had a relatively stronger tendency to engage in bodily self-stimulation while alert and content—chiefly oral behavior, and secondarily tactile self-stimulation. In active infants, oral, tactile, and kinesthetic self-stimulation usually fluctuated with their general state, increasing with behavioral arousal and decreasing with relative quiescence. Such fluctuation with general state occurred also among inactive infants, but it was almost exclusively among these babies that self-stimulation could become intense in the absence of general excitation.

SUPPLEMENTARY MATERIAL TO CHAPTER 7

Table 7.1 (Group Three)—Types of Movement during Spontaneous Activity: Individual Prominence Scores

	Whole-body				Part-body							
	FORCEFUL		GENTLE		FORCEFUL		GENTLE		MUSCLE TENSION		QUIES-CENCE	
Pair	Ac	In	Ac	In	Ac	In	Ac	In	Ac	In	Ac	In
XI	3.0	1.0	0	1.0	3.0	1.0	2.0	3.0	0	0	0	2.0
XII	3.0	0	0	1.0	3.0	0	0.5	3.0	0	0	0.5	1.0
XIII	3.0	0	1.0	2.0	2.0	0.5	1.0	3.0	0	0	0.5	1.0
XIV	3.0	1.0	1.0	1.0	1.0	1.0	2.0	3.0	0	0	0	0.5
XV	3.0	0	0	1.0	3.0	0	1.0	3.0	0	0	1.0	0
XVI	3.0	0	0	1.0	3.0	1.0	1.0	3.0	0	0	1.0	0
Totals	18.0	2.0	2.0	7.0	15.0	3.5	7.5	18.0	0	0	3.0	4.5

Ratings: 3.0 = frequent; 2.0 = medium; 1.0 = occasional; 0.5 = rare.

Table 7.2 (Group Three)—Types of Movement during Spontaneous Activity: Pair and Cross-Pair Comparison of Prominence Scores

	Ac > In		Ac < In		Ac = In		NEITHER		N COM-PARISONS	
Movement Type	Pair	Cross-Pair	Pair	Cross-Pair	Pair	Cross-Pair	Pair	Cross-Pair	Pair	Cross-Pair
Forceful whole-body *	6	6	0	0	0	0	0	0	6	6
Gentle whole-body *	0	0	5	5	1	1	0	0	6	6
Forceful part-body *	5	6	0	0	1	0	0	0	6	6
Gentle part-body *	0	0	6	6	0	0	0	0	6	6
Muscle tension	0	0	0	0	0	0	6	6	0	0
Quiescence	2	1	4	4	0	1	0	0	6	6

* $p < .05$, one-tailed test (Siegel, 1956).

Table 7.3 (Group Three)—Types of Movement during Spontaneous Activity: Summed Prominence Scores

Group	N Ratings	FORCEFUL Whole-body	FORCEFUL Part-body	GENTLE Whole-body	GENTLE Part-body	Muscle Tension	Quiescent
Active	34	18.0	15.0	2.0	7.5	0	3.0
Inactive	34	2.0	3.5	7.0	18.0	0	4.5

Table 7.4 (Group Three)—Behaviors during Spontaneous Activity: Frequency, Summed Prominence, and Age Range

Behavior	Age Range (in weeks)	N SUBJECTS SHOWING BEHAVIOR Ac	N SUBJECTS SHOWING BEHAVIOR In	Σ PROMINENCE Ac	Σ PROMINENCE In	Σ PROMINENCE Both	N Subjects in Age Range
Coordinated rolling	24–32	2	4	4	4	8	12
Prone to supine or vice versa	24–32	4	5	4	8	12	12
Prone to creeping or head-foot position	24–32	2	2	4	2	6	12
Pivoting or scooting	24–28	3	1	5	1	6	8
Creeping	28–32	3	1	6	2	8	8
Pull to standing or upright kneeling	28–32	4	1	8	2	10	8
Swinging on abdomen	24–28	1	2	2	3	5	8
Cradle rocking	24–28	0	2	0	3	3	8
Bouncing, jumping on Teeter-Babe	24–28	2	0	4	0	4	8
Bouncing, jumping supported standing	32	1	0	2	0	2	4
Other complex position change	28–32	4	4	6	5	11	8
Regard immobile person	24–32	6	6	12	10	22	12
Regard distant stationary object	24–32	2	5	3	6	9	12
Regard moving object	24–32	3	5	4	6	10	12
Reach for, contact nearby object	24–32	6	6	12	9	21	12
Reach for distant object	24–32	3	1	4	1	5	12
Manipulate small object	24–32	6	6	12	9	21	12
Regard object in hand	24–32	5	5	6	7	13	12
Attend, manipulate two toys simultaneously	24–32	4	2	6	2	8	12
Hand regard	24–28	1	3	1	3	4	8
Smiling, vocalizing at impassive person	24–32	6	4	11	7	18	12
Persistent initiation social contact	24–32	5	3	8	3	11	12
Cooing or whimpering	24–32	5	6	7	7	14	12
Squealing	24–32	6	3	12	5	17	12
Multisyllabic babbling	24–32	6	3	12	5	17	12
Single syllables	24–32	2	2	2	2	4	12
Oral behavior	24–32	6	6	8	9	17	12
Tactile self-stimulation	24–28	2	4	3	5	8	6

N patterns = 28

Table 7.5 (Group Three)—Behaviors during Spontaneous Activity: Pair and Cross-Pair Comparisons

	Ac > In		Ac < In		Ac = In		NEITHER		N COMPARISONS	
Behavior Pattern	*Pair*	*Cross-Pair*	*Pair*	*Cross-Pair*	*Pair*	*Cross-Pair*	*Pair*	*Cross-Pair*	*Pair*	*Cross-Pair*
Prone to supine, vice versa	1	2	3	3	1	1	1	0	5	6
Pivoting, scooting	3	3	1	1	0	0	2	2	4	4
Creeping	2	3	0	1	1	0	1	0	3	4
Pull to standing or kneeling	3	3	0	0	0	1	0	0	4	4
Cradle rocking	0	0	2	2	0	0	2	2	2	2
Bouncing, jumping on seat	2	2	0	0	0	0	2	2	2	2
Regard distant object	1	2	4	4	0	0	1	0	5	6
Regard moving object	1	1	4	3	0	2	1	0	5	6
Attend two toys simultaneously	4	3	1	1	0	1	1	1	5	5
Reach for distant object	3	1	1	1	0	1	2	3	4	3
Hand regard	1	0	3	2	0	1	2	3	4	3
Persistent initiation social contact	4	4	0	1	1	1	1	0	5	6
Squealing *	6	6	0	0	0	0	0	0	6	6
Multisyllabic babbling	4	4	0	0	2	2	0	0	6	6

* $p < .05$, one-tailed test (Siegel, 1956).

Table 7.6 (Group Three)—Behaviors during Spontaneous Activity: Proportion of Behaviors Focused toward Body or toward Environment

	N PATTERNS		% PATTERNS		Σ PROMINENCE		% PROMINENCE	
Behavior Focus	*Ac*	*In*	*Ac*	*In*	*Ac*	*In*	*Ac*	*In*
Body	24	34	22%	34%	38.0	48.0	21%	35%
Environment	85	66	78%	66%	139.0	89.0	79%	65%
Totals	109	100	100%	100%	177.0	137.0	100%	100%

Note: Percentages refer to the proportion of all patterns, or of total prominence scores, that were focused on the body and on the environment respectively.

Table 7.7 (Group Three)—Behaviors during Spontaneous Activity: Pair and Cross-Pair Comparison of Percentage Difference in Behavior Focus

	Ac > In		Ac < In		Ac = In		N COMPARISONS	
Body-focused	*Pair*	*Cross-Pair*	*Pair*	*Cross-Pair*	*Pair*	*Cross-Pair*	*Pair*	*Cross-Pair*
N Patterns *	0	0	5	5	1	1	6	6
Σ Prominence *	0	1	5	5	1	0	6	6
Environment-focused								
N Patterns*	6	5	0	0	0	1	6	6
Σ Prominence *	5	5	0	1	1	0	6	6

Note: Differences of 5% or less were rated as Ac = In.
* $p < .05$, one-tailed test (Siegel, 1956).

Table 7.8 (Group Three)—Behaviors during Spontaneous Activity: Frequency and Prominence of Simple and Complex Object-focused Behaviors

	Frequency								
	PROMINENT		PERIPHERAL		Total		Σ PROMINENCE		Total N
Simple Object Schemas	Ac	In	Ac	In	Ac	In	Ac	In	
Locomote toward object	3	0	1	0	4	0	7	0	4
Chest up, manipulate toy	2	0	0	0	2	0	4	0	2
Reach for, obtain nearby toy	6	4	0	1	6	5	12	9	11
Waving toy	5	1	1	2	6	3	11	4	9
Regard object in hand	1	2	4	2	5	4	6	6	9
Grasp, scratch crib side	1	0	1	2	2	2	3	2	4
Object to mouth	1	2	5	1	6	3	7	5	9
Regard distant stationary object	1	1	1	4	2	5	3	6	7
Slap or pat objects	3	0	0	1	3	1	6	1	4
Strained reaching, distant object	0	0	2	0	2	0	2	0	2
Regard moving object	1	1	0	1	1	2	2	3	3
Explore crib side with feet and hands	1	0	0	0	1	0	2	0	1
Aimless moving of blanket	0	0	1	1	1	1	1	1	2
Mouthing toy in hands	2	0	0	1	2	1	4	1	3
Mouthing bar of crib, playpen	1	1	0	0	1	1	2	2	2
Push feet against Teeter-Babe to obtain toy	1	0	0	0	1	0	2	0	1
Slap hard surfaces forcefully	2	0	0	0	2	0	4	0	2
Lift and lower toy, no release	0	0	0	1	0	1	0	1	1
Fingering object, intent regard	0	2	0	1	0	3	0	5	3
Fingering object, no regard	0	1	0	1	0	2	0	3	2
Regard only, nearby object	0	1	0	0	0	1	0	2	1
Approach object by mouth	0	1	0	0	0	1	0	2	1
Chew, suck, or lick object	0	1	0	1	0	2	0	3	2
Grasp, move own shirt or dress	0	0	0	1	0	1	0	1	1
Hold object placed in hand by adult	0	0	0	1	0	1	0	1	1
N Schemas: 25	31	18	16	22	47	40	78	58	87
Complex Object Schemas									
Drop object and retrieve repeatedly	2	1	1	1	3	2	5	3	5
Hold two toys, or reach for second one	1	0	3	2	4	2	5	2	6
Pull blanket over face	0	0	1	0	1	0	1	0	1
Bang object	4	0	0	1	4	1	8	1	5
Pull at small object (string, cord, etc.)	0	0	2	1	2	1	2	1	3
Push toy along surface	0	1	1	1	1	2	1	3	3
Transfer object from hand to hand	1	0	2	3	3	3	4	3	6
Throw toy, creep after, throw again, etc.	1	0	0	0	1	0	2	0	1
Push toy across floor while creeping	1	0	0	0	1	0	2	0	1
Shake rattle deliberately	1	0	1	2	2	2	3	2	4
Turn swivel chair	0	0	1	0	1	0	1	0	1
Vigorous pushing, tugging large object	1	0	0	0	1	0	2	0	1
Deliberate throwing, dropping objects	1	0	0	1	1	1	2	1	2
N Schemas: 13	13	2	12	12	25	14	38	16	39

Table 7.9 (Group Three)—Spontaneous Activity: Proportion of Object-related Patterns Classified as Simple and Complex

Object Schemas	*Ratings* PROMINENT		PERIPHERAL		BOTH		Σ PROMINENCE		Total N Schemas
	Ac	In	Ac	In	Ac	In	Ac	In	
Simple	31	18	16	22	47	40	78.0	58.0	25
Complex	13	2	12	12	25	14	38.0	16.0	13
Totals	44	20	28	34	72	54	116.0	74.0	38

Table 7.10 (Group Three)—Behaviors during Spontaneous Activity: Pair and Cross-Pair Comparison of Simple and Complex Behaviors by Frequency and Prominence

	Ac > In		Ac < In		Ac = In		N COMPARISONS	
Object Schemas	*Pair*	*Cross-Pair*	*Pair*	*Cross-Pair*	*Pair*	*Cross-Pair*	*Pair*	*Cross-Pair*
Number, simple	4	5	2	1	0	0	6	6
Prominence, simple	4	5	1	1	1	0	6	6
Number, complex	4	4	2	2	0	0	6	6
Prominence, complex	4	4	1	2	1	0	6	6
Total number	3	4	1	2	2	0	6	6
Total prominence *	5	5	1	1	0	0	6	6

* $p < .05$, one-tailed test (Siegel, 1956).

Table 7.11 (Group Three)—Behaviors during Need States: Patterns by Frequency

High Frequency	*Medium Frequency*	*Low Frequency*
Whimpering	Grasping foot	Tossing head
Crying	Kicking	Clutching hand
Squirming	Raising, lowering head	Raising chest from prone
Restless whole-body motions	Screaming (not crying)	Deep insertion of fingers
Scratching head, rubbing face	Rubbing abdomen	Chewing fingers
	Arching back	Scratching mattress
	Hand to mouth, no activation	Pulling lip in and out
		Diffuse mouthing
		Rubbing heels against object
		Mouthing sheet
		Cradle rocking
		Tossing legs
		Head bumping
		Squealing
		Banging toy against thigh
		Stuffing object into mouth
		Rolling
		Forced laughter
		Tight hand clasping
		Mouthing, chewing, or licking object

Note: High frequency = pattern observed 5–9 times during need states.
Medium frequency = pattern observed 3–4 times.
Low frequency = pattern observed once or twice.

Table 7.12 (Group Three)—Behaviors during Spontaneous Activity: Comparison of Behaviors Lost, Retained or Modified, and New Behaviors Developed during Need States, by Number and Percentage

	N SUBJECTS		SPONTANEOUS		Patterns: LOST				RETAINED, MODIFIED				NEW	
	Ac	In	Ac	In	Ac		In		Ac		In		Ac	In
Condition					N	%	N	%	N	%	N	%		
Hunger	4	3	97	57	82	(84%)	40	(70%)	15	(16%)	17	(30%)	15	6
Fatigue	6	6	139	118	99	(71%)	91	(77%)	40	(29%)	27	(23%)	48	21

Note: The number of patterns rated during spontaneous activity differs from totals on previous tables. It reflects the total number of behavior patterns (whether object-related, body-focused, vocalization, etc.) that received a rating during spontaneous activity. In Tables 7.4 through 7.10 individual patterns were grouped, or only categories were reported.

The number of patterns rated during spontaneous activity listed for "Hunger" includes only those seven subjects whose behavior altered with hunger.

Table 7.13 (Group Three)—Behaviors during Spontaneous Activity: Behaviors Lost, Retained or Modified, and New Behaviors Developed during Need States, by Number and Percentage

A. Hunger

	SPONTANEOUS ACTIVITY		LOST				RETAINED, MODIFIED				NEW	
	Ac	In	Ac		In		Ac		In		Ac	In
Pair	N	N	N	%	N	%	N	%	N	%	N	N
XI	24	23	22	(92%)	16	(70%)	2	(8%)	7	(33%)	4	3
XII	25	13	22	(88%)	3	(23%)	3	(12%)	10	(77%)	0	0
XIII	24	22	16	(67%)	ϕ	ϕ	8	(33%)	ϕ	ϕ	7	ϕ
XIV	18	22	ϕ	ϕ	ϕ	ϕ	ϕ	ϕ	ϕ	ϕ	ϕ	ϕ
XV	24	17	ϕ	ϕ	ϕ	ϕ	ϕ	ϕ	ϕ	ϕ	ϕ	ϕ
XVI	24	21	22	(92%)	21	(100%)	2	(8%)	0	0	4	3
Totals	139	118	82		40		15		17		15	6

B. Fatigue

	SPONTANEOUS ACTIVITY		LOST				RETAINED, MODIFIED				NEW	
	Ac	In	Ac		In		Ac		In		Ac	In
Pair	N	N	N	%	N	%	N	%	N	%	N	N
XI	24	23	11	(45%)	20	(87%)	13	(55%)	3	(13%)	7	1
XII	25	13	20	(80%)	10	(77%)	5	(20%)	3	(23%)	1	2
XIII	24	22	23	(95%)	11	(50%)	1	(5%)	11	(50%)	7	11
XIV	18	22	13	(72%)	19	(86%)	5	(28%)	3	(14%)	11	3
XV	24	17	13	(55%)	14	(84%)	11	(45%)	3	(16%)	9	0
XVI	24	21	19	(79%)	17	(81%)	5	(21%)	4	(19%)	13	4
Totals	139	118	99		91		40		27		48	21

Symbols: ϕ = No overt behavior changes occurred during the pre-feeding interval.

Table 7.14 (Group Three)—Behavior Schemas during Object Stimulation: Prominence Score and Frequency in Sample

	Pairs												Totals		
	XI		XII		XIII		XIV		XV		XVI		PROMINENCE		FREQUENCY
Behavior	Ac	In	Ac	In	Ac	In	Ac	In	Ac	In	Ac	In	Ac	In	N
Directed one-hand reaching, single object	2	1	2	2	0	2	2	2	2	2	2	2	10	11	11
Reaching with both arms, simultaneously	0	2	2	0	2	1	1	1	0	1	0	1	5	6	8
Grasping tiny object, or repeated effort	1	1	0	0	1	0	1	1	0	2	1	1	4	5	8
Reaching for distant object, or trying to	1	1	0	0	1	0	2	0	0	0	0	0	4	1	4
Slapping table or floor	2	0	0	0	1	0	0	0	0	0	0	0	3	0	2
Approach object by mouth	1	1	0	0	0	0	0	0	0	0	0	0	1	1	2
Bring object to mouth, no activation	0	1	2	1	0	1	1	2	0	1	1	2	4	8	9
Mouthing toy or edge of furniture	0	1	0	0	2	1	0	0	0	0	0	0	2	2	3
Biting, chewing or licking object	2	0	1	0	2	1	1	1	2	2	0	1	8	5	9
Object deeply inserted, mouth	0	0	0	0	2	0	0	0	0	0	0	0	2	0	1
Object held to mouth, patted with free hand	0	0	0	0	0	0	0	0	1	0	0	0	1	0	1
Banging object on hard surface	2	1	2	1	0	1	1	2	2	0	1	1	8	6	10
Waving, swinging object	0	0	2	0	0	0	1	0	2	1	1	1	6	2	6
Transferring object, hand to hand	1	2	1	2	1	1	1	1	2	1	1	1	7	8	12
Rings bell by handle	2	2	1	0	0	0	2	0	2	1	2	0	9	3	7
Shake rattle, discriminately	0	0	0	0	0	0	0	0	1	1	0	1	1	2	3
Rustle paper for sound effect	0	2	0	0	0	1	0	0	0	0	0	0	0	3	2
Purposive throwing or dropping	2	0	0	2	0	0	0	0	0	0	1	0	3	2	3
Dropping and retrieving	0	0	0	0	0	0	0	0	1	2	0	0	1	2	2
Visual inspection toy in hand	1	2	0	0	1	2	1	1	1	0	0	1	4	6	8
Simultaneous regard one object each hand	0	0	0	0	0	0	0	0	0	0	1	0	1	0	1
Rotate object to inspect all sides	0	0	0	2	0	0	0	0	0	2	0	0	0	4	2
Fingering and regarding stationary object	0	2	0	0	0	0	0	0	0	0	0	0	0	2	1
Visual attention small detail	0	0	0	0	1	1	1	0	0	1	1	1	3	3	6
Sequential reaching two toys	1	1	0	0	0	1	1	1	0	1	0	0	2	4	6
Sequential use several toys (blocks)	0	0	0	0	0	0	0	0	0	0	1	0	1	0	1
Using two toys simultaneously	0	1	0	0	0	1	1	1	1	1	2	1	4	5	8
Coordinated use two objects	0	0	0	0	0	0	1	0	0	1	1	1	2	2	4
Holds one toy, intent regard of second	0	2	0	0	0	0	0	0	0	0	0	0	0	2	1
Pushing object along table	0	0	0	0	0	0	0	1	2	0	0	1	2	2	3
Complex means-end manipulation	0	0	0	0	0	0	0	0	0	0	2	0	2	0	1
Overall activity increase only, sight of toy	0	0	1	0	0	0	0	0	0	0	0	0	1	0	1
N Schemas: 32	18	23	14	10	14	14	18	14	19	20	14	16	101	97	146

Table 7.15 (Group Three)—Behaviors during Object Stimulation and Spontaneous Activity: Comparison of Number and Prominence of Simple and Complex Object-related Behaviors

	Simple Object Schemas								*Complex Object Schemas*							
	Spontaneous Activity				*Object Stimulation*				*Spontaneous Activity*				*Object Stimulation*			
	N SCHEMAS		*Σ PROMIN.*		*N SCHEMAS*		*Σ PROMIN.*		*N SCHEMAS*		*Σ PROMIN.*		*N SCHEMAS*		*Σ PROMIN.*	
Pair	*Ac*	*In*	*Ac*	*In*	*Ac*	*In*	*Ac*	*In*	*Ac*	*In*	*Ac*	*In*	*Ac*	*In*	*Ac*	*In*
XI	8	6	13.0	8.0	6	9	9.0	13.0	3	5	5.0	5.0	6	7	9.0	10.0
XII	9	5	14.0	6.0	6	2	10.0	3.0	3	1	4.0	2.0	3	4	4.0	7.0
XIII	9	10	14.0	14.0	7	6	11.0	8.0	1	2	1.0	2.0	3	6	3.0	6.0
XIV	7	8	13.0	13.0	7	5	9.0	7.0	4	3	7.0	3.0	8	6	9.0	7.0
XV	8	6	12.0	8.0	4	5	7.0	7.0	8	0	12.0	0	8	10	12.0	13.0
XVI	7	6	12.0	9.0	3	6	4.0	8.0	6	3	9.0	4.0	11	8	14.0	8.0
Totals	48	41	78.0	58.0	33	33	50.0	46.0	25	14	38.0	16.0	39	41	51.0	51.0

Note: Sum scores is the sum of prominence scores for all patterns received by each infant, in terms of a score of 1.0 for peripheral and 2.0 for prominent behaviors.

Table 7.16 (Group Three)—Behaviors during Object Stimulation: Peripheral and Prominent, Simple and Complex Schemas, by Number and Summed Prominence

Classification	Number Schemas						Sum of Prominence Scores					
	PERIPHERAL		PROMINENT		BOTH		PERIPHERAL		PROMINENT		BOTH	
	Ac	In	Ac	In	Ac	In	Ac	In	Ac	In	Ac	In
Simple	16	20	17	13	33	33	16.0	20.0	34.0	26.0	50.0	46.0
Complex	27	31	12	10	39	41	27.0	31.0	24.0	20.0	51.0	51.0
Totals	43	51	29	23	72	74	43.0	51.0	58.0	46.0	101.0	97.0

Table 7.17 (Group Three)—Behavior Characteristics during Object Stimulation

Pair	SOCIAL AWARENESS		EXCITEMENT, MUSCLE TENSION		DELAY BEFORE RESPONSE		RESPONSE TO LOSS OF TOY	
	Ac	In	Ac	In	Ac	In	Ac	In
XI	Moderate	Strong	Mild	Strong	None	None	None	Occasional marked
XII	Moderate	Minimal	Mild	None	None	Frequent marked	Occasional moderate	None
XIII	Minimal	Moderate	Moderate	Mild	Rare	Frequent marked	Marked	None
XIV	Moderate	Absent	Minimal	Moderate	Rare	None	None	None
XV	Strong	Strong	None	Moderate	None	Occasional moderate	Very strong	Rare mild
XVI	Strong	Absent	Moderate	Minimal	None	Frequent marked	Rare marked	Rare mild

Note: Social awareness and signs of excitement were given a single rating of intensity. Delayed response and response to loss of toy were rated for relative frequency (in relation to number of occasions when response could have occurred) as well as typical intensity.

Table 7.18 (Group Three)—Patterns of Social Responsiveness

		ACTIVE		INACTIVE		TOTAL	
Behavior	*Intensity*	*N*	*Σ Prom*	*N*	*Σ Prom*	*N*	*Σ Prom*
Brief intent gaze only, transient pause, other activities	Weak	3	6	4	7	7	13
Smile only, with or without intent gaze	Weak	5	9	9	14	14	23
Casual regard, not disrupting other activities	Weak	1	2	0	0	1	2
Intent gaze observers, then turn to smile at mother	Weak	1	1	0	0	1	1
Smile at voice, person not in sight	Weak	0	0	2	2	2	2
Smile at object in response to maternal stimulation	Weak	2	2	2	4	4	6
Gaze and smile	Medium	5	8	6	9	11	17
Gaze and vocalize	Medium	1	1	3	4	4	5
Smile and vocalize	Medium	6	11	5	6	11	17
Smile, gaze or vocalize, and activity decrease	Medium	3	4	2	2	5	6
Turn to locate source of voice	Medium	1	2	2	2	3	4
Smile and activity increase	Medium	1	2	5	6	6	8
Touch partner, no smile or sound	Medium	0	0	2	2	2	2
Effort to locomote toward partner	Medium	1	1	1	1	2	2
Coo or chuckle, nothing else	Medium	0	0	1	1	1	1
Intent expectant regard and smile	Medium	1	2	0	0	1	2
Intent, prolonged "puzzled" regard	Medium	1	1	3	5	4	6
Persistent effort to obtain response	Strong	4	5	1	1	5	6
Turn to locate person touching him	Strong	1	1	0	0	1	1
Combine chuckle, laugh, squeal, grin	Strong	3	5	3	5	6	10
Laugh, chuckle, plus kicking or waving	Strong	5	5	4	4	9	9
Smile, vocalize, and touch partner's face	Strong	4	5	1	1	5	6
Gay squealing, loud babbling	Strong	1	2	2	2	3	4
Turn toward partner, touching and vocalizing	Strong	1	1	2	2	3	3
Apprehension at close playful approach	Strong	0	0	1	1	1	1
Turn to remembered position of person not perceived	Strong	2	4	1	1	3	5
Active reciprocal love games	Strong	1	2	0	0	1	2
Successful locomotion to partner, vocalizing	Strong	2	2	0	0	2	2
Activity increase, smile and vocalize	Strong	0	0	1	1	1	1
Totals		56	84	63	83	119	167

N Schemas: 29

Table 7.19 (Group Three)—Social Responses at Varying Levels of Intensity to Different Degrees of Social Stimulation: Frequency and Summed Prominence

Degree of Social Stimulation	Weak Responses				Medium Responses				Strong Responses				Totals					
	Ac		In		Ac		In		Ac		In		Ac		In		BOTH	
	N	Σ Prom	N	Σ Prom	N	Σ Prom	N	Σ Prom	N	Σ Prom	N	Σ Prom	N	Σ Prom	N	Σ Prom	N	Σ Prom
Sight only	6	12.0	3	6.0	10	15.0	11	16.0	9	13.0	3	3.0	25	40.0	17	25.0	42	65.0
Gentle	4	6.0	8	12.0	9	16.0	11	13.0	5	6.0	1	1.0	18	28.0	20	26.0	38	54.0
Medium	1	1.0	3	4.0	1	1.0	5	6.0	8	10.0	8	9.0	10	12.0	16	19.0	26	31.0
Strong	1	1.0	3	5.0	0	0	4	5.0	2	3.0	3	3.0	3	4.0	10	13.0	13	17.0
Totals	12	20.0	17	27.0	20	32.0	31	40.0	24	32.0	15	16.0	56	84.0	63	83.0	119	167.0

Table 7.20 (Group Three)—Intensity of Social Stimulation and Strength of Social Response: Pair and Cross-Pair Comparison

Response Classification	Sight Only						Gentle						Medium						Strong					
	Ac > In		Ac < In		Ac = In		Ac > In		Ac < In		Ac = In		Ac > In		Ac < In		Ac = In		Ac > In		Ac < In		Ac = In	
	Pr.	Cr.-Pr.	Pr.	Cr.-Pr.	Pr.	Cr.-Pr.	Pr.	Cr.-Pr.	Pr.	Cr.-Pr.	Pr.	Cr.-Pr.	Pr.	Cr.-Pr.	Pr.	Cr.-Pr.	Pr.	Cr.-Pr.	Pr.	Cr.-Pr.	Pr.	Cr.-Pr.	Pr.	Cr.-Pr.
Strong	6	6	0	0	0	0	3	3	0	3	3	0	2	1	1	3	1	0	1	0	0	1	1	0
Medium	3	1	2	2	1	3	3	3	2	3	1	0	0	0	3	2	1	1	0	0	2	1	0	0
Weak	3	3	0	1	3	2	0	2	5	4	1	0	1	0	1	1	2	2	1	0	0	1	1	0

Note: Not all combinations of stimulation and intensity were actually observed. The total number of comparisons is: Original Pairs N = 54
Cross-Pairs N = 49

Table 7.21 (Group Three)—Aspects of Social Behavior

	Pairs											
	XI		XII		XIII		XIV		XV		XVI	
Behavior Characteristic	*Ac*	*In*	*Ac*	*In*	*Ac*	*In*	*Ac*	*In*	*Ac*	*In*	*Ac*	*In*
Stranger response	—	—	—	+	—	—	+	+	+	—	+	+
Discrimination of mother	—	+ low	+ med.	+ high	+ med.	+ med.	+ med.	—	+ low	+ high	—	+ high
Discrimination among observers	—	—	—	+ med.	—	—	—	—	—	—	—	—
Soothability	—	φ	φ	φ	+ low	+ high	+ high	φ	φ	φ	+ high	+ high
Response to termination of play	—	—	+ med.	—	—	—	+ high	—	—	+ low	+ low	+ low
Communication	—	—	—	—	+ low	+ low	+ high	+ low	+ low	+ med.	+ high	+ low
Distractability	+ med.	+ med.	+ high	—	+ med.	+ med.	+ high	+ high	—	φ	+ med.	+ high

Symbols: (φ) = no opportunity for behavior to occur; (+) = present; (—) = absent.
Note: The notations below the + sign refer to intensity and/or prominence of the characteristic.

Table 7.22 (Group Three)—Number of Recurrent Mother-Child Contacts Typically Evoking Affect and Excitation

	Affect										N SITUATIONS	
	EXCITATORY		POSITIVE		NEGATIVE		MIXED		NEUTRAL			
Pair	Ac	In	Ac	In	Ac	In	Ac	In	Ac	In	Ac	In
XI	3	1	3	2	2	0	1	1	0	3	6	6
XII	2	0	3	3	0	0	1	0	0	1	4	4
XIII	4	0	1	1	2	0	2	2	0	1	5	4
XIV	3	2	0	4	1	1	3	0	1	1	5	6
XV	3	1	0	4	2	0	2	0	2	0	6	4
XVI	1	0	3	1	1	1	1	0	0	3	5	5
Totals	16	4	10	15	8	2	10	3	3	9	31	29

Note: The same situations received a rating for affect and, if typically present, also for their excitatory effects independent of affect. Therefore the N Situations for each child may be smaller than the sum of situations rated.

Table 7.23 (Group Three)—Number of Recurrent Social Situations Typically Involving Affect or Excitation: Pair and Cross-Pair Comparison

	Ac > In		Ac < In		Ac = In		N COMPARISONS	
Situation	Pair	Cross-Pair	Pair	Cross-Pair	Pair	Cross-Pair	Pair	Cross-Pair
Arousing excitation *	6	5	0	0	0	1	6	6
Involving pleasure	2	1	2	4	2	1	6	6
Involving unpleasure **	3	5	0	0	2	0	5	5
Involving mixed affect	4	5	0	0	2	1	6	6
Affectively neutral	1	0	4	4	1	1	6	5

* $p < .05$, one-tailed sign test (Siegel, 1954).
** p .055.

Table 7.24 (Group Three)—Bodily Self-Stimulation: Overall Prominence Ratings

	ORAL		TACTILE		KINESTHETIC	
Pair	Ac	In	Ac	In	Ac	In
XI	High	Medium	None	None	Medium +	Medium +
XII	Medium	High	Medium	Low	High	Low
XIII	High	High	None	High	High	Medium
XIV	Medium	High	Medium	Low	Low	Low
XV	Medium +	Medium −	Low	None	None	None
XVI	Low	Medium	None	Low	Medium	None

Table 7.25 (Group Three)—Patterns of Tactile Self-Stimulation: Frequency and Prominence

	Number Subjects Showing Behavior						
	PROMINENT		PERIPHERAL		TOTAL NUMBER		
Behavior Pattern	Ac	In	Ac	In	Ac	In	Both
Slapping thigh with hand or toy	0	1	1	3	1	4	5
Rubbing face	0	1	2	2	2	3	5
Stroking, rubbing own body	0	1	2	1	2	2	4
Rubbing legs against each other	0	0	0	2	0	2	2
Clutching head tightly, both hands	0	0	1	0	1	0	1
Bumping head against crib	1	0	0	0	1	0	1
Rubbing heel against hard surface	1	0	0	0	1	0	1
Tight clasping hands or foot	1	0	0	0	1	0	1
N Patterns: 9 Totals:	3	3	8	9	11	12	23

Table 7.26 (Group Three)—Tactile Self-Stimulation under Different Conditions: Incidence and Prominence

Condition	*Subject*	*Pattern*	*Prominence*	*Subject*	*Pattern*	*Prominence*
Spontaneous activity	Ac XI	Stroking own body	Low	In XII	Rubbing legs	Low
				In XIII	Rubbing own body	Medium
				In XIV	Stroking own body	Low
				In XIV	Slapping thigh	Low
Hunger and/or fatigue	Ac XII	Rubbing own body	Low	In XII	Rubbing legs	Low
	Ac XII	Rubbing heels, hard surface	Medium	In XII	Scratching face	Low
	Ac XIII	Head bumping	Medium	In XIII	Slapping thigh	High
	Ac XIV	Rubbing face	Low	In XIII	Rubbing face	Low
	Ac XIV	Scratching chest	Low	In XIV	Rubbing face	Medium
	Ac XIV	Tight hand or foot clasping	Low	In XVI	Rubbing face	Low
	Ac XV	Rubbing face	Low	In XVI	Slapping thigh	Low
	Ac XV	Scratching face	Low	In XVI		
	Ac XVI	Clutching head	Low	In XVI		
Social stimulation, gentle	Ac XII	Slapping thigh	Low	In XVI	Slapping thigh	Low

Table 7.27 (Group Three)—Patterns of Kinesthetic Self-Stimulation: Incidence and Prominence

	Number Subjects Showing Behavior						
	PROMINENT		*PERIPHERAL*		*TOTAL NUMBER*		
Behavior Pattern	*Ac*	*In*	*Ac*	*In*	*Ac*	*In*	*Both*
Sustained rolling	2	1	1	1	3	2	5
Swinging on abdomen	1	1	0	1	1	2	3
Cradle rocking	1	2	0	0	1	2	3
Rocking, bouncing on infant seat	2	0	0	0	2	0	2
Bouncing from supine	0	1	0	0	0	1	1
Bouncing, supported standing	1	0	0	0	1	0	1
Totals	7	5	1	2	8	7	15

N Patterns: 6

Table 7.28 (Group Three)—Kinesthetic Self-Stimulation under Different Conditions: Incidence and Prominence

Condition	*Subject*	*Pattern*	*Prominence*	*Subject*	*Pattern*	*Prominence*
Spontaneous activity	Ac XI	Rolling	Medium	In XI	Cradle rocking	Medium
	Ac XII	Rocking, bouncing on seat	High	In XI	Rolling	High
	Ac XII	Rolling	Low	In XII	Swinging on abdomen	Low
	Ac XIII	Swinging on abdomen	Medium	In XIII	Cradle rocking	Medium
	Ac XIII	Rolling	Low	In XIII	Swinging on abdomen	Medium
	Ac XIV	Bouncing, while standing	High	In XIV	Rolling	Medium
Hunger and/or fatigue	Ac XI	Rolling	Low	In XI	Cradle rocking	High
	Ac XII	Rolling	High	In XII	Swinging on abdomen	Medium
	Ac XII	Bouncing, supine	Medium	In XIII	Cradle rocking	High
	Ac XIV	Rolling	Low	In XIV	Bouncing, supine	Medium
	Ac XVI	Bouncing, while standing	Medium			
	Ac XVI	Rolling	Medium			
Social stimulation, gentle	Ac XII	Rocking on infant seat	Medium			
	Ac XII	Bouncing, while seated	Medium			

Table 7.29 (Group Three)—Patterns of Oral Behavior: Frequency, Classification, and Prominence

	ACTIVE		INACTIVE		BOTH		
Behavior Pattern	*N*	*Σ Prom*	*N*	*Σ Prom*	*N*	*Σ Prom*	*Classification*
Chewing or chomping object	6	10.0	3	8.0	9	18.0	Object
Sucking object	5	5.5	3	5.5	8	11.0	Object
Mouthing object, primary activity	5	12.0	2	3.0	7	15.0	Object
Biting object	1	1.0	1	0.5	2	1.5	Object
Object to mouth, no activation	5	5.0	5	6.5	10	11.5	Object
Licking toy	3	2.0	4	5.5	7	7.5	Object
Approach object by mouth	3	4.5	6	8.5	9	13.0	Object
Chewing, gnawing, chomping mother's hand	2	2.0	1	2.0	3	4.0	Object
Mouth pressed against surface	0	0.0	3	1.5	3	1.5	Object
Rubbing lips or gums with object	0	0.0	2	5.0	2	5.0	Object
Deep insertion object	3	3.5	2	3.5	5	7.0	Object
Sucking hand or fingers	5	5.0	3	2.0	8	7.0	Own body
Chewing, gnawing thumb or fingers	2	4.0	1	1.0	3	5.0	Own body
Deep insertion fingers or hand	1	2.0	3	1.5	4	3.5	Own body
Finger(s) or foot in mouth, no activation	3	1.5	4	4.0	7	5.5	Own body
Thumbsucking, prolonged	0	0.0	2	4.0	2	4.0	Own body
Thumbsucking, brief, casual	1	1.0	2	4.0	3	5.0	Own body
Moving thumb in mouth	0	0.0	1	0.5	1	0.5	Own body
Diffuse mouthing	2	2.0	3	4.5	5	6.5	Empty
Tongue play	2	1.5	2	1.5	4	3.0	Empty
Lips drawn in and out, or sucked	0	0.0	2	4.0	2	4.0	Empty
Snapping motion	0	0.0	1	0.5	1	0.5	Empty
Bubble blowing, smacking	0	0.0	2	1.5	2	1.5	Empty
Totals	49	62.5	58	78.5	107	141.0	
N Schemas: 23							

Table 7.30 (Group Three)—Oral Behaviors under Different Conditions: Prominence

	Spontaneous Activity				*Need States*				*External Stimulation*			
	ACTIVE		INACTIVE		ACTIVE		INACTIVE		ACTIVE		INACTIVE	
Pair	*N*	*Prom*	*N*	*Prom*	*N*	*Prom*	*N*	*Prom*	*N*	*Prom*	*N*	*Prom*
XI	5	5.5	5	4.0	3	7.0	1	1.0	4	5.5	6	6.0
XII	3	3.0	7	10.5	1	0.5	5	6.5	6	5.0	2	1.5
XIII	5	8.5	7	8.5	1	1.0	1	0.5	6	8.5	5	6.0
XIV	6	5.0	9	16.5	0	0.0	2	3.5	6	5.5	6	7.0
XV	2	1.0	3	4.0	9	9.5	0	0.0	1	2.0	5	7.0
XVI	1	0.5	6	4.5	1	1.0	4	2.5	2	2.5	5	4.5
Totals	22	23.5	37	48.0	15	19.0	13	14.0	25	29.0	29	32.0

Note: The prominence of each oral schema was rated separately for each of three conditions on Table 7.30. Therefore the sum of prominence scores for all subjects is not identical to the summed oral scores on Table 7.31.

Table 7.31 (Group Three)—Number of Oral Patterns and Oral Scores

	N PATTERNS		ORAL SCORES	
Pair	*Ac*	*In*	*Ac*	*In*
XI	8	11	13.5	10.0
XII	7	9	7.0	13.5
XIII	9	10	15.0	14.0
XIV	9	13	10.0	22.0
XV	12	5	13.0	9.0
XVI	4	10	4.0	10.0
Totals	49	58	62.5	78.5

Note: Oral scores are the sum of prominence ratings received by a subject for each oral schema.

Table 7.32 (Group Three)—Oral Schemas: Frequency of Each Prominence Rating, and Prominence Scores

	N RATINGS			Σ PROMINENCE SCORES		
Prominence Rating	*Ac*	*In*	*Both*	*Ac*	*In*	*Both*
Frequent	5	9	14	15.0	27.0	42.0
Medium	11	14	25	22.0	28.0	50.0
Occasional	18	12	30	18.0	12.0	30.0
Rare	15	23	38	7.5	11.5	19.0
Absent	7	0	7	0	0	0
Totals	56	58	114	62.5	78.5	141.0

Ratings: 3.0 = frequent; 2.0 = medium; 1.0 = occasional; 0.5 = rare; 0.0 = absent.

EIGHT

OVERVIEW OF HYPOTHESES AND INFERENCES

The preceding chapters combined an account of the behavior of our infant subjects with discussions of the significance of some of these behaviors for the developmental process; the comparison of active with inactive babies led to some hypotheses about the consequences of activity level for behavior. Our discussion of the implications of what was observed ranged from hypotheses to account for the consistent differences noted between active and inactive infants to the application and extension of developmental theory directed toward relating the observed phenomena to the total process of development. Our suggestions about the relevance to development of diverse behaviors and diverse events in the life of young infants are tentative and will require more extensive and specific testing with larger infant populations. The same conceptual frame of reference will be applied to the case material in Part Three, on adaptation syndromes, as a first test of how well the formulations serve their aim of treating a large aggregate of behavioral facts within a systematic framework.

In early infancy, low activity level facilitates oral activity and visual attention to the immediate environment. Between the ages of 4 and 12 weeks, active and inactive infants differ primarily in that certain behavior patterns are observed wtih greater frequency and/or intensity among inactive babies. These are non-nutritive oral behavior, visual focusing and prolonged gazing, and tactile exploration of the immediate surround. These behaviors have in common that they activate part of the body rather than the whole, and that they are focused and modulated. All of these behaviors were also seen among active babies; however, while they occurred readily and frequently in inactive infants, they were relatively rare in the active ones.

We hypothesize, then, that activity level affects the frequency with which these restricted and modulated behaviors are likely to occur. That is, even if the impulse toward oral behavior and visual focusing were equally strong in active and inactive infants, the presence of gross body movement mechanically prevents the occurrence of the more limited behavior integrations. We assume, therefore, not that low activity level is associated with a stronger impulse toward mouthing or sucking or with greater responsiveness in the visual modality, but that the relative frequency of these behaviors in inactive babies is a by-product of the circumstance that active infants spend much of their waking time engaged in massive body movement. Development during the first three months of life is affected by whether an infant has ample opportunity to give visual attention to the environment (as tends to be the case with inactive infants), and whether hand-mouth coordinations become a dominant and stable schema very early (as occurs with a proportion of inactive infants, but not with active ones at such an early age).

Active infants tend to mobilize much of their behavior repertoire in response to slight stimulation, whereas inactive infants display complex and intense behavior chiefly in response to relatively stronger and more specific stimulation. A whole array of findings can be subsumed under this general statement, but only a few of them will be recapitulated here: (1) Active infants showed better coordinated and more complex behavior during spontaneous activity than did inactive babies; further, their behavior was more frequently focused on the environment. Also, during spontaneous activity, the active infants were more often responsive to environmental stimuli at a greater distance from the infant, and their typical varieties of vocalization were both developmentally more advanced and more intense. (2) Specific social stimulation, as well as specific stimulation designated to arouse the infant's interest in objects, had a far greater impact on the behavior of inactive babies. Although both groups showed about equally mature and equally intense responsiveness to objects and to other persons, the inactive infants showed relatively advanced and intense behavior patterns almost only when aroused by specific external stimulation. The behavior of active infants, on the other hand, was of much the same order during spontaneous activity (minimum external stimulation) and at the mere sight of another person (minimal social stimulation) as it was when prodded during situations such as developmental testing (strong object stimulation) or when mothers played actively with them (strong social stimulation).

Only inactive infants tended to show prolonged and intense sucking or other mouth activity while alert, content, and not specifically stimulated (spontaneous activity), and only inactive infants were capable of self-soothing by means of oral activity. Although, after the age of 12 weeks, nonnutritive oral activity could be as intense and as frequent in active as in inactive infants, oral activity in the active babies increased as a component of general behavioral arousal, during bodily need states, or in response to external stimulation. Among inactive infants it could become a more autonomous behavior system, so that intense oral activity took place at times when there were no other signs of excitation. This difference is probably due to the fact that oral patterns can become dominant during the earliest months of life only among inactive babies. We speculate that, because stable oral schemas are available to them by the age of 3 months some inactive infants (and no active ones) are thereafter able to comfort and soothe themselves by means of sucking at their thumb or hand.

The consequences of different reaction tendencies of active and inactive infants: Our hypotheses about the developmental relevance of activity level rest on the assumption that development advances as infants engage in those behavior integrations that are their relatively most mature level of function; that is, frequent opportunities to gaze, to reach for objects and manipulate them, to vocalize in a social context, and the like, facilitate the emergence of the next more mature coordinations and discriminations. Our data demonstrate that development can and frequently does proceed at an equal rate in active and inactive infants. However, the conditions that are necessary to support developmental progress differ somewhat as a function of activity level.

The level of background stimulation given active infants in an ordinary home is generally enough to induce the frequent occurrence of behaviors that pave the way to further developmental progress—even if the infant gets little social attention beyond that entailed in routine care. Provided the infant is not in a state of distress, routine caretaking contacts with maternal persons are stimulating enough to elicit social responsiveness at whatever is the child's most mature level, even if the caretaking adult seldom combines these routine procedures with playful social interchanges. Similarly, the mere presence of objects and toys within reach and sight can elicit object-oriented behaviors from the active infant.

Inactive babies (at least up to the age of 8 months) need more specific provocation to stimulate object manipulations, more complex body coordinations, and social responsiveness beyond the simplest varieties. Therefore, if the inactive infant is to make the expected gains in visual-motor coordination, in vocalization and in communication, he requires more specific stimulation (of the variety normally provided by attentive parents) than does the active baby.[1]

Inactive babies tend to respond to hunger less intensely than active ones; in general they show less acute distress and protest less vigorously. In many homes and institutions caretakers act on the principle that young infants should be approached primarily when they appear to be in need. In such situations, inactive infants more frequently will have to wait for food after unmistakable signs of hunger (other than crying) have appeared, and will be approached and played with far less often than active infants in the same sort of environment. In addition, since inactive infants are more likely to acquire the capacity to overcome distress unaided, by sucking at their fingers or by rocking, those parents or other caretaking adults

[1] In our sample, inactive infants who received little stimulation beyond that provided by routine care made less developmental progress than active babies who were equally understimulated. Independently, Shaffer (1966) demonstrated that temporary developmental losses due to hospitalization were significantly more severe for inactive than active infants.

who respond only to clear demands for attention will not always intervene when the infant does show distress because they know that he is likely to settle down of his own accord.

For inactive infants the developmental consequences of such an environment can easily become a vicious circle in which the very infants who most require it receive a minimum of stimulation as compared with the active infants who are more likely to compel adult attention.

To put it another way: The difference between active and inactive infants, in the development of interaction patterns with caretaking adults, is that active infants are less dependent on the social and physical environment for the stimulation necessary to maintain developmental progress, while inactive infants are less dependent on the social environment for the attentions necessary to maintain relative equilibrium and equanimity and to overcome upset and distress.

Inactive infants show earlier and more sustained visual attention to the environment, and vision tends to remain an especially important modality in their experience up to at least 8 months of age. Also, inactive infants tend to discriminate the mother from all other persons at an earlier age than do active babies. Active babies, on the other hand, tend to develop responsiveness to relatively distant stimuli somewhat earlier, and acquire locomotion and the capacity for purposive manipulation of objects somewhat sooner. Almost certainly, the relative advantage that active infants have in first acquiring the active and directed use of their own body and of segments of the environment derives from the fact that during the months when these skills are acquired, they have more frequent occasion for the practice of these motor skills. By the age of 7½ months, active and inactive infants differed in terms of the *pattern* of performance on the developmental tests. By and large, the most advanced behaviors shown by inactive infants concerned discrimination among diverse visual and auditory stimuli and delicate visual-motor coordinations. The most advanced behaviors among active infants concerned locomotion and postural control.[2]

On the basis of these and related observations, we hypothesize that —in the absence of specific conditions of stimulation to counteract these trends—the course of early development tends to follow a different pattern in active and in inactive infants.

We shall now turn to suggestions and hypotheses that deal with the significance of particular events and behaviors for the developmental process.

There is a link between rudimentary ego development and recurrent arousal due to hunger and fatigue. Psychoanalysis postulates that a first awareness of the existence of an environment comes about when very young infants feel displeasure and excitement while in a state of need (chiefly hunger) and there is a delay between need state and gratification.

[2] We have reported a similar result for another sample (Escalona and Heider, 1959).

The infant is thus forced to recognize that satisfaction reaches him from "outside," and this induces vigilance in the search for need satisfaction. Analysis of conditions under which infants first show visual attention to their surroundings, and of the conditions under which they display related early capacities such as directed movement, anticipation, and discrimination among segments of the environment, showed that a state of acute bodily need leads to a generalized primitivization of behavior. That is, such capacities as the infant organism has acquired to behaviorally recognize an environment and respond to it in a reality adapted fashion is largely lost during hunger and fatigue. The early ego functions are manifested in behavior primarily during states of moderate arousal and in the absence of strong excitation or displeasure.

However, a study of the sequence of the first emergence of behaviors that reflect early ego functions, and of the range of conditions under which infants are likely to display their most advanced and complex behavior integrations, led to a formulation that assigns a centrally important role to recurrent need states and the delay of gratification. In short, we hypothesize that early ego development is best supported by a recurrent pattern of experience that provides a range of states, from alert inactivity to strong arousal, which *must include episodes of moderate animation.* Infants who are predominantly placid and who seldom experience strong excitation have little incitement to relinquish very simple and body-focused schemas of behavior. In infants who are seldom quiet and relaxed, but spend much of their waking time in a state of high arousal, the more complex and outwardly focused behavior integrations have few opportunities to emerge because high arousal leads to behavioral primitivization. Brain-damaged infants, who fail to develop the behaviors reflecting early ego functions in the normal manner, are generally infants who alternate between states of irritability and excitation and states of near lethargy; they lack the frequent moments of moderate arousal during which developmental advances in behavior organization are most typically manifested.

This way of thinking about the role of regular alternations between different degrees of arousal implies the familiar notion that structures (in this case sensorimotor schemas) tend to stabilize and to resist change if they are maintained over prolonged periods of time. Periodic *loss* of the most advanced schemas because of need states or massive excitation from without counteracts the premature stabilization of behavior schemas and therefore is a necessary component of behavior change and progressive development.

Some early ego functions emerge first in passive form during encounters with the mother, but they are actively applied and expanded during transactions with the inanimate environment before they appear as active components of social interactions. Development during the first seven months or thereabouts consists in large measure of the fact that voluntary action, intentionality, and primitive means-end structures come to guide behavior. The combined operation of early ego functions that allow the infant to initiate events that effect desired changes in the environment and to overcome obstacles is conveniently referred to as "mastery activity." In all mastery activities, the infant experiences his own voluntary actions as the causal agent of changes in the environment (*i.e.,* he shakes a rattle and creates a sound; he activates his body in creeping and obtains a previously distant toy). In our view, the oft repeated experience of effecting change and of overcoming obstacles plays a major role in mediating the awareness of a separation between the acting subject and the acted upon object; that is, these experiences lay the foundation for the infant's awareness of an objective reality, independent of himself and consisting of permanent objects in space. If this is so, mastery activities are significant not only for the development of trust in one's own powers (competence) but also for the development of a sense of self as a bounded entity.

As described in the preceding chapters the data suggest strongly that intentionality, initiatory behavior, and primitive means-end structures come to guide behavior toward inanimate objects before they are applied in social interactions. At an age when infants learn to manipulate objects and their own body to achieve anticipated ends (during about the sixth and seventh months), social responsiveness tends to remain limited to an immediate response to perceptual input. Five- and six-month-old babies smile and vocalize in response to persons, they may participate in games involving mutual imitation, and their behavior may reflect subtle discriminations in response to different varieties of social stimulation. However, definite means-end structures and intentionality by social means make their appearance, in our sample and in general, during the eighth or ninth month.[3] Children then direct responses toward other persons as a means of obtaining an effect not directly related to the person, and verbal and gestural communications begin to be understood.

At first glance, the conclusion that evolving cognitive principles enter social interactions relatively late appears to contradict a postulate widely accepted in psychodynamic theories of development—that such functions first emerge in the course of interactions with the vitally important mother, and that early cognitive development is strongly dependent on the developing mother-child relationship.[4] If this were so, one might expect that behavioral capacities developed first in interaction with the mother would later be generalized to other persons and to inanimate objects.

In order to clarify the issue we suggest that it will be useful to dis-

[3] Individual children respond to and employ communication signals earlier, but invariably after means-end structures have been applied to objects for some months.

[4] This assumption was never made by Freud, nor has it become an integral part of psychoanalytic theory since then. However, theories that derive from psychoanalysis have often assumed a direct link between the progress of the first object relationship and cognitive development.

tinguish between the *first emergence* of a function, when it is manifested in the quality of response to an immediately present perceptual stimulation, and the use or *application* of the function in mastery behavior. Intentionality and means-end organization of behavior are, of course, based upon anticipation, memory, and perceptual discrimination. These functions are indeed observed first in the direct interaction between the infant and the caretaking mother, but only in the passive mode. Sometime during the second or third month, infants cease crying at the mere sight of the mother or the bottle before the mother has touched the baby in order to pick him up or before the nipple has contacted the mouth. At this developmental stage infants respond to objects in terms of the immediate perceptual stimulation they provide, but activity with objects is not yet intentional or actively manipulatory. During the next several months anticipation and discrimination are put to use in mastery activities, as has been described. Only after directed use of the musculature and of objects in an intentional manner (however simple the intentions and expectations) has become effortless and stabilized, will the same functions be put to active use in the social sphere through the emergence of intentional communication.

The most general formulation of the issue is as follows: During early infancy new cognitive capacities are first demonstrated in the passive mode, as perceptions begin to be responded to—not in terms of the immediate sensations they provide, but as the signal of remembered associated satisfactions. The passive manifestation of the new faculty is likely to arise in the context of need states and their satisfaction, which typically occurs in direct interaction with caretaking persons. The transformation from the passive mode to the active application of the new function as mastery behavior is developed under conditions that involve less arousal than do need states and that provide maximum constancy in the effects produced by the infant's actions. The results of action applied to inanimate objects are far more consistent than the results of behavior directed toward persons, and therefore the infant's dealings with the inanimate environment become the principal arena for the development and perfection of simple mastery behavior. Once actively applying the new capacities has become a well-established and dominant mode of functioning in the relatively neutral sphere of the world of things, the same level of behavior integration (the active use of the new functions) can be applied in the more variable and more affect-laden interchanges with other human beings.[5]

[5] Our formulation addresses itself to the same issue that Hartmann (1937) speaks of as the "autonomous neutral sphere of ego functioning" which, in his view, is the sphere in which learning and mastery behavior chiefly emerge. He too emphasizes the fact that compelling pressure of need and affect counteracts the development of complex and as yet fragile cognitive structures, and that, once developed, these same structures come to operate in the more highly charged, drive-related aspects of experience. The issue of whether it is strategic to postulate an independent source of energy for learning and mastery activities, as Hartmann does, has general importance for psychological theory, but it is relatively unimportant in the narrow context of conceptualizing the events and sequences that constitute early development.

The detailed analysis of the behavior of these infants during contacts with the mother (and with caretaking adults in general) suggested the importance of some aspects of maternal functioning beyond those universally agreed upon. It was noted that, in many instances, the baby's behavior during playful interactions with the mother was either more complex (inactive infants) or both more complex and more sustained (active infants) than it was during alert activity without a social partner. The infant's actual sensorimotor experience during object play mediated by an accommodating social partner proved to be quite different from that in solitary play even with a rich variety of objects. While playing with an infant, most mothers (and other maternal persons) vary their behavior in response to what the baby does. They show or offer objects at distances and speeds adapted to the baby's changes of position. If the infant's interest flags, they introduce variations and intensify the playful actions that seem most pleasing to him. If the infant becomes overly excited or fatigued, the mother reduces her activity without terminating contact altogether. Finally, the perceptual events generated by the toys and the infant's own activity are embedded in a constant flow of social responsiveness; the infant who has difficulty in performing an action finds himself helped by a reassuring voice or touch, while his successful accomplishments produce smiles, hugs, or other forms of pleasing attention and recognition.

These observations led us to the thought that because it is these specific features of social play that promote longer attention span and experimentation with novel behavior integrations, this variety of oft repeated play may be a significant component of maternal care. Infants reared in institutions may be smiled at, spoken to, and given toys,[6] but professional caretakers seldom have the time or inclination for frequent and prolonged play of this kind. Some mothers, too, for one reason or another, are neither inclined nor able to modulate their behavior in accordance with the infant's momentary state. This hypothesis has a bearing on the enrichment programs currently being planned for children under 3 years old in day-care centers and in institutions. Toys and automated programs can be made to respond specifically to the infant's actions, but they cannot provide either the subtle variation or the familiar and rewarding social interchanges that maternal persons supply.

A related hypothesis concerns the importance for the infant of social encounters that range from the modulated and accommodating variety as described to much more rousing and excitatory play, such as is often provided by fathers and older siblings. In this kind of play, when the baby may be bounced, tickled, tossed, or teased by an offer of toys withdrawn just before they are grasped, he is usually reduced to a passive role, which may involve excited laughter, massive motion, squealing, and the like. He is not accommodated to, but must himself accommodate to mas-

[6] We here refer to more recent patterns of care in institutions, which recognize the importance of these experiences and try to provide them.

sive stimulation. However, it is one of the few life experiences of young infants that combine high arousal with high pleasure, and thus afford an ideal context in which to acquire tolerance for massive stimulation. Since we think that it is an *alternation* between mild, moderate, and strong arousals that provides an optimal setting for developmental progress and increasingly flexible adaptation, it follows that both of these types of social encounter play an important and facilitating role in early development. By the same token, our hypothesis can explain observed differences in the patterns of development and the adaptive styles of infants reared in an extremely sheltered and accommodating atmosphere and those whose experience provides a great deal of rousing social contact and relatively little sensitive accommodation.

The manner in which infants stimulate their own body has been described in great detail in preceding chapters because we think that these universal patterns of behavior are closely linked to the development of a well-defined body ego, and that they serve simultaneously as mechanisms to regulate fluctuating states of excitation.

Finding that tactile and oral self-stimulation tend to be massive and intense during hunger and fatigue—at least among infants who have developed schemas of the self-stimulating sort—we theorized that the primitivization of behavior that occurs at such times implies a loss or a reduction in the sense of the body self as a coherent entity,[7] and that the pinching and stroking of the body, as well as the sensations generated in the oral zone, serve to enhance sensorimotor awareness of the body boundary. The tactile and oral self-stimulation noted during hunger and fatigue in babies less than 8 months of age are almost certainly by-products of neurophysiologic changes. We speculate that they are a built-in adaptive device to counteract the discomfort and behavioral regression that typically accompany these need states.

For non-nutritive oral behavior, our data demonstrated for infants up to the eighth month what has already been shown for neonates: that finger and hand sucking are not specifically related to a state of hunger, but tend to accompany any excitation of comparable intensity. If anything, non-nutritive oral behavior was more frequent and intense during spontaneous activity and during fatigue than it was during hunger.

Bodily self-stimulation in the oral mode is the most universal and most intense variety. This fact can be understood on the basis of the hypothesis that infants stimulate their own bodies in the modalities that—in their previous experience—were felt vividly at moments when maternal ministrations led to a decrease in excitation and discomfort, or at moments when contact with a maternal person increased pleasurable arousal. In other

[7] This does not apply to infants during the first two or three months, for they presumably have not yet established a clear-cut differentiation between the self and the surrounding field, and in any case do not engage in sustained self-stimulation during hunger and fatigue.

words, if the mother successfully soothed the baby by rocking, he is more likely to develop bodily self-stimulation in the kinesthetic mode; if the infant was most readily aroused by touch during contacts with caretaking persons, self-stimulation in the tactile mode is likely to occur later on. The ubiquity of oral self-stimulation among infants can then be understood, as a consequence of the fact that the mouth is an especially sensitive zone in young infants and oral sensations are always associated with the feeding process.[8]

Further, the analysis of the conditions during which bodily self-stimulation waxes and wanes suggests that these activities can enter the excitation-relaxation cycle in several distinct ways. They may accompany general behavioral arousal and—like other movements—may then be regarded as discharge or overflow phenomena. Oral and kinesthetic self-stimulation (but not the tactile variety) may arise at moments of distress, serving to soothe and comfort the infant. Lastly, all varieties of bodily self-stimulation may occur when the infant is relaxed and contented, visibly increasing the infant's level of animation and arousal and tending to counteract or preclude attentiveness to the environment.

[8] These considerations do not address themselves to the broader issue of infantile sexuality in the oral mode. Our hypothesis is entirely compatible with the assumption that oral needs are dominant in infancy, that they are an early manifestation of a continuum that culminates in genital sexuality, and that they remain a component of sexuality in maturity. Neither the source of energy that activates self-stimulation nor the developmental role of orality after the first half year of life is considered in our limited formulation.

PART III

THE ADAPTATION SYNDROMES

In this last section we shall compare the infants in terms of stable patterns of experience and explore for each baby the relationship between experience patterns and overall style of functioning and adaptation.

Chapter 9 provides the general framework for this venture and is an introduction to Part Three. It may however be appropriate to explain how the individual adaptation syndromes (Chapters 13, 14, and 15) came to be written in a format rather different from the customary style of case presentations.

Our approach required that the behavior of each baby (and of each mother) be described in minute detail and that characteristics of the family and its sociocultural setting be indicated whenever such more general information was likely to have a direct effect upon the infant's life experience. However, families participated in the study with the understanding that their privacy would be respected. Case presentations therefore had to be very specific; yet they had to conceal identifying information.

For this reason family composition, the father's occupation, and similar information have deliberately been left vague, while *what* the mother and other people did with the baby and *how* they dealt with the infant are described in detail. Discretion was one of the considerations that led us to omit certain standard types of information, but not the only one. Our major hypothesis implies that it is what actually happens to the baby that is important for development, and not the circumstances that may explain how the child's experience came to be what it was.

The emphasis given to behavior in a concrete context, at the expense of material concerning parental attitudes and the broader social context, is thus in keeping with the theoretical assumptions on which this work is based.

NINE

RATIONALE AND GOALS

The attempt to describe a single personality in its totality is a familiar challenge to psychologists. Except in the literary form of the nineteenth-century novel, an adequate description of the whole personality has never been achieved. Even Henry Murray's classic *Explorations in Personality* (1938) or the descriptive studies of young children by Lois Murphy and her associates (1962) have not been able to do more than document and enumerate salient features of functioning. The more such an account refers to concrete behavior under many different circumstances, the greater is the risk of obscuring the intrinsic cohesiveness that lends unity to all behavior in a single person—infant, child, or adult.

Yet all who have attempted the study of individuals report an experience similar to our own: thorough familiarity with an individual's pattern of responsiveness in many different areas yields an impression of self-consistency. Neither parents nor investigators have the slightest difficulty in specifying that a given episode is "typical" of little Tommy, although they would have been surprised to see Mary react in the same manner. What this intrinsic unity consists of is difficult to specify. Certainly it is not a matter of similarity of behavior under diverse conditions. For instance, some of our inactive infants appeared "typically" restricted in their responsiveness under some conditions and "typically" highly reactive under others. For another example, the near-absence of oral behavior in some babies during spontaneous activity was as descriptive as the fact that oral behavior was intense during hunger or fatigue.

Nor does self-consistency mean that each child's behavior is reliably the same each time he responds to the same situation or to the same state. For instance, some babies generally tolerate the discomfort of hunger or fatigue without massive disorganization of behavior, but occasionally their distress becomes acute and its expression extreme and overt—just as older children who are ordinarily well controlled may show rare rages that are more explosive than those of children who are more easily roused to open anger. Then, it is the discrepancy between the usual pattern and the occasional extreme reaction that is individually characteristic.

After many years of experimenting with the problem, we still have not found a way of presenting comprehensive data to convey what we think we know about a particular infant or child. But the attempt to do so and our reading of the relevant literature support two assertions: First, although an aggregate of descriptive statements can yield a vivid impressionistic image of diverse personalities, it does not lead directly to a better understanding of either the genesis of individual differences or the integrating mechanisms that unify each individual's behavior. Second, it is possible to bring systematic order to diverse data by using abstractions, but *always* at a sacrifice—because whatever constitutes individuality is lost once concrete detail is replaced by categorical statements.

It has been suggested more than once that a systematic appraisal of individuality must focus on central regulatory patterns or mechanisms which can, it is hoped, be shown to operate in many different behaviors and under varied circumstances. Some efforts have been made to apply this suggestion to the characteristics of the behavior of infants and young children, though with very limited success. A number of reaction tendencies have been used for this purpose, among them general irritability and/or excitability; sensory thresholds; and a tendency toward expansiveness versus constriction (in motor behavior, range of attention, interests, and, figuratively speaking, affectivity).

In our efforts to devise a means of describing individual differences among our subjects as whole organisms, all these and many other general descriptive attributes were at first employed. It was entirely possible to determine for each baby whether he tended to be high, medium, or low in excitability, whether his behavior was highly differentiated for his age, and other similar attributes. However, condensing many behavior characteristics into constellations reflecting general behavior tendencies proved disappointing, in part because the great majority of normal, healthy children occupy a mid-position on most of these continua. Many infants were moderately excitable or moderately differentiated. However, these babies still differed widely from one another in the quality and content of behavior, demonstrating once again that summary abstraction eliminates the very thing we hope to identify—the patterns of experience as reflected in stable aspects of the infant's behavior regulation as he adapts to specific external and internal forces and conditions.

For several reasons it was necessary to find a unitary framework within which to describe how each baby tended to behave and the context in which behavior took place. The first reason has already been discussed: the need to specify individuality in systematic terms rather than impressionistically. The major purpose of the research from which this book derives was to describe individual differences in behavior style and in adaptive functioning among normal infants. But our conceptualization of the genesis of individual differences requires a further step—that we specify for each child what we term *stable patterns of experience,* since our central hypothesis is that developmental outcome (rate and pattern of development as well as individual characteristics of adaptive functioning) is directly related to such stable patterns. The hypothesis implies that neither the infant's reaction tendencies (the A factors on our diagram) nor the environmental conditions (B factors) will show a consistent and direct relationship to developmental outcome.

If we are to test the hypothesis and its corollary implications, we must first be able to assess both the reaction tendencies, which are the organism's contribution to each behavioral event, and conspicuous and fairly stable aspects of the environmental conditions to which the infant must adapt. Juxtaposing these two assessments, we must then construct and document a third level of assessment, stable patterns of experience. Only then can we determine whether a relationship exists between the reaction tendencies (A factors only) and developmental outcome; between environmental conditions (B factors) and developmental outcome; and last, between stable patterns of experience and developmental outcome.

The term "adaptation syndrome" refers to a constellation of variables that includes all the child's behavioral tendencies looked at in the context of stable patterns of experience, as well as developmental outcome. The adaptation syndromes for each child are at once a manner of describing individual infants in a coherent and systematic fashion, and the evidence to support the idea that differences in stable patterns of experience contribute to the explanation of individual differences in developmental outcome.

The search for concepts, classifications, or other abstractions that would serve both to identify reaction tendencies and to describe systematically major aspects of the environment finally led us to use a modified version of constructs first developed by Kurt Lewin. Topological and vector psychology has demonstrated that the "laws" of overt behavior can be deduced using structural concepts deriving from Gestalt psychology in juxtaposition with dynamic concepts adapted from physical field theory. The methodological virtue of Lewin's approach lies in the fact that each construct, such as "region," "boundary," and "differentiation," can be defined in stringent operational, behavioral terms.[1] We found that all of the relatively stable behavior characteristics noted in our infant subjects could be accommodated to a small number of quasi-topological constructs first employed in Lewin's work. Similarly, important components of the environmental setting, in terms of intensities of stimulation, could be conveyed through vectorial notations.

[1] Lewin believed that topological and vectorial concepts can provide a mathematical model capable of expressing psychological laws. It is doubtful whether this goal was ever achieved, but it is certain that our usage of the Lewinian terms does no more than to provide fairly stringent designations. What we have done is to borrow some of Lewin's hypothetical constructs as a means of *systematic description.*

Topological psychology treats the person, or the organism, as a bounded region encompassing subregions that correspond to components of the person that possess a degree of functional autonomy (see Fig. 9.1). The schematic topological representation of the person shows two major components or part-regions, each of which is structured into yet smaller subregions. The innermost layer (called the "inner psychological region") refers to the structural position of motives, interests, values, and generally all that determines goals, purposes, and the organized response to events and conditions. In adults this is a highly differentiated region, which includes the social, personal, intellectual, moral, and affective elements that make up the inner psychic life of each person. In infants, the inner psychological region is presumed to be relatively undifferentiated and exceedingly unstable. In a young infant a single feeling state (hunger-displeasure) or a single "intention" (reaching for a toy at a distance or resisting the intake of food) will determine all of his behavior at a given moment.

The inner psychological region is surrounded by the "motoric-perceptual region"—the totality of structures by means of which behavior is effected. The motoric-perceptual region thus occupies a boundary position between the inner psychological region and the environment. Topologically, the motoric-perceptual region is represented as surrounding the inner psychological region and as being the one and only region directly neighboring the environment because the environment can influence the state of the person and his behavior *only* by penetrating the motoric-perceptual region (perception). Simultaneously, the person can effect changes in the environment *only* through the motoric-perceptual region, *i.e.,* by activating part or all of the neuromuscular apparatus.

During ongoing behavior (when activity or change of any sort occurs), the direction and intensity of the resulting behavior will depend not only on the strength of the forces or on the degree and kind of structural differentiation that the organism has attained, but also on the ease with which the boundary or "wall" between the motoric-perceptual region and the environment can be penetrated by any force. "The individual is dynamically a relatively closed system. How strongly the environment operates upon the individual will, therefore, be determined (apart from the structure and forces of the situation) by the functional firmness of the boundaries between individual and environment" (Lewin, 1935). The same is true, by definition, of the "wall" between the inner psychological region and the motoric-perceptual region. In other words, the inner boundary is highly penetrable or functionally weak if the slightest change in state or an impulse of low intensity affects the motoric to a high degree. Similarly, someone who responds to or is affected by minimal sounds and sights in the environment would be said to possess—in this respect and at the time of such behavior—a relatively weak boundary between the person (the motoric-perceptual region) and the environment. For instance, an infant who merely tenses and frowns at a pinprick would meet the criterion for a strong outer boundary, in contrast to an infant who responds to the same pinprick with prolonged crying and thrashing about.[2]

In Lewin's application of these topological concepts, all structural aspects are considered simultaneously. That is, for any specific instance or any regular or stable pattern of behavior, topological psychology requires that one consider the degree of differentiation of the person, the type of structure (meaning which specific part-regions are adjacent to which others), the strength of the boundaries between the regions (*i.e.,* the degree of force or tension required in one region for change to occur in adjacent regions), and the plasticity of the psychic material (*i.e.,* the relative ease or difficulty with which existing structures can be broken down and replaced by a new and different structural composition—restructurization). Since the definition of all these structural properties is entirely operational, Lewin's determinations of structure were made almost entirely by the experimental method.[3] He and his associates held that both the degree and kind of differentiation are subject to change, as are the strengths of boundaries. For instance, de-differentiation or primitivization of behavior results from affective stress and generally heightened tension. The boundaries between regions become weaker as a result of fatigue, satiation and, again, affective stress.[4]

Only in the discussion of universal developmental changes does Lewin offer some formulations that exceed the limits of a particular experimental situation. On the basis of observation and of diverse experimental findings, he proposes that, in the course of early development, differentiation increases; the boundaries (between regions) or walls (between corresponding systems) become increasingly firm; the type of structure becomes more complex and hierarchical in nature; and the plasticity of psychic structures decreases. Even in the context of these broader formulations, Lewin emphasizes that, especially in children, the boundary between the environment and the person fluctuates in strength. For instance, he points out that children tend to be especially vulnerable to environmental influence and more likely to give overt expression to inner feelings and thoughts

[2] In Lewin's work, I have found no empiric application of the possibility that the same region (in this case, the motoric-perceptual) may be characterized by boundaries of different strength towards the environment on the one hand and the inner psychological region on the other. The outer boundary was usually treated as referring to "the person" as a whole, while the boundary between the motoric and the inner psychological region was considered as but one of many walls or boundaries that constitute differentiation within the person. However, Lewin's formal definitions allow for the circumstance that the inner boundary of the motoric region may be of different strength than the outer boundary of the same region.

[3] Lewin's work in the area of individual psychology dealt primarily with volitional behavior. It is no accident that the very youngest age group used in experimental work within this framework were infants upward of 6 months of age, and that the experimental situation exposed infants to an attractive toy beyond their reach. In other words, the experiment focused upon one of the earliest behaviors that is clearly goal-directed (Fajans, 1935).

[4] See Dembo (1931); Zeigarnik (1927); Karsten (1928); and Barker, Dembo, and Lewin (1943).

at bedtime, when fatigue, the removal of clothes, and the general intimacy of the situation combine to weaken the boundaries of the motoric-perceptual region (both toward the environment and toward the inner psychological systems).[5]

It was necessary to summarize this much of the original Lewinian formulation (at risk of great oversimplification) in order to make clear that, in adapting only *some* of his topological constructs, we departed from certain basic theorems and conceptions of topological and vector psychology. We found it possible and useful to use our observational data for the assessment of two structural characteristics of our infants: strength of the boundary between the environment and the motoric-perceptual region, and strength of the boundary between the motoric-perceptual region and the inner psychological region.[6]

Our operational definitions of boundary strength, like Lewin's, are based on the nature and intensity of behavior change as the result of external or internal stimulation (Lewin would have described the latter in terms of tension within a system). Unlike Lewin, we have focused on the stable and consistent behavioral reflections of boundary strength, and not on the changes in boundary strength as a function of changes in state and in field conditions. He referred to the relative strength of boundaries as one of several important sources of individual difference (Lewin, 1935), but never made these differences the subject of experimental inquiry.[7]

Fig. 9.1 is a schematic picture of selected and widely different combinations of structural and dynamic factors that may characterize an infant in his milieu.

In constellation A the motoric-perceptual region has a strong outer boundary and a weak inner boundary. The intensity of stimulation from within is typically high (as might be true, for instance, of an infant subject to recurrent gastric distress). The intensity of stimulation from without is also high, as would be true of an infant who received constant and intense stimulation from his mother and other family members, and who was seldom handled gently or left to his own devices in quiet surroundings. Schematically speaking, the high level of external stimulation should

[5] A somewhat similar observation led Freud to prescribe that analytic patients assume a recumbent position. His observation that on the couch it is easier for patients to communicate less rational and highly personal aspects of their inner life is equivalent to the statement that under such circumstances the functional boundary between innermost feelings and thoughts and the motoric (speech and gesture) is comparatively weak.

[6] It was in fact possible to assess also the degree of differentiation in several areas, such as the motoric, perceptual discrimination, affect, and the relative autonomy of some among the regions (such as oral behavior). However, these latter determinations did not add to either the description of patterns of behavior or the description of adaptive styles. They are, therefore, not presented in the text.

[7] A partial exception was the experimental comparative study of feeble-minded and normal children (Koepke, Erfurth, Saathop, and Wolmann, 1935). However, in those somewhat controversial studies the plasticity of psychic substance and the strength of boundaries were not sharply separated, nor was there an investigation of such differences within the normal range.

Outer Boundary:
Strong
Inner Boundary:
Weak
External Stimulation:
Intense, frequent
Internal Stimulation:
Intense, frequent

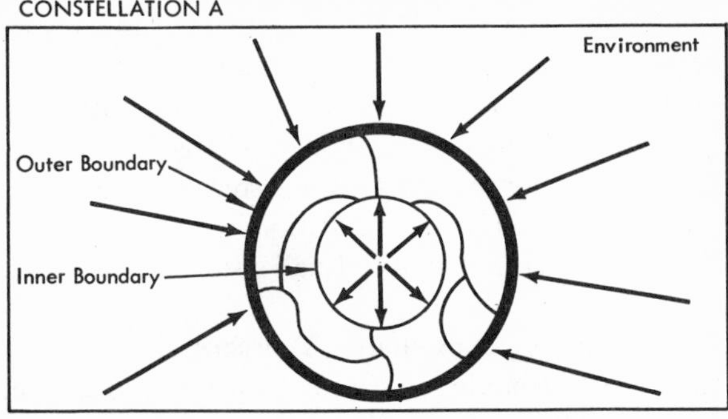

Outer Boundary:
Weak
Inner Boundary:
Strong
External Stimulation:
Low intensity and frequency
Internal Stimulation:
Low intensity and frequency

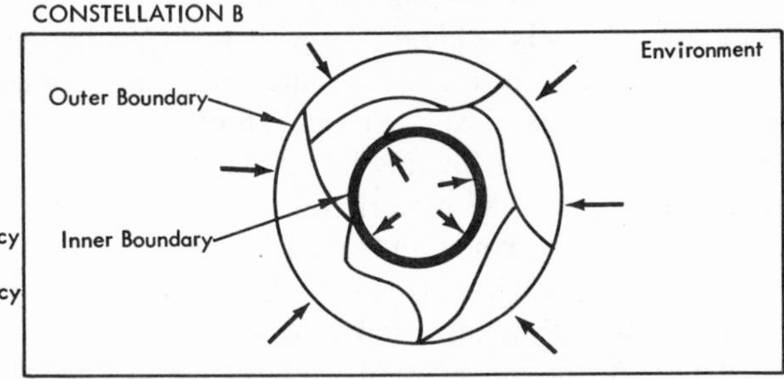

Outer Boundary Sectors:
Vision: Medium
Medium stimulation
Auditory: Weak
Medium stimulation
Kinesthetic: Weak
Low stimulation
Tactile: Strong
Intense stimulation

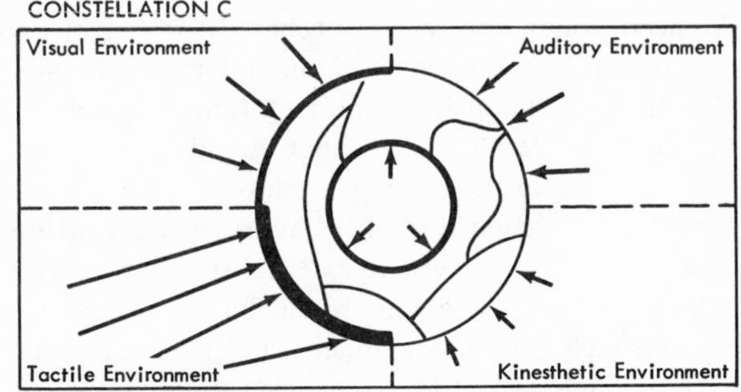

FIGURE 9.1. THREE CONSTELLATIONS OF STRUCTURAL CHARACTERISTICS AND DYNAMIC CONDITIONS.

generate for infant A only very moderate levels of excitation, as the strength of the outer boundary leaves him less affected by the objectively intense stimulation than if the boundary were weaker. In the language we have used before, such an infant would *experience* only moderate or low level excitation in response to external stimulation, although he is exposed to fairly strong excitatory forces. However, the postulated high intensity of stimulation from within would strongly affect his behavior, since the inner boundary is weak.

Among the overall behavioral characteristics of the infant described by constellation A would be these: (1) He would show fairly high levels of excitability and irritability (due to high inner stimulation in the presence of a weak inner barrier). (2) Peak levels of excitation and massive changes in state and behavior would occur predominantly as the result of stimulation from within (due to hunger, fatigue, gastric pain, and the like). (3) Overt behavior changes as the result of external stimulation would be seen only when that stimulation was fairly strong (small sounds, slight touch, or inconspicuous visual spectacles would rarely evoke behavioral responses).

In contrast, constellation B describes an infant who is highly responsive to external stimulation (weak outer boundary) and who is typically exposed to external stimulation low in frequency and intensity; *i.e.,* he is handled relatively seldom and with great gentleness, and spends much of his waking time in a shielded and quiet environment. In contrast to constellation A, low level external stimulation would yield relatively high levels of excitation for this infant, because even slight degrees of stimulation readily enter the motoric region (because of a weak outer boundary). That is, the frequency and intensity of excitation in response to external stimulation would be of comparable magnitude for A and B, although A is maximally stimulated and B is stimulated at a minimum level. In constellation B, the inner boundary is strong and the intensity of inner stimulation is low (as would be the case with an infant who has little distress in need states and who is generally free from somatic irritation). The behavioral characteristics of this infant would include the following: (1) The general intensity level and frequency of excitation and irritability would be moderate (weak outer boundary and low inner intensity of stimulation, but maximal responsiveness to such outer stimulation as occurs). (2) A large proportion of behavior changes, including peaks of excitation, would occur in response to external stimulation. (3) Relatively few massive changes in overt behavior would be the result of inner stimulation breaking through the strong inner barrier (since internal stimuli tend to be of low intensity). (4) Even very minimal external stimuli (such as low sounds, slight touch, or a visual detail) are likely to elicit overt behavioral responses.

Constellation C is a schematic representation that comes slightly closer to the complexity of observable phenomena. Although some infants are generally highly responsive and sensitive to external stimulation and some infants show general robustness in the face of all external stimulation, it is far more characteristic for the outer boundary to be variable. In the discussion of perceptual sensitivity as a dimension of infant behavior, it was mentioned that many babies were relatively more responsive in some sensory modalities than in others. It was also mentioned that mothers often place selective emphasis on some modalities in their approaches to and contacts with the infant.

Constellation C describes an infant highly responsive to sound and passive motion (weak boundary), markedly unresponsive to touch (strong boundary), and moderately reactive to visual stimulation. The consequences of such variability in the outer boundary will clearly depend upon the dosage of stimulation in each modality to which the infant is typically exposed. In this case, the most intense stimulation is provided in the strongest segment of the outer boundary, namely touch. Visual stimulation is here postulated as being of medium intensity, in combination with a medium level of reactivity. Auditory reactivity is high (weak boundary), and auditory stimulation is of medium intensity and frequency. The relatively rare and gentle kinesthetic stimulation provided by the mother produces relatively strong behavioral responses (weak boundary).

Disregarding the contribution of stimulation from within and the strength of the inner boundary (which in this example were constructed so as to minimize their functional importance by providing a strong boundary and low levels of stimulation), the behavioral and experience-pattern characteristics corresponding to constellation C would include the following: (1) The relatively largest proportion of behavior changes in response to external stimulation and high level excitations would come from auditory stimulation, alone or in association with other modalities (combination of moderately high intensity stimulation and weak boundary). (2) Visual and kinesthetic stimulation would contribute a lesser proportion of behavioral change and excitation and would very rarely reach peak levels. (The combination of medium stimulation with medium boundary strength and the combination of low intensity stimulation with weak boundary [kinesthetic] would, schematically speaking, be expected to yield comparable degrees and frequencies of behavior alteration and excitation in the child's actual experience.) (3) Despite the high intensity of stimulation in the tactile mode, this sector would account for only a small proportion of behavior activations.

The division of the environment and of the outer boundary into sectors for different sensory modalities is of course an artifact. It is employed only in order to indicate schematically an aspect of the child's reactivity and a feature of the patterns of stimulation to which he is customarily exposed. (The rating of the strength of the entire outer boundary, which is always provided, disregards the sense modalities involved and takes into account the fact that almost every episode involves multiple modalities.)

Up to this point we have discussed the schematic assessment of reaction tendencies and of conspicuous aspects of the environmental setting, the first steps in making the formal construction that determines stable patterns of experience. (The formal assessment of structural and dynamic variables by means of ratings in accordance with some topological and vectorial constructs will be referred to as the "SPE determinants.")

From the constellation of SPE determinants, we then derived selected patterns of experience (the SPE itself) which specify some of the consequences of a given combination of structural and dynamic factors. From a virtually unlimited number of experience patterns, we selected eight for systematic ratings. These eight stable patterns were chosen partly because they are considered important for infants in this age range, and partly because they lend themselves to derivation from the particular structural and dynamic assessments that we had selected as SPE determinants. In these pages we report a first attempt to relate some experience patterns to some aspects of developmental outcome. An adequate test of the usefulness of this approach rests with the selection of experience patterns that are in fact important in determining the particular developmental outcomes under study. In the discussion of adaptation syndromes we will report on aspects of experience not included in our formal SPE determinants, some of which may be more important than the ones we first selected. Further, the analysis of all formally assessed SPE's as related to the five outcome indices (Chapter 16), will show that some of the experience patterns we chose are of no relevance to the particular outcome indices we rated, though they can be of critical importance to other aspects of developmental outcome.

For better or worse, these were the patterns of experience rated for each child in terms of their prominence, intensity and/or frequency in each child's daily life:

(1) *Frequency of strong bodily arousal:* the frequency with which a child showed maximal excitation by such signs as massive poorly coordinated motion, muscle tension, loud squealing or crying, and the autonomic signs of arousal (respiratory, circulatory).

(2) *Prominence of internal somatic sensations:* the frequency and intensity with which a child was subject to bodily sensations of more than background intensity. In addition to hunger or fatigue (which may be relatively more or less disruptive), we included gastric distress, skin rashes, teething, and any other sources of behavioral arousal that come from the body, not the environment.

(3) *Balance between behavior activations responsive to internal and somatic causes and those responsive to external stimulation:* the *relative* frequency with which behavior alterations occur in each of these categories. For an infant who moves or sucks his thumb or vocalizes or does any other thing unrelated to sights, sounds, tactile, or any other external stimulation much more often than he responds to something that reaches him from the environment, the appropriate rating is "internal dominant." Both the frequency and the intensity of behavior activations are here disregarded; that is, an infant who very often shows behavior changes responsive to internal stimulation, but who equally often acts in response to external causes, would receive a rating of "equal," just as would an infant who seldom shows behavior activations of either kind.

(4) *Importance of distance receptors:* the frequency and intensity with which the distance receptors (sight and sound) are activated in the child's day-by-day experience. A rating of relatively high prominence reflects that the infant gazes often and intently and has much occasion to listen to voices and other sounds (which requires not only that he be so inclined, but that there be ample visual and auditory stimulation).

(5) *Importance of near receptors:* the frequency and intensity with which the near receptors (touch and passive motion) are activated in the child's experience. An infant whose reactivity in these modalities is low (strong boundary) is likely to receive a rating of "low" or "fairly low" prominence, even if he is touched and moved about a good deal, whereas an infant who does respond strongly (weak boundaries) in these modalities will be rated anywhere from "fairly low" to "high" in prominence, depending upon the amount and intensity of stimulation he receives.

(6) *Most prominent modality:* self-evident, but not all infants were stimulated and responded more strongly in one modality than in any other. When this was the case, the appropriate rating was "none."

(7) *Least prominent modality:* self-evident, and again a rating of "none" was applied to some infants.

(8) *Frequency of optimal states of animation:* the relative frequency with which an infant was simultaneously moderately aroused and externally stimulated at a moderate level of intensity. An infant not highly reactive to external stimulation was likely to receive a rating of "fairly prominent" (or above) only if the mother and others in the environment tended to provide ample and rather intense stimulation (which is assessed in the environmental ratings of the SPE determinants). A highly reactive infant, on the other hand, might receive a rating of "fairly prominent" or above even with environmental stimulation that was of low intensity and not especially frequent.

These patterns of experience can be read off from the constellation of SPE determinants, as they arise entirely on the basis of the particular constellation of boundary strength and external and internal stimulation. However, in each instance the derivation was made first from the SPE determinants and then confirmed or modified in terms of the infant's actual behavior (as shown in the tables in Part Two).

The last step in completing the adaptation syndrome is to determine certain characteristics of adaptation and developmental status for each infant. This was done by assessing each child's behavior in terms of five criteria that could be applied in the same manner to each one. They are very similar to the central points of any clinical and developmental assessment of a child less than one year of age: (1) developmental status (judged by means of developmental tests); (2) the adequacy of vegetative functioning (including sleep, feeding, gastric functioning, respiration, circulation, and the like); (3) excitability, which refers to the degree to which the infant is inclined to show motoric and autonomic signs of behavioral arousal [8]; (4) irritability, which was used in the everyday meaning of the term as applied to infants, referring primarily to the frequency with which excitation becomes strong enough to disrupt a comfortable state of equilibrium, and secondarily to the intensity of such discomfort; (5) alertness and pleasure in functioning (chiefly the self-generated mastery behaviors and the readiness to derive pleasure and animation from appropriate types of stimulation). This last aspect includes, but is not limited to, such familiar variables as "zest," a sense of competence, mastery, and the capacity to show appropriate ranges of affect.

These adaptive and developmental characteristics refer to some key aspects of behavior and summarize and classify where each child stands in respect to some universal components of infant adaptation. Assessment by these criteria tells little or nothing about the highly variable individual features of developmental and behavioral style. For instance, two 7-month-old infants may, to an equal degree, have reached a point in their development where they can communicate with the mother by sign or word. Yet one of these infants employs his communicatory capacities primarily in situations of conflict with the mother (when she intervenes to prevent the baby from executing behavior that corresponds to an impulse of his own), while the other infant uses his communicatory skills chiefly in situations of playful collaboration with the mother (when he indicates a wish for help in executing a difficult action he wants to perform, and when the mother incites him to pleasurable activity, as by engaging him in the game of "pat-a-cake"). The individual adaptation syndromes include a descripitve account of additional characteristic features of behavior and of adaptation. However, those qualitative aspects could not be assessed by means of formal ratings. They are appended to each adaptation syndrome in a discussion that goes beyond the explication of the formal SPE and formal rating of developmental outcome.

In the *Supplementary Material* to this chapter we provide the general definition for each structural attribute, as well as the operational definitions that specify the application of each general definition to our data. We enumerate the particular behaviors in particular situational contexts that were preselected for the determination of each structural attribute. We also list the particular behaviors and environmental circumstances (as learned through observation and the mothers' reports) that were preselected to correspond to various ratings describing conditions that prevailed in each infant's environment.

To each of these groups of definitions and criteria we have added a

[8] It is similar to but not identical with the stable pattern of experience referred to as "strong bodily arousal." The latter assesses the frequency with which peak excitation is reached for any reason, but excitability refers to the child's tendency to respond with autonomic and motoric signs of arousal, not necessarily to a high degree, nor in response to intense stimulation.

discussion section, which describes the process by which we arrived at a rating of each variable for each child, and discusses briefly the limitations of available criteria, as well as the logical relationship among the different types of rating.

For those readers who are especially interested in the development of methods adapted to the use of primary data consisting of direct and unstructured observation, the *Supplementary Material* section for this chapter is of primary importance.[9]

The assessment of several structural properties of the infant organism (and of selected dynamic variables) was undertaken not only for descriptive purposes but also to establish whether or not structural variables are related to one another, to dynamic variables, or to developmental outcome. The demonstration of such relationships is meaningful *only if the factual data that serve as the basis for one of the assessment ratings are entirely independent of the data employed in arriving at any of the other ratings.* This elementary requirement poses no difficulty for those ratings coordinated to the absence, presence, and relative frequency of certain behaviors or certain events. All the ratings dealing with conspicuous components of the child's environment are of this nature, as are the ratings of developmental outcome. However, the ratings of reaction tendencies that characterize each infant are based on inferences drawn from behavior observed under particular conditions of stimulation. The assessments of the strength of the outer boundary, the strength of the inner boundary, and the intensity of stimulation from within all are based on inferences of this nature.

The quasi-topological definitions of boundary strength on which these assessments are based imply a reciprocal relationship between the intensity of behavioral response, the intensity of stimulation, and the strength of the relevant boundary. The formal structure of this relationship is like that of an algebraic equation, in that knowledge of any two of these values makes it possible to derive the third. For example, if an infant screams at a very slight pinprick, it can be said that the boundary between the motoric-perceptual region and the environment (as mediated by pain perception) was weak. If an infant whose boundary (for pain perception) is known to be strong screams at a pinprick, it may be inferred that the painful stimulus must have been intense. And if a slight pinprick is given to an infant whose outer boundary is known to be fairly strong, it can be predicted that the behavioral response will be slight.

Elaborate procedures were devised in order to make certain that each assessment was based on portions of the data that were altogether different from the data employed in rating any of the other variables, by *deciding in advance* which behaviors and which circumstances would, by definition, be applied in the assessment of each variable.

[9] The chapters on the individual adaptation syndromes require at least occasional reference to the listing of criteria.

The *Supplementary Material* lists for each variable that enters the SPE determinants, first, the *general definition* borrowed from topological psychology; second, one or several *operational definitions* in terms of our particular data; and third, the *situational contexts* and the *specific behaviors* to which the operational definitions were applied. Thus, when the reader encounters a rating on any of these variables, he can determine from this listing what behaviors must have occurred, and under which conditions, in order to have led to the particular rating.

SUPPLEMENTARY MATERIAL TO CHAPTER 9

Rating Structural Attributes of the Infant Organism: Definitions and Criteria

I. **Strength of the outer boundary** (between the motoric-perceptual region and the environment)

General definition: The smaller the intensity of external stimulation required to produce changes in the motoric-perceptual region, the weaker the outer boundary. This definition applies to the strength of the outer boundary as a whole, as well as to the modality sectors.

Operational definition 1: The outer boundary is the weaker, the more the infant makes overt response to external stimulation of low intensity. The critical issue, in determinations based on definition 1, is not the magnitude of the response, but the fact that there is response to minimal stimulation.

Specific behavioral criteria—entire outer boundary

Criterion situations: Soothing, distraction, dressing, diapering and similar manipulations and social stimulations.

Weak outer boundary: (a) Slight soothing measures are typically effective. (b) While attention and behavior are focused in one direction (play with a toy, crying, thumbsucking, etc.), the infant typically responds to even slight distraction (sounds, movements in the visual field, etc.). (c) During feeding the infant remains alert and responsive to the environment. (d) Routine manipulations, even when performed gently and while the infant is content, typically affect his state and produce clear-cut behavior alterations. (e) The infant is often or always overtly responsive to even slight social stimulation.

Strong outer boundary: (a) Soothing must be energetic and prolonged to be effective or it is of no avail. (b) While attention and behavior are focused in one direction, visual, auditory, tactile, or other stimulation is behaviorally ignored unless such distraction is of considerable intensity. (c) During feeding the infant appears to be oblivious to the surroundings. (d) Routine manipulations do not ordinarily affect the infant's state and do not lead to overt behavior alterations. (e) The infant is responsive to social stimulation only if it is of at least moderate intensity.

Operational definition 2: The outer boundary is the weaker, the more the magnitude of response is proportionate to the magnitude of stimulation. This applies to the modality sectors as well.

Specific behavioral criteria—entire outer boundary

Criterion situations: The same as for operational definition 1.

Weak outer boundary: (a) In any of the criterion situations[1] the infant typically responds slightly to minimal external stimulation, moderately to moderate stimulation, and very strongly only to intense stimulation. (b) Intense external stimulation (prolonged forceful manipulation, vigorous play, loud sounds, etc.) typically leads to disruptive excitation and distress.

Strong outer boundary: (a) In any of the criterion situations the infant's response does not regularly vary as a function of the magnitude of stimulation (*i.e.,* behavioral response tends to have an all-or-none quality, or it varies as a function of body state). (b) Even strong external stimulation is tolerated, in that neither disruption of behavior organization nor distress occurs in response.

II. Strength of the outer boundary in the visual, auditory, tactile, and kinesthetic sectors

General definition and *operational definitions* as for I.

Specific behavioral criteria—visual sector of outer boundary

Criterion situations: Variable, all behavior while awake, alert and not massively aroused.

Weak outer boundary: (a) Visual stimuli of low intensity regularly elicit overt response (for instance, attentiveness to small details such as neutrally colored design on cloth, tiny specks on bedding, cigarette smoke at a distance, or the play of shadows on the floor). (b) Discriminatory behavior towards objects occurs on a purely visual basis (for instance, a consistent preference or aversion for the color red, or towards highly reflective surfaces such as the mirror, the metal cup, and the spoon used in testing). (c) Few of the visual spectacles that occur in the infant's perceptual range are behaviorally ignored. (A comparison of the number of visually perceptible events that occurred with the number to which there was overt response was used to rate this aspect of behavior.) (d) Intense or sudden visual stimuli regularly evoke strong excitation or distress (for instance, sharp startles, crying, or a prolonged arrest of ongoing activity in response to photographic lights, turning on of ceiling light in dark room, direct exposure to sunlight, or prolonged exposure to brightly colored mobile). (e) The visual component of social stimulation plays a decisive role in de-

[1] Definitions for relatively gentle or intense stimulation are provided in Part Two.

termining the occurrence and magnitude of social response (for instance, social response invariably occurs to approaches that involve sight of the partner's face, but it is irregular or absent when voice or touch are the chief approach modalities; or the infant can readily be made to smile, laugh and vocalize by purely visual means, as when mother silently mouths words from a distance, holds out a noiseless toy for the infant's inspection, or waves her hands in mid-air from a distance).

Strong outer boundary: (a) Visual stimuli of low intensity are behaviorally ignored on many occasions. (b) Discrimination among objects on a visual basis does not occur. (c) Comparatively few of the visual spectacles that occur within the infant's perceptual range evoke overt response. (d) Intense or sudden visual stimuli evoke small or moderate excitation and never lead to distress. (e) The visual component of social stimulation is relatively unimportant in determining the occurrence or magnitude of social response.

Specific behavioral criteria—auditory sector of outer boundary

Criterion situations: As for visual sector.

Weak outer boundary: (a) Small sounds nearly always elicit specific response (usually a brief disruption of ongoing activity, or blinking). (b) Moderately loud and/or sudden sounds, as well as very loud noise, typically evoke strong responses that may express displeasure, pleasure, or affectively neutral excitement. (c) Different voices are behaviorally discriminated while the speaker is out of sight. (d) The auditory component of social stimulation plays a decisive role in determining the occurrence and magnitude of social response (for instance, the infant makes full social response only when voice is added to sight of mother's face, or soothing is effective only when humming or singing accompanies rocking and patting).

Strong outer boundary: (a) Small sounds are behaviorally ignored unless they occur suddenly against a background of complete quiet. (b) Moderately loud or very loud sounds are usually attended, but evoke relatively slight response and do not elicit either distress or pleasure. (c) The infant's response to different human voices is not consistently different when the speaker is out of sight. (d) The auditory component of social stimulation does not consistently influence the occurrence or magnitude of the infant's response.

Specific behavioral criteria—tactile sector of outer boundary

Criterion situations: These include all direct contacts between the infant and his mother or another person, during which the baby is touched by the caretaker's hands, and by clothing, towels, utensils, and the like. In addition, the investigators made a point of lightly touching the baby while they remained out of sight and as part of playful interactions.

Weak outer boundary: (a) Even very slight and brief touch elicits some overt response (such as momentary frowning, transient smiling, or a brief arrest of activity). (b) Nearly all contacts between the infant's skin and an inanimate substance (other than background sensations of the sort associated with lying on a surface) elicit specific behavioral response. (c) Firm or prolonged touching of the infant (such as towelling after the bath, forceful rubbing of the back to elicit burping, or tickling and poking as a form of play) elicits massive behavioral response, typically accompanied by displeasure. (d) The tactile component of social stimulation plays a decisive role in determining the occurrence or magnitude of response.

Strong outer boundary: (a) Very slight tactile stimulation is not responded to overtly. (b) Of the total number of tactile events that occurred, a comparatively small proportion led to overt response. (c) Even firm or prolonged touch evokes little or no specific response. (d) The tactile component of social stimulation does not consistently influence the occurrence or magnitude of response.

Specific behavioral criteria—kinesthetic sector of outer boundary

Criterion situations: Primarily the occasions when mothers used rocking, swaying and bouncing in soothing infants or as part of social play. Also occasions when infants were moved about while placed in perambulators, swings and similar devices. Lastly, the stabilimeter has a mobile surface, and response to this variety of passive motion was noted.

Weak outer boundary: (a) Being rocked, swayed, or bounced is a *necessary* component of effective soothing. (b) Being swayed, bounced, or rocked while content causes marked pleasure or else regularly leads to overt distress.

Strong outer boundary: (a) The effectiveness of soothing does not depend upon whether passive motion is induced. (b) Being bounced, rocked, or swayed while content is no more pleasurable to the infant than other modes of social play. Also, these same varieties of kinesthetic stimulation do not lead to distress.

III. **Strength of the inner boundary** (between the inner psychological region and the motoric-perceptual region)

General definition: The smaller the internal stimulation required to evoke changes in the motoric-perceptual region, the weaker the inner boundary.

Operational definition 1: When behavioral arousals that occur in *the absence of external stimulation* range from minimal degrees through moderate and fairly strong behavior activations, the inner boundary is weak. Conversely, when behavioral arousals in *the absence of external stimulation* are limited to at least moderately strong behavior activations alternating with periods of quiescence, the inner boundary is strong.

Operational definition 1 is derived from the general definition, but the intervening steps may not be self-evident. It is assumed that behavior activations that occur in the absence of external stimulation are due to stimulation arising from within the body. If slight as well as noticeably stronger behavior alterations are observed at such times, this means—in topological terms—that slight inner stimuli are capable of penetrating the inner boundary and that the magnitude of behavior activations is a function of the intensity of stimulation from within. By the same token, if overt behavior changes due to internal stimulation are limited to at least moderately strong arousals, alternating with quiescent periods, this circumstance meets the "all-or-none" criterion that, by definition, is characteristic of strong boundaries.

It is important to note that the behavior characteristics specified in operational definition 1 are the *only* patterns that can serve to assess the strength of the inner boundary. For instance, if in the absence of external stimulation, behavior activations tended to be at least moderately strong, but quiescent intervals did not occur, such behavior could result from the presence of frequent and fairly intense stimulation from within whether the inner boundary was weak or strong. For another example, if an infant showed (in the absence of external stimulation) only periodic minor activations, an inference about the strength of the inner boundary could not be made. Intermittent minor behavioral arousals might occur if stimulation from within were intermittent and fairly intense, if the infant had a strong inner boundary. But the same behavior pattern would result if the inner boundary were weak, and intermittent stimulation from within were of low intensity. Thus, among all observed patterns of behavior activation in the absence of external stimulation, only two can serve to assess the strength of the inner boundary: a series of arousals that include minimal as well as greater activations (weak inner boundary); and the combination of only moderately strong or strong arousals with periods of quiescence (strong inner boundary).

Specific behavioral criteria—inner boundary

Criterion situations: During sleep, drowsiness, and spontaneous activity, all behavior activations (from slight muscle twitches to vocalizations and extensive motions) were classified as to whether or not they were responsive to an external stimulus that preceded or accompanied the behavior. (If during spontaneous activity the infant was attentive to any aspect of the environment, even when stimulation was only the usual perceptual background, his behavior was considered responsive to the environment.) For each infant, this left us with a number of behavior episodes (from as few as seven or eight to fifty or more) that could be ascribed to excitation from within the body.

Weak inner boundary: (a) During sleep, and while not responsive to the environment, the infant shows very minor movements, such as facial grimaces or fluttering of eyelids. He also shows somewhat larger activations, such as turning over, vocalizing, or squirming. (b) During spontaneous activity or drowsiness, and when behavior is not responsive to the environment, the infant shows very slight behavior alterations, such as head rotation, movements of fingers or toes only, or an isolated sucking motion. He also shows stronger activations, such as kicking, arm waving, squealing, thumbsucking, etc.

Strong inner boundary: (a) During sleep and while not responsive to environmental stimulation, the infant remains motionless and quiet for appreciable periods of time. Intermittently, he shows moderately strong behavior activations, such as turning over, vocalizing, or squirming. (b) During spontaneous activity or drowsiness, and while not responsive to the environment, the infant does *not* show very slight behavior activations, though marked behavior alterations and quiescent periods do occur.

Operational definition 2: The more gradual the behavior changes reflecting changes in physiological state, the weaker the inner boundary.

This definition also derives from the general one, in that it is assumed that such internal events as increasing hunger or fatigue involve a gradual change in somatic state. If overt behavior that accompanies such change reflects many degrees of excitation—that is, if behavior is different when the infant is mildly hungry, when hunger sensations increase in force, and when hunger reaches its peak—then small changes in the inner psychological region find ready and proportionate reflection in the motoric-perceptual region.

Criterion situations: Hunger, fatigue, awakening, and satiation during feeding.

Weak inner boundary: (a) When hungry, the infant typically shows a gradual transition from slight restlessness to mild discomfort, and finally to marked primitivization of behavior and possibly acute distress. (b) During fatigue the infant typically shows increasing drowsiness, increasing excitation and discomfort, or both in combination. These changes are slight at the onset and over a period of time reach behavioral expression in massive form. (c) At the beginning of feeding the infant accepts food with avidity and sucks or swallows rapidly. Then he accepts food with less eagerness, followed by a period during which satiation is shown by many pauses and slower food intake, until at last nipple or spoon is refused. (d) Upon awakening, the infant typically shows a period of drowsiness that diminishes until he becomes wakeful and alert.

Strong inner boundary: (a) The infant typically shows an abrupt transition from well-coordinated behavior and contentment to his maximal signs of hunger distress. (b) The change from complete alertness to marked fatigue (or to sleep) is typically sudden, involving few (or no) in-between states. (c) The infant accepts and consumes food at a fairly even rate until, all at once, the nipple or bottle is refused. (d) On awakening, the infant is almost at once fully alert and responsive.

Discussion

In the construction of the structural ratings, the strength of each boundary is judged on not one or two of the behavioral criteria enumerated, but on all criteria together. To reduce the probability that the rater would anticipate, on the basis of a child's behavior to one criterion, what his response to other behavior criteria was likely to be (the so-called halo effect), the procedure in arriving at these ratings was deliberately fragmented. A single behavioral criterion was assessed for all subjects in one age group; thereafter, the same procedure was followed for the next behavioral criterion, until the ratings were completed for every relevant aspect of behavior and for all subjects. In determining for one infant a rating on a single criterion (such as the proportion of activations during sleep that were unrelated to external stimuli, or whether or not he tended to respond to minimal stimulation), it was impossible to remember the behavior characteristics of the same infant to other criteria. We had to complete these criterion ratings before learning whether or not the widely different behavior tendencies would converge in such a way as to allow an assessment of boundary strength. Had it been found that the same infant typically met some of the criteria for a strong inner boundary, and equally typically met some of the criteria for a week inner boundary, the entire framework of structural assessments would have proved useless. Such a failure would have occurred if the structural variables had been inappropriate, or if logical errors had been made in the derivation of the operational definitions from the broader Lewinian definition.

In fact, different behavioral criteria relevant to a single structural variable did not yield conflicting assessments. As the more detailed material will show, what did happen was that among the diverse behavioral criteria relevant to the assessment of a single variable, a number pointed in the same direction, and a number were inconclusive or inapplicable. For example, an infant whose behavior during spontaneous activity included both small and large behavior activations unrelated to external causes, and who thus conformed to one of the operational criteria that define a weak inner boundary, was *never* found to show typical abrupt transitions from a contented state to severe hunger, or from alert wakefulness to marked fatigue—which would have met a criterion for the presence of a strong inner boundary.[2] However, an infant might demonstrate behavior characteristics defined as reflecting a weak inner boundary during spontaneous activity, but not during sleep (for instance, if he slept very quietly throughout). And again, while some of an infant's transitional behaviors were very gradual, conforming to the weak inner boundary syndrome, other transitional behaviors in the same infant might be only moderately gradual, neither confirming nor running counter to the assumption of a weak inner boundary.

If the structural concept of boundary strength as defined were intrinsically unrelated to actual behavior organization, then an assessment of boundary strength based upon half the number of available criteria should have no predictive power for the infant's behavior with respect to the remaining criteria. But after all the ratings had been made, it was found that knowing whether an infant's transitional behavior during need states was gradual or decidedly abrupt *did* permit a number of inferences about his behavior during spontaneous activity or during sleep. These inferences were negative as often as they were positive. For instance, if an infant's transitional behavior was typically abrupt, the same infant *never showed* both small and large behavior activations during spontaneous activity in the absence of external stimulation.

In our judgment, the fact that some of the central behavior regulations of individual infants are encompassed in a consistent fashion by means of these structural determinations means that the diverse behavior aspects coordinated to a single structural concept must have *a common set of determinants*. Whether the spatial language of topology provides the best conceptualization of these

[2] The one exception, which occurred in a small number of subjects, was that a drowsy interval after awakening could occur in infants who, by all other criteria, behaved to conform to the definitions for the presence of a strong inner boundary. So far as we could ascertain, drowsiness after awakening may be absent or present in the same infant, depending upon the depth of sleep. This was not true of fatigue nor of any other transitional behavior associated with changes in need states.

determinants remains an open question. The same or similar groups of behavioral criteria might be coordinated to a different set of concepts. For instance, one might prefer to think of thresholds rather than of boundaries, or one might choose to define operationally a subdivision of the organism in terms of the various rudimentary ego functions. *The inherent order and self-consistency of behavior is not altered by the name one assigns to hypothetical constructs, nor by the theoretical model that dictates the selection of key concepts.* The relative effectiveness of the topological constructs in ordering some of the phenomena of infant behavior shows only that these particular definitions have a degree of face validity and therefore offer an opportunity to investigate systematic relationships between different facets of infant behavior and between aspects of life experience and their behavioral consequences.

Rating the Dynamic Variables Affecting the Infant Organism: Definitions and Criteria

I. Intensity of stimulation from within the body

General definition: The dynamic variables refer to the objective magnitude of stimulation [3] to which the infant is typically exposed, but a further word is in order about what is meant by "stimulation from within." We assume that waxing and waning bodily need states (hunger and fatigue) involve fluctuating changes in both the kind and the intensity of perceptible body feelings; that ongoing physiological processes present a constant flow of proprioceptive stimulation; and that localized bodily occurrences such as teething, skin rashes, and gastric disturbances deliver excitatory stimuli. A rating of the *relative* intensity of stimulation from within seeks to assess both the relative frequency with which the infant is subject to rousing stimulation on a somatic basis, and the relative intensity of such arousal.

Of all the ratings that constitute the SPE determinants, the intensity of stimulation from within is the most inferential. However, there is a demonstrable difference between infants who feel physiological discomfort frequently and those whose behavior suggests a pervasive sense of bodily well-being. There is also a demonstrable difference between infants who typically reach high peaks of excitation with hunger and/or fatigue, and infants whose behavior is much less altered by such need states. (In each instance, except teething or minor but demonstrable illness, the intensity of behavioral arousal in response to stimulation from within might be ascribed to either a weak inner boundary or a relatively great intensity of proprioceptive stimu-

[3] In this respect our use of vectorial signs is a radical departure from topological and vector psychology. Lewin defined a psychological force, or the degree of tension within a psychological system, entirely in terms of the magnitude of behavior alteration it evoked. In the Lewinian frame of reference an objectively slight force acting upon a weak boundary would be represented as equal to an objectively strong force acting upon a proportionately stronger boundary. Since our interest lies in determining the conditions under which objectively equal stimulating conditions exert unequal influence upon behavior, we decided to deal with somatic and external stimulation by describing its intensity in physical (not psychological) terms.

lation. However, for a variety of reasons we chose to assume that infants are in fact subject to different intensities of stimulation from within. The unequivocal criteria for a weak inner boundary proved altogether unrelated to our criteria for the intensity of stimulation. For this reason it is feasible to treat the latter as an independent variable.)

Operational definition 1: The greater the absolute level of excitation typically evoked by bodily need states, the greater the intensity of stimulation from within.

Specific behavioral criteria—intensity of stimulation from within

Criterion situations: Fatigue, hunger, and evacuation.

Low and high levels of excitation associated with bodily need states will not be described in terms of behavioral criteria because they were presented in great detail in Chapters 5 through 7.

Operational definition 2: The more frequently and/or the more intensely the infant displays discomfort or distress due to demonstrable physiological disturbance, the greater is the intensity of stimulation from within.

This rating was based on observed behavior and on the mother's report. It is not limited to any situational context. However, episodes of discomfort were allowed to influence this rating only when they were clearly related to physical causes. We list here the most common forms of physiological distress in our sample, and their most usual manifestations.

Gastric distress: Crying and fussing when not hungry, accompanied by visible tensing and distention of the abdomen, possibly by flatulence, often relieved by burping, spitting up, or evacuation. (Reported episodes of diarrhea or true vomiting in the infant's past were included, but children suffering from such illness at the time were not retained in the sample.)

Respiratory infection: Congested nasal passages, sneezing, coughing, and general appearance indicating the common cold. (Again, some members of the sample had suffered from infectious illness in the past, but none were ill at the time of the study.)

Skin irritations: Mild eczema, heat rashes, allergic skin reactions, and the like were included. The presence of skin reactions was allowed to influence the rating only if the infant's behavior indicated that the affected areas were markedly sensitive, or that the rash caused discomfort.

Teething discomfort: Irritability when it occurred in conjunction with one or several of the following signs: intense rubbing of gums, gums swollen and reddened, a tooth visibly in process of erupting. (Intense mouthing of hand or objects was at times associated with acute teething, but if it occurred in the absence of the above signs and in the absence of other manifest bodily distress it did not influence this rating.)

II. Environmental variables

The ratings of conspicuous and fairly stable aspects of the environment in which these babies lived at the time we knew them are very different from the ratings that assess attributes of the infant organism. The environmental ratings are a descriptive account of as many different aspects of the conditions to which each infant was exposed as could reliably be ascertained for each subject. They are not derived from a construct. Our assessment of the qualities and intensities of external stimulation was limited to certain recurrent and overt features of each child's environment. These formal ratings can do no more than reduce to schematic terms the infinitely varied and complex environmental settings in which these babies lived. Some of the more subtle aspects of each child's environment will be referred to in the discussion section of the adaptation syndromes.

Nine separate assessments were made of stable components of each child's environment. Four of these deal with aspects of maternal behavior of so general a nature that they affect nearly all aspects of each child's behavior. Four additional ratings describe the relative frequency with which each mother utilized the different sense modalities (vision, touch, sound, and passive motion) in her direct interactions with the baby. One rating provides a gross characterization of the general style and quality of each family's life in terms of how much excitation it tended to generate for the baby, ranging from a tranquil and shielded existence to a turbulent and rousing style of family life.

The simplest way of conveying the basis for these ratings is to descriptively define each variable, followed by a condensed summary of the kind of maternal behavior or the kind of environmental circumstance that we took to define the extreme positions on a scale ranging from "low" to "high."

GENERAL ATTRIBUTES OF MATERNAL BEHAVIOR

1. *The frequency of mother-child contacts:* The criteria are self-evident, in that information about each mother-infant couple was scrutinized in terms of how often in the course of a day each mother interacted directly with her baby. The nature of these contacts, or the reasons for them, were altogether disregarded.

2. *The intensity of maternal behavior in relation to the infant:* Here we assessed the forcefulness with which the mother generally approached her baby and dealt with him. At one extreme are mothers who are in general energetic and emphatic persons who speak, sing, and laugh loudly, who touch their babies forcefully, who play with them "roughly," and the like. Some mothers who were also intensely stimulating during contacts with their infants appeared robust and lacking in modulation, rather than volatile or energetic. Such mothers may sharply yank the baby's body while dressing or bathing him. They appear unaware of loud noises, bright lights, or gross changes in temperature, and make little effort to shield their babies from such sharply stimulating situations.

At the extreme of "low" intensity, one finds mothers who are soft-spoken, delicate in their movements, and in general inclined to function at a "low register." Equally low in intensity are some mothers who maintain a certain "distance." Play and other interactions are carried out with a minimum of attention and energy focused upon the baby. For example, one mother often read while feeding the baby in her arms. She held him comfortably, but the infant was not touched as much, and was not provided with as much visual and auditory stimulation as the same situation usually entails.

3. *The intrusiveness of mother's behavior in relation to the infant:* Mothers who tended to intervene or interfere with ongoing behavior on the infant's part were rated high in intrusiveness. For instance, those who frequently picked their babies up while the child was perfectly content (to groom him, to check on the diaper, etc.) were judged to be more intrusive than those who usually intervened only in response to the infant's behavioral signals. Mothers who often roused their babies from sleep (either to maintain a feeding schedule or for other purposes) are more intrusive than those who awake their babies only when it is unavoidable. Finally, mothers who attempt to teach their young infants by regularly removing the thumb from the mouth, or by persistent efforts at toilet training (below the age of 8 months) are more intrusive than mothers who freely allow thumbsucking and who tolerate soiled diapers.

4. *Maternal competence:* This refers to a qualitative aspect of behavior—the mother's skill in manipulating her baby. At one extreme one sees mothers who possess unfailing skill in holding and moving their infant, providing head or back support when this is needed, giving free reign to the infant's movement impulses or restraining them in a playful fashion. Similarly, mothers who rank high on the competence dimension show a beautiful economy of motion during diapering, dressing, bathing, and similar situations. Maternal competence, as we defined the term, also shows itself in the mother's ability to adapt to the infant's changing state. Highly competent mothers often spoon-feed their babies rapidly at first and more slowly as the baby becomes less eager; they alternate from rapid to slow movement, from vigorous speech to soft low reassuring sounds, from holding the baby closely to supporting him at a distance from their own body, all as a function of small changes in the baby's behavior.

At the other extreme, one finds mothers who hold and move their babies in obviously uncomfortable postures (for instance, allowing the head to dangle or being unnecessarily confining). We include here mothers whose babies slip from their hands during the bath, who must make many attempts before they manage to get an arm through a sleeve, who often insert a spoonful of food before the baby has swallowed the last, or who toward the end of feeding hold the bottle at such an angle that milk does not reach the nipple. Similarly, mothers low in competence by our definition include those who attempt vigorous play with a desperately fatigued infant and who, in general, fail to regulate their behavior in relation to the baby's state or to his reaction tendencies. One mother, for instance, persisted in making playful hissing noises close to the baby's ear, although she herself told us that this regularly made him cry. Her stated reason was that "babies like that—my other one did when he was small." Among our mothers, high competence was rarely seen with first babies. We think that it is a mode of functioning which some, but by no means all, mothers acquire in the course of experience as they have occasion to tend more than one infant.

FREQUENCY OF MATERNAL STIMULATION IN DIFFERENT SENSE MODALITIES

All mothers provide stimulation for their babies in all modalities, and most mother-baby interactions involve multiple modalities. However, scrutiny of *all* observed mother-infant contacts shows that the majority of mothers emphasize one or several modalities at the expense of others. The frequency of stimulation a mother provided in a given modality refers to a comparison of all mothers (whose babies were of comparable ages) in terms of how often they employed a given modality in approaching their infant and in responding to him.

The procedure was to review each mother-child interaction for all cases in a given age group, noting which and how many interaction episodes involved a particular modality. We thus determined not only how often mother provided sound while in contact with her baby, but also how often she failed to employ the auditory modality, and the particular situations in which sound did not play a role. Lastly, we recorded how often one modality, such as sound, was the only one used during such a contact. Once this chore had been performed for each mother in the entire age group, and for each modality, it was possible to rank and rate mothers on this aspect of their behavior.

In addition, each record was searched for the mother's report about the use of toys, about the child's location during waking hours (playpen, crib in own room, someone's lap), about what was done when the baby became fretful, and the like. These reports were evaluated against what was observed directly. If the mother's report was congruent with what we had seen directly, it was allowed to influence the ratings. (For instance, if a mother said that when the baby fusses mildly she is apt to rock the bed or buggy in which he lies, and if we also saw her use this technique, the information affected our rating of the frequency with which passive motion was typically evoked by the mother.) Below are given some sample behavior tendencies on the mother's part, descriptive of the different use mothers made of the different modalities.

5. *Frequency of stimulation in the visual modality:* At the high extreme there were mothers who never addressed themselves to the baby without vision playing a role. That is, they never touched or lifted the baby except in face-to-face position, they never spoke to the baby while not in his sight, etc. Mothers who rated high on this variable also tended to make vision the primary or sole agent of contact. For instance, they smiled at the baby from some distance or held out an interesting object for him to look at, without speaking to him and without touching him. At the low end of the continuum were mothers who frequently approached the baby while their face (if not their hands and arms) were out of sight, and mothers who never or rarely amused or distracted their babies by visual means. We included mothers who habitually left the awake and alert baby in surroundings or positions that provided scant opportunity for visual exploration; for instance, prone in a crib or on a bassinet, with no toys in the vicinity.

6. *Frequency of stimulation in the auditory sphere:* Mothers who were rated "high" included those who seldom or never turned toward the baby without speaking or vocalizing in other ways such as humming and making clucking or blowing noises. Mothers who frequently used mechanical noises such as rattles, music boxes or turning on the radio, and mothers who were given to speaking to the baby from a distance while out of sight, also rated "high." The corresponding behaviors of mothers rated "low" in this continuum are very nearly the inverse of what has already been described. In other words, they are mothers who during many contacts with their babies did not use their

voice, and who seldom or never attracted the baby's attention by means of noise effects.

7. *Frequency of stimulation in the tactile modality:* Touch necessarily plays a large role in many mother-baby contacts. Yet the variability in how much these mothers tended to touch their baby was very great indeed. At the high end of the continuum were mothers who elaborated and prolonged the tactile component of routine procedures, by stroking, rubbing, patting, or lightly fingering the baby's body. Some mothers relied heavily on touch in play, as in tickling and poking the baby, blowing on him and kissing him, or simply holding and perhaps rubbing his hand or another body part prolongedly. At the other extreme were the mothers who never touched their babies unnecessarily. Not only did they refrain from touching the baby in the course of play, but they fed the baby as he lay supine, they were adept at dressing him quickly and with a minimum of touch, and they tended to hold the baby at some distance from their own body.

8. *The frequency of stimulation in the kinesthetic modality:* Mothers differed widely in the degree to which they tended to rock, bounce, roll or swing their babies, and in their tendency to place the baby into contrivances that mediate passive motion—buggy, stroller or crib, jumper-swing, or walker.

9. *The level of stimulation provided in the home:* The last of the dynamic variables was a very general assessment of family style for the typical degree of sound, movement, variability and general animation it provided for the baby. The rating was based on what was observed during the home visit together with the mother's descriptions of home life. At one extreme were subjects who were only children; in whose homes visitors were rare and were discouraged from approaching the baby; whose mothers maintained a regular schedule and seldom took the baby out of the home. At the other extreme were subjects who had several preschool age siblings; whose families lived in cramped quarters, with television turned on most of the day; where a large number of people were in and out of the home and were permitted to play with the baby or to help care for him; and the baby went along on most outings, including trips to drive-in theatres, church bazaars, Fourth of July parades, and shopping at the supermarket.

TEN

STRUCTURAL COMPONENTS OF THE SPE

In this chapter we shall report on the distribution of structural characteristics in our sample, and examine the relationship of the structural ratings with age range and activity level. The relationship between structural ratings and other determinants of the SPE will be reported also, as will the relationship between structural ratings and some aspects of developmental outcome.[1]

Our primary hypothesis is that a clear-cut relationship exists between the SPE and developmental outcome, but not between the latter and the separate *determinants* of the SPE. To substantiate this idea, we are under the peculiar necessity of demonstrating the *absence* of a relationship between many of our variables before presenting the positive findings.

Because there are about a hundred different possible relationships (each of six structural variables related to ten dynamic ones, to three developmental outcome ratings, and to age level and activity level), most of the numerical data have been relegated to *Supplementary Material* for this chapter. The text is limited to a summary of overall results and to a discussion of such positive trends and relationships as did emerge from the data.

Each infant received a rating on six different structural variables: the strength of the outer boundary (between the motoric-perceptual region and the environment); the strength of the inner boundary (between the motoric-perceptual region and the inner psychological region); and the strength of sections of the outer boundary corresponding to the visual, auditory, tactile, and kinesthetic sense modalities. All of the ratings were made on a three-point scale, ranging from "weak" to "strong." A rating of "strong" always means that relatively strong force or stimulation is required to penetrate the boundary and to elicit overt response. A rating of "weak" always means

[1] In this portion of data analysis, two of the outcome variables—"adequacy of vegetative functioning" and "excitability"—are omitted. Both of these refer to somatic functioning. For reasons fully discussed in Chapter 12, it was thought best to limit scrutiny of structural variables as they may affect developmental outcome to the three adaptation indices that do not manifest themselves in the form of somatic characteristics. As it happens, these three indices are a far more direct product of developmental progress and of adaptation than the quasi-somatic indices that were here omitted.

that the child typically responds to slight stimulation, and that overt response increases in magnitude proportionate to the intensity of stimulation.[2]

Structural Configurations

For the outer boundary as a whole and the inner boundary, twelve structural types or constellations are theoretically possible. They range from the most labile and highly reactive pattern (weak outer and weak inner boundaries) to a pattern of maximal imperturbability (strong outer and strong inner boundaries). Of the twelve possible structural constellations, ten are represented in our sample (see Table 10.1). As also shown in Table

Table 10.1—Structural Type Related to Activity Level and Age

STRUCTURAL TYPE BOUNDARY STRENGTH		Number of Subjects: ACTIVITY GROUP		Number of Subjects: AGE GROUP			TOTAL NUMBER SUBJECTS
Outer	Inner	Ac	In	One	Two	Three	
Strong	Strong	0	1	1	0	0	1
Strong	Medium	2	0	1	1	0	2
Strong	Weak	0	2	1	0	1	2
Medium	Strong	3	2	2	0	3	5
Medium	Medium	6	6	4	5	3	12
Medium	Weak	1	1	0	1	1	2
Weak	Strong	0	0	0	0	0	0
Weak	Medium	0	3	1	0	2	3
Weak	Weak	2	0	2	0	0	2
Variable	Strong	1	0	0	1	0	1
Variable	Medium	1	1	0	0	2	2
Variable	Weak	0	0	0	0	0	0
Totals		16	16	12	8	12	32

10.1, structural types occur in the same distribution among active and inactive infants, and also among infants in different age ranges. One important exception must be noted, however: extreme structural types were seen only among the youngest babies. Two active babies (one 4 and one 8 weeks old) showed the highest degree of lability (both boundaries weak). The single instance of minimal reactivity (both boundaries strong) occurred in a 4-week-old inactive baby.

Boundary ratings for the sample as a whole show a normal distribution (Fig. 10.1). However, differences emerge when the distribution of boundary ratings is plotted separately for each age group (see Fig. 10.2). The greatest proportion of extreme ratings occurred in infants between 4 and 12 weeks of age, whereas Group Two (16 and 20 weeks) and Group Three (24 to 32 weeks) showed much the same distribution.

[2] In Chapter 9, all variables are fully described, and all rating criteria are enumerated in the *Supplementary Material* section.

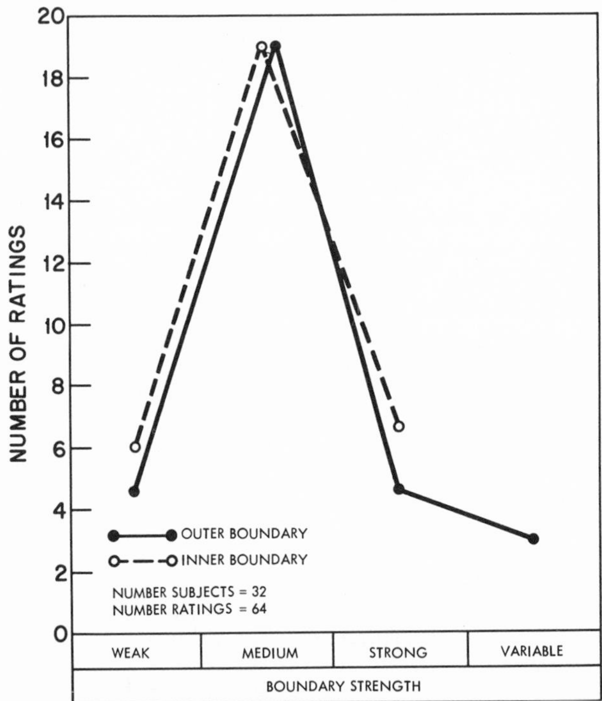

FIGURE 10.1. STRENGTH OF THE OUTER AND INNER BOUNDARIES: DISTRIBUTION OF RATINGS.

Turning to the ratings for the strength of the outer boundary in different sense modalities, we find that they bear no relationship to activity level (Table 10.3), but do seem to be influenced by age level (Table 10.2). It was again the youngest babies who contributed the largest share of extreme ratings (Fig. 10.3 and Fig. 10.4). Fig. 10.5 shows that changes with age in the visual and the kinesthetic modalities are similar to those noted for

Table 10.2—Ratings of Sectors of the Outer Boundary in Four Modalities, by Age Groups

	Rating of Boundary Strength									
	GROUP ONE			GROUP TWO			GROUP THREE			Total
Modality	Strong	Medium	Weak	Strong	Medium	Weak	Strong	Medium	Weak	N Ratings
Vision	5	3	4	3	5	0	2	8	2	32
Touch	7	1	4	3	2	3	5	6	1	32
Sound	6	0	6	1	5	2	1	5	6	32
Kinesthetic	–	–	–	1	1	3	2	7	1	15
Totals	18	4	14	8	13	8	10	26	10	111

Note: The boundary for the kinesthetic sector was not assessed in Group One. In Groups Two and Three it was assessed as "variable" in five subjects; these ratings are omitted.

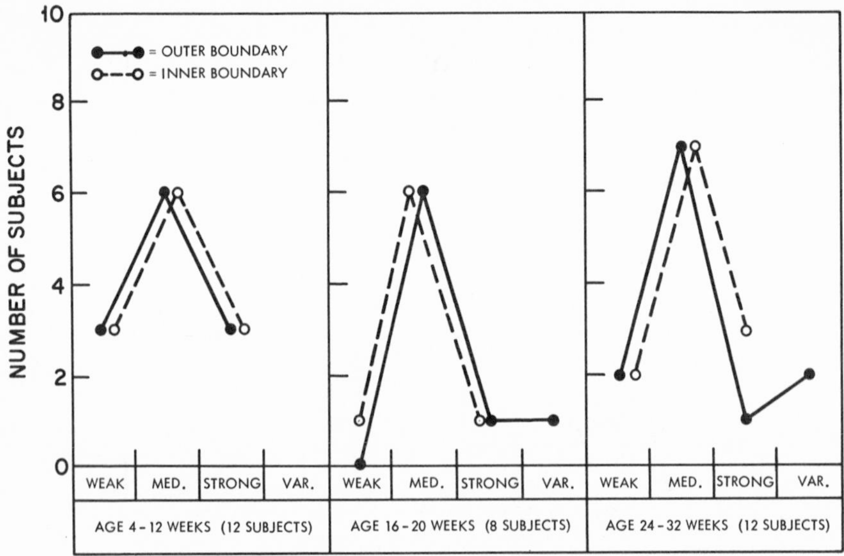

FIGURE 10.2. STRENGTH OF THE OUTER AND INNER BOUNDARIES: RATINGS FOR AGE GROUPS.

Table 10.3—Ratings of Modality Sectors of the Outer Boundary as Related to Activity Level

	Boundary Ratings								
	WEAK		*MEDIUM*		*STRONG*		*VARIABLE*		*Total*
Modality	*Ac*	*In*	*Ac*	*In*	*Ac*	*In*	*Ac*	*In*	*N Ratings*
Vision	3	3	7	9	6	4	0	0	32
Touch	5	3	3	6	8	7	0	0	32
Sound	7	7	5	5	4	4	0	0	32
Passive Motion	2	2	4	4	1	2	3	2	20
Totals	17	15	19	24	19	17	3	2	116

Note: The kinesthetic sector was not rated for subjects in Group One (4–12 weeks).

the outer and inner boundaries as a whole—that is, from an all-or-none tendency among the younger babies to an approximately normal distribution in the oldest group of infants. However, a different developmental trend is noted for the modalities of touch and sound. After the age of 16 weeks, reactivity to tactile stimulation showed a relative decrease, but the proportion of infants who proved highly reactive to sound (boundary *weak*) increased.

Our sample is too small to know whether the general lessening in the frequency of extreme reactions, the increase in strong reactivity to sound, and the decrease in strong reactivity to touch are found generally among infants between the first and the eighth months of life. However, these

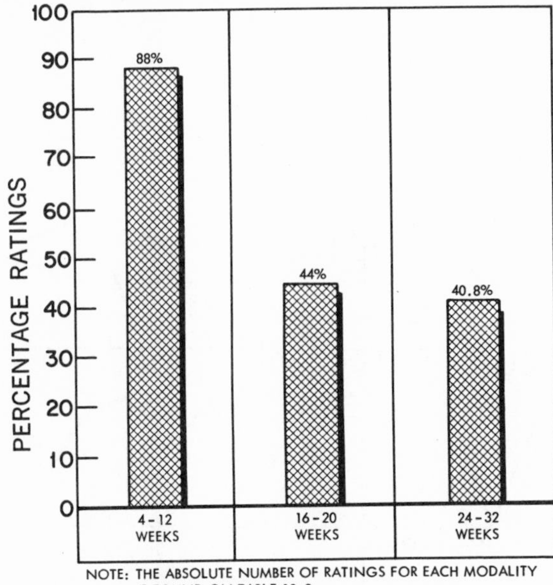

FIGURE 10.3. EXTREME RATINGS (WEAK PLUS STRONG) FOR SENSORY MODALITIES: PERCENTAGE RATINGS FOR AGE GROUPS.

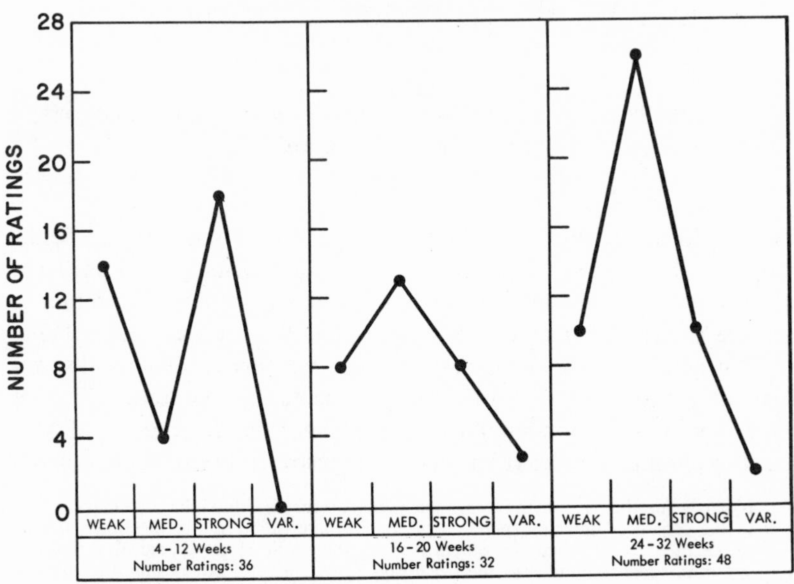

FIGURE 10.4. BOUNDARY STRENGTH FOR MODALITY SECTORS: RATINGS FOR AGE GROUPS.

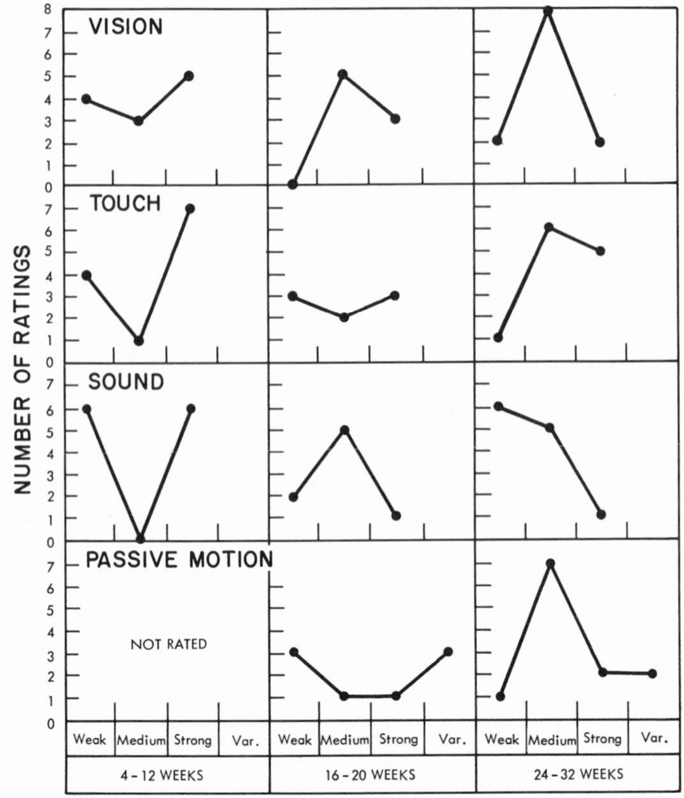

FIGURE 10.5. STRENGTH OF BOUNDARY OF FOUR MODALITY SECTORS: RATINGS FOR AGE GROUPS.

limited results are in good accord with established findings in the field of developmental neurology and of developmental physiology. In particular, the tendency of the immature organism to be either maximally or minimally responsive is well documented (Smith, 1955). We are inclined to believe that the structural ratings do assess intrinsic reaction tendencies that may well be subject to change as a function of increasing maturation.[3]

One more observation should be made about the distribution of structural ratings in this sample. It has been demonstrated in previous research [4]

[3] It is partly for this reason that we have been careful to define characteristics that are intrinsic to the organism quite independent of their origin. Some of the reaction tendencies may be the result of genetic loading, others may be the result of physiological variation on different grounds, some may alter as the organisms grow, and still others may be the consequence of alterations within the organism that came about as the result of experience and of environmental influence in the past.

[4] Lipton, Steinschneider, and Richmond (1961); Bridger (1962); Bridger, Birns, and Blank (1965); Escalona and Heider (1959); Birns, Blank, Bridger, and Escalona (1965).

that neonates and young infants differ from one another in terms of a *general* tendency to respond with characteristic intensity to external stimulation. For instance, Bridger, Birns, *et al.* (1965) found that neonates who respond strongly to auditory stimuli are also likely to respond strongly to other modes of stimulation, such as an air puff or a cold disk applied to the skin. Our ratings of the outer boundary as a whole reflect this general reaction tendency. Nevertheless, considerable variability appears to exist in the reactivity of a single infant to stimulation in different sense modalities. This may appear to be an inconsistency, since the outer boundary as a whole is, of course, composed of the same sectors that were shown to be variable in most subjects. Table 10.4 shows for each subject all of the

Table 10.4—Ratings of Whole Outer Boundary, of Sectors of Outer Boundary, and of Inner Boundary, for All Subjects

	WHOLE OUTER BOUNDARY		VISION		TOUCH		SOUND		KINESTHETIC		WHOLE INNER BOUNDARY	
Pair	Ac	In	Ac	In	Ac	In	Ac	In	Ac	In	Ac	In
I	W	St	W	St	W	St	W	W	—	—	W	W
II	St	M	St	St	W	M	St	St	—	—	M	M
III	M	St	St	M	St	St	W	St	—	—	M	St
IV	W	M	W	M	W	St	W	W	—	—	W	M
V	M	W	St	W	St	W	St	W	—	—	M	M
VI	M	M	M	W	St	St	St	St	—	—	St	St
VII	M	M	M	M	W	St	W	St	M	W	M	M
VIII	M	M	St	M	W	M	M	M	Va	W	M	M
IX	Va	M	M	M	St	W	W	M	W	St	St	W
X	St	M	St	St	St	M	M	M	Va	Va	M	M
XI	M	St	M	M	St	M	M	M	St	St	M	W
XII	M	Va	W	St	St	M	M	W	M	M	St	M
XIII	M	W	St	W	M	W	M	W	M	Va	M	M
XIV	M	M	M	M	M	St	W	M	M	M	W	M
XV	Va	M	M	M	St	M	W	W	Va	M	M	St
XVI	M	W	M	M	M	St	St	W	W	M	St	M

Symbols: W = weak; M = medium; St = strong; Va = variable or undetermined.
Note: Boundary strength for the Kinesthetic sector was not assessed for Group One (4–12 weeks).

structural ratings he received. When one compares the ratings of the outer boundary and of sectors of the outer boundary for each infant, it becomes apparent that the majority of infants show a characteristic level of reactivity in *most* modalities. Infants whose outer boundary was assessed as weak also rated weak in most of the boundary sectors, and the same consistency was noted when the outer boundary was assessed as strong. But when the outer boundary was asssessed as medium, two patterns appeared. Some of these babies also received medium ratings for most modality sectors. But in other infants, the ratings for different modality sectors ranged from weak to strong, or were about equally divided between weak and medium or between medium and strong. In this last mentioned group, an overall medium level of reactivity to external stimulation is due to the fact that most of the criterion situations involve several modalities. Marked reactivity to some components, of the stimulating situation, combined with low reactivity to others will often lead to moderate degrees of behavioral arousal. In most of our subjects a central tendency did exist, which disposed the infant to respond at a characteristic level of intensity to most varieties of external stimulation.

However, Table 10.4 also shows that in one modality many of these babies departed from their most typical level of reactivity. For example, baby Ac II had a strong outer boundary and ratings of "strong" for the visual and the auditory sectors of the outer boundary. He was exceedingly reactive to touch, however, and this sector of the boundary was rated as "weak." In many of our subjects, the responsiveness to stimulation in one of the modalities was either markedly greater or markedly smaller than in the remaining ones. The observation of differential reactivity in various modalities is therefore consistent with the observation that each infant (or rather all but three members of our sample whose outer boundaries were assessed as variable) responds to external stimulation at a typical level of intensity.[5]

It is interesting to note in passing that the tendency to respond in a unitary fashion was most pronounced among the youngest infants. The older babies showed comparatively greater variability in different sense modalities. Of the sixteen infants between 4 and 16 weeks of age, thirteen, or 81.2 per cent, received the same rating for all but one modality as they received for the entire outer boundary. Of the sixteen babies between 20 and 32 weeks of age, only seven, or 43.4 per cent, showed the same pattern. The older babies thus tended to be more variable in their typical response to stimulation in different modalities, yet they also showed a larger proportion of medium ratings for both the sector ratings and ratings of the outer boundary as a whole. Increasing differentiation and greater modulation of behavior are generally characteristic of progressive developmental change, and these findings are in good accord with the tendency of the youngest infants to respond in an all-or-none fashion.

Structural Variables, Dynamic Variables, and Developmental Outcome

Tables 10.5 through 10.9 (*Supplementary Material*) show for each structural rating the distribution of all other ratings that are also SPE determinants. Our sample is too small to demonstrate significant associations

[5] Some discrepancy between the overall level of reactivity (entire outer boundary) and reactivity in the four separate modalities is undoubtedly attributable to the fact that only some of the modalities could be assessed. For instance, thermal and olfactory components of stimulation may well have played a role in many of the criterion situations for the assessment of the outer boundary as a whole.

if they exist; however, the raw data in the form of scattergrams *can* demonstrate both the absence of correspondence and the trends that do suggest a positive relationship among some of these variables.

By and large we found that the manner in which mothers behaved with their babies was minimally influenced by those reaction tendencies of the baby assessed by the structural ratings. Specifically:

(1) None of the environmental ratings was at all related to the strength of the inner boundary (Table 10.5).

(2) Even the infant's tendency to react strongly or minimally to external stimulation (strength of the outer boundary) made little difference to maternal behavior tendencies. Although babies with weak outer boundaries were rarely dealt with in a highly intrusive or very intense manner, much the same was true of infants whose outer boundary was strong (Table 10.6).

(3) The maternal tendency to provide stimulation more frequently in some modalities than in others depended little on the degree to which the infant was reactive to stimulation in those modalities. Table 10.7 shows that all infants who were highly responsive to passive motion (weak boundary) were offered this experience with high frequency. Babies especially responsive to touch were handled either very little or more than is usual; and the large majority of infants highly responsive to sound were given auditory stimulation by their mothers with either medium or high frequency.

The intensity of stimulation from within is the only dynamic variable that deals with a characteristic of the organism itself rather than with environmental conditions. The quasi-topological model we employed postulates that the intensity of stimulation from within the body is independent of the strength of boundaries. Table 10.8 confirms this assumption. Had the manifestations of somatic arousal been confounded with the strength of the inner boundary, those babies judged to have a weak boundary would also be the babies for whom stimulation from within was judged to be at more than low intensity. The fact that such an association was not found provides assurance that we succeeded in separating criteria for strength of the inner boundary from criteria for the intensity of inner-somatic stimulation.

However, structural characteristics of the infant organism probably bear some relationship to developmental outcome.

(4) Infants who were highly vulnerable to external stimulation (weak outer boundaries) were more likely to be irritable than those more robust (Table 10.9). However, irritability can by no means be regarded as a function of perceptual sensitivity, nor sensitivity a necessary condition for irritability. Thirteen infants in the sample were judged to be irritable to some degree, yet only four of these thirteen babies had weak outer boundaries.

(5) It would appear that either marked sensitivity or a marked lack of reactivity to external stimuli (weak and strong outer boundaries) is less favorable for developmental advance than a medium level of reactivity. Ten subjects had developed at an accelerated pace (developmental status high); of these, eight had outer boundaries rated as medium. In addition, of the three infants whose developmental status was assessed as low, two had weak outer boundaries (Table 10.9).

(6) Last, the strength of the inner boundary may affect irritability and pleasure in functioning to some degree. The proportion of irritable babies was largest among those with weak inner boundaries, and smallest among those with strong inner boundaries (Table 10.10).[6] Similarly, high pleasure in functioning was relatively most frequent among infants with strong inner boundaries, and rare in those whose inner boundaries were weak.

In summary: the manner in which mothers in this sample typically behaved in direct contacts with their babies was not appreciably influenced by the reaction tendencies of the babies, insofar as these have been assessed by our structural ratings. The fact that babies who share a particular structural characteristic do not elicit similar patterns of behavioral response from their mothers does not mean that mothers fail to accommodate to the reaction tendencies of their particular infant. On the contrary, as will be shown in the adaptation syndromes, maternal style can frequently be understood as determined largely by the stable characteristics of the infant's behavior. Our finding is interpreted to mean that although the baby's structural characteristics play a role in every instance of mother-child interaction, the particular behavior style, which is (in part) an adaptation to the infant's reaction tendency, will vary from one mother-baby couple to the next.

Some patterns of association did emerge between particular structural characteristics of the infant and the three developmental outcome ratings; namely, developmental status, irritability, and pleasure in functioning. None of these relationships is strong enough to occur without exception or to do more than suggest a trend, and all conform to common sense expectation. It is hardly surprising that babies who are very vulnerable to excitatory stimuli from within or without (weak boundaries) should be more easily irritated than more robust babies. And it makes equally good sense to know that some vulnerable babies are not in the last irritable, and that some irritable babies are not in the least vulnerable to stimulation. The amount and kind of stimulation provided for the infant must necessarily play a role in shaping the consequences for behavior of great (or minimal) perceptual sensitivity, and this applies to irritability as well as to any other feature.

[6] Ratings of the strength of the inner boundary were not made on the basis of irritable behavior; see Chapter 9.

SUPPLEMENTARY MATERIAL TO CHAPTER 10

Table 10.5—Strength of Inner Boundary and Aspects of Environmental Stimulation

		STRENGTH OF INNER BOUNDARY			
Environmental Variable		*Weak* (N = 6)	*Medium* (N = 19)	*Strong* (N = 7)	N
Frequency of Mother-Child Contacts	High	3	13	4	20
	Medium	1	5	3	9
	Low	2	1	0	3
Intensity of Maternal Stimulation	High	3	6	3	12
	Medium	0	6	3	9
	Low	3	7	1	11
Maternal Competence	High	2	9	4	15
	Medium	4	9	3	16
	Low	0	1	0	1
Maternal Intrusiveness	High	0	5	1	6
	Medium	2	4	3	9
	Low	4	10	3	17
Level of Home Stimulation	High	2	4	4	10
	Medium	1	12	3	16
	Low	3	3	0	6

Table 10.6—Strength of Outer Boundary and Aspects of Environmental Stimulation

		STRENGTH OF OUTER BOUNDARY				
Environmental Variable		*Weak* (N = 5)	*Medium* (N = 19)	*Strong* (N = 5)	*Variable* (N = 3)	N *Ratings*
Frequency of Mother-Child Contacts	High	2	14	1	3	20
	Medium	2	4	3	0	9
	Low	1	1	1	0	3
Intensity of Maternal Stimulation	High	1	9	1	1	12
	Medium	2	4	2	1	9
	Low	2	6	2	1	11
Maternal Competence	High	1	11	2	1	15
	Medium	4	7	3	2	16
	Low	0	1	0	0	1
Maternal Intrusiveness	High	0	5	0	1	6
	Medium	1	4	3	1	9
	Low	4	10	2	1	17
Level of Home Stimulation	High	0	8	1	1	10
	Medium	2	9	3	2	16
	Low	3	2	1	0	6

Table 10.7—Boundary Strength of Modality Sectors and Corresponding Frequency of Maternal Stimulation

Modality	*Boundary Strength*	*MATERNAL STIMULATION* Low	Medium	High	*N Subjects*
Vision	Weak	3	2	1	6
	Medium	5	6	5	16
	Strong	3	4	3	10
Touch	Weak	3	1	4	8
	Medium	0	6	3	9
	Strong	7	6	2	15
Sound	Weak	2	6	6	14
	Medium	2	7	1	10
	Strong	1	3	4	8
Passive Motion	Weak	0	0	4	4
	Medium	4	3	1	8
	Strong	2	0	1	3

Note: The passive motion boundary was assessed only for subjects 16 weeks and above (N = 20). Of these, five received a rating of "variable" and were omitted from this table.

A separate rating was made of the relative frequency with which mothers stimulated each modality. The ratings for the frequency of maternal stimulation are therefore different from those reported on the other tables; the latter refer to the overall frequency of mother-child contacts.

Table 10.8—Strength of Inner and Outer Boundaries and Intensity of Stimulation from Within

Boundary Strength		*INTENSITY OF STIMULATION FROM WITHIN* Low (N = 18)	Medium (N = 12)	High (N = 2)	*N Ratings*
Outer Boundary	Weak	4	1	0	5
	Medium	9	8	2	19
	Strong	3	2	0	5
	Variable	2	1	0	3
Inner Boundary	Weak	4	2	0	6
	Medium	12	5	2	19
	Strong	4	3	0	7

Table 10.9—Strength of Outer Boundary and Three Indices of Adaptation

Adaptation Index		*STRENGTH OF OUTER BOUNDARY* Weak (N = 5)	Medium (N = 19)	Strong (N = 5)	Variable (N = 3)	*N Ratings*
Developmental Status	High	0	8	1	1	10
	Medium	3	10	4	2	19
	Low	2	1	0	0	3
Irritability	High	2	2	0	1	5
	Medium	2	4	1	1	8
	Low	1	13	4	1	19
Pleasure in Functioning	High	0	6	1	2	9
	Medium	2	4	1	1	8
	Low	0	3	0	0	3

Note: Pleasure in functioning was not assessed for subjects in Group One (4–12 weeks).

Table 10.10—Strength of the Inner Boundary and Three Indices of Adaptation

		STRENGTH OF INNER BOUNDARY			
Adaptation Index		*Weak (N = 6)*	*Medium (N = 19)*	*Strong (N = 7)*	*N Ratings*
Developmental Status	High	2	6	2	10
	Medium	4	10	5	19
	Low	0	3	0	3
Irritability	High	2	3	0	5
	Medium	2	5	1	8
	Low	2	11	6	19
Pleasure in Functioning	High	1	5	3	9
	Medium	2	5	1	8
	Low	1	2	0	3

Note: Pleasure in functioning was not assessed for subjects in Group One (4–12 weeks).

ELEVEN

DYNAMIC COMPONENTS OF THE SPE

The distribution of structural ratings in the entire sample proved that some structural characteristics tend to change with advancing age, that they are not associated with activity level, and that there is no association between them and any of the dynamic variables. The only positive relationships suggested by the data, aside from maturational changes, were that weak inner or weak outer boundaries increase the probability of irritability, and that an outer boundary of medium strength may be the most favorable condition for developmental progress at an accelerated rate. Even these relations were no more than trends and accounted for but a small portion of the variance.

In this section we shall describe the distribution of ratings on the dynamic components of the SPE determinants in this sample. Again, we shall examine patterns of relationships between each of the dynamic variables and age, activity level, and the developmental outcome ratings.

The Intensity of Stimulation from within the Body

The degree to which each infant is subject to stimulation emanating from within the body is part of what the organism brings into any situation. Unlike the ratings of boundary strength, it cannot be regarded as a reaction tendency. Rather, it is an attribute of the organism (an A factor in the schematic diagram) that nonetheless indicates what the organism is responding to, rather than *how* it tends to respond. Of all the ratings that determine the SPE, the intensity of stimulation from within is conceptually the least satisfactory.[1] The empirical observations on which this rating was based are unequivocal, referring to the frequency and intensity with which behavioral arousal demonstrably occurred as a product of bodily processes of some sort (need states, gastric and respiratory disturbances, and the like). Frequently, a rating above the desirable "low" reflects the presence

[1] See also Ch. 10 for a discussion of this point.

of a minor infantile ailment such as the disorder known as colic, skin rashes, or discomfort associated with teething.

As shown on Table 11.1, the majority of infants in this sample received a rating of "low," meaning that somatic processes relatively seldom led to overt disruption, or even significant alteration, of behavior. Only two infants showed enough arousal due to somatic causes to be rated high. The intensity of stimulation was the same for active and inactive babies.[2] The younger infants more often showed appreciable degrees of stimulation from within, probably because minor bodily disturbances, especially of gastric functions, are more common during the first four months of life than later on. This is another of the organismic factors that are likely to change as a function of maturation.

One might expect that in caring for babies who are often subject to somatic arousal, mothers would behave differently than in caring for babies who are relatively free from such upsets. Yet Table 11.2 does not suggest that this was the case. However, differences in the typical frequency or intensity of somatic arousal do appear to be related to developmental outcome, at least in one respect (Table 11.3). Of the twelve babies who experienced medium stimulation from within, seven, or 58 per cent, were also irritable. Of the eighteen babies for whom such somatic stimulation was rated as low, only four, or 22 per cent, were irritable. It is not surprising that such a relationship should exist, for bodily discomfort is one of the primary causes of irritability in young infants. The two babies for whom the intensity of stimulation was judged to be high were both irritable, yet as already mentioned, of the babies subject to medium levels of somatic disruption, nearly half were not at all irritable (Table 11.3).[3]

Five Aspects of Environmental Stimulation

The five dynamic variables which appraise aspects of each infant's typical environment have already been presented in terms of their relationships (or, as it turned out, the *absence* of relationship) to structural variables.

Figure 11.1 shows the distribution of these environmental ratings for the sample as a whole. It is very much in keeping with what one would expect to see in a group of healthy children cared for by their mothers under normal conditions of family life. The frequency of mother-child contacts was generally high, and only seldom low. Maternal competence was high or medium with about equal frequency, and the intensity of the mother's

[2] It was partly for this reason that we rejected the hypothesis that activity level chiefly represents different strengths of excitatory impulses from within. See Ch. 2.

[3] A full discussion of the relationship between irritability and bodily functioning is to be found in Ch. 10.

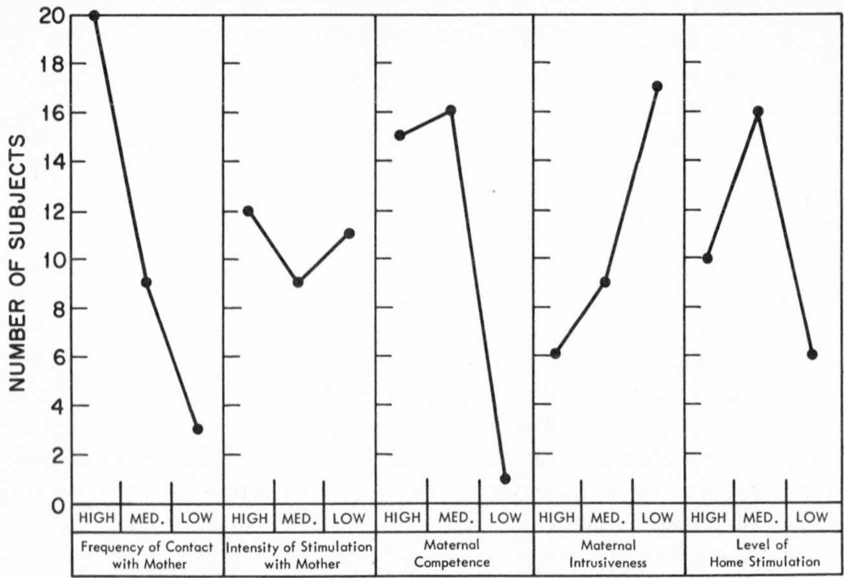

FIGURE 11.1. ASPECTS OF ENVIRONMENTAL STIMULATION: DISTRIBUTION OF RATINGS.

typical approach to her baby was distributed almost equally between high, medium, and low levels. The excitatory characteristics of family life (insofar as they directly affected the baby) showed an approximately normal distribution. Most mothers were accommodating rather than intrusive in dealing with their babies. Since intrusiveness includes, among other things, the mother's tendency to impose a schedule and in other ways interfere with spontaneous behavior (for instance, by taking measures to prevent thumbsucking), we believe that this distribution reflects the impact of what was then called "permissive" child rearing, which was at its peak in this community during the years when our observations were made (1947–1950).

From what has been reported about behavior differences between active and inactive infants, it might be expected that maternal style would vary as a function of the infants' activity level. Yet Table 11.4 shows that the formal ratings are very similar for mothers of active and of inactive babies. Although comparison of active and inactive infants showed that typical varieties of interaction are somewhat different for the two groups, the mother's contribution as assessed by these ratings does not reflect these differences.[4]

[4] There was a slight tendency for mothers of inactive infants to be judged highly competent somewhat more frequently, whereas mothers of active infants were most often judged to possess medium competence.

The ratings for maternal behavior were relative and not absolute. In other words, the same manner of dealing with a baby might be rated as of high intensity in the mother of an 8-week-old infant, but medium or even low in the mother of a 24-week-old. If we had been successful in making ratings on the basis of comparisons between babies in the same age group, the environmental ratings should not differ in their distribution within each of the three age groups. Table 11.5 shows that by and large there were no environmental differences related to age, though a completely shielded and tranquil atmosphere at home was not seen at all among the oldest group (24 to 32 weeks).

Separate ratings for different aspects of maternal style are to some extent an artifact. Each mother is characterized by a particular way of dealing with her baby, and four of the five environmental ratings are a fragmented description of a single pattern of maternal behavior. One would, therefore, expect that certain of the maternal behavior attributes would be closely associated with one another or, at least, that certain constellations of maternal behavior attributes would recur as a frequent pattern. Tables 11.6 through 11.10 show the interrelationships among the five environmental ratings in the form of scattergrams.

Taken together, these data indicate that certain maternal behavior tendencies did occur in typical combinations. However, no one aspect of maternal behavior was consistently associated with any other, in the sense that when high ratings were associated on two variables, low ratings also went together on the same variable. For instance, most of the mothers judged to be highly competent also had frequent contacts with their babies (Table 11.6), yet medium and low competence were not related to medium and low frequency of contact (Table 11.8).

In summary, Tables 11.6 through 11.10 indicate that, at least in this sample, high frequency of mother-child contacts and high maternal competence are positively related to one another, and are inversely related to intrusiveness but not to intensity. A mother's typical intensity in direct encounters with her baby tends to be in proportion to what might be called the intensity of family life—the degree to which the daily background of home experience provides direct stimulation for the infant. In constructing the patterns of recurrent concrete experience for each child, it is important to note that, with two exceptions, any one of the maternal behavior characteristics was found in combination with any other. This diversity in the patterns of maternal behavior is especially striking because our subjects came from a rather homogeneous socioeconomic level and cultural background.

From previous research with larger subject populations, we know that patterns or styles of maternal care bear a relationship to developmental outcome, even though similar environmental circumstances have a different impact upon children with different reaction tendencies. Tables 11.11

through 11.14 are scattergrams showing the relationship of each of the environmental variables to the three indices of developmental outcome. The most important overall finding is that nearly every outcome rating on each of the three indices of development could and did occur in combination with any of these widely differing maternal styles. Irritable babies could have mothers assessed as highly competent or otherwise; pleasure in functioning could be high or low whether the infants were stimulated richly or scarcely; and even high maternal intrusiveness could be seen combined with every possible position on the developmental outcome ratings.

However, the data do suggest that certain aspects of the environment tend to facilitate developmental progress. An acceleration of development (high developmental status) occurred in 50 per cent of the infants who had very frequent contacts with their mother (Table 11.11), and never otherwise. Similarly, a highly stimulating home environment was associated with high developmental status. Other studies have reported similar results. The congruence between trends in our very limited data and results obtained by others is interesting primarily because it tends indirectly to validate the ratings. But it is equally important to note that neither frequency of mother-child contacts, nor the level of home stimulation, nor the two together could have *predicted* developmental status. Our subjects were selected so as to eliminate gross obstacles to normal development (physical health, disordered family life, economic deprivation, difficulties in the birth process and the like were all screened), and it is well to remember that even statistically significant [5] relationships are limited in their power to determine outcome in individual cases.

Discussion

In reviewing the patterns of association between the various structural and dynamic variables that, in combination, provide the basis for deriving stable patterns of experience for each child, we chose to examine separately the association between any one variable and all others. This is something of a *tour de force,* in that the analysis of separate variables is appropriate only for the determination of general relationships. When the aim is to predict or to assess the conditions that lead to specific outcomes, the research design necessarily encompasses clusters or constellations of many variables. For reasons fully stated in Chapters 1 and 2, we believe that even the most complex assessment of a combination of organismic and environmental variables is not likely to lead to an understanding of the genesis of individual differences. It is understood that an equivalent of our constellations of SPE determinants could be attained if all possible

[5] Significant relationships between these variables as reported in the literature are discussed in Ch. 1.

combinations of organismic and environmental variables were studied in relation to developmental outcome. Factor analysis or a similar technique would, in principle, yield the same information as is provided by relating the SPE to developmental outcome.

It may be useful to mention at this time both the practical and the systematic reasons for relating developmental outcome to an intervening variable (the SPE), and not to the constellation of variables that determine the SPE. In the first place, if one wished to use the criteria we employed, a huge matrix of organismic and environmental variables would have to be constructed. To establish the different clusters of variables that prove to be correlated to developmental outcome, minute information would have to be obtained about large numbers of subjects. Once that had been accomplished, statistical processing of so large a matrix would produce spurious associations along with valid ones. The truth is that the accumulation of the relevant raw data for such a purpose is a practical impossibility at the present time. However, to the extent that further study validates and refines some of the variables we employed, it may in the future be possible to make similar assessments more simply and accurately.

Nonetheless, a research design that focuses on the relationship between stable patterns of concrete experience and individual differences in developmental course has certain systematic advantages, for it deals with the relevant determining variables at the resultant level. Our primary purpose in presenting the analysis of each variable that enters the SPE before reporting on the adaptation syndromes is to show that widely different combinations of organismic and environmental variables can generate highly similar patterns of concrete experience. If our hypothesis is correct, the imaginary factorial study just referred to should therefore yield the result that variable constellations of SPE determinants X, Y, and Z are equally likely to yield a particular developmental outcome. Since on this basis one would not know what X, Y, and Z have in common, even accurate prediction achieved in such a manner would be of little help in learning more about the mechanism or processes that link certain combinations of reaction tendency and environmental context to the final outcome. In our model, variable constellations X, Y, and Z, however different, would find single representation because what they have in common is that they produce similar (theoretically speaking, identical) patterns of experience. The specific nature of different patterns of concrete experience provides some clues about the processes or mechanisms that account for individual differences in subsequent development.

SUPPLEMENTARY MATERIAL TO CHAPTER 11

Table 11.1—Intensity of Stimulation from Within, by Activity Level and Age Level

Intensity of Stimulation from Within	ACTIVITY LEVEL			AGE GROUP (number of subjects)			
	Active	Inactive	Total	4–12 weeks	16–20 weeks	24–32 weeks	Total
Low	9	9	18	6	3	9	18
Medium	6	6	12	5	4	3	12
High	1	1	2	1	1	0	2
Total	16	16	32	12	8	12	32

Table 11.2—Intensity of Stimulation from Within and Aspects of Environmental Stimulation

Environmental Variable		INTENSITY OF STIMULATION FROM WITHIN (number of subjects)			N
		Low	Medium	High	
Frequency of Mother-Child Contacts	High	11	7	2	20
	Medium	6	3	0	9
	Low	1	2	0	3
Intensity of Maternal Stimulation	High	7	4	1	12
	Medium	6	2	1	9
	Low	5	6	0	11
Maternal Competence	High	8	5	2	15
	Medium	9	7	0	16
	Low	1	0	0	1
Maternal Intrusiveness	High	4	2	0	6
	Medium	4	4	1	9
	Low	10	6	1	17
Level of Home Stimulation	High	3	5	2	10
	Medium	11	5	0	16
	Low	4	2	0	6

Table 11.3—Intensity of Stimulation from Within and Three Indices of Adaptation

Adaptation Index		INTENSITY OF STIMULATION FROM WITHIN (number of subjects) *Low*	*Medium*	*High*	N
Developmental Status	High	5	5	0	10
	Medium	11	6	2	19
	Low	2	1	0	3
Irritability	High	2	2	1	5
	Medium	2	5	1	8
	Low	14	5	0	19
Pleasure in Functioning	High	7	2	0	9
	Medium	4	4	0	8
	Low	1	1	1	3

Note: Pleasure in functioning was not assessed for Group One (4–12 weeks).

Table 11.4—Aspects of Environmental Stimulation and Activity Level

Environmental Variable		N SUBJECTS *Active*	*Inactive*	N
Frequency of Mother-Child Contacts	High	11	9	20
	Medium	4	5	9
	Low	1	2	3
Intensity of Maternal Stimulation	High	6	6	12
	Medium	5	4	9
	Low	5	6	11
Maternal Competence	High	6	9	15
	Medium	10	6	16
	Low	0	1	1
Maternal Intrusiveness	High	3	3	6
	Medium	5	4	9
	Low	8	9	17
Level of Home Stimulation	High	4	6	10
	Medium	9	7	16
	Low	3	3	6

Table 11.5—Aspects of Environmental Stimulation by Age Group

	GROUP ONE: 4–12 WKS. (N = 12)			GROUP TWO: 16–20 WKS. (N = 8)			GROUP THREE 24–32 WKS. (N = 12)		
Aspect of Stimulation	*High*	*Medium*	*Low*	*High*	*Medium*	*Low*	*High*	*Medium*	*Low*
Frequency of Maternal Stimulation	8	3	1	4	3	1	8	3	1
Intensity of Maternal Stimulation	6	1	5	0	4	4	6	4	2
Maternal Competence	6	6	0	4	3	1	5	7	0
Maternal Intrusiveness	3	2	7	0	3	5	3	4	5
Level of Home Stimulation	5	3	4	2	4	2	3	9	0
Totals	28	15	17	10	17	13	25	27	8

Table 11.6—Frequency of Mother-Child Contacts and Four Aspects of Environmental Stimulation

Environmental Variable		FREQUENCY OF MOTHER-CHILD CONTACTS			N
		Low	*Medium*	*High*	
Maternal Intensity	High	0	3	9	12
	Medium	1	4	4	9
	Low	2	2	7	11
Maternal Competence	High	1	1	13	15
	Medium	2	7	7	16
	Low	0	1	0	1
Maternal Intrusiveness	High	0	1	5	6
	Medium	0	6	3	9
	Low	3	2	12	17
Level of Home Stimulation	High	0	2	8	10
	Medium	1	5	10	16
	Low	2	2	12	6

Table 11.7—Intensity of Maternal Behavior and Four Aspects of Environmental Stimulation

Environmental Variable		MATERNAL INTENSITY			N
		Low	*Medium*	*High*	
Frequency of Mother-Child Contacts	High	7	4	9	20
	Medium	2	4	3	9
	Low	2	1	0	3
Maternal Competence	High	8	4	3	15
	Medium	2	5	9	16
	Low	1	0	0	1
Maternal Intrusiveness	High	0	0	6	6
	Medium	0	5	4	9
	Low	11	4	2	17
Level of Home Stimulation	High	1	2	7	10
	Medium	5	7	4	16
	Low	5	0	1	6

Table 11.8—Maternal Competence and Four Aspects of Environmental Stimulation

Environmental Variable		MATERNAL COMPETENCE			N
		Low	*Medium*	*High*	
Frequency of Mother-Child Contacts	High	0	7	13	20
	Medium	1	7	1	9
	Low	0	2	1	3
Maternal Intensity	High	0	9	3	12
	Medium	0	5	4	9
	Low	1	2	8	11
Maternal Intrusiveness	High	0	5	1	6
	Medium	0	7	2	9
	Low	1	4	12	17
Level of Home Stimulation	High	0	5	5	10
	Medium	0	8	8	16
	Low	1	3	2	6

Table 11.9—Maternal Intrusiveness and Four Aspects of Environmental Stimulation

Environmental Variable		*MATERNAL INTRUSIVENESS* Low	Medium	High	N
Frequency of Mother-Child Contacts	High	12	3	5	20
	Medium	2	6	1	9
	Low	3	0	0	3
Maternal Intensity	High	2	4	6	12
	Medium	4	5	0	9
	Low	11	0	0	11
Maternal Competence	High	12	2	1	15
	Medium	4	7	5	16
	Low	1	0	0	1
Level of Home Stimulation	High	3	4	3	10
	Medium	8	5	3	16
	Low	6	0	0	6

Table 11.10—Typical Level of Stimulation in the Home and Four Aspects of Maternal Behavior

Environmental Variable		*LEVEL OF HOME STIMULATION* Low	Medium	High	N
Frequency of Mother-Child Contacts	High	2	10	8	20
	Medium	2	5	2	9
	Low	2	1	0	3
Maternal Intensity	High	1	4	7	12
	Medium	0	7	2	9
	Low	5	5	1	11
Maternal Competence	High	2	8	5	15
	Medium	3	8	5	16
	Low	1	0	0	1
Maternal Intrusiveness	High	0	3	3	6
	Medium	0	5	4	9
	Low	6	8	3	17

Table 11.11—Frequency of Mother-Child Contacts and Three Indices of Adaptation

Adaptation Index		*FREQUENCY OF MOTHER-CHILD CONTACTS* Low	Medium	High	N
Developmental Status	High	0	0	10	10
	Medium	3	7	9	19
	Low	0	2	1	3
Irritability	High	1	0	4	5
	Medium	0	1	7	8
	Low	2	8	9	19
Pleasure in Functioning	High	0	3	6	9
	Medium	2	2	4	8
	Low	0	1	2	3

Note: Pleasure in functioning was not assessed for subjects in Group One (4–12 weeks).

Table 11.12—Intensity of Maternal Stimulation and Three Indices of Adaptation

		INTENSITY OF MATERNAL STIMULATION			
Adaptation Index		*Low*	*Medium*	*High*	*N*
Developmental Status	High	3	3	4	10
	Medium	6	5	8	19
	Low	2	1	0	3
Irritability	High	1	1	3	5
	Medium	3	3	2	8
	Low	7	5	7	19
Pleasure in Functioning	High	1	4	4	9
	Medium	3	3	2	8
	Low	2	1	0	3

Note: Pleasure in functioning was not assessed for subjects in Group One (4–12 weeks).

Table 11.13—Maternal Competence and Three Indices of Adaptation

		MATERNAL COMPETENCE			
Adaptation Index		*Low*	*Medium*	*High*	*N*
Developmental Status	High	0	4	6	10
	Medium	0	11	8	19
	Low	1	1	1	3
Irritability	High	0	4	1	5
	Medium	0	3	5	8
	Low	1	9	9	19
Pleasure in Functioning	High	0	6	3	9
	Medium	0	4	4	8
	Low	1	0	2	3

Note: Pleasure in functioning was not assessed for subjects in Group One (4–12 weeks).

Table 11.14—Maternal Intrusiveness and Three Indices of Adaptation

		MATERNAL INTRUSIVENESS			
Adaptation Index		*Low*	*Medium*	*High*	*N*
Developmental Status	High	5	2	3	10
	Medium	10	6	3	19
	Low	2	1	0	3
Irritability	High	3	0	2	5
	Medium	4	4	0	8
	Low	10	5	4	19
Pleasure in Functioning	High	2	4	3	9
	Medium	5	3	0	8
	Low	3	0	0	3

Note: Pleasure in functioning was not assessed for subjects in Group One (4–12 weeks).

Table 11.15—Background Level of Stimulation in the Home and Three Indices of Adaptation

Adaptation Index		Level of Home Stimulation: Low	Medium	High	N
Developmental Status	High	0	5	5	10
	Medium	4	10	5	19
	Low	2	1	0	3
Irritability	High	2	2	1	5
	Medium	1	3	4	8
	Low	3	11	5	19
Pleasure in Functioning	High	0	6	3	9
	Medium	1	6	1	8
	Low	1	1	1	3

Note: Pleasure in functioning was not assessed for subjects in Group One (4–12 weeks).

TWELVE

DEVELOPMENTAL OUTCOME COMPONENTS OF THE SPE

The assessment of developmental outcome by means of formal adaptation indices consisted of five different ratings. Three of these—developmental status, irritability, and pleasure in functioning—have already been reported as they relate to structural and dynamic determinants of the SPE. The remaining two refer to characteristic somatic states—adequacy of vegetative functioning, and excitability. These indices have been omitted from the scattergrams so far presented because, although they contain important information about the functioning of each of the infants, we think there is room for doubt about their status as indications of developmental outcome.

In the clinical evaluation of infants, it is generally assumed that a thriving and well-adapted baby is one who eats well, sleeps well, and, in general, shows bodily well being. Therefore, we used the smooth integration of bodily functions as one index of adaptation. We might, with equal reason, have assumed that adequate integration of vegetative functioning is a precondition for optimal development and functioning, in which case this rating would become one of the SPE determinants. The problem is particularly obvious in this example, but in principle it applies to any of the adaptation indices, for each aspect of behavior (or of experience) can be viewed as cause, as consequence, or as a sample of ongoing behavior process. For instance, advanced developmental status is undoubtedly the result of preceding events. Yet it is also a determinant of patterns of experience, for an infant who is developmentally advanced will respond differently to the same circumstances than one who is relatively immature. Whether a given behavior characteristic is viewed as a dependent variable or as a component of the independent variables that shape the patterns of experience is a matter of research strategy and depends on the particular problem under investigation. In a cross-sectional study of young infants, we thought it strategic to consider harmonious bodily functioning as a *sign* of good adaptation. In a study looking for the relationship between patterns of experience during the early years and later patterns of adaptation, it would probably be treated as an SPE determinant.

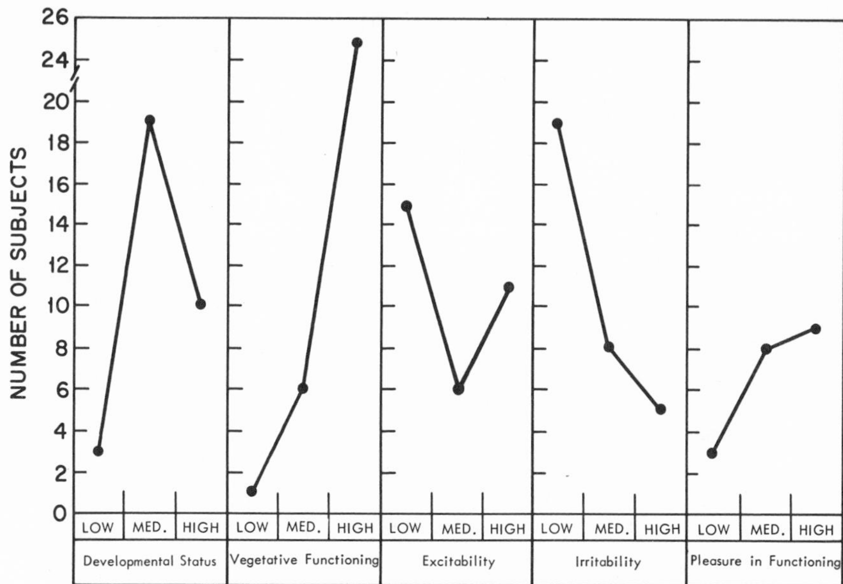

FIGURE 12.1. DISTRIBUTION OF OUTCOME VARIABLES FOR SAMPLES AS A WHOLE.

Excitability is an aspect of adaptive style, though high and low excitability also contribute to the adequacy of adaptation as a whole. We included it among the adaptation indices because we had noted that great excitability can be disruptive to the functioning of some babies, though in other subjects, it existed in combination with excellent developmental progress, high pleasure in functioning, and the absence of irritability. We were interested in discovering the conditions under which marked excitability can coexist with harmonious overall integration and hence with what Hartmann (1937) would call a "good fit" between the infant organism and his particular environment.[1]

Figure 12.1 shows the distribution of ratings for the five adaptation indices in the sample as a whole, and Table 12.1 lists the developmental outcome ratings separately for each subject. As was the case with the environmental ratings, the aggregate of developmental outcome ratings is entirely in keeping with what one would expect to see in a group of normal babies reared in ordinary families. Developmental status, as judged by test results, shows an approximately normal distribution (except that our thoroughly screened sample included a disproportionate number of babies whose development was accelerated). Generally the adequacy of vegetative

[1] Excitability also differs from the other adaptation indices because it shows a high correlation with activity level (see Table 12.2). In future studies we would be inclined to treat excitability as a qualitative aspect of infantile reaction tendencies rather than as a separate index of adaptation.

functioning was high and irritability was low; pleasure in functioning tended to be high or medium for most babies.

Excitability, however, was low in nearly half the sample, and was somewhat more often high than low for the other half. As shown on Table 12.2, all active infants were thought excitable to some degree, and only one of the inactive infants was excitable above the lowest level. Since the overall activity level varied among the active group (from 2.2 to 3.0), we wondered whether medium excitability characterizes infants who are fairly active and high excitability those who are very active. However, this was not the case. (The *average* activity level rating for highly excitable babies was 2.50, and that for moderately excitable babies was 2.44.)

These findings and the individual case studies lead us to believe that some of the very active babies are so well coordinated that energetic body motion serves to prevent strong excitation. In other words, in these infants activation of the skeletal musculature may serve to discharge tension before it reaches disruptive threshold levels, in accord with the psychoanalytic hypothesis about the role of movement in infantile adaptation. However, other active infants tend to lose coordination as activity increases; muscle tension and less competent movement patterns not only hinder the baby in achieving his postural or locomotor goals, but are themselves excitatory. The failure to sustain very high levels of activity in a coordinated and successful manner was, in our sample, quite as common among moderately active as among exceedingly active babies. Thus, the significance of excitability for adaptation lies in the manner in which active, and therefore potentially excitable, babies cope with their strong movement impulses.

For two reasons we did not assess pleasure in functioning for babies less than 16 weeks of age. Not only is it difficult to find, for the youngest babies, behavioral criteria that are independent of irritability and of the adequacy of vegetative function; also it is doubtful whether a marked tendency to respond actively to many aspects of the environment is a positive adaptive sign in tiny infants. A pattern of existence that consists of an alternation between sleeping or drowsing, feeding, and intermittent episodes during which the baby responds to maternal ministrations may well be developmentally optimal.

In any case, Table 12.2 shows that a relationship does exist between pleasure in functioning and activity level. Eighty per cent of the active babies showed high pleasure in functioning, and only one, or 10 per cent, of the inactive ones received this rating. However, most inactive babies showed a medium degree of pleasure in functioning. (The only three babies who were rated as "low" were inactive infants.) The rate of developmental progress was much the same among active and inactive subjects, except that relatively slow development was seen only in inactive ones. Nor did activity level have an influence on irritability or on the adequacy of vegetative functioning.

The adaptation indices were rated relative to the range of functioning observed within a given age group, and the ratings should, therefore, have been distributed very similarly in each. This was largely true (Table 12.3). High levels of irritability were slightly more common among the youngest babies than the rest, though the absence of irritability was about equally frequent in all age groups. Among the oldest babies, very marked pleasure in functioning was noted a bit more often than among the intermediate group. However, these differences are slight, and most of the developmental outcome distributions were much the same for all age levels.

Each of the five adaptation indices was intended to reflect one of the major characteristics that, in combination, describe the degree to which an infant functions in accordance with optimal standards of harmonious adaptation to the internal and external environment. Schematically speaking, an exceedingly well-developed and well-adapted baby should have high ratings on developmental status, adequacy of vegetative functioning, and pleasure in functioning. For such a baby, irritability should be low, and excitability might be present to any degree. By the same token, any departure from optimal behavior adaptation on the baby's part would be expected to affect the ratings for more than one of the adaptation indices. Therefore, we expected to find a fairly high degree of correlation among the five adaptation indices.

Tables 12.4 through 12.8 supply the relevant information in the form of scáttergrams. Although some association between adaptation indices was found, it was less pronounced and consistent than we had expected. The most clear-cut relationship we found was between irritability and the integration of vegetative functioning. Of those subjects whose vegetative functioning was exceedingly well integrated, 28.0 per cent showed a degree of irritability (Table 12.5). Of the six babies who received a "medium" rating, meaning they showed slight disruption of these functions or marked lability, five (or 83.3 per cent) were irritable. The single baby who showed rather poor integration of bodily functions (rated "low") was also highly irritable.

The relationship between bodily well-being and irritability has been mentioned earlier in connection with the fact that intensity of stimulation from within is associated with irritability. The criteria for the intensity of stimulation from within included the degree to which each infant was subject to physiological discomfort.[2] However, the adequacy of vegetative functioning was judged by very different criteria, such as the ease and efficiency of sleep, food intake, elimination, and the like. They also included the relative stability of some autonomic functions; namely, circulation and respiration. The relationship between the adequacy of vegetative

[2] This is the only instance where the same behavior was used (in part) for the assessment of two different variables. However, in no case was the intensity of stimulation judged solely on the criterion of physiological distress. And in no case was a judgment of irritability based solely, or even chiefly, on crying due to bodily discomfort. For details, see Ch. 9.

functioning and irritability is not immediately apparent. It occurred to us that it might be an artifact if the presence of physiological discomfort (which was considered in the assessment of the intensity of stimulation from within) always implied, in addition, some impairment in the adequacy of vegetative functioning.

A separate check was undertaken to determine whether the infants with medium or high intensity of stimulation from within were also infants whose adequacy of vegetative functioning was assessed as less than the optimal high. Such a convergence of the two ratings was not found. Thirteen infants received ratings above "low" for the intensity of stimulation from within. Of these, nine, or 70 per cent, were nonetheless rated high on the adequacy of vegetative functioning. Therefore, the association between irritability and the adequacy of vegetative function existed in a different group of infants than those for whom irritability was associated with intensity of somatic stimulation.

On the tentative assumption that a relationship between irritability and the quality of vegetative functioning can be confirmed with larger subject populations, we conclude that effortless bodily functioning may be more important to infantile adaptation than we had known. Bodily well-being is always emphasized as an important aspect of functioning in infants. But in clinical appraisal, as well as in the research literature, the absence of pain and distress in connection with bodily need states has been given primary emphasis. It may well be that a pervasive sense of well-being depends not only on the absence of pain, but also on the smooth and relatively stable regulation of autonomic functions. Such behavior manifestations as marked flushing or blanching, labored respiration, or a lack of perfect coordination between breathing and swallowing may affect young infants to a greater extent than has previously been made explicit.

Irritability also occurred with excitability to some extent. Comparing the relative proportion of irritable babies in the groups of infants judged to be low, medium or high in excitability, Table 12.6 shows that the proportion was 54.5 per cent for the highly excitable babies in comparison with 33.0 per cent for each of the less excitable groups. Table 12.7, which shows the ratings for excitability grouped in terms of the degree of irritability, confirms the relationship to some extent. Among the irritable babies, excitability was present (to medium or high degrees) in 61.5 per cent, whereas the corresponding value for nonirritable babies was 47.3 per cent.

Finally, excitability and developmental status may be interdependent to some extent (Table 12.6). Among the least excitable babies three of fifteen, or 20 per cent, showed pronounced developmental acceleration. By contrast, of the eleven highly excitable babies, six, or 54.5 per cent, had significantly superior test scores.

Again it must be said that the numerical values and the differences are too small to justify conclusions. The tendency for certain adaptation indices to occur in characteristic patterns is of descriptive interest in that they exemplify adaptation syndromes that exist. Most of the correlation trends among our adaptation indices are in good accord with what is known about normal functioning in infancy. While the positive relationships are not impressive, the tables demonstrate a fairly high degree of independence among the various indices of adaptation, which is a more important finding in its own right. In particular, behavior characteristics that carry a negative connotation in terms of our understanding of infantile well-being were quite often found to coexist with favorable developmental outcome. Superior developmental progress was quite often associated with moderate irritability (Table 12.7), and was not precluded by a low degree of pleasure in functioning (Table 12.8). In fact, we have come to think that *under certain conditions* both moderate degrees of distress and other disruptions of a comfortable equilibrium can accelerate the development of precisely those early ego functions that are tapped by developmental tests (see Chapter 16).

SUPPLEMENTARY MATERIAL TO CHAPTER 12

Table 12.1—Ratings for Five Indices of Adaptation for All Subjects

	DEVELOP-MENTAL STATUS		*ADEQUACY OF VEGETATIVE FUNCTIONING*		*EXCITABILITY*		*IRRITABILITY*		*PLEASURE IN FUNC-TIONING*	
Pair	*Ac*	*In*	*Ac*	*In*	*Ac*	*In*	*Ac*	*In*	*Ac*	*In*
I	Med.	High	High	High	High	Low	High	Med.	—	—
II	Med.	High	High	High	Med.	Low	Low	Low	—	—
III	Med.	Med.	High	High	Med.	Low	Low	Low	—	—
IV	Med.	Med.	Med.	Low	High	Low	High	High	—	—
V	Med.	Low	Med.	High	Med.	Low	Med.	Med.	—	—
VI	Med.	Med.	High	High	Med.	Low	Low	Low	—	—
VII	High	Med.	High	Med.	High	Low	Low	High	Med.	Low
VIII	Med.	Low	High	High	Med.	Low	Low	Low	High	Low
IX	High	Med.	High	High	High	Low	Med.	Low	High	Med.
X	Med.	High	High	High	High	Med.	Low	Med.	High	Low
XI	High	Med.	High	Med.	High	Low	Low	Low	High	Med.
XII	Med.	Med.	High	High	High	Low	Low	Low	High	Med.
XIII	High	Med.	High	High	High	Low	Med.	Low	Med.	Med.
XIV	High	High	High	High	High	Low	Med.	Low	High	High
XV	Med.	Med.	Med.	High	High	Low	High	Low	High	Med.
XVI	High	Low	High	Med.	High	Low	Low	Med.	High	Med.

Note: Pleasure in functioning was not assessed for Group One (4–12 weeks).

Table 12.2—Activity Level and Five Indices of Adaptation

Adaptation Index		*ACTIVITY LEVEL* Active	Inactive	N
Developmental Status	High	6	4	10
	Medium	10	9	19
	Low	0	3	3
Vegetative Functioning	High	13	12	25
	Medium	3	3	6
	Low	0	1	1
Excitability	High	11	0	11
	Medium	5	1	6
	Low	0	15	15
Irritability	High	3	2	5
	Medium	4	4	8
	Low	9	10	19
Pleasure in Functioning	High	8	1	9
	Medium	2	6	8
	Low	0	3	3

Note: Pleasure in functioning was not assessed for Group One (4–12 weeks).

Table 12.3—Age Level and Five Indices of Adaptation

Adaptation Index		*AGE LEVEL (in weeks)* 4–12	16–20	24–32	N
Developmental Status	High	2	3	5	10
	Medium	9	4	6	19
	Low	1	1	1	3
Vegetative Functioning	High	9	7	9	25
	Medium	2	1	3	6
	Low	1	0	0	1
Excitability	High	2	3	6	11
	Medium	4	2	0	6
	Low	6	3	6	15
Irritability	High	3	1	1	5
	Medium	3	2	3	8
	Low	6	5	8	19
Pleasure in Functioning	High		3	6	9
	Medium		2	6	8
	Low		3	0	3

Note: Pleasure In functioning was not assessed for Group One (4–12 weeks).

Table 12.4—Developmental Status and Four Indices of Adaptation

Adaptation Index		DEVELOPMENTAL STATUS *Low*	*Medium*	*High*	N
Vegetative Functioning	High	2	13	10	25
	Medium	1	5	0	6
	Low	0	1	0	1
Excitability	High	0	5	6	11
	Medium	0	5	1	6
	Low	3	9	3	15
Irritability	High	0	5	0	5
	Medium	2	1	5	8
	Low	1	13	5	19
Pleasure in Functioning	High	0	4	5	9
	Medium	1	5	2	8
	Low	1	1	1	3

Note: Pleasure in functioning was not assessed for Group One (4–12 weeks).

Table 12.5—Vegetative Functioning and Four Indices of Adaptation

Adaptation Index		ADEQUACY OF VEGETATIVE FUNCTIONING *Low*	*Medium*	*High*	N
Developmental Status	High	0	0	10	10
	Medium	1	5	13	19
	Low	0	1	2	3
Excitability	High	0	2	9	11
	Medium	0	1	5	16
	Low	1	3	11	15
Irritability	High	1	3	1	5
	Medium	0	2	6	8
	Low	0	1	18	19
Pleasure in Functioning	High	0	1	8	9
	Medium	0	2	6	8
	Low	0	1	2	3

Note: Pleasure in functioning was not assessed for Group One (4–12 weeks).

Table 12.6—Excitability and Four Indices of Adaptation

Adaptation Index		DEGREE OF EXCITABILITY *Low*	*Medium*	*High*	N
Developmental Status	High	3	1	6	10
	Medium	9	5	5	19
	Low	3	0	0	3
Vegetative Functioning	High	11	5	9	25
	Medium	3	1	2	6
	Low	1	0	0	1
Irritability	High	2	0	3	5
	Medium	3	2	3	8
	Low	10	4	5	19
Pleasure in Functioning	High	1	1	7	9
	Medium	6	0	2	8
	Low	2	1	0	3

Note: Pleasure in functioning was not assessed for Group One (4–12 weeks).

Table 12.7—Irritability and Four Indices of Adaptation

Adaptation Index		IRRITABILITY *Low*	*Medium*	*High*	N
Developmental Status	High	5	5	0	10
	Medium	13	1	5	19
	Low	1	2	0	3
Vegetative Functioning	High	18	6	1	25
	Medium	1	2	3	6
	Low	0	0	1	1
Excitability	High	5	3	3	11
	Medium	4	2	0	6
	Low	10	3	2	15
Pleasure in Functioning	High	6	2	1	9
	Medium	6	2	0	8
	Low	1	1	1	3

Note: Pleasure in functioning was not assessed for Group One (4–12 weeks).

Table 12.8—Pleasure in Functioning and Four Indices of Adaptation

Adaptation Index		PLEASURE IN FUNCTIONING *Low*	*Medium*	*High*	N
Developmental Status	High	1	2	5	8
	Medium	1	5	4	10
	Low	1	1	0	2
Vegetative Functioning	High	2	6	8	16
	Medium	1	2	1	4
	Low	0	0	0	0
Excitability	High	0	2	7	9
	Medium	1	0	1	2
	Low	2	6	1	9
Irritability	High	1	0	1	2
	Medium	1	2	2	5
	Low	1	6	6	13

Note: Pleasure in functioning was not assessed for Group One (4–12 weeks).

THIRTEEN

INDIVIDUAL ADAPTATION SYNDROMES: GROUP ONE

Lena, Ac I (4 Weeks)

SPE DETERMINANTS

Boundary Strength

	ENTIRE		MODALITY SECTORS			
	Inner	Outer	Vision	Touch	Sound	Passive Motion
Stimulation	weak	weak	weak	weak	weak	
Frequency of Mother-Child Contacts		high	medium	high	high	high
Intensity	low	high	→	→	medium	high
Maternal Competence		medium	→	→	→	→
Maternal Intrusiveness		low	→	→	→	→
Level of Home Stimulation		low	→	→	→	→

Activity Level: 2.4

STABLE PATTERNS OF EXPERIENCE

Frequency of strong bodily arousal: Moderate.

A markedly active infant who is extremely sensitive is, by definition, also excitable. In Lena's life, very massive arousal occurred under these conditions: when she was hungry (every 3–4 hours) when she was fatigued (only on the rare occasions when she did not quickly drop off to sleep), and when she was manipulated while already distressed by either of these causes (which mother usually managed to avoid). As compared with the other babies in the sample (of like age), she experienced very massive excitation with medium frequency, but this condition was never allowed to last for more than a very few minutes.

Internal bodily sensations: Prominent, leading to strong arousal.

A 4-week-old's behavior is necessarily dictated by changes in bodily state more than by external stimulation. Though the intensity of stimulation from within was limited to the intermittent arousals associated with bodily need states, Lena's behavior altered very markedly as a result of bodily state (weak inner boundary). Sensations from within accounted for the largest number of arousals, and for those leading to marked excitation. Occasionally, prolonged handling did lead to additional excitation.

Balance between behavior activations due to inner and to outer stimulation: Internal very predominant.

Like all 4-week-olds, Lena showed behavioral arousal chiefly in response to fluctuating somatic states. Unlike the majority, she was highly reactive to external stimulation in all modalities. Many times each day, she responded to being held, rocked, patted, spoken or sung to, but on most occasions such stimulation soothed her (and hence did not lead to behavior *activations*). The one exception was when it was necessary to carry out a routine procedure that involved handling her while she was already quite aroused and distressed. Then the handling excited and irritated her all the more, so that external stimulation did activate her to a state of arousal ranging from marked to distinctly high. However, such occasions were rare.

Importance of distant receptors: Moderate.

The SPE indicates that Lena was more responsive to sights and sounds than are most babies. In a 4-week-old this means no more than that at times when the baby was awake and fairly quiet, sounds could transiently lead to a disruption of ongoing activity or to a startle. Also, at quiet moments she could focus attentively upon a nearby visual spectacle, again reducing general activity. In Lena's case this occurred only in the mother's arms toward the end of feeding. At such times, her mother spoke to her softly but compellingly, smiled at her from close by, and sometimes even held out an object for her inspection.

Importance of near receptors: High.

All 4-week-olds experience maternal ministrations chiefly through the near receptor system. For Lena, the near receptors were even more important than usual, due to her great sensitivity and because mother handled her a great deal—very often to soothe or to feed her.

Most prominent modality: Probably touch.

During mother-child contacts both touch and sound were constantly evoked, but the SPE specifies that the mother's voice while dealing with the baby was modulated (intensity: medium) in comparison with the relative intensity of stimulation she provided in other modalities.

Least prominent modality: Vision.

In addition to the fact that vision can hardly play more than a peripheral role in the awareness of any 4-week-old, the SPE specifies that the mother evoked this modality less often than any of the others.

Frequency of states of optimal animation: Occasional.

Four-week-old infants are capable of focusing on aspects of the environment (gazing, visual following, possibly smiling in response to a sight or a sound) only during states of alertness and a low level of bodily arousal. As was already mentioned, Lena experienced such moments of quiet alertness only occasionally toward the end of feeding.

OUTCOME RATINGS

Developmental status: Medium.

The developmental status of 4-week-olds is barely measurable. All that can be said was that her movements and her attentiveness to human beings coincided with good average standards for her age. In two respects her behavior came closer to what is ordinarily seen in 8-week-olds: she could visually pursue a moving object, and she cooed responsively when smiled at and spoken to from close by. The fact that she was capable of specific responsiveness to particular components of the near environment is in good accord with the inference from the SPE that Lena had relatively frequent opportunity to be aware not only of her mother's touch, but also of the sight of her face and the sound of her voice.

Adequacy of vegetative functioning: High.

The rating of "high" was given because Lena ate well, slept well, experienced almost no gastric distress, and was not given to shallow or labored breathing or to visible and undue lability of peripheral circulation.[1]

Excitability: High.

When awake, Lena was in constant motion, almost always vigorous. She screamed loudly during both hunger and fatigue, and of course she was seldom awake except when hungry or while being handled; during maternal caretaking routines fatigue was often present. In other words, Lena was rarely seen awake without being also markedly excited. Although very high levels of bodily arousal occurred every few hours, they were not allowed to last for long. Whenever Lena cried, the mother picked her up and rocked her, swung her about, patted her, sung to her, and the like. Such vigorous soothing always succeeded in reducing the intensity of the baby's distress. But nothing except food or sleep induced quiescence. Thus, peak excitation levels occurred with medium frequency. A state of moderate excitation, manifested by quivering motion, muscle tension, considerable movement and intermittent vocalizing was very frequent indeed, whereas a calm and quiet state of alertness was rarely seen.

[1] Respiration and circulation are always somewhat labile at the age of 4 weeks. Lena showed such lability, but to a lesser degree than some other members of the sample, and not exceeding what is seen in the great majority of babies at this age.

Irritability: High.

Lena's irritability was assessed as "high" because she spent more time awake and fretful than do most 4-week-olds. The mother always tried to comfort her, and soothing was always successful in reducing the *intensity* of distress, but rarely removed it altogether. As a last resort the mother offered a bottle many, many times each day, and this always restored the baby to a state of calm, even when food intake was negligible. Thus, in Lena's case, the high irritability rating refers to frequent displays of mild discomfort, often in the mother's arms. Only immediately before feeding was Lena seen in severe distress.

DISCUSSION

Lena exemplifies one extreme structural type, in that she was highly vulnerable to both internal and external stimulation. In having to care for an extremely labile and a very active baby, Lena's mother was confronted with a difficult and perplexing task. Fortunately for both, Lena was a very healthy baby, who began sleeping through the night at the age of 3 weeks and who had never experienced gastric upsets. Nonetheless, the fact that when Lena woke she cried and thrashed about, and nothing but the bottle would content her, made the mother feel that she had a difficult baby. It also led her to wonder what she might be doing wrong.

Actually, Lena did show distress more often and more keenly than most infants, but she was nonetheless a thriving baby. The mother devoted all her energy and attention to the care of her first child. In so doing she leaned heavily on whatever advice she could obtain and followed it religiously. Thus, Lena was fed whenever she seemed hungry (on the doctor's advice), so that most of the mother's direct interactions with the baby involved feeding. When Lena woke, fussed, and soon thereafter began to cry loudly, her mother held her and soothed her as has been described, all the time trying to determine whether the baby was hungry or was crying for another reason. If Lena did not suck her fist (which her mother regarded as the most reliable sign of hunger), the mother would change a diaper, or patiently swing the baby in her arms, sing to her, and pat her. If nothing helped—if the baby subsided from screaming to intermittent crying but would not go back to sleep—she was fed anyway. The frequent feedings (sometimes as little as 1¼ hours apart, sometimes after an interval of 2½ to 3 hours) were leisurely affairs. Mother held the baby comfortably, spoke to her softly, hummed, or patted her lightly.

In her anxious efforts to accommodate to the baby, the mother prolonged the feeding process, interrupting not only to burp the baby frequently, but also when it seemed to her that Lena's attention was not on the bottle. For instance, noting Lena gazing at a nearby object, her mother withdrew the nipple until the baby's eyes began to wander. She also interrupted feedings to change the baby's diaper, even though Lena showed no response to the wet diaper.

During feedings, especially toward the end of a feeding episode, the baby gazed at the mother's face alertly and with a pleased expression, and she responded to the mother's stream of affectionate talk by cooing. (The developmental testing was performed on two such occasions, immediately after feeding when Lena did not yet seem sleepy.) Mother said that she never put Lena in her crib while she was crying, to see if she might calm down of her own accord. This was in keeping with what we could observe—the mother seemed unable to endure the baby's crying without picking her up, even at moments when observers felt that all the baby needed was a chance to go to sleep.

Thus, a mother who was neither especially skillful nor at all resourceful, and who seemed to perceive her baby as an awesome responsibility more than as an immediate source of pleasure, provided for her infant a pattern of existence that consisted of periods of sleep, periods of acute discomfort, times when distress was reduced during close bodily contact with the mother, brief periods of relatively relaxed and yet alert states during which the baby was at times responsive to visual and auditory components of the environment, and then back to sleep. Routine procedures fitted into this pattern, in that changes of clothing, diapering, and the bath were usually given at times when the baby was awake, and when it seemed to the mother that she could not yet be hungry. If Lena was markedly distressed before a procedure was begun, she screamed throughout. On most occasions, however, when she was discontent and only fairly active to begin with, caretaking routines served to soothe her (partially), much as did being held and swayed.

Since, under these conditions, Lena developed at an average pace or slightly faster and the vital functions of eating, sleeping and elimination took place easily and effectively, it may be said that the mother had made a successful adaption to her baby's needs—while Lena's contribution was limited, as yet, to her capacity to avail herself of the conditions that permitted need-gratification (by her ability to suck, to swallow, to digest, and to sleep).

Margaret, In I (4 Weeks)

SPE DETERMINANTS

Boundary Strength

	ENTIRE		*MODALITY SECTORS*			
	Inner	*Outer*	*Vision*	*Touch*	*Sound*	*Passive Motion*
Stimulation	weak	strong (−)	strong	strong	weak (+)	?
Frequency of Mother-Child Contacts		high	low (+)	medium (−)	low	high
Intensity	medium	low →				
Maternal Competence		high →				
Maternal Intrusiveness		low (−) →				
Level of Home Stimulation		high (−) →				

Activity Level: 1.4

STABLE PATTERNS OF EXPERIENCE

Frequency of strong bodily arousal: Rare.

Margaret was quite inactive, which implies by definition that bodily arousal did not occur readily. In addition, she was relatively unreactive to most varieties of external stimulation. She responded strongly to excitation arising from within, but her very accommodating and skillful mother intervened so quickly to either soothe or feed her baby that really intense arousal was forestalled. The fact that Margaret was free from gastric distress or other common ailments of early infancy also helped to prevent massive arousal.

Internal bodily sensations: Prominent.

A weak inner boundary, medium levels of stimulation from within, and relative insensitivity to external stimulation, taken in combination, imply that Margaret tended to experience changes in state primarily because of inner somatic change. For her, fatigue did not produce much arousal, though she did occasionally cry when hungry. However, she often whimpered and became restless in the crib for no apparent cause, only to become entirely content when held on someone's lap.

Balance between behavior activations due to inner and to outer stimulation: Internal very predominant.

Behavior activations, that is, arousals of any degree, occurred almost exclusively because of changes in somatic state, as noted above. Behavior changes toward quiescence were frequent in response to soothing, but this factor is not directly relevant to this particular aspect of experience.

Importance of distance receptors: Low.

The distance receptors of vision and sound were peripheral and insignificant during direct encounters with the mother, who primarily activated passive motion and touch. Though Margaret was exposed to considerable external stimulation (a high level of home stimulation) her age, in combination with the fact that only sounds elicited marked responses, explains why Margaret, when awake, was chiefly absorbed by sensations arising from within.

Importance of near receptors: Fairly high.

The fact that she was not sensitive to touch, in combination with what has been said about the role of proprioceptive stimulation, means that, as compared with other 4-week-olds, Margaret experienced changes in state mediated by the skin less sharply; yet tactile sensations were for her more vivid than those mediated by the distance receptors. Further, passive motion was so often used as part of successful soothing that it clearly added to the importance of the near receptors in her experience (though boundary strength in that modality could not be ascertained).

Most prominent modality: Unknown.

The SPE configuration permits no inference, since the auditory modality to which Margaret was most reactive received little activation, at least during contacts with the mother.

Least prominent modality: Vision.

Although inactive infants are apt to have more occasion to direct visual attention to the environment than active ones, Margaret was not highly reactive in this modality. Vision is a relatively peripheral component in the experience of most 4-week-olds, and therefore this assessment means no more than that Margaret had even less occasion than some others to experience states during which other varieties of inner or outer stimulation were so minimal as to permit the emergence of directed gazing.

Frequency of states of optimal animation: Moderate (or fairly low).

Margaret's pattern of existence was such that it is especially difficult to assess this aspect of her experience. She spent far more time than is usual on her mother's (or father's) lap, awake, quiet, and content. However, at such times she was seldom in a position to be attentive to events in the immediate environment. Both parents held the baby while they did other things (housework, watching TV, etc.). They did not speak to her or bring their faces into her view, though they might pat her lightly and occasionally shift her position. Thus, she was often in a state that may well have been conducive to optimal animation, yet much of this time she was not actually animated in response to things about as her face rested against the mother's shoulder or in the crook of her arm.

OUTCOME RATINGS

Developmental status: High.

Margaret's pattern of response to test items was unusual and especially interesting. In the motor area and in response to direct contact with another person, she behaved as is normative for 4-week-olds (by the time the developmental test was administered she was actually 5 weeks old). However, when objects were presented in a provocative manner, her behavior was distinctly mature. Her capacity to sustain visual regard toward small objects (red cube, teaspoon), while she was held in a sitting position, met average standards for 3-month-olds, and she easily followed (visually) moving objects and persons, as is expected of the average 2-month-old. The difference in her responsiveness to people and to things was striking. She could focus her gaze on the examiner's face (or her mother's face) with only the greatest difficulty, and she neither smiled nor cooed. By contrast, she immediately focused upon suitable objects (dangling ring, spoon, cube) and many times she smiled while regarding one of these toys. The presentation of objects elicited not only smiles but considerable animation—in a manner never seen in response to the mother or to the examiners. Thus developmental acceleration was significant (on the Cattell test her MA was 2.2 months at a CA of 1.1 months), but only for her response to aspects of the inanimate environment. At the age of 5 weeks, the failure to smile or coo at an animated, nearby human face does not constitute developmental retardation; but Margaret was the only infant in the sample who was able to show focused attention and definite pleasure toward objects, yet fail to do so toward people.[1]

We have suggested that the rate of developmental progress may depend in large measure on the baby's opportunity to experience states of optimal animation during which coordinated responsiveness to aspects of the immediate environment can emerge. In Margaret's case the frequency of optimally animated states was only moderate, yet developmental status was high. What has been reported about the discrepancy in her behavior when directed toward persons and toward objects fits very well with the somewhat atypical circumstances when this baby was at her most content and alert. As has been said, Margaret's mother ceaselessly soothed her baby, generally with success. She made no efforts to play with the baby, nor did she speak or sing to her; most commonly she combined housework, attentiveness to the siblings, or (in the evening) watching TV with holding and soothing the baby. Thus, during states of optimal animation, the mother's face was seldom in sight, but the baby did observe whatever happened in her immediate vicinity. We speculate that her relatively mature

[1] A fair proportion of 4-week-old infants show no focused and specific interest in either the human face or objects.

responsiveness to objects, not matched by the quality of her response to the human face, may have derived from this feature of her experience.

Adequacy of vegetative functioning: High.

Though Margaret cried and fretted more than the majority of 4-week-olds, and slept a little less during daytime hours, all vegetative processes functioned smoothly. She had no gastric troubles, she sucked well at the breast, breathing and circulation were if anything less labile than in most infants of this age, and she slept through the night and had done so since the age of 2 weeks.

Excitability: Low.

Scrutiny of the detailed descriptions suggests that this rating was given because, as expected from the SPE, external stimuli were seldom very rousing to this baby and never led to marked excitation. Any excitation from *inner* somatic causes was reduced or eliminated altogether by the mother's constant and effective soothing.

Irritability: Medium.

In this instance the rating of "medium" is an inadequate description of the actual state of affairs. If the relative amount of time spent in a restless, uncomfortable state, or spent whimpering and crying, had been the sole criterion, the appropriate rating would have been "low." However, much more often than most other babies, Margaret began to whimper (she seldom cried except when hungry), only to subside as soon as she was picked up. She spent many hours each day and evening contented in her mother's arms, but only because whenever she was placed in her crib or buggy, she fussed and the mother picked her up again. The "medium" rating here represents a compromise between the infant's strong inclination to register discomfort when awake (in the absence of discernible cause) and the mother's accommodation, which prevented the baby from remaining irritable for more than a minute or two at a time.

DISCUSSION

Margaret struck all observers as a somewhat uncomfortable baby, despite the fact that she was healthy and had developed well. Her typical day went somewhat as follows: After the morning feeding she often slept or drowsed until close to noon, though intermittently she whimpered or cried a little, whereupon her mother would hold her and walk about, or let her suck at the breast for a few minutes. During the afternoon, and until the parents went to bed, she was not content for more than about 20 minutes at a time unless she was held. Mother assumed that it was up to her to keep the baby comfortable, and so picked her up at the first sign of discontent. She had become adept at holding the baby while also doing housework, tending the other children, knitting, and watching TV. If Margaret subsided while in the mother's arms, she would try to put the baby down, usually to find that within a few minutes the baby was fussing again. If, as happened often, Margaret continued to show mild distress while held, the mother swayed her, bounced her, patted her, and walked her about. If nothing helped, the mother put her to the breast as a last resort. She knew that Margaret was not hungry, and aptly referred to these in-between feedings as "peace offerings." Once the nipple was inserted, the baby's body relaxed and her facial expression no longer reflected discontent. This was true even when she was not sucking, but merely holding the nipple in her mouth. During our observations, four such breast feedings occurred in the space of 3¼ hours, and the mother said that this was very much as usual. As has been said. In Margaret's life the feeding or sucking episodes did not involve mutual gazing or any effort by the mother to make the baby respond to her. At other times, for instance, during diapering and dressing, the mother seldom tried to get the baby to respond to her, though she might make soothing sounds.

Margaret was the fourth child in a lower middle class family, and her mother was a woman to whom child rearing seemed as natural as breathing. She possessed extraordinary ease and skill not only in manipulating her baby, but in her dealings with the older children (none of whom had yet reached school age). Somewhat to the surprise of the research staff, the mother considered that Margaret was easy to take care of, because she responded to soothing and/or feeding. It was as though, knowing she had it in her power to comfort the child, the mother remained unperturbed by the baby's frequent irritability. And it was as though holding the baby much of the day were the expected and natural state of affairs—and not a special accommodation.

Thus Margaret was one of the infants who were seldom acutely hungry (only for the first feeding of the day), and who therefore seldom experienced a change from extreme arousal to extreme quiescence. Nor did she have occasion to become sharply distressed or excited for any other cause. On the other hand, marked quiescence and bodily relaxation were less prominent in her experience than is common at the age of 4 weeks. Even while asleep (at least during observations at home and at our quarters) she engaged in a good deal of restless stirring. She vocalized and moved about both in response to sounds or vibrations and when there was no external stimulus. Similarly, during the long hours on the mother's lap she intermittently moved about, which led the mother to constantly change the baby's position in her arms. Even when Margaret was quiet, her expression had a frowning quality, and all observers commented on the fact that only during and immediately after breast feeding did she look "almost pleased." Finally, Margaret's experience lacked the brief moments of intent focus on the mother's face that we were able to observe in most 4-week-olds.

Mark, Ac II (4 Weeks)

SPE DETERMINANTS

Boundary Strength

	ENTIRE		MODALITY SECTORS			
	Inner	Outer	Vision	Touch	Sound	Passive Motion
Stimulation	medium	strong (−)	strong	weak	strong	
Frequency of Mother-Child Contacts		medium	low (+)	high (−)	low	low
Intensity	low	low	→	→	→	→
Maternal Competence		medium	→	→	→	→
Maternal Intrusiveness		low	→	→	→	→
Level of Home Stimulation		low	→	→	→	→

Activity Level: 2.3

STABLE PATTERNS OF EXPERIENCE

Frequency of strong bodily arousal: Occasional.

Mark was the kind of active baby who became very strongly aroused while hungry and while evacuating, but not with fatigue. However, his mother promptly tended to his needs, and no other kind of situation ever roused him to more than moderate excitation. Peak excitation states were relatively few in number and short in duration.

Internal bodily sensations: Medium.

The behavior of all 4-week-olds is dominated by fluctuations in body state. Mark's relative unresponsiveness to many external stimuli, along with the fact that he was not stimulated a great deal, merely mean that the frequency and intensity of moments during which he was responsive to external stimulation were less than would be found in more actively stimulated babies. Internal processes led to arousal about as often as in most 4-week-old babies.

Balance between behavior activations due to inner and to outer stimulation: Internal very predominant.

As we have said, most behavior activations shown by 4-week-olds result from fluctuating body states. In Mark's case the SPE indicates that, during contacts with the mother, he experienced strongly only the tactile contact that was involved. Since touch was used only to soothe, it seldom led to behavior activations, though it could modify his state.

Importance of distance receptors: Low.

Mark was not especially responsive to either sights or sounds, nor did his mother or his home surroundings expose him to such stimulation at all frequently or strongly.

Importance of near receptors: Fairly high.

During direct contacts, Mark's mother touched him frequently, and he was responsive to this variety of stimulation. In comparison with other infants, tactile sensations were only fairly prominent in his experience because Mark's mother did not handle him as much as some mothers do, and because she was gentle at all times.

Most prominent modality: Touch.

Least prominent modality: None.

The SPE indicates that neither sound nor vision was very important, nor was he frequently exposed to passive motion. Thus, no single modality is conspicuous for its relative insignificance in his experience.

Frequency of states of optimal animation: Fairly high.

An active infant is expected to show moderate levels of arousal even when not specifically stimulated. In the absence of disruptive somatic states (other than hunger and fatigue), and in the presence of gentle handling from the mother, Mark experienced states of comfortable wakefulness in the absence of lethargy more frequently than many other 4-week-olds. They occurred chiefly while he was in the crib and unattended, and only rarely while he was held by his mother.

OUTCOME RATINGS

Developmental status: Medium.

Mark's performance on the developmental tests conformed to high average standards for his age. At a chronological age of nearly 6 weeks (the home visit during which the tests were administered had to be postponed until nearly two weeks after the office study) his performance varied from the norm by no more than two weeks. His motor coordination and his capacity for visual pursuit corresponded to average expectations for 8-week-olds. He was among the babies whose response to appropriate social stimulation was minimal, though well within the normal range. He did regard the face of any person who smiled and talked to him from close by, but his expression did not "brighten," and he neither smiled nor cooed. Such relative lack of animation in response to the sight and sound of the human face may well reflect the fact that neither the mother nor anybody else made any effort to provoke social responses from him. In the SPE this circumstance is reflected in the fact that the distance receptors played a minimal role during contacts between his mother and her baby.

Adequacy of vegetative functioning: High.

Mark ate well, slept well, and had no gastric troubles.

Excitability: Medium.

During spontaneous activity, Mark alternated chiefly between forceful part-body activations and nearly complete inactivity. He reached peak excitation regularly when he was hungry, manifested by crying, screaming, and very forceful overall movement, interspersed with marked stiffening of the legs and fanning of the toes. However, prolonged handling by the mother, noises while awake or asleep, and many other varieties of stimulation evoked little or no visible response. In other words, hunger and such bodily events as evacuation regularly led to marked bodily arousal, including massive motion, marked muscle tension, and screaming. However, such events were relatively infrequent, and balanced by the fact that at other times he was distinctly unexcitable.

Irritability: Low.

Mark's tolerance for prolonged and awkward manipulations at the hands of an inexperienced mother was outstanding. Similarly, he could be dressed or changed without awakening from sound sleep, and during feedings "the roof could fall in" (as his mother said) without disrupting the steady rhythm of his sucking. He also was often seen awake, fairly active, and yet entirely content.

DISCUSSION

Mark is a good example of the manner in which a fairly robust baby can adapt comfortably not only to the ordinary exigencies of infantile existence, but also to an inordinate amount of very gentle manipulation as a loving but inexperienced mother works hard to accomplish routine tasks of infant care.

He was the first child of a young couple who were tremendously excited about the baby and consciously endeavored to satisfy his every need. Mother was a fervent believer in self-demand schedules, and in all current psychological thinking about the importance of a happy infancy as a foundation for healthy personality development. In this particular home such an ideology found expression chiefly in ways that did not directly affect the baby, though it dominated the life of the parents. Mother was well aware of her inexperience, but not especially concerned or troubled by this fact. She watched Mark most carefully and kept charts of his feedings, his bowel movements, and his developmental progress. While feeding him all her attention was focused on the baby, but he was held in such a way that he could not see her face. She often smiled as she held him, but almost always this occurred while she held his face to her shoulder and gently patted or stroked his body. In all other situations, too, her effort was to not disturb him, rather than to compel his attention. During caretaking routines she found it necessary to concentrate exclusively on the mechanical problems; she was so careful that she defeated her own purpose, taking several minutes to get him into a shirt or to pin a diaper, so that procedures involved a great deal more handling than most 4-week-olds receive. In part this excessive carefulness was an adaptation to his strong response to touch, for as she touched him, he often grimaced, jerked, or quivered for a moment—behaviors that she interpreted as signs of discomfort. It simply had not occurred to this mother to show the baby toys or to do anything with him for the purpose of providing pleasure.

From the point of view of Mark's adaptation it appears fortunate that this potentially excitable and markedly active baby was exposed to only moderate amounts and low degrees of external stimulation. Mothers as anxious and inexperienced as his was, and as aware of the psychological components of the early mother-child relationship, often direct to their young infants inordinate amounts of rousing attention and seek reassurance from their ability to elicit responses from the baby. Mark's mother expended enormous efforts in his behalf, but she sought and derived reassurance from carefully collected evidence of his physical well-being, and not from direct interaction with the baby.

Jackie, In II (4 Weeks)

SPE DETERMINANTS

Boundary Strength

	ENTIRE		*MODALITY SECTORS*			
	Inner	*Outer*	*Vision*	*Touch*	*Sound*	*Passive Motion*
Stimulation	medium (—)	medium (+)	strong	medium	strong	?
Frequency of Mother-Child Contacts		high	high (—)	high	high	high (—)
Intensity	low	high	———	———	———	——→
Maternal Competence		medium	———	———	———	——→
Maternal Intrusiveness		high	———	———	———	——→
Level of Home Stimulation		high	———	———	———	——→

Activity Level: 1.2

STABLE PATTERNS OF EXPERIENCE

Frequency of strong bodily arousal: Absent.

Jackie was not seen or reported as more than very moderately aroused at any time. Neither hunger nor fatigue nor massive external stimulation, which occurred frequently, elicited more than mild movement increases and perhaps whimpering.

Internal bodily sensations: Fairly low.

At the age of 4 weeks, fluctuations in bodily state are necessarily a more important determinant of behavior than are external causes. In Jackie's experience, sensations from within were not especially vivid and no more frequent than they are for most babies. Also, in his case they were supplemented by external stimulation more than is often the case.

Balance between behavior activations due to inner and to outer stimulation: Equivocal (no rating).

As has been said, changes in body state will account for most behavior changes in any 4-week-old infant. A rating of "equivocal" was made because when Jackie's behavior altered in response to inner stimulation, it was seldom allowed to run its course. More typically he was responding to body state as supplemented by active stimulation from the mother.

Importance of distance receptors: Fairly low.

During direct contacts with the mother, both vision and sound were employed a great deal. Since Jackie was relatively unresponsive in these modalities, the impact of such stimulation was nonetheless quite limited.

Importance of near receptors: High.

The mother touched her baby and moved him about a great deal. Although his response was slight in magnitude, his behavior suggested that touch especially made itself felt in his awareness at such times.

Most prominent modality: Touch.

Least prominent modality: Unknown.

Since he was about equally reactive to visual and auditory stimuli, and both modalities were evoked by the mother frequently, the SPE does not suggest that any one modality was activated less often, or experienced less keenly, than all the rest.

Frequency of states of optimal animation: Fairly high.

An inactive and not at all sensitive baby requires a fair amount of stimulation to be roused to maximal altertness, and this Jackie certainly received. A frequent sequence of events in his experience was that the mother energetically attempted to arouse his interest in her own face, in rattles placed before him, or in some other thing, and he at first focused on the stimulus with active interest—*i.e.,* showed optimal animation. As the mother persisted, the baby ceased responding, as if overwhelmed or exhausted, but without distress.

OUTCOME RATINGS

Developmental status: High.

Jackie's acceleration was chiefly in the area of visual-motor coordination in that at precisely 4 weeks of age he easily focused upon stationary objects, was able to visually follow a horizontally moving object, and could retain a rattle placed in his hand. He also listened attentively to the sound of the human voice (disrupting ongoing activity while it lasted) and his expression brightened noticeably, though he did not smile, in response to appropriate social stimulation. All of these behaviors are normative for 8-week-olds. Motor coordination otherwise, as well as vocalizations, met good average standards for his age. The mother was an energetic, volatile, and somewhat anxious person who intentionally did all she could to stimulate her baby's growth. When he was 2 weeks old, rattles were strung across his crib, and toys were frequently shown to him or placed in his hand. He was held in an upright sitting position more often than is common at that age (and far more often than is wise), and his mother tried to teach him games that involved kissing, tickling, and the like. Also, she had a way of bringing her face close to his and speaking to him intently until she had compelled his visual attention. An important part of this mother's vigorous approach to child rearing was her readiness to soothe the baby whenever he showed signs of discomfort. She persisted in rocking and swaying him, singing and talking to him at the same time, often also patting him, until he was contented. Thus Jackie had every conceivable incentive to become aware of things and people in the environment, while he was protected against more than a minimum of distress.

Adequacy of vegetative functioning: High.

All vegetative functions appeared stable and very adequate. He slept soundly and differed from most 4-week-olds by sleeping through the night without awakening (last feeding 9:30 P.M. and first feeding 4:30 A.M). He was breast-fed, receiving supplementary bottle feedings on most days.

Excitability: Low.

Jackie was described as "imperturbable," and, in fact, it was astonishing to observe his tolerance for a wide range of active manipulations. For instance, his mother more than once facilitated burping by grasping him at the ankles, dangling him upside down, and shaking him as one might a dustmop. Jackie flushed a bit, but neither grimaced nor whimpered. Also, the mother allowed a specified number of minutes for nursing at each breast. When the time was up, she quickly withdrew the nipple (to which he clung so tightly that its removal caused a plopping sound) and Jackie made no overt response. He was also accustomed to being tickled, bounced, and kissed very actively and to being picked up from sound sleep for feeding or bathing. The freedom with which both parents and the school-age sister dealt with the baby may be exemplified by the fact that he not only accompanied the family on many outings, but had also been given a bicycle ride just to see if he would like it.

Irritability: Low.

As implied in the section on excitability, Jackie was not in the least irritable. He seldom cried, and when he did his mother was as energetic in soothing him as she was at other times in rousing him. Since he proved responsive to soothing, the outcome was that Jackie fretted less and cried less than the great majority of 4-week-olds. We believe that his readiness to sleep away a large portion of the day must have played a role in protecting him from irritable states. Vigorous activities in his environment continued as he slept; his mother thought nothing of picking up the sleeping baby and taking him along on visits or shopping trips, but as often as not, he did not awaken, sleeping through many a movie in the drive-in theatre.

DISCUSSION

Jackie is another baby who exemplifies the manner in which the tendency (presumably biologically rooted) to respond to excitation by very partial motoric activation (low activity) and the biological factor of physical well-being can enable an infant to adapt comfortably to environmental conditions that are unsuitably stimulating by any standard.

Jackie's mother was a restless, tense, voluble woman who typically moved very rapidly. Though beset by anxiety and worries, she was an outgoing, warm, and intensively responsive person. She openly disliked breast feeding and looked forward to weaning Jackie to the bottle very soon; and she volunteered the information that she agreed to have this baby somewhat against her own inclination, because her husband wished for it. Yet toward both her children she maintained an attitude of deep involvement, of protectiveness, of pride, and of ambition on their behalf. Despite her apparent difficulties in living, she was an unguarded and trusting person. She spoke freely of her feelings, thoughts, and expectations, she obviously leaned on her husband and shared his interests and responsibilities, and she maintained an active and extensive social life and had many friends.

She took for granted that 4-week-old Jackie was already a personality with "good" characteristics as well as faults. Partly because she felt that she had to teach him, and partly because she derived a great deal of pleasure from his responsiveness, she controlled his life to an unusual degree. More often than not he was awakened for feeding and for his bath; his feedings were scheduled not only for certain time intervals, but also for the number of minutes he was allowed to suck. By the same token, she constantly did things to please him, to include him in the family life, and to comfort him. If he fussed, she picked him up and at first merely swayed him, patted him, and spoke to him. If this was of no avail, she intensified her efforts, and if nothing helped (which was very rare) she offered him an extra feeding. Large rattles were strung across his crib, and usually once a day she tied a toy to his wrist with a ribbon so that he might learn that his motion caused the toy to swing. When he was quiet and content, as well as at other times, she had a way of bringing her face very close to his and speaking to him in a loving and compelling manner. She also thought that she could teach him games (such as "kissing" her as she swung his body toward her until his face touched her cheek). Although she expressed concern and apprehension about many things (financial worries, health problems, and the like), she seemed supremely confident of her ability to care for both her children, and was satisfied that both were exceptionally "good" and healthy.

Under these conditions, Jackie developed more rapidly than the majority of babies. Since he was such a placid baby, his adaptation did not appear to be disrupted by a precocious awareness of aspects of the environment. As with other overly stimulated babies, we wonder about the later developmental consequences of such a pattern of existence. With advancing maturation he may be less able to, as it were, protect himself by falling alseep or by simply withholding active responsiveness.

Babette, Ac III (8 Weeks)

SPE DETERMINANTS

Boundary Strength

	ENTIRE		*MODALITY SECTORS*			
	Inner	*Outer*	*Vision*	*Touch*	*Sound*	*Passive Motion*
Stimulation	medium	medium	strong	strong	weak	?
Frequency of Mother-Child Contacts		high	low (+)	medium	low (+)	medium
Intensity	medium (−)	low →				
Maternal Competence		high →				
Maternal Intrusiveness		low →				
Level of Home Stimulation		medium →				

Activity Level: 2.4

STABLE PATTERNS OF EXPERIENCE

Frequency of strong bodily arousal: Rare.

A markedly active infant who is subject to more than ordinary degrees of inner somatic stimulation would ordinarily be expected to experience peak excitations fairly frequently. This was not the case with Babette, for reasons that are not apparent from the formal ratings. The high frequency of mother-child contacts, combined with low intensity and infrequent activation of the distant receptors, reflect the circumstance that this mother picked the baby up at the slightest sign of discomfort and never allowed peak excitation to occur.

Internal bodily sensations: Prominent.

Bodily state is a major determinant of behavior in all 8-week-olds, and Babette's SPE suggests that in her case this was especially true. She was not highly reactive to either sights or touch, and the auditory modality to which she did react strongly was seldom used by the mother during direct contacts with the baby.

Balance between behavior activations due to inner and to outer stimulation: Internal very predominant.

As has already been said, the mother's frequent contacts with the baby served to soothe rather than to arouse her. Babette's behavior activations, then, occurred chiefly in response to sensations arising from within the body.

Importance of distance receptors: Low.

Mother rarely evoked the modalities of sight and sound. To sight Babette was relatively unresponsive, but in view of the weak boundary in the auditory sector, it is likely that sounds did make themselves felt in Babette's experience. However, since the mother approached her baby very gently and was generally shielding in her approach, sound did not play an important part in the baby's day-by-day existence.

Importance of near receptors: Fairly high.

During moments of responsiveness to aspects of the environment, at least while in contact with the mother, touch and passive motion were the modalities primarily involved. However, since Babette was only moderately reactive, she did not feel sensations mediated by the near receptors as sharply as do more sensitive babies.

Most prominent modality: None.

Although she responded to sound more strongly than to other stimuli, it is unlikely that infrequent and gentle stimulation in that modality yielded any more vivid or more prominent sensations for the baby than the more frequently evoked modalities did.

Least prominent: Vision.

Frequency of states of optimal animation: Occasional.

The SPE describes an active baby who was aroused by bodily sensations fairly frequently and whose contacts with the mother were primarily soothing. Moments of animation short of strong excitation--the kind that allow the most focused and complex behavior integrations to occur—emerged occasionally when she was in the mother's arms. When left to her own devices, her strong movement impulses usually precluded states of optimal animation.

OUTCOME RATINGS

Developmental status: Medium.

Babette's protocol on the developmental tests conformed to average expectations. Unlike some of the other babies, Babette had shown exceptionally even developmental progress. Her motility, her capacity to attend visual and auditory stimuli, her vocalizations and her responsiveness to people all corresponded to standards for 8-week-olds.

Adequacy of vegetative functioning: High.

Babette ate well, slept well, and in all respects her appearance and behavior suggested the presence of bodily well-being. This was the more impressive because during early infancy (up to age 4 weeks) Babette suffered from fairly severe colic.

Excitability: Medium.

Babette received a rating of medium because, when left to her own devices in the crib, awake and even when asleep, she showed extensive restless motion and a notable degree of muscle tension. Yet she was also seen completely relaxed—always in the mother's or the father's arms, where she was held often and for long periods of time. Babette was one of the very few babies in the sample who was not seen entirely relaxed even while sound asleep or during feedings, but who did readily achieve this state when held while drowsy or while wide awake.

Irritability: Low.

Babette was not an irritable baby. She fretted or cried very rarely, despite the fact that she stayed awake for longer periods of each day than do most 8-week-olds. Her prevailing contentment can be accounted for almost entirely by the fact that both parents liked to hold her, and had learned to combine this with reading and other activities. When Babette began to stiffen her legs, to make restless quivering motions, and to vocalize in a faintly displeased fashion (not enough to be described as whimpering) one or the other parent picked her up. When the baby then became quiet, it was not necessarily taken as a signal to put her down again, but often seemed to enhance the mother's pleasure in keeping the baby in her arms.

DISCUSSION

In Babette we see a baby who, to judge by many aspects of the SPE configuration, might easily have been irritable and uncomfortable. Indeed, she proved to be a restless baby who was given to muscle tension more than the majority, and who stayed awake for longer periods of each day than is usual at 8 weeks. Her harmonious development and comfortable adaptation is intelligible only in terms of the parents' accommodation to the characteristics of their baby.[1]

Babette was the eagerly awaited first baby of a young family who lived in very modest circumstances. The mother struck all observers as a particularly relaxed and comfortable sort of person. She moved slowly and gracefully and spoke in a soft yet expressive manner. Every aspect of her dealings with the baby suggested ease and intimacy as well as enjoyment of contact with her. Despite a lack of experience in infant care, this mother took in her stride many objective difficulties. From the first day, Babette was difficult to feed, and breast feeding (which the mother desired) had to be abandoned. The baby had much gastric pain, cried a great deal, and in consequence slept very poorly. This lasted until the age of 4 weeks, when yet another change in formula seemed to correct the situation. It was during these difficult first few weeks that both parents developed the custom of holding their baby for long hours. Perhaps because she had no way of comparing her baby with other infants, Babette's mother did not seem in the least distressed at the baby's jerky motions, tremors, and restlessness that prevailed even in sleep and during feedings. Instead, she took obvious pleasure in the fact that holding the baby, swaying her slightly, and, if need be, feeding her always had the power to relax the baby.

To this mother Babette was a very important personage, but not someone from whom she expected or desired any response to herself as a person. She had not thought of tying toys to the crib, she did not hold her in the sitting position, she smiled at the baby frequently but only very rarely addressed her in a compelling manner. She realized that Babette responded to sounds, and had found that when the baby cried, a fairly sharp noise (such as knocking against a wooden surface) would, as she put it, distract her. During caretaking routines this mother was extraordinarily gentle, but not leisurely. She tried her excellent best to minimize the amount of handling, working smoothly and deftly in an effort not to disturb the baby. She seldom spoke to the baby at such times and did not compel the baby's visual attention to her own face or person.

Thus it came about that Babette, unlike the majority of babies, experienced moderate but definite arousal most of the time while left to her own devices (including while asleep). But each day she also experienced fairly long periods of drowsiness, or of a quiet but awake state, while being held by one or the other parent. Since the object was to make her comfortable, she was seldom played with at such times, but mother or father would hold the baby comfortably and at the same time read, watch TV, or occupy themselves in some other way. When Babette did show

[1] We do not imply that frequent and prolonged handling is the only way in which Babette could have functioned comfortably. But we do mean to say that a technique of infant rearing which can prove disastrous with certain kinds of babies (who become "addicted" to this situation and are unable to be content otherwise) appeared to meet the needs of this infant very adequately at the time we knew her.

discomfort from hunger or some other cause, she was picked up at once and soothed actively. If she did not quiet in response she was fed. During the day she received a bottle feeding approximately every 2½ hours (sometimes less time elapsed) while at night the intervals were 3½ hours or more. In terms of the distribution of different levels of arousal, Babette's experience pattern was far more stable than the SPE determinants would suggest. She experienced moderate arousal with each episode of hunger and definite but low level arousal while awake in the crib, but she also experienced drowsy quiescence, which most other small infants are more likely to show while unattended. Under these circumstances she developed so as to show less focused responsiveness to the environment than most active and frequently handled infants in this sample (and at this age), though no less than is normative for an 8-week-old.

Sarah, In III (8 Weeks)

SPE DETERMINANTS

Boundary Strength

	ENTIRE		*MODALITY SECTORS*			
	Inner	*Outer*	*Vision*	*Touch*	*Sound*	*Passive Motion*
Stimulation	strong	strong	medium	strong	strong	?
Frequency of Mother-Child Contacts		medium	high (—)	low	high (—)	low
Intensity	low	medium (—)	→			
Maternal Competence		high	→			
Maternal Intrusiveness		medium	→			
Level of Home Stimulation		medium	→			

Activity Level: 1.6

STABLE PATTERNS OF EXPERIENCE

Frequency of strong bodily arousal: Absent.

Sarah did not respond strongly to either internal or external stimuli, nor was she handled very often or very forcefully. Both hunger and fatigue failed to arouse her more than very slightly, and observation lent credence to the mother's statement that Sarah simply did not get upset.

Internal bodily sensations: Fairly low.

Like any other baby, Sarah, did of course experience fluctuating body states and responded to them by behavior alteration. However, prior to feeding she either slept or lay quiet and content in the crib; apparently hunger was not sharply felt, though she sucked eagerly once the nipple was in the mouth. Fatigue led to mild restlessness for a period of 3 to 6 minutes. In general, the extent to which her behavior altered in response to inner somatic stimulation was less than is usually seen.

Balance between behavior activations due to inner and to outer stimulation: Equal.

As described above, behavior activations due to somatic stimulation were of relatively small intensity in Sarah's life. Unlike a good many other 8-week-olds, she was frequently spoken to compellingly by the mother, who tended to attract the baby's gaze both to her person and to things about. Since Sarah was often very quiet to begin with, her response to such events was often a flurry of mild bodily activity. Thus, external stimulation did lead to behavior activations fairly often, though these were as small as those in response to somatic stimulation.

Importance of distance receptors: Moderate.

Importance of near receptors: Fairly low.

The mother seldom touched the baby beyond the necessary minimum, and Sarah was never rocked and hardly ever swayed. Since, in addition, her response to touch was minimal (strong boundary), this baby had relatively few occasions to feel vividly the sensations generated by the near receptors.

Most prominent modality: Vision.

Least prominent modality: Touch (and possibly passive motion).

Frequency of states of optimal animation: Moderate.

Sarah's mother made a point of speaking to her and of compelling her visual attention regularly, if not very often. During such contacts with the mother, Sarah was roused to attentiveness on many occasions. However, most mothers of young infants supplement visual and auditory stimulation by also touching the baby and moving him about. In such cases, the baby feels the mother's presence more vividly and is more likely to respond to the sights and sounds emanating from her. Sarah's mother rarely touched her baby while also speaking to her (except during some routine procedures). The sight of the mother's face and the sound of her voice frequently compelled Sarah's attention, but only occasionally did such stimulation prove arousing to an optimal degree.

OUTCOME RATINGS

Developmental status: Medium.

Sarah's test performance conformed to average standards for her age in all respects. Since her reactivity to visual stimuli had been judged to be greater than that to other modalities (medium instead of strong boundary) and she received a good deal of stimulation in that area, it is of interest to know that the *only* items on which her test behavior exceeded average standards for her age concerned visual motor-coordination (visual pursuit of circular motion of an object, steady regard of small objects while held to sitting—both 12-week items). The one area in which Sarah's behavior did not entirely meet average expectations for her age was that of vocalization. She did not make cooing sounds. Since she received a good deal of auditory stimulation, and since vocalization is so often a response to the human voice, this observation is in keeping with the fact that the outer boundary for the auditory sector was assessed as strong. Sarah was, however, highly responsive to other persons, but her responses were intent regard, often combined with a complete cessation of all movement, smiling, or sometimes a movement increase and an elaborate variety of mouthing and tonguing as she regarded the face of a person who spoke to her and smiled at her from close by.

Adequacy of vegetative functioning: High.

Sarah ate well, slept well, had no gastric problems, and in every other way demonstrated healthy and smooth bodily functioning. She did occasionally "spit up" after a feeding. However, this caused her no distress, and seemed to be the result of her mother's exceptionally conscientious and vigorous efforts to elicit burping.

Excitability: Low.

Sarah was anything but excitable. Even hunger and fatigue seldom roused her more than a very little. She responded less than most babies to ordinary handling, such as being diapered and dressed. Even her mother's custom of frequently removing the nipple while the baby was actively sucking (she thought the baby ought to burp after each ounce) led to no overt response, though on each occasion Sarah sucked eagerly as soon as the nipple was restored.

Irritability: Low.

This sturdy, robust, and healthy baby was never irritable. She spent fairly long periods unattended in the crib, where she seemed relaxed, looked about some, and engaged in very gentle motor play. She tolerated occasional vigorous manipulations (for instance, being lifted from the crib by one arm as the rest of her body dangled) without a whimper. Mild fussing occurred with hunger and fatigue, but even then she did not cry.

DISCUSSION

Sarah had made a very comfortable adaptation to a pattern of existence that was not typical in our sample, but corresponds to a pattern that was usual years ago and remains so in other cultural groups. She was an "old-fashioned" schedule baby, who was awakened for her feedings and at bath time. Her mother did not believe in holding babies, and body contact was low even during feeding, when Sarah lay along the mother's lap, her head on the mother's knees and her feet resting against the mother's abdomen. However, at this and other times, the mother kept her face in the baby's view and spoke to her warmly and continuously. When the baby gave minimal signs of restlessness, moving a bit or puckering her lips though not whimpering, the mother spoke to her and changed her position in the crib, which usually sufficed to content her.

We were interested and amused to note the contrast between this mother's description of her child-rearing techniques and the reality. Had one heard only the mother's account, one would conclude that Sarah received next to no attention except for routine care. Actually the mother was vigilant and responded to very minimal behavior clues on the baby's part. Yet it was perfectly true that Sarah was not held, walked about, or rocked, that she was not patted except to elicit a burp, and that she spent all of her waking time, which was considerable for an 8-week-old, simply lying in the crib.

Sarah's mother was a gentle, soft-spoken woman who moved in an unhurried, deliberate, and highly competent fashion. She had firm ideas about the care of her two children and seemed remarkably free from self-doubt and indecision.

In her day-by-day experience, Sarah very rarely became aroused to more than a very moderate degree. She spent much time in an awake and quiescent state during which she was likely to focus on conspicuous aspects of the environment (such as a person walking close by or a ceiling light), but all she did was gaze. This state and her sleep were punctuated by the moments when her mother cared for her or the preschool-age brother approached her with awkward vigor. At such times she either gazed and smiled so intently as to keep her body motionless, or else she slightly increased activity. However, at least while under observation, she did not activate her entire body vigorously or vocalize. It is of interest that the closest she came to fairly strong behavioral arousal was during the developmental test. The examiner made a point of touching the baby while showing her toys, and of persevering longer than would be required for testing purposes. Sarah finally stiffened her limbs, looked mildly excited, and began to mouth intensively (tongue and lip motions) as she focused on the toy.

Despite the fact that she received more stimulation of the distance modalities than most babies, Sarah's responsiveness to things about was comparatively limited. Yet, it is equally important to point out that she was alert, contented, and well developed even though her mother imposed a strict regimen and was in general not especially indulgent.

Helen, Ac IV (8 Weeks)

SPE DETERMINANTS

Boundary Strength

	ENTIRE		MODALITY SECTORS			
	Inner	Outer	Vision	Touch	Sound	Passive Motion
Stimulation	weak (+)	weak	weak	weak	weak	?
Frequency of Mother-Child Contacts		low (+)	low (−)	low	medium (−)	low
Intensity	medium	low	→			
Maternal Competence		medium	→			
Maternal Intrusiveness		low	→			
Level of Home Stimulation		low	→			

Activity Level: 2.4

STABLE PATTERNS OF EXPERIENCE

Frequency of strong bodily arousal: High.

Helen was highly reactive (weak boundaries) to both internal and external stimuli. Hunger regularly led to very marked behavioral arousal, and fatigue did so frequently but not always. In addition, because of her great sensitivity to touch and other stimuli, all prolonged caretaking routines (dressing, bathing, and usually diapering) brought marked distress and hence high levels of arousal. The rating of medium maternal competence indicates that this mother, gentle though she was, showed considerable awkwardness in manipulating her baby.

Internal bodily sensations: Prominent.

The fact that Helen experienced bodily need states very sharply suggests in itself that sensations emanating from within the body were very prominent, especially because she was highly reactive to internal stimuli. In addition, while awake and unattended, Helen often showed marked activations in the absence of external stimuli.

Balance between behavior activations due to inner and to outer stimulation: Equal.

As implied by the "weak" rating of the outer boundary, Helen was apt to respond strongly to whatever stimulation came her way. Being picked up and held or manipulated, being spoken to, hearing an incidental sound—all elicited from this baby specific behavioral response. Although the mother did not approach her very frequently, only a few of the contacts that did occur tended to be soothing. Most contacts roused Helen to greater activity, whether in the context of pleasurable animation or distress. Thus

Helen's experience differed from that of most other 8-week-olds in that the occasions when behavior activation was responsive to external stimulation were almost as numerous as the occasions when it resulted from fluctuating body states. Even more unusual, the intensity of her excitement (distress) was typically greater during maternal manipulations than during bodily need states.

Importance of distance receptors: Medium.

Helen was so responsive that even fairly infrequent activation of the visual and auditory modalities during contact with the mother clearly entered her awareness. The mere closeness of the mother or another person, before body contact occurred, was perceived and responded to by Helen more often and more strongly than one ordinarily sees in babies of this age. Similarly, movements and sounds in the environment provoked attention and response relatively often when Helen was awake and unattended.

Importance of near receptors: Moderate.

Although Helen was touched no more than necessary, and although a point was made of never rocking or swaying her, the irreducible minimum of body contact with the mother was sufficient to provide considerable excitation through one of the near receptors, namely touch. That this variety of sensation played a role in this baby's experience is also attested to by the observation that her response to visual and auditory stimuli was always magnified when light touch was added. For instance, she smiled and gazed at the sight of a smiling countenance, but if the partner very lightly touched her hand or another part of her body, Helen invariably cooed and began to move her arms and legs.

Most prominent modality: Possibly sound; possibly none.

Least prominent modality: Passive motion (?).

This baby was not rocked or swayed at all. Being lifted and manipulated did, of course, provide some kinesthetic stimulation, but of low degree.

Frequency of states of optimal animation: Moderate.

When left to her own devices, Helen alternated between periods of marked activity (chiefly kicking and waving of arms) and periods of quiescence. During the quiet moments, which seldom lasted more than about 30 seconds at a time, she inspected the environment alertly. During the active moments her behavior was not outwardly focused, but she did engage in the varieties of motor play that "practice" important coordinations. She was not seen in an alert and animated state while in the mother's arms, but very occasionally the mother bent close to the baby lying in the crib and spoke to her softly. At such times Helen responded vividly and without undue excitation, by gazing, vocalizing, and general animation clearly directed to the mother.

OUTCOME RATINGS

Developmental status: Medium.

Helen's test performance conformed closely to average standards for her age. However, her behavior approximated normal standards for 12-week-olds in one respect, that of coordinated responsiveness to visual stimuli. She easily followed the circular motion of an object, and focused readily and for long periods of time on a small stationary object (one-inch red cube). Her social responsiveness was also greater than that of most 8-week-olds, not so much in what she did (chiefly gazing, smiling, and sometimes cooing) but in her readiness to respond when occasion offered. She had developed such a selective interest in human faces that she paid no attention to test objects as long as any person was in view. Her capacity to focus, follow, and to hold an object briefly in her hand emerged only when the examiner and the observers removed themselves from her visual field.

Adequacy of vegetative functioning: Medium.

Actually, Helen ate and slept well, and was seen quite relaxed and content both awake and asleep. The "medium" score refers to occasional episodes of gastric distress, which were acute for brief periods but left no aftermath once the distension of the abdomen was relieved by burping or other means. The baby also blanched with excitement on occasion—for instance, when toys were offered for more than about 30 seconds—and she flushed a very deep red when she cried. One additional fact requires mention. During the first three weeks of life Helen suffered from fairly severe colic and cried a very great deal. Except for the brief flurries of gastric discomfort (seldom more than one a day) this had disappeared by the age of 4 weeks. Helen, who was labile in her general responsiveness, showed some lability also in the physiological realm. Yet, the vital functions of food intake and sleep were unaffected, bodily distress was limited to brief periods, and the long hours of sleep in the morning and for most of the afternoon may well have been restorative.

Excitability: High.

Helen showed pleasurable excitation when she was spoken to very gently, smiled at, and lightly touched (firm touch at such moments reduced her to tense attentiveness, and caused smiles, cooing, or pleasurable kicking to disappear). The frequency of such events was limited by the fact that mother might initiate them just before or after diapering or feeding, but rarely at other times. More often, excitation coincided with unpleasure, as will be described in the next section. Another facet of her behavior that contributed to a high rating for excitability was the fact that while she was unattended in the crib, incidental sounds or vibrations frequently led to startles, jerky or tremorous motion, and even somewhat displeased-sounding vocalizations.

Irritability: High.

Helen was a baby who could not tolerate being touched, held, or moved about without some discomfort. If she was content beforehand, she first became tense and almost always began to cry before the procedure was completed. If she was discontent she began to scream in acute distress. It must be said, however, that the mother was so anxious to avoid undue touch and generally not to upset the baby, that her overcautiousness made such procedures as diapering and dressing last much longer than is necessary.

In addition, Helen's marked distress while hungry or fatigued, which was accompanied by massive activity and pronounced muscle tension, contributed to the judgment that this was a highly irritable baby. As already mentioned, at least once a day she became tense and cried hard because of gastric pain. A bottle of warm water proved the best remedy, and was usually offered if the crying lasted for more than a few minutes.

By and large, however, the "high" rating in Helen's case refers to her pronounced intolerance for external stimulation. This is in sharp contrast to most other irritable babies, who generally show irritability by their tendency to whimper or to cry when left alone.

DISCUSSION

Helen's adaptation syndrome represents an extreme case. She was exceptionally sensitive in all respects, and she was cared for by a mother whose convictions about child care practices were extreme in their emphasis on discipline and nonindulgence. Helen's mother was a woman of few words, one who seemed somewhat stiff and constrained in her motions and who in general lacked spontaneity. She was deeply committed to one of the fundamentalist religions, and this view of life was applied to child rearing as to all else. In consequence, she was in favor of rigidity and harshness in matters that she perceived as having a moral aspect, but otherwise she was protective, gentle, and loving with the baby.

In practice this meant that Helen's mother adhered to a feeding schedule (offering water in between times to pacify the baby) and that she did not believe in rocking babies or in giving them attention when they are content and so "do not need it." It was also true that even during routine contacts she managed to touch the baby only minimally. Actually, beyond conscious intentions, this mother could express softness and affection by voice and facial expression (though she rarely allowed herself to do so), but she was unable to hold the baby comfortably or to manipulate her in a way adapted to the baby's convenience or momentary state. We think it important that the same stiffness and lack of smooth coordination was evident in her dealing with household tasks and, it would seem, in most other situations. All observers were agreed that she showed somewhat greater freedom and warmth toward the baby than she was able to muster toward us.

In some respects the mother's style of behavior suited Helen's special requirements. It is nearly certain that this very sensitive baby could not have developed as well as she did and that acute displeasure would have occurred more often had she been handled and played with as actively and as frequently as most babies are. In addition, the mother was aware of her baby's intolerance of touch and did her best to accommodate. Unfortunately, her very fear lest she upset the baby defeated her own end. As she tried to be gentle, she not only unduly prolonged procedures, but she also failed to control Helen's posture; the baby sometimes found herself dangling while held only by one arm, and at other times she slipped from mother's grasp and hit her head forcefully against the table. When this happened while we were observing the bath, the mother volunteered that "every time this happens," Helen cries very hard, so it could not have been an exceptional occurrence.

The distribution of the various states in Helen's daily life was as follows: She experienced sharp distress and behavioral arousal (fairly frequently) and moderately strong arousal in a pleasurable context (rather seldom but regularly). She spent a relatively large proportion of her time in an affectively neutral state during which she alternated between moderately strong arousal (moving massively, showing muscle tension, intermittent vocalizing) and brief periods of quiescence during which she appeared to "rest." States of optimal animation, of the kind that permit outwardly focused behavior adaptations of relatively complex nature, did occur as she lay in the crib and as her mother paid her fleeting attention, but they were brief and only moderately frequent. She spent most of the morning and a good deal of the afternoon asleep.

Under these conditions she made all the expected developmental gains and excelled in her alertness to components of the immediate environment. Especially noteworthy was the fact that Helen was strikingly responsive (though no more mature than other 8-week-olds) to any and all opportunities for social interaction. It was puzzling to observe a mother who was often serious, preoccupied, and impassive as she worked near or with her baby, while the baby gazed at the inattentive mother in a delighted manner and even smiled, though the mother did not.[1] On the basis of what we saw in Helen and in some other babies, we have come to think that markedly sensitive infants experience whatever contacts they have with the

[1] It is likely that this mother showed greater warmth and sociability with her baby when she was not observed. However, from what we came to know about her as a person, and from what we learned about the household routines, it is certain that by and large this inhibited and preoccupied mother could not at any time establish easy intimacy with her baby or spend much time in interactions beyond routine care.

mother with special vividness, and that these contacts are demarcated in their experience with special clarity when distress and agitation are also frequent in their life. Thus the mother (and at this age, anyone who behaves in a maternal manner, for Helen responded to the observers at least as strongly as she did to the mother) may become a distinguished and compelling aspect of the environment earlier in such children than is usually the case.[2]

Steward, In IV (8 Weeks)

SPE DETERMINANTS

Boundary Strength

	ENTIRE		*MODALITY SECTORS*			
	Inner	*Outer*	*Vision*	*Touch*	*Sound*	*Passive Motion*
Stimulation	medium (—)	medium	medium	strong	weak	?
Frequency of Mother-Child Contacts		high	medium	high	medium	high
Intensity	medium	high	→	→	→	→
Maternal Competence		medium	→	→	→	→
Maternal Intrusiveness		high	→	→	→	→
Level of Home Stimulation		medium	→	→	→	→

Activity Level: 1.6

STABLE PATTERNS OF EXPERIENCE

Frequency of strong bodily arousal: Rare.

Steward was a moderately inactive baby, moderately responsive to internal and external stimulation and subject to considerable excitatory stimulation both from bodily discomfort and at his mother's hands. Under these conditions peak excitations might have occurred quite readily were it not for one aspect of maternal care—his mother's discovery of the power of the pacifier. Whenever the baby was even slightly restless or uncomfortable, he was not only soothed in conventional ways, but was also given the pacifier. If this did not content him, he was nursed, regardless of the elapsed time since the last feeding. Thus Steward was never allowed to reach high levels of behavioral arousal.

Internal bodily sensations: Prominent.

In Steward's case the "medium" rating for the intensity of stimulation was made chiefly because he suffered from the gastric disorder known as

[2] Benjamin (1963), expressed a similar idea. He noted that intense gazing at the mother's face, especially during feeding, was most conspicuous when other observations led him to think that the mother-child relationship was tenuous and troubled.

colic. Repeatedly each day he fussed and cried from this cause, and so had frequent occasion to be aware of alterations in body state. Although he was moderately responsive to his mother's manipulations, the great majority of observed behavior alterations occurred in response to altered state and not to external stimulation (which is, of course, to be expected in an 8-week-old).

Balance between behavior activations due to inner and to outer stimulation: Internal very dominant.

As described in part above, Steward increased activity almost exclusively in response to gastric or other proprioceptive events. His direct contacts with the mother, which were frequent, were almost always of a soothing nature. Very occasionally, as he lay quiet in the mother's arms, he did smile and vocalize in response to her energetic fondling. These were very minor behavior activations; not infrequently, as his mother spoke to him smilingly and fondled him, Steward only looked at her and increased the vigor and tempo of sucking at the pacifier.

Importance of distance receptors: Medium.

Steward's mother quite often spoke to him both soothingly and playfully, and she also tended to place her face in his view in order to compel his attention. But during her contacts with the baby, she used touch and passive movement so massively as to overshadow the distance modalities. It was exceedingly rare for this mother to speak to the baby or to smile at him without also touching him. Nor did she tend to show him toys. However, when left to his own devices (which was rare), Steward tended to look at conspicuous objects (ceiling lights, moving curtains, etc.) with alert interest. He was more than ordinarily responsive to sounds. Small but sudden incidental noises led to startles, to blinking, or to a transient arrest of movement. Loud sudden noises caused crying or whimpering, and on a few occasions a moderate sound (such as soft ringing of a bell) made him stop crying as he listened. Thus the distance receptors did make themselves felt and evoked behavior alterations on occasion.

Importance of near receptors: Fairly high.

Steward was touched by his fond mother as much as any baby we have known. She rubbed, patted, stroked, and kissed him very often, and frequently used a laying on of hands while feeding him. He was swayed and rocked a great deal, not only when he required soothing, but because his mother thought that it gave him pleasure. However, his response to being touched was minimal, and the impact of passive motion could not be ascertained. When Steward was content to begin with, these prolonged and often quite intense maternal ministrations had no observable effect upon behavior. He looked content, kicked a bit, and occasionally focused on an object—much as he had done before the episode began. If he had been restless and uncomfortable, he always quieted in the mother's arms. However, on many such occasions he was also offered the pacifier, and it seems probable that sucking played a major role in the soothing process. Thus he must frequently have felt the sensations generated by touch and passive motion, but they may not have entered his awareness in a particularly vivid manner.

Most prominent modality: Possibly sound, in terms of vividness if not prominence.

Least prominent modality: None.

Frequency of states of optimal animation: Moderate.

This inactive baby was seen in states of alert wakefulness during spontaneous activity. At such times he did attend the visual spectacles in the immediate environment and at other times mobilized appropriate motoric schemas apparently due to mild stimulation from within. However, he was seldom left unattended unless mother thought him sleepy. During the large amounts of time when Steward was held in the mother's arms, there were occasions when she ceased vigorous physical stimulation and instead spoke to him in a pleasantly rousing manner. At such times he cooed, looked at her, and engaged in active mouthing. However, much more often (when not soothing him), the mother bounced and shook the baby or kissed him energetically. Steward looked pleased and sometimes smiled, but the situation did not permit maximal responsiveness on his part.

OUTCOME RATINGS

Developmental status: Medium.

In all areas and on both tests, Steward's performance amply met normative standards for his age, but did not significantly exceed them. There was nothing distinctive about the pattern of his test performance, for his behavior was of equal maturity in body coordination as it was in his response to things and to persons.

Adequacy of vegetative functioning: Low.

Steward's adequacy of vegetative functioning was judged to be "low," though within normal limits. The rating was assigned because, while under observation, Steward suffered from colic to a moderate degree. Several times each day he showed the typical syndrome of crying, contraction of the body, and visible signs of marked gastric distress. The large amount of rocking and holding he received, as well as the generous use of a pacifier, was due to the fact that these measures, singly and in combination, were most effective in bringing relief. In addition, Steward, who was breast-fed and whose weight gain was excellent, did not suck as steadily and forcefully as do most infants. Very contented in the mother's arms during nursing, he frequently became drowsy, and the mother had to rouse him before he would continue to feed. Even when Steward was content a slight impediment to optimal integration of vegetative functioning may have been present, in that relatively regular respiration appeared to be unduly dependent upon sucking. As he stirred in the crib, restless but far from distressed, breathing tended to become shallow and irregular and sometimes he showed a quivering motion of the lower jaw (of the sort typically seen in neonates). Then the mother often popped the pacifier in his mouth, and as Steward sucked, he breathed more evenly. It ought to be mentioned that Steward was not a sick baby when we saw him. He slept and ate normally, he was alert and responsive, tonus was good, and, overall, he looked to us and to his pediatrician like a perfectly healthy child.

Excitability: Low.

Steward tolerated his mother's endless fondling and other manipulations with perfect equanimity. Although the provocative presentation of toys aroused his interest, he was not among those inactive babies to whom this variety of challenge was markedly excitatory. As has been mentioned, hunger, fatigue and gastric pain were accompanied by an increase in activity and by crying, but these upsets were moderate in degree. It is impossible to know whether massive behavioral arousal would have occurred if mother had not intervened on each and every occasion.

Irritability: High.

This rating was not primarily due to the colic syndrome, which accounted for only a small proportion of the displeasure this baby showed. Rather, he was extraordinarily dependent on the comforting devices employed by the mother. When awake, not hungry, and not in gastric discomfort, he nonetheless was rarely content for more than 10 minutes unless he was held and played with, or had his pacifier, or both. Irritability was very mild in nature—he whimpered and stirred restlessly—and it was not allowed to continue for more than a few minutes at a time.

In this case the rating of "high" irritability reflected a behavioral characteristic that was somewhat unusual. Had one assessed only the proportion of time that Steward spent distinctly discontented, the proper rating would have been "medium." However, his adaptation when we knew him was such that either the pacifier or being held was a necessary condition for the absence of irritability when he was awake. In our judgment, this extreme dependence on maternal intervention was due largely to the mother's excessive readiness to handle him. She was unable to wait and see if he would settle down of his own accord, and she misjudged the baby's minimal restlessness by taking it as a sign of distress and at once applying vigorous remedies.

DISCUSSION

Except for the recurrent bouts of gastric distress, Steward functioned normally and his development had progressed in accordance with average expectations. Yet his adaptation syndrome differed from the optimal in some ways, and from the usual in others.

Due to some life events that occurred before Steward's birth, his mother found herself isolated from her family, and mother and baby lived alone. She was a well-educated, articulate, and responsive person, but also a very anxious one at the time we knew her. The baby was the one and only important focus of her life. Even limited acquaintance justified the assumption that her tendency to maintain constant body contact with the baby was based on the comfort and pleasure she received from fondling him, as well as on her passionate resolve to keep him happy.

Steward's existence was characterized by a very narrow range of arousal states. Even hunger was never experienced fully, as mother fed him at the slightest sign of discomfort, and often his behavior at the breast proved that he was not in need of food. Thus he experienced neither real hunger nor the sharp change in feeling state that normally occurs with satiation. Similarly, the pacifier, augmented by being held and soothingly manipulated, blurred the edges of discomfort or arousal from any cause. Further, being awake and left to his own devices was for him a break in continuity and not the background, as it is for most other babies. He had adapted well to the fact that he was kissed, stroked, patted, and otherwise handled a great deal,[1] but he seldom responded vividly or specifically to these events. The sensations of being stimulated in this manner appeared to have become an accustomed background, much as constant radio music may be responded to only when it is turned off. It adds to the total picture to know that Steward's mother did not hesitate to awaken him at will (for his bath or to show him to visitors). All in all, Steward was not only restricted in the range of arousal states he experienced, but also in his opportunity to stabilize the physiological cycles of sleep–wakefulness and hunger–feeding.

[1] It is instructive to compare Steward's adaptation to that of Jackie (In II). The two SPE's are very similar, in that Jackie was also subject to incessant maternal attention and was also of medium sensitivity in most respects. Yet he made a much more comfortable adaptation than did Steward, possibly because he slept a great deal and had no gastric troubles.

Roderick, Ac V (12 Weeks)

SPE DETERMINANTS

	Boundary Strength					
	ENTIRE		MODALITY SECTORS			
	Inner	Outer	Vision	Touch	Sound	Passive Motion
Stimulation	medium (+)	medium	strong (−)	strong (−)	strong (−)	?
Frequency of Mother-Child Contacts		high	medium	high (−)	medium (+)	medium
Intensity	high	high	→	→	→	→
Maternal Competence		high	→	→	→	→
Maternal Intrusiveness		medium	→	→	→	→
Level of Home Stimulation		high	→	→	→	→

Activity Level: 2.7

STABLE PATTERNS OF EXPERIENCE

Frequency of strong bodily arousal: Occasional.

In an exceedingly active baby who was intensely stimulated, one might have expected the regular occurrence of massive excitation, especially since Roderick was subject to more than ordinary internal stimulation. However, the SPE ratings also indicate that he was robust rather than sensitive, and that maternal competence was high. The most massive bodily arousal was observed just prior to evacuation (and his mother said that the amount of muscle tension and crying we observed was typical). He showed very high activity and crying also when hungry, but the mother was careful to feed him at once, so that he neither reached peak levels nor stayed in a state of distress for any length of time. Fatigue also was a rousing state, but mother always provided a bottle of warm water or a pacifier, which effectively reduced moderate excitation to low level restlessness. Lastly, Roderick, like most other active babies, became aroused when movement was restrained. However, the mother, very conscious of this circumstance, had become adept at so arranging things that he could kick freely while she worked with the upper portion of his body, and that his arms and shoulders were free to move as she worked with the legs. Further, if he became at all tense and irritable during dressing, she allowed frequent periods of free movement before she slipped in the next step in the procedure. Despite this baby's tendency to respond to excitation with strong muscular arousal, maximum levels of excitation occurred perhaps once or twice a day, and then briefly.

Internal bodily sensations: Prominent.

During spontaneous activity Roderick was never still. Even when content he constantly kicked, or raised extended legs, only to lower them, or waved his arms in an energetic windmill motion. Presumably, these incessant activations occurred in response to proprioceptive stimulation strong enough to penetrate the sturdy inner boundary. Roderick had earlier suffered from the colic, and when we knew him still suffered from occasional brief flurries of gastric distress, which were relieved by the offer of a bottle with warm water. Since hunger, fatigue, and evacuation also brought marked behavior alterations, it is concluded that the sensations generated by changing body states played a prominent part in Roderick's experience.

Balance between behavior activations due to inner and to outer stimulation: Equal.

A very large proportion of Roderick's behavior activations were clearly due to fluctuating body states. However, his contacts with the mother were rousing quite as often as they were soothing. As has been said, the manipulations involved in dressing and similar procedures roused him to activity. In addition, his mother frequently incited him to play with rattles or other toys, and also frequently approached him for no purpose except to elicit social responses from him. These consisted chiefly of gazing, smiling, soft cooing and sometimes waving of the arms. All in all, it proved that Roderick initiated a behavior activation in response to external stimulation almost as often as in response to internal sensations. However, response to inner somatic stimuli was much greater than to external events.

Importance of distance receptors: Moderate.

Roderick's mother, who dealt with her baby energetically, typically combined all modalities during interactions with him. She brought her face close to his and spoke compellingly, attracting his gaze to her face. Usually, this was reinforced by touching him. She valued his attentiveness to toys more than is usual, and frequently placed rattles in his hand (again combining visual, auditory and tactile stimulation). She also placed him in the sitting posture for as long as he was comfortable (up to half an hour) every afternoon, so that he had a wide range for visual exploration. To judge by his behavior, Roderick was only moderately responsive to these attentions. When unattended, he was so occupied with motor play that he responded less to sights and sounds than did some other 12-week-olds.

Importance of near receptors: Moderate.

As has been mentioned, Roderick was touched a great deal. He was also rocked and swayed, both in soothing and in play. His response to this aspect of the stimulation he received was also moderate. When uncomfortable, he often quieted in response to being rocked and patted, but his response to either toys or people was not altered when touch was added to sight and sound.

Most prominent modality: None.

Least prominent modality: None.

Frequency of states of optimal animation: Occasional.

Despite the fact that, by definition, a baby with strong outer boundaries does not experience strong and frequent stimulation as unduly arousing, Roderick had fewer opportunities to experience states of optimal animation than do many other babies. While unattended, he was, as has been said, not given to attending to the environment, though he did activate appropriate motor schemas. Since at this age the developmentally most important new behavior integrations are focused and discriminatory responsiveness to things about, spontaneous activity did not provide for periods of optimal animation in this sense. The mother's play with the baby and her social attentiveness during routine procedures provided both pleasure and animation, but not at an optimal level, because she was so vigorous as to reduce him to the role of passive respondent. As she placed one rattle in each hand, it was often she who shook it for him, holding his hand. As she spoke to him, tickled him, and moved him about, there was little Roderick could do except to regard her and smile. In addition, she often approached him in a vigorously playful manner when the observers thought that he was too sleepy or too fussy to respond. In fact, her efforts to get him to play with toys repeatedly led to tears. (Mother herself volunteered that the rattles seem to "aggravate him.") Yet the moment he began to whimper or to cry, his mother soothed him most effectively.

OUTCOME RATINGS

Developmental status: Medium.

Roderick's developmental status was of average caliber. His behavior was most mature in gross motor coordination, where he succeeded on three items at the 16-weeks level and was able to maintain his head in a steady and erect position, not usually expected until the age of 20 weeks. His response to the sight or sound of objects was entirely in accord with average expectations. However, his vocalizations, especially his behavior in response to social stimulation, were less well developed. He did coo and smile responsively, but these responses did not come readily nor were they maintained for as long as one often sees. Unlike the majority of 12-week-olds, he did not chuckle.

Despite the fact that Roderick was constantly treated as a social partner, he failed to show the special interest in the human face, and the ready social responsiveness commonly seen at this age. In fact, he was among the small minority of infants in this sample who responded more readily and with greater animation to objects than to people.

Adequacy of vegetative functioning: Medium.

Roderick slept well and soundly, but he was subject to recurrent gastric distress which was never severe. Also, feeding was an uneasy and often an uncomfortable situation for this baby, almost certainly as the result of mother's choice of technique (we believe that more appropriate ways of feeding could have prevented his discomfort). The vital process of food intake was for this baby anything but relaxed and smoothly regulated. His mother believed in propping the bottle and leaving him to, as she put it, "rassle with it." The baby sometimes choked as the milk ran too freely; at other times he whimpered as the bottle rested at such an angle that it could not flow at all; and sometimes he lost the nipple altogether. Only if he cried outright did his mother come to the rescue. In addition, mother felt that he would burp by himself if this was needed, and on several occasions we saw the baby squirm and whimper after a feeding and finally begin to cry. Thereupon, the mother would come running and very sweetly comfort him. She raised him to her arms, where burping occurred incidentally, and afterwards he settled down.

Excitability: Medium.

This rating reflects the circumstance that while Roderick was rarely seen relaxed, even in sleep, he also failed to reach peak excitation levels. Hunger distress was not allowed to reach intense degrees, a bottle or pacifier helped to get him off to sleep, and if distress from other causes became marked, mother always soothed him. However, during feeding he was often tense, during sleep he typically showed jerky motions or other signs of muscle tension in the absence of any external stimuli, and there were no quiescent intervals at all during spontaneous activity.

Irritability: Medium.

The summary of data on this point states that gastric and other bodily discomfort led to an irritable state fairly frequently but that, on the other hand, Roderick's mother was quick to provide relief when the baby's discomfort was acute. Yet she did less than many mothers to prevent irritability from arising. Inappropriate varieties of stimulation (such as overly intense play) seldom led to overt distress, but certainly did nothing to stabilize or quiet the baby. During feedings he was also mildly irritable off and on, as has been described above. It is impossible to know whether more shielding conditions could have reduced Roderick's irritability, though it seems likely.

DISCUSSION

The reciprocal relationship between Roderick and his mother, and the outstanding features of Roderick's development and adaptation exemplify with special clarity the specific behavioral consequences of the juxtaposition of a somewhat "difficult" baby with a mother who had difficulties of her own. Roderick was the first child of a couple whose life was beset by many hardships; both economic restrictions and physical illness among adult members of the family combined to make the mother feel bitter dissatisfactions, which she did not hesitate to put into words. She was the only mother in this sample whose voice and manner were altogether different when she responded to the baby than at other times. It was dramatic and a little sad to see the warmth and gentleness this woman showed whenever she turned toward the baby, in contrast to the considerable harshness and open hostility that she showed toward adult members of the family and even toward the research staff.

Everything this mother did with and for her baby conveyed the impression of affectionate devotion to the maternal role and of pride and pleasure in the baby. In our judgment, her behavior with the baby was dictated by her own needs more than by recognition of those of the baby. In this instance, her need appeared to be primarily to have one really good thing in her life and to have it all to herself. By turning *toward* the baby she turned away from other people, and her very active play and other interventions appeared to yield her direct pleasure. The practical consequence was that those of the baby's needs that she did not perceive as yielding pleasure to herself were often overlooked. Had she noticed consciously that the propped bottle interfered with smooth feeding, she would have taken steps to correct it. Similarly, she failed to perceive minimal signs of the baby's impending discomfort, only to go all out as soon as he made clear his need for care.[1] To judge by her behavior, only outright crying served as a signal of distress.

For Roderick's day-by-day experience, his mother's behavioral style meant that he experienced many pleasurable interactions with her, though usually of the kind that do not lead to *reciprocal* behavior, since she did not wait for his response and since how the baby behaved toward her did not affect her behavior toward him. He also had a great many direct contacts with the mother during which he was mildly distressed and remained so despite her ministrations. His waking hours regularly and frequently included periods during which he was restless or moderately uncomfortable when the mother was not in the perceptual field. As she did not hold him for feedings or before he fell asleep, he relatively seldom experienced contact with her during the change from unpleasurable arousal to quiescence. His adaptation to these circumstances impressed us by its positive features as well as by its shortcomings. He developed satisfactorily, real disruption of behavior integration occurred but rarely, and he was in general animated and responsive. We are inclined to think that his high ac-

[1] We have no doubt that ambivalence and related inner dynamic factors determined this mother's inability to perceive and interpret aspects of her child's behavior. In the present context we wish to emphasize all aspects of specific maternal behavior that directly affected the infant, and as much of the mother's fully conscious attitudes and perceptions as can safely be inferred from the material. We believe that an understanding in depth of the mother's motivations would explain how she came to behave as she did, but it would not add to the description of circumstances that had an immediate impact upon the baby.

tivity level, which facilitated the discharge of tension by means of vigorous movement, may have served frequently to restore relative equilibrium. The fact that he was not very sensitive to external stimuli, but rather the reverse, also worked in his favor, as it reduced the potentially disturbing impact of too much maternal stimulation at the wrong times. His somewhat advanced motor coordination, and his relatively weak and slightly less mature social responsiveness fit well with a pattern of concrete experience in which contacts with the mother tended to be overwhelming, and often unrelated to his state.

Annette, In V (12 Weeks)

SPE DETERMINANTS

Boundary Strength

	ENTIRE		*MODALITY SECTORS*			
	Inner	*Outer*	*Vision*	*Touch*	*Sound*	*Passive Motion*
Stimulation	medium	weak (+)	weak	weak	weak	?
Frequency of Mother-Child Contacts		high	high (−)	high (−)	medium	low
Intensity	low	low	→	→	→	→
Maternal Competence		high	→	→	→	→
Maternal Intrusiveness		low	→	→	→	→
Level of Home Stimulation		low	→	→	→	→

Activity Level: 1.2

STABLE PATTERNS OF EXPERIENCE

Frequency of strong bodily arousal: Rare.

Annette was a very sensitive baby whose mother stimulated her a good deal, but always very gently. In addition, Annette was markedly inactive and thus not given to strong bodily arousal. Both hunger and fatigue brought changes from minimal to slight activity, but the most conspicuous behavior change during need states was that the baby sucked avidly at her hand and fingers. The single occasion when we observed strong bodily arousal occurred when it was necessary to dress the desperately tired baby. This was atypical, because the mother usually timed her interventions in such a way that they did not disturb the baby.

Internal bodily sensations: Medium.

As mentioned, Annette's behavior while hungry and while fatigued was less aroused and less distressed than one sees in many 12-week-olds. During spontaneous activity she remained content for remarkably long times.

On all occasions she engaged in body play of a gentle sort, and cooed contentedly off and on. At irregular intervals (on some days not at all; on others, once or twice) she became very restless and began to whimper, obviously because of gastric pain, as her abdomen was distended. These upsets were not severe, and being held and patted until she burped or taking warm water from a bottle were effective remedies. Thus, like other babies, Annette had regular occasion to respond to proprioceptive stimulation but, by comparison with others, the accompanying behavior changes were not marked.

Balance between behavior activations due to inner and to outer stimulation: Equal.

During spontaneous activity Annette was a baby whose behavior was fairly often oriented toward an aspect of the immediate environment. She regarded her own hand intently, and she was seen to gaze at toys suspended above the crib and vocalize in their direction prolongedly. Thus, in a situation during which many 12-week-olds are entirely self-contained, she showed behavior activations that were responsive to external stimuli. More important was the fact that the mother treated her baby as a social partner at all times, and thus spoke to her, smiled at her and touched her lightly very often. Annette was responsive as she gazed at the mother, waved her arms and vocalized. The relatively high proportion of behavior that occurred in response to external stimulation could come about only because Annette was so sensitive to sight, sound and touch. Beyond this, it was due to three circumstances; that she slept less than most 12-week-olds (between 3 and 4 hours during the daytime); that the mother playfully approached her only at times when Annette was at her most receptive (*i.e.,* when the baby seemed drowsy or restless, mother was soothing and not stimulating with her); and that once or twice a day the mother strung large, brightly colored toys across the crib. She had noticed that Annette always "played with them" (looked at them, waved her arms vaguely in their direction, cooed and even squealed), but that the toys became "too much for her" if they were left in view for more than 20–30 minutes at a time. Thus, everything combined to maximize the occasions on which Annette could and would orient her behavior toward the environment.

Importance of distance receptors: Fairly high.

As was described above, the visual modality was often and skillfully activated by the mother. In addition, this inactive baby tended to gaze intently at her own hand and at other sights even when not in contact with the mother. She rarely failed to respond to sounds, even if they were of low intensity. Such incidental sounds as someone clearing his throat or turning a page halfway across the room caused her to blink and grimace, while moderate sounds arrested her attention as she listened alertly. Her mother had discovered that when, as a younger infant, Annette had cried with colicky discomfort, it was sometimes possible to "shock" her out of it by producing a loud and sudden sound.

Importance of near receptors: Fairly high.

The mother employed touch a great deal during contact with the baby. She held, patted and stroked her as she soothed her, and this was usually effective in the absence of swaying or any other passive motion. And the mother's play with the baby was also highly tactile. One of the very frequent patterns was for the mother to run her fingers lightly over the baby's belly, ending with a gentle poke as a sort of exclamation mark, at which baby smiled or squealed while the mother laughed. During spontaneous activity Annette rubbed and poked her own skin occasionally as part of general body play, thus providing stimulation of one of the near receptors for herself.

Most prominent modality: Probably vision.

Least prominent modality: Passive motion.

Frequency of states of optimal animation: High.

During spontaneous activity Annette was fully alert and animated much of the time. She was not sufficiently aroused to engage in relatively complex motor coordinations, but she did regard her own hand, people, or objects moving in the vicinity, and the like. And a great many of the interactions with the mother roused her to most intent focusing, as well as to vocalizations of a complex sort.

OUTCOME RATINGS

Developmental status: Low.

In Annette's case there was a discrepancy between the results of developmental testing and the quality of her behavior in areas not fully tapped in the test items for this age level. Her test performance led to a rating of "low" for developmental status, entirely because her neuromuscular coordination was delayed.[1] She was not yet comfortable when held in the sitting posture; her head control was poor; and though her arm and head motions were well articulated, leg motions were fairly infrequent and diffuse. Even her scores on the adaptive portion of this test were lowered by her unease in the sitting position. The very same objects (cube, cup, dangling ring) that elicited minimal response when she was seated in the manner required for scorable test performance elicited intense, prolonged and mature responses when they were offered as she lay supine. Another

[1] The actual test results were: Cattell Infant Intelligence Scale: CA 2.7 mos.; MA 2.8 mos.; I.Q. = 103. Gessell Schedules: CA 12 weeks (−3 days); Motor = 8 weeks+; Adaptive = 12 weeks−; Language = 12 weeks−; Personal-Social = 12 weeks.

factor that lowered test scores was that Annette was so intent upon the human face and voice that object presentation could not compete. Even when objects were presented while the examiner stood behind the child and out of sight, she looked about as if searching for a face (which, if true, would be advanced behavior for one of her age). Also, once her interest in a suspended rattle or other object was aroused, it was unusually intense, as she gazed prolongedly, made swiping motions or waved her arms, while her physiognomy suggested absorption and intense focus or she smiled.

Although Annette's responsive action was no more complex than is usual at 12 weeks (and sometimes less so), her level of discrimination among visual and auditory stimuli was unusual. This aspect of behavior, however, is not reflected in standard infant tests. Had the developmental testing been used to predict her cognitive endowment, rather than to describe present functioning, better than average intellectual potential would have been inferred from her total test performance. At the same time, Annette is a good example of the fact that adaptive (to aspects of the environment) functions in early infancy are greatly dependent on overall bodily development. Reaching for objects, which depends on both postural elements and the growing capacity to coordinate motion, is an important schema in acquainting young infants with properties of the external world, and was not yet available to Annette. Yet prolonged regard of the motions of her own hand—an equally mature behavior that is easily executed in the supine position—was a conspicuous part of her behavior during spontaneous activity.

Annette's pattern of development is intelligible only in light of the fact that she had been acutely ill during nearly one-half of her young life. Between the ages of 3½ and 9 weeks, she suffered from severe gastric disturbance of allergic origin, complicated by intolerance for several varieties of medication (to which she responded with further allergic manifestations). This condition interfered with sleep and general comfort and caused a serious loss of weight. By the time we knew her, Annette had been free from physical symptoms for three weeks, and had gained sufficient weight to be well within the normal range.

Adequacy of vegetative functioning: High.

Despite her history of significant physiological disturbance in the past, her adequacy of vegetative functioning was assessed as "high." Annette slept well, though less during the daytime than most 12-week-olds. She accepted food with eager efficiency, and showed no special lability in other physiological functions.

Excitability: Low.

Annette was not an excitable baby—but perhaps this statement should be qualified by saying that her pattern of existence was one that protected her from excitation. Her mother, who was by nature a gentle person, was so aware of her baby's sensitivity that in dealing with Annette she was extraordinarily shielding. In the home Annette was under the mother's eye at all times, and except for brief play with the father in the evening, she was kept away from contact with other people. The older brother tiptoed close to the crib to watch her daily as she slept, as did occasional visitors. She was rarely taken from the home and, as has been described, the mother not only dealt with the baby with exceeding gentleness, but she adapted the dosage of visual and auditory stimulation (toys, radio, etc.) to her judgment of the baby's tolerance. On the very rare occasions when stimulation had to be fairly strong (as when it was necessary to dress the sleepy baby in order to meet a waiting taxi), Annette demonstrated that she *could* become excited. She screamed, turned beet-red, tensed the entire body, and writhed in a manner painful to behold. Mother said that such behavior had been frequent during Annette's illness, but since then had not occurred at all.

Irritability: Medium.

We rated Annette as being irritable to a "medium" degree, though it was difficult to express the facts in a single rating. In terms of the absolute amount of discomfort or distress that Annette showed, "medium" is an overstatement. She whimpered briefly when she was hungry or from transient gastric discomfort, and also before daytime naps, but otherwise, she was contented for longer periods than most 12-week-olds, and ready to smile and coo at the slightest provocation. However, she had one prolonged "cranky" period each day, during the hour or so before she fell asleep at night. Mother had found that when Annette began to fuss and show every sign of fatigue in the evening, the usual remedies of holding or patting would not work nor would she accept a bottle right away. The usual procedure was to let her whimper and cry until, from the quality of the crying, the mother judged that the baby would now accept warm water from a bottle. Once she did, she always relaxed and subsequently slept through the night. Another characteristic we thought related to irritability was Annette's intolerance for sudden strong external stimuli. Most of the time her mother managed to protect her, but incidental traffic sounds, or turning on the light in a dark room, or a sudden jarring had the power to elicit brief crying and other transient signs of discomfort from the baby.

DISCUSSION

Annette's adaptation and development so far are an impressive illustration of the power of maternal behavior to modify the quality of an infant's experience, and of the limitations to such power. The combination of marked sensitivity and allergic tendencies strong enough to produce acute illness implies an unusual potential for the disruption of normal functioning and development. In addition, Annette was among the most inactive babies in the sample. This combination of structural and biological attributes entails the danger of excessive excitation (due to sensitivity) on the one hand, and of insufficient opportunity for active and adaptive responsiveness (due to weak impulses toward muscular activation) on the other. Indeed, Annette's ability to use her body in a coordinated fashion was somewhat impaired, and in consequence she also had not yet developed the tendency to approach objects with her hands, nor even to grasp one hand with the other (both of these normally emerge by 12 weeks). But within her motoric limitations, Annette had developed discriminatory capacities of a high order and had acquired at least age-appropriate (and possibly slightly precocious) patterns of social interaction. In view of the fact that developmental progress had almost certainly been delayed during the five and a half weeks of illness, we believe that during the three weeks prior to our study of the baby, Annette must have progressed at an accelerated pace in order to receive test scores within the normal range.

Annette was the second child born to a stable middle class family who had looked forward to her arrival with eagerness. The mother was a comfortable and empathic person who, despite her seeming lack of self-assertion, frequently found herself in positions of trust and leadership in organized neighborhood affairs. This fact is mentioned only because it is in keeping with her style of maternal behavior. She was observant of and empathic with the baby's special sensitivity, yet she took very active steps both to protect the baby and to provide rich stimulation. With all her softness, she effectively made the family and friends adapt their lives to what she thought the baby needed (especially the absence of noise), and she did not hesitate to direct aspects of the child's behavior. She was strongly opposed to thumbsucking and to the use of pacifiers. As it happened, Annette was given to a great deal of oral behavior (her oral score of 16.0 was by far the highest in her age group).[2] Whenever the mother noticed Annette's hand in her mouth, she gently but inexorably withdrew it. Since this was always combined with affectionate play, Annette never seemed to mind in the least; she merely resumed the mouthing soon afterwards.

We consider that Annette was enabled to develop a high level of responsiveness to people and to things about in large measure by the fact that the mother, without awareness of so doing, so regulated the dosage of stimulation as to prevent both too much excitation and too little stimulation.

[2] Even during the hours under observation, when mother watched the baby more consistently than she possibly could at other times, Annette spent more time sucking or mouthing her hand than any of the other babies in Group One. This was made possible in part by the mother's tendency to be either completely engaged with the baby or to remove herself entirely. She did not watch to see whether the baby would suck, but only prevented it when it occurred while her attention was turned upon the baby.

Adele, Ac VI (12 Weeks)

SPE DETERMINANTS

	Boundary Strength					
	ENTIRE		MODALITY SECTORS			
	Inner	Outer	Vision	Touch	Sound	Passive Motion
Stimulation	strong (−)	variable	medium	strong	strong	?
Frequency of Mother-Child Contacts		medium	high (−)	medium	medium	medium
Intensity	medium	high	→	→	→	→
Maternal Competence		medium	→	→	→	→
Maternal Intrusiveness		high	→	→	→	→
Level of Home Stimulation		high	→	→	→	→

Activity Level: 2.6

STABLE PATTERNS OF EXPERIENCE

Frequency of strong bodily arousal: Moderate.

Adele was a very active baby and so was prone to show strong bodily arousal, including stiffening the body and arching her back, as well as massive motion. It required at least moderately strong stimulation for her to respond at all (strong boundaries) but once she did respond, the behavior activation tended to be intense. She experienced peak excitations every 3 to 4 hours in each day, when she was hungry. Her mother did all she could in general to spare the baby distress and discomfort. However (because of a history of projectile vomiting between the age of 4 and 6 weeks), the doctor had prescribed medication to be administered 10 minutes before each feeding. Therefore the mother had to wait until Adele's behavior left no doubt that she was hungry, before she gave the atropine, after which the baby had to cry and thrash about for 10 minutes until she could be fed.

At other times Adele was frequently aroused, but both her own reactivity (strong boundaries) and the mother's constant vigilance ordinarily prevented the emergence of peak excitation levels.

Internal bodily sensations: Medium.

When left to her own devices, Adele was never still. She waved her arms and kicked forcefully, extended her neck and back while turning her head, squirmed, and not infrequently arched her back. Vocalizations also occurred at such times, often contented cooing and sometimes squealing. These activations frequently occurred when the environment provided only background stimulation but also at times when her attention was focused upon an aspect of the environment. Presumably she experienced fairly strong and continuous proprioceptive sensations. In addition, she felt hunger strongly, as has been mentioned. Fatigue, of course, altered her behavior, but since she was always given a bottle to help her go to sleep, we could not evaluate the degree to which this condition also led to vivid awareness of changes in body state.

Balance between behavior activations due to inner and to outer stimulation: Internal predominant.

As described above, a large share of Adele's behavior during spontaneous activity could not be ascribed to stimulation by the environment. Although during spontaneous activity, Adele responded to sights and sounds about her, when she focused on a nearby toy or on moving objects or people, this led her to reduce motoric activity. Since her gaze was seldom intense, these episodes of responsiveness to the environment could hardly be described as behavior activations. It is difficult to separate the calming and the arousing components of her contacts with her mother. Almost invariably, even active and strong manipulation or play at the mother's hand led to a reduction in the baby's activity and behavioral arousal. But this is not to say that she did not respond to the sight, sound and touch of the mother. She smiled a great deal, and on a few occasions was seen to turn her head toward the mother, who spoke while outside the baby's visual field. In a somewhat similar manner Adele became relatively quiet while she looked at a toy strung across the crib or at trees swaying in the wind or at her own hand. All in all, it may be said that Adele's behavior was *altered* almost as often by external as by internal stimuli, but *activations* in response to external ones tended to be less frequent and far less strong.

Importance of distance receptors: Medium.

Adele was most responsive to visual perceptions, as compared with the other modalities. Her mother had noticed that when Adele was restless (which she attributed to boredom), it was often sufficient to provide entertaining sights for her. She strung rattles on one side of the crib (and had done so since Adele was 5 weeks old), or else simply turned the baby so that the toys came into view. On the same principle she made a point of placing the baby now close to the window, now in the playpen, and now on the floor "so she will have something to look at." Also, during direct contacts with the baby, the mother always put her face in view and did not touch or lift Adele until the baby had smiled responsively. The mother also spoke to the baby softly and sang to her at times. To judge by Adele's behavior, she was normally alert to these sounds, but her behavior did not differ a great deal when the mother provided sound as well as sight and touch. Adele made almost no response to sounds other than the human voice. Not only were incidental sounds ignored, but during testing she seemed oblivious to the bell rung outside her view, and it was necessary to ring it very loudly indeed before she was moved to turn her head.[1] (Since

[1] Adele was one of the two babies in the entire sample who was observed to sleep through quite extraordinary noises without ever stirring.

she repeatedly turned to the mother's low-voiced address, this was clearly not a matter of impaired hearing.)

Importance of near receptors: Fairly low.

Adele was touched by the mother a good deal, always lightly and gently. To judge by her overt behavior, she responded minimally to this component of mother's approach. Nor was she much affected by various tactile stimuli offered by the research staff. The mother soothed the baby by briefly holding her very close to her own body, and also by rocking rather vigorously while holding the baby in that fashion. Adele nearly always responded (though she failed to respond when her mother swayed her gently and held her less confiningly). It was as though the encircling pressure of the mother's body, which prevented movement, combined with passive motion, was the only condition that soothed this baby when she was in distress. Since such occasions were not frequent, and since at other times touch did not seem to be a prominent aspect of her behavior, we concluded that the near receptors played a lesser role in Adele's experience than is usually true of 12-week-olds.

Most prominent modality: Vision.

Least prominent modality: Touch.

Frequency of states of optimal animation: Occasional.

During spontaneous activity Adele tended to be so active as to preclude intent focus on external stimuli; her response to the sights and sounds about was often brief and limited to very simple behavior patterns (usually brief gazing with reduction in activity, or arm waving while regarding something). Optimal levels of animation were also rare during contacts with the mother, although she showed a great deal of pleasure at these times. Adele's mother not infrequently brought her face close to that of the baby, and spoke to her softly and warmly. Adele would focus upon the mother, reduce activity, and smile, whereupon the mother turned her attention elsewhere. Such gentle and brief stimulation from the mother seldom led to vocalizing nor to sustained mutual gazing or other reciprocal interaction.

During routine procedures, optimal states of animation on Adele's part were not observed at all, and could not have been frequent. This was largely due to the fact that this affectionate and devoted mother was singularly awkward. Inadvertently she delivered massive doses of body stimulation, because dressing, diapering, bathing, and even spoon-feeding her wriggly baby was difficult for her. She lifted her without providing head support, and she had to make many tries before it was possible to get the baby's arm through a sleeve or slip the shirt over her head. She tended to put the baby in very awkward and seemingly uncomfortable postures and hold her firmly to make accessible whatever body part she tried to work with. All this was done in a playful and relaxed manner, and Adele smiled a great deal of the time, but she was, of course, unable to respond to the mother (or to anything else) in a coordinated manner. Thus, as compared with many other babies, Adele had relatively few occasions to practice and develop developmentally complex behavior schemas.

OUTCOME RATINGS

Developmental status: Medium.

Adele's performance on the developmental test earned scores ranging from the lower to the higher extremes of the average range.

At the time of the testing the examiner expressed some doubt as to whether these test scores fully represented Adele's abilities. She was not only a very active baby, but one given to the display of considerable muscle tension. As she became moderately excited during the presentation of test objects, involuntary movements, especially arching of the back, might have interfered with coordinated arm motions in the direction of the toys, which she failed to show. (The behaviors in question are normative at the age of 16 weeks, yet it seemed possible that, when more relaxed, Adele could have achieved some of them). In fact, during spontaneous activity she occasionally did reach for and contact an object—a behavior not seen during the test. Another factor that may have served to depreciate test scores very slightly was her overwhelming interest in the human partner. As we have seen in other 12-week-olds, she actively sought out opportunities to regard any face or human figure, and it was not easy to divert her attention to inanimate objects. Once this was accomplished, however, her interest was so intense as to produce marked muscle tension and large motion, as has been described.

Adequacy of vegetative functioning: High.

Eating, sleeping, gastric processes and all other bodily functions took place without effort or disruption. On a few occasions between the ages of 4 and 9 weeks, Adele had experienced gastric troubles in the form of projectile vomiting and occasional diarrhea. This was controlled by medication (atropine) and had never led to serious disruption in the rhythm of vegetative functioning. Very occasionally, less than once a day, Adele still experienced very brief flurries of gastric distress after feedings.

Excitability: Medium.

The rating of "medium" reflects the fact that only while hungry did Adele experience peak levels of excitation. Ordinary degrees of stimulation, such as incidental sights and sounds about her, being diapered, and the like, seldom led to behavioral arousal, as is implied in the rating for the outer boundary. If she was discontent to begin with, the mother's rather vigorous manipulation of her during routine procedures generally was soothing. Also, if Adele showed mild but definite signs of discomfort, the mother usually picked her up to rock and sway the baby in her arms, singing to her at the same time; and this did calm the baby, though less intensive soothing measures never worked. Incidentally, purely social advances were the one type of stimulation to which Adele responded with considerable excitation. Her readiness to smile at even slight stimulation, and the way in which she kicked, squealed and waved her arms in high glee when social approaches were prolonged or more intense led to the "variable" rating of the outer boundary, despite her lack of responsiveness to many types of stimulation. Since the mother almost never provided strong social stimulation (though she permitted the grandmother and the observers to do so without apparent reluctance), Adele's tendency to show massive excitement at strong social stimulation was not evoked very often.

Irritability: Low.

Adele was not an irritable baby. She was content for prolonged times while unattended, though her mother always provided toys, or placed her near the window "so she can watch the trees move in the wind," or altered her position from crib or buggy to the floor "so she won't get bored." Adele was an active participant in family life in that all her daytime hours were spent with other people; she was frequently approached and played with not only by the mother but by numerous fond relatives; she had been taken along on every outing, including shopping and the drive-in movie, since before the age of 4 weeks. All of this Adele accepted in good humor, occupying herself in vigorous body play and marked attention to toys and other sights while alone, and in eager pursuit of social exchanges when in the immediate vicinity of people. Except when hungry she very rarely cried.

DISCUSSION

Adele was a healthy, well-developed, and very lively baby. She was the first-born child of a young couple who were part of a cheerful and lively extended family. To both parents Adele was a most important little person and the object of pride and devoted care. The same was true for the grandparents and many other relatives, who were constantly about and who played with the baby freely, though routine care remained exclusively in the mother's hands.

The mother's way of caring for her baby presented an odd combination of incidental and intentional intrusiveness with constant gentleness and protectiveness. In holding and moving her wiggly active baby she had to grasp her very tightly; she allowed the baby's head to dangle; she jerked at an arm or a leg, sharply dislodging the baby; and it required what seemed like endless fumbling motions to complete an ordinary task. Throughout she was playful and warm with the baby, apparently totally confident and perhaps unaware of her lack of skill. During spoon-feeding, which she could accomplish only from above as the baby lay supine, she had to hold the baby's chin firmly for each biteful, or else she failed to reach the baby's mouth. All of this Adele tolerated not so much with equanimity as with pleasurable animation in response to the social interaction that went along with it.

Because of these maternal characteristics, as well as the mother's naivete, the recurrent contacts between the baby and her mother failed in mutual accommodation, or failed to provide for the baby conditions we believe to be desirable. Not only were solid feedings a peculiar procedure (as described above), but the baby received her bottle propped in a bottle holder, while the mother went about her business. However, she returned every few minutes to check on the baby's progress, pulling out the nipple to determine how much milk had been consumed. In many other ways this mother did not hesitate to intervene and to disrupt the baby in situations where most mothers would hesitate to do so. She regularly removed the baby's hand from her mouth, she often tried to force the baby's body into a full medial position while supine, she freely awakened her when this was convenient, and she persisted in feeding solids at times when Adele failed to swallow (that is, the baby let the food drip from the mouth, the mother scraped it off her chin and reinserted it, the baby let it overflow again, but the mother persisted until a fixed amount had been consumed). Yet each action of this sort was performed in a relaxed and softly pleasant manner, and though Adele might frown or whimper momentarily, she remained obviously pleased and smiled almost constantly. In our large experience of observing mother-baby couples we have seldom if ever seen a baby so capable of remaining comfortable in situations that would distress most babies.

Clearly, it was Adele's robust reactivity, her alertness, and her physical vigor that made such adaptation possible. But it was also the fact that while the mother often failed to adapt her actions to minimize discomfort to the baby, she simultaneously and effectively provided pleasurable and supportive stimulation on another level—social interaction. In terms of behavioral arousal states, Adele's pattern of existence contained regular high peaks of excitation (hunger) followed by relative quiescence (induced by feeding), but the change in state did not take place while the baby was in direct contact with the mother. Relaxed quiescence occurred during sleep, but was never prolonged at other times. For much of her waking time Adele was in a state of considerable (but not extreme) behavioral arousal. Contacts with the mother often reduced motility, muscle tension, and other signs of excitation to a somewhat lower level, but the baby continued to move about. Brief relative inactivity occurred fairly often as she regarded a human face or some other attractive spectacle and, for no more than a second or two, ongoing body movement ceased. She did experience moderate distress and being soothed (rocked and held) a few times each day. What she lacked, in comparison with some other babies, were opportunities for more prolonged reciprocal interaction with the mother (though for all we know she may have experienced this with other relatives). Further, her high activity level tended to counteract the occurrence of what we have called optimal states of animation—those moments in which the baby can mobilize complex new patterns of behavior integration.

These circumstances may well explain some features of Adele's development and adaptive style. She rarely vocalized during social contact with the mother, and in this respect was less mature than most 12-week-olds. (Yet when the project staff provided more prolonged and somewhat more intense social stimulation, Adele responded more intensely and in a more mature manner than she ever showed toward the mother.) Similarly, she was unable to reach toward a toy, though showing every sign of interest, nor did she regard a toy placed in her hand. (Her mother was delighted to note Adele's response to the test; she said that she had never thought of giving the baby a toy to hold, but had only offered toys convenient to the baby's view but not her reach.) Even Adele's motor coordination was not quite as well developed as that of the other active babies, apparently because muscle tension and massive body motion often took the place of more finely coordinated movement. In short, Adele's reaction tendencies, in terms of strong boundaries and high activity, played a vital role in protecting her from the disruption and discomfort that might have resulted from her mother's techniques. However, the resulting patterns of concrete experience were not as facilitating and supportive for developmental progress as they could have been. In fact, the research staff, who were far more experienced and skillful than the mother, were able to create conditions during which Adele displayed abilities (in relation to inanimate objects and to people) that her mother had not suspected to exist.

George, In VI (12 Weeks)

SPE DETERMINANTS

Boundary Strength

	ENTIRE		*MODALITY SECTORS*			
	Inner	*Outer*	*Vision*	*Touch*	*Sound*	*Passive Motion*
Stimulation	strong (—)	medium	weak	strong	strong	?
Frequency of Mother-Child Contacts		high	medium	medium	high (—)	low
Intensity	low	high	———	———	———	——→
Maternal Competence		high	———	———	———	——→
Maternal Intrusiveness		low	———	———	———	——→
Level of Home Stimulation		high	———	———	———	——→

Activity Level: 1.6

STABLE PATTERNS OF EXPERIENCE

Frequency of strong bodily arousal: Absent.

George was only moderately inactive. Though not markedly responsive to most varieties of stimulation, he was aroused by hunger, fatigue and playful contacts with other people. However, at no time was he seen to move his entire body forcefully, to become muscularly tense, to scream or to show other signs of strong bodily arousal.

Internal bodily sensations: Medium.

Like all babies, George's behavior during hunger and fatigue clearly reflected changing body states. However, as has been said, these changes were moderate in that he moved restlessly or sucked his hand, and intermittently whimpered softly. During spontaneous activity, flurries of gentle part-body motion alternated with periods of minimal activity so that proprioceptive stimulation did not lead to any but slight activations.

Balance between behavior activations due to inner and to outer stimulation: Equal.

The balance between behavior activations that were responsive to the environment and those that were not was difficult to determine because George was seldom left to his own devices while awake. During spontaneous activity, his behavior often seemed responsive to proprioceptive stimulation even when it was of a kind that also brought him into contact with things in the environment. For instance, he would finger or stroke the blanket, other things, or his own body, but paid no attention to what he touched. Most of the time he found himself in a highly stimulating field. The radio was on; children played; and adults conversed loudly in the vicinity; the dog and kitten came and went. Many of these outer stimuli were ignored, and many were responded to, though not always in the form of behavior activations (casual inspection or becoming very quiet were not uncommon).

All in all, the fact that when George had the opportunity, activations not related to environmental stimuli occurred quite frequently, and that he ignored at least as many external stimuli as he responded to, led to the judgment that the balance between internally and externally caused behavior activations was approximately equal.

Importance of distance receptors: Medium.

During direct contact with the mother, sound and sight were always evoked in combination, though sound was more persistent and intense. To judge by the baby's behavior, the visual modality was especially important in organizing his outwardly directed behavior. He smiled and cooed at the sight of an impassive face; very intent gazing was a prominent part of his response to social stimulation and to the offering of toys; and he lost no opportunity to follow with his eyes a moving person or a moving object. He also was seen to poke and scratch at a small but bright-colored design on a sofa, to turn smilingly toward a smoke ring until it dissolved, and to rouse himself from his usual placidity to respond to visual events in other ways. Since so much of his waking time was spent in circumstances that provided ample sights and sounds, and since responsiveness to vision was pronounced, at least one of the distance receptors was fairly prominent in his experience, though the other (sound) played a minor role.

Importance of near receptors: Moderate.

During his frequent direct encounters with his mother, George was often touched though seldom held. She patted and stroked him as part of soothing, to which he was not markedly responsive. In vigorous play she tickled him extensively and poked and pinched him, and the striking thing about it all was George's lack of specific response. That is, he chuckled and vocalized delightedly, but the mother's laughing face and the visible movement of her hands and person seemed to register more than the "manhandling." When his mother used energetic touch *not* in play (washing and drying him, removing mucus from his nose with a bobby pin, etc.) he made no perceptible response of any kind. George was not rocked or swayed at all except by one of the grandmothers, and then, his mother said, "he does not mind it." All in all he was touched fairly often and with vigor, but this component of his experience did not seem to have a correspondingly strong impact on his behavior.

Most prominent modality: Vision.

Least prominent modality: Passive motion.

Frequency of states of optimal animation: Moderate.

During spontaneous activity, optimal states of animation were rare for George, as he was usually too placid to engage in more than simple tactile exploration or limited movement play. However, occasionally he did regard his own hand, which for a 12-week-old is complex behavior. The one set of circumstances that did rouse him to more sustained and complex responsiveness to aspects of the environment was when vigorous efforts were made to direct his attention to a nearby stimulus (animated face or suitable object), and he was not touched or manipulated with such vigor as to prevent self-directed behavior activations. This occurred during the developmental testing, at which time he showed a number of behaviors more mature than were observed at any other time. In his daily life, however, when being dressed, and sometimes when his mother approached the crib and briefly entertained him with a toy, such states of optimal animation sometimes occurred. Many of his contacts with the mother and (so far as we could tell) all of his contacts with the lively siblings were too massive and involved too much direct body stimulation (tickling, poking, etc.) to leave room for more than passive if pleasurable responsiveness.

OUTCOME RATINGS

Developmental status: Medium.

George's test performance met high average standards for his age in all areas except gross motor coordination, which fell close to the lower extreme of the normal range. One aspect of his motor behavior, postural control in the prone posture, fell below normal standards for his age. (The mother very seldom placed him in the prone position.)

In some aspects of responsiveness to visually perceived objects, and even more in the realm of social responsiveness, his behavior was about as close to normative standards for 16-week-olds as for 12-week-olds. He was able to grasp one hand with the other and to regard a rattle in his hand; he chuckled, cooed, and even laughed aloud, and also registered excited pleasure by a panting type of exaggerated breathing that seemed to be at least partly voluntary.

Adequacy of vegetative functioning: High.

George slept very soundly, and for more of each day than some of the other 12-week-olds. He ate well, had no gastric difficulties, and in fact had not yet experienced even minor physical illness.

Excitability: Low.

George was not an excitable infant, and his behavior was described as placid and even as lethargic under many circumstances. For instance, he allowed the mother to poke about inside his nostril with a bobby pin (to remove mucus) and on one occasion he slept through the whole thing, while on another he grimaced very slightly but did not even avert his head. When he was played with very vigorously, he simply smiled but barely moved. The only occasions when he showed excitement were when object stimulation was prolonged and intense, as during the developmental test. Even then this was manifested only by more rapid and extensive motion than usual, by somewhat louder vocalizations, and by heavy breathing.

Irritability: Low.

George was not the least bit irritable. What we were able to observe lent credence to the mother's claim that he practically never cried and very rarely whimpered. His peaceful equanimity was the more striking because within the home, and while mother was not in direct contact with him, he had to cope with more than ordinary turbulence. Three older siblings, the eldest only 6, were constantly about and very interested in the baby. A favorite game, permitted by the mother, was to place him in a doll buggy and race him through the rooms. Both of the older children liked to hold him, a procedure supervised by the mother insofar as her busy life permitted. They constantly gave and took toys, played noisily nearby, tickled and poked him playfully, and the like. In addition, the house was full of relatives and friends, most of whom liked to play with him and were encouraged to unless George seemed sleepy. This was another baby who was never left at home, and he had already taken several long trips by car as well as the more usual outings to stores and relatives' homes. George's equanimity throughout was probably preserved not only because of his temperament, but also by the mother's vigilance, even when she was not close by. She knew how to interpret sounds and motions heralding stress or impending discomfort; she saw to it that he was left in peace when he seemed sleepy regardless of the hour; and she did not believe in letting a baby go hungry, and provided in-between bottles when she thought he needed them.

DISCUSSION

George was a sturdy, fairly alert, but not highly reactive baby who lived in a large and somewhat turbulent family. He was in daily contact not only with several siblings, but also with grandparents, relatives, and friends who milled about at all times. The parents were proud of their large family and, to the mother at least, child rearing and family life were a means of living up to important values and defending cherished principles. Among these principles were a rejection of conventional regimentation and conformity, an emphasis on spontaneity, and a firm belief that individual temperaments and tastes should be given maximal scope. Meal times were irregular for the whole family (the mother said she believed in self-demand schedules for adults too); all of them might climb into the car at a moment's notice and be gone for several days; and discipline of the older children emphasized chores and responsibilities, not manners or appearances.

Yet this was anything but a laissez-faire household. Mother was exceptionally competent not only in caring for her baby, but in all household work and management. She saw to it that George was fed as soon as hunger signs appeared. Believing herself to be too tense and active to hold him comfortably, she used a bottle holder but watched him very carefully. Every time the bottle seemed to slip, or the baby's posture looked less comfortable (even without a whimper on his part) she was there like a flash correcting the condition. She fully approved of the grandmother's holding him for feedings because "both of them like it." Every action with the baby was performed with practiced ease and with conscious awareness of his preferences. Children and other people in the home were allowed to play with him as they chose, which was frequently a noisy affair. For instance, she made no protest when he was put in the doll buggy and raced about the house amidst the other children's shrieks. However, the moment she thought that he was becoming sleepy, she carried him off to bed and allowed no one to approach him. Despite the turbulence and seeming irregularity of life in his family, George's existence was more protected and constant than it seemed. Even during the excursions away from home, his mother always took his preferred spoon, his customary blankets, and a carefully balanced supply of foods, so that whether he slept and ate on strange sofas or in the back of the car, constancy was preserved not only in her person, but in terms of the utensils and other objects to which he was accustomed.

Under these conditions George's pattern of existence lacked massive arousal and excitation of any sort. It also contained fewer and less intense episodes of discomfort than are common (only hunger and fatigue could lead to brief whimpering or intermittent crying). Situations that were arousing (increased motility, vocalization) and pleasurable (smiling, chuckling, occasionally even laughing) were frequent, and always occurred during interactions with another person. At least as often, he was mildly roused, yet neither displeased nor overtly pleased, by sights, sounds, and the sensations of being touched and moved. He looked at people or things moving in his vicinity, he blinked at sudden sunlight, he gazed at people speaking to him loudly or at rattles shaken by the siblings, he squirmed or waved his arms a bit as he was pulled, poked and lifted.

His excellent tolerance for massive stimulation, combined with high alertness toward visual stimuli and with prolonged gazing, may account for the excellent developmental progress made by this inactive and overstimulated infant. However, the extraordinary animation in his environment, and the fact that only some of his contacts with other persons allowed for reciprocity, may explain why he was one of the rare 12-week-olds who failed to show fascination and selective regard of the human face in comparison with other spectacles. He smiled as broadly and as readily at toys as at people, and gazed at conspicuous inanimate objects as long. In his experience, direct proximity to the mother or another person did not often mediate a change from discomfort to quiescence (bottle was propped; when fatigued he was in the crib, sucking his fingers as mother patted his back; and he rarely required soothing). Because he was seldom impelled to vigorous body movement, his postural control and neuromuscular coordination were less advanced than were his social behavior and adaptive responsiveness to aspects of the environment.

FOURTEEN

○ ○
○

INDIVIDUAL ADAPTATION SYNDROMES: GROUP TWO

John, Ac VII (16 Weeks)

SPE DETERMINANTS

Boundary Strength

	ENTIRE		*MODALITY SECTORS*			
	Inner	*Outer*	*Vision*	*Touch*	*Sound*	*Passive Motion*
Stimulation	medium	medium (−)	medium (−)	weak	weak (+)	medium (−)
Frequency of Mother-Child Contacts		high	medium (+)	low (+)	medium	low
Intensity	medium (−)	low	⟶			
Maternal Competence		high	⟶			
Maternal Intrusiveness		low	⟶			
Level of Home Stimulation		medium	⟶			

Activity Level: 2.2

STABLE PATTERNS OF EXPERIENCE

Frequency of strong bodily arousal: Moderate.

John always became exceedingly aroused with hunger. At such times he screamed, kicked, and thrashed about very actively, and showed a good deal of grossly tremorous motion. He also vigorously rubbed the heel of one foot along the opposite leg, pulled at his ear, and clasped his hands very tightly. Peak arousals also regularly occurred during routine procedures that involved more than transient handling. He cried, kicked or stiffly extended his limbs, clasped his hands, and often showed a marked tremor of the jaw when he was dressed or undressed. Mother said that even diapering caused him to become very upset, but when observed repeatedly during diapering, he cried but showed only moderate amounts of excitation.

Internal bodily sensations: Medium.

Hunger and fatigue both led to marked alterations in John's behavior, which we take to mean that internal bodily sensations were strongly felt at these times. During spontaneous activity, John was seldom still, and a relatively large proportion of his behavior activations were unrelated to any aspect of the environment. He squirmed, stiffly extended and then tightly flexed his legs, vocalized a good deal, and the like. Presumably such a constant stream of activity occurred partly in response to fluctuating body state. Thus, though John was a very healthy and comfortable baby, he felt internal bodily sensations vividly and fairly frequently—to judge by his behavior.

Balance between behavior activations due to inner and to outer stimulation: Equal.

John was highly responsive to external stimuli, but only certain categories of events led to behavior activations (as contrasted to a reduction or a disruption of ongoing activity). The sight of a moving person or the perception of a face nearby typically and very frequently led him to coo or squeal, to increase his activity, or to gaze intently. He also responded to the sight of toys strung above the bassinet with swiping motions and increased activity (lest he become too excited, his mother limited such exposure to toys to half an hour each day). A sound, a visual spectacle or some other external event arrested his attention quite as often, but did not lead to a responsive action (beyond looking), except for a reduction in activity. Thus in the course of his waking day John probably responded to external stimuli more frequently than to internal ones, but behavior activations occurred about as often in response to either source of stimulation.

Importance of distance receptors: Fairly high.

In the course of very frequent social encounters between John and his mother, both vision and sound played a large role, as the mother tended to speak to him playfully from close by, rather than to hold or pat him. In addition, John had a notable tendency to smile and vocalize at the mere sight of a nearby person (usually the mother), and he initiated many playful interactions. John also showed greater attentiveness to small sounds than do most babies. He briefly stopped whatever he was doing and sometimes blinked at such noises as the (muted) click of the camera, the turning of a page, a slight rustle of clothing, and the like. Peculiarly, his tolerance for very loud sounds was excellent, so much so that when he failed to respond overtly to the loud ringing of a bell, the research staff at first wondered if his hearing was impaired. At any rate, his behavior left no doubt that the distance receptors, especially vision, played a prominent role in shaping his behavior.

Importance of near receptors: Moderate.

As has already been described, John was exceptionally sensitive to touch and to being moved about. The mother was aware of this and did what she could to spare the baby. He spent most of his waking time strapped onto the bassinet. When he was held, every evening before bedtime, she held him loosely and minimized body contact. Similarly, she had become adept at working very swiftly during the necessary handling, knowing that he would be contented the moment that dressing or diapering had been completed. On the other hand, John's mother also capitalized on his tactile sensitivity. Occasionally, and only when he was very alert and contented, she tickled him lightly, evoking gleeful squeals, laughter, and massive movement. Correspondingly, soothing him sometimes involved gentle patting; when observed this seemed effective.

The mother told us that being rocked or even pushed in the buggy was "no good for him," in that it made him tense and uncomfortable. But she found that being held and swayed back and forth very, very slowly could be soothing when he was tired or hungry. We never saw her move the baby's body except very carefully and slowly.

In addition, John was a baby who provided a good deal of tactile stimulation for himself, though this was prolonged or intense only during hunger and fatigue. Thus, when tactile and kinesthetic stimulation came his way, John's behavior suggested that they had a strong impact and were felt vividly. On the other hand, his mother succeeded in limiting these varieties of experience so that they occurred less often and with less intensity than is usual for babies of this age.

Most prominent modality: Vision (possibly touch).

Least prominent modality: Kinesthetic.

Frequency of states of optimal animation: Fairly high.

Left to his own devices, John was so active much of the time as to preclude focused attentiveness and adaptive response to the environment, except in the simple forms of gazing, arm waving, and indistinct cooing. However, while he lay on the bassinet, as he did most of his waking time, he was approached playfully, smiled at and spoken to a great deal. At such times he showed patterns of response that were distinctly mature for a 16-week-old. The same was true when his mother strung toys across the bassinet or offered him a toy. As she provided such exposure to objects with a careful view to his tolerance, removing them as he became restless, he did experience rousing but not overwhelming stimulus to adaptive responsiveness quite often.

OUTCOME RATINGS

Developmental status: High.

Upon reviewing the rating given John, we wonder whether an overall assessment of "medium-variable" might not have been quite as appropriate. His test performance showed definite acceleration, but the acceleration was limited to a particular group of functions, while the rest of his behavior corresponded to high average standards for his age. His ability to manipulate objects in a coordinated manner (for instance, transferring an object from one hand to the other with visual regard, lifting a teaspoon from the table and bringing it to his mouth, or grasping a proffered rattle, bell, dangling ring, and one-inch cube) was like that seen in the majority of 20-week-old babies. He also squealed in a manner normative for 20 weeks (though we have found this to be a highly variable item) and smiled at his mirror image (another 20-weeks item). His gross motor coordination, his response to sounds, and other aspects of behavior were not significantly accelerated, though of excellent quality for one of his age.

From the SPE constellation one might have expected better than average ability to respond in a coordinated fashion to sound (as well as to sights), but John failed to turn his head toward either a calling voice or a bell. For reasons unknown, sounds tended to disrupt his behavior and, at times, to evoke diffuse signs of excitation, rather than to orient him to the environmental field. However, the fact that this sound-sensitive baby was able to squeal and laugh (as one expects of 20-week-olds), and that even when unattended he vocalized more often than most, is in keeping with what we have come to expect of a child who receives considerable stimulation in a modality to which he is highly reactive.

Adequacy of vegetative functioning: High.

John ate well, slept well, had no gastric distress, and had never been ill. With strong excitement he blanched and flushed deeply, and also panted, but at other times all of his behavior combined to suggest vigor and bodily well-being without undue lability.

Excitability: High.

John was a very excitable baby. As has been described, body manipulations such as being dressed were always excitatory and easily led to tears (though he loved his bath). John also responded with marked signs of bodily arousal, including muscle tension, to many pleasurable situations. Being played with actively (especially when also touched) and being shown toys always elicited such behavior. Hunger also brought high levels of excitement, though fatigue did not. The facts that even when left to his own devices he showed moderate but definite excitation (squirming, flailing, and occasional jerky motions), and that slight social stimulation evoked massive motion, tense squeals, tight clasping of the hands, and sometimes tremors contributed to the judgment that John was markedly excitable.

Irritability: Low.

Even though some body manipulations almost always brought acute discomfort, John was not at all an irritable baby when we knew him. Except when hungry or manipulated, John did not cry or whimper or manifest discomfort of any sort. Strapped to the bassinet for long periods of time, he entertained himself with body play and cooing, and responded eagerly to mother's intermittent approaches. Yet when she left him he seemed as contented as before. We have no doubt that John was potentially an irritable baby, but the combination of excellent physical health and skillful and accommodating maternal care made his pattern of existence one that seldom led to irritable behavior.

Pleasure in functioning: Medium.

In terms of our definition, a "medium" rating means that this quality was very adequately represented in the baby's behavior, yet was not so intense or so conspicuous as in some of the other babies. The rating was given because when we knew him, John's most intensely pleasurable responsiveness occurred in social interaction with other people. When left to his own devices he was more inclined than most active babies to engage in relatively primitive and self-contained behaviors rather than practice more complex coordinations. (Of the active subjects in Group Two, he showed the relatively highest percentage of simple activations during spontaneous activity; it fell close to 50 per cent.) He excelled in his ability to manipulate objects, but this was a little stressful and absorbing to him more than it yielded overt pleasure.

DISCUSSION

Up to this point we have described John's mother only in terms of the skillful care she provided. Actually, she was beset by many difficulties of the kind that often interfere with the ability to provide optimal maternal care. We should like to specify how a sensitive and excitable baby can thrive in a milieu that contains many potential hazards to a harmonious pattern of life for all involved.

The mother was an observant, vivid, and highly responsive person, much like her son in many ways. She was extraordinarily empathic, in that she often tried to imagine what the baby felt in various situations, and adapted her behavior accordingly. (For instance, she thought that he was astonished when Jello was first offered because, "It slips around in his mouth.") At the same time she was often harassed by the inconveniences of a small apartment and a smaller budget; she had many unreasonable fears about the baby's health and safety; she distrusted medical authority; and she had no hesitation about verbally expressing her anger and resentment to one and all. John was tied to the bassinet because his mother feared that otherwise he might choke or fall and hurt himself. For similar reasons, she never left him or took him out of the home except when absolutely necessary. Although her relationship to her other children (of preschool age) and to the father appeared warm and close, she deeply felt and resented the hardship of being tied to the house at all times, and of receiving little help from the father, who combined a full-time job with intensive nighttime study. It is equally important to know that she maintained an attitude of interest and responsiveness to everything about her, and had the capacity to enjoy whatever pleasures came her way. By her enthusiasm she lent to project visits a truly gay and festive quality, despite the fact that we were left in no doubt about the many hardships in her life.

Within the limitations imposed by her circumstances and her personality, she was able to maintain a consistently effective and gratifying relationship with the baby and, insofar as we could judge, also with her other children. If she kept him tied she compensated by never failing to respond —through brief playful contacts—when he vocalized or seemed restless. As has been described, she regulated her behavior with the baby almost entirely in terms of her perception of his limited tolerance and his preferences (with direct empathy rather than sound reasoning). Comparing her with other young women with similar problems, we have wondered whether her extremely open expression of fears and resentments served to keep these worries (which were not intrinsically related to the baby) from invading her direct dealings with the infant. On the baby's side, his contribution to the gratifying reciprocity was apparently enhanced by the fact that his social responsiveness to the mother (as to anyone) was so vivid and so readily obtained. Each small interaction was immediately gratifying to the mother, who appeared to perceive the direct care of her children as relief, reward, and compensation for all else that was difficult.

Under these conditions John's pattern of existence was one that contained many moments of excitation, which were accompanied by pleasure more often than by distress (though both occurred). John's experience included only one kind of occasion when distress abated while mother was close by—when hunger was followed by a comfortable breast feeding. But he also had the experience of distress disappearing without maternal aid. When fatigued he whimpered and sometimes cried intermittently and was put in the crib where, after initial restlessness, he subsided gradually as he sucked his hand and rubbed his face. Otherwise, his waking day was punctuated by frequent periods of animated contact with the mother, which tended to reduce activity rather than to increase it. While awake he very rarely experienced periods of quiet relaxation. However, his capacity to sleep very soundly during two long naps each day must have played a stabilizing role for this highly reactive baby.

The fact that John's social responsiveness was more mature than any other aspect of behavior is readily understandable in the light of his experience. Similarly, the fact that, unlike most of the other active infants, his gross motor development did not exceed average standards makes good sense in an infant who spent so much of his time in a position that allowed movement of arms and legs, but only in the supine position. John engaged in more tactile self-stimulation and in more oral activity (oral score 14.0) than the majority, though this occurred chiefly when he was hungry or fatigued. Being touched was a vivid and regular component of his experience; because his tendency to soothe himself by sucking was probably enhanced by the circumstance that, for John, need states brought marked excitation, yet the usual soothing measures (holding and rocking) were of no avail.

Peggy, In VII (16 Weeks)

SPE DETERMINANTS

Boundary Strength

	ENTIRE		*MODALITY SECTORS*			
	Inner	*Outer*	*Vision*	*Touch*	*Sound*	*Passive Motion*
Stimulation	medium (−)	medium	medium	strong (−)	strong	weak
Frequency of Mother-Child Contacts		high	high (−)	low (+)	high (−)	high
Intensity	high (−)	medium (+)	→	→	→	→
Maternal Competence		high	→	→	→	→
Maternal Intrusiveness		low (+)	→	→	→	→
Level of Home Stimulation		high	→	→	→	→

Activity Level: 1.0

STABLE PATTERNS OF EXPERIENCE

Frequency of strong bodily arousal: Occasional.

Peggy was the least active infant in the entire sample, and it is more surprising that high levels of excitation occurred at all than that they were infrequent. As the ratings indicate, she experienced rather intense stimulation from within. Peggy had extraordinary difficulty in falling asleep; each time she went through a period of extreme arousal, during which her entire body became very tense in a flexed position (unlike the other infants in similar states, she curled into a little ball rather than arching her back), and she screamed and flushed a deep red. She was subject to other kinds of bodily discomfort as well, but bodily signs of arousal were then very moderate.

Internal bodily sensations: Prominent.

Peggy was subject to recurrent flurries of gastric pain, which occurred several times each day, and briefly disrupted her usual contented, quiet state. In addition, fatigue was always massively arousing, while hunger had a lesser impact. During spontaneous activity she never showed a forceful movement, not even of a body segment, but she was also never still. A good deal of her time was occuppied with minor and uncoordinated stirring, presumably in response to proprioceptive sensations. All in all, and as compared with the other babies, it is judged that sensations emanating from within the body loomed large in Peggy's day-by-day experience.

Balance between behavior activations due to inner and to outer stimulation: Internal predominant.

For reasons already noted, this extraordinarily inactive baby roused herself to move or vocalize most often in response to internal stimuli. Each time she manifested even slight discomfort she was picked up and soothed, which was nearly always effective. Subsequent to such soothing, the mother frequently played with her, and at such times Peggy smiled, increased activity, and occasionally cooed. In addition, the mother and other family members often approached the baby when she was content, and at such times behavior activations in response to external stimulation did occur. Thus, while inner stimuli more often roused this baby to active responsiveness than did stimuli from without, the latter had a strong and frequent soothing impact on her behavior, as well as rousing her fairly frequently.

Importance of distance receptors: Medium.

During direct encounters between Peggy and her mother, both sight and sound were usually evoked, as this mother never approached the baby without placing herself in sight and inviting the baby's attention by speaking to her. The mother also had a way of holding objects so that the baby would regard them. For instance, before each feeding she held the bottle in sight but not in reach, as if to enhance the baby's interest. However, when Peggy was tired or required soothing for another reason, she was held closely to the mother's shoulder and rocked vigorously, which prevented visual focusing. During spontaneous activity the baby did regard her own hand with medium frequency, but otherwise paid scant attention to the sights and sounds about. As indicated in the SPE, she was somewhat more responsive to sights than to sounds; both were offered frequently and were obviously attended, not only during contacts with the mother but also as the baby came into contact with siblings and other people in a lively household.

Importance of near receptors: Moderate.

When upset (from fatigue or gastric distress) Peggy had to be rocked to quiet down. Such episodes occurred rather frequently each day, but were prolonged only before she fell asleep (when rocking could last as long as 25 minutes). However, Peggy's mother tended not to touch her baby more than necessary (except while holding her close during soothing). Peggy was not held for feedings; her mother was never seen to rub, pat, or stroke the baby's skin; and touch seldom occurred as part of playful episodes. When younger, Peggy had shown allergic skin irritations and, though no trace of this was left when we knew the baby, her mother still considered that the less she was touched the better. Yet, as reflected on the

SPE, Peggy made minimal responses to touch by itself; and thoroughly enjoyed the rating procedures which involved far more extensive touch by the observers (to assess muscle tonus and the like) than her mother tended to provide. All in all, the near receptors were very prominent during soothing and played a much less important role during routine caretaking procedures.

Most prominent modality: Vision (possibly passive motion).

Least prominent modality: Touch.

Frequency of states of optimal animation: Moderate.

During spontaneous activity Peggy was very quiet but usually far from lethargic. She looked at and touched nearby objects or fingered them extensively without regard, and focused on her own hand. During playful contacts with the mother, especially those occurring in conjunction with routine procedures, she showed some animation, though the more mature responsive patterns (such as cooing) were rare compared with smiling regard. However, the mother lost few opportunities to interest Peggy in suitable objects. At such times the baby was occasionally seen to reach for and grasp an object, which is a complex pattern for one of her age. According to report, other members of the family also played with the baby using rattles and the like, because the mother had made it clear that the baby was not to be picked up except for practical reasons.

OUTCOME RATINGS

Developmental Status: Medium.

Developmental progress was of good average caliber. On both tests and in all sectors Peggy's test scores conformed closely to normative standards for her age. Only in social behavior was she slightly accelerated; for instance, she smiled broadly at her mirror image (20-weeks item) and a loud and gay "belly laugh" occurred on occasion. Like a good many other 12- and 16-week-old babies, Peggy showed a selective interest in people to the detriment of spontaneous interest in inanimate objects. However, once her attention was drawn toward a suitable toy, she responded with animation and pleasure to the sight, occasionally picking it up and bringing it to her mouth.

Adequacy of vegetative functioning: Medium.

Peggy ate well, slept well, and was generally in good health. However, it was very difficult for her to go to sleep and, in addition, episodes of gastric distress were moderately frequent. These always subsided when the mother succeeded in eliciting the "bubble," or when the baby had a bowel movement.

Excitability: Low.

Even with hunger Peggy whimpered or fretted but rarely cried; muscle tension was never seen; during spontaneous activity she never went beyond gentle part-body motions; and the most severe behavioral arousal seen to occur (with gastric distress and fatigue) was still very moderate when compared with the majority of infants.

Irritability: High.

It was difficult to rate irritability for this baby, largely because its manifestations were unusual. With misgivings, the final rating of "high minus" was given, despite the fact that she cried with fatigue, but rarely at other times. Peggy was a baby who registered discomfort unmistakably, usually by irritable (the mother called them "angry") sounds that were neither squeals nor whimpers. These occurred at times for no discernible reason (possibly due to very minor gastric pain), and regularly in response to conditions that are ignored by most babies. We were able to verify the mother's report to the effect that she fussed as soon as her diapers were wet or soiled, and similarly "protested" when the milk in the bottle (or the bath water) was either warmer or cooler than usual. The same irritable reaction occurred fairly often when the mother (or anybody else) left her after a playful episode, or when she saw a person who turned away instead of responding to her gaze and smile. Lastly, as has been said, brief episodes of outright though moderate distress occurred with gastric pain (at such moments the abdomen was visibly distended), but these episodes did not last long.

Peggy's behavior might be described as intolerant rather than as irritable, for the amount of time she spent in a condition of discontent was actually small. Her mother regarded these behavior tendencies on Peggy's part as a challenge to her maternal skills and responded to relieve, distract, amuse and soothe the baby on all occasions.[1]

Pleasure in functioning: Low.

Pleasure in functioning was assessed as "low" because our definition of the term refers to spontaneous activation of relatively complex behavior patterns, and to ready and vivid responsiveness to appropriate stimulation. During spontaneous activity Peggy alternated between rather incoordinated stirring and slight movements, and primarily visual attentiveness to things about her. Even the more complex visual-motor coordinations that did occur (regarding her own hand, contacting a nearby object) were performed not so much in a state of pleasurable animation as in one of sober quiet attentiveness. She showed keen pleasure during social interactions, but unless social stimulation was prolonged and provocative, her response had a "lazy" quality. She smiled, chuckled, regarded objects, activated her arms in slight animation; in other words, she tended to employ predominantly what were

[1] We came to know this family better than many others and had more occasion to observe events in the home. While there must have been occasions when Peggy was left discontent for a bit, there is ample evidence to document the statement that this mother was able and willing to attend to the baby at any time, if not in person, then by deputizing one of the more than willing members of the family who were usually about.

for her easy and well-learned behavior schemas. Only the intensive efforts to provoke her into action that were entailed in developmental testing, and the carefully timed and imaginative playful interventions made by the mother, revealed her actual capacity for entirely appropriate behavior integrations.

DISCUSSION

In terms of her reaction tendencies and physiological state, Peggy was not a baby of whom harmonious adaptation and good developmental progress would be expected. She was both exceedingly inactive and relatively unresponsive in the modalities that are most important in mediating developmental progress, namely, vision and sound. Moreover, she had suffered from gastric distress intermittently since earliest infancy, and during her third month had been subject to painful allergic skin reactions. In addition, weaning her from the breast to the bottle had proved a tumultuous affair. Knowing that she might not have enough milk, the mother had first attempted to use supplementary bottle feedings when Peggy was 4 weeks old. However, the baby simply would not take the bottle, and it was then that allergies appeared. Peggy thus remained on breast feedings only for several more weeks. Very suddenly, when the baby was 12 weeks old, the mother stopped lactating altogether. Peggy was adamant in refusing bottle feedings as before and cried for a large part of two days (during which her mother also became upset and wept). On the third day, it was the grandmother who succeeded in feeding Peggy, and from then on the baby took her bottle feedings eagerly.

Despite these obstacles to ordinary comfort, despite her massive difficulty in going to sleep (which was also present at least as early as 5 weeks), despite her intolerance of changes in temperature and other circumstances, and despite her relative lack of response to external stimuli—Peggy developed well, enjoyed many situations, and did not cry excessively.

Her day-by-day existence when we knew her included very frequent episodes of pleasure in interaction with the mother and with many other people; many moments of slight and brief discontent almost always terminating as she saw and heard her mother nearby; and periods of minimal arousal during which she lay in the crib or buggy slightly restless and never entirely relaxed. Her daily experience also included periods of massive distress and excitation (with fatigue) that persisted for some time while she was tightly held and rocked until she fell asleep suddenly and then remained motionless and undisturbed by noises or anything else (she could be moved from place to place without awakening).

In large measure, Peggy's development and comfort were made possible by her mother's ability to accommodate to the baby's special requirements, and to capitalize on the moments when it was possible to provide for the baby pleasure mediated by playful stimulation. Peggy is among the inactive babies who would have experienced states of optimal animation very rarely had it not been for the mother's persistence in bringing them about. However, it will be remembered that even during spontaneous activity Peggy practiced relatively complex and outwardly focused behavior integrations nearly as often as most babies in her age group. Since she was not as active as other babies at such times, and was not heard to coo contentedly or show pleasurable animation we are inclined to think that it was the frequent presence of mildly rousing internal body stimulation that prevented lethargy and contributed to developmental advance. It was earlier suggested (see Chapter 8) that markedly inactive babies, not sensitive enough to respond readily to slight external stimuli, tend to progress more slowly during the early months than other babies unless either internal or external stimulation is present in dosages that will lead to moderate degrees of arousal. Even physiological discomfort can serve to propel developmental progress, provided only that it is not severe or unrelieved, and that once the baby has become aroused the environment provides appropriate varieties of stimulation. Peggy is a case in point, and we speculate that even the extraordinary skills of this mother would not have led to satisfactory developmental progress on the part of this exceedingly inactive (and relatively insensitive) baby had Peggy not also experienced frequent bodily discomfort. In proposing that physiological distress played a role in making a high average rate of developmental progress possible, we do not mean to say that frequent bodily discomfort was a positive factor for all aspects of Peggy's functioning. Not only did it lead to irritability on her part, but there is no reason to believe that the *rate* of early development necessarily correlates with the excellence of cognitive and adaptive functioning at later ages.

Cecilia, Ac VIII (16 Weeks)

SPE DETERMINANTS

Boundary Strength

	ENTIRE		*MODALITY SECTORS*			
	Inner	*Outer*	*Vision*	*Touch*	*Sound*	*Passive Motion*
Stimulation	medium (−)	medium	strong (−)	weak	medium (−)	?
Frequency of Mother-Child Contacts		medium (+)	medium (+)	low	medium (+)	low
Intensity	low	medium (−)	→			
Maternal Competence		medium	→			
Maternal Intrusiveness		medium	→			
Level of Home Stimulation		medium	→			

Activity Level: 2.2

STABLE PATTERNS OF EXPERIENCE

Frequency of strong bodily arousal: Rare.

Cecilia was a sturdy baby who, by and large, was not subject to intense or prolonged stimulation. Fairly strong signs of arousal were noted only transiently and under two conditions—first, when during spontaneous activity she attempted an action that she was unable to complete (for instance, rolling from the prone to the supine and getting stuck, or straining to obtain an object just out of reach); and second, when movement was restrained during routine procedures. At such times she could squeal loudly and angrily or cry briefly while the entire body was massively tensed and she flushed and panted heavily with effort. However, if no one came to help her when she failed in an effort, she soon began to suck her thumb, which always served to relax her. When her mother worked with her and Cecilia became upset, the mother always interrupted to comfort her effectively or to provide a pause during which she was allowed to move freely. Thus, moderate and fairly strong bodily arousals were frequent and brief, while intense levels of arousal were very rare indeed.

Internal bodily sensations: Fairly low.

Hunger and fatigue did, of course, make themselves felt and led to alterations in behavior, but Cecilia was not among the babies who showed massive or continuous discomfort at such times (in fact only the circumstance that she sucked eagerly and prolongedly convinced us that she had been hungry). Bowel movements occurred so easily that neither the mother nor the observers noted them until afterwards, and Cecilia seemed in general singularly free of bodily discomforts. She was, however, impelled to move about a good deal, even when not responding to aspects of the environment. In comparison with most of the other babies, she experienced absorbing bodily sensations from within both less frequently and less intensively.

Balance between behavior activations due to inner and to outer stimulation: External predominant.

Even during spontaneous activity most of Cecilia's behavior was responsive to an aspect of the environment (59.2 per cent). From what has been said about the low intensity of bodily sensations, and from the fact that she was very responsive to social and to object stimulation, it follows that a very large proportion of her behavior activations occurred in response to the rousing effect of sights and sounds about her. In addition, being touched always had the power to alter Cecilia's behavior; it led to marked increases of activity when touch was strong or prolonged, but to relative quiescence (not contributing to behavior activations in response to external stimulation) when it was slight.

Importance of distance receptors: Medium.

Cecilia was not especially sensitive to either sight or sound. However, her mother used these modalities whenever she was in contact with the baby, forcefully enough to compel the child's attention. Many times she was seen to smile at the baby and talk to her from a distance without touching her. In addition, Cecilia spent a large portion of her waking time propped up in a sitting position and placed so that she could see lively family activities. She had also reached the point in development where such behaviors as grasping her own foot and then bringing it into view had become possible and enjoyable, so that she provided some visual spectacles for herself.

Importance of near receptors: Fairly high.

As has been said, Cecilia was sensitive in the tactile sphere. Although her mother made every effort to touch the baby no more than was necessary, so many aspects of infant care require handling that Cecilia still frequently experienced pleasurable animation or pleasurable relaxation while being touched, but at other times prolonged touch evoked transient displeasure. With medium frequency, Cecilia held and manipulated her own foot or rubbed her face and abdomen (the latter while fatigued), providing tactile sensations for herself. She also went in for a good deal of thumb-sucking, which also provides a variety of stimulation via the near receptors.

The importance of the near receptors in Cecilia's experience was influenced by the mother's style in ways that have not yet been mentioned. This mother, while always gentle and warm in her speech and facial expressions and always careful not to provide undue touching, was very casual and almost rough in her manipulation of the baby. She yanked her about and failed to provide head support at times, and small accidents such as an inadvertent pinprick occurred occasionally. We were told reliably that Cecilia's father, who spent some time playing with the baby every day, was given to roughhousing. He would swing and toss or bounce the baby until the mother suggested that it was time to stop. All in all, we judge that sensations mediated by the near receptors were vivid and fairly frequent components of Cecilia's day-by-day experience.

Most prominent modality: Touch (?).

Least prominent modality: Passive motion.

Frequency of states of optimal animation: Moderate.

Cecilia was the kind of baby who, when left to her own devices, tended to practice complex new behavior integrations with animation and persistence. When she was in the supine position, the frequency of moderate animation leading to mastery behavior was high. However, much of her waking time was spent seated and somewhat constrained by the pillows or straps that secured her. Though the baby had much to look at that she found entertaining, her mother did not provide toys within reach while the baby was seated. (Characteristically, she was delighted to note Cecilia's readiness to play with objects during the laboratory session. When we visited the home a few days later, the mother had been shopping and said with evident sincerity that participation in the study was worthwhile because it taught her that the baby was ready to learn how to use toys.) Thus, during her typical day Cecilia had limited occasion to experience states of moderate arousal under optimal conditions. During contacts with the mother (and reportedly with the father too) Cecilia smiled, gazed, and cooed quite often, but the episodes of contact were so brief and casual that prolonged or more mature patterns of responsiveness had little chance to emerge. Or else, while being handled, she responded to body stimulation so strongly that more mature patterns of behavior barely occurred in that situation.

OUTCOME RATINGS

Developmental status: Medium.

Cecilia's test performance was of average quality. Gross motor coordination coincided exactly with norms for her age, whereas in the so-called adaptive sphere she failed to perform two items expected at her age and received a score of 16 weeks-minus. It was later found that these results did reflect her responses to standard procedures of test administration. However, if she was left with a toy for a very long time (up to 8–10 minutes) she finally, and with effort, performed as would normally be expected after brief presentation of the test object. Both her failures and her delayed success concerned the coordinated manipulation of objects (such as the dangling ring which she finally inspected in her hand, and transferred from one hand to the other). In all other respects her response to the testing situation was exactly what one most often sees at the age of 16 weeks. Although the quality of her social responses was of high average caliber, they were elicited very readily indeed and were quite vigorous.

Adequacy of vegetative functioning: High.

Cecilia slept well, ate well, and was unusually free from gastric or other bodily distress.

Excitability: Medium.

Cecilia was a moderately excitable baby. As has been described, she showed extensive movement, some distress, and flushing and heavy breathing when prevented from completing an action she had begun, or when movement was temporarily restrained. When it was impossible to avoid lengthy manipulation, as during dressing, Cecilia also manifested bodily signs of excitation. However, since bodily need states did not rouse her massively, since her mother avoided the kind of stimulation that Cecilia could not tolerate, and, last, since Cecilia soothed herself by thumbsucking on many occasions, she experienced moderately high levels of excitation every day—but no more often than many other babies and less intensively than most of the active infants in the sample.

Irritability: Low.

Cecilia was not at all an irritable baby, even though (as described under "Excitability") she became aroused and "annoyed" whenever something prevented the execution of a movement impulse, and even though her mother was not especially intent on accommodating to the baby's every need—except in relation to hunger and fatigue, which she recognized as states requiring immediate relief. On the contrary, the mother made a point of encouraging the baby to overcome obstacles or moments of upset by herself, and would smile at Cecilia from a distance as the baby squealed and whimpered. Only on the rare occasions when the baby failed to settle down of her own accord did the mother intervene. Even then she did not pick the baby up and comfort her, but rather changed her position and spoke to her briefly in a friendly but matter-of-fact way. Cecilia's capacity to overcome minor disturbances in equilibrium without maternal help was largely a function of the baby's capacity to soothe herself by means of thumbsucking. Over and over again we observed Cecilia become restless and/or irritable, only to find her thumb and thereupon become quiet and content as she sucked with vigor. The interesting thing was that—during spontaneous activity, at any rate—thumbsucking seemed to provide periods of rest and restoration. It did not diminish her inclination to engage in active body play or in the manipulation of accessible objects. After periods of thumbsucking that might last for 2 or 3 minutes, she returned to the same activity that had previously led to stress. We saw her work intermittently at such things as rolling over for periods up to 40 minutes. She expended effort to accomplish the motor feat, became unhappy as she failed, sucked her thumb for a bit, returned to the charge and again practiced the new motor coordination, erupted into angry squealing, comforted herself with her thumb, returned to the same activity, and so it went.

Mother attributed Cecilia's "independence" to the fact that aid and comfort were not offered except as a last resort—and she may well have been correct in this belief. The fact that Cecilia was not so active as to prevent mechanically the maintenance of the hand-mouth schema (gentle whole-body and forceful part-body motions were as prominent as forceful whole-body motions) allowed the sucking pattern to achieve dominance. The repeated experience of excitation and moderate distress followed by relief and relative quiescence as she sucked may well have become dominant precisely because mother did not appear on the scene. In a manner of speaking, mother had taught her baby to be self-reliant, a virtue which she valued very highly in general. However, Cecilia's disposition, as reflected in the structural ratings, lent itself to this development, not only because movement impulses were present but far from extreme, but also because many varieties of stimulation left her undisturbed, and because she was not subject to bodily discomfort except of the kind that finds immediate and complete relief (hunger and fatigue).

Pleasure in functioning: High.

What has been said about Cecilia's energetic pursuit of distant objects and the practice of new motor integrations may serve as examples for self-initiated mastery behavior. In addition, social stimulation and developmental testing proved especially enjoyable to Cecilia, who squealed, laughed, cooed, and moved about in high glee.

In short, Cecilia focused mastery activities on bodily coordinations and responded with zest and high pleasure to the opportunities to respond to things and to people that came her way. However, because of the mother's casual manner and her failure to provide much opportunity for the manipulation of small objects, Cecilia's readiness to respond with relatively mature behavior because of her high pleasure in appropriate varieties of stimulation was given limited scope in her day-by-day experience.

DISCUSSION

Cecilia's adaptation syndrome exemplifies a mutually satisfying reciprocal relationship between mother and baby, and adequate developmental progress on the baby's part—and yet falls short of what clearly was a potential for greater richness of experience and greater depth or intensity of feeling for both participants. In a manner almost comical to behold, Cecilia and her mother showed many similarities. The mother was robust, energetic, efficient, and planful to a high degree. In her movements, her speech, her range of interests, and the handling of her children she displayed much firmness and a minimum of subtlety. Nothing was to her an object of wonder, curiosity, or doubt. But whatever came her way was a challenge to her efficiency, in which she took pride and pleasure. During routine procedures she was perfectly friendly but not playful, and thought nothing of yanking the baby about rather roughly (which Cecilia tolerated well). Through most of each day Cecilia was under mother's eye while on the bassinet or propped up on the sofa. Very often the mother smiled at the baby and spoke to her from a distance, thus maintaining contact. But very rarely indeed did she come close to her, and never did she pick the baby up except for a practical reason.

These fleeting contacts with the mother were obviously pleasurable to the baby, but they did not provide occasion for anything beyond brief gazing and smiling. One important exception should be mentioned: Cecilia was a breast-fed baby, and her mother's stated reasons were highly characteristic, as she thought breast feeding economical, healthy, and efficient because it eliminated the bother of preparing formula. However, during feedings (repeatedly observed), the mother not only held the baby closely but her own posture and facial expression conveyed pleasurable relaxation and an intense and intimate focus on the baby in her arms.

Cecilia's pattern of life included a good deal of time during which she was alert, moved about a fair amount, and had many brief encounters with the mother during which she was smiled at and spoken to from some distance, which aroused mild pleasure. It also included many brief periods of distress and some excitation caused by some impediment to completing an action. Almost invariably her mother spoke to her at such times in an encouraging and comforting manner. In response Cecilia clearly attended, reduced activity while looking at the mother, and usually found her thumb and began to suck contentedly. Not infrequently she took to the thumb when apparently discomfited in the course of spontaneous activity, even before her mother had attended to her in any way. Thus mild pleasure (which also occurred before and after routines when the mother briefly played with her) and mild displeasure were both frequent in her experience. Intense pleasure was rare during contacts with the mother. During feeding she was held closely and was at her most quiet, but it was the mother who steadily gazed at the infant, while the baby did not focus on the mother's face except occasionally. According to report, the baby squealed and became excited when father played with her actively once or twice each day. Intense displeasure was very rare, as has already been described.

Her behavior at home and during part of the office visit, as contrasted to her behavior when research staff dealt with her directly, provides interesting clues about varieties of experience that were lacking in Cecilia's life. Cecilia showed both her most mature and her most intense social responses not toward the mother but toward the project staff. Similarly, during the visit at project quarters, Cecilia manipulated objects in a manner of which the mother had not believed her capable. The more intense and more mature behavior occurred only because the research staff provided more prolonged and more intensive stimulation than the mother ever did. For instance, we placed Cecilia for the first time in her life in an infant seat, which has a series of beads strung across a wire at some distance from the baby but still in reach. For fully half an hour the baby focused her attention on these beads. At first she regarded them intently, while tightly gripping the sides of the chair. Then she made innumerable attempts to approach them which, to begin with, were wholly ineffective. Frequently she became exasperated, whimpered, or squealed angrily, and then refreshed herself by thumbsucking and by smiling regard of the people in the room. Within 20 minutes she had learned to contact the beads in a smooth, well-coordinated manner, and even to push them along the wire in great contentment. Her behavior at this point was distinctly more mature than anything we observed during the developmental test. And only during the pediatric examination, the ratings, and the developmental test did we observe this baby to chuckle, laugh, and coo in a sustained fashion.

From the point of view of the genesis of individual differences well within the normal range, we wonder whether later personality characteristics such as the complexity and intensity of affective life, or introspectiveness and empathy, or the importance of cognitive activity not connected with practical problem solving may not have their origin—at least in part—in the degree to which earliest experience is varied, subtle, and vivid long before such elements find psychic representation.

Bertram, In VIII (16 Weeks)

SPE DETERMINANTS

Boundary Strength

	ENTIRE		*MODALITY SECTORS*			
	Inner	*Outer*	*Vision*	*Touch*	*Sound*	*Passive Motion*
Stimulation	medium	medium (−)	medium (−)	medium (−)	medium (+)	weak (+)
Frequency of Mother-Child Contacts		medium	low (+)	high (−)	medium	high (−)
Intensity	low (+)	low (+)	———	———	———	——→
Maternal Competence		low	———	———	———	——→
Maternal Intrusiveness		low	———	———	———	——→
Level of Home Stimulation		low (+)	———	———	———	——→

Activity Level: 1.3

STABLE PATTERNS OF EXPERIENCE

Frequency of strong bodily arousal: Rare.

In terms of what we saw and were told by both parents, it would seem that Bertram never reached high levels of excitation as judged by the usual signs of muscular or visible autonomic changes in appearance and behavior.

Except in response to passive motion he was not markedly responsive to perceptual stimulation, and he was dealt with in the most shielding and gentle fashion imaginable. Hunger and fatigue did not rouse him to much activity or to intense crying, nor did anything else. The relatively greatest levels of excitation were seen when prolonged handling (being dressed) was combined with social play. Even then, though he moved more energetically than was his wont, by comparison with other babies the degree of behavioral arousal did not exceed low medium levels.

Internal bodily sensations: Fairly low.

Except for hunger and fatigue, which did not last long or affect his behavior massively, Bertram's behavior suggested that fluctuations in body state were less extensive and less vividly felt than is usually the case. During spontaneous activity he showed prolonged periods of complete inactivity. His behavior consisted chiefly of gentle part-body motions of a simple sort, and when occasion offered he focused on interesting sights about, especially the faces of nearby persons or things and people that moved in space.

Balance between behavior activations due to inner and to outer stimulation: Equal.

This aspect of experience was somewhat difficult to assess because behavior *activations* from any cause were relatively infrequent (except during the visit to research quarters, where he received more stimulation than had ever come his way before). Of the direct encounters with the mother (and with the father, as we were told and were able to observe), the great majority were soothing, despite the fact that he was content and even lethargic to begin with. The mother treated Bertram as though he were a tiny infant and, with relatively few exceptions, her way of showing interest and affection was to rock him or to hold him at her shoulder and sway him gently. He showed behavior activations as she spoke to him and touched him extensively during routine procedures, and in response to fairly active kinesthetic play (rolling him about on the bassinet) that sometimes followed diapering. He responded also to conspicuous perceptual events nearby, though the "activation" consisted of intent gazing more than of anything else. Every effort was made to maintain a quiet environment—he had been taken outdoors only while asleep (except for visits to the Well-baby Clinic), visitors never held him or played with him, and toys had not yet been offered—so that his opportunities to respond to external stimuli were comparatively few.

Importance of distance receptors: Fairly low.

During those direct contacts with the baby when his mother spoke to him and smiled at him, Bertram responded by gazing, smiling, and cooing in a very normal fashion. However, very often his mother held him so that he could not see her face as she spoke to him, and only during some routine procedures and the brief play that sometimes followed them were mother and baby face to face. During bottle feedings he was the only baby over 8 weeks of age who closed his eyes; at all other times the sight of any face arrested his gaze. Mother spoke softly, as she did everything else, and on a good many occasions it was impossible to tell from the baby's behavior whether he was aware of slight sounds. He was not yet propped to the sitting position (nor held in that position more than momentarily), and the mother seldom moved him from one place to the other. Thus, despite his tendency to gaze intently (especially at people) and to regard his own hand (occasionally), the distance receptors seemed to play a relatively insignificant role in his experience.

Importance of near receptors: High.

During Bertram's contacts with the mother and the father, both touch and passive motion were evoked regularly. In addition to rocking, swaying and holding him at her shoulder while she walked about, the mother elaborated on the tactile aspect of any contact. She oiled and powdered him leisurely and very often, she rubbed and patted him a great deal, and on the rare occasions of active play she poked and tickled him or rolled him about on the table. Passive motion led Bertram to smile and relax and always soothed him when he was distressed (hunger only). By far his strongest social responses were seen when the mother or observer not only smiled and spoke, but also touched him.

Most prominent modality: Kinesthetic.

Least prominent modality: Unknown.

Frequency of states of optimal animation: Rare.

Bertram was so inactive that when left to his own devices he seldom showed more than very simple and constricted behavior activations. Undoubtedly this was true partly because spontaneous activity took place in surroundings (lying in his buggy or on the bassinet) that provided few attractions. As has been said, only some of his contacts with the mother were rousing, and even then direct body stimulation tended to be so dominant that sustained attention or adaptive response (other than smiling and cooing) could rarely emerge.

OUTCOME RATINGS

Developmental status: Low.

Bertram met minimal standards for performance expected at his age. He performed the great majority of items expected at the 16-weeks level, and a very few corresponding to normative standards for 20-week-olds. However, he often seemed to achieve a behavior integration (such as grasping a toy and bringing it to his mouth) with greater difficulty and after more prolonged prodding than is usual. All his near and actual failures were related to his lack of interest in inanimate objects. To appropriate stimulation he was very ready to coo, chuckle, laugh, and even squeal (the last named being a 20-weeks item). He was also attentive to the human voice (turning to locate its source) far more than to other sounds, though he noted them as well.

In Bertram's case the relationship between relevant types of experience and developmental advance (or its lack) was unusually clear. He spent most of his waking hours and a good deal of his daytime sleeping time strapped into the bassinet in the prone position. Postures in the prone position (extended arms, and the ability to lift one arm at a time to scratch the surface in front of him, both normative at 20 weeks) were the only aspects of motor coordination in which he exceeded average standards. He was neither held nor propped in the sitting posture, and was so uncomfortable in it that he failed with simple items (regard of cube or cup) if the objects were placed on a table while he was held to sitting. In the supine position, in which he was always held (even for spoon feedings) though seldom left alone, he responded easily to these and also to more complex object presentations. He had never yet been shown a toy nor offered objects in a playful manner—and he showed minimal interest and responsive activation to their sight and sound. He was smiled at, spoken to, and playfully tickled fairly often, and his social responsiveness was in perfect accord with normal expectations.

Adequacy of vegetative functioning: High.

Bertram slept readily and soundly up to eighteen hours of each day. He ate well and had no gastric troubles, and though respiration tended to become heavy and labored as he responded to his mother's occasional bouts of forceful tickling, he breathed evenly and smoothly at all other times.

Excitability: Low.

Bertram was anything but excitable. The research staff hesitated to deal with this baby in as vigorous and rousing a manner as they usually did because the mother so anxiously avoided anything (except for abrupt and brief episodes of body play) that might prove excitatory. However, during his visit at project quarters Bertram was actively shown toys for the first time in his life, was held in sitting and standing positions, and was handled a great deal more than usual. This led to greater animation than he showed while awake in the crib and while at home, but the only manifestations of excitement we could see were a playful panting type of breathing and pleasurable squealing.

Irritability: Low.

Bertram did not cry unless hungry, and was not observed or reported to whimper, fuss, or otherwise show distress at any time. With fatigue he became drowsy, mouthed a bit, cooed contentedly, and was off to sleep within a few minutes. In fact, his comparative lethargy misled the mother's perception of her baby's state. If he so much as waved his arms or vocalized or tried to alter his position, she tended to think that something was amiss. Thereupon she would rock him or pat him while trying to settle him into a fully horizontal position, effectively preventing greater animation on his part and precluding irritability.

Pleasure in functioning: Low.

Pleasure in functioning was assessed as "low" in comparison with other members of the sample. There was no question that Bertram readily showed pleasure and animation when spoken to and played with. However, often he was held so that he could not see the mother's face, and during more active play the mother did not so much invite his attention to her face or person as she created diffuse bodily arousal by tickling and rolling him about. Whether or not he was capable of showing pleasure in functioning like most other babies, the behaviors to which this shorthand term refers were infrequent and of limited variety in his experience.

DISCUSSION

It is entirely possible that, in addition to the mother's deviant methods of child rearing, some biological factors also played a role in producing for Bertram an existence that reflected perfectly comfortable adaptation, yet a comparative lack of differentiation and animation. Some evidence exists to support our interpretation that Bertram could have functioned in a different manner under different circumstances. His mother was a well-intentioned person, wholly devoted to her baby and to her husband, on whom she depended a great deal. It appeared to us that the difficulties and ineptness she showed in caring for her baby were less extensive than her awkwardness in many other aspects of living, such as housework, budgeting, or keeping up with current affairs. Her ability to recognize the baby's state was minimal, and she was one of the very few mothers in the sample who told us a good deal about how he would behave when awakening, during feedings or the bath—none of which was borne out by his actual behavior. Yet she indicated that what we observed was very much as usual.

We have not yet provided a full description of the degree to which this well-loved baby lacked the experiences commonly provided. His daytime hours, both awake and asleep, were spent strapped onto the bassinet, always in the prone position. When he was picked up it was in the manner suitable for a 4-week-old, and indeed the mother's voice and manner suggested at all times that she perceived the baby as a fragile creature who had to be protected from ordinary stimuli and from whom no responsiveness (except smiling) was yet to be expected. Even solid feedings were given as he lay supine, and in such a way that he not so much took food as swallowed what was dropped in from above. As has been said, any sign of animation, however contented, was responded to as though it were distress, and evoked gentle but persistent soothing.

Bertram's response to encounters with the project staff, the fact that in a manner of speaking he had made the most of his opportunities by making perfectly good developmental progress in the few areas where he received environmental support, and the mother's utter confusion as to what was appropriate in many situations led us to believe that the resulting syndrome was not a maternal adaptation to the baby's reactions or endowment characteristics. Rather, we thought that we saw a relatively good adaptation on Bertram's part to a life setting which, from the point of view of developmental progress, was far from optimal. We are inclined to think that had he been somewhat more sensitive, even the minimal stimulation he received would have had greater impact. Had he been an active baby, he might have developed somewhat more rapidly even in his setting, and his behavior would then have compelled the mother to deal with him differently, as he would have registered discontent while motorically confined. Even the presence of minor bodily discomfort might have aroused him to greater alertness, and thus might have served to increase his awareness of the environment.

Margo, Ac IX (20 Weeks)

SPE DETERMINANTS

Boundary Strength

	ENTIRE		MODALITY SECTORS			
	Inner	*Outer*	*Vision*	*Touch*	*Sound*	*Passive Motion*
Stimulation	strong	variable	medium	strong	weak	weak
Frequency of Mother-Child Contacts		high	high	medium	high	high (−)
Intensity	medium (−)	medium	→			
Maternal Competence		medium (+)	→			
Maternal Intrusiveness		medium (+)	→			
Level of Home Stimulation		high (−)	→			

Activity Level: 2.3

STABLE PATTERNS OF EXPERIENCE

Frequency of strong bodily arousal: Moderate.

Margo was not as active as a good many other babies in the sample, but when markedly aroused she displayed many of the typical signs of bodily excitement. Both hunger and fatigue regularly made her scream, thrash about, and turn a fiery red; with fatigue, which brought the most severe distress, she also sometimes stiffened the entire body. On rare occasions, Margo showed high excitement when she struggled to obtain a distant object, when movement was restrained more than momentarily while she was dressed, or when she lost the nipple during feedings.

Internal bodily sensations: Medium.

As has been said, hunger and fatigue made themselves felt very strongly in Margo's experience. Otherwise her behavior did not suggest that fluctuating body states were of great importance. During spontaneous activity a very large portion of her behavior was oriented toward an aspect of the environment, or else coordinated to achieve a position change.

Balance between behavior activations due to inner and to outer stimulation: External predominant.

Margo was a richly stimulated baby and a responsive one. Except while beset by bodily need states, Margo almost constantly turned toward or away from something, reached for objects or moved them about, vocalized and smiled at people, and in general regulated her activity in terms of the sights and sounds about.

Importance of distance receptors: High.

During direct encounters with her baby Margo's mother relied heavily on both the visual and the auditory modality. Not only did she speak, sing, cluck, and whistle at the baby while in view, but she also tended to pick up a toy (or any handy object) and interest the baby in playing with it. The father and many relatives who congregated in the home did much the same. In addition, Margo was always surrounded by toys, and the mother made a point of moving her from one place to another, often propped up in the sitting posture, specifically "so that she has something different to look at." One of the few things that made Margo fuss was if no one came to restore the toys that she had one by one thrown off the tray of her highchair. All in all, we have not seen another 20-week-old infant who was so consistently responsive to the frequent and rather intense stimulation she received via the distance receptors.

Importance of near receptors: Moderate.

Tactile sensations played a lesser role in Margo's experience than did the other modalities, in part because she was relatively insensitive to touch, and in part because her mother touched her baby when it was practical but tended to avoid unnecessary touching. She did not hold Margo much except to soothe or feed her, she never played tactile games, and, as a rule, she did not stroke or pat the baby.

By contrast, a great deal of passive motion was provided, and to this Margo was highly responsive. She was always rocked when fatigued, and this had to be done with considerable vigor. She was rocked at other times as well, both to comfort her when she was upset and simply because she seemed to like it. Though the parents had decided not to permit any rough play, such as tossing the baby about, both used jiggling and bouncing as a sure-fire way of getting her to laugh.

The rating of moderate prominence for the importance of the near receptors in Margo's experience is a compromise, in that touch was relatively unimportant while passive motion was decidedly prominent.

Most prominent modality: Sound.

Least prominent modality: Touch.

Frequency of states of optimal animation: High.

During spontaneous activity Margo spent a great deal of time in alert and animated responsiveness to things about her. (Both coordinated and object-related behavior schemas were more prominent in her spontaneous behavior than for any other baby in Group Two.) She strained to reach for distant objects, she moved toys about and transferred them from hand to hand, and she also squealed gaily at the sight of people and in other ways initiated social interactions by performing every trick she knew. During contacts with the mother (as well as with numerous relatives) she was involved in sustained and often complex reciprocal behavior sequences that very frequently included mutual imitation of sounds and of gesture.

OUTCOME RATINGS

Developmental status: High.

Margo's development was accelerated, and scatter was unusually wide. In the areas of both gross and fine motor coordination, she was able to perform as is normally expected of children 24, 28, 32, and even 36 weeks old. In other words, all of her behavior was accelerated, but much more so in some respects than in others. Much the same was true of the adaptive area, which at this age involves chiefly the purposive and variegated use of objects. She readily transferred objects from one hand to the other (28 weeks), reached for a second object while holding one without losing awareness of the first one (32 weeks), and even banged a small object against a larger one (36 weeks) when a juxtaposition between the two objects had been demonstrated (namely, dropping a cube into the cup). Her social behavior (as this area is delineated in the Gesell Schedules) was also markedly advanced, but showed greater uniformity in that all of her scores were distributed between the 28 and 32 weeks levels. The test report mentions that her spontaneous play with the test objects (*i.e.,* ways of using the toys that do not happen to constitute test items) was like that more often seen in children closer to six months than at Margo's age of 4½ months. Further, her attention span and resiliency to prolonged stimulation were quite exceptional for one of her age.

As will be described more fully in later sections, the mother and other members of the family did almost everything one can think of to teach the baby (by intention) and to provoke her to new types of response (for the sake of immediate pleasure in observing her). From an early age (5 weeks) Margo had been amply supplied with toys, and her mother, father, grandmother, and family friends all utilized toys in playing with her. She had also been placed in the sitting posture very early, and then for increasingly longer periods of time adapted to her tolerance. When we knew her, she regularly spent most of the afternoon seated in a safety table heaped with toys. A favorite pastime was for the baby to throw these toys one by one. Once all were gone, she squealed impatiently and someone came running to restore them. The use of sounds in interactions with this baby was of special interest to us, partly because we thought the family capitalized on one of Margo's reaction tendencies without any awareness of so doing. Mother, as well as others in the family, often imitated whatever sounds the baby produced, and thus set in motion reciprocal vocalizations until it was impossible to know who was imitating whom. Margo had been taught to produce the noise called "bubble blowing," and she was believed to imitate various sounds (though the research staff believed that it was in fact the adults who did the imitating). She was whistled at from a distance and from close by, and during soothing the mother crooned to her softly and sweetly, in a manner quite unlike her usual robust and cheerful voice. The family were also at work teaching the baby to stretch her arms before being picked up (no success as yet), and she got what was playfully called a "swimming lesson" during each bath.

Adequacy of vegetative functioning: High.

Margo slept through the night (for 9–12 hours without awakening), she ate well, she experienced no gastric distress, and with the exception of a minor cold, had never been ill. The one possible impediment to optimal bodily functioning was her difficulty in falling asleep.

Excitability: High.

Margo was considered to be a highly excitable baby because certain recurrent situations always turned into stormy episodes and provoked very high levels of excitation, though only for brief times. Margo was intolerant of movement restraint, and when this became necessary she screamed, arched her back, and stiffened her limbs, only to be completely cheerful the moment she was free to move. Her mother made every effort to provide scope for Margo's movement impulses, so that diapering and undressing seldom became difficult, but dressing and the preliminaries to breast feeding always brought eruptions of what the mother called Margo's "temper." The second type of situation that provoked Margo to unusual excitement was one that we shall have to call "frustration"—when an "intention" could not be executed. For instance, she frequently strained for toys just out of reach. As she struggled, she often squealed angrily or cried. It is of interest that the mother encouraged Margo to accomplish her aims unaided. She watched the baby fuss and squirm, spoke encouraging words from a distance, and intervened only when clearly necessary (which was often). Thus Margo very often had the experience of becoming tense while trying to change her position, to extricate a toy and the like, and to be left in such a highly aroused state for some minutes before relief was provided. (Perhaps because of this circumstance, Margo is one of the very few 20-week-olds in our acquaintance who could get back into the sitting posture after she had slumped or fallen.) Other events that produced marked excitation for Margo were when a toy was taken from her or lost inadvertently, and sometimes when the mother terminated an interlude of social play. Breast feeding was also a stormy event which regularly encompassed extreme agitation as she lost the nipple (due to massive body motion) or as she was changed from one breast to the other. Yet these same feedings also regularly included periods of nearly complete quiescence and blissful content, as she sucked steadily and gazed at the mother's face, until she obeyed another movement impulse and again lost the nipple. Finally, Margo experienced marked excitation during the last 10 or 15 minutes before she fell asleep. Restlessness mounted, she desperately tried to play as usual and to maintain social interactions by squealing and laughing in the direction of nearby persons, though she was already so tired that her movements were jerky, her head and eyelids drooped, and all of her behavior bespoke extreme fatigue. However, this only led to an increase of massive motion and, when we knew her, Margo went to sleep only as the mother rocked her forcefully for quite some time. From sobbing and squirming in the mother's arms she abruptly dropped into sleep. Once asleep, she did not even stir when placed in the crib, and slept very soundly.

Thus Margo did respond with excitation to many situations that have no such effect on other babies. Yet it needs to be emphasized that when left to herself in the safety table for long periods each day, when played with, and also when handled, she was animated but not at all excited.

Irritability: Medium.

The "medium" rating was assigned because Margo's brief spurts of irritability were counterbalanced by the sturdy and cheerful fashion in which she responded to many situations that can be disruptive to other infants. Although she was among the minority of 20-week-olds who registered distinct discomfort at first contact with a stranger, she made no protest when visiting relatives held her, and fed and diapered her. In play she was rolled about quite vigorously and responded only with enjoyment, and she remained unperturbed when mother poked about in her ear with a bobby pin, in a manner quite alarming to the observers. Margo's capacity to recover from acute displeasure, cooing, laughing, and entertaining herself as before once the cause of the disturbance had disappeared, contributed to the judgment that she was characterized by a combination of positive signs of irritability and positive signs of its opposite.

Pleasure in functioning: High.

Much of what has already been said about this child's behavior documents the fact that she showed zest and pleasure in functioning to a "high" degree. In fact, her readiness to mobilize her entire repertoire of behavior schemas on any and all occasions, her perseverance when she met with obstacles, and her eager and keen response to novel types of stimulation struck observers as the most conspicuous feature of Margo's behavior. In a child who also showed in many other ways somewhat exceptional abilities, and who lived in a maximally facilitating environment, her spontaneous tendency to practice and experiment with a large variety of action possibilities is regarded as an index not only of excellent adaptation, but also of superior endowment.

DISCUSSION

It is worthy of mention that the environment in which Margo functioned so well had some characteristics that are not in themselves positive. For one thing, both parents and the extended family were so delighted at the appearance of the first baby of this generation that extraordinary amounts and intensities of active stimulation came her way, and not the slightest thing Margo did or failed to do was ever ignored. In addition, the mother's judgment and expectations about what is appropriate for a young baby were at times grossly faulty. For instance, Margo sat with the family for all three meals beginning at the age of 5 weeks and regularly received tidbits from the table, including such unlikely substances as pickle juice. She was given toys intended for much older children (the kind that the adult activates by winding, and the like) and given little choice as to whether to respond to them. She was credited with intentions, memories, problem-solving capacities, and naughty willfulness—and therefore she was, as it were, held responsible for behaviors that were in fact unintended and often altogether involuntary. Her mother, though wholly inexperienced, trusted her own judgment on many items of physical care and diet about which it might have been appropriate to consult the staff of the Well-baby Clinic (which mother seemed to think of only in connection with the necessary "shots").

Under these conditions this robust and active child experienced day-by-day life as more excitatory than most babies do. Strong pleasure and sharp distress punctuated her waking life, occurring far more often than is usual. She cried out or squealed in anger, both when alone and while being handled, only to chuckle and squeal in high glee the next second, as someone always responded to what she did. In fact, her experience differed from that of other babies in that she almost never made a sound or performed any visible action without at once perceiving a response. At the very least she was spoken to cheerfully or comfortingly from a distance, or someone changed her position, retrieved a toy, played with her, and the like. Especially important in the social realm may be the fact that the mother and grandmother (and possibly others) greatly enjoyed imitating the baby, and fully believed that Margo imitated them. If she performed a gesture such as rhythmic banging of a toy, they were likely to answer in kind. If she squealed or cooed or panted playfully, they reciprocated, waited for her to repeat the same sound, echoed it back, and thus enabled Margo to experience situations in which what she did led to predictable and specific events in the environment.

It is probably important that Margo also experienced states of thorough relaxation. When she was awake, these occurred only during breast feedings. As has been mentioned, feeding typically consisted of an alternation between periods of nearly complete relaxation as she sucked and gazed at the mother's face, and periods of marked irritability as she lost the nipple, only to become altogether quiet as sucking was resumed. She was also a baby who, once asleep, slept for long periods very quietly (she slept more than 10 hours without awakening each night).

We think that many another baby would not have been able to thrive as well as Margo did under these conditions. Her disposition was one that enabled her, so to speak, to give as good as she got. She left her parents in no doubt as to the limits of her tolerance, protesting with sufficient vigor to influence what the mother did for her and how it was done. She made no overt response to a good deal of the fondling and almost "kneading" she received, peacefully focusing on the human partner or on a toy as she was kissed and juggled. Her impressive muscular strength and bodily resiliency—along with the capacity for relaxation and sound sleep—also enabled her to survive without strain what might have been a taxing pattern of existence for a less vigorous child not yet 5 months of age.

Joella, In IX (20 Weeks)

SPE DETERMINANTS

Boundary Strength

	ENTIRE		*MODALITY SECTORS*			
	Inner	*Outer*	*Vision*	*Touch*	*Sound*	*Passive Motion*
Stimulation	weak (+)	medium (+)	medium (−)	weak	medium	strong
Frequency of Mother-Child Contacts		low	low	low	low	low
Intensity	medium	low	———	———	———	——→
Maternal Competence		high	———	———	———	——→
Maternal Intrusiveness		low	———	———	———	——→
Level of Home Stimulation		low	———	———	———	——→

Activity Level: 1.2

STABLE PATTERNS OF EXPERIENCE

Frequency of strong bodily arousal: Absent.

This inactive and understimulated baby was not seen or reported ever to show really massive excitation. Neither hunger nor fatigue nor any other circumstance brought more than a mild degree of restlessness and discomfort. The nearest she came to the display of bodily arousal was in a situation that had no counterpart in her ordinary experience—during the developmental testing, when she moved more extensively and in a jerky fashion, and her face was flushed and excited. However, though this was a high state of arousal for Joella, it was still no more than moderate by comparison with other babies.

Internal bodily sensations: Medium.

The degree to which internal body feelings influenced Joella's behavior was difficult to assess, because while known changes in body state such as hunger and fatigue led to mild behavioral manifestations, she frequently stimulated her own body during spontaneous activity, not in response to anything in the environment. She sucked her hand or thumb intensely and prolongedly, rubbed or stroked her own skin, rubbed one leg against the other, and pulled at her hair. On the assumption that some proprioceptive stimulation must have led to these behavior activations, the relative prominence of internal bodily sensations was thought to be moderate.

Balance between behavior activations due to inner and to outer stimulation: Internal predominant.

During spontaneous activity, a good deal of Joella's behavior was oriented toward an aspect of the immediate environment (58.1 per cent), though in large measure she focused on a part of her own body (her hand or her feet); her response to the sights and sounds about consisted largely of intent regard, which is not so much an activation of behavior as an arrest of other activity. During direct encounters with the mother, she tended to show mild increases in activity and sometimes vocalized. However, direct contacts with the mother were relatively rare, and Joella had very few contacts with other people. Her siblings understood that the baby was not to be approached, and only the parents dealt directly with the baby (her father played with her briefly when he returned from work). Joella spent a good deal of her waking time in the crib in a room by herself, though for about an hour and a half each afternoon she was brought into the living room, still in the prone position, and was observed but not played with. Our best estimate is that most of the relatively intense behavior activations were due to internal stimulation (chiefly oral and tactile self-stimulation), but that many of the slight behavior changes were responsive to something in her immediate environment. Most important is the fact that, compared with other babies, Joella was extraordinarily placid and showed a lesser number of behavior activations (that is, observable *changes* in behavior) than most infants at this age.

Importance of distance receptors: Fairly low.

What has been said implies that Joella had comparatively little to look at and to listen to. Not only was she usually placed in the prone position, but she was seldom offered toys (the home contained a single rattle), and her mother was not given to playfulness, with or without the use of objects. The baby was, of course, spoken to during routine procedures, but less so and with less animation than is usual. The radio was not often used, and the other children, who did create a certain amount of animation, were only sometimes in the same room with the baby, and then on condition that they not be noisy. Although Joella was fairly responsive to visual spectacles, and tended to gaze intently at things and people that were conspicuous (she did not explore visual details), she had limited opportunity to do so.

Importance of near receptors: Fairly high.

Joella was touched as much as necessary and not one bit more, and, so far as we could learn, she was not rocked or swayed. However, she did generate considerable tactile stimulation for herself, not only through the behaviors we have defined as tactile and oral self-stimulation, but also by clasping her hands tightly, clutching her head, and grasping her own feet.

Most prominent modality: Touch.

Least prominent modality: Kinesthetic.

Frequency of states of optimal animation: Occasional.

During spontaneous activity Joella was not so much lethargic as she tended to alternate between fairly intense bodily self-stimulation and coordinated action consisting of rather simple schemas such as gazing, indistinct cooing, and gentle arm waving. However, occasionally she struggled to attain the shift from the prone to the hand-knee creeping posture, or (when supine) reached for her foot and brought it into view. During brief routine procedures, which were performed with a minimum of playfulness, she was contented and wide-eyed, but showed minimal animation. Being dressed and bathed did elicit higher and more coordinated types of behavior (apparently because touch was prolonged). While under observation she rarely showed optimal levels of animation while unattended or in contact with the mother, but in interactions with the research staff this state occurred quite frequently. This mother may have been somewhat more spontaneous with her baby when unobserved, but it is certain that states of optimal animation could not have been more than an occasional event in Joella's experience.

OUTCOME RATINGS

Developmental status: Medium.

On both tests, Joella's scores closely conformed to average standards for her age. Some unevenness in her performance was noted, although this finds only partial reflection in the protocol. For instance, unlike most 20-

week-olds, Joella could not hold her head steady while pulled to sitting; nor did she, in the prone position, support her upper body on extended arms. However, while lying down she performed complicated actions primarily involving her legs. For instance, in the prone she raised the pelvis and lower abdomen off the mattress and thus achieved the hand-knee creeping posture, and when supine she lifted her legs high in extension, grasped her feet, and managed to get the toes into her mouth. Joella spent a large portion of her waking time in a horizontal position in her own crib or on the parents' large bed; the different level of motor coordination when she was in the accustomed position by contrast to the upright posture is almost certainly a reflection of that aspect of her experience.

Joella's interest in object manipulations was high. In what was for her a very active manner she reached for toys presented invitingly and attempted to manipulate them. Her movements at these times (and at no other) were fumbling and excited. While she did succeed on a number of items slightly above her chronological age level, she did not perform them as smoothly and competently as is usual once an infant has learned to perform them at all. Here again, her pattern of day-by-day experience amply accounts for the deficiency. We understand her test performance as reflecting perfectly normal readiness to respond to specific visual and auditory stimulation, but infrequent occasions for the practice of the relevant visual-motor coordinations.

Her social responsiveness met average expectation in terms of formal scoring, but was in some respects immature and was described by all as "feeble." She was heard to laugh aloud only once, she smiled at the sight of the human face but not at her mirror image, she vocalized relatively seldom, and behaviorally she made no discrimination between the mother and unfamiliar persons, nor did she manifest a reaction to the first encounter with a stranger. Her mother very seldom addressed herself to the baby as a social partner (she said that she *never* played with her, but that is hardly credible). In a highly capable, gentle, and perfectly friendly fashion this mother cared for her baby, but usually she did not speak to her except for incidental comments, which were not specifically addressed to the baby. On more than one occasion we observed the mother gaze at the baby in a warm, half-smiling fashion, but each time her position was such that the baby could not see her. Joella received her bottles propped in the crib (the late evening bottle was given while the baby remained asleep!) and it was then that we saw mother contemplate her baby in a pleased fashion. During grooming procedures and spoon-feedings, and on many other transient occasions, Joella of course saw her mother's face, heard her voice, and felt her touch. The baby appeared to make the most of these occasions, smiling and gazing for all she was worth. At least while under our observation, the mother's occasional smiles were always responsive to action initiated by the baby, who got things going by smiling first. The fact that social responses that occur primarily during interactions, especially vocalizing, were underdeveloped in Joella, and that, unlike most babies of her age, she failed to respond to the sound of the human voice, must be related to a pattern of experience that invited such responses to a minimal degree.

Adequacy of vegetative functioning: High.

Joella ate and slept well, had no gastric distress, and had never been ill at all. She did have a tendency to hiccup, which the mother usually stopped by offering a bottle of warm water. However, the hiccups did not appear to disturb the baby in the least, nor were they allowed to last for more than a few minutes at a time.

Excitability: Low.

Joella was assessed as being not at all excitable. Her manner of behaving when aroused seldom included the motoric and autonomic signs that, for rating purposes, were by definition coordinated to excitability. Except for moderately rapid motions and some loss of coordination during the developmental test, she showed no muscle tension whatsoever. Body movements did not increase in amount or forcefulness with hunger or fatigue, nor did she cry on these occasions, though she might whimper. What she *did* do, to quite an unusual extent, was stimulate her own body. She rubbed, poked, and vigorously scratched her own skin not only when left to her own devices, but also when spoken to or playfully touched, and during occasions such as the physical examination. She also rubbed one leg against the other, pulled at her hair, and tightly clutched her own head, though only in the absence of external stimulation. Oral behavior, chiefly hand and thumbsucking, was also very conspicuous during spontaneous activity, as were scratching and fingering nearby surfaces without visual regard. Thus, if our definition for excitatory behavior had included rather intense self-stimulation, the appropriate rating would have been "medium," especially because of her tendency to *scratch herself* in response to moderately active social approaches that included being touched among other modalities.

Irritability: Low.

As we already know, Joella was not irritable. She almost never cried even with hunger or fatigue, she remained content in the crib or wherever she was put down while awake, and she showed animation and often mild pleasure while the mother took care of her. It should be mentioned that Joella's mother was extraordinarily deft and gentle despite her impersonal manner. She could remove clothing swiftly and with a minimum of body contact, and when she had occasion to hold the baby she held her comfortably yet very loosely—in a manner not at all confining or encircling. Even during the much more sustained stimulation provided by the research staff (and, we were told, occasionally by the father) the baby did not show displeasure, but scratched herself with such vigor as to leave deep red impressions on her skin.

Pleasure in functioning: Medium.

A "medium" rating was assigned because while it was true that Joella spent a large proportion of her time in a self-contained manner, applying easy and primitive behavior schemas such as sucking, it was also true that whenever stimulation came her way, she responded eagerly. For instance, mere contact with the mother, however impersonal by our standards, evoked what were for her among the most complex social responses (smiling first, and sometimes slight vocalizing). Similarly, when toys were offered, she at once turned toward them with animation and exerted maximum effort to reach and manipulate them. Last, some of her patterns of bodily self-stimulation were not primitive, developmentally speaking. For instance, grasping her own feet and bringing them to the mouth entails what are advanced motor coordinations for her age, and she brought objects to the mouth when this was not an easy thing to do.

DISCUSSION

Joella is another baby who showed, on the whole, good developmental progress under circumstances that are unusual (at least in this culture) and that do not, on the surface, provide some of the elements thought desirable in the life of young infants. Her mother combined great practical skill with a genuinely distant attitude. She was a woman of few words, with us as well as with the baby. Her general manner was preoccupied though not withdrawn, in the sense that she was alert to all that was said and done, but responded minimally and with seeming reluctance. One felt that all aspects of her relationship with the baby showed the same qualities as her relationship with the project staff (though she had volunteered to participate) and possibly also with her husband. It was as though nothing interested her very much, as though whatever feelings she may have had were not so much held in check as prevented from emerging. In other words she appeared to be inhibited and a bit anxious, impassive rather than resentful.

From the beginning she did everything required to care for a baby, and she did it very well. However, such pleasure as we guessed she was actually feeling, especially at the baby's positive responses toward her, she kept to herself; she looked pleased, but not *at* the baby, and she was not seen to elaborate upon interactions or to do anything with the baby just for pleasure. So far as we could learn, Joella never experienced mutual gazing during feedings, and only very transiently at other times. Seldom was she "answered" when she vocalized, and then in ordinary language instead of the more usual cooing and crooning sounds. She was not picked up (except when practically necessary), nor did her mother maintain casual contact from a distance, as some other mothers do. No relatives lived near, visitors were reported to be rare, and when Joella was taken along to visit friends, the mother usually placed her in a separate room to sleep.

Joella had perfected the art of providing for herself much of the "external" stimulation that other infants receive from the environment. She made good use of her hands and feet as manipulanda, she evoked tactile sensations so energetically that we wondered whether pain might be involved, she used her eyes whenever there was anything to look at. Equally striking was her capacity to use thumbsucking as a means of self-soothing. When hungry or fatigued she lay almost motionless, sucking avidly.[1] In situations that lead most babies to show some displeasure (nipple loss during feeding, loss of a toy, termination of a social contact), she looked momentarily displeased and then brought her hand to the mouth and become content and very quiet. The mother was able to say and demonstrate more than once that the baby needed no attention when she fussed a bit, for she would soon settle down of her own accord.

In terms of immediate adaptation to an objectively impoverished environment, Joella's use of bodily self-stimulation certainly served both to provide animation and to counteract displeasure and discomfort. Whether such self-sufficiency is advantageous for later development is a different matter. Certainly Joella failed to show the vivid brightening and enhancement of all faculties during pleasurable contacts with the mother (or with anybody) that one often sees. Certainly she did not yet overtly manifest any distinctive mode of responding to very familiar persons, as many 20-week-olds do. She had in fact very little occasion to perceive a direct connection between relief from discomfort and her mother's proximity. The baby's behavior, though perfectly normal in all ways, lacked variety and modulation as compared with other infants of like age. And it certainly was limited in range, including neither peak distress nor intense pleasure, neither marked activity nor complete quiescence (except while sucking strenuously). Even during feeding and sleep her postures remained somewhat stiff; for instance, her hands were often fisted or her ankles sharply averted. Joella maintained a reasonably comfortable adaptation through what we consider an overuse of bodily self-stimulation, but at the cost of missing out, even at this early age, on much experience that, whether pleasurable or painful, lends evocative and stable qualities to persons and things in the environment. The mechanisms that underlie such adaptive regulation are presumably mediated by the central nervous system, and are physiological or biological phenomena. Yet they have manifest consequences for behavior and for the pattern, and possibly the scope, of psychological development as well.

[1] Oral behavior was not rated as increased during need states because it was also very prominent during spontaneous activity. However, the quality of oral behavior while the baby was alert and content was more varied, and sucking was prolonged but not avid at these times.

One speculates whether later psychological mechanisms are in part influenced by peculiarities of functioning in early infancy. Neurotic mechanisms that operate at later ages serve also to avoid discomfort (chiefly anxiety) and, by definition, they prevent the personality from realizing some of its potentials. It is possible that extreme behavioral self-sufficiency in very early infancy increases the probability that in meeting the conflicts and anxieties of childhood, the person will be more inclined to seek relief by autoerotic means, through phantasy, and generally in a fashion that does not involve outwardly directed action and reciprocal involvements with other people. If something of the sort is true, the manner in which preferred defenses are sometimes transmitted from one generation to the next may be exemplified by Joella and her mother. Although we have no clinical understanding of the mother's personality, even brief contacts left no doubt that she was not leading a satisfying life, that she was markedly burdened by anxiety, and that in consequence she restricted contact with other human beings and was severely limited in her ability to enjoy casual pleasures of everyday life. Her dealings with the baby were in large measure dictated by her limitations. She could not offer soothing—and by the time we knew Joella, the child certainly did not require it. She reduced body contact and touching of the baby as much as possible—and when we knew her, Joella touched herself a very great deal. She seldom spoke to the baby—and Joella vocalized much less than other babies. She did not play with her baby—and Joella played with herself. Thus, quite inadvertently, this mother may have imposed on her accommodating baby a pattern of infantile existence that predisposes her towards defense mechanisms similar to those of the mother herself.

Walter, Ac X (20 Weeks)

SPE DETERMINANTS

Boundary Strength

	ENTIRE		*MODALITY SECTORS*			
	Inner	*Outer*	*Vision*	*Touch*	*Sound*	*Passive Motion*
Stimulation	medium (+)	strong (−)	strong (−)	strong	medium (+)	?
Frequency of Mother-Child Contacts		medium	medium (−)	low (+)	medium	low (+)
Intensity	low	medium	→			
Maternal Competence		medium (+)	→			
Maternal Intrusiveness		medium	→			
Level of Home Stimulation		medium	→			

Activity Level: 2.2

STABLE PATTERNS OF EXPERIENCE

Frequency of strong bodily arousal: Rare.

Walter was a robust, energetic, and only moderately active baby who seldom received stimulation intense enough to yield high levels of excitation. He showed massive and poorly coordinated motion, considerable muscle tension and loud crying only when he was hungry. He responded to the developmental testing with very marked excitement, but since such prolonged and energetic play did not take place at home, it is concluded that very high levels of bodily arousal occurred regularly but infrequently.

Internal bodily sensations: Prominent.

Both hunger and fatigue brought massive alterations of behavior. During spontaneous activity and during sleep, Walter was never entirely relaxed or quiescent. When awake, much of his behavior was focused upon an aspect of the environment (62.8 per cent), but he also rolled about a great deal, raised and lowered his stiffly extended legs, clasped his hands, and engaged in a good deal of mouthing. During sleep, muscle twitching and jerky motions were frequent, even when he was in a darkened, quiet room. These activations are thought to reflect proprioceptive stimulation of some sort.

Balance between behavior activations due to inner and to outer stimulation: Equal.

As described above, Walter rather often initiated some sort of movement apparently in response to fluctuating body states. However, the sight and sound of things about elicited activity increases and movements of approach or of avoidance very regularly. Although some of his contacts with the mother were distinctly soothing, the great majority led to behavior activations.

Importance of distance receptors: Medium.

Walter tended to startle at sudden sounds, though in other ways he was not especially attentive or sensitive to sound. Visual stimuli such as the sight of persons or of toys nearly always aroused his interest, provided they were close by or otherwise conspicuous. His mother often spoke to him playfully, but seldom in a compelling or sustained fashion, and while she saw to it that toys were close by, she did not seek to attract his visual attention to her face except during routine procedures that necessarily created face-to-face contacts (such as diapering).

Importance of near receptors: Low.

Walter's mother did not hesitate to touch her baby for practical purposes, and when he required soothing (which was rare), she held him very close to her body. However, during most contacts with the baby, tactile components were minimized. Except for burping, he was not patted or stroked. She held him loosely in her arms and seldom touched him playfully; nor was she given to affectionate gestures that involved touch. Similarly, he was not swayed or rocked at all (which accounts for the fact that his reactivity to kinesthetic stimulation could not be rated). Except for mouthing (objects more often than his own hand), oral and tactile self-stimulation were rare. While one must assume that his rolling in the crib generated some kinesthetic stimulation, both of the near receptor systems seemed less important in his experience than is usual.

Most prominent modality: None.

Least prominent modality: Touch.

Frequency of states of optimal animation: Moderate.

During his waking periods and when unattended in the playpen, on the floor, or propped up sitting on a sofa, Walter was alert and active much of the time. He frequently engaged in complex behavior integrations, primarily in the form of motor play; and less often in the form of reaching for and manipulating toys. During contacts with the mother he was attentive, but often his response consisted of the simple acts of smiling, arm waving, and cooing. The mother's contacts with the baby tended to be casual and brief, so that sustained reciprocal behavior sequences developed only occasionally. When they occurred, Walter's contribution frequently was to reach for portions of the mother's face or clothing and grasp so tightly that she had to unclench his hand. Since the father was seldom at home when Walter was awake, and since this was not a sociable family, it is safe to conclude that optimal states of animation occurred occasionally in a social context, but were more typically present during spontaneous activity when the baby was under his mother's eye, but not in direct contact with her.

OUTCOME RATINGS

Developmental status: Medium.

Test results placed Walter in the high average category. Gross motor coordination was slightly advanced, as he was able to roll efficiently from the prone to the supine position, to lift his legs high in extension, and to retain a rattle, as well as to retrieve it when it dropped from his hand to an easily accessible place (all of these are normative at 24 weeks). In the adaptive area of the Gesell Schedules he failed to perform one item at his own age level, but achieved one of the 24-weeks items. It is of interest that his capacity to produce differentiated sounds and to respond to sounds (by locating the source) was also slightly accelerated compared with his response to visual stimuli. It will be remembered that the outer boundary in the auditory sector had been rated "medium," whereas that for vision had been assessed as "strong." Walter was comparatively expert in the purposive manipulation of objects. It was in discriminatory behavior and in the capacity to attend more than one object at a time that his performance was somewhat less mature.[1]

Adequacy of vegetative functioning: High.

When we knew Walter he no longer experienced gastric distress, though in earliest infancy (first 6 weeks of life) he had pyloric spasms and received sedation. At that time he was said to have been tense and irritable and, for that reason, was kept in a quiet room away from the family. However, he was considered to be completely well by 7 weeks, and by the time we knew him he was a healthy, sturdy baby.

Excitability: High.

Walter was assessed as a highly excitable baby partly because he was never seen really relaxed and quiescent except during feedings, and not always then. His sleep was usually restless, not only when we could observe it, but, according to his mother, always. He showed so many jerky movements, muscle twitches, and squirming motions that it was impossible to know what proportion was related to external stimuli. However, the high mobility in sleep was present even in a darkened, entirely quiet room. Further, his strong excitement when objects were playfully presented and sometimes when he spontaneously approached and manipulated a nearby toy influenced the rating.

It is important to specify that in Walter's experience moments of high excitation were very rare. What he did show frequently was fairly strong excitement, as indicated by jerky motions, heavy panting breathing, and sometimes muscle tension. The failure to become extremely excited may also be ascribed to his lack of sensitivity; he failed to become aroused in a good many situations that prove excitatory to other babies. The mother's rather rough manner of manipulating him, the loss of the nipple during feeding, the removal of a toy, termination of a playful episode—these and similar situations sometimes led to a mild and composed response and at other times they found no expression in overt behavior.

Irritability: Low.

Walter was not at all irritable. He enjoyed direct encounters with the mother, which took place mostly during routine caretaking procedures. He spent many hours each day contentedly in the playpen, and shorter periods propped in a sitting position on the sofa. He entertained himself with toys

[1] The pattern of Walter's test performance is nearly identical with that of Cecilia (Ac VIII) whose SPE ratings are strikingly similar to his. The developmental outcome ratings are very similar for these two babies in all respects.

that were always nearby, watched the other people in the room (he was kept with the family unless asleep), and responded well to the unfamiliar setting and strange people at the research quarters, showing nothing but pleasure in response to far more attention and manipulation than he was accustomed to.

Walter's mother was perfectly willing to soothe her baby when she thought he was in pain, but felt strongly that she ought not to intervene when he showed discontent without "good reason." She described herself as lacking the patience to play with the baby and comfort him as she saw other mothers do. Actually she did herself an injustice. Although her self-report seemed accurate as far as it went (he really was not held or played with much), she was seen to distract and comfort the baby when he showed minor episodes of distress. Often she spoke to him pleasantly from a distance, to which he was responsive. Or else she approached him, smiled at him, handed him a toy, or changed his position, which—when observed—always served to content him. This moderately active and rather tense baby might well have been somewhat irritable had it not been that his mother adapted his position and his physical location to his momentary state and also intervened readily and briefly in ways that improved his mood.

Pleasure in functioning: High.

The "high" rating was given because, when left to his own devices, Walter was very alert to things about him, and engaged in fairly complex motor play. He often rolled from prone to supine in a coordinated fashion, he clasped and unclasped his hands with intent regard, he reached for and grasped nearby objects, he looked prolongedly both at people and at distant objects. In addition, he responded to object stimulation and to social play with eagerness and obvious pleasure when they came his way.

DISCUSSION

Walter developed and functioned well even though he had gotten off to a poor start due to illness (pyloric spasm) in early infancy. During the first 6 weeks of life, he cried a great deal, had to be fed at intervals of no more than 2½ hours both day and night, and on the doctor's advice was kept in a darkened and very quiet room at all times. However, from the age of 7 weeks he had been in robust health, as he was when we knew him.

During contacts with his mother, Walter received less of the prolonged and finely attuned varieties of stimulation than do most babies, and body contact was less prolonged and intimate than is usual. He was held for feedings and, although he sucked vigorously and steadily, the situation was not as relaxed and peaceful as it might have been. He kicked and wriggled a good deal and frequently grasped the mother's finger or her blouse very tightly. His mother often looked at him intently, mostly to gauge the position of the nipple, but there was no mutual gazing whatsoever. She removed the nipple rather often, at which Walter became very active but did not cry.

As Walter was on a regular schedule, he almost always experienced marked distress before feeding. Fatigue also led to intermittent crying and marked restlessness, though of moderate degree. Typically, he was placed in the crib and left alone at such times, and went to sleep after fussing from 20 to 30 minutes. As has been said, sleep did not bring muscular relaxation to this baby (his mother reported that he moved about as much in the night as we saw him do during several daytime naps). Because she was inexperienced, and probably for other reasons as well, the mother's manipulation of her baby during routine procedures was neither gentle nor accommodating, though perfectly friendly. She handled him rather roughly, yanking him about, and lifted or dropped him rather suddenly. This did not appear to disturb the baby, but it did preclude either relaxed or intense social interchanges. Both mother and baby appeared to derive most pleasure from each other at moments when they were not in close body contact, and when the mother laughed at his antics, provided toys, or lifted him into a more comfortable posture.

Under these conditions, Walter's experience provided high states of excitation with distress (but not often) and fairly strong arousal that could be pleasurable, distressing or affectively neutral (very often). His experience lacked periods of relaxation and quiet contentment, and provided few occasions for the type of social interaction in which each partner's behavior is delicately attuned to that of the other and which lasts long enough for reciprocal patterns to emerge.

Walter's pattern of development and adaptation seems to us to reflect these circumstances. His motor coordination was somewhat advanced, and he had both the opportunity and the inclination for considerable body play. Toward objects his behavior was vigorous, but less discriminatory and less complex (he could not attend more than one toy at a time) than is often true at this age. His social behavior also lacked discrimination and was described as stereotyped and not at all subtle. He responded to the strange observers as he did to the mother, except for the fact that he responded to them more strongly (by laughing and squealing) simply because their play with him was more energetic and sustained than he was used to. If one assumes that differentiated and discriminatory responsiveness to people and things emerges as an infant is responded to in a discriminatory and subtly responsive fashion, it makes good sense that Walter's lack of these characteristics came about because he had less occasion for varied and intense affective and perceptual experience than most babies do.[2]

[2] This is another striking similarity to Cecilia (Ac VIII) who, for very different reasons, also lacked this component of life experience, and who, like Walter, was vigorous but somewhat stereotyped in her response to people and to things.

Hanna, In X (20 weeks)

SPE DETERMINANTS

	Boundary Strength					
	ENTIRE		*MODALITY SECTORS*			
	Inner	*Outer*	*Vision*	*Touch*	*Sound*	*Passive Motion*
Stimulation	medium (−)	medium	strong (−)	medium	medium	?
Frequency of Mother-Child Contacts		high	high (−)	medium (−)	medium (−)	high (−)
Intensity	medium (+)	low (+)	→	→	→	→
Maternal Competence		high	→	→	→	→
Maternal Intrusiveness		low	→	→	→	→
Level of Home Stimulation		medium	→	→	→	→

Activity Level: 1.3

STABLE PATTERNS OF EXPERIENCE

Frequency of strong bodily arousal: Rare.

Hanna was so inactive that each of the few times when she showed strong or fairly strong excitement surprised the observers. Only one situation typically led to energetic and tense body movements accompanied by loud squealing and by tremors and/or arching of the back—just before feeding. Hanna was entirely placid during the preliminaries to feeding, but once the breast was bared she lunged toward it, squealing impatiently or crying, and moving the entire body so tensely that it was difficult to help her grasp the nipple. This never lasted more than a second or two but, according to what her mother said and what we saw, it occurred regularly when she was fed.

Internal bodily sensations: Medium.

This aspect was difficult to assess. Hanna was generally quiet and usually contented during spontaneous activity. However, she was given to prolonged and intense spurts of sucking (either objects or her own hand). One presumes that the exceptionally strong impulse toward oral self-stimulation (oral score: 20.0) reflected some sort of internal body tension. Her behavior justified the inference that much of the time sucking or mouthing was for her a condition of well-being. When the toy or hand was separated from the mouth, she tended to become restless and whimper, only to relax again as she resumed the mouthing. In other ways body state did not affect her behavior very strongly. Both hunger and fatigue led to very moderate arousal, she had no gastric troubles, and she was able to remain almost motionless yet fully alert for prolonged periods of time. Another complicating factor was that Hanna suffered from mild but recurrent eczema. Insofar as we and the mother (who was an excellent observer) could judge, the rash was not painful to the baby, except when it was touched. Thus, Hanna did experience bodily discomfort when her clothing or the mother's hand contacted the affected areas, but this did not come from within the body, but in response to external (tactile) stimulation.

Balance between behavior activations due to inner and to outer stimulation: Equal.

If thumb or object sucking is considered an activation, even though it tended to decrease motility while it lasted, the best estimate is that internal and external stimulation led to behavior activations with approximately equal frequency. Hanna was frequently approached and spoken to or played with, not only by the mother but by other members of the family and by visitors. If such contacts were very brief and casual, they did not lead to behavior activations, as Hanna merely gazed at the other person in a friendly fashion. However, much more often she smiled, cooed, reached for an object, and the like. In other words, small but definite activations occurred rather frequently to both inner and outer stimulation.

Importance of distance receptors: Fairly high.

Hanna was spoken to and played with or otherwise attended very often indeed, though usually rather gently. Vision in particular was an important component of her experience despite the fact that she was relatively unreactive, because her mother was exceptionally skillful and persistent in cultivating Hanna's visual responsiveness. She offered the sight of her own face and person in a gentle but compelling manner, and very often offered the baby a toy or an object to look at, timing her interventions to elicit maximal responses. For instance, if she saw the baby's glance rest on a nearby object (such as a can of food, a piece of clothing or a toy) she was repeatedly seen to move the object playfully, encouraging Hanna to reach for it or at least to follow it with her eyes.

Importance of near receptors: Prominent.

Although her mother tried not to touch the baby unnecessarily for fear of causing pain, the necessary routines do involve considerable touch; more often than not, Hanna responded by whimpering and mild restlessness. The skin condition made it necessary to change diapers even more frequently than the mother would otherwise have done. Hanna was also rocked and swayed a good deal, both in play and in soothing. We could not rate her sensitivity to this variety of stimulation because passive motion was never provided except in association with patting, holding, being spoken to, and the like. During soothing Hanna almost always also sucked her thumb, so that when she quieted we never knew whether she was responding to being rocked or to the sucking.

Most prominent modality: None.

Least prominent modality: Sound.

Frequency of states of optimal animation: Fairly high.

Despite her quietness and her tendency to spend much time just mouthing, Hanna was roused to responsiveness and animation frequently by the mother and also by others in the home. As has already been described, the mother had a way of playing with the baby that tended to elicit relatively complex responsiveness, at least to objects. Whenever Hanna showed even slight restlessness, she was attended to, and both parents frequently held her on their laps for rather long periods of time, because in that position she was especially content. The mother, though not the other members of the family, always remained responsive to the baby, even if most of her attention was directed toward the siblings or something else. She retrieved toys that the baby dropped, she helped the baby achieve position changes without imposing them, and in many other ways facilitated Hanna's outwardly directed responsiveness.

OUTCOME RATINGS

Developmental status: High.

Hanna's test performance placed her in the superior range. Gross motor coordination was in exact accord with average standards for her age. However, her capacity and her interest in reaching for and manipulating objects were that of the average 24-week-old, and she was able to achieve two items that become normative only by 28 weeks (transfer objects, retain bell). Similarly, her vocalizations conformed to ordinary standards for 24-week-olds, and she occasionally uttered polysyllabic sounds (a 28-weeks item on the Gesell Schedules). Hanna was among the babies whose accelerated developmental status could not have been expected from behavior observations in situations other than the test itself. The protocol makes special mention of the fact that less mature (though normative for her age of 20 weeks) behavior patterns dominated even during the test. Still, occasionally, and in response to the special prodding provided in the course of test administration, she demonstrated unequivocally her capacity for more mature behavior integrations.

As will be discussed more fully later on, Hanna's rate of developmental progress was apparently made possible by two features of her experience that are not specified in the formal ratings. One was the mother's remarkable skill in providing appropriate stimulation at exactly the right time. Her frequent though usually brief sociable contacts with the baby used toys (or booties, utensils, cans of food, whatever happened to be handy) not as a substitute for social attention but as an integral part of it. She also actively supported actions with toys that the baby had initiated. For instance, when Hanna had grasped a toy and was clearly trying to bring it to her mouth but could not quite accomplish this, the mother slightly lifted the toy from beneath, enabling the baby to complete the action but not really doing it for her.

The second feature that created many occasions for Hanna to deviate from very simple, stereotyped behavior patterns, which were characteristic while she was entirely content and unattended, was her eczema. By the time we knew the baby the eczema was mild, but still sufficient to produce moderate but distinct discomfort many times each day. As she became mildly fretful and somewhat more active than was her wont, and as her mother promptly attempted to relieve her by position changes, talking to her, rocking her or diverting her through play, the baby was sufficiently aroused to respond more strongly to gentle external stimulation than she did at other times.

Adequacy of vegetative functioning: High.

The adequacy of Hanna's bodily functioning cannot be condensed into a single rating. With the exception of the eczema, or perhaps one should say, despite it, the adequacy of vegetative functioning was "high." She ate well, slept well, had no gastric troubles whatsoever, and, except for a cold during the third month, had never been ill. She did experience irritation and discomfort from the skin condition, especially during the hot and humid Kansas summer days when we observed her. Thus, disruption and discomfort due to bodily sensations were far more frequent in Hanna's life than is usual, but they did not affect the adequate integration of any of the vital body functions.

Excitability: Medium.

The "medium" is due primarily to the consequences of the eczema for Hanna's experience. Body manipulations of the sort required in diapering and dressing a baby often proved irritating to Hanna. Her mother reduced the discomfort involved by her deft motions and by providing a constant stream of comforting and mildly playful speech, but nonetheless Hanna usually whimpered or cried before the procedure was completed. In addition, on the rare occasions when stimulation was distinctly intense, Hanna manifested excitement by squeals, by jerky, quivering, rapid motions, and by a flushed face. To everyone's surprise, she behaved in this manner during the developmental test when objects were offered in a far more vigorous and intrusive way than the mother would have known how to use. As described earlier, Hanna also was excited for a very brief moment just before breast feeding began, if she was quite hungry at the time. Once the feeding was under way, she became very still, sucking avidly at first and more leisurely thereafter. In other words, she was more excitable than other very inactive and not especially sensitive babies, but by comparison with the sample as a whole she showed only a very moderate degree of excitability.

Irritability: Medium.

Hanna showed irritability only when her behavior clearly suggested the presence of painful skin sensations. On her "good" days she never whimpered or cried except very briefly during some manipulations. For the greatest portion of each day she was content, placid when alone and mildly animated when in contact with other people. Hanna was another baby who effectively used thumbsucking or sucking at objects to soothe herself. She failed to show much discomfort during hunger and fatigue, but sucked avidly. If she lost her thumb she became restless and fussy, only to return to relative quiescence as thumbsucking began again. Much the same behavior was observed when the mother held Hanna on her lap because she had shown discomfort. There the baby sucked contentedly, more often on a toy provided by the mother than on her thumb. When the toy dropped from her hands she looked displeased, and moved restlessly though not extensively until it was restored and put again to oral use. Scrutiny of the observational data leaves little doubt that this frequently uncomfortable baby showed relatively little irritability (by comparison with other babies with eczema or with recurrent gastic distress) not only because of her mother's skillful care, but also because self-initiated sucking very often soothed her effectively. In Hanna's life, encounters with the mother were very frequent nonetheless, and the baby often calmed herself by sucking while at the same time mother succeeded in arousing at least her visual interest in something in the environment.

Pleasure in functioning: Low.

Left to her own devices, Hanna spent more of her time in the activation of primitive behavior schemas than any other infant in her age group (57.6 per cent in terms of prominence scores). She was the only infant above 16 weeks of age who did not manipulate objects in any way during spontaneous activity. Instead she waved her arms, rolled about a bit, sometimes clasped her hands in midline, or regarded nearby persons or her own hands. A great deal of the time she mouthed and sucked her hands and fingers, and occasionally went so far as to grasp her foot. In responding to the mother she smiled, gazed, and vocalized softly; only very seldom did she demonstrate the capacity she proved to have for more vigorous and more mature behavior, such as squealing, laughing, and the production of complex polysyllables. As shown during the developmental testing and on the few occasions when the mother's (and especially the father's) play became more vigorous, she could manifest pleasurable excitement while experimenting with new coordinations, but much of the time she employed relatively simple, well-learned behavior schemas. (It was for this reason that the research staff and the mother felt real surprise when Hanna showed what she could do during the test).

DISCUSSION

Hanna provides a good example of the manner in which a not especially responsive infant, plagued by recurrent bodily distress, can nonetheless make excellent developmental progress and function in a predominantly comfortable manner. In her case, the acceleration of development was present only in some ego functions, whereas other aspects of behavior remained at the level normally expected of 20-week-old babies. Specifically she excelled in that she was one of two infants in her age group (the eight subjects in Group Two) who in their behavior distinguished the mother from all other persons; moreover, she did this to an unusual degree. It was as though the sight, sound, and touch of the mother had greater power than anybody else's. Hanna smiled more quickly and broadly and vocalized more readily at the mother than at others who addressed her with equal gentleness, and she was one of the very few babies in the entire sample who could be soothed only by the mother. If anybody else performed the very same actions, she cried as if in anger or distress. We were especially interested in the fact that she showed slight but definite discomfort when the irritated portions of her skin were touched by the mother, but when one of the observers did so, she cried as if in real pain.[1]

The second area of acceleration was Hanna's superior ability to reach for and hold objects. Yet here, too, her behavior in dealing with objects (except to obtain them) was undistinguished. She showed no interest in their color, texture, or noise-generating properties. Her object manipulations did not exploit the potentials of each thing for shaking, banging, or producing visual effects. Instead, everything within reach was treated in the same manner—as something-to-bring-to-the-mouth. However, her movements in implementing the object-to-mouth schema were exceptionally well adapted to the size, shape, and spatial position of the objects that aroused her interest.

In short, although the test scores placed her in the superior range, based upon superior performance in isolated areas, Hanna did not show the behavior characteristics often associated with exceptionally high endowment. What has been said so far leads to the suggestion that in Hanna's case, partial acceleration of development occurred because the combination of somatic discomfort and arousal on the one hand and maximal facilitation from the mother on the other forced upon her an early awareness of some selective aspects of the environment.

Her pattern of experience was one that very often indeed combined a reduction in discomfort (or a change to pleasurable feelings) with the

[1] The only other eczema baby in the sample, Clara, In XVI, showed precisely the same intolerance for touch by anyone but the mother. Yet social behavior and discriminatory power were not shown in other spheres. Both showed no response to a first encounter with strange persons, but at once smiled and vocalized in response to the unfamiliar research staff (though less intensively than when responding to the mother). Nor were their facial expressions, vocalizations or movement patterns highly articulated or differentiated.

physical proximity of mother. As Hanna was in discomfort frequently, the mother was of especially great functional importance. We think that she came to behaviorally recognize her mother (*i.e.*, discriminate her person) earlier and more sharply than many other babies because greater or more frequent stress compelled vigilance toward the primary sources of relief and comfort. Her partial acceleration in the capacity to obtain and manipulate objects can be understood in a similar manner. Probably because object-mouthing had soothing power, the object-to-mouth schema dominated her behavior. In other words, the mere sight of an object almost always led her to reach for it, grasp it, and promptly bring it to the mouth in an unbroken sequence. The sight of suitably manipulatable objects also had the functional significance of signalling (leading to the sensorimotor anticipation of) relief or some variety of need gratification. Since different objects at different distances cannot be attained and brought to the mouth by means of exactly the same movement patterns, Hanna learned to adapt her movements to the different physical properties of objects and of the spatial field, in the direct service of immediate bodily gratification.

Freud (1913) suggested that partial precocity in the development of early ego functions may be a determinant of a predisposition toward obsessive-compulsive defense structures at a later age. We have been at pains to discriminate between partial developmental acceleration and uniform precocity, in part because Hanna's constellation of concrete experience may illustrate the manner in which such a predisposition can come about. At any rate, relative acceleration of some functions while the remainder of behavior is organized in a less mature manner is not necessarily advantageous to subsequent development and adaptation.[2]

[2] See also discussion of this point in Ch. 8.

FIFTEEN

INDIVIDUAL ADAPTATION SYNDROMES: GROUP THREE

Robert, Ac XI (24 Weeks)

SPE DETERMINANTS

Boundary Strength

	ENTIRE		MODALITY SECTORS			
	Inner	*Outer*	*Vision*	*Touch*	*Sound*	*Passive Motion*
Stimulation	medium	medium (+)	medium	strong	medium (−)	strong
Frequency of Mother-Child Contacts		high	medium	low (+)	medium (−)	strong
Intensity	low (+)	high	→	→	→	→
Maternal Competence		medium	→	→	→	→
Maternal Intrusiveness		high	→	→	→	→
Level of Home Stimulation		medium	→	→	→	→

Activity Level: 2.9

STABLE PATTERNS OF EXPERIENCE

Frequency of strong bodily arousal: Rare.

Robert was a sturdy and exceedingly active infant who became quite excited in response to the parents' provocative play or sometimes when he encountered obstacles in executing a movement impulse. However, he was not seen to reach levels of arousal high enough to produce marked distress or to lead to a marked loss of coordination. Even hunger distress built up gradually, and his mother fed him long before it became intense. Thus he was often aroused to a moderately high degree, but was not seen (or reported) to reach the state we have designated as peak excitation.

Internal bodily sensations: Fairly low.

Except for hunger and fatigue, which affected his behavior fairly strongly, changes in body state seemed to exert less influence on Robert's behavior than is true for many 24-week-olds. During spontaneous activity he was never still, but most of his behavior was oriented toward an aspect of the environment or consisted of fairly complex motor coordinations.

Balance between behavior activations due to inner and to outer stimulation: External very predominant.

As has been mentioned, even when left unattended, Robert busied himself responding to the sights and sounds about him, including the perception of his own feet and hands, though occasionally he began to roll, kick, and mouth in the absence of external stimulation. In addition, he was played with and manipulated a great deal by the mother, and spent much of his time in situations that tended to provoke his active interest (*i.e.,* the family dog, mother doing housework close by, many toys). To all of this he responded by movements of approach or pursuit, by loud vocalizing, and by kicking and bouncing. The great majority of behavior activations thus occurred in response to external stimulation, though external events could also quiet him and activations due to internal causes did occur.

Importance of distance receptors: Fairly high.

Though he was not especially reactive to either sight or sound, both of these modalities (especially vision) played a large role in shaping Robert's behavior. During direct encounters with the mother the distance receptors were not the primary modalities, but his mother constantly and systematically exposed him to interesting spectacles. Not only did she provide a rich array of toys, but she placed his infant seat strategically (to face outdoors, toward the kitchen, etc.) because "he likes it when there is something interesting to look at."

Importance of near receptors: High.

Both mother and father used primarily the kinesthetic mode in playing with their baby. He was bounced and juggled, "elevator" was a preferred game (rapid lifting and lowering in mid-air), and his father tossed him and caught him like a ball. In addition, the baby generated for himself a good deal of kinesthetic stimulation in the course of forceful movements during play and at other times. Touch in its own right was provided less frequently by the mother, but it was, of course, part of the active playful manipulations we described.

Most prominent modality: Vision (and/or kinesthetic).

Least prominent modality: Touch.

Frequency of states of optimal animation: Fairly high.

Like many of the active infants, Robert showed optimal animation in his execution of fairly complex and mature behavior coordinations while unattended, playing on the floor or in his infant seat. With impressive energy and persistence he propelled himself toward things by pivoting, he dropped and retrieved objects, he dealt with more than one object at a time, he played "peek-a-boo" with himself by covering his face and chuckling as he removed the blanket, and engaged in similar activities. During contacts with the mother his behavior was generally fairly simple, clearly because she was so energetic that there was little he could do except laugh, squeal, squirm, or roll and kick.

OUTCOME RATINGS

Developmental status: High.

Robert's test performance was accelerated in all areas; at the age of 24 weeks he performed every single item normative at 28 weeks, and slightly more than half of the items not generally achieved until 32 weeks. His test performance in different areas was rather uniform (relatively little scatter), so that motor coordination, discriminatory behavior, vocalizations, and modes of social responsiveness were all of approximately equal caliber from a developmental point of view. His interest in test objects was immediate, intense and well sustained. As the test continued he became quite excited and showed a good deal of muscle tension. One of his outstanding characteristics, also noted in other situations, was persistence in the face of difficulty. In such situations as attaining a toy that was attached to a string (the toy itself being out of reach) he continued very active efforts, squealing impatiently and moving tensely, but with unabated interest, until he succeeded.

His vigorous and enthusiastic young mother treated her baby in ways designed to encourage "independence" and rapid learning. In large measure this was due to ignorance, in that she had little knowledge of what may be expected of a young infant, and found out by experiment. She tried to teach him to hold his own bottle when he was less than 3 months old, she had placed rattles in his hand long before he could reach for them, and by the age of 10 weeks he was regularly placed in a sitting position several times a day. She also provided small problems for him to solve—watching his efforts and intervening only when he proved helpless. For instance, prior to feeding, she would place the bottle just beyond reach, encouraging him to obtain it, and she removed the tray from the infant seat (the tray provides support and prevents the infant from propelling himself forward by stemming his feet against the floor). She then actively encouraged him to move while seated, and was delighted to believe that he had learned to use the gadget as a walker, though it seemed to us that the resulting movements were incidental. At any rate, Robert not only tolerated the rather intense stimulation reflected in the SPE, but responded to an accelerating environment by developing many skills rather earlier than is usual.

Adequacy of vegetative functioning: High.

Robert was a radiantly healthy baby. He had never experienced gastric distress, had never been ill except for a very minor cold, and ate and slept exceedingly well. In a manner quite unusual among our very active infants, he even went to sleep very easily; he whimpered and moved restlessly but showed no real distress and required no soothing in order to fall asleep.

Excitability: High.

Robert was judged to be "highly" excitable, though the notes indicate that "high-minus" or "fairly high" would have been more accurate. Robert showed bodily signs of excitation fairly often, but he was never seen to reach extremely high peaks of excitation. During play with the mother, in response to movement restraint, during the developmental test and at other times, Robert stiffened his limbs, arched his back, panted heavily, and not infrequently abandoned all other activity in favor of very forceful mouthing of whatever object came to hand. Yet these signs of bodily arousal were accompanied either by signs of pleasure or no specific affect. The fairly frequent excited episodes were thus not of an extreme nature and did not lead to distress; on the contrary, they were almost always part of a pleasurable episode.

Irritability: Low

As one would expect from what has been said about excitability, Robert was not the least bit irritable. On the contrary, he gave the impression of positive well-being and could respond with zest and pleasure to nearly every situation. Both mother and father enjoyed "roughhousing" with him, and Robert smiled and squealed in pleasure as he was tweaked, bounced, tossed, and even thrown into the air and caught again (by father only). He cried very rarely indeed (his mother said never, except when he hurt himself) and was described by observers in such terms as "robustly cheerful" and "unusually good natured."

Pleasure in functioning: High.

Pleasure in functioning was a conspicuous feature of Robert's behavior. During spontaneous activity he spent much of his time in performing fairly complex motor coordinations, in manipulating objects, and in responding to the sights and sounds of the people who constantly surrounded him. Gentle social stimulation (which was rare) and playful presentation of objects elicited mature behavior patterns as well as strong signs of pleasure. When social play became intense, as it often did with his parents, his responses lost in complexity but not in pleasure. The same was true of prolonged and vigorous object stimulation, which was observed only during the psychological test.

DISCUSSION

Robert was most certainly a thriving baby, and one who made excellent developmental progress under conditions that might easily have been disruptive to many another child. Certain aspects of his behavior have not yet been described, though they are of interest in terms of the particulars of his day-by-day experience. He was the only 24-week-old whose behavior toward the mother was indistinguishable from his responsiveness to the observers, the grandmother, or anyone else who approached him appropriately. He also failed to manifest even a transient response to first encounters with strange persons. However, he shared this latter characteristic with the majority of 24-week-old infants. Despite his interest in toys, he never responded to the loss of a toy as several of the others did. The descriptions—not of what he did, but of *how* he smiled, squealed, laughed, or manipulated objects—emphasized over and over again a relative lack of nuances and of fine discrimination. He looked pleased in much the same way whether he was spoken to, bounced about, or shown a toy. His face registered a smaller number of different expressions than one ordinarily sees, and he showed none of the tentativeness or the gradual development from a small smile to a broad grin and laughter that most 24-week-olds are capable of showing. Toys, once obtained, were usually banged with force (regardless of what object happened to be in his hand) or mouthed or sometimes transferred. In short, his behavior had an "on-and-off" quality and lacked modulation. It was vigorous, effective, and appropriate but, to quote one observer, "not especially interesting, and of the stereotyped kind one associates with advertisements for baby products." Thus, some qualitative aspects of his behavior impressed experienced observers as unusual in a child whose development had proceeded at an accelerated pace. A relative lack of differentiation in movement patterns, physiognomic expressiveness, and vocalization was seen in a number of babies whose perceptual sensitivity was not pronounced. However, as has already been described for some other babies, the mother's contribution to the patterns of interaction that develop may well be the crucial factor.

Robert's mother was, as we have said, young and inexperienced. Not only with the baby, but also in general conversation, in response to the research staff, and while observed at home when other relatives were also present, she reminded one of a child who plays at keeping house. On the surface at least, she was warm, outgoing, and full of goodwill. She enjoyed her home and baby, did a great many things for her own pleasure and that of others, and functioned in an entirely responsible manner. Yet one felt that she had as yet remained untouched by much that is important in the lives of most adults. Her enthusiastic and loving care of the baby was not guided by much sensitivity to his momentary state, and her perfectly good capacity for observing his behavior appeared to be employed only in the service of selected practical aims. For instance, she had begun toilet training when the baby was 2 weeks old, and aimed to "catch him" not only for bowel movements but also for urination. Often she succeeded, because she watched for the signs of impending elimination and also carried him to the toilet very frequently after meals. It was typical of this mother-baby couple that Robert rather enjoyed the endless trips to the bathroom, because it so happened that as he was held above the receptacle, he could see himself and his mother in a mirror and found this entertaining. In a similar manner, he adapted to many of the mother's interventions. Whether she was trying to hold him in a standing position, or tweaking his nose, or placing the bottle nearby to see if he could get it, the two of them maintained a constant stream of mutual smiles, reciprocal vocalizations, and generally pleasant contact.

Robert's day-by-day experience chiefly provided changes from moderate to fairly high levels of arousal. He was not seen in an entirely relaxed state while awake, though he slept very quietly and in adequate amounts. He was one of the very few extremely active babies who did not become highly aroused, partly because bodily discomfort was very nearly absent and partly because he was not especially reactive in any sensory modality. In addition, he had hit on avid mouthing (of the biting and chomping variety, usually applied to toys) as a means of containing (though not reducing) strong excitation. When hungry or fatigued, or when he encountered difficulty in accomplishing a movement, he would bring something to the mouth, and though he continued to squirm or show muscle tension and squeal in annoyance, it seemed that intense oral activation served to prevent the diffuse motoric actions and the severe crying that other equally active babies show at such moments.

Rose, In XI (24 Weeks)

SPE DETERMINANTS

Boundary Strength

	ENTIRE		*MODALITY SECTORS*			
	Inner	*Outer*	*Vision*	*Touch*	*Sound*	*Passive Motion*
Stimulation	low (+)	high (−)	medium (−)	medium (−)	medium (+)	high
Frequency of Mother-Child Contacts		medium	low	medium (+)	low (+)	low (+)
Intensity	low	high	——————→			
Maternal Competence		medium	——————→			
Maternal Intrusiveness		medium	——————→			
Level of Home Stimulation		medium	——————→			

Activity Level 1.5

STABLE PATTERNS OF EXPERIENCE

Frequency of strong bodily arousal: Rare.

Rose was fairly inactive and, in addition, she was less responsive to external stimuli than most babies. Although her mother was very vigorous in dealing with the baby (high intensity), and although a preschool age sibling who was allowed free access to the infant made for many lively moments, she remained placid much of the time. Since neither hunger nor fatigue led to marked behavioral arousal, and since she experienced no other bodily discomforts, she was not seen or reported to become very excited for any cause. The one exception (which led to a rating of "rare" rather than "absent" for this variable) was as puzzling to the research staff as to the parents. No more than once a week, and usually less frequently, Rose cried long and hard for no apparent reason. We had been told about this and, by chance, were present once when it occurred. The details are described elsewhere. In the present context, all that is relevant is that without any evidence of bodily pain, Rose cried hard, flushed, showed tense squirming motions, and could not be soothed for about 25 minutes.

Internal bodily sensations: Fairly low.

Rose showed less behavioral response to fatigue and to hunger than the majority, and she was not subject to bodily discomforts of other sorts. Though of course she felt and responded to fluctuating body states, she had less occasion than many other babies to experience (or at least to register behaviorally) strong inner somatic sensations.

Balance between behavior activations due to inner and to outer stimulation: External predominant.

When left to her own devices Rose spent most of her time in activity focused upon sights and sounds about her. Very often she showed very slight activations, but her occasional spurts of cradle rocking, rolling, or kicking—relatively more extensive behavior activations—appeared unrelated to external events. Direct contacts with the parents or the sibling also led to an increase in activity on most occasions (though she could be soothed readily on the rare occasions when it was necessary). On the whole, changes in the direction of behavior *activation* were responsive to external stimulation somewhat more often than not. But since external stimulation also led to the reduction or inhibition of ongoing activity (while gazing at something or during soothing), and since some of her more prominent behavior schemas while unattended seemed unrelated to anything in the environment, this difference was relatively slight.

Importance of distance receptors: Medium.

Rose was not markedly reactive to either sight or sound, and during direct contacts with the mother, touch was so vigorous and prominent as to overshadow the other modalities. However, Rose's mother provided her baby with a multitude of toys, and Rose spent her waking time with the family, so that she could see the activity of the sibling and the mother. In addition, Rose (like many of the inactive babies) was a baby who often and to inspect them thoroughly as she moved them about. While she was normally alert to sound, this modality seemed to affect her behavior to a lesser extent. In particular, mutual vocalizing with the mother was a rare event, perhaps in part because this mother rarely, if ever, spoke to the baby in a soft, warm, or playful fashion.

Importance of near receptors: Prominent.

During Rose's encounters with her mother, touch was by far the most important modality. The mother was extraordinarily vigorous when she burped, rubbed, towelled, and otherwise manipulated the baby—so much so, that observers used the term "manhandling," and were amazed that no matter how hard the baby was kneaded and rubbed, she remained undisturbed. When mother played with Rose it was always in the tactile and kinesthetic mode. She kissed the baby, poked, tweaked, and tickled her unrestrainedly; and also rolled her about or lifted and lowered her rapidly in the "elevator" game. The importance of the near receptors in Rose's experience was enhanced by the fact that she engaged in a good deal of cradle rocking, both in play and while hungry or fatigued.

Most prominent modality: None.

Least prominent modality: Sound.

Frequency of states of optimal animation: Occasional.

During spontaneous activity Rose was not lethargic, but neither did she show the vigor or the interest in complex behaviors seen in many other babies. Occasionally she practiced complex motor coordinations, such as bringing the foot to the mouth, but this was more than counterbalanced by her tendency to cradle rock or roll about in a self-contained manner. Direct contacts with the mother seldom allowed the emergence of optimal animation, primarily because maternal interventions were so massive as to preclude complex, subtle and reciprocal interactions.

OUTCOME RATINGS

Developmental status: Medium.

In Rose's case the "medium" rating is not based on average performance in most areas, but reflects failure on a number of test items at her own age level and success on a fairly large number of items that are normative for the ages of 28 and 32 weeks. Some aspects of gross motor coordination were relatively immature though within normal limits. As was also noted in some other inactive babies, she sat relatively poorly and had difficulty in compensating the position of her head when she was pulled to the sitting position. Coordinated motion of arms and legs, as well as position changes while lying down, met average expectations. In the adaptive sphere, which includes chiefly the capacity to respond to small objects in a purposive and discriminating manner, her behavior was very uneven. She failed three of six items at her own age level of 24 weeks, but achieved seven of eight items at the 28-weeks level, and one (holding one object while also paying attention to another) at the 32-weeks level. Her pattern of test scores was puzzling to the examiner, since no particular group of functions seemed accelerated or retarded. In other words, attention span, discriminatory powers, and fine coordination were advanced in some test situations and of less than average caliber in others. Yet Rose showed positive pleasure in response to the examiner and to the toys, and was not fatigued. Most of the items that seemed to present undue difficulty used red 1-inch cubes or a red wooden ring. The mother volunteered that Rose disliked the color red—and it is true that when a metal cup was substituted for the standard red ring, she achieved two items that she had failed before (and failed again later when the ring was again used). Unlike other babies who were strongly influenced by color (or by brightness), Rose did not show active aversion or displeasure; she merely failed to use red objects as extensively or with as much coordination as she was capable of in other contexts. (The SPE implies that her reactivity to visual stimuli in general was not particularly sensitive.) In the area of vocalizations and patterns of social responsiveness, Rose's behavior met high average standards for her age and scatter was minimal. All in all, the test protocol concluded that the scores may not fully reflect the child's developmental level, except in the motor area in which she was definitely not advanced.

A more detailed description of the mutual adaptation between this mother and her baby will given in the discussion section. It may be relevant to Rose's test performance that her mother very seldom placed her in the sitting posture. The baby had her long naps in the buggy and spent her waking time lying in the playpen. In the playpen, toys were always provided; but according to observation and the report of both parents, no one played *with* the baby using toys or other objects. Nor was the mother at all playful or even socially attentive during routine procedures, which were performed with dispatch and in an objective "no-nonsense" sort of way.

Adequacy of vegetative functioning: Medium.

Rose slept well, ate small but adequate amounts, and was generally healthy. The medium rating was assigned for two reasons: first, when moved about after a feeding she tended to "spit up" (*i.e.,* not true vomiting but the regurgitation of small amounts without visible distress); and second, she occasionally had skin rashes that were not severe and cleared readily without medication. The fact that she accepted food, but showed no real eagerness (she did not cry when hungry and often the mother had to move the nipple within the baby's mouth in order to stimulate her to renewed sucking) also was considered a slight but definite departure from the optimum with respect to one vegetative function.

Excitability: Low.

Rose was not an excitable baby. As has been mentioned, the mother tended to be remarkably vigorous in performing some of her caretaking functions. Rose's tolerance was excellent. Caretaking routines, which were not in the least playful, brought neither pleasure nor distress. In response to the infrequent episodes of vigorous play, Rose almost always seemed hugely pleased, smiling and vocalizing, but not excited. It should perhaps be mentioned that while Rose was not seen in a state of strong bodily arousal, neither was she often seen in complete relaxation. While she slept very soundly indeed, she occasionally moved about or rocked in her buggy without awakening, in the absence of any external stimulus. During feeding she maintained rather tense body postures, and in the mother's arms she did not relax as most other babies do, so that we understood what her mother meant when she described the baby as "not at all cuddly."

Irritability: Low.

Irritability was assessed as low, though, had a more differentiated rating been attempted, "low-plus" might best describe the actual state of affairs. As a rule Rose remained placid or moderately animated throughout her day. However, on rare occasions (once a week or less) she had spells of severe crying that lasted from 10 to 30 minutes, during which she could not be comforted by any means her mother had been able to devise. She was neither hungry nor sleepy at these times, there was no indication that she was feeling gastric or other bodily pain, and the pediatrician, rightly or wrongly, advised that these spells had no somatic cause. We observed one such episode, which was said to be milder than usual. The baby certainly did not flex the body and thrash about as in an attack of colic or of earache, nor was her abdomen distended. She was not teething, and the observers were as mystified about the immediate cause as were the parents. However, it should be emphasized that this occurred on rare occasions and that in general Rose was noteworthy for a lack of irritability.

Pleasure in functioning: Medium.

During spontaneous activity Rose did "practice" certain motor skills, such as bringing her foot to her mouth, and played with a rattle or another toy in an absorbed manner. However, in comparison with other 24-week-olds, the range of such activities and the energy expended were on the modest side. A good proportion of Rose's time when awake and alert was devoted to such activities as cradle rocking and rolling about, with little attention to things around her. Many of the everyday situations that bring pleasure and animation to most babies failed to do so in Rose's life. In other words, being bathed, dressed, and played with often left her in an apparently neutral affective state and did not elicit behavior changes. To the variety of stimulation provided during the developmental test, she responded with unexpectedly strong signs of pleasure and very marked arousal. However, during playful interludes with the mother, the stimulation she received was so intense and so focused upon bodily sensations (tickling and the like) that she laughed and squealed in pleasure and moved about more than usual, but the more complex patterns of behavior did not typically emerge.

DISCUSSION

What has been described of Rose's functioning so far, and much more that has not yet been mentioned, suggests that her pattern of existence was for the most part comfortable, and certainly one that enabled her to develop normally, if slightly unevenly. But it also suggests that her existence lacked certain kinds of experience and pleasure that are common in the lives of most babies. Seldom did she have the experience of feeling discomfort or distress which disappeared while she was in direct contact with the mother. (She did not especially welcome the bottle or the spoon-feedings, though she accepted them; she fell asleep in a separate room when the mother judged the time had come and carried her to bed; she was very rarely soothed and never rocked or held prolongedly—partly, at least, because she did not require soothing.) Nor were recurring contacts during routine procedures made an occasion for social interaction, as Rose's mother made a strict division between "business"—during which she did not invite the baby's attention by smiles or speech or any other means—and "play" which intentionally took place on separate occasions. Lastly, the feeding situation, which is visibly relaxing and gratifying to most babies and provides intimate body contact with the mother for many, lacked these features for Rose. She was fed while strapped to the bassinet. The mother stood close by, watched the baby to gauge her food intake, and once in a while reactivated sucking by touching the baby or by moving the bottle. Rose did focus on the mother's face repeatedly, and occasionally mutual gazing was present, but there was none of the close reciprocal responsiveness so often seen in this situation.

In this instance, the lacks in Rose's pattern of concrete experience are considered to be very largely due to the nature of the mother's contribution to the interaction. Rose's mother provided excellent care for her baby in an objective and at times somewhat distant fashion, but we could detect few signs of warm and easy spontaneity in her behavior with the baby. In fact, she was one of the two mothers in the entire sample whose quality of speech and quality of movement when she was caring for the baby appeared indistinguishable from her usual manner. She was so conscious of this fact that, it seemed to us, her very awareness of some lack of maternal feeling further added to her difficulties and prevented her from finding ways of dealing with the baby that might have been better suited to the needs of both. She was an intellectually alert woman, wholly cognizant of recently popular knowledge about the psychological importance of the early mother-child relationship. She regarded both herself and Rose as "nervous," though in the baby's case it was difficult to know what she might have meant. Several times a day she picked up the baby and played with her as described, quite deliberately because she knew that babies need affectionate attention. Thus she regarded the baby's emotional needs as of the same order as the need for cleanliness and food, and by and large provided for them in addition to physical care, not integrated with it. Our conviction that Rose would have been able to participate in the more usual forms of interaction comes from her response to research staff. In the arms of each observer Rose did cuddle and relax—which the mother clearly noted but did not comment on. When the pediatric examination was performed in a playful manner, Rose responded with animation, and the same was true when observers employed the usual visual and auditory incitements to attentiveness and directed response to the environment.

In terms of the specific criteria we employed for the assessment of developmental progress and the quality of overall adaptation, the indications that Rose's pattern of concrete experience was not altogether favorable are few and uncertain. She had developed well, but as judged by test performance, somewhat less evenly and harmoniously than most babies. She did have minor physiological upsets in the absence of a recognized physical cause (the frequency with which she spat up part of a feeding unless kept very quiet), though weight gain was adequate and general health excellent. She was the only baby in the sample who cried severely for no cause that anyone could discern, but this occurred on rare occasions.

More impressive are the positive (from a developmental point of view) aspects of her functioning. In addition to her capacities shown on psychological testing, she demonstrated the capacity for learning. During the test she was given an unfamiliar object—a bell. At first she dealt with it as she did with most other objects, in terms of familiar schemas such as waving, transferring, and intent regard. Then she discovered incidentally (without demonstration) that when held by the handle and moved, it produced a sound. Thereafter, she only grasped it by the handle, swung it, and listened with obvious pleasure to the result. There can be little doubt that whatever her experience may have lacked, there was no significant impairment of either the capacity or the readiness to engage in age-appropriate behaviors, including those that mediate further learning.

Her social responsiveness was adequate but in no way remarkable. Like most of the 24-week-olds she responded more readily and intensively to the mother than to anyone else. There was no trace of a specific reaction to contact with strangers, nor was she especially discriminating or expressive in other ways. In this realm of behavior the developmental level of her behavior was very much in accord with average expectations, but compared with some of the other babies her responses were somewhat colorless and somehow blunt.

Richie, Ac XII (24 Weeks)

SPE DETERMINANTS

Boundary Strength

	ENTIRE		*MODALITY SECTORS*			
	Inner	*Outer*	*Vision*	*Touch*	*Sound*	*Passive Motion*
Stimulation	strong (−)	medium	weak (+)	strong	medium (+)	medium (+)
Frequency of Mother-Child Contacts		high	high	low (+)	medium (+)	medium
Intensity	low (+)	low	→			
Maternal Competence		high	→			
Maternal Intrusiveness		low	→			
Level of Home Stimulation		medium	→			

Activity Level: 2.5

STABLE PATTERNS OF EXPERIENCE

Frequency of strong bodily arousal: Rare.

Richie was a distinctly active baby who demonstrated the capacity for fairly extreme behavioral arousal (arching of back, tremors, muscle tension) while under observation. However, such peak excitations were observed in situations that had no counterpart in his daily life; namely, when feeding was delayed in order to permit some research procedures, and toward the end of developmental testing. Observation in the home and the mother's report convinced us that normally Richie was fed as soon as hunger signs were clear, and that no one played with him more than momentarily in the provocative manner that is necessary for developmental testing.

Bodily need states did not yield high levels of excitation for this infant. He was singularly free from bodily discomfort otherwise, and he was handled in a gentle and accommodating manner by his mother. Moderate and fairly strong behavioral arousal occurred frequently in his life (almost always associated with strong pleasure), but peak level arousals were rare indeed.

Internal bodily sensations: Low.

Richie's behavior was of course affected by hunger and fatigue and by fluctuating body state in general, but rather less than is the case with many other babies. During spontaneous activity almost all of his behavior was in response to an aspect of the environment, and even during fatigue he was hardly seen in the self-absorbed state so characteristic of that condition.

Balance between behavior activations due to inner and to outer stimulation: External very dominant.

Richie was the kind of infant who responds actively to almost every stimulation. Very rarely did he reduce activity while looking at a person or a thing, as many others did. Inner somatic events rarely roused him, his mother provided a pacifier when he became restless with fatigue, and he neither needed nor received soothing at other times. Thus, nearly all behavior activations (ranging from large movement to squealing or reaching only) occurred in direct response to external stimulation.

Importance of distance receptors: High.

Richie was highly reactive to visual events, and the mother cultivated this modality beyond all others. He spent large amounts of his waking time on the floor or in his infant chair surrounded by a large array of toys. Many of the mother's interactions with the baby occurred at some distance, and in the visual mode. For instance, she waved her highly polished fingernails at which he squealed and laughed, she bobbed her head in his direction, made "funny faces" at him, or mouthed words soundlessly as he gazed at her animated face. When manipulating the baby and playing with him, she also spoke to him softly and warmly a great deal, or else whistled, clucked, or sang for his entertainment. The radio was played a good deal, and the parents included Richie in their frequent sessions of listening to recorded music, and were not altogether joking when they said that it was not too early to direct his interest to good music. All in all, the distance receptors played a large role in shaping Richie's behavior.

Importance of near receptors: Fairly high.

Richie's mother did not hesitate to touch her baby, but they were light deft contacts of brief duration, usually in the context of routine care. In play she occasionally touched him momentarily, as when she brought her extended finger slowly toward his face (primarily a visual game) and, for a climax, allowed the fingertip to touch the baby's nose (at which point both erupted into laughter). He was rocked or bounced by both parents on occasion, not for soothing but during animated play.

In Richie's case, the near receptors, especially kinesthetic experience, were lent a degree of prominence more by self-initiated actions than by what others did. As part of generalized pleasure, and also when displeased, Richie often bounced and rocked with considerable vigor. When his mother's face came close enough, it was often the baby who reached for and touched the mother, who responded warmly but not by touching him in return.

Most prominent modality: Vision.

Least prominent modality: Touch.

Frequency of states of optimal animation: High.

Richie spent his waking time in some sort of contact with the mother and other members of the family, although, as has been said, prolonged close physical contact was not particularly frequent. During spontaneous activity he was often in a state of animation that facilitated the emergence of complex behavior integrations; along with simpler modes of play, he entertained himself by placing a diaper over his face and removing it with gay squeaks, or dropping objects just to retrieve them. The mother's style of dealing with the baby was important in this connection, but in a different way than has been described for several other babies. During direct interactions between the two, subtle and complex reciprocal adaptations did occur occasionally, but it was not primarily at such times that states of optimal animation were observed. Instead, the mother's vigilance when Richie was playing by himself tended to forestall discomfort and to support pleasurable mastery activity. When he strained to reach a distant toy and uttered irritable sounds, she typically came and placed the toy within reach—but did not put it in his hands. In other words, she tended to alter his immediate environment (or his position) so as to help him complete action impulses successfully on his own. Similarly, noting that he had become slightly restless in the propped-to-sitting posture, she either adjusted his position or put him on the floor or provided a different set of toys. The high frequency of states of optimal animation during spontaneous activity was to some extent the result of Richie's active disposition, but the mother's way of facilitating and supporting his behavior aims by *indirect* intervention was a crucial factor.

OUTCOME RATINGS

Developmental status: Medium

Richie's test protocols indicated developmental progress in accord with high average standards for his age, though in some respects his behavior was somewhat accelerated. In his case scoring of test items was especially conservative, and a judgment of "high" might have been equally appropriate. In his manipulation of small objects he happened to be in a transitional stage between the modes of grasping and transferring normative at 24 weeks and the more complex patterns not generally achieved until the ages of 28 or 32 weeks. For instance, he no longer used a radial palmar grasp in lifting a small cube, but attempted to pick it up with two or three fingers; since he had not yet mastered this skill, the cube fell from his hand. Thus some of his "failures" with 24-week items are to be discounted, in that they actually reflected fairly high levels of maturity. (However, in the interest of greater objectivity in the assessment of each child, these qualitative features were disregarded both in scoring the tests and in rating developmental status.)

Richie was alert throughout the test, showed eagerness and pleasure in response to all toys and to the examiner, and tended to be vigorous and quick rather than highly discriminatory in his behavior. The examiner described him as tough and sturdy rather than sensitive or passively receptive. The scores on the Gesell Schedules and observation at other times showed that this baby was more advanced in his interpersonal behavior (vocalizations and physiognomic responses) than in the area of motor coordination, both gross and fine.

Though Richie was the first baby in the family, his mother had previous experience in the care of infants and was far more deft and certain in her handling of the baby than most young primaparas are. She was not one of the mothers who by their behavior try to hasten the development of their infants, but she was quick to respond to any signs that he was ready for new experiences. A good supply of suitable toys was always nearby, but the mother never initiated their use. Finding that he was more content in an upright posture, she placed him in a Teeter-Babe for some time each day, comfortably padded and securely tied into the seat. He had never been held to standing, and when this was done in the course of testing he flexed his legs, and his facial expression was astonished but not displeased. He spent most of his waking hours where he could see and hear the mother even though he was not in physical contact with her. We think it relevant to his developmental progress that his mother rarely lost contact with him.

As has already been described, mother made frequent casual contact with the baby from some distance, and Richie typically responded by smiling, squealing, turning toward her, and the like. The baby was thus consistently and frequently invited to attend to visual and other aspects of the environment, yet these episodes typically occurred while he was not especially aroused and while he was not in direct bodily contact with the mother.

Adequacy of vegetative functioning: High.

It is difficult to imagine a baby who could excel Richie in both general health and positive signs of bodily well-being. He slept through the night and had done so since the age of 3 weeks. His appetite was excellent and he had never had any gastric distress or any illness. His movements were vigorous but seldom tense, he was capable of muscular relaxation, and in all ways his behavior and appearance radiated health.

Excitability: High.

Such excited behavior as Richie showed occurred in conjunction with signs of high pleasure. In the mother's arms he often initiated forceful bouncing, squealing, and laughing in an excited manner. During the playful conduct of the pediatric examination he arched his back and squirmed, but also laughed and cooed. During play with toys, as the test progressed, he became somewhat tense and banged whatever object came to hand very forcefully, not at all troubled by the sharp sounds he created as metal objects hit the metal table. His postures, movements, breathing, and facial expression combined to reflect considerable bodily excitation with a mixture of absorption and pleasure.

In the course of day-by-day experience Richie ranged from moments of nearly complete relaxation through various degrees of animation to fairly but not extremely high excitation.

Irritability: Low.

Though Richie occasionally showed mild displeasure or what his mother called a "temper," these episodes were so brief and mild that his behavior could not be described as irritable even then. He made protesting sounds when movement was restrained during routine procedures, but neither cried nor whimpered. He fussed momentarily when a toy was removed from his hand, but almost at once turned his attention elsewhere and was content again. And on the rare occasion when a feeding was delayed, or briefly while fatigued, he combined active bouncing with loud squeals that had pleasurable as well as discontent components, but he was neither seen nor reported to cry or otherwise show overt distress at such times.

Pleasure in functioning: High.

Richie spent most of his waking time in the active pursuit of motor skills or in exploiting nearby toys or persons for whatever action potential they offered. Pleasure in functioning was not only inferred from his tendency to practice various behavior integrations and to persevere in the face of obstacles but was also shown by the gay squeals, chuckling, and laughter that accompanied most of these behaviors. Mention was made of the fact that when playing peek-a-boo with himself, he typically squealed and laughed as he removed the diaper from his face, though his gaze did not encounter the face of another person. The same was true as he bounced joyously in his Teeter-Babe, as he obtained a toy, and on similar occasions.

DISCUSSION

This healthy, active, well-developed baby was an important member of a family who, to all appearances, were also singularly well adapted and well functioning as a social unit. More than many of the families in this sample, the parents were people with interests beyond immediate family life, though deeply immersed in the task of building a home and a family. Both parents combined a quality of reserve and, as it were, self-discipline with ready responsiveness and considerable spontaneity. The mother thoroughly enjoyed talking freely about the baby, and about all aspects of family life that she thought relevant. But she volunteered no information about herself and seemed to have no need to unburden herself in a situation that rather invited this. Possibly for this reason both she and her young husband (both were in their mid-20's) struck all observers as more mature and reflective persons than most of the project families.

Some aspects of Richie's pattern of adaptation and of characteristic patterns of interaction with the mother have not yet been mentioned. For instance, the baby was highly reactive to all visual stimuli, and his mother lent selective emphasis to this modality. Since in many other ways this mother clearly adapted her behavior to Richie's reaction tendencies (for instance, she was very adept at reducing movement restraint to a minimum), it seems possible that her tendency to rouse the baby by visual means also was a response to his differential reactivity in various sense modalities. At any rate, the facts that Richie was so discriminately responsive to social interactions in the visual mode and that his physiognomic expressiveness was of an exceptionally high order for so young a baby make good sense in light of the fact that he spent so much time in pleasurable interactions of this kind.

It may be relevant that the interplay between Richie and his mother struck us as being more finely regulated by a flow of reciprocal behavior clues than is common. Further, we were interested in the fact that on many occasions contact between this mother and baby seemed very intense though the behavior of both participants was somehow modulated. One might say that mother and baby seldom had occasion to make forceful demands on one another. Richie was fed, put to sleep, or playfully approached at the first sign that he might need attention, and so he rarely felt acute excitation or distress that disappeared as mother came close. On the other hand, he frequently had occasion to perceive her proximity as part of an action (or an impulse) that he could not complete unaided. If she saw him slide from the propped sitting posture and struggle to sit up again, she came and seated him securely. If he started bouncing on her lap she grasped his trunk and actively supported and extended the movement pattern.

On his part, Richie conveyed his momentary states and desires clearly. When he felt uncomfortable he uttered protesting squeals and was responded to. He looked about the room until he had located the mother's face and then began to smile and vocalize. When an observer who was holding him turned him around to face the mother who stood close by, arms extended to receive him, he moved toward the mother so forcefully that the observer felt she had helped him "jump," rather than having placed him in the mother's arms.

Against this general background it is impressive to note that in Richie one could observe with special clarity the operation of an ego function often not visible until at a later age—he had learned to provide for himself varieties of experience that previously had been provided for him by the parents. For instance, when he was younger the mother had frequently played peek-a-boo with him (always using a diaper), and when we knew him she reported, and we were able to confirm, that "now he does it mostly by himself." Similarly, he spent a good deal of time in rhythmic bouncing motions, both while seated in the Teeter-Babe and when in the supine position. The motions involved were very similar to rocking, and while he rock-bounced often when entirely content, it was also a behavior conspicuously associated with hunger, fatigue, and strong social stimulation (the latter was fairly often provided by the father). During the first three months of life he had been rocked frequently, as a soothing device and at other times. The parents then decided to rock him only rarely, so as to prevent him from becoming spoiled and demanding of this variety of attention. We were told credibly that his tendency to bounce and rock himself had become prominent after the parents limited their rocking (which, however, they still did on occasion). Thus it would seem that Richie could and did provide for himself certain kinds of experience that had at first been a prominent and pleasurable part of his direct contacts with the mother.

Debbie, In XII (24 Weeks)

SPE DETERMINANTS

	Boundary Strength					
	ENTIRE		*MODALITY SECTORS*			
	Inner	*Outer*	*Vision*	*Touch*	*Sound*	*Passive Motion*
Stimulation	medium	variable	strong	medium	weak	medium
Frequency of Mother-Child Contacts		high (−)	high	medium (+)	high	medium
Intensity	low	low (+)	→	→	→	→
Maternal Competence		high	→	→	→	→
Maternal Intrusiveness		low	→	→	→	→
Level of Home Stimulation		medium	→	→	→	→

Activity Level: 1.1

STABLE PATTERNS OF EXPERIENCE

Frequency of strong bodily arousal: Absent.

Debbie was an exceedingly inactive baby who seldom showed bodily signs of arousal and never reached high levels of excitation at all. Her behavior during hunger was nearly indistinguishable from that at other times, though she ate eagerly once food was offered. Fatigue led to a degree of restlessness and discomfort, but almost at once she took to her thumb and thereafter remained drowsy and quiescent until she fell asleep. The mother dealt with her baby very gently, and only the school-age sibling occasionally exposed the baby to loud noise and vigorous touch.

Internal bodily sensations: Medium.

As has been said, fatigue (which usually lasted for 20 to 30 minutes until she dropped off to sleep) markedly affected Debbie's behavior in that she became inattentive and unresponsive to the environment, whereas while hungry she remained amiable and alert to things about. Debbie was free from minor bodily discomforts, and though episodes of mouthing or gentle motion occurred in the absence of external stimulation, her behavior on the whole suggested that internal bodily sensations were a constant background rather than a massive influence.

Balance between behavior activations due to inner and to outer stimulation: Equal.

When awake, content, and unattended, Debbie was typically highly alert to her surroundings, but manifested it chiefly by gazing, by fluctuating physiognomic expression, and by gentle and delicate exploratory movements of the hands. Intermittently she gave the appearance of "resting" as she sucked her thumb or engaged in other oral play and lost interest in her surroundings. The mother was in contact with her baby very often, and her gentleness matched that of the baby. As mother compelled the baby's visual attention and spoke to her and as she introduced toys or performed routine caretaking tasks, not all of Debbie's responses could be described as *activations* of behavior. She gazed and smiled a good deal; less often she kicked or waved her arms, vocalized or reached for a toy. In other words, Debbie's behavior activations were minimal in range and intensity, and were aroused quite as often by something in the environment as by changes in somatic state.

Importance of distance receptors: High.

Debbie was highly reactive to auditory stimuli, and during contacts with the mother, they were provided constantly, though vision was almost always activated at the same time. Even though Debbie was not alert to slight visual impressions or particularly affected by strong lights or colors (strong boundary), vision played a prominent part in much of her behavior. Her most intense and prolonged response both to people and to things was gazing, which was for her an absorbing activity in its own right. Mother capitalized on this fact (and was herself a visually oriented person) and their social interactions used primarily the visual mode. She also amply provided toys and saw to it that Debbie spent a fair amount of time in a position that provided interesting things to look at (by placing the Teeter-Babe facing toward family activity or outdoor spectacles).

Importance of near receptors: Fairly low.

Debbie's mother touched her baby freely in her customary delicate and deft fashion. But we could see no sign that Debbie's behavior during social interactions differed markedly depending on whether or not touch was involved. Nor did the mother cultivate the tactile varieties of play, though of course she did pat and lightly kiss the baby. Similarly, swaying and gentle bouncing games occasionally came the baby's way, especially from the father, but these were not the occasions when Debbie showed her greatest animation, nor were they frequent or intense.

Most prominent modality: Vision.

Least prominent modality: Probably kinesthetic.

Frequency of states of optimal animation: Moderate.

In Debbie's case this rating was difficult to make. If optimal states were judged by altertness only, one would say that they were characteristic both during spontaneous activity and at other times. However, she so rarely mobilized complex behavior integrations of which she proved capable, and the element of active responsiveness and body mastery was so inconspicuous, that such a judgment would prove misleading.

OUTCOME RATINGS

Developmental status: Medium.

Developmental status was of good average caliber. Debbie's test protocol, as well as her behavior during the testing situation, showed a distinct and somewhat unusual pattern. She was far less roused and excited by provocative presentation of a series of toys than most babies are, yet she gazed at each object prolongedly, and there was typically a marked delay between intent regard and such motoric response as she finally made. However, in reaching for objects and in manipulating them, the skill and delicacy of her finger and hand motions were impressive. Unlike the majority of 24-week-olds (actually she had reached the age of 25 weeks when the tests were administered during the home visit) she always reached with one hand only. She attempted to grasp a tiny pellet, and at no time did she show the groping or swiping motions commonly seen at this age, nor did she ever "overshoot the mark" in reaching for a toy. On the other hand, test responses that require a tendency to manipulate objects actively or to achieve some sort of effect were elicited not at all or with considerable difficulty. She held the rattle by the handle easily, but was not interested in shaking it to produce a sound. With intense and prolonged prodding she transferred objects from one hand to the other, but was never seen to do so spontaneously, any more than she was inclined to wave or bang objects as most other babies do at this age. She was so content and interested while regarding one object in her hand that it was difficult and at times impossible to direct her attention to a second one. Her entire approach was described as passive to an unusual degree; simple goal striving (reaching for something at a distance, changing position, etc.) was remarkable for its near-absence and for its lack of vigor when it did occur.

It was also interesting that gross motor coordination in the prone position was somewhat advanced (she was able to pivot at will), but was distinctly immature in the supine (she was unable to roll from the supine to the prone). Debbie had shown a definite preference for the prone position since an early age, and her waking time was spent almost entirely lying on her stomach or sitting with support in the Teeter-Babe.

Debbie's social responsiveness and her vocalizations were quite mature for her age (conformed to average standards for 28-week-olds), but lacked vigor to some extent. She produced well-differentiated polysyllabic vowel sounds, but though she was able to squeal she did so rarely, and never in a manner conveying strong pleasure or marked annoyance or impatience as other babies are apt to do. Yet, despite the lack of out-going social responsiveness, Debbie's behavior in this realm was unusually discriminatory. As will be described more fully later on, she not only discriminated among persons, but her response varied systematically with how close the partner came to her, how playful and animated the social response was and even (we thought) with the kind of affect (intimate warmth to casual cheerfulness) the adult brought to the situation.

A detailed discussion of patterns of interaction between Debbie and her mother is reserved for a later section. Here it is sufficient to mention that this mother was rarely seen to teach or challenge her baby. Both solid feedings and being placed in a sitting posture commenced late, as compared with other babies in the sample. In fact, at 24 weeks Debbie still spent a good deal of her waking time in the crib and lying down. However, a large array of toys was always provided, and the mother often brought these to the baby's attention, though seldom in the form of active play. Yet the mother had a way of very gently inviting her baby to active responsiveness. For instance, she brought the rim of the cup close to the baby's lips and waited patiently until Debbie moved her head to initiate the act of drinking by herself. Where another mother might hold a bottle at a distance to induce reaching, Debbie's mother placed the nipple on the baby's lips to induce the baby to seize the nipple with her mouth. Or she gently prodded the baby to close her fingers upon a toy, to turn her head in order to locate mother's face, etc., etc. The behavior activations that the mother provoked (instead of imposing them as many mothers do) all concerned minute behavior integrations and actions that were already well within the baby's repertoire.

Adequacy of vegetative functioning: High.

Debbie slept well, and rather more than a good many babies of her age. She accepted food readily, and had experienced gastric distress but once in her life and then for a period of only two days. Muscle tension, labored breathing and the like were never seen at all, and altogether Debbie was a healthy and comfortable if somewhat placid baby.

Excitability: Low.

Debbie was noteworthy for a lack of excitability. Even the relatively most rousing situations she experienced—the 5-year-old sibling's attempts to play with her and occasional bouts of vigorous body play of the bouncing, swinging and rolling variety—elicited delighted squealing, and somewhat more extensive body movement than she usually showed, but none of the signs of excitation in terms of which this variable was rated.

Irritability: Low.

Debbie was not the least bit irritable. Very occasionally her vocalizations had a slightly discontented querulous quality, but this was not observed or reported to turn into whimpering or crying. Mother said that Debbie cried very seldom indeed, though on those rare occasions she cried long and hard (her mother thought she cried only when she had hurt herself or when the other child inadvertently caused her pain). We did not happen to witness such an episode, but since the mother was an excellent observer we assume that the description she provided was accurate.

Pleasure in functioning: Medium.

During spontaneous activity Debbie spent only a small portion of her time in fairly complex or recently acquired types of behavior. It was also true that to many varieties of external stimulation her responses were restricted, in the sense that they involved visual, tactile and auditory contact raher than coordinated motorically implemented action. "Medium" was nonetheless considered the appropriate rating because of her high level of alertness, and because within a narrow range of behaviors she showed prolonged attention and complex patterns of exploration focused upon aspects of the environment. Although she rarely waved, banged or transferred objects, even during developmental testing, she was quite often seen to hold an object while regarding it, systematically rotating it to inspect all sides and simultaneously exploring each visible aspect of the toy by gentle rubbing motions with her fingertips. Similarly, she seldom energetically reached for objects, nor did she throw them away with force. But fairly often she gently dropped a small toy, only to retrieve it deftly, never losing sight of it from the beginning to the end of such an episode.

DISCUSSION

Whether or not Debbie could have been more vigorous and energetic under other circumstances we shall never know. But it is certain that she developed very well, that she experienced much pleasure and very little discomfort, and that she was an active participant in a continuously maintained and mutually gratifying relationship with the mother and possibly with others as well. Debbie's pattern of adaptation is of interest because it represents an extreme in several respects: low activity as judged by body movements; the relative absence of active outwardly directed behavior in any sense; and a highly modulated, low-intensity quality that was as true of her physiognomic expressions as it was of her vocalizations and motions. The only aspect of her behavior that could be called intense was gazing.

Debbie's mother was a singularly gentle and composed person. Her own clothes, the furnishings of her home, the baby's toys, and all else over which the mother had control were notable for a soft and muted quality. In all our contacts with the family we did not see a single strong color or a glossy surface. But the effect of blended pastels was cheerful and harmonious, not in the least drab. Similarly, the mother spoke in a soft voice, moved delicately and fairly slowly, and her effect upon the observers was to make them feel a little crass by comparison. In her quiet way the mother was communicatory about the baby, responsive to all aspects of her contact with us, and generally well informed. Insofar as we could learn this was an unusually stable family who knew exactly what they wanted from life, made long-range plans accordingly, and had every expectation of achieving their aims. Observers could not help but feel that such a level of calm and contentment was an improbable state of affairs, but nothing was noted or sensed that suggested the undercurrents we suspected must exist nonetheless.

In the interactions between Debbie and her mother it was usually the mother who initiated and prolonged them, and quite often it was Debbie who terminated them. Perhaps because Debbie's responses were so inconspicuous, mother had become adept at noting and responding to minimal behavior changes in the baby. The manner in which she offered nipple, cup, or toy for Debbie to take, rather than giving them to her, has already been described. Mother showed a similar combination of protectiveness and subtle challenge in other ways as well. She never lost an opportunity for social interaction during caretaking procedures, she never approached the baby without first placing herself in view and speaking to her, and she was never hurried or abrupt. Moreover, on the very frequent occasions when she spoke to the baby playfully, the mother seldom contented herself with the baby's first and slight response. After Debbie smiled or vocalized softly in response to mother's approach, the latter tended to persevere by continuing to speak to the baby, gently touching her, and the like, continuing until Debbie smiled more broadly, chuckled, or uttered syllabic sounds. On most of the observed occasions, Debbie amiably turned away after such interaction had lasted for a while, whereupon the mother made no further effort to prolong the interlude.

A last example typifies the manner in which the mother tended to take the initiative in creating close involvement with the baby, and yet avoided intrusiveness. She had a way of participating in some of Debbie's bodily processes. For instance, when Debbie was in the process of moving her bowels the mother grasped the baby's feet and helped by pushing. At the same time she bent closely over the child and made encouraging grunting noises very similar to those the baby herself had produced. Our impression is that Debbie was not particularly sensitive, but on the whole a placid baby. Yet she was in the hands of an unusually subtle and sensitive mother who, while she failed to rouse the baby strongly, constantly elaborated and supported whatever responsive behavior Debbie was disposed to show.

Debbie's pattern of day-by-day experience showed a narrow range of excitation (from relaxed quiescence to infrequent moderate arousal); it involved frequent mild pleasure and very rare episodes of distinct distress; and it nonetheless provided for active interchanges with the human and inanimate environment much of the time. Under these conditions she developed and functioned well, yet differed from the majority in her lack of forcefulness, and in that she was highly discriminatory and alert toward the near environment, but relatively unresponsive to more distant portions of the perceptual field. In the terminology we have used before, her effective environment was constricted in comparison with those of her peers, just as the effects she produced in the environment were relatively slight.

It is instructive to compare Debbie's adaptation syndrome with that of Richie (Ac XII). Despite their different dispositions, the SPE constellations of these children are highly similar, as were their outcome ratings. Yet Richie's effective environment was extensive and he typically achieved considerable alterations (in his position, by creating sound effects and manipulating objects) in the circumstances that surrounded him. When, in other contexts, we spoke of individual differences in the style of adaptation and development, we had in mind the kind of differences in the adaptation syndrome shown by these two infants. Assuming that each infant's pattern of experience was supportive of his developmental potential, part functions that were either prominent or peripheral differed widely for the two, as did the range of sensations and behaviors shown by each. In addition to the factors already mentioned, Richie often "demanded" the mother; Debbie often experienced the mother's spontaneous appearance. One wonders whether differences such as these have consequences beyond a different sequence in the acquisition of new behaviors. Since in later childhood and maturity people differ in their inclination to manipulate the environment actively, and also differ in the amount of physical activity, the intensity of overtly expressed affect, and the subtlety of discrimination, it seems possible that such differences in character and personal style have their roots in some of the early and specific patterns of adaptive behavior that we have described.

Harry, Ac XIII (28 Weeks)

SPE DETERMINANTS

	Boundary Strength					
	ENTIRE		MODALITY SECTORS			
	Inner	*Outer*	*Vision*	*Touch*	*Sound*	*Passive Motion*
Stimulation	medium (+)	medium	strong	medium	medium	medium
Frequency of Mother-Child Contacts		high	medium (+)	high	medium (−)	low
Intensity	low	medium	→	→	→	→
Maternal Competence		high	→	→	→	→
Maternal Intrusiveness		low	→	→	→	→
Level of Home Stimulation		medium	→	→	→	→

Activity Level: 2.8

STABLE PATTERNS OF EXPERIENCE

Frequency of strong bodily arousal: High.

Harry's day-by-day experience was punctuated by moments of very intense excitation that occurred not only with distress but also with high pleasure. During nursing at the breast, he was so eager and so active as to repeatedly lose the nipple. At such times he extended and arched the entire body, squealed very loudly, squirmed, and stiffened. But these episodes were very brief, and the next moment he sucked comfortably and his movements became smooth, relaxed, and intermittent. High arousal states occurred most frequently when free movement was restrained, in response to which the baby usually squealed, stiffened, arched his back, and showed other signs of muscle tension. Both hunger and fatigue were responded to very strongly and led to behavior much like that described above. When we knew Harry, he spent much time striving to stand upright (holding onto something); if he failed to achieve it, or if he slid, wobbled, or fell down and was unable to sustain the posture, he again showed every sign of high behavioral arousal. Other recurring events during which he briefly reached peak excitation levels included the following: straining for an object too far away to reach; having a toy removed from his hand; and at the climax of pleasurable games with his mother (especially immediately after nursing).

Internal bodily sensations: Medium.

Harry was a radiantly healthy baby whose behavior of course reflected fluctuating body states, but no discomfort except during hunger or fatigue. A rating of moderate prominence was assigned for two reasons. Hunger and fatigue both regularly led to massive arousal, and during spontaneous activity both oral and kinesthetic self-stimulation were shown frequently. Though most of the time he was responding to aspects of the environment (oral activity consisted chiefly of chomping at objects), he also engaged in vigorous rolling, and swinging on the abdomen. These episodes of body play alternated with other activity, and he remained alert and in a happy mood throughout.

Balance between behavior activations due to inner and to outer stimulation: External predominant.

During his waking hours, Harry was almost always responsive to portions of the environment. A large share of the behavior activations observed occurred as he responded to the mother, the very active preschool age sibling, or some other person. Quite as conspicuous was his tendency to approach large objects in order to pull himself erect and smaller ones in order to manipulate them in a variety of ways. In short, behavior activations apparently due to somatic state did occur, but far more characteristic was his impulse to respond to the sight and sound of things and of people by vigorous activation.

Importance of distance receptors: Fairly high.

Although he was no more reactive to sights and sounds than the majority of babies, Harry's behavior was governed to a large extent by visual and auditory events. During the frequent interactions with his mother, touch almost always followed visual invitation, so to speak; that is, the mother brought her face or body close, and in response to this sight the baby reached for her. Or else, mother lightly touched him in the course of play, in which mutual regard remained a primary element. As has been described, his spontaneous activity consisted chiefly of adaptive action to both the near and the far environment, as registered by means of the distance receptors.

Importance of near receptors: Fairly high.

During contacts with the mother, especially play and soothing, the tactile component was very prominent indeed. The mother accommodated to Harry's tendency to explore her face and other portions of her body, to bury his face in her neck, and the like. She also lightly patted him or simply placed her hand on his body as a means of comforting and soothing him. He was not rocked at all, but he at times initiated bouncing and other movement games, which his mother then sustained by moving his body in the pattern he had begun. In addition, his constant efforts at locomotion or at posture change, as well as the swinging and rolling already described, provided kinesthetic sensations of considerable magnitude.

Most prominent modality: None.

Least prominent modality: Probably kinesthetic.

Frequency of states of optimal animation: High.

As has been implied throughout, Harry's behavior during spontaneous activity was generally animated and highly coordinated. Except when he encountered obstacles in carrying out a complex motor coordination, he was alert and responsive, yet not overly aroused. In addition, a great many of his encounters with the mother were of such a nature as to induce and maintain precisely the level of excitation that enhances outwardly directed responsiveness but remains well modulated. (As will be described more fully later, the typical sequence was an episode during which rather gentle reciprocal responsiveness gradually intensified and finally culminated in pleasurable excitement so great that it exceeded the condition we have called optimal.)

OUTCOME RATINGS

Developmental status: High.

Harry's test performance was accelerated to a significant degree. In all respects and on both tests, he accomplished every item that is normative at 32 weeks (his chronological age was 28 weeks). In addition, his ability to obtain and manipulate objects as well as his postural control, conformed (in part) to what is more usually seen at the age of 8 months. He could pull himself to a standing position by holding on to the railing of the crib and was able to creep (both 40-weeks items on the Gesell). He was able to bang one object against another in mid-air and grasp a tiny pellet using a two-finger scissor grasp (both 36-weeks items). His vocalizations and some of his social responses were also advanced, but not to the same degree (they conformed to normative standards for 32-week-olds).

Harry responded to the playful offer of toys with immediate and strong interest. In fact, so great was his excitement as the test continued that he lunged toward the object with his entire body and nearly always reached with both arms, though perfectly capable of using one hand only. He also resisted the removal of toys from his hand and required a little time before —with equal intensity—he approached the substitute that had been offered.

As will be described more fully later, this mother was not seen to teach the baby skills nor did she leave him to his own resources when he encountered obstacles. Rather, this very energetic youngster received constant support and protection in the course of his nearly continuous efforts to move about, to reach for things, and to actively manipulate everything in sight. This aspect of the mother's style is mentioned here because it may have contributed to Harry's exceptionally rapid development. Mother tended to direct his attention toward the sights and sounds about him and, more important, when he attempted a new coordination of which he was not yet capable, she neither left him to his own devices nor did she take over. Instead she cushioned his fall (rather than changing him to a less precarious position) or she assisted by partially supporting him. Thus his efforts to achieve difficult actions met with success more often than they would have otherwise.

Adequacy of vegetative functioning: High.

Harry slept well, ate eagerly and efficiently, had no gastric troubles whatsoever, and in general radiated a sense of bodily well-being. During his first few weeks he did show a colic syndrome which, according to mother's report, must have been of moderate severity. However, this had disappeared entirely by the age of 4 to 5 weeks. With very strenuous muscular exertion, such as arching his back at moments of high excitement or while straining to achieve a difficult postural change, he flushed a deep red and panted. However, this was not considered to indicate special lability, since both skin color and respiration remained relatively even at all other times.

Excitability: High.

Arching of the back, loud squealing, and energetic thrashing movements of the entire body were highly characteristic of this baby. Almost invariably these states occurred when movement was restrained, or when his eagerness for food (in mother's arms immediately before being offered the breast) or sleepiness led to large movements that actually interfered with completing an intended action (*i.e.,* reaching the nipple when hungry, maintaining an upright posture while fatigued). Muscular signs of excitation became marked at moments of distress, but also at moments when he squealed gleefully or when there were no overt signs of affect.

Irritability: Medium.

Harry showed annoyance and distress during situations such as when he could not maintain a standing posture, when he was placed in the horizontal position during diapering, and when a toy was removed from his hand. It was equally characteristic of Harry that he remained unruffled in many situations that elicit distress from other babies. Very frequently he fell or bumped his head, but proceeded undisturbed. He spent prolonged periods in contented play while unattended, and he responded pleasurably to almost every situation that came his way, provided only that it did not involve the restraint of movement or loss of an upright posture. In fact, Harry was one of the babies who quite often showed irritability and pleasure side by side. For instance, as mother dressed or diapered him, she made every effort to allow scope for his movements and, knowing his dislike for restraint, maintained a stream of cheerful and comforting conversation and playful activity. Harry might then arch his back, cry or squeal angrily, but also smile and babble in a pleasurable and responsive manner, only to be completely happy the moment he was free to move.

Pleasure in functioning: Medium.

In this instance, rigid adherence to pre-defined criteria led to a lower rating than might have resulted from a qualitative and unrestrained assessment of the child's behavior. Harry showed maximal pleasure in functioning in connection with the persistent and joyous practice of motor skills, and intense pleasure in the use of fairly complex patterns of social interaction. But he did not spend as much time and energy in the exploration and manipulation of objects (toys) as do some other babies. As has already been described, he thoroughly enjoyed the use of objects during the psychological test, and he often reached for objects at other times as well. However, during spontaneous activity, interest in object manipulation was subordinated to motor play and tended to be relatively simple.

DISCUSSION

Harry was an exceedingly active infant, at a developmental level when forceful motoric impulses necessarily lead to friction with the environment, who developed exceedingly well, and whose day-by-day experience yielded frequent high peaks of pleasure, frequent episodes of sharp but brief distress, and more intense, prolonged and varied interactions with another person than is common among 6-month-olds. We were interested in noting the specific ways in which the mother responded to her impatient and energetic baby primarily because, in other mother-baby couples, we had seen very similar reaction tendencies on the baby's part produce a far less harmonious pattern of adaptation (see, for instance, Billy, Ac XV).

The mother combined considerable vigilance in relation to the baby with what might be described as confidence in his resiliency and in his essential "good nature" (as she thought of it). One or two descriptions of characteristic episodes may exemplify what we have in mind: When Harry was fatigued and, in addition, had been handled a great deal (pediatric examination immediately after the developmental test), he began to cradle rock with increasing vigor and, in a manner that seemed deliberate, he bumped his head against the crib side very forcefully. The mother did not interfere, but placed her hand against the inner railing of the crib to soften the impact, while watching to see if he would calm down of his own accord. Similarly, when he arched his back and stiffened in her arms and seemed in danger of falling off her lap, she did not prevent the motion, but rather supported it by holding his trunk firmly and securely at sufficient distance to allow the baby to reach a fully extended position. Somewhat surprisingly to the observers (who had never seen this behavior dealt with in just this manner), Harry on many occasions then stopped crying or squealing as his body relaxed while still extended. Only then did mother gather him closely to her body or place him in the crib.

She was similarly given to the support and, as it were, elaboration of action patterns that the baby set in motion during play and during soothing or comforting. When she held him on her lap he typically shifted his position—from standing first facing her and then facing the room, to sitting either close to her body or far from it, and from reclining sideways in her arms to lying along her lap, his head on her knees and his feet touching her abdomen. We saw literally hundreds of such shifts, all initiated by the baby, and in each case the mother's grasp upon his body and her posture shifted responsively to continue and facilitate what the baby had begun. A third dominant characteristic of the mother's style has already been mentioned; namely, her proclivity to engage in vivid and quite stimulating play with him, though always in situations that began with a sort of invitation from the mother, who approached the baby closely and smiled at him. If and (while observed) only if the baby then responded actively—by babbling, touching her face, or by burying his face in her neck—did she elaborate and intensify the contact.

We shall now describe Harry's characteristic patterns of experience and functioning, for it seems to us that qualitative aspects of his style of adaptation are intelligible in the light of his reaction tendencies operating in the setting that the mother provided. It will be remembered that Harry's development was most accelerated in the same areas that also yielded for him an exceptionally high proportion of excitation and of affect—gross motor coordination and locomotion, and social interaction. In Harry's social behavior, it was the complexity and duration that were advanced, not the discriminatory aspects. He did consistently discriminate mother from the observers, in that he turned toward her more often and more intensively and showed toward her behaviors that were never shown toward the observers, even at moments of highly pleasurable play with them. But he showed not the slightest response to a first encounter with a stranger (as two of the four 28-week-olds did). The inanimate part of the environment held for him less fascination, and his behavior with objects (while also somewhat advanced in terms of the actions he could perform) was not nearly so advanced. We think that this pattern came about largely because in Harry's experience, as compared with that of other equally active babies, the distress associated with futile straining was minimized, and the sequence beginning with effortful activation of the entire muscular apparatus and ending with a new and pleasurable postural equilibrium was maximized. Similarly, Harry very often experienced a variety of social interaction that is uncommon—it was *his* behavior, again in the form of body movement, that both initiated and terminated intense reciprocal play with the mother. We saw Harry's mother pay him fleeting playful attention not in direct response to a socially oriented action on his part. But unlike the majority of mothers in the sample whose babies were 6 or 7 months of age, Harry's mother was never seen to turn to him and commence active play, more or less compelling him to respond. On the other hand, she went further than most in following his lead and maintaining contact for what seemed relatively long periods of time. And she seemed to thoroughly enjoy the intrusive nature of his play. She encouraged him to poke his fingers into her mouth and nostrils, she let him poke, squeeze and rub her breast during play intermittent with feeding, and while she reciprocated intimate physical contact (nibbling his fingers or toes, blowing at his neck), this was always gentle and brief, compared with his vigorous assaults upon her person. The situation which we previously called "vigorous reciprocal love games" was for Harry one in which he, at 6 months, functioned in the conventional male role of playful aggressor, while the mother accommodated to him but showed only a calm sort of pleasure. Harry's experience during playful intimacy with the mother thus usually left him in a relatively calm and well integrated state.

Harry was a baby whose exceptional excitability did lead to irritability, but the presence of frequent episodes of overt distress and something like impatience did not interfere with the full use of all his capacities, or with the ability to remain content when left alone, and the capacity to recover equilibrium unaided, as well as the development of a selective and obviously pleasure-yielding relationship with the mother. It may not be superfluous to again point to the fact that Harry's pattern of adaptation cannot be viewed only as the result of especially appropriate maternal behavior. Had this very active baby also been markedly sensitive in one or several modalities, the same environmental conditions would have yielded excitation levels beyond those he actually experienced. The same would have been true had he been subject to more frequent somatic distress. It is also likely that Harry was an exceptionally well-endowed child, and that his rapid progress in acquiring new skills helped to shape his experience so that, comparatively often, marked effort and consequent stress terminated in successful action.

Sibyl, In XIII (28 Weeks)

SPE DETERMINANTS

Boundary Strength

	ENTIRE		*MODALITY SECTORS*			
	Inner	*Outer*	*Vision*	*Touch*	*Sound*	*Passive Motion*
Stimulation	medium (−)	weak (+)	weak (+)	weak (+)	weak (+)	?
Frequency of Mother-Child Contacts		low	low	medium	medium (−)	medium (−)
Intensity	low	medium (+)	⟶	⟶	⟶	⟶
Maternal Competence		medium	⟶	⟶	⟶	⟶
Maternal Intrusiveness		low (+)	⟶	⟶	⟶	⟶
Level of Home Stimulation		medium	⟶	⟶	⟶	⟶

Activity Level: 1.7

STABLE PATTERNS OF EXPERIENCE

Frequency of strong bodily arousal: Absent.

Sibyl was only moderately inactive and highly sensitive—yet she was not seen or reported to become aroused beyond very moderate degrees at any time. Hunger produced no overt behavioral change, though she accepted food quite eagerly when it arrived on schedule. Fatigue affected her behavior a great deal, but what she showed was restlessness, moderately extensive movement, and intermittent whimpering. In short, no state or situation ever led her to exceed very moderate levels of excitation.

Internal bodily sensations: Medium.

As has been said, fatigue affected Sibyl's behavior to a high degree and, in addition, it persisted for long periods of time before she could fall asleep. (Fifty minutes of severe fatigue before both nap and nighttime sleep was the estimated average, and her mother could not remember an occasion within the last month or so when it had taken less than half an hour.) Beyond this, it is difficult to assess the prominence of inner somatic sensations in Sibyl's life. She did not suffer from gastric or other bodily discomforts, but she did spend a disproportionate amount of time in intense and varied forms of bodily self-stimulation. However, though such body play was probably initiated in response to some impulse originating from within (it certainly was not responsive to any external stimulus), during it she was attentive to bodily sensations that she herself produced and that were thus external rather than intrinsic.

Balance between behavior activations due to inner and to outer stimulation: Equal.

Sibyl's behavior was noteworthy for the fact that behavior *activations,* as distinct from other modes of response, were very rare. The sight and approach of another person almost invariably led to intent gazing and often to smiling, vocalizing, and even slight increases in activity. Yet she experienced the proximity of mother or anybody else less often than do most babies of her age. Bodily self-stimulation (primarily oral and tactile but also kinesthetic) was the most frequent type of behavior activation noted; it occurred in response to fatigue or during spontaneous activity (inner stimulation), and in response to social approaches if they were at all prolonged, but these were rare occasions. The fact that behavior activations occurred about equally often in response to outer and to inner provocation is less descriptive of Sibyl than the fact that she did so much less reaching for, manipulating, vocalizing, and moving about than most babies do.

Importance of distance receptors: Medium.

Sibyl was highly reactive to both sights and sounds. Intent gazing was a prominent component of her response to persons as well as to things—

and more often than not it was her sole response. She was attentive to small visual detail, and very bright light (as well as sharp sounds) elicited discomfort and aversion. Many of the ways in which her sensitivities were manifested showed that the distance receptors did not so much govern or shape adaptive response as they qualified and even limited behavior. Sounds led to blinking, startling or a transient interruption of ongoing activity far more often than they led her to localize their source or attend to them. And her disinclination to shake, wave, or bang toys seemed related to her obvious dislike of the resulting sounds. Since contacts with the mother and with people generally were comparatively infrequent, the fact that the distance receptors were of obvious importance during social contacts did not mean that they achieved much prominence in her day-by-day experience. However, the mother provided an ample supply of toys and generally placed the baby in positions that invited visual exploration (seated in a safety table or on a jumper swing).

Importance of near receptors: High.

During direct contacts with the mother (and the father), energetic touch and passive motion were the prominent features as she was rolled about, swung and tickled. While these episodes were limited in number, they were important because they were the only times when Sibyl was seen to chuckle, squeal, and move with some vigor. Routine procedures also involve a fair amount of touching, and Sibyl's behavior at such times left no doubt that it was the manipulation of her body that animated her (and sometimes brought discomfort), especially as her mother was not the least bit playful or even, as a rule, socially attentive. The near receptors were especially prominent in Sibyl's experience because she was given to extensive, prolonged, and frequent bodily self-stimulation. Much of the time when most babies are responding to things about them or to another person, she was entirely content and absorbed in attending to the sensations generated as she stroked, hit or pinched her own skin, as she swung to and fro or cradle rocked, and as she sucked or mouthed any nearby object (rarely her own hand).

Most prominent modality: Touch.

Least prominent modality: None.

Frequency of states of optimal animation: Occasional.

During Sibyl's contacts with the mother, optimal states of animation as we defined them did not occur at all while we observed, and must have been very rare at other times. Either the mother played with the baby somewhat roughly, which led to pleasure but not to attentiveness to nearby things or to any but very simple responsive behaviors; or else she dealt with the baby deftly and considerately, but in an impersonal and somewhat remote manner. During spontaneous activity the baby was often so quiet as to preclude more than minimal animation as she gazed about her soberly. At other times she was wholly absorbed by self-contained body play. But there were occasions when, during spontaneous activity, she gently fingered a toy while also inspecting it with great intensity, or delicately pushed an object along a surface, watching both it and the motion of her own hand. It appeared to be chiefly or only at such times that this baby employed her energy and coordinating capacities in the manner we have defined as optimal.

OUTCOME RATINGS

Developmental status: Medium.

Sibyl's performance on both developmental tests conformed to high average standards for her age. Her test pattern was remarkably even in that, except for the adaptive part of the Gesell Schedules, almost all of her behavior conformed to norms for 28-week-olds (chronological age was exactly 28 weeks at the time of testing). However, she was better able to deal with several objects at once than is expected at her age. For instance, she could imitatively bang a block against a cup (a 36-weeks item) and found it easy to remain attentive to two and even three objects at a time (four of the five 28-weeks items on the adaptive portion of the Gesell refer to this aspect of behavior). On the other hand, she did not manipulate rattles and the bell as most 6-month-olds do. This was ascribed to her apparent dislike of sharp noise, which was manifested also when the examiner used sound-generating toys.

The most outstanding aspect of Sibyl's behavior during the test was her tendency to interpose delay between perception of a toy and responsive action. She would look in an alert and intense fashion, showing neither pleasure nor aversion, and only after from 10 to about 40 seconds had elapsed would she reach for the toy or move it. A second noteworthy characteristic of her response to the testing situation was the fact that she remained tentative, exploratory, and somehow lacking in vigor throughout. She fingered toys, held them up for visual exploration, very gently pushed them along the table and the like. She was not seen to bang or wave toys, as 6-month-olds usually do, and she never reached for an object at a distance or registered annoyance when a toy was taken from her. The same characteristics were noted in all her dealings with objects, during spontaneous activity and at other times.

Adequacy of vegetative functioning: High.

Sibyl ate and slept exceedingly well. She was an altogether healthy baby, skin tonus was excellent, and respiration and peripheral circulation (as judged by skin color) were markedly stable.

Excitability: Low.

Were it not for her frequent and intense bodily self-stimulation, Sibyl would have been described as an exceptionally placid baby. Still, she showed less animation and far less excitement in the sense of bodily arousal than the great majority of infants. As has been mentioned, prolonged and provocative presentation of toys elicited interest but not excitement. She was rarely seen to attempt an activity in the face of obstacles and so was spared the occasions when stress and excitation result from an encounter with physically restraining conditions. During most of the caretaking routines Sybil remained impassive though contented. Only while being dressed and undressed, which involves prolonged handling, did she show considerable fanning of the toes, tight fisting of the hands, and occasional stiffening of the body, while she looked displeased and vocalized irritably. The formal rating of the mother's style is not fully descriptive of her manner, for she was exceedingly skillful manually. She was quick and deft so that diapering and other routines involved a minimum of handling. Although her other contacts with the baby (soothing and play) were distinctly vigorous, she actually provided a minimum of stimulation during caretaking procedures.

Irritability: Low.

Sibyl was not an irritable baby, though she did not show as much pleasure or relaxed contentment as one sees in many babies. As already described, only prolonged handling was disturbing to her, and then only briefly. Many situations that are annoying to other babies either did not occur or were tolerated impassively. She frequently fell from a sitting posture and placidly remained in the position to which she had fallen. She did not mind having toys removed from her grasp; she was not in the least cranky, although a tooth was in the process of erupting. Occasionally, she cried or vocalized in a protesting manner when put down after she had been in a parent's arms, or when she was moved from a sitting to a horizontal posture. However, the parents made a point of not going to her at such times, knowing that she would soon calm down of her own accord (which we observed on numerous occasions). Mother was able to take great pride in the fact that her baby did not cry except for "good reasons" (fatigue or pain).

Pleasure in functioning: Medium.

This rating was arrived at with much difficulty, and the final judgment does not fully describe the actual state of affairs. During spontaneous activity Sibyl very seldom activated complex behavior involving objects (less often than any baby in her age group). She engaged in a great deal of bodily self-stimulation of all varieties. But one of her most prominent patterns, cradle rocking, utilizes a fairly complex pattern of muscular coordination for one of her age. In her response to social situations, Sibyl had comparatively little opportunity to display pleasure in applying relatively novel and discriminatory patterns of behavior. As has been described, her mother did not tend to provide gentle and prolonged episodes of interaction and did not use toys or other objects in her contacts with the baby. The "medium" rating was assigned because of Sibyl's impressive capacity to make the most of opportunities that came her way. Unless she was fatigued, she always brightened at the sight of the mother. A brief smile from the mother (or from others) was sufficient to elicit from the baby prolonged and complex patterns of vocalization (clearly enunciated syllabic sounds with varied and expressive inflection). Not infrequently the baby made a full and clearly pleasurable response to the mother at times when the latter's attention was primarily directed elsewhere. Thus, we considered that Sibyl had fewer occasions than many other babies to experience pleasure in functioning, but that her behavior, when opportunity arose, suggested a marked readiness to respond pleasurably to appropriate stimulation.

DISCUSSION

The formal ratings of developmental outcome describe Sibyl as a baby who had developed normally, who was neither irritable nor excitable as compared with other babies of like age, and who took normal and healthy pleasure in the exercise of behavior integrations still in the process of being learned. In other words, she was a thriving baby. Even more than in many other instances, these perfectly accurate descriptive statements fail to convey much that seems important and individually characteristic. After a brief description of noteworthy aspects of her behavior, we shall attempt to see what aspects of her experience pattern may help to explain how she came to function as she did.

Sibyl spent a good deal of her waking time in a safety table, the playpen, the crib, or a jumper swing. At such times she was surrounded by toys and under the mother's eye, but not in direct contact with the mother. The baby was content enough as she fingered or gently moved nearby toys; let her gaze travel all over the room and fix with interest as she sighted a person or a moving object; and changed her posture frequently from prone to supine, from either of these positions to the hand-knee creeping posture, and from the latter to a sitting position. Such very simple object play and gentle but usually well-coordinated motor play were frequently interrupted by prolonged episodes of bodily self-stimulation. She mouthed furniture and toys (less often her own hand), she swung rhythmically on her abdomen with chest and legs raised off the mattress, and she rocked on her hands and knees (cradle rocking), often for prolonged periods of time. In addition, she had a way of rubbing her own skin with her hand, exerting a fair amount of pressure as the hand moved over her chest, abdomen, or thigh. Most of the time she was neither gay nor discontented nor lethargic. Rather, her facial expression ranged from alert interest (as she inspected the environs) to a somewhat sober self-absorbed expression. She vocalized occasionally, and observers commented that the sounds she produced sounded mildly discontented, though they were neither plaintive nor protesting. They appeared to be as expressive of her state as were the movements, and her behavior at such times did not suggest that these vocalizations were of a social nature (*i.e.,* they were not accompanied by visual or body orientation toward the environment).

In comparison with other babies, Sibyl showed less pleasure and animation, less excitement and annoyance, and a marked preoccupation with her own body at the expense of attention toward any but the most immediate environment. Yet, as implied in the ratings of the outer boundary, sounds and sights were rarely ignored, but the behavioral response to slight external stimuli often consisted of blinking, a brief interruption of ongoing activity, or transient flexion of the hands, rather than directed action. The exception was the sight of a person, which always caused alert regard and often led to smiling and a sociable cooing, even when the other person's attention was not on the baby.

Another noteworthy feature of Sibyl's behavior was her impassive response to situations that are likely to arouse most babies of this age. She frequently fell from sitting, and simply continued to play in the new position. She made no visible response when toys were taken from her hand or when mother removed her thumb from the mouth. Again, the one exception involved social interactions. She was observed and reported to fuss when put down after she had been held. In her experience, such response did not lead to renewed social contact. Her mother first waited to see whether Sibyl would calm down, which she often did within a very few minutes—almost always as she began to swing or to rock. If she continued to squeal or whimper, the mother rocked the crib (if that was where the baby had been put) or else placed her in the "jumper swing" (a canvas seat suspended from the ceiling) and helped the baby to set it in motion. Being rocked and swung was said to either content her or make her go to sleep (unless she was hungry), and we had repeated occasion to verify this report.

As has been mentioned, Sibyl was carefully tended and supervised by her efficient mother, but she was played with relatively seldom; in particular, the mother seldom created or prolonged episodes of mutual smiling, mutual gazing, or other sustained social episodes. It was to us impressive to observe this mother as she diapered, dressed, fed or put her baby to sleep, and maintained a sober, attentive and impersonal facial expression most of the time. Yet, to judge by Sibyl's behavior, these were nonetheless social interludes. She focused on the mother's face intently, smiled and vocalized as it came near, and was generally more animated than usual. Mother did of course look at her baby's face, smile occasionally, and also speak to her. But her social responses to the baby at such times were slight and, at least while under observation, lacked warmth and animation. It was Sibyl who made the most of each encounter, and often her mother seemed unaware of the baby's responses as she spoke to someone else or concentrated on a piece of clothing.

As has been mentioned, the mother played with Sibyl on occasion, her father played with her every evening about supper time, and various relatives frequented the home. Both parents, according to what we saw and according to the father's own description, went in for very energetic body play. Mother tickled the baby, poked her, rolled her about and blew into her neck. Father did the same, but also swung and bounced the baby, and tossed her about. There was no doubt of Sibyl's enjoyment of such play—she laughed, chuckled and squealed in high glee. But these playful episodes did not allow for the gradual and modulated social interactions that have been described for many of the other babies in the sample.

Sibyl's most direct encounters with other people, whether during soothing (when mother sometimes combined swinging or rocking with very forceful patting of the back) or during play, were such as to generate strong bodily sensations. Or else (during routines) she was highly aware of the social partner, but there was very little interaction. And at other times (during spontaneous activity) the creation of fairly strong bodily sensations also loomed large in her experience.

One last characteristic of Sibyl's behavior needs to be mentioned in this connection. She was one of the very few babies in the entire sample who tended to respond to moderately strong external stimulation by activity that further stimulated her own body. Both when the mother played with her, and when staff members did so (for instance during the pediatric examination which was playful and leisurely), Sibyl responded not only by smiling, chuckling, and vocalizing, but also by firmly rubbing her own skin in the region of the groin and forcefully hitting her own thigh with a toy or her open hand. This was most marked when she was being touched, as though tactile stimulation provided by another person led to an impulse to intensify the same variety of body feeling.

Sibyl's mother was an efficient woman who took pride in her baby and in her home. She struck all observers as lacking in spontaneity and gentleness. This was equally true during her contacts with the research staff, even though she had chosen to participate and showed great interest in the study, to which she later referred numerous other mothers on her own initiative. During conversations with the staff her face was strikingly immobile, as was her posture when she was not busy. She rarely smiled or laughed, and occasionally she looked tense and uncomfortable, giving the impression of someone attempting to subdue strong emotion. Observers found her puzzling because often they could not guess what she might be feeling. In the home, and in the presence of the father, she showed brief flashes of anger (when he appeared to contradict her), always contained and always directed toward her husband. She was a firm believer in a strict schedule (to which Sibyl seemed very comfortably adapted), she was resolved to prevent the baby from thumbsucking, and she made it clear that too much attention only serves to spoil a baby and interfere with the development of "independence" (by which she meant the capacity to overcome minor upsets unaided). Like some other mothers in the sample, she defiantly exaggerated her own harshness. For instance, she claimed that—unless the baby were tired, hungry, or in pain—she would let her cry for at least 20 minutes before going to her. During the home visit she was seen to do nothing whatsoever while the baby fussed in the playpen, but within about 10 minutes she had found a practical reason that made it necessary to pick the baby up. Similarly, she described herself as forcefeeding pablum, which Sibyl disliked, because babies "have to learn to eat what is good for them." However, we were able to learn (ten days later and in another context) that soon thereafter she switched to another cereal. It is also probable that while not under observation this mother could show greater warmth. However, her striking stiffness in even the most neutral circumstances (such as dealing with the mailman at the door), her inability to show ordinary animation in superficial social contexts, and the way she spoke both to and about her husband—all suggest that compared with other women, Sibyl's mother had little capacity for free and intimate responsiveness to others, her baby included.

In this setting Sibyl developed normally in terms of coordination, discrimination, vocalization and related functions. And if her manipulation of objects was less vigorous than that of most babies and less oriented toward achieving specific effects (she rarely shook a rattle or banged an object), she made up for this by prolonged visual regard, attentiveness to several things at the same time, and gentle tactile exploration of each thing with which she came in contact. She had also come to differentiate the mother from all other people, responding to the sight and sound of her more strongly than to the perception of others. A reaction to strangers (shown by half of our babies at this age) had not yet occurred. Her behavior differed from that of most other babies in that she showed overt affect much less often than is usual (both pleasure and distress). More typically, and for longer periods of time than most babies, she was in a state of moderate arousal as she swung, rocked, scratched or rubbed her skin, and mouthed nearby objects. At these times she appeared to be attentive to sensations emanating from her body; insofar as her behavior was focused upon aspects of the environment, it was responsive only to that which was within easy reach or very close. Even the very strong response to the sight of a person occurred when someone came close to her, and very seldom across distances of more than about three feet. Her effective environment was thus comparatively narrow in scope.

Sibyl's case is an especially clear example of the manner in which specific features of a baby's behavioral style can be understood in the light of specific features of concrete experience. She was sensitive to perceptual stimuli in all modalities. During direct contacts with the baby, the mother seldom used the visual modality (though she often placed the baby so as to provide scope for visual exploration). Presumably for this reason, Sibyl was relatively unresponsive to the aspects of the environment that are perceived by visual means. The mother did speak to the baby more than she encouraged visual contact, though quite often she was out of sight and spoke in a matter-of-fact fashion not especially suited to interest the baby. And Sibyl's sensitivity to sound manifested itself chiefly in shrinking from loud or sharp noise. Seldom did Sibyl respond to a sound as a clue or signal for something in the environment to be identified visually or responded to in an outwardly directed manner. Fairly strong tactile sensations were a conspicuous element of the only rousing and fairly intense contacts between Sibyl and her mother. And Sibyl provided a great deal of tactile stimulation for herself, both when left to her own devices and when socially stimulated fairly strongly. The mother used rocking and swinging as a device to soothe the baby or to help her get off to sleep. She gave such kinesthetic stimulation in a strikingly impersonal manner, by placing the baby in the swing and pushing it from behind, or by rocking the crib (again while out of sight), or by holding the baby in her arms without speaking and without placing herself in the baby's view. That these forceful kinesthetic sensations did make themselves felt in the baby's experience is attested to by the fact that being rocked was the only thing that did enable her to go to sleep. Again, Sibyl provided for herself a great deal of rocking and swinging motion, but seldom in conjunction with either pleasure or displeasure.

We think that if Sibyl had been less reactive to perceptual stimuli, it is unlikely that she could have developed as well as she did under circumstances that provided so little incitement for the integration (or combined activation) of the various modalities in pleasurable contact with another person. Similarly, had she not been a sensitive baby, we think it unlikely that she would have developed such a strong selective responsiveness to the mother, in view of the relative infrequency of direct contact between the two, and of the lack of variety and prolonged interchange that characterized these episodes. From the point of view of developmental advance, it may have been her high reactivity that enabled Sibyl to progress despite a relative lack of maternal facilitation.

The exceptional prominence of bodily self-stimulation in her behavior —at the expense of outwardly directed adaptive action—is understandable because strong body stimulation is what she experienced at the hands of her mother (and father), at the expense of the activation of the distance receptor systems in a social context. And yet it may have been her strong reactivity to visual impressions that enabled her to make animated social responses unilaterally, when mother was in contact physically but did little to sustain the interpersonal aspect of the situation. The mother's lack of intimacy with her baby, manifested in the scarcity of mutual gazing, smiling and vocalizing, is clearly reflected in Sibyl's behavioral style. She did not register overt discomfort or protest on occasions when other babies do so, but turned to bodily self-stimulation instead, which meant that relatively seldom did she experience the cessation of distress in conjunction with the mother's appearance in her perceptual field. Similarly, the relative infrequency of affective arousal makes good sense as one realizes how rarely Sibyl's mother participated in affective exchanges with her baby (or, it would seem, with anyone).

Grace, Ac XIV (28 Weeks)

SPE DETERMINANTS

	Boundary Strength					
	ENTIRE		*MODALITY SECTORS*			
	Inner	*Outer*	*Vision*	*Touch*	*Sound*	*Passive Motion*
Stimulation	weak (+)	medium	medium	medium	weak (+)	medium (−)
Frequency of Mother-Child Contacts		high	high (−)	medium (+)	high (−)	high
Intensity	medium	high	——————→			
Maternal Competence		medium	——————→			
Maternal Intrusiveness		medium	——————→			
Level of Home Stimulation		high	——————→			

Activity Level: 2.7

STABLE PATTERNS OF EXPERIENCE

Frequency of strong bodily arousal: Fairly high.

This active and robust baby, who was subject to fairly strong internal stimulation and to frequent and intense stimulation from without, often became sufficiently excited to arch her back, show marked muscle tension by stiffening and squirming, flush deeply, and breathe in a panting fashion. Always these episodes were accompanied by loud squealing and by other signs of affect, mostly consisting of displeasure but sometimes of high glee.

Grace always experienced intense bodily arousal and acute distress before she was able to fall asleep. Fatigue showed itself in mounting restlessness, agitation, and prolonged unhappy squealing as well as crying, and was accompanied by all the bodily signs of arousal described above. This difficulty had been present since early infancy, and the mother could not remember an occasion when Grace had been able to go to sleep without spending at least 45 minutes (often more than an hour) in distress. Always, the mother rocked her forcefully and patiently until the baby fell asleep, quite suddenly "knocked out" by fatigue.

Grace's daily life included many other brief episodes of peak excitation —when she was put down after someone had played with her; when she was changed from an upright to a horizontal position; when she strained to reach a distant object; or when she rocked or bounced during spontaneous play, increasing the intensity until she flushed, squealed loudly, and became generally very tense though not at all unhappy.

Internal bodily sensations: Medium.

The massive impact of fatigue was by far the most important occasion when Grace responded primarily to arousal clearly due to internal somatic sources. Hunger brought no observable behavior change. A better way of putting it might be to say that she was on a self-demand schedule, and hunger distress was not allowed to develop (though she accepted food eagerly and even with impatience when it came).

Otherwise, almost all of Grace's behavior appeared primarily responsive to events in the environment, the possible exception being her proclivity to engage in bouts of vigorous bouncing while seated in the Teeter-Babe.

Balance between behavior activations due to inner and to outer stimulation: External very predominant.

Except when tired, Grace was exceedingly responsive to everything about her, though she was not a baby who focused on inconspicuous elements or who showed marked perceptual discrimination. As will be detailed later on, she was in nearly constant contact with a lively, noisy, affectionate family, who intruded upon her awareness and compelled her responsiveness. Even when playing alone, usually seated on the Teeter-Babe, she always had an audience, so that when she dropped toys someone ran to restore them, when she vocalized insistently someone answered, and when she slumped in her seat or otherwise became uncomfortable, someone noted and corrected the condition. During spontaneous activity bodily self-stimulation (except for joyous bouncing) was nearly absent, and she was never seen in a self-absorbed state.

Importance of distance receptors: High.

As has been implied, Grace was exposed to very high levels of visual and auditory stimulation, both in direct contact with the mother and other family members, and across distances or impersonally through toys, playful sounds, and the constant presence of a family who pursued their lives in an active, vigorous, noise-generating fashion.

Importance of near receptors: Fairly high.

Grace's mother touched her baby without hesitation during routine procedures as well as in play. But visual, auditory, and movement elements were nearly always dominant, and it did not appear that either mother or baby elaborated on the tactile component of the interaction. Moreover, Grace's responsiveness to the mother or to anyone else was much the same whether or not touch was involved. Passive motion was a prominent aspect of this baby's experience. Not only was prolonged and forceful rocking the only thing that enabled her to sleep, but she provided for herself rhythmic kinesthetic sensations by bouncing and rocking. Many of the established and repetitive games that family members played with her also used the same movement patterns.

Most prominent modality: Sound.

Grace was more reactive to sound than to other stimuli, and the family seemed to capitalize on this fact. Most of her toys were sound producing ("she likes them best," her mother said); she was sung to, whistled at, and entertained by other sounds; and last, not least, the permanent members of the family all tended to imitate her vocalizations, in the firm belief that Grace was imitating them (which may well have been true part of the time).

Least prominent modality: Touch.

Frequency of states of optimal animation: High.

For this rather robust baby the excitatory yet accommodating style of mother and others in the family provided many occasions when she was somewhat aroused and her behavior was focused entirely on an aspect of the environment, not passively, but by approaching, manipulating, and other responsive activations. In addition, when left to her own devices, though within sight of others, she frequently maintained the same state of responsiveness, directed at nearby objects or at the achievement of complex motor feats. (During spontaneous activity she showed a larger proportion of complex behavior schemas than any other baby in her age group.)

OUTCOME RATINGS

Developmental status: High.

Grace's performance on both tests proved that she had developed at an accelerated pace. At a chronological age of 28 weeks (6.7 months) she succeeded on all items that are normative only by the age of 32 weeks. In the areas of neuromuscular coordination, vocalization, and patterns of social responsiveness, scatter was not pronounced. She passed a single item at the 36-weeks level in the so-called language area of the Gesell Schedules. In view of what has been said about the importance of the auditory sphere in her experience, it is of interest that she was the only baby of her age (in this sample) who clearly and readily imitated sounds. In the adaptive sphere (of the Gesell Schedules) she was markedly advanced, but scatter was pronounced. Here too, she met normative standards for 32-week-olds in all respects. At the 36-week level she succeeded on only one of five items, yet she was able to perform three of eight 40-week items. She excelled in the deliberate and forceful manipulation of objects, especially if this manipulation led to sound effects (banging cube against cup, 36 weeks; purposive ringing of the bell, 40 weeks). She was also attentive to visual detail. However, more delicate motions (such as using the index finger in approaching a small object) were not her forte. Her progress with respect to fine coordination was not delayed. Rather, she excelled in other aspects and failed to do so in this one area.

Grace responded to the testing situation in an eager, vigorous, active, and manipulatory manner. She was not a baby who merely gazed at a toy before approaching it. Rather, she seized upon each toy offered and at once proceeded to wave or bang it, to mouth it or to transfer it from one hand to the other. As long as a substitute was provided, Grace never minded having a toy removed from her grasp. Her social responsiveness, of a piece with the rest of her behavior, was vigorous and not especially differentiated. She squealed, laughed, chuckled, and smiled broadly, but finer nuances and transitions were lacking.

It is interesting that Grace was able to develop in such an all-around superior fashion despite the presence of a significant chronic difficulty in going to sleep, and despite the fact that she received more and more intensive stimulation than would seem desirable. We attribute this partly to the fact that she was not an especially sensitive baby, partly to the fact that she was exceptionally robust physically, and partly to the fact that the mother combined forceful intrusiveness with consistent accommodation to the baby's preferences and needs. Grace was fed when her mother judged her to be hungry, she was never awakened, and the mother did what she could to provide scope for her strong movement impulses. The mother's intrusiveness took the form of often and forcefully approaching the perfectly contented baby, apparently for the sheer pleasure she took in playful contacts. She poked at the baby's body, spoke to her loudly and cheerfully, and often moved toys close to the baby's face or placed them in her hand. That is to say, she intruded by compelling the baby's attention to her person or to objects, but she did not often interfere with an action sequence initiated by the baby. Since Grace was as forcible in her response as the mother was in her approach, these frequent intrusions into the baby's awareness were seldom disruptive; they probably furthered rather than hindered the consolidation of developmental gains.

Adequacy of vegetative functioning: High.

Despite her difficulty in going to sleep, Grace slept soundly and in adequate amounts. She ate eagerly, had no gastric troubles, and conveyed by appearance and behavior a prevailing sense of bodily well-being.

Excitability: High.

It was difficult to decide whether a "medium" or a "high" rating was more appropriate in this case. A number of situations that provoke excitation in many other babies evoked from Grace moderate signs of bodily arousal. On the other hand, she was given to arching of the back, to tense body postures, and to loud excited squealing more frequently than most babies. This was true even during spontaneous activity, when she at times engaged in a rocking or bouncing motion while she looked flushed and squealed loudly; and at other times became tense and excited as she exerted all her strength in efforts to approach an object actually beyond her reach. Also, as has been said, muscle tension and other signs of bodily arousal were very intense indeed when she was tired.

Irritability: Medium.

Much of her waking time Grace was either gay or entirely contented, but she also cried and fussed more than most babies. Again the marked irritability when fatigued and unable to go to sleep was a major factor. However, Grace also cried or squealed angrily when put down after having been played with, when placed in a horizontal (rather than upright) position, and when too many people actively tried to play with her at once (which regularly happened during frequent get-togethers of a large and lively extended family).

Pleasure in functioning: High.

As described earlier, Grace showed overt pleasure in interaction with people and with toys more often and more intensively than many other babies. Mother's varied use of toys (or everyday objects treated as toys) in direct play with her elicited complex patterns of response in the context of high pleasure generated by the social aspect of the situation. In fact, Grace's behavior provided especially clear-cut examples of what is meant by pleasure in functioning. For instance, during the test she was handed a bell (a variety of object she had not seen before). To begin with she treated it as she did most other objects. Grasping it at the bowl and not the handle, she waved, banged, and mouthed it with enjoyment. The examiner removed it from her grasp and demonstrated only once how to hold it by the handle and produce the ringing sound. Grace's face lit up, she grasped it by the handle and rang it as she had been shown, with an expression of excited glee. From that time on she used the bell only in this fashion, choosing it from among other available toys and repeating the performance for as long as she had the opportunity.

DISCUSSION

It seems to us that Grace's style of adaptation and the pattern of her development remain inexplicable except in the light of the particular quality of her family's life.

Grace was an eagerly awaited first baby and a most important personage to her parents and to a large family group, all of whom had daily contact with her. The family shared a home with one set of grandparents, and innumerable relatives lived close by and were constantly in and out of the home. Grace was responded to throughout her waking day. No new "trick" on her part remained unnoticed as family members vied with one another to get Grace to reproduce the new sound or new movement patterns. Almost always they performed the same action they had noticed in the baby, hoping that Grace would imitate them in turn. Thus, mutual imitation, both immediate and delayed, was a particularly important element in Grace's day-by-day experience. Because of their delight in Grace's every action, family members were also unusually alert to her likes and aversions. Often, when an incidental occurrence proved to amuse the baby, it was transformed into a family ritual. For instance, she laughed when, by accident, she found herself bounced up and down while seated on the stomach of a portly uncle. Henceforth, he habitually placed her on his stomach and let her "ride" it. Grace's high pleasure and vigorous participation in so many playful episodes must have been enhanced by the fact that whatever happened aroused strong interest and response from everyone about. During a single episode of this kind, she thus experienced not only the bouncing and the interaction with the uncle, but the laughter and general animation of an audience; she was aware of them and squealed or laughed as she looked from one face to another.

It is important to know that Grace's family behaved toward one another much as they did toward the baby. The mother thoroughly enjoyed contacts with the research project both because she could show off her baby and because she enjoyed new people, watching the use of equipment, the small courtesies extended toward her during sociable coffee drinking, and the like. She and, it would seem, others of the family, were given to immediate affective response to all that occurred. Mother easily showed anger at a delayed taxi, alarm at a minor illness of a relative, or indignation at the inconsiderate behavior of a neighbor. Similarly, she expressed joy and excitement about such things as a nice new apartment acquired by a friend or any other occasion for vicarious rejoicing. Like most of the family members, she was demonstrative and action-oriented. In this extended family group it was customary and natural for each person to intervene and to share in many aspects of the other's life. The intensity of responsiveness to the baby was part of an established pattern of family functioning. It did not, as in some other families in the sample, reflect the presence of inordinately strong adult needs or emotions focused upon the baby.

Grace's day-by-day experience shared many features with that of the adults. She experienced frequent episodes of pleasure and displeasure, and still more frequent states of vigorous activation and marked pleasure without strain. Many of these involved prolonged, intimate, reciprocal social contact with the mother and with an array of familiar quasi-maternal persons. Grace did experience the mother (and, it seemed, only the mother) as a soothing agent and as the agent of bodily need satisfaction (since it was the mother who always fed her and put her to sleep).

Under these conditions Grace not only functioned and developed very well, but evolved a style of behavior comically similar to her mother's. As it happened, there was a marked physical resemblance between the two. But far more impressive was the fact that both were vigorous, well coordinated, and not the least bit subtle. Both were roused to pleasure easily and often, both easily became annoyed, both were impatient, both took delight in novelty per se. It is further of interest that this sound-sensitive baby, in a setting that strongly emphasized the auditory mode, was most strikingly accelerated in her capacity to produce differentiated sounds and to respond to them by imitation; also she displayed the most complex use of objects with those that created sound effects. What was lacking in her experience is well reflected in those aspects of her behavior that were less advanced or absent. She was relatively indiscriminate in relation to social and to general perceptual components of the environment (except for a definite discrimination of mother from all others). Delicate and finely coordinated motion, subtle physiognomic expression, thorough exploration of an object—all these behavior attributes were not represented in Grace's repertoire. And she was a baby who was given little opportunity or encouragement in these directions. During social interactions at any rate, what she was offered was so vivid and compelling that subtleties and minute behavior accommodations could hardly have emerged.

Peter, In XIV (28 Weeks)

SPE DETERMINANTS

	Boundary Strength					
	ENTIRE		*MODALITY SECTORS*			
	Inner	*Outer*	*Vision*	*Touch*	*Sound*	*Passive Motion*
Stimulation	medium (−)	medium	medium	strong	medium	medium
Frequency of Mother-Child Contacts		high	medium (−)	high	high	low (+)
Intensity	low	high	⟶			
Maternal Competence		high	⟶			
Maternal Intrusiveness		high	⟶			
Level of Home Stimulation		high	⟶			

Activity Level: 2.0

STABLE PATTERNS OF EXPERIENCE

Frequency of strong bodily arousal: Absent.

Although Peter was not a markedly inactive baby, both observation and report indicated that significant levels of bodily arousal simply did not occur. Neither hunger nor fatigue nor the extensive and forceful manipulations to which he was subjected led to more than very moderate movement increase, vocalization, or changes in autonomic functioning (insofar as these are visible).

Internal bodily sensations: Fairly low.

In Peter, hunger produced no observable behavior changes, and fatigue led to a brief period of mild restlessness and intermittent whimpering. When we knew him he was entirely free from gastric or other bodily distress, so that, compared with other babies, he felt strong internal bodily sensations less often and less vividly.

Balance between behavior activations due to inner and to outer stimulation: External predominant.

Peter was the sort of baby who became less responsive as the stimulation to which he was exposed grew stronger. Since stimulation emanating from the outside was frequent and exceedingly intense, it often failed to lead to a behavior activation. When left to his own devices, which happened rarely and never lasted long, he reached for and manipulated objects much as most other babies do, and engaged in body play such as rolling and reaching for his feet. At these moments behavior activations occurred predominantly in response to external sights and sounds. Such occasions, though, were the exception rather than the rule during his waking hours. He did, of course, respond to both internal and external events and sensations, but chiefly by ceasing whatever activity had been present or by reducing behavior activations to a minimum.

Importance of distance receptors: Fairly high.

Peter was moderately alert to sights and sounds about him, and, far more than most babies, he was exposed to all manner of visual impressions and to auditory effects of all sorts. His responsiveness to visual and auditory stimulation often took a different form from what is observed in most 6-month-olds. This was true largely because sounds and sights were often overshadowed by simultaneous strong tactile stimulation, and because he tended to withhold active response when stimulation became intense. For him, the distance receptors often mediated a reduction in behavior output, in addition to the more usual behavior activations. Nonetheless, social responsiveness and the occasional episodes of quiet play provided a good deal of opportunity for him to apprehend a situation first by means of vision, and for his subsequent behavior to be guided by visual clues (as in reaching, in smiling or in crying at the approach of strangers). However, unlike many of the inactive babies, he was not given to intent and prolonged gazing, nor was he especially attentive to sounds.

Importance of near receptors: High.

Peter was fondled, tickled, massaged and vigorously moved about very frequently by the mother, whose attention to her baby was maintained chiefly by direct body contact. Peter would smile or even laugh at the onset, but then became rather sober and impassive, though not at all distressed. The sheer amount of waking time during which he was moved about and touched, and the fact that his behavior changed in consequence (though not by becoming actively responsive) lead to the judgment that the near receptors (touch more than passive motion).loomed large in his everyday experience.

Most prominent modality: Touch.

Least prominent modality: None.

Frequency of states of optimal animation: Occasional.

When left to his own devices Peter was sometimes content to engage in very simple and limited behaviors, prominently the mouthing of objects, but he also engaged in coordinated efforts to move or to change his posture. However, much of the time he had to accommodate to the mother's forceful and affectionate attention and to her incessant efforts to teach him things. What made these moments of social interaction (during which mother incited him to act upon objects) less than optimal from the point of view of his participation was that the mother's behavior was seldom regulated by the baby's state or by his activity of the moment. She did not so much *invite* him to execute an action (such as reaching or maintaining an upright posture with support) as she *imposed* the behavior—moving or holding his body for him, placing toys in his hand, or telling him in words what she expected him to do (not at all dismayed by his failure to comprehend or comply). All this was done in a comfortable and loving manner, and the baby showed a pleased or neutral expression, but it rarely enabled Peter to perform at his most mature level (as observed at moments of lesser or more accommodating stimulation).

OUTCOME RATINGS

Developmental status: High.

Peter's performance on both tests reflected definite acceleration. Actually, he was not quite as advanced as several of the other babies who received the same rating, though at the age of 28 weeks he performed all items that correspond to normative standards for 32-week-olds. However, he achieved only three isolated items at the 36- and 40-weeks level. Although an acceleration equivalent to one month's growth is moderate in extent, a rating of "high" was judged to be appropriate because of the extraordinary uniformity of his behavior. No aspect of Peter's functioning (of those functions tapped by either of the tests) had remained at the level ordinarily seen in 6-month-olds.

Despite what has been said about the overly compelling quality of this mother's dealings with her baby, Peter's advanced developmental status must have come about in part because she did everything conceivable to teach him skills. In her written response to our questionnaire, when asked to describe what she understood by the phrase "spoiling a baby," she denied that there was such a thing and added "they can't learn to sit or to talk unless someone teaches them." Her behavior bore out this attitude to an extreme degree. She was not seen to offer the bottle without first holding it out to the baby and urging him to obtain it for himself. She often approached him with outstretched arms, urging him to "come on," and would not pick him up until he had begun to stretch his arms in her direction. Characteristically, she initiated relatively mature techniques of care at the earliest possible moment. Toys were strung across his crib on the first day after they came home from the hospital, and a rattle was pressed into his hand on the same day. He was tied into a highchair and sat with the family for his main meals beginning at 8 weeks; solid feedings, cup feedings, being given a cracker to munch by himself, and being equipped with a spoon of his own while mother fed him all began earlier than usual (sometimes in defiance of the pediatrician's explicit advice).

More will be said about how Peter was able to tolerate constant intrusions of this sort and to adapt to a generally turbulent style of existence. For the moment, it may be sufficient to recall his capacity to withhold responsiveness, and to point out that he slept away a larger portion of each day than the majority (no less than 18 hours of every 24), thus reducing the sum total of excitatory experience with which he had to cope.

Adequacy of vegetative functioning: High.

As has been said, Peter slept a great deal and very soundly. He took pleasure in movement, his tonus was excellent, and there was no visible lability of respiration or of circulation. His extraordinarily good appetite had become a family legend.

Peter's physical well-being was the more impressive because during the early months of life he had experienced bodily discomfort and acute illness. Up to the age of 9 weeks, gastric pain and vomiting occurred daily. (The mother vigorously denied that he had colic, but the symptoms she described conformed to the classic definition of the syndrome.) During his fourth month he had an acute infection with high fever and apparent pain, and during the fifth month he caught a severe cold. However, when we knew him Peter was in splendid health, and had been entirely well for at least six weeks.

Excitability: Low.

Peter was anything but excitable. It was astonishing to see the degree to which his body remained relaxed and his movements retained their co-ordination while he was moved, tickled, subjected to loud playful noises close to his ear, or pulled this way and that by his preschool age siblings. He did manifest excitement by a change in voice quality to sharp, loud squealing. In a manner not observed in other babies in this sample, Peter responded to prolonged and massive stimulation by fatigue. As mother continued to play with him actively, he simply changed from at first responding maximally to at last responding almost not at all. Whereas at the beginning of such an episode, he squealed, laughed, and looked at mother's face intently, later on he smiled in response to each new approach, but often rested his gaze on a nearby object rather than his mother; on some occasions we saw him being kissed and mauled while he was nearly motionless, and his face reflected impassivity but not displeasure. One example may illustrate the discrepancy between the objective strength of stimulation and Peter's response. On occasion, mother grasped the baby by his ankles and dangled him upside down (a procedure she had invented when he was 3 months old and had gastric distress, for she found that it induced vomiting and so relieved the pain). Peter's body did not tense as he was suspended upside down; he flushed a bit, but registered no displeasure, and as he was lifted to a more normal position observers felt that his facial expression registered at most mild relief.

Irritability: Low.

Enough has been said to convey a sense of this baby's remarkable imperturbability. Nor can his lack of irritability be ascribed to his capacity for self-soothing. He engaged in a great deal of oral behavior (during spontaneous activity as well as in response to external stimulation), but sucking was not one of his patterns, and on the only occasions when he was distressed (during fatigue), bodily self-stimulation stopped altogether. In situations that in many other babies lead to mounting tension or to increased bodily self-stimulation, Peter looked a bit overwhelmed and became very quiet.

Pleasure in functioning: High.

In this realm too, the quality of Peter's behavior was somewhat different from that of most other babies who received the same rating. While left to his own devices (a rare and brief event), Peter did play with nearby objects, but this was not a conspicuous aspect of his behavior. However, he worked assiduously at mastering a few movement patterns that still presented difficulty for him. He engaged in a great deal of oral behavior, mouthing and engulfing toys, chomping at hard objects and rubbing them against his mouth. But, while this much mouthing affected other babies during spontaneous activity, it did not interfere with Peter's other activity.

He often mouthed a toy while grasping his feet, accomplishing a postural shift, or alertly watching persons and smiling and vocalizing in their direction. His tendency to respond with pleasure and adaptive movements to the sight and sound of things about him was most manifest during the developmental test and on the rare occasions when his mother's contact with him was fairly gentle.

DISCUSSION

Peter's pattern of experience and his style of functioning present an interesting extreme. What has been said so far does not provide an accurate picture of either the mother's behavior with her baby, or of the setting in which he had acquired such a distinct pattern of adaptation.

Peter's mother was a young woman who enjoyed her home, her children, social activities, and every opportunity to enlarge her experience, including the research sessions. Peter was the third child, and his mother was extraordinarily deft and skillful in handling him. The siblings were still very young (2 and 3 years old) and Peter's mother was equally active and intense and positive in her dealings with all three children. Despite small living quarters and stringent budget limitations, she ran a relaxed yet orderly home. Without help she managed to dress the children exquisitely, provide them with better than average medical care, and join many of her husband's athletic and social interests, and yet she did not seem harassed. An outstanding feature of her behavior with Peter was that, with a few exceptions, what she did and when she did it was almost unrelated to the baby's behavior at the moment. Except for feeding him when she had reason to believe him hungry, putting him to bed when he was sleepy, and picking him up when he seemed uncomfortable, she approached him when she felt like it. For instance, a favorite game was to tickle him, yet the mother herself commented that, unlike her other children, it seldom made him laugh. She picked him up to dance with him to phonograph music, she squeaked toys for him, she got the older children involved in playing with him, or she decided that it was time for him to learn to stand and held him to an upright posture at moments when he sat or lay in great contentment. All of this and a great deal more was done not only lovingly, but with a high level of interest in the baby as a social partner. She always placed herself in view and spoke to him, and she watched his smiles and sounds eagerly.

In terms of what we saw in other mother-baby couples, the combination of what struck us as a sort of blindness to behavioral clues provided by the baby, with impressive skill in maternal tasks and enormous pleasure in the baby, seemed incongruous. In view of Peter's ready responsiveness to mild and moderate approaches, and his tendency to become inert when stimulation was provided at high levels of intensity, the mother's pervasive tendency to do too much too often was also puzzling, especially since she was an accurate observer and often told us quite correctly how he would behave next. One sensed that this mother was compelled to overstimulate her baby by some needs not really related to maternal functioning. Even on relatively short acquaintance, she showed herself to be a person beset by anxieties and inner problems. She was inordinately fearful of bodily injury and illness (when the baby's back seemed sensitive to touch she was terrified at the thought that he had polio, and a slight respiratory difficulty was interpreted as a sign of asthma). She could not tolerate inactivity; when ill, she refused to remain in bed, she made the obstetrician discharge her three days earlier than he thought proper, and she was always busy doing something.

Neurotic difficulties of this sort are often observed to interfere with a satisfying mother-infant relationship, and, of course, with a well-adapted and satisfying style of life. If this was true of Peter's mother, it was so to a minimal degree.

Peter's experience involved frequent and pleasurable encounters with the mother, during which he did not reach peak excitation. Crying or other signs of overt distress occurred very rarely, so that he alternated between states of moderate animation as he played by himself for brief periods; states of distinct pleasure; rare and brief moments of discomfort; and long intervals of oblivion during sleep. He thus had few occasions to experience the mother in the context of relief from distress and, despite their frequent contact, Peter had little opportunity to experience true reciprocity with his mother. We never once saw either of Peter's parents imitate the baby or attempt to elicit imitative behavior from him. In other ways as well, Peter seldom had the experience that his action of the moment produced predictable or regular alterations in the behavior of the social partner. Whether he merely smiled or laughed aloud, whether he reached for the mother's face or averted his head, he was kissed, tickled, given toys, or played with anyway. He was offered constancy, in the sense that mother made herself felt in his awareness in particular and pleasure-yielding ways, but he met no reflection of his particular state or momentary behavior through what he saw or heard his mother do in consequence.[1]

These specific aspects of Peter's life experience may well explain aspects of his developmental course that have not yet been mentioned. Peter

[1] It is instructive to compare Peter's adaptation syndrome with that of Grace (Ac XIV). In reactivity and in the environmental setting, these two 28-week-olds had much in common. Both were developmentally advanced (Grace was more so), but in other ways their experience and their behavior differed widely. Peter's experience illustrates what we have called a *divergence* between maternal style and the infant's pattern of reactivity, in that mother provided chiefly the variety of stimulation (in this case intensity) to which he was least responsive. In Grace's case, the *convergence* between maternal style and the infant's reaction pattern was very marked. We think it not impossible that the great similarity between Grace and her mother arose on this basis, whereas Peter's style could not have been more different from that of his mother: she was volatile and energetic, he was imperturbable. Yet Peter's behavior can plausibly be regarded as an adaptation to the mother's style, just as Grace's patterns were thought to be a response to her mother.

showed marked distress during his first encounter with the strange observers, but once the stranger effect had been overcome he was the only baby in his age group who responded to the observers exactly as he did to the mother. In fact, his behavior with the observers was more animated and somewhat more mature, simply because the observers recognized that gentle but prolonged interchanges were most likely to maintain his interest. Similarly, Peter was among the babies whose capacity to participate in the exchange of communicatory signals was very limited. Unlike several of the other 28-week-olds, he did not turn toward mother when she was out of sight and address her with complaining or provocative sounds, nor did he respond to verbal signs from her unless she was close by and in view.

In summary, Peter's pattern of experience, as reflected by overt behavior regularities and by the kind, frequency and intensity of overt affect expression, was relatively stable, narrow in range, and characterized by the near absence of peak excitation—despite the fact that he lived in an objectively turbulent environment. His pattern seems possible only because he was not particularly reactive to stimulation in any sensory modality and because sensations from within the body rarely yielded excitation or distress (at least by the time we knew him). As neither oral activations nor other forms of bodily self-stimulation led to self-generated soothing, and as his mother's ways of comforting him are better described as distracting than as soothing (he had never been rocked, she said), his tendency to reduce responsiveness without losing all contact with the environment played a major role in his adaptive functioning. One wonders whether such partial withdrawal had a chance to emerge as a dominant mechanism precisely because this mother was so active and intrusive (according to self-report) at an age when infants often respond to excitation by drowsiness, sleep, or autistic withdrawal.

Billy, Ac XV (32 Weeks)

SPE DETERMINANTS

Boundary Strength

	ENTIRE		*MODALITY SECTORS*			
	Inner	*Outer*	*Vision*	*Touch*	*Sound*	*Passive Motion*
Stimulation	medium	variable	medium (—)	strong	weak (+)	?
Frequency of Mother-Child Contacts		high	low (+)	low (+)	high (—)	medium (+)
Intensity	low (+)	high	⟶	⟶	⟶	⟶
Maternal Competence		medium	⟶	⟶	⟶	⟶
Maternal Intrusiveness		high (—)	⟶	⟶	⟶	⟶
Level of Home Stimulation		medium	⟶	⟶	⟶	⟶

Activity Level: 3.0

STABLE PATTERNS OF EXPERIENCE

Frequency of strong bodily arousal: Medium.

More than any other baby in the sample, Billy experienced intense anger and distress as well as excited joy many times each day. However, in this child very extreme affect did not lead to all of the bodily signs of excitation that served us as criteria. It was his voice and facial expression and his patterns of motility that altered massively as he became extremely angry or very gay. Although he might flush and tightly fist his hands at such times, he did not arch his body, nor stiffen it, nor did he squirm or develop tremors. Thus his behavior, though obviously very aroused, did not fully meet the pre-defined criteria for peak levels of excitation.

Billy became very distressed and angry on each and every occasion when free movement was restrained. Since he was so very active, his entire day was punctuated by occasions when either a parent or a physical obstacle (playpen, door, sofa, etc.) prevented him from creeping, climbing, standing, or reaching for things as he was constantly impelled to do. Each routine caretaking procedure (except eating) turned into a battle because he would not hold still, and in the course of free play he constantly encountered physical obstacles to which he responded exactly as he did to restraining persons. When he did succeed in a difficult motor coordination (such as achieving the upright standing posture or climbing on a piece of furniture), he literally shrieked and jumped for joy—showing nearly as much excitement as in distress. Furthermore, playful interludes with either parent could also generate massive pleasure and excitation. Billy thus experienced an exceptionally large number of excited (though not usually at absolute peak levels) episodes each day, both of distress and of pleasure, and involving inanimate obstacles almost as often as they involved other human beings.

Internal bodily sensations: Fairly low.

What we observed in Billy conforms to the expectation based on the SPE constellation, which indicates low levels of inner somatic stimulation combined with an inner boundary of medium strength. Hunger brought no observable behavior change, though he ate eagerly once food was offered. Fatigue was typically prolonged (90 minutes was not exceptional) and greatly altered the quality of his behavior. However, this change took the form of restlessness, of increased oral behavior, and of intermittent drowsy spells during which he was very quiet. There was some whimpering or soft crying, but he did not show marked distress and he was rather more relaxed while sleepy than at other times. He did not engage in bodily self-stimulation (except while tired and then it did not occupy all of his attention), and he had none of the minor bodily ailments of infancy.

Balance between behavior activations due to inner and to outer stimulation: External very predominant.

Billy's behavior activations almost invariably occurred in response to the sight, sound and feel of things about him. Fatigue, as has been said, led to a reduction of behavior activations and to a change in pattern, but even then he remained alert and responsive to the environment most of the time. The single exception was his behavior during the daytime nap. He moved restlessly throughout; jerks and grimacing were frequent and occurred spontaneously as often as in response to sounds. (We were reliably assured that at nighttime he slept very soundly.)

Importance of distance receptors: High.

Billy was normally reactive to visual impressions and exceptionally sensitive to sound. In his turbulent environment he was not only exposed to all manner of visual and auditory events, but he was frequently and forcefully compelled by means of these modalities. His parents spoke to him constantly during all direct contacts, as well as from a distance. Not only did his mother happen to have a strident voice, but this modality was also emphasized by her use of voice quality more than word meaning to communicate. He heard her be playfully provocative, impatient, angry, anxiously pleading, commanding, and so forth—and when he vocalized, the parents often answered him in kind, imitating his vocal productions. Although vision was less prominently used by the mother, she was in view and highly expressive during their many contacts, and he was often shown toys and objects. He was not a baby given to intense regard as an activity in its own right, but almost all of his behavior was guided or incited by visual impressions.

Importance of near receptors: Fairly low.

This aspect of Billy's day-by-day experience was difficult to judge. It is certain that his mother did not emphasize the tactile modality though, of course, she touched and held him as was necessary for practical reasons. Billy was not seen to finger persons or objects as if to make or prolong tactile contact, nor did he show overt behavior changes in response to touch. Undoubtedly his vigorous activity created a constant background of kinesthetic sensations. But in the situation that allows one to assess reactivity—when mother rocked him—he was among the babies whose state and behavior did not alter in response (except as he fought the movement restraint it involved). All in all, it seemed to us that the near receptor systems were relatively unimportant in Billy's day-by-day experience.

Most prominent modality: Sound.

Least prominent modality: Touch.

Frequency of states of optimal animation: Moderate.

During direct encounters with his mother, Billy seldom if ever experienced optimal states of animation because, whether unhappy or joyous, they were always excitatory and too intense to permit the emergence of either complex integrations or harmonious reciprocity. However, when left to his own devices, Billy was often content, active, and intent on the practice of complex and novel bodily coordinations. These episodes of optimal animation occurred readily, but they were limited because his proclivity to attempt actions that he could not complete and his parents' mode of dealing with him soon put an end to periods of contented play.

OUTCOME RATINGS

Developmental status: Medium.

Billy's development corresponded to high average standards for his age in most respects and was advanced in one. His vocalizations and patterns of social responsiveness were in accord with average standards, while gross motor coordination was advanced. It should perhaps be mentioned that the examiner considered Billy capable of performing some of the items that were scored as failures. The baby became very excited during the test, not so much in response to continued presentation of toys as in response to their repeated removal from his grasp. He was a remarkably impatient baby and responded to the removal of objects as to an insult, screaming angrily each time. His intermittent irritability appeared to prevent him from the execution of fine motor coordinations of which he was in fact capable. The examiner recorded her clinical judgment that Billy probably possessed superior endowment that, due to marked fluctuations in mood, was not fully reflected in his test performance. A healthy and vigorous infant who is also very active has more than the usual opportunity to develop gross motor skills, and Billy's acceleration in this sphere was in no way surprising. The unevenness in other aspects of his development, especially his difficulty in performing actions that require the delay or partial inhibition of movement impulses, was probably related to some aspects of his day-by-day experience that have not yet been mentioned.

Billy's self-initiated adventures in exercising all his faculties on any accessible aspect of the environment were augmented and modified by the mother's very frequent efforts to direct his behavior and to teach him skills. Two aspects of her behavior seem especially relevant to the pattern of development we saw in Billy. One was that her high rating for intrusiveness was based on behavior that would be better described by the term "coercion." She frequently approached the baby and attempted to get him to perform a particular action quite unrelated to whatever he was doing, and without first motivating him in the desired direction. She would approach him and tell him in all seriousness to roll his ball, to say "dada," to stand, to leave a certain portion of the room, etc. She was affectionately energetic on these occasions, but if he initiated some other activity, she made no playful adaptation. She simply interrupted what he was doing and did her best to make him understand what she wanted. When observed (which was very often) the mother usually lost the game, in the sense that Billy either had no way of comprehending what she wanted or was not inclined toward that particular activity. Although many of these episodes were accompanied by smiles and laugher, and though they involved mutual regard and almost constant speech directed toward the baby, they necessarily involved intermittent irritability on both sides, and most certainly an absence of reciprocal behavior regulation. From the mother's point of view at least, they were a failure of communication.

The second characteristic aspect of the mother's behavior was more disruptive. She was teasing and provocative on many occasions, and we thought that she was totally unaware of the way in which she produced the very storms she said she was trying to prevent. What happened very frequently indeed was that she directed the baby's attention to a toy or an object, whereupon he of course moved toward it and tried to grasp it. When he was well under way she would remove the toy from his reach, and when he fussed she would try to direct his attention elsewhere. No sooner had she succeeded in so doing than she would again show the first toy, and as he eagerly approached it she would say reproachfully, "I told you you can't have it" and take it away. Her teasing went so far that she was seen to hand him something (for instance, a keyring), then take it from him ("You better not play with that") but leave it in sight, respond to his fussing by returning it, only to take it again, saying, "No, it's not a toy after all." In consequence, Billy frequently had the experience of failing to complete an action sequence, and more importantly, vigorous protest and bodily struggle were often his only means of getting back something that had been taken from him.

The fact that Billy's patterns of social responsiveness were relatively less advanced makes sense in view of the frequent failure of communication between him and his mother. From the point of view of Billy's experience it is important to note that for a good portion of each day he was cared for not by the mother (who was employed part time) but by the father (whose working hours had been adjusted to this necessity). In many respects, Billy's behavior and experience with his father were very similar to those with the mother. However, the father, who was nearly as stimulating as the mother, was never seen to tease or provoke the baby in this fashion. During that portion of each day, the number of occasions when Billy's irritation or excitement stemmed from provocative inconsistency on the parents' part was markedly reduced.

Adequacy of vegetative functioning: Medium.

Billy was a very healthy baby who avidly consumed exceptionally large amounts of food. The basis for judging vegetative functions to be less than optimally integrated was this: Although Billy slept soundly, at the age of 7 months he had not yet been able to sleep through a single night. He regularly awakened crying about one hour after his last bottle and went back to sleep after he had been burped. And again, he regularly awoke crying during the early morning hours (between 4:00 and 5:00 A.M.), at which time he had to be fed if he was to go back to sleep. In addition, each time he was fatigued, Billy experienced considerable difficulty and distress before he could finally go to sleep. During daytime naps he slept very lightly and restlessly.

Excitability: Medium.

By more general and common sense standards Billy would be described as a very excitable baby. As has already been described, at times of high pleasure and at times of annoyance and distress he squealed very loudly, he panted heavily, and his movements, though not tremulous, were very simple and maximally forceful actions, such as slapping his open hand against a hard surface or his own body so sharply that one felt it must have produced pain. Both pleasurable and distressing arousals were very frequent indeed, but the rating of "medium" was thought appropriate because loud squealing or enraged screaming were the most prominent signs of excitation. In his case excitement found overt bodily expression, but it was manifested vocally more than through the gross muscle system.

Irritability: High.

Billy was one of the very few distinctly irritable babies in the sample. As has already been reported, he responded with overt distress and active protest whenever movement was restrained. Equally consistent and even more intense was his anger when an object was removed from his grasp (and since he tended to approach and grasp any object in sight this was a frequent occurrence). Fatigue often led to irritable crying or squealing, as did the offer of a new variety of food on occasion. Finally, Billy reacted with intense annoyance whenever he attempted an action that he could not achieve. As with other active babies, this applied to his efforts to grasp an unattainable object (for instance, when he tried to pluck from the sofa fabric a highly colored area depicting a flower), to overcome a barrier such as the bars of the playpen or a closed door, or to climb up on a piece of furniture. Thus, Billy's waking day was punctuated by frequent episodes of irritable behavior, very often induced not by what the parents did or failed to do, but by the discrepancy between his vigorous action impulses and his motoric capacities. The intensity of such distress varied from moderate to extremely high, but its duration always was brief. Typically, he squealed or cried angrily, and mother came and succeeded in diverting him by active play or by putting him in a situation that allowed unhampered locomotion. Or he fussed and cried as he failed to reach a particular object or position, but within less than a minute he had initiated some other and pleasurable type of activity. As will be described more fully later, routine caretaking situations nearly always led to distress and irritability on Billy's part.

Pleasure in functioning: High.

Billy's zest and pleasure in applying all his energy to an activity that presented real difficulty was extraordinary. He derived intense pleasure from unhindered locomotion, which he pursued whenever possible. For instance, he was often seen to throw a toy, creep after it very rapidly, pick it up, bang it forcefully, throw it again, and follow it at once. This was accompanied by gleeful squeals, and often he briefly turned to anyone who was nearby and smiled broadly or laughed aloud. He was equally delighted when he succeeded in pulling himself to a standing position or in walking while holding onto something with both hands. Again, upon accomplishment he often turned his head until he located the mother or one of the observers, whom he regarded in a delighted and, as it were, triumphant manner. All observers agreed with a statement made by both parents—that Billy was at his very happiest at moments when he had succeeded in a difficult feat of bodily coordination.

DISCUSSION

Billy has been described as a well-developed and healthy infant whose pattern of adaptation and functioning was unusual, and less than optimal. Despite frequent episodes of friction with the social and physical environment, and the attendant distress for all concerned, Billy was regarded by his parents and by the research staff as a difficult but thriving baby. During encounters with the parents and with the inanimate environment he experienced joyous excitation as often as distress, and he availed himself of every opportunity for directly gratifying experience. What he lacked, and what we think led to the unevenness of developmental progress, was recurrent periods of very moderate animation that might have served to consolidate developmental gains and to facilitate the development of self-regulating mechanisms that could have enabled him to better tolerate delay and frustration.

The stormy nature of his day-by-day experience and the relative lack of reciprocal exchanges in a pleasurable context affected aspects of his development other than cognition, and must have played a large role in producing a high level of irritability. He did show a negative response to first encounters with a stranger, but thereafter he showed less behavioral discrimination between the mother and all other persons than do most 7-

month-old babies (in this sample, as well as in general). In fact, such discrimination as he showed appeared to be responsive to the mother's behavior at the moment (which was markedly different from that of all others), more than it was selective on his part. Further, he lacked variety and resourcefulness in many situations, as well. He laughed and squealed gaily when pleased and squealed angrily or screamed when distressed, but more subtle or transitional facial expressions were rare. He was not seen to evade or circumvent obstacles (either physical or social), but met them head-on, and he rarely had available more than one means of achieving a desired end. Despite its vividness, his behavior thus had a somewhat stereotyped quality, and despite his impressive physical competence, he was more dependent on parental help than are a great many of his peers.

These disadvantages to smooth adaptation were matched by many aspects of parental style. Billy was the firstborn child of young parents who were devoted to one another and to the baby, but who had to cope with a good many internal and external difficulties. The mother obviously was what she described herself to be, a tense and anxious person. The real difficulties of combining part-time work with running a home and managing a baby were somewhat overwhelming to her. She openly voiced concern about her ability to control the baby and to give him a happy childhood, such as she herself had not enjoyed. She spared no trouble, enjoyed the baby, and was proud of him, while at the same time she was impatient and easily angered. These conflicting feelings found expression not only in her tendency to tease and provoke, which has been described, but also in many other ways. She lacked resourcefulness and the capacity to adapt means to ends flexibly—just as the baby did. For instance, both she and the father found it necessary to completely immobilize Billy during all procedures except feeding. Not uncommonly, it took both parents to hold down the baby while one of them pulled articles of clothing on or off. This appeared to us a matter of ineptness, in that the mother did not seem to have the knack of allowing extensive movement of part of his body, nor did either parent know how to distract his attention at such times. (On the single occasion when one of the observers managed to partially clothe him without the mother's help, Billy fussed intermittently, but most of the time he happily played with an object and seemed reasonably content kicking his legs while being maneuvered into the sleeves.)

Another aspect of family style may be important in understanding how Billy's pattern of adaptation came about. As has been said, the parents had so arranged their working schedules that they completely shared his care. There was no aspect of maternal care that Billy did not receive from the father as often as from the mother, whether it was being fed, put to sleep, toiletted, or bathed. The parents were so intent on maintaining consistency that even when both were present, nothing was done without consultation. In consequence, observers felt that in this household parental roles were not only merged in external ways, but neither parent was able to respond to the baby quite spontaneously, because each of them was so conscious of their contract to deal with any situation that arose in accord with techniques decided in advance.

In Billy we observe an example of convergence between infantile reaction patterns and parental style that failed to yield mutual accommodation in many ways. He was sound-sensitive and was spoken to loudly and in an affect-laden manner almost continuously. He was dependent on body movement as a condition of well-being, and he experienced a confusing mixture of no restraint whatever and unduly stringent restraint on some occasions. He tended to be roused beyond optimal levels in the course of self-generated activity, and nearly every contact with the parents led to further excitation. He was not highly discriminating perceptually, and his life experience was one that, at least in important social relationships, was less differentiated than is usual.

In the adaptation syndromes of other highly stimulated babies in the sample, it has been possible to identify behavior regulations on the infant's part that served to modulate or reduce excitation. In some (for instance, Peter—In XIV), the ready appearance of fatigue and a tendency to sleep more than most appeared to serve this function. In other babies (for instance, Grace—Ac XIV) bodily self-stimulation in the form of oral behavior and rocking served to partially screen the baby from continued external stimulation or to contain the discharge of bodily excitation. In yet others, certain maternal soothing techniques were effective; for instance, being rocked in the crib, a swing, or the mother's arms. Billy appeared to lack both the capacity to evade excessive stimulation and the capacity for self-soothing. His mother frequently attempted to quiet him by energetic rocking in her arms (this is what led to a medium rating for the frequency of kinesthetic stimulation). Yet when observed, Billy never quieted in consequence. Whether thumbsucking could have served to soothe, we do not know, for the parents had agreed to always remove his thumb from the mouth. For whatever reason, Billy showed less bodily self-stimulation than many other babies, and such mouthing as he did occurred almost only when he was fatigued and then had no quieting effect.

Martin, In XV (32 Weeks)

SPE DETERMINANTS

Boundary Strength

	ENTIRE		*MODALITY SECTORS*			
	Inner	*Outer*	*Vision*	*Touch*	*Sound*	*Passive Motion*
Stimulation	strong	medium	medium	medium	weak	medium
Frequency of Mother-Child Contacts		medium	low (+)	medium (+)	medium	medium
Intensity	medium	high (−)	→	→	→	→
Maternal Competence		medium	→	→	→	→
Maternal Intrusiveness		medium	→	→	→	→
Level of Home Stimulation		high (−)	→	→	→	→

Activity Level: 1.6

STABLE PATTERNS OF EXPERIENCE

Frequency of strong bodily arousal: Absent.

Martin was not seen or reported to show maximal bodily arousal in any situation. Hunger did not lead to any observable behavior change (he was well adapted to a 4-hour schedule); fatigue brought restlessness and whimpering of very short duration (seldom more than 5 minutes); he experienced no pain or discomfort due to other somatic factors; and the exceedingly vigorous manner in which he was dealt with by both parents and an active preschool age sibling was distinctly arousing to him, but not to an extreme degree.

Internal bodily sensations: Low.

As has been said, neither hunger nor fatigue brought massive or prolonged behavior changes. He had no bodily discomforts, and even the fact that a tooth was in the process of erupting did not seem to make itself felt (mouthing was not intense, he was not irritable or restless in the least). He was reported to cry out occasionally as if in pain, but "bubbling" or a position change always brought relief.

Balance between behavior activations due to inner and to outer stimulation: External very predominant.

Martin was seldom left to his own devices for any length of time—the highly sociable and intensely stimulating parents and the active sibling saw to that. However, even during the brief periods of spontaneous activity, Martin's behavior was generally directed toward aspects of the environment, including his own feet (which he grasped and manipulated much as he did some toys). Behavior activations typically occurred in response to both the social and the inanimate environment. Only rarely did sounds or sights inhibit ongoing activity, and soothing did not occur (because he did not become distressed).

Importance of distance receptors: Fairly high.

Martin was highly reactive to sound, and his mother used her voice as well as other sounds (kissing, clucking, noise-generating toys) with fair frequency and with exceptional intensity. The baby was not given to prolonged intent gazing, nor did he respond to inconspicuous visual details. However, his orientation to the environment was guided by visual perceptions, and not only were his surroundings highly animated, but he was supplied with toys and placed in positions that encouraged visual exploration (*i.e.,* the highchair or the playpen were placed in such a way that he could readily observe family activities).

Importance of near receptors: Fairly high.

During direct contact with the mother (as well as the father), he was rolled, tickled, bounced and generally moved about a great deal, and the mother's style of performing routine caretaking tasks was very rough. Tactile and kinesthetic sensations must have been vivid at such times. Martin did not show tactile or kinesthetic self-stimulation at any time, and the number of direct body contacts with the mother was not exceptionally great.

Most prominent modality: Sound.

Least prominent modality: None.

Frequency of states of optimal animation: Moderate.

Left to his own devices, Martin was not lethargic, but content in employing easy and well-learned behavior integrations of very limited scope. However, despite the mother's vigorous manner, her interactions with the baby almost always roused him to high levels of animation and responsiveness. The same could not be said of the sibling's approaches to the baby, nor of the father's.

OUTCOME RATINGS

Developmental status: Medium.

Martin was in fact somewhat advanced in several areas, but the discrepancy between his score and standards for his age was moderate. He achieved all items at his own age level, a number of items at the 36-week level, and a few isolated items not usually achieved until the age of 40 weeks. Delicate manipulation of small objects and discriminatory attention were relatively less advanced than were fairly simple manipulations that produce clear-cut effects. For instance, he disregarded the pellet inside a glass bottle (36 weeks), but he quickly learned how to grasp the bell by the handle in order to produce a ringing sound. His vocalizations and the pattern of his social response did not exceed average standards for his age, nor did gross motor coordination.

Martin responded to the testing situation with pleasure, animation, and ready interest in each object offered. Throughout, he thoroughly enjoyed the social interaction with the examiner and never showed a complete absorption in play with the objects, as some other babies do. He was pleased rather than excited, and he showed no annoyance when toys were removed from his grasp, provided he was spoken to or given a substitute.

We see in Martin a fairly inactive baby who made excellent developmental progress in a family setting that provided him with a great deal of stimulation. Although his mother's direct contacts with the baby were not as frequent as in many other baby-mother couples, she maintained constant vigilance toward him. She did not believe in unnecessary holding or in rocking, and she went to comfort him only if he failed to settle down of his own accord. She was one of the mothers who thought it desirable to teach a baby "independence" by encouraging him to overcome minor upsets without help. She also was a didactic mother who attempted to teach her baby specific skills, apparently with some success. For instance, she thought that he ought to be standing, and repeatedly each day placed him in that position and verbally encouraged him to "hang on" to the railing. She put the bottle just beyond his reach, urging him to "come and get it" and the like.

This inactive baby was relatively most advanced in behaviors involving vigorous manipulations to produce clear-cut perceptual effects, and not so far along (though within the normal range) in fine coordinations and discriminations. His developmental pattern may well be related to the circumstance that so many of his interactions with the mother were reciprocal in the sense that the mother adapted her behavior to the infant's mode of response, but they rarely involved modulated or subtle exchanges. Mutual gazing was not observed except momentarily; mutual imitation of vocal patterns never developed fully because the mother's contribution soon drowned the baby's sounds; she was not seen to show him a toy merely to look at, and so forth.

Adequacy of vegetative functioning: High.

Martin ate well, slept well, and had no painful gastric troubles; his skin color was excellent and his behavior and appearance were such as to lead observers to describe him as "vibrant with life." His bodily well-being was the more impressive because throughout the first six months of life, he had experienced a good deal of illness and bodily discomfort. During the first three months he vomited extensively (projectile). He had also had a number of severe colds and the chicken pox (between three and six months), as well as occasional skin rashes. We were impressed by the fact that although his gums were swollen due to teething, and although he had a few skin lesions in the region of the groin, and although his most recent cold had ended only a week before, none of the vital vegetative functions appeared to be impaired in any way.

Excitability: Low.

As has already been described, Martin responded to the mother's rough and ready handling with pleasure and some animation, but no signs of strong bodily arousal. The same was true when he was played with forcefully and during the pediatric examination and the ratings, which involved prolonged handling of a gentler sort. He manifested a degree of muscle tension on only one occasion. This was when mother, to demonstrate his good nature, removed the nipple from his mouth as he was sucking, and hid the bottle behind her back. Martin looked at her tensely, puckered up his face, extended both arms which then trembled markedly, and finally began to cry.

Martin's day-by-day existence yielded brief periods of low level animation (spontaneous activity) and moderately frequent states of high animation, but only moderate excitation as judged by the usual bodily manifestations. Relatively strong excitation occurred almost always together with high pleasure, though occasionally (with the sibling) it entailed short-lived periods of distress.

Irritability: Low.

As implied in what has already been said, Martin was notable for the absence of irritability. He not only tolerated vigorous manipulations of his person, but showed remarkable equanimity in general. Though acutely teething, he was content and not the least bit restless. What we observed was in complete accord with the mother's claim that Martin was exceptionally good natured and never cried except in pain (a condition that had occurred in the past when he was ill, but not during the time when he was under observation).

Pleasure in functioning: Medium.

When left to his own devices (which was seldom, because the sibling was near even when the mother was not close by), he occupied himself in the exercise of simple well-learned schemas. He regarded and fingered nearby objects, but neither reached for distant ones nor moved objects about in space. Occasionally he grasped his feet and pulled at the booties, or briefly attained the hand-knee creeping posture. However, his response when someone offered playful attention was vivid and highly pleasurable; he babbled, reached for the partner, and made other relatively mature responses. Similarly, when mother held out a toy only to place it just beyond his reach (as she often did to encourage locomotion) he again showed not only pleasure but persistence in his efforts to obtain it, activating quite advanced patterns of coordination. The same was true to a striking degree during the developmental test. In other words, pleasure in functioning, as it refers to the spontaneous tendency to activate mastery activities, was minimal. But in response to appropriate environmental prodding, his tendency to respond in ways that constitute learning and lead to mastery was impressive.

DISCUSSION

Martin's adaptation syndrome is noteworthy in several respects. He was a baby who was in poor health during much of early infancy, yet he developed well and harmoniously (by which we mean that development was uniform and his functioning in general was stable). In addition, he was exposed to more massive and intrusive stimulation than most babies, yet he appeared to thrive on it (whereas several of the other overstimulated babies developed protective devices or responded with irritability).

Martin's mother was a husky, vigorous, and outgoing young woman. In spite of the fact that the family was poor and likely to remain so, and in spite of significant health problems in the family, she thoroughly enjoyed her children and planned to have more as soon as possible. Our interest in babies seemed perfectly natural to her, and she made the most of the outings to project quarters, responding to us, to the equipment in the office, to our visits to her home with vivid curiosity about who we were and what we did—not about why we did it or what it might lead to. She was equally free to express discouragement and fearfulness when occasion warranted—for instance, when Martin was unwell, the weather was bad, and it just seemed impossible for her to do what needed to be done that day. This description may help make intelligible some features of this mother's behavior that, we believe, played a major role in enabling Martin to adapt to a rather turbulent pattern of existence.

As has been said, she related to both her children in an active, responsive, affectionate, didactic manner. Although she failed to respond to minor behavioral clues emanating from the baby, she was continually and spontaneously responsive to his state and his needs as she perceived them. She was aware of his sensitivity to sound and even to the implications of his low activity level ("he is lazy"). Her typical response was not to accept these behavior tendencies but to counteract them. For instance, she volunteered that when Martin was a tiny baby, noises frightened him. She decided that he must get used to noises and deliberately made whistling or clucking sounds close to his ear. Proudly she said that the same things that used to make him cry now made him laugh. Moreover, she kept the radio on all day because she had noticed that "if it is too quiet he'll jump at every little noise, but when the radio is on he doesn't notice." Similarly, if the baby was disinclined to locomote or to put toys to active use, it was up to her to provoke him lovingly but firmly to more extensive activity. In Martin's experience an action sequence, once begun, was rarely thwarted.

And each time he succeeded in obtaining a toy, in standing momentarily, and the like, his success was greeted with intense pleasure by both the mother and the father. If he seemed uncomfortable (for instance, while sliding from the sitting posture, while standing with support and unable to get down, or as his leg was caught between the bars of the crib), he was neither ignored nor immediately relieved. Instead, the mother spoke to him encouragingly and did not come to his rescue until she had got him at least to try to overcome the difficulty. If she teased him, as by holding out the bottle to the hungry baby, it was always in a context that terminated in a manner highly gratifying to him. Many of Martin's contacts with the mother were of a kind that briefly delayed need gratification but did not withhold it; that aroused action impulses but did not frustrate them. In a baby who was spared arousal and distress in consequence of the dissonance between spontaneous action impulses and physical barriers, many maternal interventions (which in the case of other children can lead to overstimulation and distress) thus served to rouse him to age-appropriate and pleasure-yielding behaviors.

Another aspect of the mother's style accounts for the circumstance that in this baby's experience such a very large proportion of encounters with the mother (and equally with the father) led to overt and intense pleasure. During play and at other times, the mother used a vigorous manner. She yanked him about, up-ended him at will, and bounced, poked, and tossed him about freely. Throughout she laughed and spoke to him in a rousing manner. Yet during these encounters the behavior of each partner was attuned to that of the other. As the baby smiled, chuckled, squealed, and reached for her, the mother would repeat the same procedure to evoke the same response, or else she would elaborate and intensify the game until it reached its climax, accompanied by laughter on both sides. Although subtle and minute behavioral exchange was lacking, reciprocal behavior on a cruder level was a significant element in Martin's life. The pattern of achievement on developmental test items makes good sense viewed in this light; for his dealings with inanimate objects and the perceptual environment were of the same quality as both his and her behavior during highly pleasurable mother-baby contacts.

We think that the quality of Martin's experience had additional consequences for the course of his development. For instance, in comparison with other babies of the same age (with the exception of Curt, Ac XVI, whose development was significantly advanced in all respects), Martin was conspicuous for his ability to employ and respond to communicatory signals. When he whimpered and his mother spoke to him pleasantly, he became content and looked at her expectantly. And mother was able to demonstrate to us that he responded to "No, no," although it must have been the mother's tone of voice that conveyed the prohibition. He was quite often seen to turn around until he had sighted the mother, and then to address her by sound and gesture unmistakably "asking" her to approach. In a manner unusual in one so young, he more than once turned around while he was playing with a toy and held it out in her direction while smiling broadly, as if to show her what he was doing or somehow involve her in a situation that was clearly gratifying to him. In other words, the mother's tendency to communicate with him at moments when his attention and energy were outwardly focused (encouraging him to approach the bottle or to accomplish a position shift, and also prohibiting certain actions) and her tendency to rely on the spoken word (from the baby's point of view, characteristic voice inflections), combined with his sensitivity to sounds, may have set the stage for a comparatively early emergence of the capacity to respond to (and use) conventional communication signals. This notion finds some support in the fact that Martin was among the babies who not only responded to a voice when the speaker was out of sight, but also responded differentially to the mother's voice and those of the women observers. Yet Martin was the only one of the 32-week-old babies who made no response whatsoever to first encounter with strange persons (though he discriminated mother from all others). In the social realm as well, the more differentiated and less immediate varieties of responsiveness were less well developed than was the type of behavior that is a specific response to the impact of immediate perceptual input, and that evokes familiar and immediate consequences.

Curt, Ac XVI (32 Weeks)

SPE DETERMINANTS

Boundary Strength

	ENTIRE		*MODALITY SECTORS*			
	Inner	*Outer*	*Vision*	*Touch*	*Sound*	*Passive Motion*
Stimulation	strong	medium	medium	medium	strong	weak
Frequency of Mother-Child Contacts		high	medium (+)	medium (−)	medium	high (−)
Intensity	low	medium (−)	⟶	⟶	⟶	⟶
Maternal Competence		high	⟶	⟶	⟶	⟶
Maternal Intrusiveness		low	⟶	⟶	⟶	⟶
Level of Home Stimulation		medium (+)	⟶	⟶	⟶	⟶

Activity Level: 3.0

STABLE PATTERNS OF EXPERIENCE

Frequency of strong bodily arousal: Rare.

Curt cried or whimpered and showed considerable restlessness both when hungry and when tired. However, peak level excitations as we defined the term were not seen to occur, nor were they reported. In part this was because he was highly responsive to soothing (by rocking) and his mother intervened before massive arousal could take place. Like other extremely active 7-month-olds, Curt registered annoyance and distress when he was unable to complete an action or encountered obstacles. However, instead of very high levels of arousal, he usually showed moderate distress, plaintive rather than protesting in quality, and quickly overcome. So far as we could ascertain, massive excitation occurred only on the very rare occasions when he encountered obstacles while also fatigued, and when his mother was not immediately available to comfort him.

Internal bodily sensations: Low.

Fatigue and hunger did affect Curt's behavior, but not massively nor for long. He was exceedingly healthy, and even acute teething, which was present while we knew him, may have increased the amount of oral play but did not interfere with comfortable and alert responsiveness to all situations that came his way.

Balance between behavior activations due to inner and to outer stimulation: External very predominant.

This aspect of experience is less relevant for infants above the age of 6 months than for younger ones (except for extreme cases in which internal sensations loom unusually large). Curt remained responsive to the environment even during bodily need states. The perception of things and of people about characteristically led to movements of approach or to manipulation, *i.e.,* to behavior activations. During his frequent contacts with his mother, he often became less active than he had been before (in soothing and in some playful episodes), but on many occasions such a lessening of excitation led to a change in the *kind* of behavior activation, rather than to a suppression of active responsiveness.

Importance of distance receptors: Fairly high.

As is to be expected by the age of 32 weeks, a very large portion of Curt's behavior was guided by visual and auditory components of the total situation. At times contact between the mother and the baby was maintained by vision, or by voice and vision only. But during most of his encounters with the parents, both distance and near receptors came into play. Except for rare but intense moments of mutual gazing, Curt was not given to visual regard as a primary activity. And, except in a social context, he behaviorally ignored all but very sharp sounds.

Importance of near receptors: High.

This mother touched her baby freely, and very occasionally and lightly introduced tactile varieties of play, but prolonged or intense touch was not a conspicuous component of the interaction. Nor was Curt a baby who tended to create tactile contact, though he did at times vigorously manipulate part of the mother's body (by grasping hard, or inserting his fingers into her mouth). However, the kinesthetic modality was primary during both playful episodes and the frequent soothing contacts. He was not rocked, but rhythmic and forceful bouncing and swaying were constantly used. In addition, bouncing was one of Curt's dominant schemas (both when happy and with discomfort) and he frequently provided this sensation for himself, whereas tactile self-stimulation did not occur.

Most prominent modality: Kinesthetic.

Least prominent modality: None.

Frequency of states of optimal animation: High.

Curt was the sort of baby who, when left to his own devices, was very often animated, outwardly focused, and yet exceedingly well integrated, thus meeting the criteria for optimal states of animation. In addition, the mother tended to sustain and intensify this very state during direct interactions with the baby, often calming him by helping him perform a highly coordinated action or by removing distracting circumstances or obstacles.

OUTCOME RATINGS

Developmental status: High.

Curt's development was distinctly accelerated in all but one area of functioning. At the age of 7½ months, his motor coordination, both gross and fine, corresponded to normative standards for 9-month-old infants. He crept easily and rapidly, pulled himself to standing, and could "walk" by holding on to a piece of furniture with both hands. One of his favorite pastimes was to walk across the room with both hands held by an adult. To a degree seldom seen in babies less than 8 months of age, the supporting hands served only to maintain his balance, while he himself performed the coordinated walking motions. He had no difficulty grasping a small pellet or a thin piece of string using thumb-index finger opposition (40-week items on the Gesell) so that fine coordination was also advanced. When it came to the sustained use of several objects at one time, his performance was closer to average standards, though he succeeded with three of five such items at the 36-weeks level (Gesell Schedules). He was attentive to visual detail on some occasions; for instance, he noted small holes in a large pegboard and explored them with extended fingers (a 10-months item on the Cattell scale). In other contexts, for instance, a small pellet inside a glass bottle, he may have noted the inconspicuous object but was more interested in vigorous play with other things. It was the examiner's distinct impression that in a situation such as being given several blocks, he was capable of some of the coordinations that are normative at 36 and 40 weeks, but was so fascinated by the game of throwing with the expectation that the toy would be restored that he failed to perform them.[1]

The one area in which Curt's behavior did not exceed average standards for his age was vocalization. Neither single syllables nor multiple ones were heard (these are 32- and 36-weeks items). Instead, he uttered expressive vowel sounds and squealed frequently. He was capable of imitating sounds (a 36-week item), but what he imitated were particular singsong-like inflections and not specific combinations of consonants and vowels. We thought this relative lack in the use of differentiated sound of special interest in a baby whose SPE specifies the auditory modality as least vivid in his experience.

Curt responded to the testing situation with delight and considerable excitement. Throughout, he remained highly responsive to the examiner and to the mother, alternating between socially oriented behavior and vigorous use of the toys. No sooner did he see an object than he moved toward it (no delay between perception and motoric response), and he preferred banging, waving, and the like to more contemplative modes of dealing with the toys. The shiny cup and mirror and the bright metal bell, which he rang delightedly for as long as he was permitted, were far more interesting to him than small objects and those of neutral coloring. On most occasions he was unperturbed when a toy was taken from his hand, and at once turned to the substitute provided. However, he cried each time the bell was removed from his grasp, showing a very strong reaction to the loss of this particular toy.

Adequacy of vegetative functioning: High.

All bodily processes seemed to function with exceptional smoothness and adequacy in this child. He was still breast-fed and nursed eagerly and well, and welcomed solid feedings also. He had never experienced gastric troubles nor illness of any sort. He fell asleep easily, slept soundly, and had slept through the night since the age of about 6 weeks. In short, it would be difficult to find a child whose behavior conveyed a sense of bodily well-being more consistently than did Curt's.

Excitability: Low.

Curt was not an excitable baby, which is rare in an exceedingly active infant. However, this rating must be understood in light of the particular criteria that had been selected for the definition of excitability. Curt did show excitement by loud squealing and by vigorous coordinated bouncing and jumping. However, muscle tension was not observed, nor arching of the back, nor a loss of motor coordination. In his case, bodily arousal found expression in well-contained behavior activations and did not lead

[1] This first clinical impression was borne out by the formal behavior analysis performed more than ten years later. Certain complex object schemas, such as bringing two objects into contact with one another and attending three objects at the same time, occurred fairly frequently during spontaneous activity, and rarely or not at all during the developmental test.

to the disruption of muscular coordination specified by our criteria. In addition, the low rating for excitability was based on the fact that certain events that can provoke strong excitation in many babies failed to do so in his case. This was particularly true of situations when he came to grief as he fell in the course of vigorous play or was unable to complete an action successfully. At such times, he was observed to cry or whimper (and not to squeal or scream angrily), and at once he crept toward the mother who was nearly always able to comfort him.

Irritability: Low.

Curt played contentedly for prolonged periods of time; routine caretaking procedures such as being dressed or diapered were nearly always pleasurable episodes, despite the transient restraint of movement they involved. In fact, when mother performed caretaking routines, they usually induced a calmer state than that which had prevailed before. He was teething at the time, and though his mother thought this made him fussy, he showed displeasure or discomfort so seldom and so briefly that a rating of "low" was still appropriate.

In large measure, Curt's good nature and his capacity to be extraordinarily active and yet seldom massively excited were made possible by the mother's remarkably skillful accommodation to his behavioral style. She minimized the movement restraint in caretaking routines in many ways. For instance, while dressing him she allowed brief pauses during which he moved about freely, confident that he would return to her as she called him. Even during nursing she allowed him to slip off her lap, creep about a while, and then return for a second or third helping. Also, before any major step in a procedure (sleeves, trouser legs, tying his shoelaces, etc.), she initiated some sort of game that held his attention long enough for her to accomplish the task. Her sheer manual skill in "catching him on the run" and her easy confidence and relaxed manner, even when he was being difficult, contributed to the fact that what developed was not a struggle but an animated, largely pleasurable, yet rather casual episode of social interaction.

Pleasure in functioning: High.

Curt was notable for the amount of energy he expended in practicing new and as yet difficult behavior integrations and for the pleasure he derived from mastery activities in general. Locomotor feats, such as pulling himself to standing and walking with support, were dominant while we knew him. Yet they did not replace an interest in the varied and vigorous manipulation of objects and in the exploration of their properties. Typically he combined the two. For instance, he especially enjoyed pulling himself to standing by holding on to a side table or a chair. As often as not, he arrived at this position toy in hand and, once upright, he banged or slapped the toy upon the hard surface, rhythmically and so as to produce a maximum of sound. While so doing he beamed happily, looked at various persons in the room, and squealed at them gaily, unmistakably conveying a sense of keen pleasure and something akin to pride or triumph. For another example, he was remarkably persistent in the exploration of unfamiliar objects. He crept toward the tangle of electric cords located beneath the stabilimeter table, and, patiently, his mother retrieved him on many occasions (usually by holding out an attractive object and calling him persistently). In addition, each time he moved in the direction of the table, everyone present tried to deflect him from his course by providing attractive alternatives. But even though he allowed himself to be distracted if an adult acted soon enough, he managed to explore the dangerous area thoroughly by dint of returning to it many times. What he did was to move so quickly that no one realized what he was doing until he had already crept beneath the table. He maintained this interest for 2½ hours, returning to it after long intervals.

As has already been described, Curt also showed a great deal of zest in responding to appropriate and specific stimulation, and at such times showed complex patterns of behavior; for instance, during the developmental test, when the mother played with him using objects, and during relatively intense episodes of social play with the mother. As an example of the latter, it may be mentioned that he had been taught to perform the motions that go with "pat-a-cake," "bye-bye," and "so big." The mother compellingly said the appropriate words, and Curt would look sober and somewhat tense as she assumed a waiting attitude and repeated the purely verbal clue. Finally, he brought his hands together in a clapping motion (or stretched both arms upward for "so big") and then smiled very broadly and looked somehow relieved as his mother beamed approval. The formal ratings of the prominence of complex object schemas in his behavior reflect the same state of affairs. The prominence of complex object schemas during spontaneous activity was the second highest among the babies in Group Three, and during object stimulation he received the very highest prominence score for complex object schemas.

DISCUSSION

Curt was an exceptionally well-developed and well-functioning infant, and the only exceedingly active baby in our sample who was neither irritable nor excitable. His pattern of adaptation lends itself to comparison with that of Billy (Ac XV), who was of the same age and who was equally active. Yet, the moment-by-moment and the day-by-day experience of these two babies was very different indeed—as was developmental outcome.

Curt, like Billy, was dependent on gross motor activity as a condition of well-being, and spent most of his waking time on the floor. Also, like Billy, the sight of objects (and in Curt's case, frequently of persons) at once led to movements of approach and to active manipulation where this was possible. He constantly got into situations that endangered household furnishings and, of course, himself. Both mothers were continually extricating the baby from precarious situations. And both children registered distress when they fell down or when they were unable to perform a motoric feat too difficult for them. The manner in which Curt's mother dealt with this situation was remarkable for the way in which she avoided friction. For instance, we witnessed at least a hundred episodes of maternal intervention and never once heard the word "no." Mother often initiated an activity that proved more beguiling to the baby than what he had been about to do just before. Interestingly, these distracting maneuvers almost always utilized behavior schemas that were very prominent in Curt's repertoire. For instance, Curt liked to bang objects on hard surfaces, and we repeatedly saw his mother divert his interest from dangerous activity by banging any handy object on a convenient surface—inviting him, by her manner and her words, to join her and to take over. Quite often, she did not physically approach the baby, but called to him in a compelling and inviting manner, usually holding out an interesting object, or else telling him to come so that she could "change his breeches" or give him a drink of water. (Although Curt could not understand the content of her words, he was surely affected by the circumstance that she never focused attention, verbal or otherwise, on the forbidden thing, but only on the alternative.) If it was necessary for mother to act very quickly, she called out to him in a friendly manner while moving toward him and then initiated one of the sure-fire games, such as letting him walk or holding his hands and bouncing him. When Curt did come to grief in his conflicts with the inanimate environment, he tended to show more distress than annoyance. At such times, he crept toward the mother to be comforted.[2]

In fact, the major differences in the manner in which Curt and Billy experienced the consequences of their extraordinary need to move are intelligible in light of the different ways in which each one experienced contact with his mother. Curt would not have been likely to approach his mother when he was distressed unless he had frequently felt relief from discomfort while she held him. Indeed, Curt was rated as highly soothable because each time the mother sought to calm and comfort him, she succeeded. The frequency of successful soothing cannot be ascribed entirely to the mother's skill, for Curt was rated as having a weak outer boundary for the kinesthetic sector. Rocking, swinging, and bouncing always altered his behavior, more frequently toward quiescence, but on occasion also to provoke pleasure combined with a degree of excitement. (It will be remembered that Billy's mother rocked her baby when he was distressed, but

[2] We recognize a tendency to wax lyric in the description of this mother, as well as in some others. No doubt at times she used direct prohibition and otherwise departed from the patterns of behavior described in the text. However, the behavior episodes we did observe cannot be produced at will. The mutual responsiveness between this mother and her baby must have developed over time as the result of the totality of encounters between these two people.

to no avail.) Beyond the act of soothing, Curt's frequent direct encounters with the mother nearly always led to a decrease in activity accompanied by signs of partial relaxation. All of Billy's contacts with his mother—including the highly pleasurable ones (except feeding)—increased his excitation level. Thus, in Curt's repetitive experience, his mother functioned to induce relative calmness, whereas Billy's mother functioned to arouse him. This fact does seem to be largely the consequence of maternal style, in that Curt's mother was neither intense nor vigorous in her manner, and anything but intrusive, while Billy's mother was highstrung, coercive and provocative. Even here a difference in reaction tendency may have played some role, for Curt had exceptional tolerance for sound (strong boundary), whereas Billy was vulnerable in the same area (weak boundary).

Another facet of the interaction pattern between Curt and his mother is important. A large number of the contacts between these two seemed casual, though mutually pleasurable. However, for brief moments we observed very intense and intimate contact also. In such situations as diapering, and typically toward the end of breast feeding, mother brought her face close to that of the baby, quietly smiling. Curt's eyes were riveted on his mother's face, he became nearly immobile, and during such mutual gazing and smiling episodes, neither partner moved nor made a sound. When observed, these "love scenes" never lasted more than about 30 seconds, but during them both mother and baby were totally absorbed and seemed unaware of their surroundings.

One last circumstance should be mentioned as contributing to the sharp difference in the stable patterns of experience for these two babies. Curt had almost no experience of bodily discomfort. Even hunger and fatigue seldom led to overt distress, he was singularly free from gastric troubles, and he had never been ill. Billy, on the other hand, had been colicky during his first three months and had suffered several fairly severe respiratory infections. Further, fatigue regularly brought prolonged acute distress for Billy, whereas Curt fell asleep easily. Thus, Curt rarely experienced disruptive somatic stimulation, whereas Billy did so on occasion.

In the case of other active infants, we have tried to describe the behavior regulations initiated by the baby or provided by the environment that enabled the infants to evade or counteract massive excitation and distress. Billy's partial maladaptation and uneven developmental course may have come about because he could neither be soothed, nor soothe himself, nor contain and simultaneously discharge excitation in coordinated movement patterns. In Curt, distressing levels of excitation were prevented in part by the fact that he did respond to soothing and that his mother frequently provided it. In a sense, he also provided relief for himself by moving toward the mother when he was distressed. However, Curt was also seen to deal with displeasure and heightened arousal by himself. While hungry or sleepy he pulled himself to the standing position and bounced up and down with vigor. This activity was not rhythmic nor did it totally screen him from external stimuli (as was true of cradle rocking for some of the babies). However, it did take the place of more complex activity, it was not directed at any aspect of the environment, and it repeatedly occurred at moments when all observers expected him to cry. After bouncing for a while, he sometimes returned to his usual outwardly directed and more highly organized behavior. At other times, it preceded going to sleep (without maternal aid) or being fed.

Clara, In XVI (32 Weeks)

SPE DETERMINANTS

	Boundary Strength					
	ENTIRE		*MODALITY SECTORS*			
	Inner	*Outer*	*Vision*	*Touch*	*Sound*	*Passive Motion*
Stimulation	medium (−)	weak (+)	medium (−)	strong (−)	weak	medium (−)
Frequency of Mother-Child Contacts		medium (+)	medium (+)	medium	high (−)	low (+)
Intensity	medium (+)	medium (+)	→	→	→	→
Maternal Competence		medium (+)	→	→	→	→
Maternal Intrusiveness		medium	→	→	→	→
Level of Home Stimulation		medium (+)	→	→	→	→

Activity Level: 1.3

STABLE PATTERNS OF EXPERIENCE

Frequency of strong bodily arousal: Rare.

This very inactive and distinctly sensitive baby showed moderate arousal fairly often, but she showed no muscle tension, no stiffening or arching, and no loud squealing or crying at any time. As she was subject to disruptive bodily sensations on occasion and exposed to fairly rousing life situations (especially for one so sensitive), this is somewhat surprising. As will be seen, Clara had developed specific and rather extreme behavior patterns that served to forestall maximal excitation at times when it could have been expected to occur.

Internal bodily sensations: Medium.

Clara suffered from recurrent eczema (which was not acute while we observed her). Although painful skin sensations are not really internal in origin, the discomfort they caused on occasion is the major reason for our judgment that her behavior was dictated by bodily state relatively more often than is true of most 7-month-old babies. More directly relevant is the fact that she typically experienced distress and became unresponsive to the environment both during fatigue and for at least ten minutes after awakening, before she overcame the drowsiness and mild irritability that always followed sleep.

Balance between behavior activations due to inner and to outer stimulation: Equal.

This rating was given not because behavior activations often occurred in the absence of external provocation, but rather because a fairly large proportion of external events led to the inhibition of ongoing behavior or to transient disruption. Even when Clara's response to sights and sounds about her was one of positive interest, it often took the form of intent gazing while all movement ceased, which—at the age of 7 months—cannot be considered an *activation* of behavior.

Importance of distance receptors: High.

Clara was highly reactive to sound and rather alert to vision, and both modalities were evoked with regularity by the mother (sound more so than vision). Sights or sounds about her often led to smiling, moving, reaching and other adaptive responses, as they do in all babies. But in addition (and this is the factor that made these modalities prominent), the sight and/or sound of people or objects was inhibitory or disruptive for her, leading to simple movements of aversion far more often than one sees in most babies.

Importance of near receptors: Fairly low.

During direct encounters with the mother, the near receptor systems were evoked less frequently and less strongly than the distance ones. Except for the areas of eczema, Clara was not seen to respond to the mother's or anybody else's touch unless it was very firm (a characteristic she shared with the other eczema baby in the sample). Mother did offer soothing on occasion, but was much more likely to divert her by sights and sounds than to pat or rock her. Nor was Clara a baby who engaged in tactile or kinesthetic self-stimulation, except to a minimal degree.

Most prominent modality: Sound.

Least prominent modality: Kinesthetic.

Frequency of states of optimal animation: Fairly frequent.

During spontaneous activity Clara was content enough as she regarded objects and people, moved toys about in a somewhat stereotyped fashion (waving, shaking, gently pushing objects) or changed her postures. That she was in a state that permitted more active and complex responsiveness was apparent from her response to more specific stimulation, but in its absence the background level of perceptual stimulation (toys in reach, visual access to family life, and the upright sitting posture) rarely evoked behavior integrations or, for that matter, affect expressions of more than very moderate intensity.

During the moderately frequent contacts with the mother, Clara did rouse herself to more active and vivid responsiveness, but typically these were brief occasions, terminated not by the mother but by the baby, as will be described.

OUTCOME RATINGS

Developmental status: Low.

Clara's performance on the developmental tests was self-consistent, but unusual in pattern. In her case, the rating finally arrived at does not describe the actual situation. In some respects her behavior barely met average standards for 28-week-olds (she was exactly 32 weeks of age on the day she was tested), yet she achieved a fair number of items that are normative for the ages of 36 and 40 weeks. This wide scatter occurred both within and between particular areas of functioning, as these are divided on the Gesell Schedules (Motor, Adaptive, Language, and Personal-Social). For instance, in motor coordination she was markedly advanced in postural behavior; she could sit steadily for an indefinite period of time (40 weeks), could easily change from sitting to the prone position (40 weeks), and was exceptionally adept at changing her position by means of pivoting (a means of locomotion that in more primitive form is normative at 32 weeks; but the more mature execution of the motion was not seen at all in about half of Gesell's population, and those infants who did develop it achieved it by about the age of 40 weeks). On the other hand, she was not interested in the upright standing posture, and when placed to standing with her hands on the railing of the crib she could not maintain it (36 weeks). Nor did she stand when her hands were held (32 weeks) or attain the hand-knee posture as most 7-month-olds do. In the manipulation of small objects the discrepancies were even more pronounced. She grasped the bell by the handle and used it spontaneously only in order to ring it (40 weeks), she delicately pushed one cube with another (36 weeks), and she was able to obtain a ring out of reach by pulling the string attached to it (32 weeks). Yet she would not or could not hold a cube in each hand more than momentarily (28 weeks), nor deal with more than one object at a time in the various ways normative at the age of 32 weeks.

Clara's vocalizations were of the kind expected at her age, and test scores referring to "Personal-Social" behavior conformed to average standards for 36-week-olds. However, it so happens that the three items at this age level in this area (on the Gesell) all refer to persistency and interest in obtaining single toys and not to patterns of interpersonal behavior. Actually, she was highly responsive socially, but rarely, if ever, showed patterns of response that could be regarded as developmentally advanced. She responded differently to the mother than to all others; she showed a definite but minimal response to first encounter with the strange observers; she smiled broadly, vocalized in the form of gentle squeals, and sometimes activated her arms or legs as part of a social response. What she did during social interactions was thus appropriate for one of her age. However, in some ways she was more discriminating than many other babies. For instance, she responded pleasurably to the research staff (after they were no longer strangers) only if they maintained a physical distance of about two feet. When they came closer, she looked at them soberly, intently and perhaps anxiously, and became immobile and unresponsive. (This was not at all like her behavior with the mother.) In a child for whom sound was the most important modality, it is of interest that although she always smiled, or turned around and smiled when the mother spoke to her while out of sight, she never once did more than blink or transiently interrupt her activity when someone else spoke to her in a similar manner, though it was tried frequently.

All in all, Clara's development was well within normal limits, but distinctly slow in some areas and distinctly advanced in others.

Adequacy of vegetative functioning: Medium.

Clara was a perfectly healthy baby who ate well and slept soundly. However, she was subject to allergic skin rashes; with varying severity (very slight during the week she was observed), some portions of the skin were irritated and sensitive to touch. Yet, as was the case with the other eczema baby in the sample (In X), unaffected portions of the skin were not sensitive, and touch was responded to only if it was intense, and then not very strongly. In addition, Clara occasionally had the hiccups (once or twice a day, her mother said). When observed, they did not seem to trouble her, but were nonetheless an interruption in the smooth functioning of respiration. Not infrequently, she spat up a little soon after a feeding. This was not vomiting and did not cause distress. It should also be mentioned that whenever Clara became fatigued, she spent some time fussing or crying softly until she fell asleep.

Excitability: Low.

When left to her own devices and even when stimulated fairly strongly, Clara was responsive and alert. She gazed with exceptional intensity, she often interposed a delay between perception of a stimulus (toy or smiling countenance) and motoric response, and her movements were described as "deliberate," "unhurried," and "smooth." When the external circumstances and the quality of her response reached what was for her maximal intensity, and one expected signs of excitation to develop, she consistently showed a quite unusual behavior in one so young. She simply ceased to move and vocalize and became transiently so rigidly immobile as to remind observers of catatonic postures. This lasted for no more than a second or two, and if the stimulating approach from someone in the environment continued, she averted her eyes and head, effectively preventing herself from further responsiveness. The same mechanism was seen not only in response to what may have been uncomfortably high levels of arousal, but also in situations where she cut short very moderate levels of animation. For instance, her mother often initiated vigorous and rousing play with her baby. At first Clara smiled delightedly, and sometimes went so far as to squeal, laugh, and wave her arms or kick her legs in pleasure. However, after a very short period of time, it was Clara who turned away. She looked entirely content as she thus abandoned the social partner or a proffered toy. It was as though she were using her capacity for voluntary movement (of body and of eyes) to regulate the dosage of excitatory play.

Irritability: Medium.

This rating was based upon the circumstance (both observed and reported) that during spontaneous activity Clara quite often produced sounds that unmistakably conveyed some displeasure or annoyance. She did not whimper or cry, but somehow sounded angry or at least decidedly displeased. Neither the parents nor the observers were able to determine what brought on these brief and mild episodes of irritability. They did not typically occur when she encountered difficulties in manipulating objects or in changing her posture; in fact, she was rarely seen to initiate an activity that she could not readily complete. Usually she was entirely content both before and after each such episode, and each time she either settled down of her own accord or was restored to a pleasant mood by transient contact with the mother or with another person. Occasionally, mild but definite discontent occurred even in the mother's arms, for no reason that could be discerned. The fact that she was irritable for 10 to 20 minutes before she could go to sleep has been mentioned. In addition, we observed and were told that Clara was always cranky for a while after awakening, while still somewhat drowsy. At no time was she seen in great distress, and the mother said that except when ill or in pain, Clara never cried hard or screamed.

Pleasure in functioning: Medium.

When unattended on the sofa, in the playpen or in the Teeter-Babe, Clara "practiced" behavior integrations that had not yet been completely mastered; for instance, bringing her feet to her mouth (in the supine), pivoting in all directions, or lowering herself from the sitting posture to the prone. However, she showed none of the interest in achieving an upright posture that is commonly seen at this age, and she made no efforts to locomote from one point in space to another. She could persistently reach for an object at the periphery of her grasp, but never expended a great deal of effort in the process. On achieving success with this or any other enterprise, she looked mildly pleased but did not show the marked joy or satisfaction one sees in many other babies. As has already been described, her response to appropriate varieties of stimulation was often pleasurable, and it did elicit some relatively complex behavior integrations (at least in the manipulation of toys). However, her dominant responses (especially in social interactions) took the form of simple and well-learned behaviors. More important in this context was her tendency to cut short such episodes by actively avoiding further contact.

DISCUSSION

Clara was a well-functioning and fairly well-developed baby who lived in an environment that, so far as we could judge, offered much that was supportive and facilitating. Her behavioral style represents an extreme example of the use of adaptive regulations that can emerge only in inactive infants, though they are not a necessary consequence of inactivity.

She was a valued member of an active, well-organized family who lived in comfortable circumstances. The mother, who had raised three much more active children, thought of Clara as both alert and lazy. She made it clear that she tried to rouse Clara's interest in many activities that she knew to be age-appropriate, because her other children had spontaneously engaged in them or had "demanded" them. Her manner with the baby, as well as with the other children, was vigorous, cheerful, and comforting in turn. She was skillful in holding the baby and in caring for her, but she did not show the spontaneous intimacy and the subtle responsiveness to behavior clues emanating from the baby that we saw in a good many of the other mothers. Withal, she was a woman who had firm notions of how things ought to be done, and who valued order and efficiency. For instance, though Clara was said to be on a self-demand schedule, she was awakened every evening for her supper; because otherwise her bedtime would not have coincided with that set for all the children. Similarly, Clara was spoon-fed in the flat supine position to prevent the mess made by spilled food. Thus the mother's approach to Clara was often guided by what was most convenient or efficient for all concerned, and not by the baby's behavior at the moment.

From what has been said so far, it may not be apparent that the relationship between Clara and her mother was intense and intensely pleasurable to both. Clara spent all her waking hours in the mother's company. As she sat in the Teeter-Babe surrounded by toys, or in the playpen, she had free access to the sight and the sound of the mother, of the siblings who were usually nearby, and of the frequent visitors in this lively household. Each time she saw the mother, Clara's face lit up as she smiled and often vocalized. The mother, in turn, never passed the baby without speaking to her and smiling, though she might not come close enough to touch her for as long as an hour at a time. Very frequently, the mother, while at a distance from the baby, made active contact with her by speaking, singing, or making funny clucking noises for her entertainment. Clara watched these antics intently, gave every sign of pleasure, and then turned away, to respond with interest and quiet pleasure the next time she encountered the mother's gaze or voice. In Clara's experience all routine caretaking situations were also episodes of pleasurable social play. In between times, the mother also played with her for the fun of it and to teach her things. She played pat-a-cake, though Clara as yet could not perform the clapping motion on verbal clues alone. She playfully held her to standing, and Clara smiled complacently as she dangled more than she stood. Mother even crouched on the floor next to the baby, urging her verbally and in other ways to "come on," hoping that the baby would creep. Clara focused on the mother and activated her arms, legs, and trunk as if about to get up on her hands and knees, but collapsed almost at once looking sober but not at all displeased.

Yet in certain situations, interactions developed so that Clara remained far more impassive than might have been necessary. During feedings, for instance, she lay flat on the mother's lap (not in the usual half-raised position), and mother inserted the spoon or nipple. Never did the mother place a nipple or spoon close to the baby's mouth and wait for her to seize it. Nor did she hold a toy close to the baby's hand. She either placed it in her hand or put it within reach. Thus, unlike at least some mothers of inactive babies, Clara's mother did not capitalize on the small ways in which the baby might have been incited to greater reciprocity. Mother provided pleasure, comfort, and stimulation—but in such a way that this alert but rather passive infant responded but did little to sustain the interaction or influence its course. There was one exception: Clara did act to terminate social episodes, and also exerted herself in resisting unwelcome influence. It was striking to note that Clara showed her most vigorous bodily activity and greatest intensity of affect while avoiding and resisting—rather than in approach activities. For instance, though she allowed food to be placed into her mouth and sucked or swallowed it once it was there, she became very active when she wanted no more. She then pushed the bottle or spoon in ridding motions, clamped her lips, averted her head, and kicked and squirmed. Much the same type of behavior occurred during the developmental test. Although most toys aroused her interest and she dealt with them by well-coordinated and rather slow movements, she obviously disliked having her attention compelled toward several objects at once. At these times also, she pushed toys away, squealed in brief displeasure, closed her eyes, and averted her head (so much so that the examiner wondered whether her behavior in response to some of these items should be scored as "refusal" rather than as failure).

In summary, the inactive Clara was cared for by a mother who lacked subtle attunement to the inconspicuous aspects of her infant's behavior, but who maintained active and mutually pleasurable contact with the baby. Clara's stable patterns of experience included many episodes of apparently keen pleasure at contact with the mother; prolonged periods of contentment and low levels of animation as she engaged in motor play or play with toys; frequent but mild and brief episodes of displeasure for unknown reasons; and more prolonged periods (10–20 minutes) of mild distress each time before she went to sleep and for about 10 minutes after awakening. Mother had learned that once Clara showed fatigue, it was best to put her in the crib and let her fuss until she dropped off to sleep. During the cranky period after naps, mother always held her and played with her until she was "fully awake." Compared with most other 7-month-old babies, Clara's stable patterns of experience lacked moments of high arousal (both joyous and distressed). Also lacking were sustained periods of intimate interaction with the mother, at least of the variety that is mediated by small gestures, inflections, reciprocal changes in physiognomic expression, and the like.

Under these conditions, Clara had developed a style of behavior in which discrimination and vigilance were more prominent than action to achieve effects (mastery). Her gaze was more intent and prolonged than that of any other child in the sample and was in itself a major response. She was highly alert to sights and sounds about though affective response and turning toward a voice were pronounced only in response to her mother. She had become adept at aversion, resistance, and partial withdrawal in situations that seldom elicit such behavior from other infants. It is in keeping with this pattern that Clara still took three naps a day. Her adaptive style shows some similarity to that of Peter (In XV), who also protected himself from undue excitation by ceasing to respond; and who also was a baby who slept more than most. However, while Clara at times showed determined resistance and displeasure, Peter merely became impassive. It may be more than chance that Peter's experience (which on the whole was far more rousing and excitatory than Clara's) also lacked high peaks of excitation and subtle and sustained interactions with the mother.

SIXTEEN

PATTERNS OF EXPERIENCE AND DEVELOPMENTAL OUTCOME

In the chapters on adaptation syndromes, we presented for each infant a rating for each of eight different aspects or patterns of recurrent experience. We used these ratings in the discussion of each baby's course of development and of conspicuous features of his functioning and adaptation. Yet in every instance we found it necessary to include many additional features of each child's recurrent experience—regularities and patterns that were not included in the original eight ratings. For the most part, these additional patterns concerned aspects of the interaction between mother and child; for instance, the degree to which each infant experienced his mother (or other familiar persons) as immediate agents of need satisfaction and relief from distress; the degree to which each infant experienced sustained reciprocal interactions with mother or other persons; and many more. In a good many instances, these more qualitative and specific patterns proved at least as illuminating and important as the more schematic patterns specified in the formal ratings.

The eight formal ratings were selected *before* we had begun the process of exploring each subject's individual characteristics of behavior in relation to the totality of individually characteristic patterns of experience. They were selected partly on an a priori basis and reflected some of our hypotheses about variables likely to be important in shaping the course of development. Beyond this, the selection of patterns for formal ratings was dictated by the author's interest in exploring the potential of assessing behavior in terms of structural dimensions, as compared with the variables that describe content aspects of experience. The attempt to link certain patterns of experience with specific aspects of developmental outcome is an experiment performed retrospectively with descriptive data. Clearly, success in relating SPE configurations to developmental outcome must depend entirely upon success in identifying those components of infant experience that are in fact significant determinants of the developmental outcomes under investigation. The eight formal ratings are no more than a first attempt to delineate and put to preliminary test a very few of the stable components of experience that may be important. The primary purpose of the work reported in these pages is to suggest a model that can be used in future studies, and that we believe will prove effective in investigating the manner in which early experience molds development and adaptation. As will become apparent in what is to follow, some of the formal SPE ratings were consistently associated with some of the outcome variables, and some were not.

Similar limitations exist also for what we have called the developmental outcome variables. As fully discussed in Chapter 3, the analysis of cross-sectional data led to a hypothesis that can be tested only if experience patterns are related to developmental and other behavior characteristics observed at a later point in time. However, we consider that behavior characteristics noted in these babies are also products of development over time. On the assumption that the patterns of experience we observed have a degree of stability, it seemed worthwhile to determine whether the rate of developmental progress, irritability, and pleasure in functioning could be tied to them. Of the original five outcome variables, only the three mentioned above lent themselves to the purpose. The other two, excitability and the adequacy of vegetative functioning, might more strategically have been treated as one of the SPE determinants. Excitability correlates highly with activity level (which was considered one of the SPE determinants) and the adequacy of vegetative functioning was high for the great majority of subjects, so that it failed to distinguish among them.

With all their limitations, our SPE ratings reflect actual differences in the lives of these babies, of a kind that has not previously been described. As we have done for the other variables, we shall begin by describing the distribution of SPE ratings in the sample, and then explore their relationship to age and to activity level.

Table 16.1 shows the frequency distribution of each SPE for the group as a whole. For many of these patterns it can be said that one or two positions on the scale are modal for the group, and a proportion of the subjects depart from this mode. Below we summarize the modes and ranges for the five SPE's that show this characteristic:

	Mode	*Range*
Frequency of strong bodily arousal	rare	absent—high
Prominence of internal bodily sensations	medium	low—high
Prominence of distance receptor systems	high, medium	low—high
Prominence of near receptor systems	high	fairly low—high
Frequency of states of optimal animation	high, medium	low—high

Balance between behavior activations due to inner and to outer stimulation	equal	internal very dominant—external very dominant

No such regularity is noted for the most prominent and least prominent sensory modalities. Passive motion was very rarely the most important one, and it was an exceptional circumstance if either vision or sound was least important.

Experience patterns are the product of the organism's state and capacities under whatever environmental conditions happen to exist. Since the organism changes with advancing age, one expects to see changes in SPE from one age level to the next. Table 16.2 confirms this expectation for our sample. The major changes may be summarized as follows:

(1) The prominence of behavior activations due to inner somatic events decreased with advancing age. (2) Similarly, the older the infants, the greater the proportion of behavior activations responsive to the environment. (3) By the same token, the prominence of the distance receptor systems increased with age. (4) However, the near receptor systems tended to remain prominent at all age levels, which is not surprising in a group of babies none of whom had yet reached the age of 8 months. (5) The frequency of states of optimal animation increased a very little with advancing age, and the most and least important modalities were unrelated to it.

It was to be expected that changes in the organism's capacities and state due to advancing age would alter patterns of experience. Table 16.2 shows that this is the case. There remains the question of whether other organismic variables also affect experience patterns. Activity level is one of the organismic factors, and Table 16.3 shows the following relationships between it and the SPE's:

(1) The frequency of strong bodily arousal was far greater for active than for inactive babies. (2) The frequency of states of optimal animation was more often "high" or "moderate" for active babies, though low positions on this continuum did not differentiate between the groups. (3) Touch was the least important modality for more active than inactive babies. (4) Behavior activations were predominantly responsive to external stimuli more often among active infants.

These results are in good accord with the material reported in Part Two, which demonstrated that the probability that certain behavioral events will occur (or occur frequently) depends significantly upon activity level.

Turning now to the relationship between SPE's and the adaptation indices, we are confronted by the technical dilemma that we have used a large variety of SPE ratings for each of a small number of subjects. The primary hypothesis is that individual differences in developmental course and adaptation are the result of specific *constellations* of SPE.

From the outset we were reconciled to the fact that our data lend themselves more to quantitative description than to statistical manipulation. Insofar as the descriptive findings support the hypothesis, they will have served our purpose, which is to point to relationships between facts that merit further and more rigorous study. For the structural and dynamic determinants of the SPE we presented scattergrams (Chapters 10 and 11) to show for each separate variable the degree of association it showed with each of three adaptation indices. Of the eight SPE determinants, only two showed such a relationship consistently, and both of these with respect to only one of the adaptation indices—namely, irritability. In short, irritability was related to the strength of the inner boundary, in that the proportion of infants who were irritable was greatest among those with weak boundaries, intermediate for those whose inner boundary was assessed as medium, and smallest for those with strong inner boundaries. Similarly, irritability was found to be proportionate to the intensity of stimulation from within.[1]

In the *Supplementary Material* for this chapter, scattergrams are again presented for each experience pattern in relationship to the five adaptation indices. Below we summarize the more important findings.

Frequency of Strong Bodily Arousal (Table 16.4)

Developmental Status: The greatest proportion of advanced developmental status ratings occurred among children for whom the frequency of bodily arousal was "high" or "moderate" (50 per cent). Conversely, average developmental status was predominantly associated with frequency ratings of "occasional," "rare," and "absent" (63 per cent). The few instances of slow developmental progress were found in children for whom strong bodily arousal was a rare event.

Irritability: The proportion of markedly irritable babies was greatest when the frequency of strong bodily arousal was "high" or "moderate" (37 per cent), and smaller when strong bodily arousal was "occasional" or less (8 per cent). Irritability was low predominantly among children for whom strong bodily arousal was "rare" or "absent" (76 per cent), and low irritability was not seen at all in infants for whom strong arousal was a frequent occurrence (rating "high").

[1] A number of additional associations between structural and dynamic SPE determinants and adaptation indices were reported in Chs. 10 and 11, but they were not consistent. For instance, developmental status was high relatively often where the frequency of mother-child contacts was also high. However, lesser frequencies of mother-child contact did not show an inverse relationship to developmental status.

Internal Bodily Sensations (Table 16.5)

Irritability: Both high and medium levels of irritability occurred almost only when inner somatic stimulation was "medium" or "marked" in prominence; all but one of the infants for whom the prominence was "fairly low" or "low" were not irritable at all.

Pleasure in Functioning: A large proportion of those infants for whom inner somatic stimulation was rated "fairly low" or "low" in prominence were infants whose pleasure in functioning was "high" (66 per cent); a "medium" prominence of inner somatic stimulation was most often accompanied by "medium" pleasure in functioning (66 per cent).

Balance between Behavior Activations due to Inner and to Outer Stimulation (Table 16.6)

Developmental Status: The proportion of subjects showing developmental acceleration was highest when external sources of stimulation were very dominant or dominant (54 per cent) and lower when the balance was equal (16 per cent). With the exception of one 4-week-old infant, advanced developmental status was not seen when internal sources of stimulation were dominant.

Excitability: When behavior activations are very predominantly due to external stimulation, marked excitability (rating "high") was more likely to be present (63 per cent) than when the balance was equal (8 per cent) or when internal stimulation was dominant (15 per cent).

Pleasure in Functioning: When external sources of stimulation were very dominant, pleasure in functioning was usually "high" (83 per cent); it decreased (to 60 per cent) when external dominance was less pronounced; a "medium" degree of pleasure in functioning was most characteristic when the balance was equal (57 per cent). Only three infants showed "low" pleasure in functioning; for them the balance was equal or in favor of internal sources of stimulation.

Importance of Distance Receptors (Table 16.7)

Developmental Status: Accelerated developmental status was most often present when the prominence of the distance receptors was rated "high" or "fairly high" (57 per cent), but did not occur at all among infants for whom the distance receptors were of "medium" prominence. A "low" prominence of the distance receptors was found in only six infants, of whom two (33 per cent) were advanced developmentally. In keeping with this distribution, all of the infants for whom the distance receptors were of "medium" prominence showed average developmental progress. However, of the three babies whose development had proceeded at a slow pace, two experienced the distance receptors with more than medium prominence.

Although the number of subjects in whom a "fairly high" or "high" prominence of the distance receptors was associated with relatively slow developmental progress is small, this finding appears to run counter to a major trend and thus to contradict a hypothesis which was discussed throughout Chapters 13, 14, and 15. In fact, the two "exceptions" confirm the rule, because in both instances the quantitative test results (which were the sole criteria for developmental status ratings) failed to reflect the actual state of affairs. Subjects In V and In XVI both had atypical test score profiles that reflected an acceleration of discriminatory functions, but relative immaturity in neuromuscular development (In V) or in the capacity to focus on more than one object at a time (In XVI). The developmental *diagnosis,* as contrasted with the numerical IQ or DQ, was reported as "superior endowment" for In V and as "at least good average endowment" for In XVI. A glance at their respective adaptation syndromes will show that both were highly sensitive (weak outer boundary) and that both responded to moderate amounts of stimulation by disruption and distress. Therefore, in both these infants, atypical and overly discriminatory behavior tendencies prevented optimal performance under the standard conditions of developmental examination.

Pleasure in Functioning: When the prominence of the distance receptors was rated "high," pleasure in functioning tended to be "high" (66 per cent), and lesser prominence levels were associated with a lesser tendency for high pleasure in functioning. A trend in the same direction but far less consistent was present in the association of "medium" ratings for pleasure in functioning with "medium" or "fairly high" prominence of the distance receptors (42 per cent).

Importance of Near Receptors (Table 16.8)

Developmental Status: The proportion of babies showing advanced developmental status varied with the prominence of the near receptor systems (ranging from 55 per cent for "high" prominence to 27 per cent and 33 per cent, respectively, for "fairly high" and "moderate" prominence, to none at all when prominence was "fairly low"). "Fairly high" and "moderate" prominence of the near receptors were associated with "medium" but not with "high" developmental status.

Frequency of States of Optimal Animation (Table 16.9)

Developmental Status: Developmental acceleration occurred by far the most often when the frequency of optimal states of animation was "high" or "fairly high" (72 per cent as contrasted to 8 per cent and 13 per cent when the frequency was "moderate" and "occasional"). Similarly, "moderate" and "occasional" frequency of optimal states of animation were associated with average developmental status (93 per cent and 87 per cent, respectively). Two of the three instances of slow developmental progress, however, failed to conform to the pattern.[2]

Pleasure in Functioning: Pleasure in functioning showed much the same relationship to the frequency of states of optimal animation as did developmental status. Again, "high" pleasure in functioning tended to occur most often when the frequency of optimal states was "high" (80 per cent), or "fairly" or "moderately high" (40 per cent), and seldom when optimal states of animation were "occasional" or "rare" (20 per cent). "Medium" pleasure in functioning seldom occurred when the frequency of optimal states of animation was "high," but the distribution was inconclusive when optimal states of animation fell in the range from "fairly high" to "occasional."

On the whole, we found that several of the experience patterns reflected in the formal ratings of the SPE are related to the rate of developmental progress, to the degree to which infants display pleasure in functioning, and to irritability. We have said earlier that the primary value of relating patterns of experience to developmental outcome lies in the possibility of gaining more specific information about the aspects or components of an infant's existence that promote, retard or otherwise modify particular aspects of the developmental process. In what manner is developmental progress affected by the frequency of strong bodily arousal, or by the balance between activations due to stimulation from within the body and those responsive to the environment? When we selected stable patterns of experience, the choice was guided by our understanding of the nature of development during early infancy. Many of the concepts and hypotheses that are central to our thinking have already been discussed, as they were relevant to the differences seen between active and inactive infants, and in connection with the adaptation syndromes. It may not be amiss to specify at this point how we interpret our findings, and some of their implications.

Every one of the SPE ratings addresses itself to the central theme of waxing and waning arousal and excitation. Its intensity (frequency of strong bodily arousal and frequency of optimal states of animation); what evokes

[2] These are the same two infants discussed in some detail earlier (In V and In XVI), and the discrepancy is an artifact.

it (balance between internally and externally aroused behavior activations); the combination of intensity and source (prominence of inner somatic stimulation) and the particular body systems most prominently activated (prominence of distance and of near receptors, most and least prominent sensory modalities). In keeping with most developmental theories, we assume that the infant organism changes and develops in accordance with a ground plan that is shared by all members of the species. Like all living organisms, infants are constantly responsive to fluctuating alterations in physiological state, and to varied and fluctuating stimulation that affects them through the perceptual apparatus. It is in the process of responding and of adapting to a degree of dissonance and constant change that behavior alters and achieves increasing complexity and integration. Piaget has described this process in terms of the organism's simultaneous accommodation to sensory input, and assimilation that transforms the organism (or its behavioral capacities) in consequence of the act of accommodation. The development of thought processes and their operation at any level of maturity are then viewed in the context of disequilibrium, which necessitates action and thought, and transient relative equilibrium that pertains as closure, solution, or appropriately effective action are achieved.

The psychoanalytic view of development is very similar in this respect. Pushed from within by needs of instinctual origin, and pushed from without either by obstacles to need satisfaction or by noxious and pleasurable stimulation, the infant is impelled to directed action and to thought. In psychoanalytic theory as well, homeostasis is a central notion, and the absence of disequilibrium or tension is viewed as absolute negation of life and growth (the Nirvana principle).[3]

Consistent with such a view of development, we have assumed that *normal* development and effective adaptation must depend on arousal or activation occurring in dosages sufficient to compel constantly modified patterns of accommodation and new, increasingly complex behavior integrations. We have assumed also that the impetus to activation must not be so intense or so continuous as to be disruptive and therefore prevent effective action; that is, prevent the transient fitness between action impulse, action capacity, and the specific adaptive demand of a situation. Lastly, normal development would then require that the incitement to behavior activation be of such a kind as to support the development of *all* the necessary functions that, jointly and in coordination, are required to maintain normal functioning at higher levels of maturity. If discrimination is strongly developed, but integrative patterns or ego synthesis are weak, maladaptation is sure to follow. If one or several sensory systems are rarely brought into use, those ego functions or behavioral capacities that are most readily

[3] The Nirvana principle implies an equation between the absence of tension and the absence of life and growth, but it goes beyond this. It asserts that all living organisms contain an inner impulsion toward death and disintegration, and that in man this tendency finds psychic representation.

or uniquely mediated by the sense modality in question will suffer. (For instance, blind infants have lesser opportunity to recognize cause and effect in the external world, and are much slower to acquire a sense that outer reality exists independent of their own action and perception.)

Individual differences within the normal range may then be attributed to variations in the intensity, the rhythm, and the kind of activation or arousal experienced by the infant. In consequence of such differences in experience, certain cognitive functions may receive more support (what Piaget calls *aliment*) than others; accommodation to certain bodily states and affects may rarely be required; and in consequence certain varieties of adaptation may be developed at slower speed or less effectively. For instance, infants who very rarely experience acute pangs of hunger and delay may be under less pressure to develop ways of actively seeking need satisfaction or of overcoming obstacles, and will thus be more vulnerable to frustration and less resourceful in some varieties of problem-solving.

In speaking of different patterns of experience in terms of the intensities and kinds of behavior activation that occur, we do not mean to imply that the infant organism is passive and pliant to such stimulation as comes its way. With Buehler, Freud, Piaget, and many others, we take for granted that infants are prone to generate animation, to seek stimulation actively, and to practice developmentally relevant behavior activations. We do not think it necessary to postulate a special "need to function" or a "drive toward mastery" or competence. It seems simpler to assume that self-generated spontaneous behavior activation—the selection of and active search for suitable action opportunities—is one of the built-in modes of reactivity that normally receives behavioral expression. The infant who kicks and grasps his foot, who entertains himself by reaching for and regarding objects, or who practices a newly learned sound until it is fully mastered is responding to something. A barren environment, poor physical health, or a constant state of overstimulation can reduce mastery activation to a minimum. Thus, a tendency for repetitive and exploratory activity attuned to the developmental schedule may be regarded as one of many functions that, like respiration or cognition, result from the biological properties of the organism evoked in response to internal and external processes and events that arouse it.

The sequence, intensity, distribution and variety of behavioral arousals that constitute patterns of experience in our sense are not a function of the objective external conditions of stimulation alone, nor of stimulation from within, but—as has been said so often in these pages—are the resultant of both of these as they affect organisms that are differently constituted and hence vary in their reactivity to excitatory and soothing stimulation.

In noting the particulars of infant behavior under many different circumstances and in many different states (as described in Part Two), we came to focus our attention on differences in the kind and intensity of behavior activations, and these differences are summarized in the eight stable patterns of experience that received formal ratings.[4]

The results we reported early in this chapter lend support to the general view that has been briefly sketched. Among the adaptation indices, developmental status probably comes closest to a true outcome variable, as it reflects the degree of developmental change that has taken place over the infant's entire lifetime. Finding that accelerated development was more likely to occur when strong bodily arousal was "moderately frequent" or higher, and was unlikely to occur when such peak excitation was "occasional" or even less frequent, may be understood to mean that when massive arousal is rare, the organism is under less pressure to develop coordination, discrimination among aspects of the environment, and early forms of voluntary action—all of these being functions tapped by developmental tests. It does not have to mean that one could induce more rapid progress in infants who develop slowly by providing a larger number of episodes of peak excitation. It can suggest as well that infants who are exceptionally well endowed are also those who are not impassive to external stimulation, but readily aroused. As we have mentioned earlier, we speculate that it may be the alternation between states of fairly high arousal, periods of lesser arousal, and periods of relative quiescence that facilitates the replacement of already acquired schemas by more complex behavior integrations.

The positive relationship between developmental status and a pattern of experience in which the balance of responsive behavior is in favor of external stimulation fits into the same picture. By and large, developmental change reflects increasingly complex adaptations to the world. Behavior not responsive to the environment most often consists of either random movements or easy, well-learned actions (arm-waving, rolling, kicking, bodily self-stimulation); whereas a child who is focusing on a visual stimulus, turning to localize a sound, or responding socially to a human face is more often under the necessity to modulate his behavior as a function of the nature (size, position, etc.) of that to which he is responding. He thus is likely to have more experience with precisely those behavior activations that mediate developmental advance.

Developmental status also proved related to the relative intensity and frequency with which the distance receptor systems were activated in the child's experience. It is sound and vision that primarily acquaint the infant with continuity in space and with the properties of the wider environment

[4] Of course, our focus on which components of the bodily apparatus are activated and to what degree can be appropriate only for very young infants. To the degree that mental content emerges and achieves some autonomy, behavior comes to be guided by anticipation, memory, stable perceptual organization, and the affective connotations of each situation and the like—to that degree, behavior activations must be defined in psychological terms. It is for this reason that even in our sample, such patterns of experience as social reciprocity were shown to be of primary importance for the older babies (see the Adaptation Syndromes, Chs. 13, 14, and 15).

in general. It is not surprising that those babies who, as it were, used their eyes and ears more often and more intensively than others also tended to be the ones whose test performances were superior for their age. Again, the *prominence* of the visual and auditory spheres in an infant's day-by-day experience is only partly dictated by the richness of stimulation in these modalities. Vision especially, may be employed intensively in relation to parts of the body and to components of a constant background environment that do not specifically provoke visual attention. It is partly for this reason, we believe, that superior development was nearly as frequent among the inactive as the active babies, although strong bodily arousal was much less common in the inactive group. And it is also on this basis—the fact that infants differ in the degree to which they utilize opportunities—that we understand the fact that fairly strong bodily arousal, prominence of the distance receptor systems, and other experience patterns that facilitate more rapid developmental advance were associated with advanced developmental status, but were also found present when developmental progress was of good average caliber. Optimal facilitation provides the impetus for accelerated development to infants who—by virtue of endowment and the absence of retarding or disruptive experience—have the potential for rapid development. For those less well endowed, facilitating patterns of experience may make the difference between what we have called "good average" well-consolidated development and a position nearer the low extreme of the normal range.[5]

That a fairly high prominence of the near receptor systems equally makes superior developmental progress more likely is intelligible if one considers that touch and passive motion determine bodily state and awareness of the own body and its boundaries. Much of the learning taking place in infancy centers on growing control over body motions, and on coordinating body feelings (including affects) and body movements to stable and "recognized" perceptual configurations. In addition, infants can change their level of arousal and consequent behavior activation by delivering stimulation to their own bodies. By rolling, bouncing, rocking, creeping, and the like, they can generate heightened perceptions of their own body while also changing the contents of the perceptual field. Conversely, sucking, rocking, and other bodily self-stimulation can be a means of lessening arousal, just as the touch of another person or being rocked can be. We are not inclined to think that bodily self-stimulation is functionally equivalent to the experience of receiving tactile and kinesthetic stimulation from a caretaking person. But having noted (see Adaptation Syndromes, Chapters 13, 14, 15) that those infants most given to tactile self-stimulation are those whose mothers touched them less than is usual, we consider that, at

[5] Our sample provided no way of examining the implied assumption that infants whose development is fairly slow or retarded will be found significantly lacking in many of these facilitating experiences.

least with respect to excitation, self-stimulation can alter experience (or modify behavior) in a similar manner.

The definition of states of optimal animation attempts to specify the degree of arousal that is most directly conducive to the practice and the emergence of new and relatively more mature behavior patterns. The more frequent and prominent this intermediate state, the more likely is rapid developmental advance. It will be remembered that optimal states of animation arise in many different contexts. For some infants they occur chiefly during social interactions with caretaking persons, for others the condition we called spontaneous activity is most conducive, and for all the presence of bodily discomfort or perceptual monotony reduces the likelihood of their occurrence. The state of optimal animation was defined in absolute terms (moderate levels of arousal while content and alert), but the degree to which complex behavior occurs during these states is relative. Some inactive infants, who otherwise limited behavior to exceedingly simple and, for their age, primitive patterns, responded by performing behavior integrations of only slightly greater complexity, far below those they produced in response to more intense stimulation. Other infants, and usually active ones, displayed during optimal animation the most mature behavior of which they were capable at any time.

For the former, states of optimal animation do provide learning opportunities, but their frequency may not affect developmental progress as much as more intense and specific stimulation does. If this were the case, the frequency of states of optimal animation ought to be relatively more important—as a determinant of developmental pace—for active than inactive infants. A separate check showed that this is probably the case, though the number of subjects in each activity group is so small that observed differences may be due to chance. For what it is worth, among the inactive babies whose development was accelerated, two of four experienced optimal animation with "moderate" or "occasional" frequency, and both of them received at least moderately intense stimulation fairly often. Among the active babies, the six who were accelerated experienced states of optimal animation frequently or fairly frequently. None of the active babies for whom optimal animation was of "medium" frequency or less had developed at better than an average rate.

Both pleasure in functioning and irritability refer to important aspects of adaptation, but both are behavior characteristics that may vary over time, though they may also be typical of particular infants over months and years. It is plausible to assume that both of these attributes are determined by fluctuating aspects of experience as much as by its more stable components. For instance, a limited period of discomfort due to teething is likely to have the immediate effect of increasing irritability and reducing pleasure in functioning, even in infants who in general are not irritable. There is little doubt that pleasure in functioning and irritability make a difference to overall development and adaptation over time, but the degree to which this is the case can be learned only from longitudinal study.[6]

Pleasure in functioning was found to be associated with the frequency of optimal states of animation, though to a lesser extent than might have been supposed. It was assessed by more than just the infant's tendency to engage spontaneously in mastery activities and derive pleasure from so doing. Had this been the criterion, "frequency of optimal animation" and "pleasure in functioning" would have referred to the same phenomenon, at least in active infants who often reached optimal animation levels while left to their own devices. The eagerness and pleasure with which infants responded to suitable varieties of stimulation (social and object play) were the primary consideration. From the adaptation syndromes it will be remembered that there was an appreciable number of infants who were highly responsive to arousing stimulation and showed dramatic pleasure and effort on those occasions, yet such episodes were relatively rare in their everyday experience.

An especially strong and consistent link was found between the relative importance of the distance receptor systems (but *not* the near receptors) and pleasure in functioning. A "high" prominence of the distance receptors was almost always associated with high pleasure in functioning, while "fairly high" and "medium" prominence were equally likely to be accompanied by high and medium levels of pleasure in functioning. By the same token, it was the infants for whom behavior activations responsive to external stimulation dominated who were most likely to develop high pleasure in functioning. A closer look at the circumstances under which babies simultaneously exert effort and display pleasure (or display pleasure when effort is rewarded by successful action) makes the relationship intelligible. Mastery behavior addresses itself almost exclusively to environmental challenges. The manipulation of objects, the use of locomotion to approach and to avoid, or the active participation in pleasurable social interchange all require the adaptation of the body to sights and sounds about. It makes good sense to find that proportionately more experience utilizing the distance receptors should be accompanied by proportionately greater intensity and positive affect when they come into play.

Lastly, the relative prominence of inner somatic stimulation is inversely related to pleasure in functioning. Inner somatic sensations beyond the necessary minimum are almost always due to disruptive bodily states. In infants at this age level, they refer to the degree to which hunger, fatigue, gastric distress, teething and similar causes affect behavior. And the effects

[6] In principle this statement applies to all adaptation indices that might be devised, but while developmental status is something like a result of *all* that has happened up to this point, this is not true to the same extent of zest and irritability.

of such body feelings are usually in the direction of displeasure, reduced responsiveness to the environment, and a primitivization of behavior.[7]

Irritability related to the experience patterns in a different manner than did the other indices. It is the only one that refers to an interference with good adaptive functioning, which might lead one to expect that it would correlate with a relative lack of the experience patterns that were found to be supportive of good adaptation and development. But for the most part, this was not the case. When the frequency of strong bodily arousal was "occasional" (or less), irritability was unlikely to be present (70 per cent not irritable); but with higher frequencies of strong bodily arousal, irritability could range from high to low.

The relationship between irritability and the frequency of optimal states of animation is of special interest, for high irritability occurred most often in association with "medium" frequency of optimal animation. When states of optimal animation were "frequent," irritability was most often present to a medium degree; while, with some exceptions, "occasional" frequencies of optimal animation tended to go with the absence of irritability. Elsewhere we commented on the circumstance that irritability is but one variety of arousal—it differs from pleasurable excitation only in the accompanying affect, which, in turn, affects the behavior integrations that occur in consequence. When one considers only the difference between irritable and non-irritable babies, it is not surprising that children who relatively seldom experience even moderate levels of arousal are also seldom irritable.

Why a moderate frequency of optimal levels of arousal should be more conducive to high levels of irritability than a high frequency opens a wide field for speculation. Assuming that this relationship can be confirmed on other samples, the combination of a marked tendency to become aroused (high irritability) and only a moderate opportunity to experience optimal states of animation suggests the possibility that these are infants in whom there is some discrepancy between the dosage or kind of stimulation they receive and their requirements. Events that yield pleasurable and moderate degrees of excitation for other infants lead instead to disruptive episodes for them. A glance at the SPE determinants of the four infants who combined medium frequency of moderate arousal with high irritability lends support to this speculation. Ac IV was an exceptionally sensitive infant (outer and inner boundary assessed as weak). She was an infant for whom even very moderate stimulation generated maximal and thus displeasurable excitation. Though her mother was able to adapt to this by minimizing stimulation of most kinds, it was necessary to touch the baby a good deal in the course of routine caretaking procedures. As the baby was overly reactive

[7] The prominence of inner somatic stimulation also depends upon the relative prominence of all varieties of *external* stimulation. It could receive a rating of "medium" even in the absence of disruptive body states, if the baby was grossly understimulated in general. The consequence of such a state of affairs for the emergence of pleasure in functioning would be much the same.

to touch, this meant that most procedures involved displeasure for the baby, as fully described in her adaptation syndrome (see Chapter 13).

Baby In IV, on the other hand, had a mother who was excessively intense and intrusive in all her dealings with the baby. In addition, he experienced moderate amounts of gastric distress, which—together with chronic overstimulation at the mother's hands—reduced the occasions when he could be content, alert, and yet animated. As described in the adaptation syndrome (Chapter 13), the chief factor that counteracted optimal states of animation was the mother's anxious tendency to intervene too much, too soon, and too energetically. In VII was a very inactive baby, tended by an attentive and competent mother. In this baby's experience, intense somatic sensations loomed very large (intensity of stimulation from within was "high"). A chronic and severe difficulty in falling asleep, and other sorts of less severe bodily discomfort, interfered with this baby's optimal responsiveness to the perfectly ordinary environmental conditions (see Chapter 14).

Ac XV was an exceedingly active and excitable infant, whose parents were more intensely overstimulating and intrusive than any others in the sample. The adaptation syndrome (Chapter 15) describes the way in which the mother's provocative and coercive manner, combined with the infant's unusual impetus toward large motor action, made the frequent contacts with both parents an energetic and angry struggle most of the time. In this instance, the amount and kind of parental stimulation would have been excessive for any baby, but was especially unsuited to this one's requirements because his parents lacked resourcefulness and tended to provoke the very storms they feared.

The relationship between irritability and the intensity of somatically aroused sensations requires no discussion, as in young infants irritable behavior is chiefly associated with bodily discomfort.

In summary, we found that of the eight SPE patterns that received formal ratings, six bear a direct relationship to developmental status, four bear a direct relationship to pleasure in functioning, and three bear a relationship to irritability. These three adaptation indices are sufficiently independent of one another that different components of stable experience have primary relevance to each. By contrast, the SPE *determinants* showed no consistent relationship to developmental status and to pleasure in functioning. Two of the eight SPE determinants, however, showed a consistent relationship to irritability.

In view of the great dispersion of SPE determinants among infants who share one or several patterns of experience, we take this preliminary finding as support for our central hypothesis to the effect that development and adaptation can be anticipated better on the basis of *what actually happens* to infants than on the basis of organismic or milieu factors, which nonetheless account for these patterns of experience. Further, the fact that formal properties of the arousal and relaxation patterns that characterize each infant's life are related to the adaptation indices, especially to the results of developmental testing, is highly congruent with those developmental theories that emphasize the activation of the organism as the primary mechanism underlying and compelling developmental change.

SUPPLEMENTARY MATERIAL TO CHAPTER 16

Table 16.1—Stable Patterns of Experience: Distribution in the Sample

	ABSENT		(LOW) RARE		(FAIRLY LOW) OCCASIONAL		MEDIUM		(FREQUENT) PROMINENT		TOTAL	
	N	%	N	%	N	%	N	%	N	%	N	%
Frequency of Peak Arousal	8	25.0	13	40.6	3	9.3	4	12.5	4	12.5	32	99.9
Internal bodily sensations	0	0	3	9.4	8	25.0	13	40.6	8	25.0	32	100
Importance of Distance Receptors	0	0	3	9.4	3	9.4	12	37.5	14	43.7	32	100
Importance of Near Receptors	0	0	0	0	6	18.7	6	18.7	20	62.5	32	99.9
Frequency of Optimal Animation			1	3.1	8	25.0	12	37.5	11[a]	34.4	32	100

	INTERNAL VERY DOMINANT		INTERNAL DOMINANT		ABOUT EQUAL		EXTERNAL DOMINANT		EXTERNAL VERY DOMINANT		TOTAL	
	N	%	N	%	N	%	N	%	N	%	N	%
Balance between Behavior Activations, Inner–Outer[b]	5	16.0	3	9.7	12	39.0	5	16.0	6	19.3	31	100

	TOUCH		PASSIVE MOTION		VISION		SOUND		NONE		TOTAL	
	N	%	N	%	N	%	N	%	N	%	N	%
Most Prominent Modality	7	21.9	2	6.2	9	28.1	7	21.9	7	21.9	32	100
Least Prominent Modality	9	28.1	9	28.1	3	9.4	2	6.2	9	28.1	32	99.9

[a] The ratings of "fairly frequent" and "frequent" were combined on this table.
[b] The balance between behavior activations responsive to inner versus outer stimulation could not be rated for Infant In II.

Table 16.2—Stable Patterns of Experience and Age

Experience	Age Group							
	4–12 WKS.		*16–20 WKS.*		*24–32 WKS.*		*TOTAL*	
	N	*%*	*N*	*%*	*N*	*%*	*N*	*%*
Frequency of Strong Bodily Arousal								
Absent	3	25.0	1	12.5	4	33.3	8	25.0
Rare	4	33.3	4	50.0	5	41.7	13	40.6
Occasional	2	16.7	1	12.5	0	–	3	9.3
Moderately frequent	2	16.7	2	25.0	0	0	4	12.5
Frequent	1	8.3	0	–	3	25.0	4	12.5
Total	12	100	8	100	12	100	32	99.9
Frequency of Optimal Animation								
Rare	0	–	1	12.5	0	–	1	3.1
Occasional	4	33.3	1	12.5	3	25.0	8	25.0
Moderately frequent	5	41.7	3	37.5	4	33.3	12	37.5
Fairly frequent	2	16.7	2	25.0	1	8.3	5	15.6
Frequent	1	8.3	1	12.5	4	33.3	6	18.7
Total	12	100	8	100	12	99.9	32	99.9
Internal Bodily Sensations								
Low	0	–	0	–	3	25.0	3	9.3
Fairly low	2	16.7	2	25.0	4	33.3	8	25.0
Medium	4	33.3	4	50.0	5	41.7	13	40.6
Prominent	6	50.0	2	25.0	0	–	8	25.0
Total	12	100	8	100	12	100	32	99.9
Balance Activations due to Inner and Outer Stimulation								
Internal very dominant	5	45.4	0	–	0	–	5	16.1
Internal dominant	1	9.1	2	25.0	0	–	3	9.7
About equal	5	45.4	4	50.0	3	25.0	12	38.7
External dominant	0	–	2	25.0	3	25.0	5	16.1
External very dominant	0	–	0	–	6	50.0	6	19.3
Total	11[a]	99.9	8	100	12	100	31[a]	99.9
Importance of Distance Receptors								
Minimal	3	25.0	0	–	0	–	3	9.4
Fairly low	1	8.3	2	25.0	0	–	3	9.4
Moderate	7	58.4	3	37.5	2	16.6	12	37.5
Fairly prominent	1	8.3	2	25.0	5	41.7	8	25.0
Prominent	0	–	1	12.5	5	41.7	6	18.7
Total	12	100	8	100	12	100	32	100

Table 16.2 (continued)

Experience	Age Group							
Importance of Near Receptors	4–12 WKS.		16–20 WKS.		24–32 WKS.		TOTAL	
	N	%	N	%	N	%	N	%
Fairly low	2	16.7	1	12.5	3	25.0	6	18.7
Moderately prominent	3	25.0	3	37.5	0	–	6	18.7
Fairly prominent	5	41.6	2	25.0	4	33.3	11	34.4
Prominent	2	16.7	2	25.0	5	41.7	9	28.1
Total	12	100	8	100	12	100	32	99.9
Most Prominent Modality								
Touch	3	25.0	2	25.0	2	16.7	7	21.9
Passive motion	0	–	1	12.5	1	8.3	2	6.2
Vision	4	33.3	2	25.0	3	25.0	9	28.1
Sound	2	16.7	1	12.5	4	33.3	7	21.9
None	3	25.0	2	25.0	2	16.7	7	21.9
Total	12	100	8	100	12	100	32	100
Least Prominent Modality								
Touch	2	16.7	3	38.0	3	25.0	9	28.1
Passive motion	3	25.0	3	38.0	0	–	3	9.3
Vision	3	25.0	0	–	1	8.3	2	6.3
Sound	0	–	1	12.0	4	33.3	9	28.1
None	4	33.3	1	12.0	12	99.9	32	99.9
Total	12	100	8	100	4	33.3	9	28.1

[a] One subject could not be rated.

Table 16.3—Experience Patterns and Activity Level

Experience Pattern	ACTIVE		INACTIVE		TOTAL	
	N	%	N	%	N	%
Frequency of Strong Bodily Arousal						
Absent	0	–	8	50.0	8	25.0
Rare	6	37.5	7	43.7	13	40.6
Occasional	2	12.5	1	6.2	3	9.3
Moderately frequent	4	25.0	0	–	4	12.5
Frequent	4	25.0	0	–	4	12.5
Frequency of States of Optimal Animation						
Rare	0	–	1	6.2	1	3.1
Occasional	4	25.0	4	25.0	8	25.0
Moderate	4	25.0	8	50.0	12	37.5
Frequent	8	50.0	3	18.7	11	34.4

Table 16.3 (continued)

Experience Pattern	ACTIVE N	ACTIVE %	INACTIVE N	INACTIVE %	TOTAL N	TOTAL %
Internal Bodily Sensations						
Low	2	12.5	1	6.2	3	9.4
Fairly low	3	18.7	5	31.3	8	25.0
Medium	6	37.5	7	43.8	13	40.6
Prominent	5	31.3	3	18.7	8	25.0
Balance between Activations due to Inner and to Outer Stimulation [a]						
Internal very dominant	3	18.7	2	13.3	5	16.1
Internal	1	6.2	2	13.3	3	9.7
Equal	4	25.0	8	53.3	12	39.0
External	3	18.7	2	13.3	5	16.1
External very dominant	5	31.3	1	6.6	6	19.3
Importance of Distance Receptors						
Low	2	12.5	1	6.2	3	9.4
Fairly low	0	–	3	18.7	3	9.4
Moderate	6	37.5	6	37.5	12	37.5
Prominent	8	50.0	6	37.5	14	43.7
Importance of Near Receptors						
Fairly low	3	18.7	3	18.7	6	18.7
Moderate	4	25.0	2	12.5	6	18.7
Prominent	9	56.2	11	68.7	20	62.5
Most Prominent Modality						
Touch	3	18.7	4	25.0	7	21.9
Passive motion	1	6.2	1	6.2	2	6.2
Vision	4	25.0	5	31.3	9	28.1
Sound	4	25.0	3	18.7	7	21.9
None	4	25.0	3	18.7	7	21.9
Least Prominent Modality						
Touch	7	43.7	2	12.5	9	28.1
Passive motion	4	25.0	5	31.3	9	28.1
Vision	2	12.5	1	6.2	3	9.4
Sound	0	–	2	12.5	2	6.2
None	3	18.7	6	37.5	9	28.1

[a] One inactive infant could not be assessed.

Table 16.4—Frequency of Strong Bodily Arousal and Five Adaptation Indices

ADAPTATION INDEX	FREQUENCY OF STRONG AROUSAL					N SUBJECTS
	Absent	Rare	Occasional	Moderate	High	
Developmental Status						
High	2	4	0	2	2	10
Medium	6	6	3	2	2	19
Low	0	3	0	0	0	3
Vegetative Functioning						
High	8	10	1	4	2	25
Medium	0	2	2	0	2	6
Low	0	1	0	0	0	1
Excitability						
High	0	4	0	3	4	11
Medium	0	3	2	1	0	6
Low	8	6	1	0	0	15
Irritability						
High	0	1	1	1	2	5
Medium	0	4	1	1	2	8
Low	8	8	1	2	0	19
Pleasure in Functioning						
High	1	5	0	1	2	9
Medium	4	2	0	1	1	8
Low	0	2	1	0	0	3

Table 16.5—Internal Bodily Sensations and Five Adaptation Indices

ADAPTATION INDEX	INTERNAL BODILY SENSATIONS				N SUBJECTS
	Low	Fairly Low	Medium	Prominent	
Developmental Status					
High	1	3	5	1	10
Medium	2	4	6	7	19
Low	0	1	2	0	3
Vegetative Functioning					
High	3	6	12	4	25
Medium	0	2	1	3	6
Low	0	0	0	1	1
Excitability					
High	2	2	4	3	11
Medium	0	1	3	2	6
Low	1	5	6	3	15
Irritability					
High	0	1	0	4	5
Medium	0	0	6	2	8
Low	3	7	7	2	19
Pleasure in Functioning					
High	2	4	2	1	9
Medium	1	1	6	0	8
Low	0	1	1	1	3

Table 16.6—Balance between Activations due to Internal and External Stimulation and Five Adaptation Indices

ADAPTATION INDEX	BALANCE IN BEHAVIOR ACTIVATIONS					N SUBJECTS
	Internal Very Dominant	*Internal Dominant*	*Equal*	*External Dominant*	*External Very Dominant*	
Developmental Status						
High	1	0	2	3	3	9[a]
Medium	4	3	7	2	3	19
Low	0	0	3	0	0	3
Vegetative Functioning						
High	4	2	9	4	5	24[a]
Medium	0	1	3	1	1	6
Low	1	0	0	0	0	1
Excitability						
High	1	0	3	2	5	11
Medium	2	1	2	1	0	6
Low	2	2	7	2	1	14[a]
Irritability						
High	2	1	1	0	1	5
Medium	1	0	4	2	1	8
Low	2	2	7	3	4	18[a]
Pleasure in Functioning						
High	0	0	1	3	5	9
Medium	0	1	4	2	1	8
Low	0	1	2	0	0	3

[a] One infant could not be assessed.

Table 16.7—Importance of Distance Receptors and Five Adaptation Indices

ADAPTATION INDEX	IMPORTANCE OF DISTANCE RECEPTORS					N SUBJECTS
	Low	*Fairly Low*	*Medium*	*Fairly High*	*High*	
Developmental Status						
High	1	1	0	6	2	10
Medium	2	1	12	1	3	19
Low	0	1	0	1	1	3
Vegetative Functioning						
High	3	3	7	8	4	25
Medium	0	0	4	0	2	6
Low	0	0	1	0	0	1
Excitability						
High	0	0	3	4	4	11
Medium	2	0	3	1	0	6
Low	1	3	6	3	2	15
Irritability						
High	0	0	4	0	1	5
Medium	1	0	1	3	3	8
Low	2	3	7	5	2	19
Pleasure in Functioning						
High	0	0	2	3	4	9
Medium	0	1	2	3	2	8
Low	0	1	1	1	0	3

Table 16.8—Importance of Near Receptors and Five Adaptation Indices

ADAPTATION INDEX	IMPORTANCE OF NEAR RECEPTORS				N SUBJECTS
	Fairly Low	Moderate	Fairly High	High	
Developmental Status					
High	0	2	3	5	10
Medium	5	4	7	3	19
Low	1	0	1	1	3
Vegetative Functioning					
High	4	3	10	8	25
Medium	2	3	0	1	6
Low	0	0	1	0	1
Excitability					
High	2	3	3	3	11
Medium	1	1	3	1	6
Low	3	2	5	5	15
Irritability					
High	1	2	1	1	5
Medium	1	2	4	1	8
Low	4	2	6	7	19
Pleasure in Functioning					
High	2	1	3	3	9
Medium	2	1	3	2	8
Low	0	1	0	2	3

Table 16.9—States of Optimal Animation and Five Adaptation Indices

ADAPTATION INDEX	FREQUENCY OF STATES OF OPTIMAL ANIMATION					N SUBJECTS
	Rare	Occasional	Moderate	Fairly High	High	
Developmental Status						
High	0	1	1	4	4	10
Medium	0	7	10	1	1	19
Low	1	0	1	0	1	3
Vegetative Functioning						
High	1	6	7	5	6	25
Medium	0	2	4	0	0	6
Low	0	0	1	0	0	1
Excitability						
High	0	1	3	2	5	11
Medium	0	3	1	2	0	6
Low	1	4	8	1	1	15
Irritability						
High	0	1	4	0	0	5
Medium	0	1	2	1	4	8
Low	1	6	6	4	2	19
Pleasure in Functioning						
High	0	1	3	1	4	9
Medium	0	3	3	1	1	8
Low	1	0	1	1	0	3

Table 16.10—Most Prominent Modality and Five Adaptation Indices

ADAPTATION INDEX	MOST PROMINENT MODALITY				N SUBJECTS	N SUBJECTS NONE
	Touch	*Passive Motion*	*Vision*	*Sound*		
Developmental Status						
High	2	1	2	2	7	3
Medium	5	0	6	4	15	4
Low	0	1	1	1	3	0
Vegetative Functioning						
High	7	2	8	3	20	5
Medium	0	0	1	3	4	2
Low	0	0	0	1	1	0
Excitability						
High	1	1	3	4	9	2
Medium	2	0	1	0	3	3
Low	4	1	5	3	13	2
Irritability						
High	1	0	1	3	5	0
Medium	0	0	1	3	4	4
Low	6	2	7	1	16	3
Pleasure in Functioning						
High	2	1	2	3	7	2
Medium	2	0	2	2	6	2
Low	0	1	1	0	2	1

Table 16.11—Least Prominent Modality and Five Adaptation Indices

ADAPTATION INDEX	LEAST PROMINENT MODALITY				N SUBJECTS	N SUBJECTS NONE
	Touch	*Passive Motion*	*Vision*	*Sound*		
Developmental Status						
High	3	2	1	1	7	3
Medium	6	5	2	1	14	5
Low	0	2	0	0	2	1
Vegetative Functioning						
High	7	7	3	1	18	7
Medium	2	2	0	1	5	1
Low	0	0	0	0	0	1
Excitability						
High	6	3	1	0	10	1
Medium	1	1	1	1	4	2
Low	2	5	1	1	9	6
Irritability						
High	2	1	1	0	4	1
Medium	2	3	1	1	7	1
Low	5	5	1	1	12	7
Pleasure in Functioning						
High	6	1	0	0	7	2
Medium	0	5	0	1	6	2
Low	1	0	0	1	2	1

o o
o

REFERENCES

AHRENS, R. Beitrag zur Entwicklung des Physiognomic-und Mimikerkennens. *Z. d. exp. u. angew. Psychol.,* 1954, 2, 412–454.

AINSWORTH, M. D. The development of mother-infant interaction among the Ganda. In B. M. Foss (Ed.), *Determinants of infant behavior,* Vol 2. New York: John Wiley, 1963. Pp. 67–112.

AINSWORTH, M. D. Patterns of attachment behavior shown by the infant in interaction with his mother. *Merrill Palmer Quarterly,* 1964, 10, 51–58.

AINSWORTH, M. D., and BOWLBY, J. Research strategy in the study of mother-child separation. *Courier,* 1954, Vol. 4, No. 3.

AMBROSE, J. A. The development of the smiling response in early infancy. In B. M. Foss (Ed.), *Determinants of infant behavior,* Vol. 2. New York: John Wiley, 1963. Pp. 179–195.

AMES, L. B. The constancy of psycho-motor tempo in individual infants. *J. genet. Psychol.,* 1940, 57, 445–450.

APPELL, G., and DAVID, M. A. A study of mother-child interaction at thirteen months. In B. M. Foss (Ed.), *Determinants of infant behavior,* Vol. 3. New York: John Wiley, 1965.

ASERINSKY, E., and KLEITMAN, N. A motility cycle in sleeping infants as manifested in ocular and gross body movement. *J. appl. Physiol.,* 1955, 8, 11–18.

AUSUBEL, D. P. *The psychology of meaningful verbal learning.* New York: Grune and Stratton, 1963.

BARKER, R. G. On the nature of the environment: Kurt Lewin Memorial Address. *J. Social Issues,* 1963, XIX, No. 4, 17–38. (a)

BARKER, R. G. *The stream of behavior.* New York: Appleton-Century-Crofts, 1963. (b)

BARKER, R. G. Explorations in ecological psychology. *American Psychologist,* 1965, Vol. 20, No. 1.

BARKER, R. G., DEMBO, T., and LEWIN, K. Frustration and Regression. In R. G. Barker, J. S. Kounin, and H. F. Wright (Eds.), *Child behavior and development.* New York: McGraw-Hill, 1943.

BARKER, R. G., and WRIGHT, H. F. Psychological ecology and the problem of psychosocial development. *Child Development,* 1949, Vol. 20, No. 3, 131–143.

BAYLEY, N., and SCHAEFER, E. S. Relationship between socio-economic variables and the behavior of mothers toward young children. *J. genet. Psychol.,* 1960, 96, 61–77.

BAYLEY, N., and SCHAEFER, E. S. Correlations of maternal and child behaviors with the development of mental abilities: data from the Berkeley Growth Study. *Monographs of the Society for Research in Child Development,* 1964, Ser. No. 97, Vol. 27, No. 6.

BELL, R. Q. Retrospective and prospective views of early personality development. *Merrill Palmer Quarterly,* 1959/60, Vol. 6, 131–144.

BELL, R. Q., and DARLING, J. F. The prone head reaction in the human neonate: *Child Development,* 1960, 31, 463–477.

BELL, R. Q. Three tests for sex differences in tactile sensitivity in the newborn. *Biol. Neonat.,* 1964, 7, 335–347.

BELL, R. Q. Developmental psychology. *Ann. Rev. Psychol.,* 1965, Vol. XVI.

BELL, R. Q., and DARLING, J. F. The prone head reaction in the human neonate: relation with sex and tactile sensitivity. *Child Development,* 1965, 36, 943–949.

BENDA, C. E., SQUIRES, N. D., OGONIK, J., and WISE, R. Personality factors in mild mental retardation. Part I: Family background and socio-cultural patterns. *Amer. J. ment. Defic.,* 1963, 68, 24–40.

BENJAMIN, J. D. Methodological considerations in the validation and elaboration of psychoanalytic theory. *Amer. J. Orthopsychiat.,* 1950, Vol. XX.

BENJAMIN, J. D. Prediction and psychopathological theory. In L. Jessner and E. Pavenstedt (Eds.), *Dynamic psychopathology in childhood.* New York: Grune and Stratton, 1959.

BENJAMIN, J. D. Some developmental observations relating to the theory of anxiety. *J. Amer. Psychoanal. Ass.,* 1961, IX, 652–688. (a)

BENJAMIN, J. D. The innate and the experiential in development. In H. W. Brosin (Ed.), *Lectures in experimental psychiatry.* Pittsburgh: University of Pittsburgh Press, 1961. Pp. 19–42. (b)

BENJAMIN, J. D. Further comments on some developmental aspects of anxiety. In H. S. Gaskill (Ed.), *Counterpoint: Libidinal object and subject.* New York: International Universities Press, 1963. Pp. 121–153.

BERES, D., and OBERS, S. J. The effects of extreme deprivation in infancy on psychic structure in adolescence: A study in ego development. *The PSA Study of the Child,* Vol. V. International Universities Press, 1950.

BERGMAN, D., and ESCALONA, S. K. Unusual sensitivities in very young children. *The PSA Study of the Child,* Vol. III/IV. New York: International Universities Press, 1949.

BERLYNE, D. E. The influence of the albedo and complexity of stimuli on visual fixation in the human infant. *Brit. J. Psychol.,* 1958, 49, 315–318.

BERLYNE, D. E. *Conflict, arousal and curiosity.* New York: McGraw-Hill, 1960.

BERLYNE, D. E. Curiosity and exploration. *Science,* 1966, Vol. 153, No. 3731, 25–33.

BERNSTEIN, A. Some relations between techniques of feeding and training during infancy and certain behavior in childhood. *Genet. Psychol. Monographs,* 1955, 51, 3–44.

BIRNS, B. Individual differences in human neonates' responses to stimulation. *Child Development,* 1965, Vol. 30, No. 1, 249–256.

BIRNS, B., BLANK, M., and BRIDGER, W. H. The effectiveness of various soothing techniques on human neonates. *Psychosomatic Medicine,* 1966, XXVIII, No. 4, Part 1, 313–322.

BIRNS, B., BLANK, M., BRIDGER, W. H., and ESCALONA, S. K. Behavioral inhibition in neonates produced by auditory stimuli. *Child Development,* 1965, Vol. 36, No. 3, 639–645.

BLANK, M. Some maternal influences on infant's rates of sensori-motor development. *J. Child Psychiat.,* 1964, 3, 668.

BLAU, T. H., and BLAU, L. R. The sucking reflex: The effects of long feeding versus short feeding on the behavior of a human infant. *J. abnorm. soc. Psychol.,* 1955, 51, 123–125.

BLAUVELT, H. Capacity of a human neonate reflex to signal further response by present action. *Child Development,* 1962, 33, 21–28.

BLAUVELT, H., and MCKENNA, J. Capacity of the human newborn for mother-infant interaction. II. The temporal dimension of neonate response. *Psych. Res. Reports,* 1960, 13, 128–147.

Blauvelt, H., and McKenna, J. Capacity of the human newborn for orientation. In B. M. Foss (Ed.), *Determinants of infant behavior,* Vol. 1. New York: John Wiley, 1961. Pp. 3–28.

Bower, T. G. R. The visual world of infants. *Scientific American,* 1966, Vol. 215, No. 6, 80–97.

Bowlby, J. *Maternal care and mental health.* World Health Organization Monograph Series No. 2, 1951. Geneva.

Bowlby, J. The nature of the child's tie to his mother. *Int. J. Psychoanal.,* 1958, Vol. XXXIX, Part V, 1–23.

Bowlby, J. Separation anxiety. *Int. J. Psychoanal.,* 1960, 41, 1–25.

Bowlby, J., Ainsworth, M., Boston, M., and Rosenbluth, D. The effects of mother-child separation: a follow-up study. *Brit. J. Med. Psychol.,* 1956, 29, 211–247.

Boyer, L. B. On maternal overstimulation and ego defects. *The PSA Study of the Child,* Vol. IX. New York: International Universities Press, 1956. Pp. 236–256.

Brackbill, Y. Extinction of the smiling response in infants as a function of reinforcement schedule. *Child Development,* 1958, 2a, 115–124.

Braine, M., Heimer, C., Wortis, H., and Freedman, A. Factors associated with impairment of the early development of prematures. *Monographs, Society for Research in Child Development,* 1966, Vol. 31, No. 4.

Brazelton, T. B. Psychophysiologic reactions in the neonate: effect of maternal medication on the neonate and his behavior. *J. Pediatr.,* 1961, 58, No. 4, 513–518.

Brazelton, T. B. Observations on the neonate. *J. Child Psychiatry,* 1962, Vol. 1, No. 1.

Brazer, M. Panel discussion. *J. Child Psychiatry,* 1962, Vol. 1, No. 1, p. 64.

Bridger, W. H. Sensory habituation and discrimination in the newborn. Amer. *J. Psychiat.,* 1961, 117, 991–996.

Bridger, W. H. Sensory discrimination and autonomic function in the newborn. *J. Amer. Acad. Child Psychiatry,* 1962, 1, 67.

Bridger, W. H. The effects of hunger and arousal on the sucking activity of newborn infants. Presented at the annual meeting of the Society for Research in Child Development, March 16, 1966.

Bridger, W. H., Birns, B., and Blank, M. A comparison of behavioral ratings and heart rate measurements in human neonates. *Psychosom. Medicine,* 1965, Vol. XXVII, No. 2, 1965.

Bridger, W. H., and Reiser, M. F. Psychophysiological studies of the neonate: an approach toward the methodological and theoretical problems involved. *Psychosom. Med.,* 1959, 21–265.

Bridges, K. M. B. Emotional development in early infancy. *Child Development,* 1932, 3, 324–341.

Brody, S. *Patterns of mothering.* New York: International Universities Press, 1956.

Brody, S., and Axelrod, S. Anxiety, socialization and ego formation in infancy. *Int. J. Psychoanalysis,* 1966, Vol. 47.

Brown, J. States in newborn infants. *Merrill Palmer Quarterly,* 1964, 10, 313–327.

Brownfield, E. D. Activity variable in neonates. Unpublished doctoral thesis, Cornell University, 1956.

BRUNSWICK, E. *Systematic and representative design of psychological experiments.* Berkeley: University of California Press, 1947.

BUHLER, C. *The first year of life.* New York: John Day, 1930.

BUHLER, C., and HETZER, H. Individual differences among children in the first two years of life. *Child Study,* 1929, 7, 11–13.

BURGERS, J. M. Curiosity and play: basic factors in the development of life. *Science,* 1966, 154, No. 3757, 1680–1681.

CALDWELL, B. The usefulness of the critical period hypothesis in the study of filiative behavior. *Merrill Palmer Quarterly,* 1962, 8, 229–242.

CALDWELL, B., HERSHER, L., LIPTON, E. L., RICHMOND, J. B., STERN, G. A., EDDY, E., PRACHMAN, R., and ROTHMAN, A. Mother-infant interaction in monomatric and polymatric families. *Amer. J. Orthopsychiat.,* 1963, 33, 653–64.

CALL, J. D., and MARSCHAK, M. Styles and games in infancy. *J. Child Psychiat.,* 1966, Vol. 5, No. 2, 193–209.

CASLER, L. Maternal deprivation: A critical review of the literature. *Monographs, Society for Research in Child Development,* 1961, No. 2.

CATTELL, P. *The measurement of intelligence in infants and young children.* New York: Psychological Corp., 1940.

CHARLESWORTH, W. R. Development of the object concept: A methodological study. Paper presented at annual meeting of the American Psychological Association, Sept., 1965.

CLARKE, A. D. B., and CLARKE, A. M. Recovery from the effects of deprivation. *Acta Psychol.,* 1959, 16, 137–144.

CLAUSEN, J. A. Family structure, socialization and personality. In L. W. Hoffman and M. L. Hoffman (Eds.), *Review of child development research,* Vol. 2, New York: Russell Sage Foundation, 1966.

COLBY, K. M. *Energy and structure in psychoanalysis.* New York: The Ronald Press, 1955.

COLEMAN, R., and PROVENCE, S. Environmental retardation (hospitalism) in infants living in families. *Pediatrics,* 1957, 19, 285–292.

DAMBORSKA, M., and STEPANOVA, P. Problems of adaptability of institutionalized children. *Cesk Pedist.,* 1962, 17, 600–606.

DARWIN, C. A biographical sketch of an infant. *Mind,* 1877, No. 7, 285–294.

DAVID, M., and APPELL, G. A study of nursing care and nurse-infant interaction. In B. M. Foss (Ed.), *Determinants of infant behavior,* Vol. 1. New York: John Wiley, 1961. Pp. 121–136.

DAVIDS, A., HOLDEN, R. H., and GRAY, G. B. Maternal anxiety during pregnancy and adequacy of mother and child adjustment eight months following childbirth. *Child Development,* 1963, 34, 993–1002.

DE LISSOVOY, V. Head banging in early infancy: a study of infancy. *Child Development,* 1962, 33, 43–56.

DEMBER, W. N., and EARL, R. W. Analysis of exploratory, manipulatory and curiosity behaviors. *Psychol. Rev.,* 1957, 64, 91–96.

DEMBO, T. Anger as a dynamic problem (1931). In K. Lewin, *A dynamic theory of personality.* New York: McGraw-Hill, 1935.

DENNIS, W. Causes of Retardation Among Institutionalized Children. In C. R. Stendler (Ed.), *Readings in child development* (2d ed.). New York: Harcourt, Brace & World, 1964.

DENNIS, W., and NAJARIAN, P. Infant development under environmental handicap. *Psychol. Monogr.,* 1957, 71, No. 436.

DITTRICHOVA, J., and LAPACKOVA, V. Development of the waking state in young infants. *Child Development,* 1964, 35, 365–370.

Dubos, R. Humanistic biology. *American Scientist,* 53, 1965.

Engen, T., Lipsit, L. P., and Kaye, H. Olfactory responses and adaptation in the human neonate. *J. Comp. Physiol. Psychol.,* 1963, 56, 73–77.

Erikson, E. H. *Childhood and society* (2d ed.). New York: W. W. Norton, 1963.

Escalona, S. K. The psychological situation of mother and child upon return from the hospital. *Problems of infancy and early childhood.* Josiah Macy Jr. Foundation, Transactions of the Third Conference, 1949.

Escalona, S. K. Emotional development during the first year of life. *Conference on infancy and early childhood.* Transactions of the Josiah Macy Jr. Foundation, 1953.

Escalona, S. K. The case of Jerry. In K. Soddy (Ed.), *Mental health and infant development.* New York: Basic Books, 1955.

Escalona, S. K. The study of individual difference and the problem of state. *Child Psychiatry,* Vol. 1, No. 1, 1962.

Escalona, S. K. Patterns of infantile experience and the developmental process. *The Psychoanalytic Study of the Child,* Vol. XVIII, 197–244. New York: International Universities Press, 1963.

Escalona, S. K. Some determinants of individual differences in early ego development. *Transactions of the N.Y. Acad. of Sciences,* May 1965, Ser. II, Vol. 27, No. 7, 802–817.

Escalona, S. K., and Heider, G. *Prediction and outcome: A study of child development.* New York: Basic Books, 1959.

Escalona, S. K., and Leitch, M. The reaction of infants to stress. In *The psychoanalytic study of the child.* New York: International Universities Press, 1949.

Escalona, S. K., Leitch, M., and others. Early phases of personality development: a nonnormative study of infant behavior. *Monographs of the Society for Research in Child Development,* 1953, Vol. XVII, Serial No. 54, No. 1.

Fairweather, D. V. J., and Illsley, R. Obstetric and social origins of mentally handicapped children. *Brit. J. Prev. Soc. Medicine,* 1960, Vol. 14, No. 4, 149–159.

Fajans, S. Success, persistence and activity in the infant and the small child (1933). In K. Lewin, *A dynamic theory of personality.* New York: McGraw-Hill, 1935.

Fantz, R. L. A method for studying depth perception in infants under 6 months of age. *Psychol. Rec.,* 1961, 11, 27–32.

Fantz, R. L. Visual perception from birth as shown by pattern selectivity. In H. E. Whipple (Ed.), *New Issues in infant development. Annals of the N.Y. Academy of Sciences,* 118, 793–814, 1965.

Fantz, R. L. The critical early influence: mother love or environmental stimulation. *Am. J. Orthopsychiat.,* 1966, 36, No. 2, 330–331 (Abstract).

Fantz, R. L., Ordy, J. M., and Udelf, M. S. Maturation of pattern vision in infants during the first six months. *J. Comp. Physiol. and Psychol.,* 1962, 55, 907–917.

Flavel, I. H. *The developmental psychology of Jean Piaget.* Princeton: Van Nostrand, 1963.

Foss, B. M. (Ed.). *Determinants of infant behavior.* New York: John Wiley, 1961, 1963, 1965. 3 vols.

Fraiberg, S., and Freedman, D. A. Studies in the ego development of the congenitally blind child. *The Psychoanalytic Study of the Child,* Vol. XIX, 113–169. New York: International Universities Press, 1964.

FRAIBERG, S., SIEGEL, B. L., and GIBSON, R. The role of sound in the search behavior of a blind infant. *The Psychoanalytic Study of the Child,* Vol. XXI, 327–357. New York: International Universities Press, 1966.

FRANK, G. H. The role of the family in the development of psychopathology. *Psychological Bulletin,* 1965, Vol. 64, No. 3, 191–205.

FREEDMAN, D. G. The infant's fear of strangers and the flight response. *J. Child Psychol. and Psychiatry,* 1961, 2, 242–248.

FREEDMAN, D. G. Hereditary control of early social behavior. In B. M. Foss (Ed.), *Determinants of infant behavior,* Vol. 3. New York: John Wiley, 1965. Pp. 149–159.

FREEDMAN, D. G., and KELLER, B. Inheritance of behavior in infants. *Science,* 1963, 140, 196–198.

FRIES, M. E., and WOOLF, P. J. Some hypotheses on the role of congenital activity type in personality development. *The Psychoanalytic Study of the Child,* Vol. VIII, 48–62. New York: International Universities Press, 1953.

FRIES, M. E. Some hypotheses on the role of congenital activity type in personality development. *Int. J. Psychoanal.,* 1954, Vol. XXXV, Part 6.

FREUD, A. Child observation and prediction of development. A memorial lecture in honor of Ernst Kris. *The Psychoanalytic Study of the Child,* Vol. XIII. New York: International Universities Press, 1958.

FREUD, A., and BURLINGHAM, D. T. *Infants without families.* New York: International Universities Press, 1944.

FREUD, A., and DANN, S. An experiment in group upbringing. *The Psychoanalytic Study of the Child,* Vol. VI, 127–168. New York: International Universities Press, 1951.

FREUD, S. *The interpretation of dreams* (1900). *Collected works* (standard ed.), Vol. 5. London: Hogarth Press, 1958.

FREUD, S. *The disposition to obsessional neurosis* (1913). *Collected works* (standard ed.), Vol. 12. London: Hogarth Press, 1958.

FREUD, S. *Three essays on sexuality:* II. *Infantile sexuality* (1905). *Collected works* (standard ed.), Vol. 7. London: Hogarth Press, 1957.

FREUND, B. On satiation in and between menstrual periods (1930). In K. Lewin, *A dynamic theory of personality.* New York: McGraw-Hill, 1935.

FUNK, J. The chemical nature of the substance which cures polyneuritis in birds induced by a diet of polished rice. *J. Physiol.,* 1911, Vol. 43.

GEBER, M. The psycho-motor development of African children in the first year of life and the influence of maternal behavior. *J. Soc. Psychol.,* 1958, 47, 185–195.

GESELL, A. Early evidence of individuality in the human infant. *Science Monthly,* 1937, 45, 217–225.

GESELL, A., and HALVERSON, H. Development of thumb opposition in the human infant. *J. genet. Psychol.,* 1936, 48, 339–361.

GESELL, A., and AMATRUDA, C. *Developmental diagnosis* (2d ed.). New York: Hoeber, 1947.

GEWIRTZ, J. L. A learning analysis of the effects of normal stimulation, privation and deprivation on the acquisition of social motivation and attachment. In B. M. Foss (Ed.), *Determinants of infant behavior,* Vol. 3. New York: John Wiley, 1965. (a)

GEWIRTZ, J. L. The course of smiling by groups of Israeli infants in the first eighteen months of life. In *Scripta Hierosolymitana,* Publication of the Hebrew University, Jerusalem. Vol. XIV: *Studies in psychology.* Jerusalem: The Magnus Press, 1965. (b)

GEWIRTZ, J. L., and GEWIRTZ, H. B. Stimulus conditions, infant behaviors, and social learning in four Israeli child-rearing environments: A preliminary report illustrating differences in environment and behavior between the 'only' and the 'youngest' child. In B. M. Foss (Ed.), *Determinants of infant behavior,* Vol. 3. New York: John Wiley, 1965.

GIFFORD, S. Sleep, time and the early ego. *J. Amer. Psychoanal. Assn.,* 1960, 8, 5–42.

GILLILAND, A. R. Socio-economic status and race as factors in infant intelligence tests. *Child Development,* 1951, 22, 271–273.

GORDON, N. S., and BELL, R. Q. Activity in the human newborn. *Psychol. Reports,* 1961, 9, 103–116.

GOUIN-DECARIE, T. *Intelligence and affectivity in early childhood.* New York: International Universities Press, 1965.

GRAHAM, F. K. Behavioral differences between normal and traumatized newborns. I. The test procedures. *Psychol. Monogr.,* 1956, 70, No. 20.

GRAHAM, F. K., ERNHART, C. B., THURSTON, D., and CROFT, M. Development three years after perinatal anoxia and other potentially damaging newborn experiences. *Psychol. Monogr.,* 1962, 76, No. 3.

GUNTHER, M. Infant behavior at the breast. In B. M. Foss (Ed.), *Determinants of infant behavior,* Vol. 1. New York: John Wiley, 1961.

HALVERSON, H. M. An experimental study of prehension in infants by means of systematic cinema records. *Genet. Psychol. Monogr.,* 1931, 10, 107–286.

HARLOW, H. F. Mice, monkeys, men and motives. *Psychol. Rev.,* 1953, 60, 23. (a)

HARLOW, H. F. Motivation as a factor in the acquisition of new responses. In M. R. Jones (Ed.), *Current theory and research in motivation.* Lincoln: University of Nebraska Press, 1953. (b) Pp. 24–48.

HARTMANN, H. Comments on the psychoanalytic theory of instinctual drives. *The PSA Quarterly,* 1948, 17, 368–388.

HARTMANN, H. Psychoanalysis and developmental psychology. *The Psychoanalytic Study of the Child,* Vol. V. New York: International Universities Press, 1950.

HARTMANN, H. Mutual influences in development of ego and id. *The Psychoanalytic Study of the Child,* Vol. VII. New York: International Universities Press, 1952.

HARTMANN, H. Notes on the reality principle. *The Psychoanalytic Study of the Child,* Vol. XI. New York: International Universities Press, 1956.

HARTMANN, H. *Ego psychology and the problem of adaptation.* New York: International Universities Press, 1958.

HARTMANN, H., KRIS, E., and LOEWENSTEIN, R. Comments on the formation of psychic structure. *The Psychoanalytic Study of the Child,* Vol. II. New York: International Universities Press, 1946.

HARTMANN, H., KRIS, E., and LOEWENSTEIN, R. Notes on the theory of aggression. *The Psychoanalytic Study of the Child,* Vol. III/IV. New York: International Universities Press, 1949.

HEBB, D. O. *The organization of behavior.* New York: John Wiley, 1949.

HEBB, D. O. Drives and the CNS (conceptual nervous system). *Psychol. Rev.,* 1955, 62, 243–254.

HEIDER, G. M. Vulnerability in infants. *Bull. Menninger Clinic,* 1960, 24, 104–114.

HEINICKE, C. M. Some effects of separating two-year-old children from their parents; a comparative study. *Human Relations,* 1956, 9, 105–176.

HEINSTEIN, M. I. Behavioral correlates of breast-bottle regimes under varying parent-infant relationships. *Monographs, Society for Research in Child Development,* 1963, 28, No. 4.

HELD, R., and HEIN, A. Movement produced stimulation in the development of visually guided behavior. *J. Comp. Physiol. Psychol.,* 1963, 56, 872–876.

HELLMAN, I. Sudden separation and its effect followed over 20 years: Hempstead Nursery follow-up studies. *The Psychoanalytic Study of the Child,* Vol. XVII. New York: International Universities Press, 1962.

HENDRICK, I. Instinct and ego during infancy. *Psychoanal. Quart.,* 1942, XI, No. 1.

HENDRY, L. S., and KESSEN, W. Oral behavior of newborn infants as a function of age and time since feeding. *Child Development,* 1964, 35, 201–208.

HOFFMAN, M. L., and HOFFMAN, L. W. (Eds.). *Child development research,* Vol. 1. New York: Russell Sage Foundation, 1964.

HOPPER, H. E., and PINNEAU, S. R. Frequency of regurgitation in infancy as related to the amount of stimulation received from the mother. *Child Development,* 1957, 28, 229–235.

HUNT, J. McV. Experience and the development of motivation: some reinterpretations. *Child Development,* 1960, 31, 489–504.

HUNT, J. McV. *Intelligence and experience.* New York: Ronald Press, 1961.

HUNT, J. McV. Piaget's observations as a source of hypotheses concerning motivation. *Merrill-Palmer Quarterly,* 1963, Vol. 9, No. 4. (a)

HUNT, J. McV. Motivation Inherent in Information Processing and Action. In O. Harvey (Ed.), *Motivation and social interaction.* New York: Ronald Press, 1963. (b)

INHELDER, B. Criteria of the Stages of Development. In I. M. Tanner and B. Inhelder (Eds.), *Discussions on child development,* Vol. I. Geneva: World Health Organization, 1953.

IRWIN, O. C. The amount and nature of activity of newborn infants under constant stimulating conditions during the first 10 days of life. *Genet. Psychol. Monogr.,* 1930, 8, 1–92.

IRWIN, O. C. The effect of darkness on the activity of newborn infants. University of Iowa *Studies in Child Welfare,* 1934, 9, 163–175.

IRWIN, O. C. The effect of strong light on the body activity of the newborn. *J. Comp. Psychol.,* 1941, 32, 233–236.

JACKSON, E., KLATSKIN, E. H., and WILKIN, L. C. Early child development in relation to degree of flexibility of maternal attitude. *The Psychoanalytic Study of the Child,* Vol. VII. New York: International Universities Press, 1952.

KAGAN, J., and MOSS, H. A. *Birth to maturity: A study in psychological development.* New York: John Wiley, 1962.

KARSTEN, S. Psychical Satiation (1928). In K. Lewin, *A dynamic theory of personality.* New York: McGraw-Hill, 1935.

KESSEN, W. Research in the psychological development of infants: an overview. *Merrill-Palmer Quarterly,* 1963, 9, 83–94.

KESSEN, W., HENDRY, L. S., and LEUTZENDORFF, A. M. Measurement of movement in the newborn. *Child Development,* 1961, 32, 95–105.

KLACKENBERG, G. Studies in maternal deprivation in infants' homes. *Acta Paediatrica,* 1956, 45, 1–12.

KLATSKIN, E. H. Intelligence test performance at one year among infants raised with flexible methodology. *J. Clin. Psychol.,* 1952, 8, 230–237.

KLATSKIN, E. H., JACKSON, E. B., and WILKIN, L. C. The influence of degree of flexibility in maternal child care practices on early child behavior. *Amer. J. Orthopsychiat.,* 1956, 26, 79–93.

KLEITMAN, N., and ENGELMANN, T. G. Sleep characteristics of infants. *J. Appl. Physiol.,* 1953, 6, 269–282.

KNOBLOCH, H., and PASAMANICK, B. The relationship of race and socio-economic status to the development of motor behavior patterns in infancy. *Psychiat. Res. Rep.,* 1958, No. 10.

KNOBLOCH, H., and PASAMANICK, B. Syndrome of minimal cerebral damage in infancy. *J.A.M.A.,* 1959, 170, 1384–1387.

KNOBLOCH, H., RIDER, R., HARPER, P., and PASAMANICK, B. Neuropsychiatric sequela of prematurity: a longitudinal study. *J.A.M.A.,* 1956, 1961, 581.

KOEPKE, ERFURTH, SAATHOP, and WOLMANN. Studies on feeblemindedness. In K. Lewin, *A dynamic theory of personality.* New York: McGraw-Hill, 1935.

KORNER, A. F. Some hypotheses regarding the significance of individual differences at birth for later development. *The Psychoanalytic Study of the Child,* Vol. XIX. New York: International Universities Press, 1964.

KORNER, A. F., and GROBSTEIN, R. Visual alertness as related to soothing in neonates: Implications for maternal stimulation and early deprivation. *Child Development,* 1966, Vol. 37, No. 4, 867–877.

KUHLEN, R. G., and THOMPSON, G. G. (Eds.) *Psychological Studies of Human Development.* New York: Appleton-Century-Crofts, 1963.

KUNST, M. S. A study of thumb and fingersucking in infants. *Psychol. Monographs,* 1948, 62, No. 3.

LAMPL DE GROOT, J. On defense and development: Normal and pathological. *The Psychoanalytic Study of the Child,* Vol. XII. New York: International Universities Press, 1957.

LENNEBERG, H. H., REBELSKY, F., and NICHOLS, J. The vocalization of infants born to deaf and hearing parents. *Human Development,* 1965, 8, 23–37.

LESSER, G. S., FIFER, G., and CLARK, D. H. Mental abilities of children from different social class and cultural groups. *Monographs, Society for Research in Child Development,* 1965, Vol. 30, No. 4.

LEVY, D. M. The infant's earliest memory of innoculation: A contribution to public health procedure. *J. genet. Psychol.,* 1960, 96, 3–46.

LEWIN, K. *A dynamic theory of personality.* New York: McGraw-Hill, 1935.

LEWIN, K. *Principles of topological psychology.* New York: McGraw-Hill, 1936.

LEWIS, M., BARTELS, B., FADEL, D., and CAMPBELL, H. Infant attention: The effect of familiar and novel visual stimuli as a function of age. Read at the 37th Annual Meeting of Eastern Psychological Association, April, 1966, New York.

LIPSIT, L. P., ENGEN, T., and KAYE, H. Developmental changes in the olfactory threshold of the neonate. *Child Development,* 1963, 34, 371–376.

LIPSIT, L. P., and LEVY, N. Electrotactual threshold in the neonate. *Child Development,* 1959, 30, 547–554.

LIPSIT, L. P., and SPIKER, C. C. (Eds.) *Advances in child development and behavior,* Vol. 1. New York: Academic Press, 1963.

LIPTON, E. L., STEINSCHNEIDER, A., and RICHMOND, J. B. Autonomic function in the neonate. II. Physiological effects of motor restraint. *Psychosom. Med.,* 1960, 22, 57–65.

LIPTON, E. L., STEINSCHNEIDER, A., and RICHMOND, J. B. Autonomic function in the neonate. IV. Individual differences in cardiac reactivity. *Psychosom. Med.,* 1961, 23, 472–484. (a)

LIPTON, E. L., STEINSCHNEIDER, A., and RICHMOND, J. B. Autonomic function in the neonate: III. Methodological considerations. *Psychosom. Med.,* 1961, 23, 461–471. (b)

LUSTMAN, S. L. Rudiments of the Ego. In *The psychoanalytic study of the child,* Vol. II. New York: International Universities Press, 1956.

MAAS, H. S. Long term effects of early childhood separation and group care. *Vita Humana,* 1963, 6, 34–56.

MACCOBY, E. E., DOWLEY, E. M., and HAGEN, J. W. Activity level and intellectual functioning in normal preschool children. *Child Development,* Vol. 36, No. 3, 1965.

MARSCHAK, M. A method for evaluating child-parent interaction under controlled conditions. *J. genet. Psychol.,* 1960, 97, 3–22.

MCGRADE, B. J., KESSEN, W., and LEUTZENDORFF, A. Activity in the human newborn as related to delivery difficulty. *Child Development,* 1965, 36, 73–79.

MEILI, R. *Anfänge der Charakterentwicklung.* Bern and Stuttgart: Verlag Hans Huber, 1957. (a)

MEILI, R. Angstentstehung bei Kleinkindern. *Schweiz. z. Psychol.,* 1957, 14, 195–212. (b)

MOORE, T., and UCKO, L. E. Night waking in infancy. *Arch. Dis. Childh.,* 1957, 32, 333–342.

MOSS, H. A. Methodological issues in studying mother-infant interaction. *Amer. J. Orthopsychiat.,* April 1965, Vol. 35, No. 3, 482–486.

MURPHY, L. B. *Personality in young children.* New York: Basic Books, 1956.

MURPHY, L. B. *The widening world of childhood.* New York: Basic Books, 1962.

MURPHY, L. B. Some aspects of the first relationship. *Int. J. Psychoanal.,* 1964, Vol. 45, Part 1.

MURRAY, H. A. *Explorations in personality.* New York: Oxford University Press, 1938.

NAGERA, H. Sleep and its disturbances approached developmentally. *The Psychoanalytic Study of the Child,* Vol. XXI. New York: International Universities Press, 1966. (a)

NAGERA, H. Early childhood disturbances, the infantile neurosis and the adulthood disturbances. *The Psychoanalytic Study of the Child,* Monograph No. 2. New York: International Universities Press, 1966. (b)

NEILON, P. Shirley's babies after fifteen years. In R. C. Stendler (Ed.), *Readings in child behavior and development* (2d ed.). New York: Harcourt Brace and World, 1964.

ORLANSKY, H. Infant care and personality. *Psychol. Bull.,* 1949, 46, 1–48.

OURTH, L., and BROWN, K. B. Inadequate mothering and disturbance in the neonatal period. *Child Development,* 1961, 32, 287–295.

PAPOUŠEK, H. The development of higher nervous activity in children in the first half year of life. *Society for Research in Child Development, Monographs,* 1965, Vol. 30, No. 2.

PARMELEE, A. H., WENNER, W. H., and SCHULZ, H. R. Infant sleep patterns from birth to 16 weeks of age. *J. Ped.,* 1964, 65, 576–582.

PATTON, R. G., and GARDNER, L. J. *Growth failure in maternal deprivation.* Springfield, Ill.: Charles C Thomas, 1963.

PEIPER, A. *Cerebral function in infancy.* New York: Consultant's Bureau, 1963.

PETERSON, C. H., and SPANO, F. L. Breast feeding, maternal rejection and child personality. In *Character and Personality,* Vol. 10, 62–66, 1941.

PIAGET, J. *The origins of intelligence in children.* New York: International Universities Press, 1952.

PIAGET, J. *The construction of reality in the child.* New York: Basic Books, 1954. (a)

PIAGET, J. Panel discussion in J. M. Tanner and B. Inhelder (Eds.), *Discussions of child development,* Vol. 2. New York: International Universities Press, 1954. (b)

PIAGET, J. The general problems of the psychobiological development of the child. In J. M. Tanner and B. Inhelder (Eds.), *Discussions on Child Development,* Vol. 4. New York: International Universities Press, 1956.

PINNEAU, S. R., and HOPPER, H. E. The relationship between incidence of specific gastro-intestinal reactions of the infant and psychological characteristics of the mother. *J. genet. Psychol.,* 1958, 93, 3–13.

PRECHTL, H. F. R. The directed head turning response and allied movements of the human body. *Behavior,* 1958, 13, 212–242.

PRECHTL, H. F. R. The mother-child interaction in babies with minimal brain damage (a follow-up study). In B. M. Foss (Ed.), *Determinants of infant behavior,* Vol. 2. New York: John Wiley, 1963.

PREYER, W. *The mind of the child.* Part I: the Senses and the Will. New York: Appleton, 1890.

PROVENCE, S. Disturbed personality development in infancy: a comparison of two inadequately nurtured infants. *Merrill-Palmer Quarterly,* 1965, II(2), 149–170.

PROVENCE, S., and LIPTON, R. C. *Infants in institutions.* New York: International Universities Press, 1962.

PRZELACNIKOWA, M., BUTERLEWICZ, H., and CHRZANOWSKA, D. The mental development of children aged from 9 months to 3 years, brought up in crèches or at home. *Psychol. Wych.,* 1963, No. 1, 2–16.

PULVER, W. Spannungen und Störungen im Verhalten des Säuglings. *Beiträge z. Genet. Charakterol.,* 1959, No. 2, 5–123.

RADKE-YARROW, M. The elusive evidence. *Newsletter, Division of Developmental Psychology,* Fall, 1963.

REICHSMAN, F. ENGEL, G. L. HARWAY, V., and ESCALONA, S. Monica, an infant with gastric fistula and depression; an interim report on her development to the age of four years. *Psychiatric Research Reports,* 1958, 8 (American Psychiatric Association).

RHEINGOLD, H. L. The modification of social responsiveness in institutional babies. *Monographs of Society for Research in Child Development,* 1956, 21, No. 63 (No. 2).

RHEINGOLD, H. The measurement of maternal care. *Child Development,* 1960, 31, 565–575.

RHEINGOLD, H. L. The effect of environmental stimulation upon social and exploratory behavior in the human infant. In B. M. Foss (Ed.), *Determinants of infant behavior,* Vol. 1. New York: John Wiley, 1961.

RHEINGOLD, H. L. Controlling the infant's exploratory behavior. In B. M. Foss (Ed.), *Determinants of infant behavior,* Vol. 2. New York: John Wiley, 1963.

RHEINGOLD, H. L. The development of social behavior in the human infant. *Monographs, Society for Research in Child Development,* 1966, Vol. 31, No. 5.

RHEINGOLD, H. L., and BAYLEY, N. The later effects of an experimental modification of mothering. *Child Development,* 1959, 30, 363–372.

RHEINGOLD, H. L., Gewirtz, J. L., and Ross, H. Social-conditioning of vocalizations in the infant. *J. Compar. Physiolog. Psychol.,* 1959, 52, 68–73.

RIBBLE, M. *The rights of infants.* New York: Columbia University Press, 1943.

RICHMOND, J. B., and CALDWELL, B. M. Child rearing practices and their consequences. In A. J. Solnit and S. A. Provence (Eds.), *Modern perspectives in child development.* New York: International Universities Press, 1963.

RICHMOND, J. B., and LIPTON, E. L. Some aspects of the neurophysiology of the newborn and their implications for child development. In L. Jessner and E. Pavenstedt (Eds.), *Dynamic Psychopathology in Childhood.* New York: Grune and Stratton, 1959.

RICHMOND, J. B., LIPTON, E. L., and STEINSCHNEIDER, A. Observations on differences in autonomic nervous system function between and within individuals during early infancy. *J. Child Psychiatry,* Vol. 1, No. 1, 83–91.

RITVO, S., MCCOLLUM, A. T., OMWAKE, E., PROVENCE, S. A., and SOLNIT, A. J. Some relations of constitution, environment and personality as observed in a longitudinal study of child development. In A. J. Solnit and S. A. Provence (Eds.), *Modern perspectives in child development.* New York: International Universities Press, 1963.

ROSENBLITH, J. F., and DELUCIA, L. A. Tactile sensitivity and muscular strength in the neonate. *Bio. Neon.,* 1963, 5, 266–282.

ROSS, S., FISHER, A. E., and KING, O. Sucking behavior: a review of the literature. *J. genet. Psychol.,* 1957, 91, 63–81.

SANDER, L. W. Issues in early mother-child interaction. *J. Amer. Acad. of Child Psychiatry,* 1962, Vol. 7, No. 1, 141–165.

SANDLER, A. M. Aspects of passivity and ego development in the blind child. *The Psychoanalytic Study of the Child,* Vol. XVIII. New York: International Universities Press, 1963.

SAYEGH, J., and DENNIS, W. The effect of supplementary experiences upon the behavioral development of infants in institutions. *Child Development,* 1965, 36, 1, 81–90.

SCHAEFER, E. S., and BAYLEY, N. Maternal behavior, child behavior, and their intercorrelations from infancy through adolescence. *Monographs, Society for Research in Child Development,* 1963, Vol. 28, No. 3.

SCHAFFER, H. R. Objective obervations of personality development in early infancy. *Brit. J. Med. Psychol.,* 1958, 31, 174–183.

SCHAFFER, H. R. Some Issues for Research in the Study of Attachment Behavior. In B. M. Foss (Ed.), *Determinants of infant behavior,* Vol. 2. New York: John Wiley, 1963.

SCHAFFER, H. R. Changes in developmental quotient under two conditions of maternal separation. *Brit. J. Soc. Clin. Psychol.,* 1965, 4, 39–46.

SCHAFFER, H. R. Activity level as a constitutional determinant of infantile reaction to deprivation. *Child Development,* 1966, Vol. 37, No. 3, 595–602. (a)

SCHAFFER, H. R. The onset of fear of strangers and the incongruity hypothesis. *J. Child Psychol. Psychiatry,* 1966, Vol. 7, 95–106. (b)

SCHAFFER, H. R., and CALLENDER, W. M. Psychological effects of hospitalization in infancy. *Pediatrics,* 1959, 24, 528–539.

SCHAFFER, H. R., and EMERSON, P. E. The development of social attachments in infancy. *Monographs, Society for Research in Child Development,* 1964, 29, No. 3.

SCOTT, J. P. The process of primary socialization in canine and human infants. *Monographs, Society for Research in Child Development,* 1963, Serial No. 85, Vol. 28, No. 1.

SHIRLEY, M. M. *The first two years, a study of twenty-five babies.* Vol. 1. *Postural and locomotor development.* Minneapolis: University of Minnesota Press, 1931.

SHIRLEY, M. M. *The first two years, a study of twenty-five babies.* Vol. 2: *Intellectual development.* Minneapolis: University of Minnesota Press, 1933. (a)

SHIRLEY, M. M. *The first two years, a study of twenty-five babies.* Vol. 3: *Personality manifestations.* Minneapolis: University of Minnesota Press, 1933. (b)

SIEGEL, S. *Nonparametric statistics for the behavioral sciences.* New York: McGraw-Hill, 1956.

SKEELS, H. M. Adult status of children with contrasting early life experiences. *Monographs, Society for Research in Child Development,* 1966, Vol. 31, No. 3.

SKINNER, B. F. The phylogeny and ontogeny of behavior. *Science,* 1966, Vol. 153, No. 3741, 1205–1213.

SMITH, C. The newborn patient. *Pediatrics,* 1955, Vol. 16, No. 2.

SODDY, K. (Ed.). *Mental health and infant development.* (2 vols.) New York: Basic Books, 1956.

SOLOMONS, G., and SOLOMONS, H. Factors affecting motor performance in 4 months old infants. *Child Development,* 1964, Vol. 35, No. 4, 1283–1295.

SPIKER, C. C. The concept of development: relevant and irrelevant issues. *Monographs, Society for Research in Child Development,* 1966, Vol. 31, No. 5, 40–54.

SPITZ, R. Hospitalism: an inquiry into the genesis of psychiatric conditions in early childhood. *The Psychoanalytic Study of the Child,* Vol. I, 53–74. New York: International Universities Press, 1945.

SPITZ, R. Hospitalism: a follow-up report on investigation described in Volume I, 1945. *The Psychoanalytic Study of the Child,* Vol. II, 113–117. New York: International Universities Press, 1946.

SPITZ, R. The role of ecological factors in emotional development in infancy. *Child Development,* 1949, 20, 145–155. (a)

SPITZ, R. Autoeroticism: some empirical findings and hypotheses on three of its manifestations in the first year of life. *The Psychoanalytic Study of the Child,* Vol. III/IV, 85–120. New York: International Universities Press, 1949. (b)

SPITZ, R. *No and yes.* New York: International Universities Press, 1957.

SPITZ, R. *The first year of life.* New York: International Universities Press, 1965.

SPITZ, R., and WOLF, K. The smiling response: a contribution to the ontogenesis of social relationships. *Genet. Psychol. Monogr.,* 1946, 34, 57–125. (a)

SPITZ, R., and WOLF, K. Environment versus race—environment as an etiological factor in psychiatric disturbances in infancy. *J. Nerv. Mental Dis.,* 1946, 103, 520–521. (b)

SPITZ, R., and WOLF, K. Anaclitic depression: an inquiry into the genesis of psychiatric conditions in early childhood. II. *The Psychoanalytic Study of the Child,* Vol. II, 313–342. New York: International Universities Press, 1946. (c)

STEINSCHNEIDER, A., LIPTON, E. L., and RICHMOND, J. B. Auditory sensitivity in the infant: effect of intensity on cardiac and motor responsivity. *Child Development,* 37, 233–252, 1966.

STENDLER, C. B. (Ed.) *Readings in Child Behavior and Development* (2d ed.). New York: Harcourt Brace & World, 1964.

STERN, W. *Psychology of Early Childhood up to the Sixth Year of Age.* New York: Henry Holt, 1926.

STOTT, L. H. The persisting effects of early family experience upon personality development. *Merrill Palmer Quarterly,* 1957, 3, 145–159.

STOTT, L. H. An empirical approach to motivation based on the behavior of a young child. *J. Child Psychol. Psychiatr.,* 1961, 2, 97–117.

TANNER, J. M. Physical and physiological aspects of child development. In J. Tanner and B. Inhelder (Eds.), *Discussions on child development,* Vol. I. New York: International Universities Press, 1953.

TANNER, J. M., and INHELDER, B. *Discussions on child development,* Vol. I. Proceedings of Meetings of the World Health Organization Study Group on the Psychobiological Development of the Child. New York: International Universities Press, 1953.

TANNER, J. M., and INHELDER, B. *Discussions on child development,* Vol. II. 1954.

TANNER, J. M., and INHELDER, B. *Discussions on child development,* Vol. III. 1955.

TANNER, J. M., and INHELDER, B. *Discussions on child development,* Vol. IV. 1956.

TENNES, K. M., and LAMPL, E. E. Stranger and separation anxiety in infancy. *J. Nerv. Ment. Dis.,* 1964, Vol. 139, No. 3.

TENNES, K. M., and LAMPL, E. E. Some aspects of mother-child relationship pertaining to infantile separation anxiety. *J. Nerv. Ment. Dis.,* 1966, Vol. 143, No. 5, 426–437.

THOMAS, A., BIRCH, H. G., CHESS, S., HERTZIG, M. E., and KORN, S. *Behavioral individuality in early childhood.* New York: New York University Press, 1963.

WALTERS, R. H., and PARKE, R. D. The Role of Distance Receptors in the Development of Social Responsiveness. In L. P. Lipsit and C. C. Spiker (Eds.), *Advances in child development and behavior,* Vol. 2. New York: Academic Press, 1965.

WARNER, W. W., MEEKER, M., and EELS, K. *Social class in America—a manual of procedure for the measurement of social status.* Chicago: Science Research Associates, 1949.

WEISBERG, P. Social and non-social conditioning of infant vocalizations. *Child Development,* 1963, Vol. 34, No. 2, 377–388.

WENAR, C., and WENAR, S. C. The short-term prospective model, the illusion of time, and the tabula rasa child. *Child Development,* 1963, Vol. 34, No. 3, 697–708.

WERNER, H. *Comparative psychology of mental development.* (rev. ed.) New York: Follett, 1948.

WERNER, H., and KAPLAN, H. *Symbol formation.* New York: John Wiley, 1963.

WERTHEIMER, M. Psychomotor coordination of auditory and visual space at birth. *Science,* 1961, 134, 1692.

WHIPPLE, H. E. (Ed.). New issues in infant development. *Annals of the N.Y. Academy of Science,* 1965.

WHITE, B. L. Plasticity in perceptual development during the first six months of life. Read to the American Association for the Advancement of Science, December 30, 1963.

WHITE, B. L., CASTLE, P., and HELD, R. Observations on the development of visually directed reaching. *Child Development,* 1964, 35, 349–364.

WHITE, R. W. Motivation reconsidered: The concept of competence. *Psychol. Rev.,* 1959, 66, 297–333.

WHITE, R. W. Ego and reality in psychoanalytic theory. *Psychol. Issues,* III, 1963, No. 3, Monograph No. II.

WILLIAMS, J. P., and KESSEN, W. Effects of hand-mouth contacts on neonatal movement. *Child Development,* 1961, 32, 243–248.

WILLIAMS, J. R., and SCOTT, R. B. Growth of Negro infants: IV. Motor development and its relationship to child rearing practices in two groups of Negro infants. *Child Development,* 1953, 24, 103–121.

WOLF, K. Observation of individual tendencies in the first year of life. *Problems of Infancy and Childhood.* Transactions of the Sixth Conference of the Josiah Macy Jr. Foundation, 1953.

WOLFF, P. H. Observations on newborn infants. *Psychosom. Med.,* 1959, New Series Vol. XXI, No. 2, 110–118.

WOLFF, P. H. The developmental psychologies of Jean Piaget and psychoanalysis. *Psychol. Issues,* 1960, Monogr. No. 5, Vol. II, No. 1.

WOLFF, P. H. Observations on the early development of smiling. In B. M. Foss (Ed.), *Determinants of infant behavior,* Vol. 2. New York: John Wiley, 1963. (a)

WOOLF, P. H. The natural history of a family. In B. M. Foss (Ed.), *Determinants of infant behavior,* Vol. 2. New York: John Wiley, 1963. (b)

WOLFF, P. H. The pertinence of direct infant observation for psychoanalytic theory. Presented at midwinter meetings of the American Psychoanalytic Association, 1964.

WOLFF, P. H. The development of attention in young infants. In H. E. Whipple (Ed.), *New issues in infant development. Annals of the N.Y. Academy of Science,* 118, 815–830, 1965.

WOLFF, P. H. The causes, controls, and organization of behavior in the newborn, *Psychol. Issues,* 1966, Vol. V, No. 1, Monogr. 17.

WOLFF, P. H., and WHITE, B. L. Visual pursuit and attention in newborn infants. *J. Am. Acad. Child Psych.,* 1965, Vol. 4, No. 3, 473–484.

WOODWARD, M. The behavior of idiots interpreted by Piaget's theory of sensorimotor development. *Brit. J. Educat. Psychol.,* 1959, 29, 60–71.

WOODWARD, M., and STERN, D. J. Developmental patterns of severely subnormal children. *Brit. J. Educat. Psychol.,* 1963, 33, 10–21.

YARROW, L. J. The relationship between nutritive sucking experiences in infancy and non-nutritive sucking in childhood. *J. genet. Psychol.,* 1954, 84, 149–162.

YARROW, L. J. Maternal deprivation: toward an empirical and conceptual reevaluation. *Psychol. Bull.,* 1961, 58, 459–490.

YARROW, L. J. Research in dimensions of early maternal care. *Merrill Palmer Quarterly,* 1963, 9, 101–114.

YARROW, L. J., and GOODWIN, M. S. Some conceptual issues in the study of mother-infant interaction. *Amer. J. Orthopsychiat.,* April 1965, Vol. 35, No. 3.

ZEIGARNICK, B. On the retention of completed and uncompleted activities (1927). In K. Lewin, *A dynamic theory of personality.* New York: McGraw-Hill, 1935.

INDEX